JOURNALISTS PRAISE MURRAY WAAS'S INVESTIGATIVE JOURNALISM

"MURRAY WAAS FILLED IN another piece of the prewar propaganda puzzle."
–FRANK RICH, *The New York Times*

"WAAS BROKE THE STORY of I. Lewis 'Scooter' Libby saying President Bush had authorized him to leak classified information about Iraq in 2003."
–HOWARD KURTZ, "Media Notes," *The Washington Post*

"HE'S A DOGGED REPORTER with an amazing capacity
to get sensitive documents."
–DOUGLAS FRANTZ, *Los Angeles Times*

"[WAAS'S] JOURNALISM WILL CONTINUE to draw attention to him. Waas's exhaustive *National Journal* stories on special prosecutor Patrick Fitzgerald's inquiry into the leak of Plame's name to reporters have been praised by media critics and White House watchers."
–LIZ HALLORAN, *U.S. News & World Report*

D1114576

THE
UNITED
STATES

v.

I. LEWIS
LIBBY

THE

UNITED STATES

v.

I. LEWIS LIBBY

EDITED AND WITH REPORTING BY

MURRAY WAAS

ADDITIONAL EDITING AND REPORTING BY

JEFF LOMONACO

UNION SQUARE PRESS
An imprint of Sterling Publishing Co., Inc.

New York / London
www.sterlingpublishing.com

STERLING and the distinctive Sterling logo are registered trademarks of
Sterling Publishing Co., Inc.

Library of Congress Cataloging-in-Publication Data Available

10 9 8 7 6 5 4 3 2 1

Published by Sterling Publishing Co., Inc.
387 Park Avenue South, New York, NY 10016
Trial transcript materials © 2007 by Sterling Publishing Co., Inc.,
as a unique assembly of public documents
Introduction ©2007 by Murray Waas
Commentary and additional reporting
©2007 by Murray Waas and Jeff Lomonaco

Distributed in Canada by Sterling Publishing
c/o Canadian Manda Group, 165 Dufferin Street
Toronto, Ontario, Canada M6K 3H6
Distributed in the United Kingdom by GMC Distribution Services
Castle Place, 166 High Street, Lewes, East Sussex, England BN7 1XU
Distributed in Australia by Capricorn Link (Australia) Pty. Ltd.
P.O. Box 704, Windsor, NSW 2756, Australia

Sterling ISBN-13: 978-1-4027-5259-9
ISBN-10: 1-4027-5259-8

Interior design by Sherry Williams, Oxygen Design

For information about custom editions, special sales, premium
and corporate purchases, please contact Sterling Special Sales
Department at 800-805-5489 or specialsales@sterlingpub.com.

Editor's Note

In editing the trial transcript, strenuous efforts have been made to maintain fidelity to the record of the court reporters while providing readers with an accessible and useful book.

THERE IS TALK ABOUT a cloud over the Vice President. There is a cloud over the White House as to what happened. Don't you think the FBI, the Grand Jury, the American people are entitled to a straight answer?

—PATRICK FITZGERALD, February 20, 2007

CONTENTS

TIMELINE

February 2002: Joe Wilson travels to Niger at the request of the CIA to investigate reports that Iraq was pursuing an agreement with Niger for yellowcake uranium. Wilson is told the trip is in response to interest in the Niger story from the Office of the Vice President (OVP).

March 5: Wilson returns from Niger and reports orally to the CIA that his excellent contacts in Niger have made it clear no such agreement took place. This view is corroborated by other U.S. government officials.

March 8: CIA distributes a report based on Wilson's trip. The report gets normal and wide distribution. Wilson is not named as the source in the report.

September: The British publish a white paper publicly making the uranium claim. CIA official express doubts about it to Congress in October.

October 1: Intelligence community produces a National Intelligence Estimate on Iraqi weapons of mass destruction programs. Buried in the text is the claim that Iraq "began vigorously trying to procure uranium and yellowcake." The main basis turn out to be forged documents.

October 5–7: The CIA intervenes and gets the White House to remove the uranium claim from an important speech Bush is to give in Cincinnati on October 7. Two memos are sent to the White House, and Tenet personally intervenes with Deputy National Security Adviser Stephen Hadley. The reference is removed.

October: The United States government receives, from Italy, documents purporting to cover Iraq's pursuit of uranium in Niger. They are not examined carefully. State Department analyst sees them as transparent forgeries at the time.

January 28, 2003: President Bush's State of the Union address proclaims these sixteen words: "The British government has learned that Saddam Hussein recently sought significant quantities of uranium from Africa."

February 5: Colin Powell delivers UN presentation on intelligence on Iraqi WMD, and notably does *not* use the uranium claim.

March 7: On the eve of war, the International Atomic Energy Agency, having received the Niger documents from the United States, easily detects and declares them to be forgeries.

March 19: Iraq war begins.

May 6: Nicholas Kristof publishes "Missing in Action: Truth," which recounts Wilson's Niger mission for the first time in public, without naming Wilson, who is a source for the column. The column is especially critical of President Bush and Secretary of State Colin Powell.

May 29: Libby asks Marc Grossman if he knows anything about a retired ambassador's travel to Niger to look into the question of yellowcake. Grossman asks Richard Armitage about it; Armitage knows nothing of it either. Grossman queries two assistant secretaries.

May 29: Having received preliminary information identifying Wilson as the ambassador from the bureaus where the two assistant secretaries worked, Grossman reports back preliminarily to Libby identifying Wilson and promising a fuller report. Grossman had called Joe Wilson as well, and believes he told Libby that Wilson thought the trip had been at the request of the Office of the Vice President. Grossman also requested a report be written up on the matter.

June 8: Condoleezza Rice appears on *This Week* on ABC and is pressed by George Stephanapoulos about the Niger story and Kristof's month-old column on Wilson's trip.

June 9: Libby's notes show that Bush expressed interest in Kristof's column and the State of the Union.

June 9: Numerous documents marked classified are faxed from the CIA to the Vice President's office, to the attention of Libby and Hannah, bearing on Wilson's mission, though Wilson is nowhere identified by name. Cheney and Libby make notes in the margins identifying Wilson by name in relevant portions of the documents.

June 10 or 11: Grossman, who had been out of the country for a week, receives the so-called INR memo on Wilson's role and the Niger story more generally. The INR memo, and the underlying memo from a participant in the February 19 meeting, identifies Wilson's wife, whom it refers to as "Valerie Wilson," as a CIA WMD manager and a CIA WMD managerial type.

Around June 11: Cheney tells Libby that Wilson's wife works in the Counterproliferation Division (CPD) of the CIA. Libby understands Cheney's source to be at senior levels of the CIA.

June 11: Libby contacts Robert Grenier of the CIA to ask him about Wilson's mission. Grenier reports back to Libby in a phone call about Wilson's trip, and mentions that Wilson's wife works in the unit of CPD that sent Wilson.

June 11: Cathie Martin, having been told by CIA press spokesman Bill Harlow that Wilson's wife worked for the CIA, relays that information to Cheney and Libby.

June 11 or June 12: Grossman tells Libby more extensively about Wilson's trip and tells him that Wilson's wife works at the CIA.

June 12: Walter Pincus publishes "CIA Did Not Share Doubt on Iraq Data" in *The Washington Post,* using both Wilson and Libby as anonymous sources. The article serves to aggravate the battle between the White House and the CIA over prewar claims about Iraqi WMD.

June 13: Nicholas Kristof publishes another column on the Niger matter, this time highly critical of the Vice President, whom Kristof places at the center of the affair.

June 13: Richard Armitage becomes first known Bush administration official to disclose Plame's identity to a reporter, telling Bob Woodward that Wilson's wife is a WMD analyst at the CIA.

June 14: At his morning intelligence briefing, Libby mentions Joe and Valerie Wilson to Craig Schmall, his CIA briefer, and asks why the Ambassador was told mission arose from a Vice President's Office question.

June 23: Libby meets with Judith Miller of *The New York Times* in his office in the Old Executive Office Building and tells her that Wilson's wife works in a bureau, which Miller understands to mean a unit within the CIA that dealt with nonproliferation.

June 27: Bob Woodward interviews Libby. Libby uses language from the NIE. Woodward may have notes with him touching on Wilson's wife; he has no recollection of mentioning her to Libby and Libby says nothing about the matter.

July 2: David Sanger interviews Libby about the prewar intelligence controversy, and Libby does not bring up Plame. Libby discusses the October 2002 NIE.

July 6: *The New York Times* publishes Wilson's op-ed, "What I Didn't Find in Africa" concluding "some of the intelligence related to Iraq's nuclear weapons program was twisted to exaggerate the Iraqi threat." The same day, an article about Wilson appears in the *Washington Post* and Wilson himself appears on NBC's *Meet the Press*.

July 7: A copy of Wilson's column is printed out for Libby, who underlines it.

July 7: OVP sends talking points to White House spokesman Ari Fleischer, which he uses at a press gaggle that morning, where he also for the first time refuses to reassert that the White House is standing by the sixteen words, causing an uproar among the press.

July 7: Libby has lunch with Fleischer, and tells Fleischer that Wilson's wife works in the Counterproliferation Division of the CIA and also, Fleischer believes, that her name is Valerie Plame. Libby tells him the information is "hush-hush" and "on the QT."

Around July 7: Cheney takes notes on a copy of Wilson's op-ed. He writes, "Have they done this sort of thing before? Send an Amb. to answer a question? Do we ordinarily send people out pro bono to work for us? Or did his wife send him on a junket?" Cheney directs Libby to leak classified information to rebut Wilson to Judith Miller of *The New York Times*. After Libby expresses concern, Cheney gets authorization for the leak from President Bush and conveys that to Libby. Libby later told the grand jury it had to do with the NIE.

July 7: The INR memo, identifying Valerie Wilson as a CIA employee, is faxed to Colin Powell aboard Air Force One on a presidential trip to Africa.

July 7–8: Overnight, the traveling White House puts out a statement to the press backing off of the sixteen words.

July 7 and 8: At a senior staff meeting, Karl Rove and others discuss the need to get a message out about Wilson and express frustration about him.

July 7 or 8: In a conversation in his small office, Libby confirms with OVP Counsel David Addington the President's powers to declassify information by authorizing its disclosure and asks Addington what paperwork would exist at the CIA if a spouse of an employee was sent on a mission.

July 8: In a morning meeting at the St. Regis Hotel, after asking Miller to identify him only as a "former Hill staffer," Libby tells Miller that Wilson's wife works at the CIA and discloses information from the October 2002 NIE.

July 8: Cheney dictates new talking points to Cathie Martin for OVP to use; the new primary talking point raises the question of who authorized Wilson's mission.

July 8: Richard Armitage tells Robert Novak that Wilson's wife works in the Counterproliferation Division of the CIA and suggested her husband for his mission to Niger. Shortly thereafter, Novak calls and leaves messages for Rove and Libby.

July 8: Late in the day, Cathie Martin tells Cheney and Libby she'd heard from the CIA spokesman that Andrea Mitchell of NBC and David Martin of CBS were working on stories on the controversy. Cheney dispatches Libby to call them back to put out OVP's side of the story, and on her way out of the office, Martin sees Libby talking to one of them about the NIE (which he has in front of him), which she thinks is still classified. Later that day, Mitchell runs a report on White House criticism of CIA.

July 8 or 9: Karl Rove confirms for Novak that Wilson's wife works at the CIA and suggested Wilson for his mission.

July 9: At a morning meeting, Hadley reproaches communications people, including Martin in particular, about finger-pointing and blaming the CIA in Andrea Mitchell's report the previous evening. Libby does not take responsibility for having spoken with Mitchell the previous day. Martin and other communications people in the White House are thereafter excluded from senior-level discussions of how to deal with the sixteen words controversy.

July 9: Novak talks with Libby but, according to his testimony, Libby does not bring up Plame.

July 10: David Martin of CBS reports that CIA officials warned the White House before the State of the Union that the intelligence underlying the sixteen words was not good.

July 10: With Steven Hadley acting as go-between, Cheney and Libby participate in negotiations with the CIA over whether George Tenet would make a public statement, and what the substance of the statement would be, accepting some or all responsibility for the sixteen words. Libby brings Cathie Martin back into the loop of communications strategy to talk about Tenet's statement and how OVP should proceed with its own defense. Martin suggests, among other things, having Cheney go on *Meet the Press*, the best way to "control message"; leaking an exclusive to a reporter; or have someone outside OVP write an op-ed.

July 10 or 11: Following Mary Matalin's advice, Libby calls Tim Russert to complain about coverage of the OVP on Chris Matthews' *Hardball* on MSNBC. It is this conversation that Libby would later claim was where he effectively learned about Wilson's wife. Russert denies that he knew about or told Libby about Wilson's wife.

July 10 or 11: Rove tells Libby that he had spoken with Novak about Wilson's wife and that Novak would be publishing a column.

July 11: In a press gaggle, Condoleezza Rice puts the blame for the sixteen words on Tenet and the CIA.

July 11: White House Communications Director declares, in Fleischer's presence, that Wilson's wife works at the CIA and sent him on his mission while reading the INR memo.

July 11: Fleischer either tells reporters David Gregory and John Dickerson that Wilson's wife sent him on the trip, or hints at it.

July 11: Karl Rove volunteers to reporter Matt Cooper that Wilson was suggested for the trip by his wife, who works at the CIA, and that information to that effect would be coming out.

July 11: Novak's column goes on the wire, meaning it arrives in newsrooms but is embargoed until the following Monday.

July 11: Late in the day CIA releases Tenet's statement taking responsibility for the sixteen words, but also subtly pointing blame back at the White House as well. As the White House and OVP recognize, the statement will not end the controversy.

July 12: Libby travels with Cheney and others back and forth to the dedication of an aircraft carrier on Air Force Two, and discusses media strategy with Cheney on the ride back. Cheney gives Libby a rare on-the-record statement to give the press, as well as what to say not on the record.

July 12: Fleischer tells Pincus of the *Post* in a phone call that Wilson's wife works at the CIA.

July 12: Libby talks to a number of reporters. He discusses Plame with Matt Cooper of *TIME*, and Judith Miller of *The New York Times*.

July 14: Robert Novak publishes syndicated column publicly blowing Plame's cover: "Wilson never worked for the CIA, but his wife, Valerie Plame, is an Agency operative on weapons of mass destruction. Two senior administration officials told me Wilson's wife suggested sending him to Niger to investigate the Italian report."

July 14: Cheney asks CIA briefer Schmall if he had read the Novak column.

July 18: Luncheon with Cheney at his residence for conservative columnists, who have been invited mainly by Libby and also by Cathie Martin. It is intended to coincide with the press conference Dan Bartlett gives on background at the White House to shape the reception of the officially declassified October 2002 NIE, released in redacted form that day. During the luncheon, Cheney responds to Wilson's allegations but does not mention his wife.

July 22: Bartlett and Stephen Hadley hold a press conference at which Hadley, having been forced to acknowledge the evidence that the CIA had forcefully intervened with him to get the uranium claim taken out of Bush's Cincinnati speech in October 2002, accepts responsibility for the mistake of letting the sixteen words into the State of the Union.

End of July: CIA sends a criminal referral to the Department of Justice with regard to the disclosure of Plame's CIA employment.

September 26: Department of Justice opens a criminal investigation into the potential unauthorized disclosure of classified information in the disclosure of Plame's employment at the CIA to reporters. NBC reports on it shortly thereafter.

September 28: *The Washington Post* publishes a story reporting that "a senior administration official said that before Novak's column ran, two top White House officials called at least six Washington journalists and disclosed the identity and occupation of Wilson's wife." *The Washington Post* later identifies its source as a senior White House official.

September 29: In a telephone conversation, Robert Novak assures Rove, one of his sources for his column outing Plame publicly, that he does not give up his sources and that Rove would not get burned. The same day, White House spokesman Scott McClellan says, having spoken with Rove, that the notion that Rove was involved in Plame's outing was a "ridiculous suggestion."

October 1: Armitage tells Colin Powell that he had told Novak about Plame, and shortly after is interviewed by the FBI about it.

October 1: Scott McClellan declines to specifically clear Libby as he had cleared Rove at a press briefing.

Early October: Having unsuccessfully intervened with McClellan and Bush's Chief of Staff Andy Card to have the White House publicly clear him, Libby gets Vice President Cheney to intervene with the White House to do so. Libby crafts a carefully parsed statement for McClellan, and Cheney notes, "Has to happen today," and "Not going to protect one staffer + sacrifice the guy ["this Pres" crossed out] that was asked to stick his neck in the meat grinder because of the incompetence of others." The defense suggests that President Bush himself was directly involved in Cheney's efforts.

October 6: Asked if the President would fire anyone on his staff found to have leaked classified information, Scott McClellan states, "I think I made that very clear last week. The topic came up, and I said that if anyone in this administration was responsible for the leaking of classified information, they would no longer work in this administration. This is a very serious matter."

October 7: President Bush says, "I have no idea whether we'll find out who the leaker is: partially because, in all due respect to your profession, you do a very good job of protecting the leakers." The same day, McClellan publicly clears Libby. Speaking of Libby and two others, he says, "I spoke with them, so that I could come back to you and say that they were not involved."

Fall 2003: FBI pursues investigation. Concerns mount, among Democrats, on the one hand, and among career Department of Justice employees, on the other, that Attorney General John Ashcroft, who is receiving briefings on the progress of the case, should not be in charge of the investigation and should recuse himself, largely on account of his close ties to Karl Rove, who is one of the focuses of the investigation.

October 14 and November 26: Libby is interviewed by the FBI and tells his story, which would remain consistent, that he effectively learned about Plame from Russert, having forgotten completely his conversation in June with Cheney, and that he only relayed information about Plame to reporters as unconfirmed journalistic rumor.

December 30: In part because of conflicts of interest, Ashcroft recuses himself from the investigation, and his Deputy James Comey names Patrick Fitzgerald, US Attorney in Illinois, as special prosecutor.

January 2004: Fitzgerald moves quickly and aggressively in the investigation, and a federal grand jury begins hearing testimony and issuing subpoenas for documents.

March 5 and 24: Libby's grand jury appearances.

By June 4: Vice President Cheney has been questioned by Fitzgerald by this time.

June 24: President Bush is questioned by investigators.

Spring–Fall: Fitzgerald pursues the testimony of a number of journalists, and works out arrangements with most of them.

July 6, 2005: Judith Miller goes to jail for contempt of court for refusing to comply with a subpoena she had battled in the courts and lost.

September 12: Fitzgerald writes a letter to Libby's lawyer explaining that news reports suggest there may be a misunderstanding on Libby's part keeping Judith Miller in jail. Fitzgerald cites a report in *The American Prospect* by Murray Waas.

September 29: Miller gets out of jail, and testifies before the grand jury the next day.

October 12: Miller testifies again, having discovered notes that indicate that she was in fact told about Wilson's wife by Libby in an earlier, June 2003 conversation that the special prosecutor had asked her about inher first appearance.

October 28: Scooter Libby is indicted on 5 counts of obstruction of justice, perjury and false statements, and resigns from his job at the White House.

November 3: Libby pleads not guilty.

November 16: Bob Woodward publicly reveals that he had a source who leaked to him about Valerie Plame earlier than any other known leak, and that he had been deposed by Fitzgerald two days earlier.

May 12, 2006: As part of the extensive pretrial phase, Fitzgerald discloses a key piece of evidence, Vice President Cheney's copy of Wilson's op-ed, on which Cheney has written notes expressing his concern that Wilson's wife sent him on a junket.

June 13: Karl Rove's lawyer discloses that Fitzgerald has decided not to pursue charges against Rove. Rove had testified before the grand jury five times.

July 12: Robert Novak formally discusses a fact long known: that Karl Rove was his confirming source for his original column publicly blowing Plame's cover.

September 7: Richard Armitage, long recognized by observers of the case as Robert Novak's first source on Plame, officially comes forward to explain his role. Novak's two sources – Armitage and Rove – have thus been identified.

September 27: As part of the pretrial phase, the Court begins what would turn out to be several months of arduous hearings to deal with the possible use, by Libby's defense, of classified information at trial under the auspices of the Classified Information Procedures Act (CIPA).

January 16, 2007: Jury selection begins in the trial of Scooter Libby.

January 23: The trial begins in earnest with opening statements.

February 21: The legal teams having presented their cases and done their closing statements, the jury begins deliberations.

March 6: The jury reaches a verdict: Libby is found guilty of one count of obstruction of justice, two counts of perjury and one count of making a false statement; Libby is found not guilty of one count of making a false statement.

KEY FIGURES

U.S. District Court Judge Reginald Walton

DEFENDANT:

I. Lewis (Scooter) Libby: Chief of Staff and National Security Advisor to Vice President Cheney, as well as Assistant to the President.

WITNESSES CALLED BY THE PROSECUTION:

Marc Grossman: The third highest-ranking official at the State Department, Grossman testifies that on June 11 or 12, 2003, he told Scooter Libby that the wife of Ambassador Joseph Wilson worked at the CIA.

Robert Grenier: The former CIA official was the Agency's Iraq manager. He testifies that on June 11, 2003, he told Libby about Valerie Plame in response to a request from Libby.

Craig Schmall: Libby's CIA briefer also sometimes briefed Vice President Cheney. He testifies that Plame and Joseph Wilson were discussed during Libby's briefing on June 14, 2003; and on July 14 Cheney or Libby asked him if he'd read Robert Novak's column, "Mission to Niger," published that day.

Cathie Martin: Cheney's former press spokeswoman, Martin testifies that sometime before July 6, 2003, probably June 11, she told Libby and Cheney that Wilson's wife worked for the CIA. She also testifies that on July 12, 2003, after a flight back to Washington, D.C., from Norfolk, Virginia, she was with Libby when he made a phone call to *TIME* magazine reporter Matt Cooper.

Ari Fleischer: President Bush's press secretary at the time Valerie Plame's CIA employment was disclosed, Fleischer recalls Libby telling him about Plame over lunch on July 7, 2003, and saying the information was "hush hush and on the QT." Fleischer later gives that information to reporters. He was granted immunity from prosecution in exchange for his testimony.

David Addington: Counsel to Vice President Cheney (and later Libby's replacement as Chief of Staff), Addington testifies that Libby asked him whether any paper trail would exist if a CIA employee's spouse was sent overseas by the Agency, and about the president's declassification powers. Addington reports that when the investigation began Libby asked him if someone could know whether a CIA officer was undercover. He also made the cryptic remark to the vice president's counsel, "I didn't do it."

Judith Miller: Then with *The New York Times*, Miller says Libby discussed Plame with her on June 23 and July 8 of 2003, before Libby testifies he first learned about Plame. After Vice President Cheney urged President Bush to instantly declassify the October 2002 National Intelligence Estimate, Libby leaked portions of it to Miller. She claims she urged *The New York Times* to do a story on Plame and Wilson. Miller served 85 days in jail after she refused to name her source in the case, Scooter Libby.

Matthew Cooper: A former *TIME* magazine reporter, Cooper said that Libby confirmed to him off-the-record that he had also heard that Wilson's wife was involved in sending her husband on the trip to Niger. Defense lawyers maintain that Libby told Cooper only that he had heard the same from other reporters and did not know whether it was true.

Deborah Bond: On Oct. 14 and Nov. 26 of 2003 Bond was part of the FBI team that interviewed Libby. She testifies that Libby told them he'd first learned Wilson's wife worked for the CIA from Cheney on or about June 12, 2003, but had later forgotten that conversation. Libby told the FBI agents he thought he was hearing the information for the first time from NBC reporter Tim Russert on July 10 or 11 of 2003.

Tim Russert: The head of NBC's bureau in Washington, D.C., and host of *Meet the Press* testifies that Libby called him to complain about Chris Matthews's coverage of the sixteen words controversy, and that Plame never came up in their July 2003 phone call with Libby. Libby testified to the grand jury in March 2004 that Russert told him "all the reporters know" Plame worked for the CIA. Libby also told grand jurors that he passed the information on to other reporters based on Russert's comment.

WITNESSES CALLED BY THE DEFENSE:

Walter Pincus: The longtime *Washington Post* reporter spoke with Libby in preparation for his June 12, 2003, article that also cited comments by an unnamed ambassador who had gone to Niger on a fact-finding mission. The national security and intelligence reporter testifies that Fleischer told him that Plame worked at the CIA, while the topic never came up in discussions with Libby.

Bob Woodward: An assistant managing editor at *The Washington Post* and best-selling author, Woodward testifies that in June 2003, Deputy Secretary of State Richard Armitage told him that Plame worked at the CIA. Woodward did not recall the topic coming up in any of his interviews with Libby.

David Sanger: A *New York Times* reporter, Sanger testifies that he talked to Libby in July 2003 and Libby did not bring up Plame.

Robert Novak: His "Mission to Niger" column of July 14, 2003, identified Valerie Plame as "an agency operative on weapons of mass destruction." Novak testifies that he had two sources: Armitage and White House political

guru Karl Rove. He added that Libby was not a source, although they did speak before his column was published.

Glenn Kessler: A *Washington Post* diplomatic affairs correspondent, Kessler testifies that he interviewed Libby on the same day as Cooper but that Libby never brought up Plame.

Evan Thomas: A *Newsweek* reporter, Thomas testifies that he is certain Libby never told him Plame worked for the CIA.

Carl W. Ford, Jr.: The former assistant secretary of state for intelligence and research (INR), Ford testifies very briefly, saying that he prepared the memo on Wilson for Marc Grossman that said his wife worked for the CIA.

Jill Abramson: The *New York Times* bureau chief in Washington, D.C., Abramson testifies that she did not recall Judith Miller ever urging her to pursue a story on Valerie Plame, though she noted that she sometimes tuned out the reporter. The defense hoped this would suggest that Libby hadn't really told Miller about Plame.

John Hannah: He also worked in the Office of the Vice President (OVP); he testifies to Scooter Libby's poor memory and the fact that in 2003 he was routinely dealing with many diplomatic crises and terrorist threats worldwide. On cross examination by Patrick Fitzgerald, Hannah admitted that if Scooter Libby took two hours out of his busy day—as he did to meet with Judith Miller on July 8, 2003, at the St. Regis Hotel—it surely indicated that he considered the issues raised by Joe Wilson's trip to Niger very important.

THE
UNITED
STATES

v.

I. LEWIS
LIBBY

INTRODUCTION

THE LAST COMPARTMENT

LATE IN THE MORNING OF JULY 12, 2003, Vice President Dick Cheney stood atop the pier at Naval Station Norfolk in Virginia awaiting the commissioning of the nuclear-powered Nimitz-class aircraft carrier, the USS *Ronald Reagan*. The carrier had taken eight full years to construct and stood twenty stories high. More than 15,000 people waited under clear skies to participate in the pomp and ceremony. As Nancy Reagan christened the carrier by breaking a bottle of champagne across its bow, she told the crowd: "I only have one line: Man the ship and bring her alive!"

A *Washington Post* reporter painted the scene: "With those time-hallowed words, hundreds of crew members wearing dress whites ran aboard the 20-story *Reagan* and lined the flight deck while four fighter jets flew overheard and every crane, radar, whistle, and alarm aboard was turned on simultaneously."

Once the fanfare quieted, Cheney himself took to the podium. As he spoke, the crowd grew subdued and a bit somber: "The *Ronald Reagan* sets sail in a world with new dangers," he intoned. "The outcome is certain. There will be victory for the United States."

The moment of triumph, however, would prove to be illusory. Few Americans had any idea that the war in Iraq, then not even four months old, would take a turn for the worse; that nearly 3,300 American service members would have died in the line of duty by the time of this writing; that "liberated" Iraq would spiral down into sectarian violence and civil war; and that the war would not only divide the Iraqi nation but the American republic as well.

On the flight back to Washington, D.C., the Vice President was suddenly sullen, and focused. For virtually the entire flight north, Cheney sat alone with I. Lewis "Scooter" Libby, his then-Chief of Staff and National Security Advisor.

Six days earlier, on July 6, 2003, former ambassador Joseph C. Wilson IV had leveled explosive charges in a *New York Times* op-ed. He wrote that the Bush administration had "twisted" intelligence to make its case for invading Iraq, and claimed first-hand knowledge of his own that refuted the President's words in his latest State of the Union address.

Wilson had undertaken a CIA-sponsored trip to Niger in February 2002 to investigate reports that Saddam Hussein was attempting to procure uranium from the African nation. Wilson returned home from the Niger mission and gave an oral briefing to a CIA reports officer, stating on several grounds that the uranium claim was almost certainly untrue. Moreover, his findings corroborated earlier fact-finding by both the U.S. Ambassador to Niger, Barbro Owens-Kirkpatrick, and four-star Marine Corps General Carleton Fulford. Nevertheless, President Bush cited the claim in his

2003 State of the Union speech as evidence of an Iraqi program to build an atomic weapon, a key justification for taking the nation to war.

As the charge gained public currency in the days following publication of the op-ed, undermining Wilson's accusation became a personal mission for Cheney. In fact, though, even before Wilson began speaking out, the administration's case for war had been faltering. Despite their pre-war certainty, forcefully repeated many times, that weapons of mass destruction would be found in Iraq, U.S. forces and UN weapons inspectors had been unable to find any evidence of them.

After Wilson's column appeared, Cheney and Libby became preoccupied with attempting to undercut his allegations and discredit him personally. Special prosecutor Patrick J. Fitzgerald told the jury during his January 23, 2007 opening statement at the Libby trial that Wilson's column was viewed by Cheney as "a direct attack on the credibility of the President and Vice President. And it was on an issue that could not be more important." President Bush and Vice President Cheney had been "accused of lying about the justification for war."

As the Vice President and his Chief of Staff strategized on how best to discredit Wilson and his allegations, the rest of their staff were excluded, much to the consternation of at least one of them, Cathie Martin, Cheney's press aide.

And so the two men sat alone in the front compartment of the plane on the flight back to Washington D.C. following that morning's ship christening. Whether by happenstance or design, no one but the two of them would ever be able to know what transpired between them that early afternoon. No other White House staff. Not prying FBI agents or federal prosecutors. Not historians who would one day search through archives. Not reporters eager to find traces of the truth.

Whatever Dick Cheney did or did not tell Scooter Libby to do was figuratively and physically compartmentalized.

EARLIER THAT MORNING, as Cheney spoke aboard the aircraft carrier, Libby had stood off to the side as his boss spoke. The most powerful aide to the most powerful Vice President in the nation's history was adept at avoiding the spotlight. He always understood that he was staff. His proper place was off to the side, behind the scenes.

Those who had worked with Libby, or had worked at cross purposes with him, as was often the case in the divisive first term of the Bush administration, said that Libby understood that the limelight was not where the real power was to be wielded. As the man behind one of the principals, he could wield power on the same levels as many of the principals themselves. Behind the scenes, he waged bureaucratic war against Secretary of State Colin Powell—and often won. He would routinely attempt to circumvent the Director of the Central Intelligence Agency, George Tenet—and often succeed at that.

"At deputies' meetings, Libby would sit there and say absolutely nothing at all," Lawrence Wilkerson, the-then Chief of Staff to then-Secretary of State Colin Powell, told me. Because of the behind-the-scenes influence that Cheney wielded with the President, Libby "knew that he was always going to have several bites at the apple. Unlike anyone else in government, he knew that the OVP [Office of Vice President] could argue their brief to the President time and time again—from the smallest thing to whether or not to go to war with Saddam Hussein."

But, above all, he was a loyal staffer, not one known to go beyond what his boss wanted. One longtime friend of Libby's, who worked with him in government more than a decade earlier, told me: "He's no freelancer. It's incomprehensible that the Scooter we all knew [would] one day turn into some sort of loose cannon." Others I interviewed described him as deliberative, meticulous, and careful to a fault.

The *New York Times* similarly said of Libby in a profile: "Paradox seems to define I. Lewis Libby . . . By all accounts a first-rate legal mind and a hyper-cautious aide whose discretion frustrated reporters," he did not seem the type to go off on his own and so indiscreetly leak the identity of Valerie Plame to the media.

Paul Wolfowitz, who was once Libby's political science professor at Yale and served alongside him as Deputy Secretary of Defense, said of his indictment on criminal charges: "He's always been excruciatingly careful, which is ironic in this situation."

The Republican operative, Mary Matalin, who was in charge of Cheney's public relations affairs for the early part of his tenure as Vice President, said that Libby was "Cheney's Cheney," and that he was "an absolutely salient translator" for Cheney.

Though the irony may be lost on these supportive individuals, in attempting to serve as character witnesses for Libby in the court of public opinion, Wolfowitz, Matalin, and other administration officials who spoke in his favor and on his behalf were also serving as fact witnesses against the Vice President. If Scooter Libby was not someone apt to go off on his own against the wishes of his boss but rather was his "salient translator," how likely could it be that Libby would—entirely on his own— leak the identity of Valerie Plame to the media?

*

AS LIBBY STOOD ATOP THE PIER in Norfolk that summer day of 2003, it is doubtful that he had the slightest clue that events later that exultant day would cause him to endure him repeated trips to the dreary and windowless confines of a room in a federal court house where a grand jury was expecting answers.

In the grand jury room on March 5, 2004, Libby, on the instruction of his attorneys, told his story impassively to twenty-three equally expressionless grand jurors.

The grand jurors wanted to know what role, if any, Libby had played in leaking the identity of a CIA officer to the media. They also wanted to know what he knew about any role that Cheney may have had in encouraging him to unleash the leak about Plame. In the end, the grand jurors did not believe the answers that he gave them.

On October 28, 2005, the federal grand jury would return an indictment against I. Lewis "Scooter" Libby, charging him with five felony counts of making false statements to the FBI, perjury before the grand jury, and obstruction of justice.

The criminal charges alleging that he misled the FBI and grand jury sprung from events that occurred after he disembarked from Air Force Two after his discussions with the Vice President that fateful day of July 12, 2003.

It was only six days before the flight to Norfolk that Wilson had made his charges in the pages of *The New York Times*. For the first few months following the State of the Union address on January 28, 2003, with its now-infamous "sixteen words"—"The British government has learned that Saddam Hussein recently sought significant quantities of uranium from Africa"—Wilson had been urging the administration to correct the record from within, but these efforts were unavailing. Beginning with a *New York Times* column by Nicholas Kristof on May 6, the traces of his story began appearing in the press, although he was not named as a source in any of this early coverage. Meantime, Cheney and Libby became determined to find out everything they could about the unnamed ambassador.

Signs of their determination can be found as early as June 11, 2003, according to notes of Libby's made public at his trial, when Cheney told Libby that Wilson's wife worked at the CIA: "Wife works at C.P.," Libby wrote in reference to the CIA's Counterproliferation Division, which was part of the Clandestine Directorate of Operations. Over time, both Cheney and Libby would learn as well that Plame may have played a role in her husband's selection for the Niger mission.

First, Libby spoke to Marc Grossman, Undersecretary of State for Political Affairs, the third-highest ranking official in the department, whom Libby asked what he could find out about Wilson's mission to Niger. Making inquiries of his own, Grossman was told that Wilson's wife, Plame, may have played a role in selecting him to go on the mission to Niger.

"It was kind of an interesting tidbit, if you will," Grossman testified.

Grossman also testified: "I thought it was odd and remarkable that she worked at the Agency, and secondly, that she had been involved in the organization of the trip . . . It didn't seem right somehow that the spouse of someone would be organizing their spouse's trip." Grossman testified that he told Libby about Plame on either June 11 or June 12, 2003.

It should be noted here that, nine days after Libby's conviction, and more than three years after her CIA employment was revealed, Plame spoke in public for the first time. "I'm delighted that I am under oath as I reply to you," Plame said during her sworn testimony before Congress before continuing:

"In February of 2002, a young junior officer, who worked for me, came to me, very concerned, very upset. She had just received a telephone call, on her desk, from someone, I don't know who, in the Office of the Vice President, asking about this report of this alleged sale of yellowcake uranium from Niger to Iraq. She came to me and as she was telling me this story—what had just happened—someone passed by, another officer, [and] heard this. He knew that Joe had already—my husband—had already gone on some CIA missions, previously, to deal with other nuclear matters. And he suggested, 'Well, why don't we send Joe?' He knew that Joe had many years of experience on the African continent. He also knew that he had served well and heroically, in the . . . embassy in Baghdad, during the first Gulf War. . . . I was somewhat ambivalent. We had two-year-old twins at the time, and all I could envision was me, by myself, at bedtime, with a couple two-year-olds. So I wasn't overjoyed with this idea.

"Nevertheless, we went to my branch chief, our supervisor. My colleague suggested this idea and my supervisor turned to me and said, 'Well, when you go home this evening, would you be willing to speak to your husband, ask him to come in to head-quarters next week, and we'll discuss the options, see if—what we could do?' 'Of course,' I said. And as I was leaving, he asked me to draft a quick email to the chief of our Counterproliferation division, letting him know that this was—that this might happen. I said of course.

"And it was that e-mail, Congressman, that was taken out of context, a portion of which was used in the Senate Select Committee on Intelligence report of July 2004, that makes it seem as though I had suggested or recommended him."

AS IN THE JUVENILE GAME of "telephone," Plame's role would become altered and amplified with each subsequent retelling. The notes of the State Department analyst that formed the basis for Grossman's understanding in the INR report described Plame "apparently convening" the meeting with Joe Wilson, when she had actually left the room by the time the analyst came in to the meeting.

Around the same time Grossman was telling Libby what he had learned, Libby had Robert Grenier, a senior CIA official who was the agency's Iraq manager, called out of a meeting to talk about Wilson and Plame, whereupon Grenier also told Libby that Wilson's wife worked in the unit that sent Wilson to Niger. Cathie Martin, Cheney's press secretary, next testified that, roughly around the same time, she learned about Plame. She immediately told Cheney and Libby, who were together at the time.

A few days later, on June 14, 2003, Libby questioned his CIA briefing officer, Craig Schmall, about Wilson and Plame. Prosecutor Peter Zeidenberg pointed out to the jury that Schmall was the "fifth person that Mr. Libby discussed Wilson's wife with in a three day period." (Yet, during two interviews with the FBI and during two appear-ances before a federal grand jury, Libby claimed that he did not remember anything at all about any of these conversations when purportedly told about Plame by Tim Russert a month later.)

After reading Wilson's July 6, 2003 *New York Times* op-ed, Cheney scribbled in the margins of the column: "Have they done this sort of thing before? Send an Amb. [sic] to answer a question? Do we ordinarily send people out pro bono to work for us? Or did his wife send him on a junket?"

Questioned before the grand jury, federal prosecutor Patrick Fitzgerald approached Libby with a copy of the marked-up column and asked if he recalled the Vice President expressly raising the same issues with him.

"Do you recall ever discussing those issues with Vice President Cheney?"

"Yes, sir."

"And tell us what you recall about those conversations," Fitzgerald pressed Libby.

"I recall that along the way he asked, 'Is this normal for them to just send some-body out like this uncompensated, as it says?' He was interested in how did that per-son come to be selected for this mission. And at some point, his wife worked at the

Agency, you know, that was part of the question." But Libby testified that the issue of Wilson's wife came up only after Libby had heard about her from Tim Russert.

The extraordinary amount of time and energy that Cheney personally devoted to the issue, as well as his intensity of emotion regarding it, is underscored by this exchange between a federal prosecutor and Libby during his testimony before the grand jury:

"Was it a topic that was discussed on a daily basis?" Fitzgerald asked.

"Yes, sir," answered Libby.

"And it was discussed on multiple occasions each day, in fact?"

"Yes, sir."

"And during that time did the Vice President indicate that he was upset that this article was out there which falsely in his view attacked his own credibility?"

"Yes, sir."

"And do you recall what it is the Vice President said?"

"I recall that he was very keen to get the truth out. He wanted to get all the facts out about what he had or hadn't done—what the facts were or were not. He was very keen on that and said it repeatedly. 'Let's get everything out.' "

Libby's testimony vividly underscores the intense effort that the Vice President and his Chief of Staff engaged in for several weeks, zealously directing the administration's efforts to discredit Wilson. Cheney took charge of devising talking points for Libby and other administration officials to use when speaking to the press. The Vice President worked closely with then-Deputy National Security Advisor Stephen J. Hadley to draft with CIA director George Tenet a statement that Tenet was to release. In it, the CIA would take much of the blame for the uranium allegations ending up in the State of the Union. Cheney also sought out the President for secret presidential authorization to have Libby leak classified information to the media that they hoped would also lay blame on the CIA. Cheney also was aware of each conversation that Libby had with reporters during which Libby surreptitiously provided that information to journalists.

On the day after the Wilson column appeared, July 7, 2003, Libby had lunch with then–White House Press Secretary Ari Fleischer. It was Fleischer's last week working at the White House and much of his morning was devoted to answering questions about the Wilson mission to Niger. Fleischer relied on talking points in large part formulated by Cheney and Libby.

At the lunch, Fleischer would testify, Libby told him, "Ambassador Wilson was sent by his wife. His wife works for the CIA." At that point, Libby was so familiar with the subject, Fleischer testified that Libby even referred to Wilson's wife by her maiden name, Valerie Plame. "He added it was 'hush-hush, on the QT,' and that most people didn't know it."

On the following day, July 8, 2003, Libby met with Judith Miller of *The New York Times* to further his efforts and to do what Cheney told him to do: "get everything out."

Among other things, Libby disclosed to Miller the contents of the still-classified National Intelligence Estimate (NIE)[1], indicating the Bush administration had been told by the intelligence community that Saddam had weapons of mass destruction.

What Miller didn't know was that Libby did this on the authorization of the President and Vice President of the United States.

When Libby expressed reservations to Cheney as to whether he could leak the classified document to Miller or other reporters, Cheney told him that he had spoken to the President and that he had authorized Libby to disclose it. Libby, the "hyper-cautious" staff aide, still had reservations. He sought out Cheney's counsel, David Addington, according to both Libby's grand jury testimony and Addington's testimony at the criminal trial, to make sure that the President had indeed authorized him to disclose the classified document.

In disclosing the NIE to Miller, only the President, Vice President, and Libby knew that he was doing it.

"So far as you know, the only three people who knew about this would be the President, the Vice President, and yourself," Libby was asked by special prosecutor Patrick Fitzgerald during one grand jury appearance.

"Correct, sir," Libby responded.

Libby testified that he, Cheney and Bush had decided to keep secret from the President's other top advisors that he had been authorized to leak the NIE to Miller. Among those kept in the dark, according to Libby's testimony, were then-National Security advisor Condoleezza Rice, then-deputy national security advisorStephen Hadley, and then CIA director George Tenet.

Another compartment.

Miller testified to the federal grand jury, and during Libby's trial, that during the same July 8, 2003 meeting at which he spoke about Wilson's mission to Niger, Libby told her that Wilson's wife worked at the

"So far as you know, the only three people who knew about this would be the President, the Vice President, and yourself," Libby was asked.

CIA. Among other things, Miller testified, she agreed during this meeting to a request by Libby that she identify him, regarding anything he might say about Wilson or Plame, as a "former Hill staffer" to mask the fact that he worked at the White House.

Like so much else in the CIA leak case, there is an ironic twist about the declassification and release of the NIE: the document contained decidedly mixed opinions on the uranium claim, and did not definitively endorse it. For instance, the State Department's intelligence arm, the Bureau of Intelligence and Research (INR)—the same part of the bureaucracy that generated the memo for Libby that brought Valerie Plame into the affair—called claims that Iraq was pursuing uranium in Africa "highly dubious." This dissent was relegated to the back pages of the document, far from other, more robust conclusions.

---

[1] A report issued by a consortium of 16 intelligence agencies giving their consensus on issues of national security.

In fact, within days of the completion of the NIE in October 2002, the CIA had intervened forcefully to have the uranium claim deleted from an important speech on Iraq that President Bush was to give on October 7 in Cincinnati . The CIA sent memos about this to White House staffers, including then-National Security Advisor Condoleezza Rice. Eventually Tenet himself called then-Deputy National Security Advisor Stephen Hadley to insist that the reference be removed from the speech. The CIA clearly did not want the president to be a fact witness on the claim. (Hadley would later say he did not remember this incident when he was coordinating the State of the Union three months later.) The CIA also told Congress that they had doubts about the British claim—made in a public White Paper—that would later be part of the sixteen words in the address.

It was, of course, those sixteen words that would later erupt in Wilson's op-ed. On July 10 or 11, struggling to exercise damage control, Libby spoke with Tim Russert, the NBC News Washington Bureau Chief and moderator of *Meet the Press.*

According to Libby's version of events, when he spoke with Russert, it was Russert who disclosed to him that Wilson's wife worked at the CIA. Libby claimed that he had completely forgotten that he learned a month earlier from the Vice President that Plame worked for the CIA. He also claimed that, while speaking with Russert, he remembered nothing at all about his conversations about Wilson and Plame with Grossman, Grenier, Martin and Schmall. Libby said that he was "taken back" upon hearing from Russert that Plame worked for the CIA. When he expressed his surprise, or so Libby testified to the federal grand jury that later indicted him, Russert told him that "all the reporters know."

Libby testified to the grand jury: "On July 10 or 11 I learned, I thought anew, that the wife—that the reporters were telling us that the wife worked at the CIA. And I may have had a conversation with the Vice President either late on the 11th or on the 12th in which I relayed that reporters were saying that."

That Libby heard about Plame from Russert and not from Cheney or someone else

> *"On July 10 or 11 I learned, I thought anew, that the wife— that the reporters were telling us that the wife worked at the CIA. And I may have had a conversation with the Vice President either late on the 11th or on the 12th in which I relayed that reporters were saying that."*
>
> LIBBY'S GRAND JURY TESTIMONY

in the government was a cover story devised to shield him from criminal charges, Fitzgerald said in his opening statement at the trial. Disclosing information about a covert CIA officer's status that he had learned from the Vice President or other government officials might be regarded even by Libby as potentially a criminal act. In contrast, simply passing along gossip from one reporter to another would have been a mere indiscretion.

Deputy Special Prosecutor Zeidenberg said in his closing statement that the story told by Libby about his conversations with Russert was "made up" and "never happened."

Testifying as a prosecution witness, Russert claimed that Libby's account of their conversation was a fabrication as well. Asked if it was possible that he was misremembering his conversation with Libby, Russert testified: "That would [have been] impossible because I don't know who that person was until several days later." According to Russert, the first that he ever learned that Wilson's wife, Plame, was a CIA officer was when columnist Robert Novak revealed that information in a column published a few days later, on July 14.

As to what they actually did discuss, Russert testified that the conversation revolved around complaints about coverage of the Niger controversy by Chris Matthews, the host of the MSNBC program, *Hardball.* Russert regarded Libby's phone call as a "consumer complaint"—albeit one made at a higher level then he ordinarily received.

Libby's faulty memory played a central role in the defense's argument, but the government maintained Libby's "misrecollections" were hard to believe. This wasn't a case simply of two men—Russert and Libby—with different memories of a single phone call. As Zeidenberg pointed out in closing arguments, Libby told grand jurors that he didn't remember learning about Plame from Grossman, or Grenier, or Martin, or about talking of her to Schmall. Zeidenberg told the jury, "You heard witness after witness take that stand, raise their hand, take an oath, and testify about one conversation after another that they each had with Mr. Libby about Valerie Plame…during the time period that Mr. Libby claimed to the FBI and the grand jury that he had no memory of Mr. Wilson's wife."

Zeidenberg noted that Libby claimed "that he forgot nine separate conversations with eight individuals over a four-week period about Joseph Wilson's wife." In the end, as jurors in the criminal trial explained after they found Libby guilty on four counts out of five, it was impossible to believe that all eight of those witnesses were lying or mistaken, or that Libby had possibly forgotten his conversations with each and every one of them.

*

ON THAT FATEFUL FLIGHT FROM NORFOLK to D.C. following that morning's ship christening, Libby and Cheney, excluding everyone else, sat alone in the front cabin of the plane and plotted strategy as to how best to further discredit Wilson. At one point, the Vice President dictated to his Chief of Staff what he wanted said. They also spoke about which reporters Libby was going to talk to. Cheney told Libby exactly what he wanted said, what he wanted done.

After landing at Andrews Air Force Base, Libby and press aide Cathie Martin scrounged around for a telephone to use. They eventually found one in an empty lounge.

Libby was anxious, however, to get home. It was his ten-year-old son's birthday. The family had all traveled together to Norfolk, but there was a party to be thrown, cake to be eaten, pictures snapped. But he was pressed to make the telephone calls—from below and above. Questioned during the trial by Libby defense attorney Ted Wells as to whether she "nagged" Libby to make the calls, Martin said that she did not disagree with that characterization. "Bugged" was her word in front of the jury. And, of course, Libby's boss urgently wanted Libby to make the calls. Cheney wanted no one but Libby to do it; he had made that very clear to his chief of staff.

From the airport lounge, Libby spoke with *TIME* magazine reporter Matthew Cooper. Almost to the word, Libby spoke according to the script written out for him by Cheney. Later, from home, he did much the same thing with Judith Miller. Except that Libby deviated from that script (written on a card that was preserved and entered into evidence during the trial) in one major way: He discussed with both reporters that Valerie Plame worked for the CIA and that she had played a role in sending her husband to Niger.

One last compartment. An unanswered question that lingers is whether Libby decided to speak about Plame on his own, or whether he did it with the knowledge of the Vice President and direction from him. As of this writing, only Scooter Libby (and Vice President Cheney) knows what happened in that last compartment. Unless he someday talks, we may never know. Meantime, inquiring historians and enterprising journalists will surely continue digging for the truth.

At the conclusion of the trial, a jury of Scooter Libby's peers gave their verdict. This volume—which supplements an edited version of the prodigious trial transcript with reporting and commentary— is an opportunity for the public to further its collective understanding and, ultimately, to render judgment on this shrouded chapter in the presidency of George W. Bush.

Murray Waas
Washington, D.C.
April 13, 2007

INDICTMENT

IN THE UNITED STATES DISTRICT COURT FOR
THE DISTRICT OF COLUMBIA

Holding a Criminal Term

Grand Jury Sworn in on October 31, 2003

UNITED STATES OF AMERICA v. I. LEWIS LIBBY,
also known as "SCOOTER LIBBY"

Count 1: Obstruction of Justice (18 U.S.C. Section 1503)

Counts 2-3: False Statements (18 U.S.C. Section 1001(a)(2))

Counts 4-5: Perjury (18 U.S.C. Section 1623)

COUNT ONE
(Obstruction of Justice)

THE GRAND JURY CHARGES:

1. At times material to this indictment:

Defendant's Employment and Responsibilities

a. Beginning on or about January 20, 2001, and continuing through the date of this indictment, defendant I. LEWIS LIBBY, also known as "SCOOTER LIBBY," was employed as Assistant to the President of the United States, Chief of Staff to the Vice President of the United States, and Assistant to the Vice President for National Security Affairs. In the course of his work, LIBBY had frequent access to classified information and frequently spoke with officials of the U.S. intelligence community, as well as other government officials, regarding sensitive national security matters.

b. In connection with his role as a senior government official with responsibilities for national security matters, LIBBY held security clearances entitling him to access to classified information. As a person with such clearances, LIBBY was obligated by applicable laws and regulations, including Title 18, United States Code, Section 793, and Executive Order 12958 (as modified by Executive Order 13292), not to disclose classified information to persons not authorized to receive such information, and otherwise to exercise proper care to safeguard classified information against unauthorized disclosure. On or about January 23, 2001, LIBBY executed a written "Classified Information Nondisclosure Agreement," stating in part that "I understand and accept that by being granted access to classified information, special confidence and trust shall be placed in me by the United States Government," and that

"I have been advised that the unauthorized disclosure, unauthorized retention, or negligent handling of classified information by me could cause damage or irreparable injury to the United States or could be used to advantage by a foreign nation."

The Central Intelligence Agency

c. The Central Intelligence Agency (CIA) was an agency of the United States whose mission was to collect, produce, and disseminate intelligence and counterintelligence information to officers and departments of the United States government, including the President, the National Security Council, and the Joint Chiefs of Staff.

d. The responsibilities of certain CIA employees required that their association with the CIA be kept secret; as a result, the fact that these individuals were employed by the CIA was classified. Disclosure of the fact that such individuals were employed by the CIA had the potential to damage the national security in ways that ranged from preventing the future use of those individuals in a covert capacity, to compromising intelligence-gathering methods and operations, and endangering the safety of CIA employees and those who dealt with them.

Joseph Wilson and Valerie Plame Wilson

e. Joseph Wilson ("Wilson") was a former career State Department official who had held a variety of posts, including United States Ambassador. In 2002, after an inquiry to the CIA by the Vice President concerning certain intelligence reporting, the CIA decided on its own initiative to send Wilson to the country of Niger to investigate allegations involving Iraqi efforts to acquire uranium yellowcake, a processed form of uranium ore. Wilson orally reported his findings to the CIA upon his return.

f. Joseph Wilson was married to Valerie Plame Wilson ("Valerie Wilson"). At all relevant times from January 1, 2002 through July 2003, Valerie Wilson was employed by the CIA, and her employment status was classified. Prior to July 14, 2003, Valerie Wilson's affiliation with the CIA was not common knowledge outside the intelligence community.

Events Leading up to July 2003

2. On or about January 28, 2003, President George W. Bush delivered his State of the Union address which included sixteen words asserting that "The British government has learned that Saddam Hussein recently sought significant quantities of uranium from Africa."

3. On May 6, 2003, *The New York Times* published a column by Nicholas Kristof which disputed the accuracy of the "sixteen words" in the State of the Union address. The column reported that, following a request from the Vice President's office for an investigation of allegations that Iraq sought to buy uranium from Niger, an unnamed former ambassador was sent on a trip to Niger in 2002 to investigate the allegations. According to the column, the ambassador reported back to the CIA and State Department in early 2002 that the allegations were unequivocally wrong and based on forged documents.

4. On or about May 29, 2003, in the White House, LIBBY asked an Under Secretary of State ("Under Secretary") for information concerning the unnamed ambassador's travel to Niger to investigate claims about Iraqi efforts to acquire uranium yellowcake. The Under Secretary thereafter directed the State Department's Bureau of Intelligence and Research to prepare a report concerning the ambassador and his trip. The Under Secretary provided LIBBY with interim oral reports in late May and early June 2003, and advised LIBBY that Wilson was the former ambassador who took the trip.

5. On or about June 9, 2003, a number of classified documents from the CIA were faxed to the Office of the Vice President to the personal attention of LIBBY and another person in the Office of the Vice President. The faxed documents, which were marked as classified, discussed, among other things, Wilson and his trip to Niger, but did not mention Wilson by name. After receiving these documents, LIBBY and one or more other persons in the Office of the Vice President handwrote the names "Wilson" and "Joe Wilson" on the documents.

6. On or about June 11 or 12, 2003, the Under Secretary of State orally advised LIBBY in the White House that, in sum and substance, Wilson's wife worked at the CIA and that State Department personnel were saying that Wilson's wife was involved in the planning of his trip.

7. On or about June 11, 2003, LIBBY spoke with a senior officer of the CIA to ask about the origin and circumstances of Wilson's trip, and was advised by the CIA officer that Wilson's wife worked at the CIA and was believed to be responsible for sending Wilson on the trip.

8. Prior to June 12, 2003, *Washington Post* reporter Walter Pincus contacted the Office of the Vice President in connection with a story he was writing about Wilson's trip. LIBBY participated in discussions in the Office of the Vice President concerning how to respond to Pincus.

9. On or about June 12, 2003, LIBBY was advised by the Vice President of the United States that Wilson's wife worked at the Central Intelligence Agency in the Counter Proliferation Division. LIBBY understood that the Vice President had learned this information from the CIA.

10. On June 12, 2003, *The Washington Post* published an article by reporter Walter Pincus about Wilson's trip to Niger, which described Wilson as a retired ambassador but not by name, and reported that the CIA had sent him to Niger after an aide to the Vice President raised questions about purported Iraqi efforts to acquire uranium. Pincus's article questioned the accuracy of the "sixteen words," and stated that the retired ambassador had reported to the CIA that the uranium purchase story was false.

11. On or about June 14, 2003, LIBBY met with a CIA briefer. During their conversation he expressed displeasure that CIA officials were making comments to reporters critical of the Vice President's office, and discussed with the briefer, among other things, "Joe Wilson" and his wife "Valerie Wilson," in the context of Wilson's trip to Niger.

12. On or about June 19, 2003, an article appeared in *The New Republic* magazine online entitled "The First Casualty: The Selling of the Iraq War." Among other things, the article questioned the "sixteen words" and stated that following a request for information from the Vice President, the CIA had asked an unnamed ambassador to travel to Niger to investigate allegations that Iraq had sought uranium from Niger. The article included a quotation attributed to the unnamed ambassador alleging that administration officials "knew the Niger story was a flat-out lie." The article also was critical of how the administration, including the Office of the Vice President, portrayed intelligence concerning Iraqi capabilities with regard to weapons of mass destruction, and accused the administration of suppressing dissent from the intelligence agencies on this topic.

13. Shortly after publication of the article in *The New Republic,* LIBBY spoke by telephone with his then Principal Deputy and discussed the article. That official asked LIBBY whether information about Wilson's trip could be shared with the press to rebut the allegations that the Vice President had sent Wilson. LIBBY responded that there would be complications at the CIA in disclosing that information publicly, and that he could not discuss the matter on a non-secure telephone line.

14. On or about June 23, 2003, LIBBY met with *New York Times* reporter Judith Miller. During this meeting LIBBY was critical of the CIA, and disparaged what he termed "selective leaking" by the CIA concerning intelligence matters. In discussing the CIA's handling of Wilson's trip to Niger, LIBBY informed her that Wilson's wife might work at a bureau of the CIA.

The July 6 "Op Ed" Article by Wilson

15. On July 6, 2003, *The New York Times* published an Op-Ed article by Wilson entitled "What I Didn't Find in Africa." Also on July 6, 2003, *The Washington Post* published an article about Wilson's 2002 trip to Niger, which article was based in part upon an interview of Wilson. Also on July 6, Wilson appeared as a guest on the television interview show *Meet the Press.* In his Op-Ed article and interviews in print and on television, Wilson asserted, among other things, that he had taken a trip to Niger at the request of the CIA in February 2002 to investigate allegations that Iraq had sought or obtained uranium yellowcake from Niger, and that he doubted Iraq had obtained uranium from Niger recently, for a number of reasons. Wilson stated that he believed, based on his understanding of government procedures, that the Office of the Vice President was advised of the results of his trip.

LIBBY's Actions Following Wilson's July 6 "Op Ed" Column

16. On or about July 7, 2003, LIBBY had lunch with the then White House Press Secretary and advised the Press Secretary that Wilson's wife worked at the CIA and noted that such information was not widely known.

17. On or about the morning of July 8, 2003, LIBBY met with *New York Times* reporter Judith Miller. When the conversation turned to the subject of Joseph Wilson, LIBBY asked that the information LIBBY provided on the topic of Wilson be attributed to a "former Hill staffer" rather than to a "senior administration official," as had been the understanding with respect to other information that LIBBY provided to Miller during this meeting. LIBBY thereafter discussed with Miller Wilson's trip and criticized the CIA reporting concerning Wilson's trip. During this discussion, LIBBY advised Miller of his belief that Wilson's wife worked for the CIA.

18. Also on or about July 8, 2003, LIBBY met with the Counsel to the Vice President in an anteroom outside the Vice President's Office. During their brief conversation, LIBBY asked the Counsel to the Vice President, in sum and substance, what paperwork there would be at the CIA if an employee's spouse undertook an overseas trip.

19. Not earlier than June 2003, but on or before July 8, 2003, the Assistant to the Vice President for Public Affairs learned from another government official that Wilson's wife worked at the CIA, and advised LIBBY of this information.

20. On or about July 10, 2003, LIBBY spoke to NBC Washington Bureau Chief Tim Russert to complain about press coverage of LIBBY by an MSNBC reporter. LIBBY did not discuss Wilson's wife with Russert.

21. On or about July 10 or July 11, 2003, LIBBY spoke to a senior official in the White House ("Official A") who advised LIBBY of a conversation Official A had earlier that week with columnist Robert Novak in which Wilson's wife was discussed as a CIA employee involved in Wilson's trip. LIBBY was advised by Official A that Novak would be writing a story about Wilson's wife.

22. On or about July 12, 2003, LIBBY flew with the Vice President and others to and from Norfolk, Virginia, on Air Force Two. On his return trip, LIBBY discussed with other officials aboard the plane what LIBBY should say in response to certain pending media inquiries, including questions from *TIME* reporter Matthew Cooper.

23. On or about July 12, 2003, in the afternoon, LIBBY spoke by telephone to Cooper, who asked whether LIBBY had heard that Wilson's wife was involved in sending Wilson on the trip to Niger. LIBBY confirmed to Cooper, without elaboration or qualification, that he had heard this information too.

24. On or about July 12, 2003, in the late afternoon, LIBBY spoke by telephone with Judith Miller of *The New York Times* and discussed Wilson's wife, and that she worked at the CIA.

The Criminal Investigation

25. On or about September 26, 2003, the Department of Justice authorized the Federal Bureau of Investigation (FBI) to commence a criminal investigation into the possible unauthorized disclosure of classified information regarding the disclosure of Valerie Wilson's affiliation with the CIA to various reporters in the spring of 2003.

26. As part of the criminal investigation, LIBBY was interviewed by Special Agents of the FBI on or about October 14 and November 26, 2003, each time in the presence of his counsel. During these interviews, LIBBY stated to FBI Special Agents that:

a. During a conversation with Tim Russert of *NBC News* on July 10 or 11, 2003, Russert asked LIBBY if LIBBY was aware that Wilson's wife worked for the CIA. LIBBY responded to Russert that he did not know that, and Russert replied that all the reporters knew it. LIBBY was surprised by this statement because, while speaking with Russert, LIBBY did not recall that he previously had learned about Wilson's wife's employment from the Vice President.

b. During a conversation with Matthew Cooper of *TIME* magazine on or about July 12, 2003, LIBBY told Cooper that reporters were telling the administration that Wilson's wife worked for the CIA, but that LIBBY did not know if this was true; and

c. LIBBY did not discuss Wilson's wife with *New York Times* reporter Judith Miller during a meeting with Miller on or about July 8, 2003.

27. Beginning in or about January 2004, and continuing until the date of this indictment, Grand Jury 03-3 sitting in the District of Columbia conducted an investigation ("the Grand Jury Investigation") into possible violations of federal criminal laws, including: Title 50, United States Code, Section 421 (disclosure of the identity of covert intelligence personnel); and Title 18, United States Code, Sections 793 (improper disclosure of national defense information), 1001 (false statements), 1503 (obstruction of justice), and 1623 (perjury).

28. A major focus of the Grand Jury Investigation was to determine which government officials had disclosed to the media prior to July 14, 2003 information concerning the affiliation of Valerie Wilson with the CIA, and the nature, timing, extent, and purpose of such disclosures, as well as whether any official making such a disclosure did so knowing that the employment of Valerie Wilson by the CIA was classified information.

29. During the course of the Grand Jury Investigation, the following matters, among others, were material to the Grand Jury Investigation:

a. When, and the manner and means by which, defendant LIBBY learned that Wilson's wife was employed by the CIA;

b. Whether and when LIBBY disclosed to members of the media that Wilson's wife was employed by the CIA;

c. The language used by LIBBY in disclosing any such information to the media, including whether LIBBY expressed uncertainty about the accuracy of any information he may have disclosed, or described where he obtained the information;

d. LIBBY's knowledge as to whether any information he disclosed was classified at the time he disclosed it; and

e. Whether LIBBY was candid with Special Agents of the Federal Bureau of Investigation in describing his conversations with the other government officials and the media relating to Valerie Wilson.

LIBBY's Grand Jury Testimony

30. On or about March 5 and March 24, 2004, LIBBY testified before Grand Jury 03-3.

On each occasion of LIBBY's testimony, the foreperson of the Grand Jury administered the oath to LIBBY and LIBBY swore to tell the truth in the testimony he was about to give.

31. In or about March 2004, in the District of Columbia,

I. LEWIS LIBBY, also known as "SCOOTER LIBBY,"

defendant herein, did knowingly and corruptly endeavor to influence, obstruct and impede the due administration of justice, namely proceedings before Grand Jury 03-3, by misleading and deceiving the grand jury as to when, and the manner and means by which, LIBBY acquired and subsequently disclosed to the media information concerning the employment of Valerie Wilson by the CIA.

32. It was part of the corrupt endeavor that during his grand jury testimony, defendant LIBBY made the following materially false and intentionally misleading statements and representations, in substance, under oath:

    a. When LIBBY spoke with Tim Russert of *NBC News,* on or about July 10, 2003:

        i. Russert asked LIBBY if LIBBY knew that Wilson's wife worked for the CIA, and told LIBBY that all the reporters knew it; and

        ii. At the time of this conversation, LIBBY was surprised to hear that Wilson's wife worked for the CIA;

    b. LIBBY advised Matthew Cooper of *TIME* magazine on or about July 12, 2003, that he had heard that other reporters were saying that Wilson's wife worked for the CIA, and further advised him that LIBBY did not know whether this assertion was true; and

    c. LIBBY advised Judith Miller of *The New York Times* on or about July 12, 2003 that he had heard that other reporters were saying that Wilson's wife worked for the CIA but LIBBY did not know whether that assertion was true.

33. It was further part of the corrupt endeavor that at the time defendant LIBBY made each of the above-described materially false and intentionally misleading statements and representations to the grand jury, LIBBY was aware that they were false, in that:

    a. When LIBBY spoke with Tim Russert of *NBC News* on or about July 10, 2003:

        i. Russert did not ask LIBBY if LIBBY knew that Wilson's wife worked for the CIA, nor did he tell LIBBY that all the reporters knew it; and

        ii. At the time of this conversation, LIBBY was well aware that Wilson's wife worked at the CIA; in fact, LIBBY had participated in multiple prior conversations concerning this topic, including on the following occasions:

        • In or about early June 2003, LIBBY learned from the Vice President that Wilson's wife worked for the CIA in the Counter Proliferation Division;

        • On or about June 11, 2003, LIBBY was informed by a senior CIA officer that Wilson's wife was employed by the CIA and that the idea of sending him to Niger originated with her;

        • On or about June 12, 2003, LIBBY was informed by the Under Secretary of State that Wilson's wife worked for the CIA;

        • On or about June 14, 2003, LIBBY discussed "Joe Wilson" and "Valerie Wilson" with his CIA briefer, in the context of Wilson's trip to Niger;

        • On or about June 23, 2003, LIBBY informed reporter Judith Miller that Wilson's wife might work at a bureau of the CIA;

        • On or about July 7, 2003, LIBBY advised the White House Press Secretary that Wilson's wife worked for the CIA;

        • In or about June or July 2003, and in no case later than on or about July 8, 2003, LIBBY was advised by the Assistant to the Vice President for Public Affairs that Wilson's wife worked for the CIA;

        • On or about July 8, 2003, LIBBY advised reporter Judith Miller of his belief that Wilson's wife worked at the CIA; and

  • On or about July 8, 2003, LIBBY had a discussion with the Counsel to the Office of the Vice President concerning the paperwork that would exist if a person who was sent on an overseas trip by the CIA had a spouse who worked at the CIA;

b. LIBBY did not advise Matthew Cooper, on or about July 12, 2003, that LIBBY had heard other reporters were saying that Wilson's wife worked for the CIA, nor did LIBBY advise him that LIBBY did not know whether this assertion was true; rather, LIBBY confirmed to Cooper, without qualification, that LIBBY had heard that Wilson's wife worked at the CIA; and

c. LIBBY did not advise Judith Miller, on or about July 12, 2003, that LIBBY had heard other reporters were saying that Wilson's wife worked for the CIA, nor did LIBBY advise her that LIBBY did not know whether this assertion was true;

In violation of Title 18, United States Code, Section 1503.

COUNT TWO
(False Statement)

THE GRAND JURY FURTHER CHARGES:

1. The Grand Jury realleges Paragraphs 1-26 of Count One as though fully set forth herein.

2. During the course of the criminal investigation conducted by the Federal Bureau of Investigation and the Department of Justice, the following matters, among others, were material to that investigation:

  a. When, and the manner and means by which, defendant LIBBY learned that Wilson's wife was employed by the CIA;

  b. Whether and when LIBBY disclosed to members of the media that Wilson's wife was employed by the CIA;

  c. The language used by LIBBY in disclosing any such information to the media, including whether LIBBY expressed uncertainty about the accuracy of any information he may have disclosed, or described where he obtained the information; and

  d. LIBBY's knowledge as to whether any information he disclosed was classified at the time he disclosed it.

3. On or about October 14 and November 26, 2003, in the District of Columbia,

  I. LEWIS LIBBY, also known as "SCOOTER LIBBY,"

defendant herein, did knowingly and willfully make a materially false, fictitious, and fraudulent statement and representation in a matter within the jurisdiction of the Federal Bureau of Investigation, an agency within the executive branch of the United States, in that the defendant, in response to questions posed to him by agents of the Federal Bureau of Investigation, stated that:

During a conversation with Tim Russert of *NBC News* on July 10 or 11, 2003, Russert asked LIBBY if LIBBY was aware that Wilson's wife worked for the CIA.

LIBBY responded to Russert that he did not know that, and Russert replied that all the reporters knew it. LIBBY was surprised by this statement because, while speaking with Russert, LIBBY did not recall that he previously had learned about Wilson's wife's employment from the Vice President.

4. As defendant LIBBY well knew when he made it, this statement was false in that when LIBBY spoke with Russert on or about July 10 or 11, 2003:

a. Russert did not ask LIBBY if LIBBY knew that Wilson's wife worked for the CIA, nor did he tell LIBBY that all the reporters knew it; and

b. At the time of this conversation, LIBBY was well aware that Wilson's wife worked at the CIA;

In violation of Title 18, United States Code, Section 1001(a)(2).

COUNT THREE
(False Statement)

THE GRAND JURY FURTHER CHARGES:

1. The Grand Jury realleges Paragraphs 1 and 2 of Count Two as though fully set forth herein.

2. On or about October 14 and November 26, 2003, in the District of Columbia,

I. LEWIS LIBBY, also known as "SCOOTER LIBBY,"

defendant herein, did knowingly and willfully make a materially false, fictitious, and fraudulent statement and representation in a matter within the jurisdiction of the Federal Bureau of Investigation, an agency within the executive branch of the United States, in that the defendant, in response to questions posed to him by agents of the Federal Bureau of Investigation, stated that:

During a conversation with Matthew Cooper of *TIME* magazine on July 12, 2003, LIBBY told Cooper that reporters were telling the administration that Wilson's wife worked for the CIA, but LIBBY did not know if this was true.

3. As defendant LIBBY well knew when he made it, this statement was false in that:

LIBBY did not advise Cooper on or about July 12, 2003 that reporters were telling the administration that Wilson's wife worked for the CIA, nor did LIBBY advise him that LIBBY did not know whether this was true; rather, LIBBY confirmed for Cooper, without qualification, that LIBBY had heard that Wilson's wife worked at the CIA;

In violation of Title 18, United States Code, Section 1001(a)(2).

COUNT FOUR
(Perjury)

THE GRAND JURY FURTHER CHARGES:

1. The Grand Jury realleges Paragraphs 1-30 of Count One as though fully set forth herein.

2. On or about March 5, 2004, in the District of Columbia,

I. LEWIS LIBBY, also known as "SCOOTER LIBBY,"

defendant herein, having taken an oath to testify truthfully in a proceeding before a grand jury of the United States, knowingly made a false material declaration, in that he gave the following testimony regarding a conversation that he represented he had with Tim Russert of *NBC News,* on or about July 10, 2003 (underlined portions alleged as false):

.... And then he said, you know, did you know that this—excuse me, did you know that Ambassador Wilson's wife works at the CIA? And I was a little taken aback by that. I remember being taken aback by it. And I said—he may have said a little more but that was—he said that. And I said, no, I don't know that. And I said, no, I don't know that intentionally because I didn't want him to take anything I was saying as in any way confirming what he said, because at that point in time I did not recall that I had ever known, and I thought this is something that he was telling me that I was first learning. And so I said, no, I don't know that because I want to be very careful not to confirm it for him, so that he didn't take my statement as confirmation for him.

Now, I had said earlier in the conversation, which I omitted to tell you, that this— you know, as always, Tim, our discussion is off-the-record if that's okay with you, and he said, that's fine. So then he said—I said—he said, sorry—he, Mr. Russert said to me, did you know that Ambassador Wilson's wife, or his wife, works at the CIA? And I said, no, I don't know that. And then he said, yeah—yes, all the reporters know it. And I said, again, I don't know that. I just wanted to be clear that I wasn't confirming anything for him on this. And you know, I was struck by what he was saying in that he thought it was an important fact, but I didn't ask him anymore about it because I didn't want to be digging in on him, and he then moved on and finished the conversation, something like that.

3. In truth and fact, as LIBBY well knew when he gave this testimony, it was false in that:

a. Russert did not ask LIBBY if LIBBY knew that Wilson's wife worked for the CIA, nor did he tell LIBBY that all the reporters knew it; and

b. At the time of this conversation, LIBBY was well aware that Wilson's wife worked at the CIA;

In violation of Title 18, United States Code, Section 1623.

COUNT FIVE
(Perjury)

THE GRAND JURY FURTHER CHARGES:

1. The Grand Jury realleges Paragraphs 1-30 of Count One as though fully set forth herein.

2. On or about March 5, 2004 and March 24, 2004, in the District of Columbia,

I. LEWIS LIBBY, also known as "SCOOTER LIBBY,"

defendant herein, having taken an oath to testify truthfully in a proceeding before a grand jury of the United States, knowingly made a false material declaration, in that he gave the following testimony regarding his conversations with reporters concerning the employment of Joseph Wilson's wife by the CIA (underlined portions alleged as false):

a. Testimony Given on or about March 5, 2004 Regarding a Conversation With Matthew Cooper on or About July 12, 2003:

> Q. And it's your specific recollection that when you told Cooper about Wilson's wife working at the CIA, you attributed that fact to what reporters—
>
> A. <u>Yes.</u>
>
> Q. —plural, were saying. Correct?
>
> A. <u>I was very clear to say reporters are telling us that because in my mind I still didn't know it as a fact. I thought I was—all I had was this information that was coming in from the reporters.</u>
>
> . . . .
>
> Q. And at the same time you have a specific recollection of telling him, you don't know whether it's true or not, you're just telling him what reporters are saying?
>
> A. <u>Yes, that's correct, sir. And I said, reporters are telling us that, I don't know if it's true. I was careful about that because among other things, I wanted to be clear I didn't know Mr. Wilson. I don't know—I think I said, I don't know if he has a wife, but this is what we're hearing.</u>

b. Testimony Given on or about March 24, 2004 Regarding Conversations With Reporters:

> Q. And let me ask you this directly. Did the fact that you knew that the law could turn, the law as to whether a crime was committed, could turn on where you learned the information from, affect your account for the FBI when you told them that you were telling reporters Wilson's wife worked at the CIA but your source was a reporter rather than the Vice President?
>
> A. <u>No, it's a fact. It was a fact, that's what I told the reporters.</u>
>
> Q. And you're, you're certain as you sit here today that every reporter you told that Wilson's wife worked at the CIA, you sourced it back to other reporters?
>
> A. <u>Yes, sir,</u> because it was important for what I was saying and because it was—that's what—<u>that's how I did it.</u>
>
> . . . .
>
> Q. The next set of questions from the Grand Jury are—concern this fact. If you did not understand the information about Wilson's wife to have been classified and didn't understand it when you heard it from Mr. Russert, why was it that you were so deliberate to make sure that you told other reporters that reporters were saying it and not assert it as something you knew?
>
> A. I want—I didn't want to—I didn't know if it was true and I didn't want people—I didn't want the reporters to think it was true because

I said it. I—all I had was that reporters are telling us that, and by that I wanted them to understand it wasn't coming from me and that it might not be true. Reporters write things that aren't true sometimes, or get things that aren't true. So I wanted to be clear they didn't, they didn't think it was me saying it. I didn't know it was true and I wanted them to understand that. Also, it was important to me to let them know that because what I was telling them was that I don't know Mr. Wilson. We didn't ask for his mission. That I didn't see his report. Basically, we didn't know anything about him until this stuff came out in June. And among the other things, I didn't know he had a wife. That was one of the things I said to Mr. Cooper. I don't know if he's married. And so I wanted to be very clear about all this stuff that I didn't, I didn't know about him. And the only thing I had, I thought at the time, was what reporters are telling us.

. . . .

Well, talking to the other reporters about it, I don't see as a crime. What I said to the other reporters is what, you know—I told a couple reporters what other reporters had told us, and I don't see that as a crime.

3. In truth and fact, as LIBBY well knew when he gave this testimony, it was false in that LIBBY did not advise Matthew Cooper or other reporters that LIBBY had heard other reporters were saying that Wilson's wife worked for the CIA, nor did LIBBY advise Cooper or other reporters that LIBBY did not know whether this assertion was true;

In violation of Title 18, United States Code, Section 1623.

A TRUE BILL:
FOREPERSON
PATRICK J. FITZGERALD
Special Counsel

JANUARY 23, 2007

OPENING STATEMENT ON BEHALF
OF THE GOVERNMENT

MR. FITZGERALD: MAY IT PLEASE THE COURT, the defense team, the government team, members of the jury. Good morning.

It's Sunday, July 6th, 2003. It's the last day of a three-day Fourth of July weekend.... The fireworks are over, except a different kind of fireworks are about to begin. When people wake up, they open up the Sunday paper, the Sunday *New York Times*. On the page opposite the editorial page appears a column, a column written by a man named Joseph Wilson.

Wilson served his career in the State Department and rose to rank of ambassador. And in this column he made an explosive charge. Mr. Wilson claimed that he had personal knowledge that would indicate to him that the Bush administration may have twisted the intelligence used to justify the war in Iraq. Mr. Wilson leveled a direct attack on White House credibility, an attack on the Office of the Vice President in particular.

Mr. Wilson's allegations were not limited to the Sunday *New York Times* that day. He was interviewed for a story in *The Washington Post*, and he appeared on a national TV program, NBC's *Meet the Press*. In all three places, Mr. Wilson made the same charges about the administration twisting the intelligence to justify the war.

These claims came in the fourth month of the war in Iraq, the fourth month when weapons of mass destruction had not been found. Coming as they did, they ignited a media firestorm. At first, the White House was stunned. A day later, the White House admitted that some of the things it said before the war about Iraq's efforts to get nuclear weapons should not have been said.

But then the White House began to push back. People in the White House, and particularly people in the Office of the Vice President, looked at Wilson's claim and said, "You know what, we don't agree. We don't think all the facts are there. We don't think all the logic is there. We think some of his accusations are unfounded and unfair." So they pushed back. And people in the White House said things to the newspapers, using their names, saying, "Here is why we disagree with Wilson."

But some people pushed back in a different way. They said things about Wilson to the newspapers on the understanding that the newspapers wouldn't print their names. And in the shooting back and forth between Wilson and the White House, at one point Wilson's wife got dragged into it. Some officials told some reporters that Wilson's wife worked at the CIA, and some reporters printed that in the paper.

As a result of those disclosures, a very serious criminal investigation began. First, the FBI, and then later a Grand Jury, had to look into whether the laws protecting classified information, and whether the laws protecting covert CIA employees had been broken by any government officials who talked to reporters about Wilson's wife working at the CIA.

The FBI and the Grand Jury had an important but tough job...They had to figure out who were these officials who knew that Wilson's wife worked at the CIA? How did they learn it? What did they learn? What did they understand about the information? And, more importantly, what did they do with it? Did they talk to reporters about it? What did they say? Why? Did they want the story to appear in the paper?

That's what they had to do. To make it simple, they had to find the truth.

This case is about how the defendant, "Scooter" Libby, then the Chief of Staff to the Vice President of the United States, obstructed that search for truth. It's about how the defendant obstructed the search for truth by lying repeatedly to the FBI while it was doing its investigation. It's about how the defendant appeared before a federal Grand Jury in this courthouse, raised his right hand, took an oath, swore to tell the truth, and then violated that oath repeatedly by lying to the Grand Jury both about how he had learned that Wilson's wife worked at the CIA and what he did with that information. The evidence in this case will show that the defendant lied repeatedly both to the FBI and the Grand Jury.

In short, what the evidence will show is that the defendant learned that Wilson's wife worked at the CIA directly from the Vice President himself, and that the defendant discussed the fact that Wilson's wife worked at the CIA with multiple government officials in June and July 2003, and he also talked to more than one reporter on more than one occasion about Wilson's wife working at the CIA, and also gave the information to the White House Press Secretary, a man whose job it was to talk to the press.

When the FBI and the Grand Jury asked questions about what he did, the defendant lied. He made up a story. He told the FBI and the Grand Jury that all he told reporters was stuff he had heard from other reporters, rumors he was told that he didn't even know if they were true.

In fact, you will learn that the defendant went so far as to say that he first learned—or learned it as if it were new—on Thursday, July 10, 2003, from Tim Russert that Wilson's wife worked at the CIA. He said he was startled by this information and taken aback.

You will also learn through the course of this trial, that on Monday, July 7th, the defendant told the White House Press Secretary, Ari Fleischer, that he had hush-hush information that Wilson's wife worked at the CIA.

On the morning of Tuesday, July 8th, the defendant told *New York Times* reporter Judith Miller that Wilson's wife worked at the CIA. You can't learn something startling on Thursday that you are giving out on Monday and Tuesday.

How do we get to the point where the Chief of Staff to the Vice President of the United States is lying repeatedly to the FBI and to a Grand Jury? Well, that's the story of this case.

. . . You will hear a fair amount of names and a fair amount of dates. It's not important that you get them exactly right as you listen to the opening. We will spend plenty enough time together in this courtroom with the witnesses before you that you will figure out the names and dates later. So think of this as [if you] are about to take a trip. Someone gives you a heads-up beforehand—look out for this landmark, look out for that landmark.

Well, to really understand the context of this case, we have to go back from July 2003 several months before, to almost exactly this time in January 2003.

…[On] January 28th, [2003], President Bush delivered his annual State of the Union address. Every time a President delivers the State of [the] Union address, it's important. People pay attention to what he has to say. But in 2003, it was especially important. The possible war in Iraq loomed large. People were wondering, are we going to war? Should we go to war?

In the 2003 State of the Union address, President Bush laid out the case for war, why it was that we needed to go to war to protect our country from Iraq. And part of that case was a claim by the President that Iraq was believed to have weapons of mass destruction and was trying to get more, including nuclear weapons.

During the course of the State of the Union address, the President made one particular statement, a sentence that had sixteen words in it that have since become known as "the sixteen words." And those sixteen words are up here. President Bush stated, "The British government has learned that Saddam Hussein recently sought significant quantities of uranium from Africa."

Now, we all know that, following the State of the Union, in March 2003 the war in Iraq began. As the days passed, then the weeks passed, then the months passed, the stockpiles of weapons of mass destruction were not found. People began asking questions: When will they be found? Will they be found? Where are they? Where were they? Were they ever there? If we got it wrong and they weren't there, was that a mistake? Did people slant the intelligence? Did people lie about it?

Let me stop right there and remind you of something very, very important. You won't be asked to decide nor consider in this case whether or not the war in Iraq was a good thing or a bad thing, or whether or not the case made for the war in Iraq was made properly or not. That's just the background of this case.

You will be asked to decide whether or not the government proves beyond a reasonable doubt the defendant's guilt of the five charges in the indictment. You need to understand the background.

So now it's…early May and June 2003. And the press accounts began to report a trip taken by a former ambassador over to a country in Africa, Niger, where this former ambassador went to investigate whether or not Iraq had obtained uranium from Niger. These press accounts were describing Joe Wilson, but they didn't name him.

In these press accounts, it was alleged that the trip was taken at the request of the Vice President, [by] this former ambassador…[who] proved…Iraq didn't obtain uranium from Niger, and people wondered how those sixteen words could be said in the State of the Union.

This got some attention. People in the government began asking questions. Who is this former ambassador? What did he do? Where did he go? Who sent him? The defendant was one of those people asking those questions. And because he was focused on this trip by this former ambassador, you will learn that in the course of June 2003, the defendant had multiple conversations where he learned that the former ambassador was Joseph Wilson, and that the ambassador's wife worked at the CIA.

The first conversation we will discuss was a conversation between the defendant and the Vice President in the Vice President's office. Sometime shortly before June 12th, 2003—I think we will put it on the calendar as around June 11, but it was just before a June 12th *Washington Post* article—there had been questions in *The Washington Post* about this trip. The defendant met with the Vice President. The Vice President told the defendant that he had learned that this former ambassador had a wife who worked at the CIA in the Counterproliferation Division, meaning she worked against the spread of nuclear weapons.

The defendant understood that the Vice President had gotten this information from the CIA itself, perhaps from the director of the CIA himself. And the defendant wrote it down. He wrote in his notes that the Vice President had told him that the wife worked in the Counterproliferation Division.

Marc Grossman talks to the defendant on the side at a White House meeting. He tells the defendant what he learned, that [the wife of] the former ambassador, Joseph Wilson,... worked at the CIA.

At about the same time, the defendant had another conversation with the number-three man in the State Department who will be the first witness at this trial, Marc Grossman.

Marc Grossman had also seen these news stories and was asked by the defendant, "What do you know about this former ambassador who took a trip?" Grossman is number three at the State Department. He is scratching his head. He can't figure out, "how come I don't know about this trip? I'm with the State Department. I would think I would know if a former ambassador traveled."

The defendant, Chief of Staff to the Vice President, is asking him to find out. So he finds out. He comes to learn that this former ambassador is Joseph Wilson. Marc Grossman knows Joseph Wilson. They were both in the State Department together. They were both ambassadors to different countries at the same time.

He does some further investigating, and on June 11th or June 12th, Marc Grossman talks to the defendant on the side at a White House meeting. He tells the defendant what he learned, that [the wife of] the former ambassador, Joseph Wilson, . . . worked at the CIA.

You will also learn of another conversation. A high-ranking CIA official, Bob Grenier, the Iraq mission manager at the CIA, was called by the defendant also in the same time frame, June 11th. The defendant was trying to get answers so that he could respond to press inquiries about this trip.

The defendant had called up Grenier to find out why this ambassador was sent on this trip. Was it only because the Vice President had asked questions? Or did other people—other cabinet people—ask questions? And, if so, could the CIA make a statement to the press indicating that it wasn't just because of the Vice President that this ambassador took a trip?

So Mr. Grenier set out to find out what he could. Mr. Grenier did not get back to the defendant fast enough. At a late afternoon meeting at the CIA, Mr. Grenier was pulled out of the meeting because the defendant wanted his answers. Mr. Grenier told the defendant that he had learned that the ambassador, Joe Wilson, had a wife who worked at the CIA and that she worked in the unit responsible for sending Mr. Wilson on the trip.

Now, in addition to speaking about Wilson's wife working at the CIA with the Vice President, the number three at the State Department, and this high-ranking official at the CIA, you will also learn that the defendant learned about Wilson's wife working at the CIA from a woman named Cathie Martin. She was the Assistant to the Vice President for Public Affairs, the main Public Affairs person in the Office of the Vice President.

The date of this conversation is unclear, but I think by the end of the trial, the evidence will show that this likely occurred right around the same time in June. It occurred no later than early July. Cathie Martin learned from the CIA that Wilson's wife worked there. She went straight to the Vice President and the defendant together and told them that she had just learned that Wilson's wife worked at the CIA.

And, finally, you will learn about a fifth conversation with a government official in June 2003, involving the defendant discussing Wilson's wife. You will learn that every day, or six days out of the seven days of the week, the defendant received a morning intelligence briefing. Someone from the CIA would come to the defendant, spend 40 minutes with the defendant or the defendant and the Vice President together, and brief them on what the morning intelligence showed. That person is called the morning intelligence briefer. Craig Schmall was the morning intelligence briefer assigned to the defendant in June 2003.

On Saturday, June 14th, 2003, the defendant and Mr. Schmall were alone at a briefing, and the defendant discussed with Mr. Schmall this trip to Niger, this ambassador, Joe Wilson, and Valerie Wilson by name. In short, you will learn, on multiple occasions in June 2003, the defendant was focused on learning about this ambassador's trip. He had learned from high-level government people that Wilson's wife worked at the CIA.

You will also learn that, in June 2003, the defendant also discussed Wilson's wife working at the CIA with someone outside the government.

June 23rd: Judith Miller, then a reporter for *The New York Times*, met with the defendant in his office in the Old Executive Office Building. The defendant was talking about the controversy in the press about the intelligence supporting the war. The defendant was complaining that he thought the CIA was leaking unfairly. And during the course of the conversation, the defendant discussed with reporter Miller his view of Joseph Wilson. And during that conversation, he mentioned that Wilson's wife worked at the CIA.

Now, to be very clear, the defendant never wanted to see his name in print…If information he gave was used in a story, it wouldn't be attributed to "Scooter" Libby. It wouldn't be attributed to the Vice President's Chief of Staff. It wouldn't be attributed to the Office of [the] Vice President. It would be attributed to "a senior administration official."

Now, there things stood in June 2003. And then again, we get to July 6th, 2003, when Joseph Wilson appeared everywhere, in the newspapers and on TV but as you will see, other people in the government, including the defendant, had been focused on Joe Wilson before.

On July 6th, 2003, the op-ed appeared in *The New York Times*…The title was "What I Didn't Find in Africa." It was by Joseph Wilson. Mr. Wilson said, "I took this trip over to Niger to investigate what I could about whether or not Iraq had obtained uranium from Niger." Uranium is used to make nuclear weapons.

He said he did some investigation and became convinced that it was impossible for Iraq actually to have obtained uranium from Niger.

He said he took this trip because he understood that there had been a question raised by the Vice President. He said that he didn't write a report about his trip, but he told both the CIA and the State Department what he had found. Mr. Wilson said, "I assume that if the Vice President asked a question, they gave him an answer." So he assumed that the Vice President had been told his findings and wondered aloud how it was that if the Vice President knew what he had found in Niger, the President could be saying the sixteen words in the State of the Union.

WHEN THIS HAPPENED, it was a firestorm. The sixteen words were heard by the country in January 2003, but now everyone was paying attention to the sixteen words in July 2003.

In fact, within a day, the White House did something extraordinary. They issued a statement saying that the sixteen words should not have been in the State of the Union address in the first place.

Now, the evidence will show if the defendant was focused on the issue of Wilson . . . in June 2003, he became really focused on it after July 6th, 2003, when [Wilson's] article appeared in the paper. And you could understand why. The evidence will show that Mr. Wilson was accusing the Vice President of allowing the President to mislead the country. It was a direct attack on the credibility of the President and the Vice President. And it was on an issue that could not be more important: Someone being accused of lying about the justification for war.

The Vice President took note of this article. The defendant took note of this article literally. You will learn that the Vice President cut out from the newspaper a paper copy of the Wilson op-ed in *The New York Times,* underlined it and wrote handwritten notes at the top of the page of his thoughts. And he kept that paper copy . . . It was found months later in the office of the Vice President. You will also learn that the defendant had…a printed-out copy of the same Wilson op-ed, and he underlined it. They were frustrated by what Wilson was saying.

The Vice President wasn't going to take it lying down, nor was the defendant. The defendant was the Vice President's right-hand man. He was his Chief of Staff, and he also had the job of National Security Advisor to the Vice President. The defendant worked very, very closely with the Vice President on many issues, including the war in Iraq. Wilson's charges hit close to home.

You will see that the defendant spent significant time in the period following July 6th working on issues involving Wilson, the sixteen words controversy, and how to handle the press. At times, the defendant directly inserted himself in dealing with the press at the direction of the Vice President. Day, after day, after day, after day, he focused on this controversy.

LET'S GO THROUGH THE CALENDAR. Let's start on July 7th, the Monday following Wilson's op-ed. That's the same day that the White House issued a statement saying that the sixteen words should not have been in the State of the Union.

That day, the defendant had lunch with Ari Fleischer, then the White House Press Secretary. Ari Fleischer was about to...go overseas to Africa with the President and a number of other officials on an official delegation to various African countries. Ari Fleischer would be traveling with...the reporters who cover the White House, overseas to Africa. It was also Fleischer's last week in the White House. He was going into private business.

Over lunch, the defendant and Ari Fleischer talked. They talked about what Ari Fleischer would do once he left the White House. They talked about football. They are both Miami Dolphins fans. And they talked about Joseph Wilson.

And during the lunch, the defendant told Ari Fleischer that he had some information that was hush-hush. And, remember, he is talking to the White House Press Secretary, someone whose job it is to talk to the press. The defendant told Ari Fleischer that Wilson's wife worked at the CIA.

The seed that was planted worked. You will learn that, in Africa, Ari Fleischer had conversations with reporters about Wilson's wife that he should not have had.

Let's turn to the next...morning. On Tuesday, July 8th, the defendant met with reporter Judith Miller of *The New York Times* once again, this time not in his office in the Old Executive Office building, but outside the White House complex. They met at the St. Regis Hotel in the dining room and spent an hour or two together talking.

The defendant talked to reporter Judith Miller about various information concerning intelligence that was used to support the war in Iraq, and the defendant shared that information with the reporter on the grounds that he be treated as a senior administration official. If she published it, it wouldn't say "Scooter" Libby; it would say "senior administration official."

But then the conversation turned to Joseph Wilson, and the defendant asked to change the rules. "Senior administration official" wasn't good enough. The defendant asked to be treated as a "former hill staffer" because, years ago, the defendant once worked on the staff in Congress. With the understanding that the defendant would be treated as a former hill staffer, the defendant discussed Wilson. During that conversation, he once again mentioned to reporter Judith Miller that Wilson's wife worked at the CIA.

Now, in addition to this conversation [at his] Monday afternoon lunch with Ari Fleischer, and Tuesday morning with Judith Miller, you will learn about a third conversation. The defendant spoke with a man by the name of David Addington. He was a lawyer—the lawyer in the Office of the Vice President. His title was Counsel to the Vice President... Mr. Addington had started his career as a lawyer over at the CIA.

During this week, probably on July 8th, the defendant talked to Mr. Addington in a small office outside the Vice President's office in the West Wing of the White House. And the defendant asked Mr. Addington what paperwork there would be if someone who worked at the CIA sent a spouse on a trip.

Now, to be clear, the defendant didn't mention the name Wilson, Joe Wilson, or Valerie Wilson to Mr. Addington, but he asked about a person at the CIA sending a spouse on a trip during the very week that the Wilson controversy raged.

. . . [I]n addition to these conversations, you will learn the defendant was very focused this week on a statement that was to be issued by then Director of the CIA George Tenet. If you remember, earlier in the week, you have this extraordinary statement where the White House says that there were sixteen words . . . in the State of the Union address that should not have been said. Now, if people thought the media controversy would die down with that statement, it did the opposite. People began asking the question, well, if the President shouldn't have said it, how did it get in there? Who is responsible? Who checks these things? Whose fault [is it]?

It was understood that week that Director Tenet of the CIA would accept responsibility. And the defendant and the Vice President were very focused on what Director Tenet would say. They wanted Director Tenet to make a full statement. They wanted him to make it promptly. And they wanted the statement to be as full as possible in making clear that Tenet was responsible, and also in making clear that the President and Vice President were not . . .

Now, during the week, you will learn, in fact, that people in the White House were letting the defendant know where the statement stood, what the drafts looked like, what Director Tenet was expected to say. The defendant was pushing to put additional language into Director Tenet's statement to better protect the President and the Vice President.

Now, during... this same week, there is an aside. The defendant ends up calling Tim Russert on July 10th, the Thursday. That's important for two reasons. The first one I will discuss now, the second reason later.

During the week, there was lots of coverage... in the newspapers, [on] TV, and radio about this controversy about what Mr. Wilson said. But one of the shows that focused a lot on the Wilson controversy and focused on criticizing the Vice President and even the defendant by name was a show called *Hardball*. It's a show on MSNBC The host is Chris Matthews.

You may or may not know about the *Hardball* show or Chris Matthews, but the evidence will show that the defendant knew about it in July 2003. He kept up-to-date on transcripts of the *Hardball* show. He was very upset about what Mr.

Matthews was saying about him and the Vice President. He thought it was unfair, and he was ticked off.

So he picked up the phone and he called Tim Russert. Now, Tim Russert is host of *Meet the Press.* He appears on the *Today* show. He is also the Washington bureau chief for *NBC News.* He is not directly in line with Chris Matthews. He is not his boss and doesn't control him. But the defendant thought if he called up Tim Russert and let him know how upset he was, that maybe Tim Russert could help out with what Chris Matthews was saying.

It didn't work.

Well, Friday, July 11th rolls around, and finally the Tenet statement comes out. It comes out late in the evening on Friday. One of [the] things that, if you don't know, you will learn, is that the last thing you want to do if you want to get attention for a big press statement is to issue it late in the day on a Friday before the weekend starts. Not good timing.

...the Tenet statement comes out. It comes out late in the evening on Friday. One of [the] things that, if you don't know, you will learn, is that the last thing you want to do if you want to get attention for a big press statement is to issue it late in the day on a Friday...

The defendant was frustrated by the timing. He thought it should be out earlier in the week and certainly not when the weekend began. The defendant and the Vice President were frustrated by what it said. They didn't think it went far enough.

Meanwhile, other reporters were still asking questions. One of the reporters was Matt Cooper of *TIME* magazine. Matt Cooper had e-mailed Cathie Martin, the woman I told you who was in charge of public affairs in the Office of the Vice President, and e-mailed her questions on July 11th about this whole controversy, about uranium, about Niger, and about the role of the Office of the Vice President.

Cathie Martin told Matt Cooper, "I will try to get you an answer tomorrow, Saturday." Saturday is the closing day for magazines. Things go into print. If you can make the Saturday deadline, you can make the Monday morning magazine.

So July 12th rolls around. It's a Saturday. It's actually an enjoyable Saturday morning. The Vice President has been invited to Norfolk, Virginia, to...commission a ship, the USS *Ronald Reagan,* an aircraft carrier. The Vice President takes the defendant, other officials, and people's families down to Norfolk, Virginia, for the ceremony.

On the way back, Cathie Martin has this e-mail...from Matt Cooper of *TIME* magazine asking these questions. She shows it to the defendant. They sit in the back of the plane while the Vice President is in the front of Air Force Two, and they work through the questions, what they should answer, and how they should answer it. They have a preliminary talk. Then the defendant leaves the public affairs person and goes forward to the front of Air Force Two to meet alone with the Vice President to discuss how to respond to this media inquiry.

The defendant then comes back. He tells Cathie Martin that the Vice President has directed that the defendant, "Scooter" Libby, not the public affairs person, will deal with the press. The Vice President wants the defendant to make an on-the-record statement in his own name to Matt Cooper of *TIME* magazine and others. The Vice President has dictated that statement.

The Vice President has also told him to say certain things not on the record, but on background, that could appear in the newspapers but not be quoted to the Office of Vice President. And the defendant wrote that down.

So the defendant goes with Cathie Martin…and another assistant…into an office at the air force base when Air Force Two lands…

In that room, they make phone calls. The defendant is speaking to Matt Cooper on the telephone; it's on a telephone without a speaker, so the people in the room can hear what the defendant has to say, but they can't hear what Matt Cooper has to say. The defendant goes through that statement, the statement written on a card, describing the Vice President's position on these issues.

And after he is finished relaying all that the Vice President had told him to say, Matt Cooper asked him a question. He says, ["]What have you heard about Wilson's wife being involved in sending him on the trip?["]

And the defendant says, "I have heard that, too."

For Matt Cooper, he has confirmation. He has a second source telling him that Wilson's wife worked at the CIA, because he had learned from his first source in the White House a day before.[2]

So Matt Cooper printed an article which states that Wilson's wife worked at the CIA. It appeared on-line on July 17th. But it wasn't the first article. Three days before, there was an article by a person by the name of Robert Novak. On July 14th, he ran a column indicating that Wilson's wife worked at the CIA.

One thing should be very clear. Mr. Novak relied upon two sources. Neither of those sources are the defendant.

Let's move forward to the fall of 2003. If in July 2003, things were hot with this controversy about whether or not the intelligence had been twisted, and all that was going on because of the Wilson controversy, in the fall of 2003 it got hotter. At the end of September 2003, it was announced that there would be a criminal investigation as to whether senior government officials had broken the law protecting classified information, and had broken the law protecting covert CIA employees by disclosing to the press the fact that Wilson's wife worked at the CIA.

Immediately, there was another firestorm. The President was being asked questions when he traveled, or when he spoke, or when he went near a reporter…: What had

---

[2] Evidence later submitted to the jury will show this initial source was Karl Rove.

gone on? Was the White House involved? Who did it? What happened? What's going to happen to the people who did it?

And the White House Press Secretary—well, there was a new White House Press Secretary. Ari Fleischer had left; Scott McClellan was in. Scott McClellan did daily press briefings. He would [stand] behind a podium with a blue background and the White House seal and take questions from the press. And for the first two weeks in October, he should have brought a helmet to work, because they kept bombarding him with questions: What's going on? Is the White House involved? Who did this? What's going to happen?

You will learn that Scott McClellan made it clear that there was no White House involvement in people telling the press about Wilson's wife working at the CIA. In fact, you will learn that on September 29th, Scott McClellan, the White House Press Secretary, denied any White House involvement in leaking classified information about Wilson's wife and also said, if any one in this administration was involved in it, they would "no longer be in this administration."

Scott McClellan laid down a marker—no one in the White House is involved in this—and laid another marker—if it turns out anyone is, they are gone.

Well, that didn't end the press firestorm. Questions continued to be asked. And reporters then began asking about specific names. Reporters said, what about Karl Rove? Was Karl Rove involved in leaking information to the press about Wilson's wife? Scott McClellan gave an answer. He said, "I talked to Karl Rove. Karl Rove is not involved. It is ridiculous to suggest that he's involved.". . .

Reporters began to go to other names. The next name they asked about was the defendant. They asked whether or not the Vice President's Chief of Staff was involved in leaking information about Wilson's wife. And McClellan wouldn't answer, not because he knew anything about what the defendant had done or not done, what he knew or what he said, but McClellan decided, "I can't go down a list and go name, by name, by name, so I'm just drawing a line after Rove."

As you can imagine, the defendant was not happy. The defendant did not like seeing his name in print. He certainly didn't like to see his name in the press concerning this. So the defendant decided to go to someone to see if he could get help, to get the White House Press Secretary to clear him the way Rove had been cleared. The defendant went to his boss, the Vice President.

You will see during this trial that the defendant took out a piece of paper and wrote out a note, wrote out the words that he wanted the White House Press Secretary to tell the world to make clear that he was not involved.

You will also see that the Vice President wrote on that note, and the Vice President wanted to make sure that the White House Press Secretary did for the defendant what had been done for Karl Rove. You will also learn that the White House Press Secretary came through on more than one occasion.

For example, you will learn that on October 7th, the White House Press Secretary was asked these questions and gave these answers:

Question: "Scott, you have said that you personally went to 'Scooter' Libby, Karl Rove and Elliott Abrams to ask them if they were the leakers. Is that what happened?

Why did you do that? Can you describe the conversations you had with them? What was the question you asked?"

Answer: "Unfortunately, in Washington, D.C., at a time like this, there are a lot of rumors and innuendoes. There are unsubstantiated accusations that are made. That's exactly what happened in the case of these three individuals. They are good individuals. They are important members of our White House team, and that's why I spoke with them, so that I could come back to you and say that they were not involved. I had no doubt of that in the beginning, but I like to check my information to make sure it's accurate before I report back to you exactly what I did."

Question: "So you're saying—you're saying categorically those three individuals were not the leakers or did not authorize the leaks; is that what you're saying?"

Answer: "That's correct. I've spoken with them."

So we have a remarkable turn of events. The end of September 2003, a high-profile criminal investigation, and less than two weeks later, the White House has cleared people publicly, saying these people are not involved.

But the evidence will show that the defendant had a problem. He was involved in leaking information about Wilson's wife to reporters. He had talked to Judith Miller about it on June 23rd, 2003, July 8th, 2003, and July 12th, 2003. He confirmed it to Matt Cooper in that phone conversation from the air force base. And he also told it to the White House Press Secretary, someone whose job it was to talk to the press...

THE EVIDENCE WILL SHOW that, at the time of the interview, there was an active criminal investigation where the FBI was looking to determine whether or not the laws protecting classified information had been broken. There was a press controversy. The White House had insisted that no one in the White House was involved, and anyone involved would be fired. And at the defendant's insistence, the White House had told the world he had nothing to do with this.

You will learn that, during that FBI interview, the defendant lied. He made up a story. He told a story that he wasn't relying on any of the information that came from government officials in telling the reporters what he told them. That he told them just what he heard from other reporters. Rumors, rumors—he didn't even know if they were true.

Now, one other thing. Remember I mentioned there was a note the defendant wrote in June [with] what the Vice President told him. He wrote down that the Vice President told him that the wife worked at the CIA.

The defendant knew that note was in his file, but the defendant's story took care of that. It wiped out all the prior information from the government, and wiped out that note because the defendant's story was that he had forgotten all that. He was learning the information all over again, as if it were new, from Tim Russert.

The defendant's claim was that, on July 10th, he is on the phone with Tim Russert, complaining about Chris Matthews, and Tim Russert says, "Hey, did you know that Wilson's wife works at the CIA?"

And what does the defendant say? "No, I don't know that"

And then Tim Russert tells him, "Sure, all the reporters know it."

And the defendant says, again, "I don't know that."

According to the defendant, Mr. Russert both becomes a source for his information to give out later…[and] this conversation proves—he had forgotten everything that happened before.

The other part of the defendant's story: he said that when he told reporters Cooper and Miller the information, he didn't tell it to them as if it were government information; he passed it along as rumors and he told them he didn't know it was true; he didn't want them to rely upon him.

So his story was essentially this: "I am learning from Tim Russert this information, and as I'm learning it, I'm saying, I don't know this." And then, as he takes the information and passes it on to the other reporters, he says, "I am just giving you rumors from another reporter; I don't know if it's true."

Well, what about Tim Russert? Tim Russert will walk into the courtroom during this trial, take that witness stand, swear to an oath and testify. Tim Russert will tell you that he did not tell the defendant on July 10th, 2003, that Wilson's wife worked at the CIA Tim Russert will tell you that he didn't ask the defendant on July 10th, 2003, ["D]o you know if Wilson's wife worked at the CIA?" Tim Russert will tell you he didn't tell the defendant that "all the reporters know" that Wilson's wife worked at the CIA. In fact, Tim Russert will tell you that he knows of one journalist on July 10th, 2003, who did not know that Wilson's wife worked at the CIA: Tim Russert. Tim Russert didn't know it on July 10th. Tim Russert couldn't have told the defendant on July 10th.

What's more, the evidence will show that earlier that week, the defendant had told Ari Fleischer, the White House Press Secretary, the very same information he claims he was taken aback to learn on Thursday in his conversation with Tim Russert.

I submit to you the evidence will show that the conversation the defendant claimed took place between him and Tim Russert about Wilson's wife never happened. And even if it had happened, the defendant couldn't have been surprised to learn what he was giving out on Monday and Tuesday to a White House Press Secretary and a reporter.

Now, the evidence will show that after this first FBI interview, the defendant had planted his feet and was stuck. He was interviewed again six weeks later by the FBI, and he told the same story. Once again, he said, ["n]one of this information from the government did I give out or remember. I just took rumors from reporters that I didn't know if they were true, and told the other reporters that these are rumors."…

And then, January 2004, a federal Grand Jury investigation began. A federal Grand Jury are citizens drawn from the district who sit to determine whether or not crimes have been committed. They sit in this courthouse. They try to determine whether or not the laws have been broken.

And this Grand Jury had two missions. The first mission was to do what the FBI was also trying to do: to determine whether or not any government officials had broken the law protecting classified information, and protecting covert CIA employees, by talking to reporters about the fact that Wilson's wife worked for the CIA they had to do the same thing of finding out who knew what when, how the officials learned the information, what they understood about Valerie Wilson and her work, and what they did with the information: who did they tell? Did they tell the press and what did they say?

They had a second mission. The second mission was to see if there had been a cover-up, whether or not any of the people who had been talking to the FBI had been lying about what they did or others did. And that was the Grand Jury investigation.

In early March 2004, Mr. Libby appeared before the Grand Jury. He was given all the constitutional rights that every other citizen is given. He was told the nature of the investigation. He was told that he was a subject of the investigation. He was advised of his constitutional rights. He was advised of the consequences of perjury. He had the assistance of counsel. An attorney was allowed to be outside the room, and he could consult with him as he needed to.

The defendant raised his hand, swore to an oath, promised to tell the truth, and violated that oath repeatedly. He told the same story about this Russert conversation and told that under oath to the Grand Jury . . .

WHAT I WOULD LIKE TO DO NOW is play for you the charged statements in the Grand Jury where the defendant is charged with lying. The first section involves the allegation that he lied about his conversation with Tim Russert...

The evidence, we submit, will show that he never talked to Tim Russert about Wilson's wife, but during his testimony he made clear that he said Mr. Russert had told him and that he had said out loud, "I don't know this to be true."

Audiotape played as follows:

"And then he said, ['Y]ou know, did you know that this—excuse me. Did you know that Ambassador Wilson's wife works at the CIA?['] And I was a little taken aback by that. I remember being taken aback by it. And I said—he may have said a little more, but that was—he said that. And I said, ['N]o, I don't know that.['] And I said, ['N]o, I don't know that['] intentionally because I didn't want him to take anything I was saying as in any way confirming what he had said, because at that point in time I did not recall that I had ever known this, and I thought this is something he was telling me that I was first learning. And so I said, 'No, I don't know that,' because I want to be very careful not to confirm it for him so that he didn't take my statement as confirmation for him.

"Now, I had said earlier in the conversation, which I omitted to tell you, that this—you know, as always, 'Tim, our discussion is off the record, if that's okay with you.' And he said, 'That's fine.'

"So then . . . Mr. Russert said to me, ['D]id you know that Ambassador Wilson's wife, or his wife, works at the CIA?['] And I said, ['N]o, I don't know that.' And then he said, ['Y]eah—yes, all the reporters know it.['] And I said, again, [']I don't know that.' I just wanted to be clear that I wasn't confirming anything for him on this. And, you know, I was struck by what he was saying in that he thought it was an important fact, but I didn't ask him any more about it because I didn't want to be digging in on him, and he then moved on and we finished the conversation, something like that."

Now, you will also learn that, in the indictment, the defendant is not only charged with lying about how he learned this information in the first place, this claim that this was some startling information he learned from Tim Russert on July 10, 2003, and that he had forgotten everything else he had learned in June and July and discussed with people as late as July 7th and July 8th. You will also learn the defendant is charged with lying to the Grand Jury about what he told reporters Cooper and Miller, because the other half of saying all you are doing is taking rumors from one reporter to another is to make clear that you are telling the reporters that you are giving the information out to that it came from other reporters, and you don't know if it's true.

The defendant is charged with lying about that. And this is his testimony about his conversations, particularly with reporter Matt Cooper, but more generally with all reporters where he claims that every time he told a reporter this information, he said it's just something he didn't know if it were true . . .

We are about to play the next section of the Grand Jury transcript. And, again, this is Mr. Libby testifying about the way he relayed the information to reporter Matt Cooper of *TIME* magazine and also how he generally described it to other reporters, which would include Judith Miller.

Audiotape played as follows:

FITZGERALD: "And it's your specific recollection that when you told Cooper about Wilson's wife working at the CIA, you attributed that fact to what reporters—"

LIBBY: "Yes."

FITZGERALD: "—plural, [']were saying,['] correct?"

LIBBY: "I was very clear to say, [']reporters are telling us that['] because, in my mind, I still didn't know it as a fact. I thought I was—all I had was this information that was coming in from the reporters."

FITZGERALD: "And at the same time, you have a specific recollection of telling him, you don't know whether it's true or not; you're just telling him what reporter are saying?"

LIBBY: "Yes, that's correct. And I said, [']Reporters are telling us that. I don't know if it's true.['] I was careful about that because, among other things, I wanted to be clear, I didn't know if Mr. Wilson. I don't know—I think I said, [']I don't know if he has a wife, but this is what we're hearing.[']"

MR. FITZGERALD: Now, you will learn that the defendant was also asked by the Grand Jury in the next session, which was on March 24th, just—roughly three weeks later—he was asked a direct question basically about whether or not he was changing his story to make it appear that the information he was giving out to reporters came from reporters' rumors, not from the Vice President.

And listen to that question and answer which are charged as false statements. Audiotape played as follows:

FITZGERALD: "And let me ask you this directly. Did the fact that you knew that . . . the law as to whether a crime was committed could turn on where you learned the information from, affect your account for the FBI when you told them that you were telling reporters Wilson's wife worked at the CIA, but your source was a reporter rather than the Vice President?"

LIBBY: "No. It's a fact. It was a fact. That's what I told the reporters."

FITZGERALD: "And you're certain, as you sit here today, that every reporter you told that Wilson's wife worked at the CIA, you sourced it back to other reporters?"

LIBBY: "Yes, sir, because it was important for what I was saying and because it was—that's what—that's how I did it."

And the final section we will play for you today, which again you will hear in the course of the longer Grand Jury testimony later on in this trial, concerns a question that was actually asked by a grand juror. The question focuses on why it is that if the defendant thought this information wasn't anything special, or sensitive, or classified, he claimed to be so careful about what he did with it.

Audiotape played as follows:

FITZGERALD: "The next set of questions from the Grand Jury . . . concern this fact. If you did not understand the information about Wilson's wife to have been classified and didn't understand it when you heard it from Mr. Russert, why was it that you were so deliberate to make sure that you told other reporters that reporters were saying it and not assert it as something you knew?"

LIBBY: "I want—I didn't want to—I didn't know if it was true, and I didn't want people—I didn't want the reporters to think it was true because I said it. I—all I had was that reporters are telling us that, and by that I wanted them to understand it wasn't coming from me and that it might not be true. Reporters write things that aren't true sometimes, or get things that aren't true. So I wanted to be clear they didn't—they didn't think it was me saying it. I didn't know it was true, and I wanted them to understand that. Also, it was important to me to let them know that because what I was telling them was that I don't know Mr. Wilson. We didn't ask for his mission. That I didn't see his report. Basically, we didn't know anything about him until this stuff came out in June. And among the other things, I didn't know he had a wife. That was one of the things I said to Mr. Cooper. I don't know if he's married. And so I wanted to be very clear about all this stuff, that I didn't— I didn't know about him. And the only thing I had on it, I thought at the time, was what reporters are telling us."

Members of the jury, the evidence you will see in this case from the witness stand will show you that the defendant knowingly and intentionally lied to the FBI and lied after taking an oath before the Grand Jury.

This is not a case about bad memory. This is not a case about forgetfulness. Having a bad memory is not a crime. The defendant is not charged with having a bad memory. The government will meet its burden to prove beyond a reasonable doubt the defendant knowingly and intentionally lied by trying to shift the information he gave to reporters away from where he really learned it and to blame it on a conversation with Russert that never happened.

Now, remember, the burden of proof is at this table. It is always at this table. We accept that responsibility. We welcome that responsibility. And we commit to you that at the end of the evidence in this case, we will stand up before you and we will be able to look you in the eye and tell you that the evidence will have convinced each and every one of you beyond any reasonable doubt that the defendant is guilty of each of the charges in the indictment . . .

I ask you, as you sit here during this trial, to remember one thing. The most important thing you brought to the courtroom today is your life experience and your common sense. When you check into whatever room you eat in and leave your coats in, leave your coats there every morning, but bring your common sense into the courtroom.

You all have a lifetime of experience in sizing people up, knowing when you are being talked to straight and when you are not, knowing when someone is telling you the truth, knowing when someone makes a mistake, and knowing when someone is telling you a lie.

I submit to you if you keep an open mind during this trial, if you pay attention to the evidence, if you follow the instructions of the law that Judge Walton will give you and you apply your common sense, each and every one of you will be convinced of what happened here.

Something important needed to be investigated: Whether the laws protecting covert agents and classified information have been broken. And to do that on behalf of the citizens, the FBI and the Grand Jury needed the truth. What the evidence will show is that the defendant obstructed that search for truth. The defendant lied to the FBI, and he stole the truth from the Grand Jury.

Thank you.

OPENING STATEMENT ON BEHALF OF THE DEFENDANT

MR. WELLS: Judge Walton, members of the prosecution team, ladies and gentlemen of the jury: As you learned a few days ago, my name is Ted Wells, and I speak for "Scooter" Libby. "Scooter" Libby is innocent. He is totally innocent. He did not commit perjury. He did not commit obstruction of justice. He did not give any false statements to the FBI . . . He has been wrongly and unjustly and unfairly accused.

There will be no witness who takes that stand during this trial who takes the oath, swears to God and says, "I know 'Scooter' Libby lied. I know 'Scooter' Libby intentionally gave false statements." There is no such witness.

There will be no witness who will take the stand and produce a document that shows that "Scooter" Libby lied or intentionally made any false statements. There will be no scientific evidence that he lied or gave a false statement. No documents, no scientific evidence, no witness who says " 'Scooter' Libby told me he lied, 'Scooter' Libby told me he was going to lie, 'Scooter' Libby said he had lied."

This is a weak, paper-thin, circumstantial-evidence case about he said/she said. No witness, no documents, no scientific evidence.

People do not lie for the heck of it. When somebody tells an intentional lie, it's because they have done something wrong. They are trying to cover something up. And what you will learn from the evidence is "Scooter" Libby . . . had nothing to cover up. He was an innocent person, and there was no reason to lie . . .

You will find "Scooter" Libby was not out pushing any reporter to write any stories about Valerie Wilson. Now, there will be some people at the White House—at the White House, not the Office of the Vice President—who you will learn may have pushed reporters to write stories about Ms. Wilson. There may be people at the State Department, even, who pushed reporters to write stories about Ms. Wilson. But "Scooter" Libby did not push any reporter to write a story about Ms. Wilson. Yet the man who pushed no one is sitting here in this courtroom.

You will also learn that "Scooter" Libby did not have any knowledge that Ms. Wilson's job was covert or classified before July 14th, when Mr. Novak's article was published. There will be no witness who takes that stand who says he or she told "Scooter" Libby that Ms. Wilson had a classified job or had a covert job. He was never told that…As Judge Walton told you, that's not an issue in this case. And as I stand here right now, I can't tell you whether she was or whether she wasn't. Judge Walton has decided it's irrelevant, so we are not going to get into that.

. . . There will be newspaper articles that may suggest she was, but . . . we are not going to have any testimony of any witnesses on that issue. So no one is to assume that she was classified. No one is to assume she was covert . . .

Now, Mr. Fitzgerald suggested that Mr. Libby might have a motive to lie because Mr. McClellan, the President's Press Secretary, went on T.V. and said, ["]Anybody involved in leaking classified information, you are going to lose your job.["] . . . Well, you will find that Mr. Libby was not concerned about losing his job in the Bush administration . . . He was concerned about being set up. He was concerned about being the scapegoat for this entire Valerie Wilson controversy.

And Mr. Libby, you will learn, went to the Vice President of the United States and met with the Vice President in private. Mr. Libby said to the Vice President, "I think . . . people over there in the White House"—not the Office of the Vice President—people in the White House—"are trying to set me up. People in the White House are trying to sacrifice me. People in the White House want me to be a scapegoat. People in the White House are trying to protect a man named Karl Rove, the President's right-hand man."

And the Vice President made a note of what Mr. Libby said in private to the Vice President. The note shows Mr. Libby telling the Vice President, ["]I did not leak any classified information...I was not involved with the leak to Mr. Novak. I had nothing to do with the Novak leak. I did not leak any classified information. But I am concerned I am being set up. I am concerned people are trying to use me as a scapegoat."

Let me show you one sentence of what the Vice President wrote—and you will get to see it in the Vice President's own handwriting...He kept it. Maybe it never was supposed to be seen.

The Vice President wrote, "not going to protect one staffer and sacrifice the guy that was asked to stick his neck in the meat grinder because of the incompetence of others."

And you will learn from the evidence that...the person who was to be protected...was Karl Rove. Karl Rove was President Bush's right-hand person in terms of political strategy. Karl Rove was the person most responsible for making sure that the Republican party stayed in office. He was viewed as a political genius. His fate was important to the Republican party if they were going to stay in office. He had to be protected.

And the person who was to be sacrificed. "Sacrifice the guy"—that's "Scooter" Libby. "Scooter" Libby was to be sacrificed. Karl Rove was to be protected...The person whose neck had been put into the meat grinder, you will learn, was "Scooter" Libby.

Mr. Libby was asked by the Vice President [to] go out and rebut the allegations made by Mr. Wilson. Nothing to do with his wife. Respond to Wilson on the merits. And Mr. Libby was asked to go out there and deal with those reporters. That's what's meant by Mr. Libby's neck was put into the meat grinder, because Mr. Libby's job was not to deal with reporters. That was not his normal job. Mr. Libby was the National Security Advisor for the Vice President of the United States. Mr. Libby's job involved terrorism. It involved homeland security. It involved dealing with foreign crises . . . I am not even permitted to talk about most of what he did because it is so top secret. I am going to have to later read a script to you about what his job was all about, his day job.

He started at 7:00 in the morning, every morning, dealing with the most important national security issues of this country...They are going to make me read a script because I can't even talk about the details, but there is no dispute . . .

My client had a day job. And he had one of the most serious day jobs of anybody in this country, a 16-hour-a-day day job. But they took him off his day job and said, ["G]o into the meat grinder and deal with the press.["]

But while Mr. Libby was dealing with the press in this meat grinder, the national security problems didn't just go away...He still had to deal [with] Al-Qaeda. He still had to deal with various threats, some on Washington, D.C., some on New York. He had to deal with these things while he was also dealing with this sixteen-word controversy.

So we're going to put things into perspective because, when you just listen to the charges, you would think that Ms. Wilson was some big deal. She became a big deal when the criminal investigation started. But in real time, in June and July, in terms of "Scooter" Libby, Ms. Wilson [and] where she worked was no big deal to him . . .

And when the note by the Vice President refers to the incompetence of others, you will learn that refers to the fact that this whole controversy over the sixteen words had been caused in great part by the incompetence of people at the CIA who let the words get into the speech in the first place.

And so Mr. Libby, because of the incompetence of the CIA, had to go into the meat grinder. And so in late September, early October, he was put in the spot where he is sitting in private with the Vice President saying, ["T]hey are trying to set me up. They want me to be the sacrificial lamb. I didn't do anything. I am not going to stand for it.["]

And you will learn that the Vice President, because Mr. Libby said to him, "I am innocent and I demand—I will not be sacrificed so Karl Rove can be protected"—the Vice President takes steps and forces the White House to go out and say to the press the same thing that had been said about Karl Rove.

But unlike Karl Rove, you will learn Mr. Libby had not been out pushing stories about Ms. Wilson. You see, the innocent person was to be sacrificed; somebody who had done something, he was to be protected. But, again, Mr. Libby was just a staffer. He was just a guy working on national security. He was an important staffer, but Karl Rove was the lifeblood of the Republican party.

Mr. Libby was just a staffer. He was just a guy working on national security. He was an important staffer, but Karl Rove was the lifeblood of the Republican party.

Now, you will learn that, about two weeks after that note was written by the Vice President, Mr. Libby was interviewed by the FBI. He was interviewed on October 14, 2003 . . . He came voluntarily, prepared to answer any and all questions . . . His lawyer said right up front—he said, ["Y]ou have not permitted Mr. Libby to talk to any of his staff before he comes to this interview. You have not permitted him to review any of the notes that his staff would keep of his various activities. And I want to let you know, Mr. Libby has a horrendous schedule. He is dealing with multiple issues. And the way he would normally refresh his recollection about what had taken place, he would sit down with his staff, and you haven't done that. So I want to let you know right upfront, he is going to do his best, but some of what he may say may be inaccurate because you said he should not talk to his staff.["] So that was said right upfront.

And the FBI said,["N]o, we don't want you to talk to anybody. We would rather hear it fresh. Nobody should talk to anybody.["] And Mr. Libby said, ["T]hose are the rules. Okay. But I want to let you know right up front["]—his lawyer tells them—"some of it may be inaccurate."

. . . You will learn he did his best to recollect what had taken place . . . but I want you to understand, when the interview takes place, it's October, and they are asking him about some telephone calls that took place in July, three months earlier.

This case is about three telephone calls. That's what he had been charged with, three telephone calls: one call to Matt Cooper, one call with Tim Russert, and one call with

Judy Miller. Three telephone calls. So three months later he is being asked, "What do you recall, with specificity, with details, about what was said on a telephone call, about a snippet of a conversation that may have involved the wife that may have taken 20, 30 seconds at most."

. . . Forget that he is a busy person. Forget he is dealing with national security issues. If you were young and vibrant, right out of college—you get out of school in June, you enjoy the summer, and you go back to school in September. Mid-September, some-body says, tell me about a telephone conversation you had in June. You would look at somebody like they had two heads. I mean, that's what we are talking about. Three calls, a few seconds, three months later: what do you recollect?

Mr. Libby has no notes of the calls. Mr. Russert has no notes of the calls. Mr. Cooper has some notes of the calls, but he has testified already and will testify in this case that his notes do not reflect anything about any conversation concerning the wife. So for all practical purposes, he has no notes.

Russert has no notes. Cooper has no notes concerning the wife. And Ms. Miller has testified repeatedly she has got a fuzzy, speculative memory, and her notes are cryptic. The only notes she has are, like, two words. So that's what the case is about. It's not about the war. It's not about whether the Bush administration lied to the American public about the war.

. . . I am here to defend "Scooter" Libby for three telephone calls. And as interesting as it is to be in a case with the backdrop of the war and to have all these people here, ultimately, what you all are going to have to focus on and decide is a very narrow ques-tion having nothing to do with the war, but about three phone calls, three reporters, what somebody recollected three months later, and what some other people recollected three months later where there are no notes, no recordings. He said/she said . . .

You will find, for example, with respect to Mr. Cooper, the debate between Mr. Cooper and Mr. Libby is over about four words. Mr. Cooper says, "I have heard Valerie Plame was involved in sending her husband on a trip. Have you heard that?". . . Mr. Cooper says Libby says, "I heard that, too." Mr. Libby says, "I heard that from reporters, but I don't know if it's true."

. . . As I said, if you look at Mr. Cooper's notebook, there is no reference . . . to any discussion about the wife, which is totally consistent with the concept of what Mr. Libby was saying. Forget the particular words. The concept that Mr. Libby said he communicated to everybody was, "I am not confirming anything. I am not confirm-ing anything. I don't know if it's true."

And one way to know if a person who is talking to a reporter has not confirmed something is to look at the notes because the confirmation is something that is impor-tant to reporters. And if somebody has . . . said something that's not confirmation, it's probably not in the notes. If somebody has said something that's confirmation, it will be in the notes . . .

Now, in a lot of respects, we already have accomplished the most important part of this case. We chose you . . . Most juries are selected in a couple hours. We took days to select you.

Under our system of justice, we bring people in from the community who sit as impartial judges of the facts to make a decision. And it is an enormous power that you have to sit in judgment of another human being. But with that enormous power also comes enormous responsibility. It's a responsibility to do the very best that you can to return a fair and a just verdict, a verdict based on the evidence.

... We asked you these questions about how you feel about the war because, just as it was wrong what the White House was trying to do to "Scooter" Libby in terms of sacrificing him to protect Rove, it would be wrong for any of you to let your feelings about the war interfere with "Scooter" Libby getting a fair trial. "Scooter" Libby cannot be sacrificed for how somebody feels about the war . . .

Now, "Scooter" Libby is 56 years old. He was born August 1950. He is trained as a lawyer. He went to Yale College undergrad, Columbia Law School. He has been "Scooter" since he was a little baby because he would scoot around, and his parents nicknamed him "Scooter," and it stuck. And everybody calls him "Scooter" and we will call him "Scooter" during this trial. He has always been "Scooter" because he's just moving.

AFTER LAW SCHOOL, HE WENT and got a job at a law firm. But what interested him was policy issues, and "Scooter" Libby left the law and he went and worked in the State Department. Then, later on, he took a job at the Defense Department.

And during the administration of the first President Bush, Bush 1, Vice President Cheney was the Secretary of Defense, and "Scooter" Libby worked at the Defense Department. That's how he got to know Vice President Cheney in terms of a close working relationship.

And when Vice President Cheney became the Vice President under Bush 2, he asked "Scooter" Libby if [he] would be his National Security Advisor and Chief of Staff . . . He had to oversee both foreign and domestic issues. But his main job, in addition to doing all that, was national security issues . . .

I want you to understand when the note talks about the meat grinder, that was in addition to his day job. And we're going to go through what was going on in his life during this week of July 6th, 7th, 8th, 9th and 10th and 11th—in addition to the meat grinder [of his] day job.

And what you will find is that in terms of what was going on—the wife [was] not something of importance. So there is this disconnect because people—Mr. Libby and others—months later are being asked questions about the wife because now there is a criminal investigation; it has become important, when in real time, it was like a slither; it was like a piece of gossip.

I just want to [make] certain key points that the evidence will show:

One, that he gave his best, good faith recollection . . . .

Second, that any misstatements by Libby were innocent mistakes. If you make a mistake in this country, God bless, that does not make you a criminal . . . everybody can have a misrecollection, even a misrecollection that you believe with a degree of confidence, and you can find out later that you may have been mistaken . . .

Third point. Libby had no knowledge that Valerie Wilson's job status was classified. No witness will say that they told "Scooter" Libby before July 14th that Ms. Wilson had a classified or a covert job.

Libby did not push reporters to write about Valerie Wilson . . . Libby did not leak to Robert Novak. Richard Armitage did.

Robert Novak wrote an article that was published on July 14th in *The Washington Post*. That is the article that said to the world "Ambassador Wilson's wife works at the CIA" . . . and as the prosecutor said in his opening, there is no dispute that Mr. Libby was not . . . the source for Robert Novak. The source for Robert Novak was Richard Armitage, who worked at the State Department.

And you will learn that when Mr. Libby was interviewed by the FBI, it was Mr. Libby's understanding that the investigation was about who leaked to Robert Novak. And he did not get that understanding based on a dream or going to a fortune-teller. He got that understanding because the Justice Department wrote a letter to the White House that said the investigation is focusing on Robert Novak. And that letter was given to Mr. Libby before he was interviewed by the FBI so that's where he got the notion— the understanding that the investigation was about who leaked to Robert Novak.

He is innocent and [had] no motive to lie. As I say, we're going to focus on motive, and he had no motive to lie because he had not done anything wrong.

THE TELEPHONE CALLS that are the subject of the indictment take place on July 12th, and the Russert call takes place either on the 10th or the 11th. Mr. Russert will testify that it's on the 10th or the 11th. The 11th, you will learn, is a very important day.

In terms of the three reporters, the evidence will show that what you have to decide relates to Mr. Libby's recollection, from at least October 14th forward, about calls that had taken place three months earlier . . .

Now… before I go to Mr. Russert, I want to make something clear because I'm not sure it came across in the Government's opening.

When I listened to the opening statement, at times it seemed to suggest that Mr. Libby heard it for the first time from Mr. Russert. That's not what happened. Mr. Libby told the FBI on October 14th within the first few minutes of the interview, "I learned it from the Vice President. I have a note that I have produced that shows that the Vice President told me about the wife on or about June 12, 2003. That note refreshes my recollection. And it's clear to me the Vice President told me about Mrs. Wilson on or about June 12."

He said that from the very beginning. He's never wavered from it . . . He said it to the Grand Jury in both sessions . . . He produced a note that showed it. He said, with respect to Mr. Russert, again, looking back, when he was being interviewed in October, he said, ["B]ut when Mr. Russert told it to me on the 11th, I felt a sense of surprise.["] That's what he said.

He said that sense of surprise . . . made him look back and say, ["W]ell, maybe I forgot." But in terms of how he learned it, he said from day one, the Vice President of the United States told me on or about June 12 . . .

I don't want anybody to have [the] suggestion from the government's opening that Mr. Libby said, ["O]h, I first heard it from Tim Russert.["] That is not what happened . . .

Now, I'm going to talk in a minute about each one of the reporters. I'm going to walk you through what they recollect, what Mr. Libby recollects. And I want to make clear right now, I do not contend that any of those reporters, Mr. Russert, Mr. Cooper or Ms. Miller, are going to come into this courtroom and give false testimony or lie. They're going to give, I believe or assume, their good faith recollection based on their oath. And they're going to do their best. I do not contend any of them are lying.

They may, however, be mistaken, just like Mr. Libby may be mistaken. Mr. Libby, for example, in his Grand Jury [testimony], he talks about Tim Russert. He makes clear, he thinks Tim Russert is one of the most respected reporters in the United States . . .

But Mr. Libby had a different recollection than Tim Russert. And maybe Mr. Libby's recollection, it will turn out, was incorrect, although made in good faith. Maybe Mr. Russert forgot, too. Tim Russert is a great reporter, but he's a human being . . . He could be confused and make an innocent mistake just like anybody else. So can Matt Cooper. So can Judy Miller. And you don't have to conclude that anybody is lying to acquit Mr. Libby.

It's not, "well, if I believe Russert, then Libby must be guilty" . . . The question is, did someone tell an intentional lie. That's the sole issue in the case.

It may turn out, in some of these situations, Mr. Libby and the reporter both got it wrong because nobody has any notes. Again, people trying to think about a snippet of a telephone conversation, not even face-to-face, no notes, three months later. Somebody might be right. Somebody might be wrong. It may be some combination where some of them got a little bit right, some a little bit wrong, who knows? . . .

Mr. Libby is being told, go out and talk to reporters. Even though that's not your day job, go out and talk to reporters.

You're going to find that Mr. Libby talks, not only to Mr. Cooper, Ms. Miller and Mr. Russert. Mr. Libby talks to Pincus, [Mr. Kessler and] . . . Bob Woodward from *The Washington Post,* Mr. Sanger from *The New York Times,* Mr. Novak from the *Chicago-Sun Times,* Andrea Mitchell from NBC, [and] Evan Thomas from *Newsweek...*

We're going to produce evidence to show you that Mr. Libby is talking to these reporters. He's talking about the war in Iraq. He's talking about the Wilson allegations and how the Vice President was not involved in terms of Mr. Wilson. He's talking to all these reporters. You're going [to] see, . . . Mr. Libby is not out saying anything about the wife. He's not out pushing any story. It just didn't happen.

Okay. Let's talk about Russert . . . The Russert conversation takes place, as I said, . . . either on July 10 or July 11. I think the evidence will show that it took place on July 10th and 11th because there are actually two telephone conversations. And it's Mr. Libby's recollection that Russert asked . . . if Libby was aware that Wilson's wife worked for the CIA. So Libby remembers Russert asking him a question about the wife.

And that Libby responded that he did not know. And Russert replied, all the reporters know. So that's what Mr. Libby testified to in the Grand Jury. That was his position when he first went to the FBI.

Mr. Russert said, he didn't ask Libby whether he knew that the wife worked at the CIA. And Russert said he did not know what Wilson's wife did. He did not know that Wilson's wife did work at the CIA until the morning of July 14th when he read it in the *Post*.

Now, let's start for a minute in terms of the facts as to how Libby got on the phone in the first place with Tim Russert. NBC was . . . covering the Wilson issue very intensely. When Mr. Wilson wrote his article on Sunday, July 6th, he appeared that day on *Meet the Press*.

Both Tim Russert and Andrea Mitchell were following this story from the beginning.

One of the NBC reporters who was covering it was Chris Matthews, who is the moderator of a show called *Hardball*.

Matthews, you'll learn, was being very aggressive in his reporting about the Vice President being involved in terms of the Wilson issue. He was saying the Vice President knew about Wilson. The Vice President must have gotten a report. The Vice President must have sat on the report. All incorrect information that you will learn in this case, [is] incorrect reporting by Chris Matthews.

And Mr. Libby calls Tim Russert about Chris Matthews to complain . . . It's not a call where Mr. Libby is calling Tim Russert as a reporter. He's basically calling Tim Russert in his job as the head of the NBC Washington Bureau. [It's] like you bought a defective product and you're making a customer complaint . . . He's saying, "Can't you do something? Can't you stop him? It's wrong what he's saying."

Mr. Libby says it's during that telephone call that Russert raises the issue of the wife. And Russert says, when asked, I don't think it happened because I didn't know anything about the wife until July 14. So that kind of sets the stage. That's how Mr. Libby gets on the phone with Russert.

Now, in terms of the evidence that Russert may have been mistaken, we want to start with the basic proposition that Mr. Russert has no notes of the conversation either.

Mr. Libby has no notes . . . So, there's not going to be any notes, any recordings. There's no other party who was a witness to the conversation. It is a classic case of he said/she said and what two people remembered three months later about a conversation that took place in July.

You'll find, as I said, that Tim Russert and NBC were all over this story. They were covering it. They were out, digging for information. So, the fact that Tim Russert might have heard either a rumor or a fact that the wife did work at the CIA is not something that would be unusual.

That would be his job. That would be the job of his reporters, out digging, trying to figure out, who is this unnamed ambassador. Who is this guy Wilson? So people are out digging. That's what's going on this week . . .

Now, you also learned that two of Russert's key NBC colleagues were working with Russert on the story. David Gregory, who is the NBC White House correspondent, was part of . . . Russert's team that was focusing not only on the Wilson story but the whole issue of whether the Administration had been candid with the American public about the reasons for going to war.

Andrea Mitchell, also the top foreign correspondent for NBC, she was working with Russert on this story. So Russert's two top people are working with Russert on the story. And the evidence will show that they were both working on the story. And that, if Andrea Mitchell knew or David Gregory knew, then it's likely Tim Russert knew. And I think the evidence will show that from the stand. There won't be any dispute about that . . .

[W]ith respect to David Gregory, . . . the evidence will show that on July 11, 2003, in time for Russert to get the information before he talks to Libby on July 11, in the African country of Uganda, that Ari Fleischer, . . . who at that time was serving as the Press Secretary to President Bush, . . . discloses, according to Mr. Fleischer, . . .to David Gregory that Ambassador Wilson's wife worked at the CIA.

Mr. Fleischer testifies to that and tells the Government that before Mr. Libby is ever indicted. So Mr. Fleischer says to the Government, I told David Gregory. And you'll find that, in terms of the time, Uganda is eight, nine hours ahead of U.S. time. So, it would have been time for Mr. Russert to have known.

Now, Andrea Mitchell, you'll learn, she goes on TV, on October the 3rd, 2003, on a TV show, and Andrea Mitchell says on a TV show that it was widely known among the reporters who covered the intelligence community that Ambassador Wilson's wife worked at the CIA, widely known before July 14th by certain reporters, including herself.

Okay? She says it on TV that she and other reporters knew before July 14. And, as I said, if Andrea Mitchell knew, doggone it, Tim Russert knew.

And it's very interesting because you'll find later on, Ms. Mitchell retracts her statement after Mr. Libby had been indicted: "Oh, I know I said it on TV. I must have made a mistake. I don't know what I was thinking."

And then Mr. Russert . . . goes on the *Imus in the Morning* radio show . . . It's 7 o'clock in the morning, [and Imus, the guy] with the cowboy hat, he asked Mr. Russert, "Well what do you think about what Ms. Mitchell said?" Mr. Russert's like, "Well she misspoke. She misspoke. I don't want to talk about it."

You're going to see powerful compelling evidence that both David Gregory knew and Andrea Mitchell knew. Yet, Mr. Russert, when he was questioned by the Government about his knowledge and his recollection of the conversation between he and Mr. Libby, Mr. Russert was only questioned for 22 minutes. Twenty-two minutes.

Mr. Russert was not even required to go down to court and appear before the Grand Jury. They interviewed Mr. Russert in a law office . . .

During that 22 minutes, Mr. Russert was not asked one question about what he knew about possibly David Gregory knowing. He wasn't asked one question about Andrea Mitchell knowing . . . Not one question.

Mr. Fitzgerald says the FBI was concerned about getting to the truth . . . Well, you're going to see that Tim Russert had a deal . . . with the Government whereby he would only be questioned about his conversation with Scooter Libby and he couldn't be questioned about anything else . . . We'll explore that deal when Mr. Russert comes to court. But in terms of getting at the truth? They didn't ask Mr. Russert about Mitchell. They didn't ask Mr. Russert about Gregory.

Now, you will find that the Government went out and did ask David Gregory and Andrea Mitchell if they would submit to an interview. And both of them told the Government, we don't want to be interviewed. We don't want to talk about it.

What did the Government do? They did not subpoena Andrea Mitchell. They did not subpoena David Gregory. They just said we don't want to be interviewed. That was the end of it. Twenty-two minutes with Russert, they don't ask him. David Gregory, I don't want to be interviewed, no subpoena. Andrea Mitchell, I don't want to be interviewed, no subpoena.

Now, Andrea Mitchell, she goes on the Imus radio show and talks about what she knew readily, but she doesn't talk to the Government. I mean so we have this perverse situation where Imus on the radio is asking the tough questions. He's asking the tough questions, the guy with the cowboy hat, yet, neither Gregory nor Mitchell are subpoenaed . . .

One of the things you should ask yourself during this case [is] why would Mr. Libby concoct the story. That's what Mr. Fitzgerald said he did. Why would Mr. Libby concoct a story with Tim Russert? What you will learn from the evidence is Mr. Libby had no personal friendship with Tim Russert . . .

Mr. Russert, as I said, is one of the most respected reporters in the United States. So if you're going to cook up a story, why would you cook up a story about a phony conversation that you had with one of the most respected reporters in the country who you have no personal friendship with, who you know would be called, well, what happened, and they would say it was a cooked up story? Well, it didn't happen. Mr. Libby was a very busy man, but he wasn't stupid. Nobody's going to tell you he was a nut. It makes no sense.

The Russert conversation had nothing to do with a reporter/source relationship. It was just Mr. Libby on the phone talking to Tim Russert in his capacity as the manager, complaining about Chris Matthews. So that never was going to be a protected conversation.

So again, there would be no reason in the world for Scooter Libby to make up a lie based on Tim Russert, no friendship, it wasn't a protected conversation . . .

Now, let me tell you, I think the evidence will show that Mr. Russert made a mistake. But, as I said, there will be no claim that Mr. Russert is lying . . . It also may be, as the evidence will show, that Mr. Libby made a mistake. That all Mr. Libby did was get the name Tim Russert confused with another reporter who asked the very same question that he thought Mr. Russert asked of him. Did you know the wife worked at the CIA?

And the evidence is going to show that Mr. Robert Novak, who happens to write the article that exposes Mrs. Wilson publicly, that Mr. Novak is going to take the stand and he's going to say, at around the same time that Mr. Libby says he talked to Mr. Russert, Mr. Novak talked to Mr. Libby.

And that Mr. Novak had learned that the wife worked at the CIA from Mr. Armitage. And Mr. Novak is going tell you that it is very possible when he had Libby on the telephone that he said to Libby, do you know the wife works at the CIA. And he will also say that Mr. Libby did not confirm anything to him.

So maybe . . . all that has happened is that Mr. Libby has gotten Russert and Novak confused . . . because the questions, you will learn, are basically the same questions in the same time period.

You will also learn that Mr. Cooper, who I will talk about in a minute, his question to Mr. Libby is very close to what Libby remembers Mr. Russert saying. Mr. Cooper says, do you know the wife was involved in sending him on the trip? Very close question, similar question.

Mr. Cooper is going to say he raised it to Mr. Libby, just like Mr. Libby thought Mr. Russert raised it. And he's going to say, Mr. Libby said I've heard that, too. That's Cooper's recollection . . .

And Mr. Cooper is going to testify that, when Mr. Libby said, according to Cooper, I heard that too, that Mr. Cooper did not know whether he heard it on the radio or saw it on the TV. He will say he had no idea in the world about the reliability of where he heard it.

. . .But I want you to understand, there will be evidence suggesting that Tim Russert, rather than Scooter Libby, got it wrong, has a misrecollection. It may be that Mr. Russert is entirely right. Maybe Andrea Mitchell just misspoke on the TV show.

Maybe David Gregory wasn't told by Mr. Fleischer as they walked down the road in Africa. Maybe Mr. Libby just got Tim Russert and Robert Novak confused. And Mr. Novak will take the stand and say that that's possible in terms of what he said to Mr. Libby . . .

Now, Matthew Cooper, according to Mr. Libby, Mr. Libby said he heard other reporters were saying Wilson's wife worked for the CIA and said he did not know whether this was true. Cooper says he asked Libby if he knew Wilson's wife was involved in sending Wilson to Niger, and Libby replied something to the effect of yeah, I heard that, too. Now, if you get into a textual analysis of the words you see, we're talking about a small difference in words, only a few words different.

ON SATURDAY JULY 12, Mr. Libby and his entire family—he has a wife named Harriet, two kids, who are now 13 and 10, a boy and a girl . . . [H]is wife of 15 years and Mr. Libby, they go on a plane that morning, Saturday morning, with the children.

They go on Air Force Two with the Vice President, with Cath[ie] Martin and they leave Andrews Air Force base and they fly to Norfolk, Virginia. They fly because a ship is going to be commemorated in the name of former President Ronald Reagan, and they're going there for the ceremony.

It's a Saturday. It's like a day off, okay? He's taking his kids . . . It's his son's tenth birthday. This is supposed to be a trip to take his son to see the commissioning of that ship. Mr. Libby is not focused on calling Matt Cooper.... .

But Ms. Martin is on the airplane, and Ms. Martin has been called by Matt Cooper. Ms. Martin is nagging Mr. Libby. I got this reporter. He wants to do a story. His deadline is Saturday afternoon. You need to give a response . . .

Ms. Martin's going to tell you, Mr. Libby was trying to get off the phone because he had the wife and the two kids, the boy's birthday, sitting in the next room at

Andrews Air Force base after the plane had landed . . . He didn't want to be on the call. He was trying to get off the call.

. . . Mr. Cooper says, in an effort just to keep the conversation going, he throws out this statement about the wife. What do you know about the wife being involved in the trip? That's where the dispute starts because Mr. Libby doesn't dispute that they had the call. Mr. Libby recollected that he just said, I heard that, too, but I don't know if it's true.

Mr. Cooper says differently. Now, what you're going to find is Mr. Cooper took notes of the conversation . . . We're going to look at Mr. Cooper's notes.

You will not see in those notes . . . there's not one word about the wife. The notes do not support Mr. Cooper's recollection at all . . . And right after he gets off the call with Mr. Libby, Mr. Cooper does an e-mail to his editor, setting forth his conversation with Mr. Libby, and there's nothing in the e-mail about Mr. Libby saying anything about the wife.

But Mr. Cooper will tell you also that Mr. Karl Rove . . . the President's right-hand man, the chief political strategist, the person that was to be protected, . . . had told Mr. Cooper the day before about the wife. And if you look at Mr. Cooper's notes from the day before, when Mr. Karl Rove told Mr. Cooper about the wife, you see it. It's right there about the wife. Then Mr. Cooper comes back and types an e-mail to his editor. You see it right there in the e-mail[,] about the wife.

But you look at the notes involving Scooter Libby, there's nothing about the wife. And remember, what Scooter Libby is really saying in terms of Matt Cooper is forget the specifics of the words. Whatever I said, it was to communicate. I'm not confirming anything. That's what—I've heard that too from reporters, but I don't know if it's true. It's the kind of thing a reporter wouldn't write down because it's not confirming anything and it's not written down, which suggests Mr. Libby's recollection is correct.

Next slide. This is the last reporter, Judith Miller . . .

Mr. Libby, you will learn, talked to Ms. Miller on multiple occasions . . . The call that's the subject of the indictment occurs on July 12 . . . Libby has a recollection that they did discuss the wife on that call and that Libby said to Miller the same thing he said to Cooper. I heard it from reporters, but I don't know if it's true . . .

Mr. Fitzgerald told you in his opening that what Scooter Libby wanted to do was to make up a phony story about having a conversation with Tim Russert so that, when he was asked questions about Ms. Miller and Mr. Cooper, he could say, oh, I didn't get the information from Mr. Cheney. I learned it from Tim Russert. So he could say, well, I just was repeating what a reporter had told me. So that he makes up the Tim Russert conversation.

Now, what the evidence is going to show is that that theory is both illogical and intellectually flawed. And it's intellectually flawed because, on the same day that Mr. Libby talks to Tim Russert, . . . on July 11th, Mr. Libby is told by Karl Rove that Robert Novak has already written a story about Valerie Wilson, saying that Valerie Wilson works at the CIA, and the story has been written. Mr. Libby testifies to it in the Grand Jury. He says, as of the 11th, I understood that Novak had written a story and that the story was coming out that weekend.

So if Mr. Libby needed a reporter on the 11th so that he could say to Miller or Cooper, I've heard it from reporters, he didn't need to invent any phony story with Tim Russert. He testified in the Grand Jury that he had heard on the same day that Robert Novak had written the story.

So all he would have to say, if that's what he wanted to, is well, I've heard that from Robert Novak or I've heard a reporter has already written a story. No need to make up any false, phony story from Tim Russert. Mr. Libby told the truth as he recollected it.

And the entire premise, the theory of the prosecution's case that he had to make up Tim Russert, to put some reporter in between him and Miller and Cooper, it's just stupid. It's just stupid . . .

. . . In terms of evaluating Mr. Fleischer's testimony, Mr. Fleischer is in a different position than any other witness in this case. Mr. Fleischer was the Press Secretary to President Bush. And when the FBI asks to speak to Mr. Fleischer, Mr. Fleischer asserted the Fifth Amendment. Mr. Fleischer refused to testify. He said I plead the Fifth. I will not testify about anything unless I am immunized. I want complete protection from anything.

. . . After being immunized, Mr. Fleischer then testifies and says he has this recollection of this conversation with Mr. Libby.

Now, what you will learn from the evidence is that Mr. Fleischer, while in Africa with the President of the United States, Secretary Powell, Condoleezza Rice, [and] Mr. Bartlett, the head of Communications, they all go on July 7 to Africa . . . Now, while on the plane, Mr. Fleischer says he has a conversation with a Mr. Bartlett.

And he says Mr. Bartlett tells him about the wife working at the CIA . . .

And Mr. Fleischer then says that, right after Mr. Bartlett tells him about the wife, right after the head of White House Communications says something about the wife, then Mr. Fleischer then goes out and has his conversation with David Gregory and perhaps other reporters where he discloses that the wife works at the CIA.

And you'll find that the timeline is interesting because Mr. Fleischer says, Mr. Libby told him about the wife at the lunch. And if it's a passing comment, so be it, on July 7th. And then Mr. Bartlett that evening gets on the airplane to go to Africa with the President. And reporters are on the plane.

Mr. Bartlett doesn't say anything to any reporter on the 7th. Doesn't say anything to any reporter on the 8th. Doesn't say anything to any reporter on the 9th. Doesn't say anything to any reporter on the 10th. But right after Mr. Bartlett says to him that the wife works at the CIA, that's when Mr. Fleischer goes and has conversations with reporters about the wife.

So what you'll see, in terms of the evidence concerning these six witnesses, that all of these witnesses have their own personal recollection problems, or, like Mr. Fleischer, may have issues where their credibility should be questioned because they have an arrangement . . .

Now . . . I want to go to a different area . . .

I want to tell you how the world looked through Scooter Libby's eyes. I want to take you to that week of July 6, from Sunday right through that Saturday. Because the question is well, what did Mr. Libby recollect three months later about what happened on July 10, 11 and 12? That's the issue in the case.

Let's talk about what was going on in his life. Let's try to see what the evidence will show in terms of putting things in context because, again, when you start off thinking this case is about the wife, the wife is naturally just blown out of proportion . . .

This is critically important: there's a huge difference between discussions about Mr. Wilson and the Wilson allegations and discussions about the wife. Mr. Wilson's allegations that the Vice President of the United States had, in some way, suppressed information, lied to the American public concerning his knowledge of Mr. Wilson's trip to Niger were extraordinarily important. There's no dispute about that, nor will there be.

But in terms of the wife, the wife did not have that importance. You should not let the two issues be conflated . . . Some people have said, and you'll see some newspaper articles to the effect, that there was a plan in the White House to retaliate against Mr. Wilson, to punish Mr. Wilson for being a critic of the war by outing his wife . . .

Whether such a plan existed in the White House or not, I don't know. But Scooter Libby was not part of any such plan . . .

And you'll learn that the Vice President asked Libby to help him respond to the sixteen-word controversy, and that's what is meant by the Vice President's note neck in the meat grinder. That's what's meant by the note. He was thrown into this . . .

In October of 2002, there had been an NIE published that dealt with issues dealing with Iraq and weapons of mass destruction. It was an extraordinarily high secret document. Some of the NIE had been publicly disclosed to the public. Other parts had been kept secret.

. . . Shortly before July 8th, President Bush makes a decision that he is going to declassify certain parts of the NIE.

It is a decision that is made and that is not published or publicized and only three people at that time already know about the decision by President Bush to declassify certain portions of the NIE, President Bush himself, Vice President Cheney and Scooter Libby.

Secretary of State Powell is not told. Mr. Hadley is not told. Condoleezza Rice is not told. The President has decided I want to declassify certain portions of this NIE. He tells that to the Vice President of the United States. The Vice President says to Mr. Libby, the President has declassified certain portions of this document.

And I, the Vice President, want you, Mr. Libby, to talk on a selective basis to certain reporters to get the story out. Give them an exclusive. You are to tell no one anything about the declassification process or how it came about. It's supposed to be top secret.

Now, you'll learn, in this case, there is no dispute that the President has the authority to make the declassification decision on his own. He has the authority, if he wishes as he decided to do, to make the disclosure on a selected basis. And there is no dispute, in this case, that President Bush did it with respect to disclosures made by Mr. Libby on July 8th.

There is no dispute that it was done by the President and that, what Mr. Libby did, in terms of what he did on July 8th, was appropriate. But Mr. Libby, on July 8th, was basically put in the spot. This is still part of the meat grinder, where he was engaged for him. This was not normal business. He was being tasked by the President to the Vice President to go talk with Judy Miller.

He meets with Judy Miller at a hotel in Washington, D.C. He makes disclosures to Ms. Miller with respect to the NIE because the President and the Vice President had made the decision that this story needs to get out . . .

[T]here are going to be discussions where Mr. Libby, for example, is in the presence of Mr. Hadley, one of the top intelligence officers in the country. And Mr. Hadley is sitting there talking about we need to declassify the NIE.

Mr. Libby has to stay silent. He can't even tell Mr. Hadley that the President already declassified it for secret purposes for me to talk to certain reporters. He has to be quiet. Vice President is there too. He has to be quiet. They have to follow the President's instructions that this not be discussed, that this not be disclosed.

But it has nothing to do with the wife . . .

So what are we going to do? We're going to give you a complete picture. We're going to give you a full picture. And we're going to show you that he's totally innocent. He didn't do anything. This is, as I said, a circumstantial evidence case based on he said/she said. We're going to put things in context. I want to conclude now, just by highlighting again. These are the key points:

Good faith recollection. Innocent mistakes. No knowledge that Wilson's job status was classified. Didn't push reporters to write about Wilson. Did not leak to Robert Novak. He's innocent and [had] no motive to lie.

I want to focus you back on that note. Not going to protect one staffer and sacrifice the guy that was asked to stick his neck in the meat grinder because of the incompetence of others.

During this trial, you will learn . . . how the Vice President of the United States ordered him to stick his neck in the meat grinder. But being in the meat grinder . . . did not involve saying anything about Valerie Wilson. Did not . . .

I want to conclude by saying what I said earlier. You promised you would be fair. Any feelings about the war in Iraq, you would put to the side. You promised. The only way I lose this case is if somebody starts to interpret the evidence based on your feelings about the war. They have no evidence. They have no case. He is innocent and, at the end of this trial, I will ask you to return a verdict of not guilty on each and every count.

Thank you.

*

MARC GROSSMAN

THE FIRST WITNESS THE GOVERNMENT CALLS is Marc Grossman, who was the Undersecretary of State for Political Affairs, the number three position in the State Department, at the time of the outing of Valerie Plame. As such, he worked closely with Richard Armitage, the Deputy Secretary of State to Colin Powell. He also interacted several times a week with Scooter Libby, generally at Deputies' Committee meetings. In that context, according to his testimony, in May 2003 he was asked by Libby about Joe Wilson, a former ambassador who traveled to Niger, before Wilson had publicly identified himself. In order to respond, he requested information from two units within the State Department, and had the INR report produced, which included the fact that Wilson's wife worked in the CIA on weapons of mass destruction. He reported back to Libby first about Wilson himself and then, in early June as part of a more detailed account, about the fact that Wilson's wife worked at the CIA. Grossman testified that he thought what he learned about Wilson's wife's purported role in her husband's mission was irregular. The defense cross-examined Grossman about his memory of those events, and also about the fact that in October 2003, Richard Armitage, Grossman's immediate superior, came to him the night before Grossman was to be interviewed by the FBI and told him that he, Armitage, had leaked information about Plame to Robert Novak. The defense hoped, thereby, to suggest some inappropriate conduct on Armitage's part and possibly on Grossman's, giving him a bias against Libby.

Even before Grossman begins testifying, there is a dispute over whether the defense should be allowed to cross-examine him on Armitage's conduct with Grossman at the time of Grossman's interview with the FBI in October 2003. As Wells describes the issue for the judge:

MR. WELLS: Your Honor, what Mr. Grossman says is the following. Mr. Grossman is interviewed by the FBI about my client, Mr. Libby, on October 17th. The night before he is to be interviewed by the FBI, he is visited by Richard Armitage [who] tells Mr. Grossman there are some things I think you ought to know. He then discusses with him, I want you to know that I was the one who leaked to Mr. Novak.

Discussion is had about whether what was leaked was confidential, was classified for not. Mr. Armitage has said in the 302[3] itself . . . "that Mr. Grossman was mixed up," that's in quotes . . .

I personally interviewed Mr. Grossman [who] said that he recognized at the time of the conversation that meeting with another witness on the night before . . . his interview could be construed as "cooking the books." Those are his words, not mine.

---

[3] Standard FBI document, used to make a record of an interview.

. . . After they meet, the night before, . . . he goes into [an] interview . . . concerning Mr. Libby . . . [T]hen Mr. Grossman, goes back and reports to Mr. Armitage what took place at the FBI interview.

I have every right to go after Mr. Grossman with respect to whether or not he was engaged in inappropriate conduct, whether he engaged in what could be construed as obstruction, whether or not he and Mr. Armitage had discussions that impacted what he says about Mr. Libby in this trial.

He will testify that every time he talked to Mr. Libby he went back and reported to Mr. Armitage. Every time there was a conversation between Mr. Grossman and Mr. Armitage, he first went back and reported it. That Mr. Armitage gave him authorization as to what to say and what should be said.

And in a meeting the night before the interview and talking about subjects that are part of the FBI interview, and he has admitted that he knows full well it could be viewed as cooking the books, I have every right. This is cross-examination. I'm going right after him. I have every right to do that.

THE COURT: Let me just ask. In reference to the specific conversations that Armitage had with him, how would that somehow be relevant on your suggestion of motive or whatever?

MR. WELLS: They come out with a story, Your Honor, that Mr. Libby is the one who caused the State Department to do what's called an INR report. And that all started because Scooter Libby asked for it. So, it's all on Mr. Libby. I don't accept it . . .

THE JUDGE ACCEPTS the defense's contention, and Grossman is brought in. In response to questioning from prosecutor Peter Zeidenberg, Grossman explains who he is and his role as number three in the State Department under Powell and Armitage during the events at issue in the trial, as well as how he interacted with Libby several times a week at Deputies' Committee meetings. Zeidenberg asks Grossman about a conversation Grossman had with Libby before or after the May 29, 2003 Deputies' Committee meeting:

Q *Can you tell the ladies and gentlemen what you recall about that conversation?*
A Yes. I recall that Mr. Libby just asked me if I knew anything about the travel of a retired ambassador, a former ambassador to Africa to look into the question of yellowcake, and I said that I did not.

Q *Was that anything that you were familiar with?*
A No, sir.

Q *What was your reaction to the question?*
A Well, first of all, I told him that I would be very glad to look into it. And I was, I guess, a little bit embarrassed that I didn't know because I should have . . .

Q *Why do you say that?*
A Well, I think that if the Chief of Staff of the Vice President asks you a question

and it's about a retired ambassador, it made some sense that maybe I would have known about it.

Q *What did you say you would do?*

A I said I would look into it and report back to him . . .

Q *Now, did you discuss a time frame as to when you were going to get back to him?*

A No, sir. I said I would just get back to him. I think he had every right to assume I would do so as quickly as possible . . . I took it as a perfectly legitimate and right question from the Chief of Staff of the Vice President.

Q *What did you do upon returning to your office after that Deputies Committee meeting?*

A . . . [S]ince I did not know anything about this specific question, I went and asked Mr. Armitage if he knew anything about it. I figured I had better sort of check up first, so I didn't get myself into any trouble.

Q *Why would you say you wouldn't get yourself into any trouble?*

A Well, there are programs in the government that only Deputy Secretaries of State and Secretaries of State know about. I didn't want to go thrashing around inside the bureaucracy if this was something that other people shouldn't have been aware of.

Q *What was Mr. Armitage's reaction when you asked him if he knew about it?*

A He said he knew nothing about it either. I went back to my office is my recollection, and I sent an e-mail to the two . . . Assistant Secretaries [I thought were responsible], the Assistant Secretary for Intelligence and Research and the Assistant Secretary for African Affairs. I said "I have this question. Does this ring any bells with anybody?"

Q *Did you get a response back?*

A Yes, I did . . . I got two responses . . . They both said yes, they knew all about it, and they had known about it. They said that they had known that . . . retired Ambassador Joe Wilson had gone to Africa. That he had gone to check into this allegation about the yellowcake. That they knew he had reported back to the government.

Q *What did you do with this information?*

A Well, the first thing I did was I went back to Mr. Armitage, and I said well, here's some pretty interesting information. Does this make you recall it? He said no. And then my recollection . . . is that, having sort of gotten a little bit of this information at least that I then put in a call to Mr. Libby and said I've got . . . some of the answer here. I may have apologized that I didn't know. I said I'd give him a fuller report when I had it.

Q *Did you reach out yourself to Mr. Wilson?*

A I did, yes, sir.

Q *Can you tell the ladies and gentlemen about that? First, when did you do that?*

A I think I did it on that same day. And when I was visiting Rich, Mr. Armitage, I said look, I happen to know Joe Wilson. Maybe I'll just call him up. Is that okay with you. And he said sure, go ahead.

Q *How did you happen to know Joe Wilson?*

A We had known each other kind [of] on and off in the foreign service, and . . . he and I both went to the University of California in Santa Barbara. He had been, over the years, active in the alumnae association and had involved me in a couple of events.

Q *How often did you have contact with Mr. Wilson?*

A Maybe twice a year.

Q *What was Mr. Armitage's reaction when you suggested maybe you should just call Mr. Wilson up yourself?*

A Told me to go right ahead . . .

Q *Can you tell us what happened when you did that?*

A Yes. He told me all about the trip. He said that he had gone. He had made contact, and he visited with people in Africa, come back and reported to the government . . .

Q *Now, do you have a memory, present memory today whether you spoke to Mr. Wilson before or after you spoke to Mr. Libby on May 29th?*

A My recollection is I spoke to Joe Wilson before and told Mr. Libby about it.

Q *What do you recall telling Mr. Libby about your conversation with Ambassador Wilson?*

A Simply that I had known him. Thought it was best to go directly to the source, and so I did. I told him about my conversation.

Q *. . . Did you talk to Mr. Wilson about who Mr. Wilson thought instigated the trip?*

A . . . Mr. Wilson said that he thought the trip had been at the request of the Office of the Vice President.

Q *Did you relay that information to Mr. Libby?*

A I believe so.

Q *Did Mr. Libby have a reaction to that?*

A No, sir.

Q *Now, . . . you testified a few minutes ago that you told Mr. Libby that you were going to try and get a fuller report?*

A Correct.

Q *Why is it you wanted to get a fuller report?*

A . . . I . . . felt that the information that I had received just didn't all add up to me. I had a sense that there was some other information yet to be had.

Q *So, what did you do?*

A . . . I said, ["A]ll right. We've got sort of different parts of the government, different parts of the State Department who know about this. Let's write it all down and make sure everybody knows what everybody else knows.["] So I asked that a memo be written to me with everything that we knew at the State Department about this issue . . .

Q *Did you ultimately get a report?*

A Yes, sir.

Q *When did you get it?*

A I got it either late on the 10th or the 11th of June . . .

Q *Can you tell us about that report?*

A Well, the report was a more full compilation of . . . what the department knew. And it was also a rendition of what our people had been involved with, which were meetings at the Agency in order to get the trip organized.

Q *And the trip we're talking about is Mr. Wilson's trip to Niger?*

A Yes, sir.

Q *In that report, it came from what department or agency?*

A It came from the Bureau of Intelligence and Research.

Q *Is there an abbreviation that goes with that?*

A INR, sir . . . It is the State Department's internal research organization and the organization that has interfaced with the intelligence agencies around town.

Q *Now, do you recall when you read the INR report, information about Joseph Wilson's wife?*

A Yes, I do.

Q *Can you tell the ladies and gentlemen of the jury what it is you recall reading in that report?*

A I recall reading that Valerie Wilson was employed at the CIA.

Q *Can you explain the context in which it came up in the report?*

A Yes. As I recall, the context was that, a number of, some of our people had gone to a meeting to . . . help organize Ambassador Wilson's trip. And that Mrs. Wilson, as the report referred to her, was the chair of those meetings. And that she was described in that memo as a WMD, Weapons of Mass Destruction manager type.

Q *Did it indicate in that report or did you have an understanding after reading the report, what role she may have played in Mr. Wilson's trip?*

A According to the report, she was the organizer of Ambassador Wilson's trip.

Q *Do you recall your reaction to reading this?*

A I thought this was pretty interesting.

Q *When you say "interesting," what do you mean?*

A I thought it was kind of odd and remarkable that she worked at the Agency, and secondly, that she had been involved in the organization of the trip.

Q *Did you recall thinking whether or not, in your own mind, whether or not it was appropriate or not?*

A I thought that it was not appropriate . . . .

Q *What struck you about it?*

A It seemed to me that it didn't seem right somehow . . .that the spouse of someone would be organizing their spouse's trip.

Q *Did you have a subsequent conversation with Mr. Libby about this information?*
A I did.

Q *Can you tell the ladies and gentlemen when that was?*
A My recollection is it was at the next time we saw each other at a Deputies Committee meeting, sir.

Q *If we could go to June 11th, can you tell the ladies and gentlemen what Deputies Committee meeting you would have attended on June 11th, that Mr. Libby would also have been present at?*
A I can say that I attended a meeting on June 11th on Afghanistan at 12:00.

Q *Is that one that Mr. Libby would typically attend?*
A I believe so. As I say, it's my recollection that I told him, I had a second conversation with him at the next Deputies Committee meeting . . .

Q *And if we could go to June 12th. Is there a Deputies Committee meeting there that you would have attended?*
A Yes, there are two. One on Indonesia and one on Iraq.

Q *What times are they?*
A One at 12:00 o'clock and one at 12:45, sir.

Q *In your mind, sitting here today, can you recollect whether your subsequent conversation with Mr. Libby was either on June 11th or June 12th?*
A I can only tell you that I believe it was on one of those days.

Q *Okay. Can you tell the ladies and gentlemen what happened when you saw Mr. Libby at that next Deputies Committee meeting?*
A I just went up to him and I said that I wanted him to recall the question he had asked me. That we knew that Ambassador Wilson had made this trip. That he has reported back to the government. And I said there was one other thing that you['ve] got to know and that is that his wife worked at the Agency . . .

> *And I said there was one other thing that you['ve] got to know and that is that his wife worked at the Agency . . .*

Q *How is it . . . , to the best of your recollection, you phrased that when you told him?*
A . . . I recall that I said that there was one other thing I thought he needed to know, which was that Mrs. Wilson, or that Joe Wilson's wife worked at the Agency.

Q *When you said Agency, what were you referring to?*
A The CIA.

Q *Is Agency a way that you would typically refer to the CIA?*
A Yes, sir.

Q *Now, when you say, said to Mr. Libby there is one other thing I think you need to know, why did you phrase it that way?*

A Well, I phrased it that way because he was senior to me. I felt it was my responsibility to make sure that he had the whole context. I didn't think it was right . . . to not tell him the whole story.

Q *Now, what was Mr. Libby's reaction?*

A [He] thanked me and he said in response that he wanted to tell me something, which was that he wanted me to know that the Office of the Vice President had nothing to do with organizing Mr. Wilson's trip. I thanked him and that was that . . .

Q *Did you have any subsequent conversation with Deputy Secretary of State Armitage about your conversation with Mr. Libby?*

A I don't recall. It would have been normal for me to tell him that I closed the loop with [Mr. Libby].

ZEIDENBERG TURNS TO QUESTIONING Grossman about his FBI interview and Armitage's intervention the evening before, hoping to blunt the force of the defense's upcoming questioning:

Q *Now, were you subsequently interviewed by the FBI in connection with this investigation?*

A Yes, sir.

Q *And prior to the FBI coming to see you, were you visited by Deputy Secretary Armitage?*

A I was.

Q *What was the—tell us about that?*

A Well, you know the night before or the day that the FBI came to visit me, Mr. Armitage asked me to see him . . . He told me that, before I saw the FBI, he wanted me to know . . . that he had told Mr. Novak about Joe Wilson's wife.

He told me it was sort of unbelievable—he said it was the dumbest thing he had ever done in his life. That he had done it just as Mr. Novak was leaving. That he hadn't mentioned any names but that he had felt terrible about it. That he offered to quit. And that he had reported it fully to the FBI.

Q *Did he tell you why he was telling you?*

A He told me that he thought it was—he told me that he didn't want me to go to my FBI interview without knowing this fact.

Q *How did you take—what was your impression, your feeling when he told you this?*

A I was really shocked. I was shocked and I was disappointed. But I thought, for me anyway, that he had given me, it was clearly a matter of, he had given me a piece of professional courtesy and I appreciated it.

Q *At your FBI interview, did you relay the information about what Secretary Armitage had told you?*

A Yes, sir.

Q *How did you do that?*

A They asked me at one point if I knew anybody who might have told Mr. Novak anything. I said well yes, actually I do. And I told them about the conversation I had had with Mr. Armitage . . .

MR. ZEIDENBERG: I have no further questions, Your Honor.

ON CROSS-EXAMINATION, Grossman confirms that the conversation with Libby in which he disclosed the fact that Wilson's wife worked at the CIA was very brief. Picking up on Grossman's testimony that he informed Armitage of Libby's interest in the mission to Niger the day Libby initially asked him, May 29, 2003, the defense raises the Nicholas Kristof article of May 6, 2003, which, using Wilson as an anonymous source, is highly critical of the President and also of the Secretary of State Powell. Grossman says he never read the column nor heard about it from Armitage:

By Mr. Wells:

Q *Do you find it strange that there would be an article published on May 6 in* **The New York Times** *about an unnamed ambassador that was highly critical of the State Department in the article and that neither you, the number three person in the State Department, nor Mr. Armitage, the number two person in the State Department, would know [anything] about the article. Do you find that unusual?*

A It seems sort of unusual now that this is such a big deal. But all I can tell you, sir, is that at that time, as my calendar shows, I had about a billion other things to do. . . . I recognize this doesn't sound so smart now. But I just . . . couldn't be troubled with stuff that had happened in the past. My whole job and everybody's job at that time was to make sure that what we were doing in Iraq and Afghanistan was working out.

THE DEFENSE HIGHLIGHTS GROSSMAN'S long familiarity with Joe Wilson, before eliciting testimony about the INR report that Grossman requested. Grossman confirms that he shared the INR report with Armitage, which is presumably how Armitage learned of Plame. Armitage shared the information with reporter Bob Woodward two days later on June 13th, becoming the first known Bush administration official to blow Plame's cover to a reporter:

Q *When you got the report, you indicated on June 10th or 11th you reviewed it, right?*
A I did.

Q *That was the first time you learned about the wife, right?*
A Yes, sir.

Q *Then you had a conversation with Mr. Armitage about the report, correct?*
A Correct.

Q *And Mr. Armitage had a copy of the report also, correct?*
A Yes.

Q *You and Mr. Armitage sat and you discussed what was in the report, right?*
A Correct.

Q *One of the things you discussed was the fact that the wife worked at the CIA, right?*
A Correct.

THE DEFENSE ENTERS the INR memo into evidence and gets Grossman to confirm that it does not indicate that Libby or the Office of the Vice President requested information on the matter, before turning to the report's mention of Wilson's wife. It is disputed elsewhere that Valerie Wilson actually chaired the meeting described below:

Q *Now, the report refers to Ms. Valerie Wilson in the second paragraph, correct?*
A Yes, sir.

Q *The second paragraph reads, "From what we can find in our records, Joe Wilson played only a walk-on part in the Niger/Iraq uranium story. In a February 19, 2002, meeting, convened by Valerie Wilson, a CIA Weapons of Mass Destruction manager and the wife of Joe Wilson, he previewed his plans and rationale for going to Niger but said he would only go if the [State] Department thought his trip made sense."*
  So in the report, Ms. Wilson is described as a CIA Weapons of Mass Destruction manager, right?
A Correct.

Q *And the report also indicates that it was Ms. Valerie Wilson who convened the meeting with respect to her husband possibly going on a trip, correct?*
A Correct.

Q *Was that a meeting with persons from the State Department and the CIA?*
A Well, I assume so because later on, there's a kind of a record of that meeting, yes, sir.

Q *We'll get to the record in a minute. It's fair to say though that, based on the evidence you received in the INR report, there is absolutely no indication that the Office of the Vice President had anything to do in terms of requesting Mr. Wilson to go on that trip, right?*
A That's correct.

Q *. . . There was no evidence that Vice President Cheney personally received a report concerning what Mr. Wilson found on his trip, right?*
A No, sir . . .

THIS IS PART OF LIBBY'S DEFENSE that he was responding to Wilson on the merits of his claims, not smearing him. The defense then elicits testimony that Grossman kept Armitage apprised that he was going to talk to Libby about the report. After asking Grossman about how onerous the preparation for Deputies Committee meeting was, the defense asks Grossman about his own view of the importance of

Wilson's wife's role:

Q *In terms of how you viewed the importance of the wife back on June 10th or 11th, how would you describe it?*

A I actually, with respect to how I viewed the whole thing is was just not very important at all.

Q *Did you view the wife as zero or less than zero importance?*

A I thought the whole business was of less than zero importance. I thought the wife was kind of an interesting tidbit if you will.

Q *Now, when you talked to Mr. Libby on June 11th or 12th, it was a face-to-face meeting, correct?*

A Uh-huh.

Q *And it's fair to say that at no time did you tell Mr. Libby in any way, shape or form that the employment status of Ms. Valerie Wilson was classified or covert?*

A No, sir.

Wells tells the judge this is a good place to stop for the day, and Judge Walton recesses the court for the day.

JANUARY 24, 2007

MARC GROSSMAN (continued)

THE DEFENSE RESUMES CROSS-EXAMINATION of Grossman, and begins by bringing out the fact that there are no documents associated with any of Grossman's interactions with Libby about the Wilsons. The defense also contends that Libby did not himself receive a copy of the INR report, and then delves into the details of the memo. One particularly interesting line of questioning brings up the dispute between the CIA and the State Department over the Niger intelligence, in the context of the decision to send Wilson on the mission in February 2002:

Q *And it is fair to say that based on your review of the documents, you came to understand that there was a disagreement between how the CIA viewed the issue of Iraqis possibly buying uranium from Niger and how the people in INR viewed the issue, correct?*

A From the document, yes, sir.

Q *Okay. And the people at the CIA took the possibility of Iraqis trying to buy uranium from Niger much more seriously than the people at the State Department, correct?*

A I don't know that, sir. I only know what's written here, sir.

Q *Okay. Well, at least in terms of verifying whether or not there was any truth to the possibility that Iraqis were trying to buy uranium from Niger, it was the position of the people at INR and the State Department that it wasn't necessary to send Ambassador Wilson there, but rather that the State Department's embassy in Niger could deal with the issue?*

A I would say, to be fair, sir, . . . that's the position of the people who went to that meeting. I have no idea what the position of the senior leadership of INR was, but that is certainly what I read from the paragraph, sir.

GROSSMAN CONFIRMS THAT THE INR report containing information about Wilson's wife was faxed to Colin Powell on Air Force One on July 7, 2003, and the document is entered into evidence. Grossman is asked about a conversation he had with Joe Wilson on June 9, 2003 and another on June 10:

Q *Okay. So on June 9th, which was a Monday, you had a conversation with former Ambassador Wilson concerning his reaction to having seen Condoleezza Rice on* Meet the Press *on June 8th, right? . . .*

A Yes, sir.

Q *And what he told you was that he was furious at the comments of Condoleezza Rice on* **Meet the Press** *that Sunday?*

A Yes, sir. He was really mad…[A]s I recall it, …he was very mad at the way he had been described and that people were not taking him seriously, sir.…[H]e [said] he had been described as some low-level person, and he was very upset by that, sir.

Q *And did he also tell you that he was considering going public in order to correct what he thought was a misimpression caused by the statements of Condoleezza Rice? . . .*

A Yes, sir.

Q *Okay. And then you talked to Mr. Libby on June 11 or 12 about his concerns about the unnamed ambassador, right?*

A Yes, sir.

Q *And you have made absolutely no mention to Mr. Libby of the fact that you had talked to Mr. Wilson on June 9th and that he was furious and might go public, correct?*

A I think that's true, yes, sir.

Q *You kept the comments that Mr. Wilson was furious and might go public . . . to yourself, right?*

A Yes, sir.

Q *You didn't tell anybody, did you?*

A No, sir, I did not.

Q *Now, is it correct that on June 10 you placed a telephone call to Mr. Wilson concerning the background with respect to the Niger trip?*

A Sir, I can't recall now whether these are one call or two, but I know I did call him to continue to get information, yes, sir.

Q *Is it possible that the first time you called him to get information was, in fact, on June 10, 2003?*

A As opposed to the 29th of May?

Q *Yes, sir.*

A That's not my recollection, sir . . .

THE DEFENSE PRODS GROSSMAN to acknowledge that in fact the June 10 conversation—and not the May 29 conversation, as Grossman testified—was his first with Wilson. But Grossman insists that the May 29 conversation really happened. Grossman is asked about what he did after his conversation with Libby in June:

Q *Okay. Mr. Grossman, with respect to your June 11 or 12th conversation with Mr. Libby during which you disclosed to him that Mrs. Wilson worked at the CIA, did you advise Secretary Powell that you had had such a conversation with Mr. Libby?*

A I believe I did, yes, sir . . .

THE DEFENSE PRESSES GROSSMAN on the fact that when he was initially inter-viewed by the FBI in fall 2003, he stated that his conversations with Libby about the Wilsons were over the phone, not in person. The defense raises other memory issues in order to undermine Grossman's testimony.

Q *I want you to look at page 2 of your October 17, 2003 interview. Read paragraph 1 and see if that refreshes your recollection.*

A Okay, sir.

Q *Does that refresh your recollection that during your October 17, 2003, interview with the FBI that you told the FBI that in terms of giving Mr. Libby information concerning Mr. Wilson's trip and Valerie Wilson, that you had two or three tele-phone conversations with Mr. Libby and that you made absolutely no reference to a face-to-face meeting with Mr. Libby?*

A Sir, I don't know how to explain this. All I can tell you is that today, as I look back on this, my recollection is that they were face-to-face meetings . . . I don't know what else to tell you, sir.

Q *I have a very limited question: Having looked at the FBI interview, does it refresh your recollection that you told the FBI something different in October of 2003 than what you told this jury?*

A No, sir.

Q *. . . Do you deny that you made the statement to the FBI?*

A I believe I made the same statements I have made to the jury, sir . . .

GROSSMAN CONTINUES TO RESIST the defense's implications, but does acknowledge that he has changed his story over time with regard to what he shared with Armitage and Powell:

Q *Now, you told the jury yesterday that you discussed with Mr. Armitage the INR report, correct?*

A Yes, sir.

Q *And you said that Mr. Armitage had a copy of the report, correct?*

A Yes, sir.

Q *Do you recall telling the FBI on October 17, 2003, that you had no knowledge regarding whether the INR report was disseminated to Mr. Armitage?*

A I don't recall. I don't deny that.

Q *You don't deny that you said it?*

A Yes, sir.

Q *So you recognize that what you said to the FBI on October 17, 2003, is different from what you said to the jury yesterday?*

A Right. Yes, sir.

Q *Now, you told the jury a few minutes ago that you recall having a conversation with Secretary Powell concerning your conversation with Mr. Libby on June 11 or 12 [about] Mrs. Wilson's employment by the CIA, correct?*

A I think so, yes, sir.

Q *Do you recall that in your FBI interview of February 24, 2004, you stated that you did not discuss with Secretary of State Powell your June 12, 2003, conversation with Mr. Libby?*

A I am sorry. I don't recall that.

Q *Do you deny that you said that to the FBI?*

A I do not deny that, no, sir.

Q *You don't deny it?*

A No, sir.

Q *Okay. So you accept the fact that you told the FBI something different on February 24, 2004, than you told this jury a few minutes ago?*

A Yes, sir . . .

THE DEFENSE THEN SHARPLY QUESTIONS Grossman about the fact that Richard Armitage talked to Grossman the day before Grossman's first interview with the FBI about Armitage's own role and testimony in the case:

Q *Now, in terms of verifying the accuracy of your conversations with Mr. Ford and Mr. Kansteiner, prior to being interviewed by the FBI on October 17, 2003, you did not go and talk to either Mr. Ford or Mr. Kansteiner about your recollection and its accuracy of what had happened, correct?*

A Yes, sir.

Q *And the reason you did not do that is you understood it was improper and would have been inappropriate for you to go talk to a potential witness of the criminal investigation prior to the time that you were about to be interviewed by the FBI, right?*

A No, sir. I think I didn't do it because I was sure that there would be these e-mails and it would all just be all there.

Q *Well, did you recognize that it would be inappropriate for you to talk to a person who might also be a witness in the criminal investigation prior to the time that you were going to be interviewed by the FBI?*

A No, sir.

Q *You did not realize that was inappropriate?*

A No, sir.

Q *. . . Did you realize it could be construed as possibly cooking the books by having such conversations with other potential witnesses in the criminal investigation?*

A No, sir. I simply thought the e-mails were there and that that would take care of it.

Q *. . . Do you recall stating, during your interview with myself and other lawyers and* *a State Department attorney, that you recognized that if you had met with Mr. Ford and Mr. Kansteiner about their recollections of what happened on the eve of your being interviewed by the FBI, that that might be construed as cooking the books?*

A No, sir.

Q *You have no recollection of making that statement? …*

A The recollection I have is a very clear one, which is you asked me if I thought that was true about my conversation with Mr. Armitage. With respect, I don't think and I do not recall in our conversation at your offices that we talked about Mr. Kansteiner or Mr. Ford at all.

Q *Okay. Do you recall that with respect to Mr. Armitage, in our discussions that you used the term that your meeting with Mr. Armitage on the eve of your FBI interview might be viewed as "fishy"?*

A You said to me that some people could see it that way, and I said that was true, yes, sir . . .

Q *And on the night before your interview with the FBI on . . . October 17, 2003, you had a private meeting with Mr. Armitage, right?*

A Either the night before or that morning, yes, sir.

Q *And it happened right before the FBI interview was supposed to take place, correct?*

A Yes, sir.

Q *And it was a private meeting, right?*

A I believe so, yes, sir.

Q *Just you and Mr. Armitage one-on-one, correct?*

A Yes, sir.

Q *And Mr. Armitage understood that you were going to be interviewed shortly by the FBI, correct?*

A Yes, sir . . .

Q *He told you he thought there were certain things that you should know before your FBI interview, right?*

A Yes, sir.

Q *And he said to you he wanted you to know before the FBI interview that he, Richard Armitage, had disclosed the fact that Valerie Wilson worked for the CIA to a journalist by the name of Robert Novak, right?*

A He said to me he wanted me to know he had disclosed that to the FBI, yes, sir.

Q *And before he said he disclosed it to the FBI, he said he had first disclosed it to Mr. Novak…right?*

A No. My recollection is that the conversation started with his reporting on his conversation with the FBI, sir.

Q *Okay. And what he told you was that he, Mr. Armitage, had told the FBI that Mr.*

Armitage had disclosed to Robert Novak that Mrs. Wilson worked for the CIA?

A Yes, sir.

Q *And you knew at that time that there was an ongoing criminal investigation with respect to who had disclosed Mrs. Wilson's work status at the CIA to Mr. Novak, correct?*

A Yes, sir.

Q *And you knew when Mr. Armitage made that disclosure to you, that he was a subject of that investigation, correct?*

A I knew he had been interviewed by the FBI, yes, sir.

Q *And Mr. Armitage discussed with you the fact that he did not view Mrs. Wilson's employment at the CIA as being covert or classified, correct?*

MR. ZEIDENBERG: Objection.

THE COURT: Sustained. Approach.

(Sealed bench conference.)

By Mr. Wells:

Q *Mr. Grossman, is it correct that after you met with Mr. Armitage and he disclosed to you the fact that he, Mr. Armitage, had been the person to disclose information concerning Ms. Wilson's employment at the CIA to Mr. Novak, that you then were interviewed by the FBI? Correct?*

A Yes, sir.

Q *And is it correct that, after you were interviewed by the FBI, you went back and met with Mr. Armitage and discussed with him some of the things that took place during your FBI interview?*

A I went back to him and reported that the subject had come up, yes, sir.

Q *Okay. And you described to him what questions they had asked you and how you had responded?*

A I told him that I had conveyed to them the substance of what he had told me about his FBI interview, yes, sir.

MR. WELLS: Okay. I have no further questions . . .

THE BRIEF REDIRECT by the prosecution includes this:

Q *. . . [O]n your cross-examination yesterday, I believe, you said that the issue of Joseph Wilson and his trip to Niger and the wife was—I forget exactly how you put it. It wasn't really on your radar screen. It wasn't an important issue to you. Is that correct?*

A To me, no, sir.

Q *And if it was so relatively unimportant to you, can you tell us why you tasked INR to come up with a report about it?*

A I was trying to answer Mr. Libby's question.

MR. ZEIDENBERG: I have nothing further, Your Honor.

THE JURY HAS A FEW minor questions on the State Department's role in Wilson's trip, which Grossman minimizes, and the first witness in the trial is excused.

ROBERT GRENIER

ROBERT GRENIER WAS A LONGTIME EMPLOYEE on the clandestine, operations side of the CIA who, in the spring-summer of 2003 was the Iraq mission manager, the CIA's point person on Iraq. He regularly attended Deputies Committee Meetings on Iraq in the Situation Room at the White House, where he interacted with Scooter Libby.

Grenier was one of several government officials to testify that he told Libby that Joe Wilson's wife worked at the CIA in June 2003. Grenier testified that Libby called him on June 11, 2003 asking for information on Joe Wilson. Libby, whom Grenier said sounded aggrieved and accusatory toward the CIA, told Grenier that Wilson was telling reporters and others that he had gone to Niger for the CIA on a mission that called into question prewar claims about WMD, and that the mission was in response to a request from the Office of the Vice President. Because Libby was a senior government official, Cheney's Chief of Staff, and because he sounded accusatory, Grenier wanted to be as helpful as possible. When Libby had Grenier pulled out of an important meeting later that day, Grenier told him what he had learned about Wilson's mission, including the fact that Wilson's wife worked in the unit of the Counter Proliferation Division of the CIA that had sent Wilson.

Grenier testified that he immediately felt guilty for having disclosed the identity of a CIA officer when it was not absolutely necessary, and it was that feeling and his efforts to rationalize it away that ultimately triggered his memory of having told Libby about Plame—a memory that had grown fuzzy and uncertain by the time Grenier was interviewed by the FBI in fall 2003 and the Grand Jury in January 2004. Grenier changed his testimony in July 2005. Libby's defense exploited Grenier's changing memory in their cross-examination.

Prosecutor Peter Zeidenberg does the direct examination of Grenier:

Q *Now, I would like to direct your attention to June 11, 2003. Do you recall receiving a phone message that Scooter Libby called you that day?*

A I received a phone message. I couldn't have told you on my own that it was June 11th, but of course I have seen a slip indicating that we had received that call at my office, which is dated June 11th . . .

Q *And can you tell the ladies and gentlemen whether or not it was unusual or typical for you to get phone calls from Scooter Libby?*

A That was the—that was the first time that it ever happened.

Q *And do you recall—the time on that slip is—could you translate that? It says 1315.*
A 1315, which means 1:15 p.m.

Q *And can you tell us to the best of your recollection approximately when you believe you actually received that message?*
A I believe it was fairly shortly after that time, but I can't tell you precisely when.

Q *And did you call Mr. Libby when you got that note?*
A Yes, I did.

Q *Can you tell us about that?*
A Well, I placed the call to Mr. Libby, and we talked . . . He told me that there was an individual by the name of Joseph Wilson, a former ambassador, who, as he said, was going around town speaking to people in the press and claiming that he, Ambassador Wilson, had been sent on a mission by the CIA to the country of Niger in Africa to try to determine whether there was any truth to previous reports that Iraq had attempted to purchase uranium from Niger.

Q *And what else, if anything, did he tell you during that conversation?*
A Well—and he also said that Mr. Wilson was claiming that he, Mr. Wilson, had been told by his contacts in the CIA that the only reason that they were following up in this manner—the only reason that they were dispatching him to Africa was because of interest in this issue that had been expressed by the Office of the Vice President.

Q *And did Mr. Libby—did he tell you what it was he wanted?*
A Yes. He wanted two things. He wanted me to verify for him whether or not there was truth to that story, whether, in fact, the CIA had sent Ambassador Wilson to Africa on this mission, and, secondly, whether it was, in fact, true that the only reason that the CIA had done so was because of interest expressed by the Office of the Vice President.

Q *How did he refer to the individual who went to Niger, by name or by title?*
A It was by name. Joe Wilson, as I recall.

Q *And did he say anything about what Mr. Wilson was saying? [What] his basis of knowledge was for his claim?*
A The claim that they—the Office of the Vice President sent him. Oh, that it was people in the CIA who had told Mr. Wilson this.

Q *And what was Mr. Libby's tone of voice on the telephone?*
A Well, I think it was pretty even. He was—he was concerned about this. He was clearly serious about it. I think, on that particular issue, as I recall, he sounded a little bit aggrieved. There was a slightly accusatory tone in his voice when he mentioned about the story that people in [the] CIA had stated this to Mr. Wilson, i.e., that it was only because of interest on the part of the Vice President that they were doing this. And the way that he said it, it suggested to me that CIA people had perhaps been complaining about the Office of the Vice President.

Q *Did Mr. Libby talk to you in the course of that conversation about the press?*

A I recall that he mentioned that Joe Wilson was repeating the story to the press.

Q *And did he tell you what it is he wanted you to do?*

A Again, he wanted—he wanted for me to try to verify whether or not the two parts of the story were true, i.e., that first we had sent Mr. Wilson off to Africa, and secondly,—whether or not it was true that we had only done so because of interest on the part of the Office of the Vice President. I vaguely recall in the course of that conversation saying to him something to the effect that, well, I don't know what people might have said to Mr. Wilson, if, in fact, these conversations took place, but I can find out whether or not—you know, what was the reason why we dispatched him on that visit, and was it only because of the Vice President.

Q *And what, if anything, did you know about Ambassador Wilson and his trip to Niger at that point, June 11th, during this telephone call?*

A That was complete news to me. I had never heard of it before.

Q *Did Mr. Libby say how quickly he wanted answers to these questions?*

A He didn't specify, but it was pretty clear from the context that he wanted answers as quickly as I could get them.

Q *And when you say from the context, what context do you mean?*

A Again, it was unusual for him to be calling me in the first place. He was serious about getting an answer. It was probable that I was going to see him in the next day or two. I am not sure when the next Deputies Committee meeting was scheduled for. So that indicated that he wanted an answer certainly sooner than that. And to me, at least in the way that I reacted, when he mentioned that Mr. Wilson was speaking to the press, it suggested—although he didn't say—that he would need to have this information sooner rather than later so that he could potentially get out in front of this story that was perhaps going to appear in the press.

Q *What did you do after you got off the phone with Mr. Libby in regards to his questions?*

A Well, I attempted to call an individual who I thought would have information about this.

Q *And where does this individual work?*

A This—the individual was working in the Counterproliferation Division [CPD] of the CIA.

Q *And who—if we could just refer to that individual by a first name—who was it you were trying to contact?*

A I believe I was trying to contact Kevin.

Q *And what was Kevin's position at the Counterproliferation [Division] within the CIA?*

A There was a unit within the Counterproliferation Division that was devoted to the issue of Iraq weapons of mass destruction. And Kevin was the deputy chief of that unit.

GRENIER DIDN'T REACH KEVIN, but he did get all the information on Wilson's mission later that afternoon from someone else:

Q *And what did this person explain to you?*

A Well, the person explained to me that, in fact, we, the CIA, had sent Ambassador Wilson to Niger to get information to determine whether or not Iraq had attempted to purchase uranium from that country.

Q *Did they give you any more information other than that bare fact?*

A Yes—well, in fact, explained in a fair amount of detail how we did it, when he went, where he went, who was supposed to meet with him, and a number of those details.

He was also able to tell me that, in fact, while the Office of the Vice President had been very interested in getting more information on this topic, in fact, interest had been expressed also by the Department of State and the Department of Defense.

Q *And this information was significant to you in terms of the question that Mr. Libby had asked you?*

A Yes. I felt that I had all the information and more, in fact, that had been requested by Mr. Libby.

Q *And did the individual that you spoke to at CPD—did they also bring up the subject of Ambassador Wilson's wife?*

A Yes. The person mentioned to me that, in fact, Ambassador Wilson's wife was working in the unit within CPD that had sent Ambassador Wilson there, and clearly indicated that that's where the idea had came from. That's why they knew about Ambassador Joseph Wilson and the fact that he had contacts in Africa.

Q *Did the individual name, to the best of your recollection, the Ambassador's wife's name?*

A No. I am certain that the person did not tell me the name, only that it was Ambassador Wilson's wife.

Q *Was that information that was new to you?*

A Yes.

Q *Did you immediately contact Mr. Libby with this information and fill him in with what you had learned?*

A No, I didn't speak with Mr. Libby right away. I may have attempted to call his office preliminarily, but . . . I don't specifically recall. I had a following meeting that was scheduled for 4:15 that afternoon. And so, as I say, I may have tried to call back to his office before 4:15, but I know that I didn't get through to him.

Q *What type of meeting did you have at 4:15?*

A Well, at 4:15 we were having one of our regular Iraq-update meetings where we briefed the Director of Central Intelligence on the latest from Iraq.

Q *So did you have a choice to make in terms of going to the meeting or making the phone call? …[E]xplain what your situation was in regard to your choices there.*

A Right. There was some tension in my mind as to whether or not I should stay and try to make sure that I got back to Mr. Libby in as timely a manner as I could, but I really had no intention of missing that meeting at 4:15. So I remember feeling a little bit uncomfortable, ["I]f I don't get back to him until after the 4:15 meeting is over, it's going to be late in the afternoon. Is there a chance that I could miss him?["] So I was a little bit concerned about it.

Q *What did you end up doing?*

A I ended up going to the meeting at 4:15.

Q *And at some point while you were in the meeting, did something happen?*

A Yes. Someone came to the door and beckoned me out. And so I went out of the conference room, and I was handed a note indicating that I should call Mr. Libby.

Q *And can you recall any other occasions when you have been called out of such a meeting before?*

A I don't think I had ever been called out of the meeting with the Director either before or since.

Q *And what was your reaction when you saw the note was from Mr. Libby?*

A I was a little bit chagrined. I thought, ["O]h, dear. I would have much preferred that I would initiate the next contact rather than him having to get back in touch with me."

Q *And why was it important to you to appear particularly responsive and forthcoming with Mr. Libby?*

A Well, I think there were at least two reasons. One is—I mean, he was a senior government official, the Chief of Staff to the Vice President, and obviously anytime you are dealing with a senior person in the administration, you want to be as forthcoming as you possibly can. And, secondly, there was the issue, again, where it seemed that Mr. Libby perhaps had reason to believe that CIA people had behaved badly, if you will, vis-à-vis Mr. Wilson and perhaps [had] spoken negatively about the Office of the Vice President. So that made me all the more eager to, again, be responsive.

Q *So what did you do once you got this note outside the meeting?*

A I called back to Mr. Libby's office.

Q *Did you get in touch with him?*

A Yes. I spoke with him.

Q *And can you tell us about that conversation, please?*

A Yes. I told him that, in fact, it was true, that the CIA had sent Ambassador Wilson to Niger in order to acquire this information. And how much else I said about it, I really don't recall. I may have mentioned that he was debriefed and that a report was written as a result. But the second major point that I made was that, in fact, the people within—or the people with whom I had spoken—had verified that it wasn't only the Office of Vice President that was driving all of this, that there had been inquiries as well from State and Defense.

Q *And what was his reaction when you told him about the information that you had learned that the Department of State and the Department of Defense were also interested and somewhat responsible for instigating the trip?*

A Right. He asked whether the CIA would be willing to reveal that publicly.

Q *And in your conversation with Mr. Libby, did you also talk to him about the information you had learned from the individual at CPD about Wilson's wife?*

A I believe I did.

Q *And can you tell us about that?*

A Well, I mentioned it only in passing. I believe that I said something to the effect that—in fact, Ambassador Wilson's wife works there, and that's why—that's where the idea came from.

Q *And when, in the context of the conversation, did you mention Mr. Wilson's wife?*

A When, in the context of that conversation?

Q *Yes.*

A In terms of the sequence, I am pretty certain that the first thing I told him was that, yes, this trip had occurred and that we had sent Ambassador Wilson. The specific sequence after that is very difficult for me to say.

Q *And why was it you felt that that was a piece of information that was—should be passed on to Mr. Libby?*

A Well, I am not sure that it should have been passed on to Mr. Libby, but the reason that I said it at the time was, again, I wanted to be as forthcoming as I possibly could. And, to me, it was an explanation as to, you know, why we had done this in the first place. You know, why did we, you know, find this Ambassador Wilson and send him off to Africa. So, again, it was—I thought it was—germane to the story and something that I related.

Q *And how was, in your mind, it germane to the story that his wife—Wilson's wife—worked at CPD in the context of explaining why he was sent?*

A Well, because not only was she working in CPD; she was working in the specific unit that had decided to send Ambassador Wilson. So I guess there would have been some question, not that he would have posed it, as to, you know, well, how do we know about Ambassador Wilson, and why him, et cetera, et cetera? Well, the reason why him and the reason why we knew about him was because his wife worked there.

Q *What was Mr. Libby's response to the information you provided him?*

A He—the only response that I clearly remember, again, was when I revealed to him that, in fact, there were others in government who were interested in this information, that he asked me if the CIA would be willing to reveal that publicly.

Q *And what did you respond when he asked you if the CIA would reveal this publicly?*

A I said that I thought perhaps we could, but that I would have to check with our director of public affairs . . .

Q *The note and the two phone calls from Mr. Libby all occurred the same day, June 11th?*

A Oh, yes.

Q *Okay. A few days later... did you see Mr. Libby at a Deputies Committee meeting?*

A I remember seeing Mr. Libby again at a meeting. I believe it was a Deputies Committee meeting.

Q *And did he say anything to you in regards to your telephone calls?*

A Yes. He thanked me for the information and said that it had been useful.

THE PROSECUTION NEXT ASKS GRENIER about his initial interview with the FBI in fall 2003 and his testimony before the Grand Jury in January 2004. This was an attempt to preempt an anticipated defense move; Grenier had initially testified that he thought he had relayed information about Wilson's wife to Libby but he could not clearly recall. Grenier explained that as he thought back on the guilty feelings he had had, his conviction that he had indeed told Libby about Plame grew stronger. Grenier still didn't come to think it was relevant to the investigation until spring 2005, when he read published reports that whether Libby learned from the press or elsewhere was a relevant issue, at which point Grenier came forward to investigators.

Q *And when you were feeling guilty, . . . what part of the information that you revealed to Mr. Libby were you having some concerns about?*

A Specifically having mentioned . . . that Mr. Wilson's wife worked in the CIA . . . I didn't know her name, so I . . . obviously didn't indicate the name, but . . . in indicating the relation, by saying that Joe Wilson's wife was working in the CIA, in effect, I was revealing the identity of a CIA officer.

Q *And why would you have qualms about having such a discussion with the National Security Advisor and Chief of Staff to the Vice President?*

A Because it wasn't absolutely necessary for me to have said that, and that is information that we normally guard pretty closely. And, in the CIA, our habit is that if you don't need to say something, you generally don't.

THE PROSECUTION FINISHES its questioning by asking a question designed to elicit the fact that there was information Grenier thought could be released publicly about Wilson's mission at the time of his conversation with Libby, but it specifically did not include the information about his wife:

Q *Just so it is clear, Mr. Grenier, jumping back now to your conversation with—outside the meeting room when you had Mr. Harlow and Mr. Libby on the phone—*

or you were about to call back Mr. Libby, what was it that . . . you thought could be said publicly about the trip?

A Only that—well, again, because it was Ambassador Wilson who, in effect, had outed himself, that that was not—under normal circumstances, we would have protected that. We would not, . . . the CIA would not have wanted to reveal Ambassador Wilson as a source. He had already revealed that publicly, so I didn't anticipate that there was going to be a problem with that. That was already out there.

And the only additional information that we would provide was that he was sent as a result of interest expressed not just by the Office of the Vice President, but also State and Defense.

AND WITH THAT, the morning session concludes.

*

THE DEFENSE TAKES UP its cross-examination that afternoon.

The defense initially elicited testimony from Grenier that in spring 2003 the CIA was embarrassed by the failure to find WMD in Iraq and there was finger-pointing between the CIA and the Bush administration. The defense questions Grenier about Walter Pincus's June 12, 2003 article in *The Washington Post*, which dealt with the Niger story and used Joe Wilson as an anonymous source, notwithstanding Grenier's mistaken assumption that Wilson was identified:

A I do recall an article dealing with this issue did come out from Mr. Pincus the following day. Of course, to me, it was the fact that it made reference, as I recall, to Ambassador Wilson and to allegations Ambassador Wilson was making. So given the comments from the day before, I understood where this was coming from . . .

Q *Did you tell the Deputy Director of Central Intelligence that you regarded that article as attempting to take the responsibility for the investigation away from, for Wilson's trip, away from the Office of Vice President and put it on the CIA?*

A Not precisely. Yes, I remember thinking, and I'll tell you in a minute what it was that I was thinking at the time, and I might very well have said that to the Deputy Director. I don't really specifically recall that conversation. But my belief at the time, was that the stories that came out in the press reflecting information that had come from the Administration, was that the Administration was trying to suggest in effect that, well, had they only known that it was the eminent Ambassador Joseph Wilson who had [inquired, we] would come to the conclusion that there had been no attempt made on the part of Iraq to acquire uranium from Niger, that they, the White House, would have felt that that was very compelling. And the fact that this report was not highlighted to them, therefore, was a failing or was an error on the part of the CIA, which I thought was unfair[,] by the way.

THE DEFENSE THEN PRESSES Grenier on what he had told the FBI in his interview of fall 2003.

Q   *Didn't you opine to Deputy Director McLaughlin that this article was an effort by the Office of the Vice President to take the onus of Wilson's trip off of the Vice President and put it on the CIA?*

A   Not precisely. I'm not trying to be difficult here. I guess I thought that this was an attempt on the part of someone in the White House, perhaps the Office of the Vice President, to place blame on the CIA for not having warned them, that is at the White House, that there was compelling evidence that in fact Iraq had made no attempt to acquire uranium from Niger. I would not have regarded that report in question as being compelling evidence.

THE REPORT IS THE ONE THE CIA produced as a result of Wilson's trip. Grenier explains that in his view Wilson's mission was unlikely to ferret out the truth. Grenier also confirms that the CIA was embarrassed for not having recognized the Niger documents as forgeries. The defense then raises the Robert Novak column that publicly outed Plame:

Q   *And do you recall again believing that that article was White House finger-pointing at the CIA?*

A   Well, it seems to me, if I recall the Novak article correctly, that that signaled a shift in the public relations strategy[,] whereas, early on at the time of the Pincus article, the suggestion that appeared to be being made was that Ambassador Joe Wilson was, you know, a source of eminent repute, and that had only the White House known that it was Ambassador Wilson who had made this report, that that would have been persuasive to them and it would have kept them from continuing down the path of error.

At the time of the Novak column, it seemed that there was a different path that was being taken. Instead, quite the opposite one, which was saying in effect, "Well why should anyone believe this Mr. Wilson?" That's what I took from it.

Q   *Did you discuss the Novak article with Bill Harlow, the CIA press spokesman, on the day it appeared?*

A   I don't recall if it was on the day that it appeared. I think I may very well have discussed it with him.

Q   *Did you tell Mr. Harlow that, again, with respect to the Novak article, that you thought the Novak article reflected the White House's motivation to throw the blame at the CIA in order to avoid taking responsibility for Wilson's trip?*

A   Again, not to avoid taking responsibility for Wilson's trip. I think they were trying to avoid responsibility for positions that they took with regard to the truth about whether or not Iraq had attempted to acquire uranium from Niger. So, to me, the idea about who was taking responsibility for Wilson's trip, that didn't particularly matter at all. The issue was who was going to stand up and take the blame for having alleged, against a fair amount of counter evidence, that Iraq had attempted to acquire uranium from Niger.

THE COURT: Ladies and gentlemen, the same thing I said about the Pincus article equally applies to this article and any other news articles this witness will be questioned about. The information contained in those articles are not before you for their truth, only for the purpose of you assessing what impact those articles would have had on this witness's state of mind . . .

Q   *But what you talked to Mr. Harlow about was the nepotism argument, right? You had a question about Wilson's wife having worked for the CIA?*
A   Right.

Q   *And you interpreted Novak's article, which didn't name any sources, as an effort by the White House to throw at the CIA, right?*
A   Yes.

Q   *So you made an assumption when you read that Novak article that the source for Mr. Novak was in the White House; Is that right?*
A   I was strongly suspecting that he had received information from the White House, yes.

THE POINT OF THIS QUESTIONING is to suggest that the CIA had an animus against the White House, and the Office of the Vice President in particular, which might discredit the testimony of CIA witnesses against Libby. It also set up the defense's point that the White House was not solely responsible for the Novak column—Richard Armitage in the State Department, widely reputed to be hostile to the neoconservatives in the White House, was in fact Novak's initial source on Plame.

The defense asks Grenier about being questioned on July 31, 2003 about his June 11 discussions with Libby, during which Grenier did not mention Wilson's wife. On redirect questioning from the prosecution, however, Grenier confirms that the subject of the July 31 investigation was not about the outing of Plame, but rather about the forged documents. The defense went on to cast more doubt on Grenier's recollection, and got him to acknowledge at one point:

A   I will say that, in fact, my recollection of the conversation with Mr. Libby has a fair amount of vagueness attached to it as well.

THE DEFENSE PRESSES GRENIER on the fact that he did not initially tell the FBI or the Grand Jury that he had told Libby about Plame in June 2003. The defense confronted Grenier with the fact that in his first Grand Jury appearance, he had testified that he did not even recall being told about Plame by the CPD officer. In his subsequent Grand Jury testimony a year and a half later, Grenier changed that part of his testimony and firmed up to some degree his testimony that he had told Libby about Plame. The defense highlighted the elusive nature of Grenier's changing memory and his lack of notes to refresh his recollection. The defense also seeks to suggest that Grenier's executive assistant had a record of Grenier being asked about Wilson's mission by the Deputy Director of Central Intelligence the day before his conversation with Libby about it, suggesting that Libby was not the impetus for Grenier's inquiries about Wilson. But Grenier resists all these suggestions, and affirmed that he had not talked with the DDCI about the issue.

After attacking Grenier's claim that he felt guilty for having revealed Wilson's wife's identity to Libby, the defense verifies that Grenier had not told Libby that Plame's status was classified or that she was covert:

Q   *When you did see Mr. Libby, . . . a day or two, three, whatever it was, after your conversation with him, did you say something to him about, you know, "Maybe I shouldn't have mentioned anything about Joe Wilson's wife the other day. I hope you'll keep that confidential." Did you say something like that to him?*
A   No, I don't think I did.

Q   *By the way, you didn't mention the name of Wilson's wife to Mr. Libby, correct?*
A   That's right.

Q   *You didn't mention anything to Mr. Libby concerning whether Wilson's wife was classified or covert?*
A   No.

Q   *And covert, in simple terms, means undercover, correct?*
A   Yes.

Q   *While the CIA does have undercover employees, it has thousands of employees who are not, right?*
A   That's true.

Q   *When you learned that Ambassador Wilson's wife was employed by the CIA, what you heard was that she was a staff person in the Counterproliferation Division, correct?*
A   Well, no. All I heard was that she was working in that unit. So, that could have meant any number of things. [It c]ould have meant that she was a staff director of operations officer who was working in that unit. It could have meant that she was an analyst from the Director of Intelligence who was essentially on loan and working in that unit. It could have meant a number of different things, and I didn't ask for clarification.

Q   *. . . Did you testify to the Grand Jury the second time, July 29, 2005, that the clear implication of what you learned from the person in the CPD was that Mr. Wilson's wife was "an individual who was employed as a staff person in the Counterproliferation Division." Did you tell the Grand Jury that?*
A   Yes.

Q *Now, that did not tell you, in itself . . . that she was a classified or covert employee, correct?*

A No.

JEFFRESS ENDS HIS CROSS EXAMINATION by bringing out that, on June 11, Grenier passed the phone to Harlow, who talked to someone named Cathie, most likely Cathie Martin, in the OVP. This set up the defense's contention that Cathie Martin learned from Harlow about Plame on June 11 and conveyed the information to Cheney and Libby at that time, not later, in July 2003, closer to the occasion on which Libby purportedly learned from Russert. This looks ahead to Martin's testimony.

On redirect examination, the prosecution asks Grenier a question about what Grenier had been told about Plame:

Q *Finally, Mr. Grenier, if the person at the CPD that you spoke to did not tell you that Wilson's wife was covert or undercover or classified, why were you feeling uncomfortable later when you were recounting that conversation you had with Mr. Libby in your mind?*

A Well, in part because I knew that there was a good chance that that person could be undercover. After all, we were talking about a unit, Counteproliferation Division, which is in the Directorate of Operations, the vast majority of whose employees are undercover.

MR. ZEIDENBERG: I have nothing further, Your Honor.

CRAIG SCHMALL

C RAIG SCHMALL, A LONGTIME CIA EMPLOYEE, was Scooter Libby's morning intelligence briefer from summer 2002 until fall 2003. Beginning in early 2003, he split duties with Cheney's briefer providing the daily morning briefing to both Cheney and Libby. In the passages below Schmall testifies with regard to his notes from June 14, 2003, which indicated that Libby had asked Schmall a question about Joe Wilson and his wife, whom Libby called Valerie Wilson. Schmall also testifies that on July 14, 2003, either Libby or Cheney asked him whether he'd read Bob Novak's column outing Valerie Plame, which had just been published that day. This indicated that Cheney and Libby were focused on the Plame issue the day Novak's column appeared, even asking Schmall if he had read it. (Schmall recalls under questioning that he had not done so.)

Schmall explains that he typically carried a briefing binder, which would actually be destroyed after the fact, and a table of contents. Fitzgerald questions Schmall about the notes Schmall took on his table of contents during the briefing with Libby on June 14,

2003 and a month later, when briefing Libby and Cheney, on July 14, 2003, the day Novak's column was published.

Q *When you briefed the Vice President and Mr. Libby together, as between the two of them, did one of them tend to do more of the talking?*

A Well, the Vice President tended to. It was really his briefing session.

Q *Would you make notes on the table of contents as the briefings happened?*

A Yes, I would.

Q *Can you describe the type of things you would note on the table of contents?*

A Okay. I would note the reaction that they had to reading the items. And I would mark off if they had read that item or if they had skipped it. I might mark that down. General reactions to the analysis. So I could provide feedback back to headquarters. And if they had any questions.

Q *What would happen if they asked you a question that you felt comfortable you could answer on the spot?*

A Well, I would answer on the spot. I generally would record those.

Q *What if they asked you a question that you did not feel comfortable that you could give an answer on the spot?*

A Well, I would write it down and judge whether we needed to turn that into a task or something where I would take it back to headquarters, and we would task that question out to the analyst answerer.

Q *You were marking to note that something was, what you would call, a tasker?*

A Right. Things that we determined either in briefing in talking to the Vice President or Mr. Libby where they really wanted a formal answer, I would mark it with a "T" and then put a circle around it. I wrote a lot on these table of contents. And doing that mark made it easier for me to find out which questions needed a tasking.

Q *When in time would you write down any questions that you were asked? Was it during the briefing or was it later?*

A Yeah, it was right after the question was asked.

Q *During these briefings, would you ever offer your personal opinions on matters?*

A No, only if invited to . . .

Q *Now, sir, prior to testifying, have you had occasion to look at a redacted version of your table of contents for the June 14, 2003, briefing?*

A Yes, sir, I have.

Q *Understanding that that was a Saturday, where would that, who would that briefing involve?*

A That would typically involve Mr. Libby at his home.

Q *Okay.*

MR. FITZGERALD: If I may approach the witness, Your Honor, with what has been marked for identification as Government's Exhibit 702?

THE COURT: Very well . . .

Q *Finally, do you have a recollection, having looked at the document, do you specifically recall the conversation referred to in a third section of that document?*

A I didn't have an independent memory of that, sir.

MR. FITZGERALD: Your Honor, I would offer the document pursuant to 8013 . . . This is 702. If we could publish Exhibit 702. It is now in evidence. [Exhibit GX702 appears in the appendix.]

Q *Can we go to the upper left corner and look at the third section. Can you read your handwriting to the jury?*

A Yes. "Why was the"—it should say 'ex-ambassador'—"told this was a V.P. office question, Joe Wilson, Valerie Wilson."

Q *As you sit here now, do you have a specific recollection of this conversation going back and forth in your mind?*

A No, I don't.

Q *When you write a question down, is it a question you ask the people you brief or is it a question the person being briefed asks you?*

A It generally comes from the principal.

Q *Who else was present in the room that day?*

A Just Mr. Libby and myself.

Q *Prior to this occasion, do you have any specific recollection of ever hearing the name Joe Wilson or Valerie Wilson before?*

A No, I don't . . .

Q *. . . [A]re you familiar now with a column written on July 14, 2003, by a columnist named Robert Novak?*

A Yes, sir.

Q *And just so we're clear, have you looked at the July 14, 2003, table of contents prior to testifying?*

A Yes, sir, I have.

Q *Having looked at that document, can you bring to your mind and specifically if you remember any conversation that's described in those notes?*

A No, sir . . .

MR. FITZGERALD: If we could publish Government's Exhibit 703 [see appendix]. And if we could enlarge the line in the upper left corner.

Q *Can you read the writing on the left?*

A Yes, sir. It says, "Did you read the Novak article?" Then there's a dash, it says, "Not your problem …"

Q *By the way, there is a circled "T" there.*

A That has to do with the redacted portion underneath.

Q *So we're clear that "T" for tasks doesn't relate to that question?*

A Correct.

Q *As we sit here now, is it your best recollection, had you read the Novak column prior to your morning briefing on July 14th?*

A I don't believe that I had.

Q *As you sit here now, do you have a specific recollection of who asks the question at that meeting, have you read the Novak article?*

A Not a specific recollection, no.

Q *Is it your understanding that the briefing on Monday, July 14, that it involved the Vice President and Mr. Libby?*

A It probably had both of them. It certainly had the Vice President since he's listed on the table of contents.

Q *So, you can't specifically identify which of the two would have asked the question between the Vice President and Mr. Libby?*

A No, not specifically.

Q *Is it fair to say that the Vice President did more talking in these meetings than Mr. Libby?*

A That's fair.

Q *Can you specifically tell us who said the words "not your problem"?*

A No, I can't.

Q *Is it fair to say that you can't reconstruct the conversation now in your mind other than to say that's what you wrote down during the briefing?*

A That's correct.

Q *And did there come a time when you later read the Novak article?*

A Yes, sir.

Q *Did there come a time when you ever discussed the Novak article with either the Vice President or Mr. Libby or both?*

A The issue, yes.

Q *Can you tell us when that occurred?*

A Well, it was some time after the Novak article was published. I don't recall the specific date.

Q *Do you have any notes reflecting this conversation specifically?*

A No, I do not.

Q *Can you tell us anything you recall about the circumstances under which the conversation took place in terms . . . that would help fix a date?*

A Right. Well, it was during a time when the issue of the leak was being talked about very heavily in the press and by pundits. I also remember that the conversation took place at the Naval Observatory. Both the Vice President and Mr. Libby were present. We were wearing suits.

Q *And knowing that the conversation took place at the Naval Observatory, what information does that give you about dates? Does it rule any dates out?*

A Yes, it does. It would rule out the month of August because the Vice President goes out to his home in Jackson Hole, Wyoming, for the whole month and that's where we conduct those briefings.

Q *What do you recall was said about the Novak article at that time during this conversation?*

A I remember that I was invited to offer my opinion on what I thought on the issue of the leak.

Q *And as you sit here now, let me make it clear, did you know . . . Valerie Wilson Plame personally?*

A No, sir. I did not.

Q *Have you ever met her?*

A No, sir.

Q *Do you have any actual knowledge of what her status was within the CIA at the time of this conversation?*

A No, sir . . .

Q *Is it fair to say that you had no actual knowledge of what damage might or might not be caused by naming her as an employee?*

A Her specifically, no.

> *I thought there was a very grave danger to leaking the name of a CIA officer. And I talked about how, now that Valerie Wilson's name is out in the press, foreign intelligence services in countries where she served now have the opportunity to investigate everyone she came in contact [with] while she was in those countries. And, in many countries, those people, innocent or otherwise, can be harassed along with their families.*

Q *With that in mind, can you tell us what you said in this conversation?*

A Well, I noted that the press and pundits were mostly talking about the damage to Valerie Wilson and her career. And also people were saying that, well this is really no big deal. There is no danger involved here. I thought there was a very grave danger to leaking the name of a CIA officer. And I talked about how, now that Valerie Wilson's name is out in the press, foreign intelligence services in countries where she served now have the opportunity to investigate everyone she came in contact [with] while she was in those countries. And, in many countries, those people, innocent or otherwise, can be harassed along with their families. They can lose their jobs. They can be arrested, tortured or killed. So in my mind, it was a very grave danger involved.

Q *Do you recall if anyone said anything in response to what you said?*
A No, I don't recall that.

Q *Did there come a time when you were interviewed by the FBI in connection with the investigation of this matter?*
A Yes, sir.

Q *Do you recall exactly when the interview was?*
A Not exactly, no, sir.

Q *When you were interviewed, had you reviewed any documents to prepare for the interview?*
A No, sir.

Q *What was the state of your memory during the first interview?*
A I would say it was pretty poor.

Q *Had you reviewed either of the two documents that are exhibits before you when you were first interviewed by the FBI?*
A No, sir, I hadn't.

Q *Did you describe either of the two conversations such as they're reflected on those documents when you were first interviewed by the FBI?*
A I don't believe that I did.

MR. FITZGERALD: If I may have a moment, Your Honor.
THE COURT: Yes.
MR. FITZGERALD: Nothing further.
THE COURT: Approach for a minute.
(Bench conference is sealed and redacted.)
(Open Court.)

THE COURT: Ladies and gentlemen, in reference to what was just said, I need to give you an instruction again. It was one of the instructions I gave you during my preliminary instructions. No evidence will be presented to you as to Valerie Plame Wilson's status with the Central Intelligence Agency, also known as the CIA, and whether or not disclosure of that status would pose a risk of damage to national security or Ms. Wilson herself. That is because, what her actual status was, or whether any damage will result from the disclosure of her status are totally irrelevant to your assessment of the defendant's guilt or innocence on the charges for the offenses the defendant has been charged with in this case.

You must therefore not consider those matters in your deliberations or speculate or guess about them. You may consider, however, what if anything Mr. Libby knew or believed about her status and any damage disclosure of her status could cause in assessing what his state of mind was when he spoke to the FBI agents and testified before the Grand Jury.

AFTER THE JUDGE'S INSTRUCTION, the defense begins its cross-examination of Schmall. The defense manages to introduce some of its memory defense through Schmall, They question him about the volume of intelligence he handled on alarming situations, including terrorism, and by extension, what Libby had to deal with.

The defense goes on to bring up Eric Edelman, Libby's chief deputy in spring 2003, getting Schmall to testify that he had faxed some documents to Edelman as a follow-up to a conversation they had had about Nicholas Kristof's May 6, 2003, *New York Times* op-ed column, which described Joe Wilson's Niger mission. The defense also introduces into evidence a series of documents that Schmall faxed to the Office of the Vice President (OVP) on June 9, 2003, concerning Wilson, his mission, and the Niger story. The documents were faxed to the attention of Libby and his Acting Deputy, John Hannah, who would later testify for the defense.

The defense then bears down on something that Schmall had already acknowledged—that he had no independent memory of the June 14 and July 14 meetings with Libby, with reference to Schmall's first interview with the FBI in January 2004, and his interview with investigators on April 22 of that year:

Q *During that January 8th, 2004, interview, you didn't say anything about the "not-your-problem" note on your July 14, 2003, table of contents, correct?*
A That's correct.

Q *During that interview, you didn't say anything about the Joe Wilson and Valerie Wilson note on your June 14, 2003 table of contents, right?*
A That's correct.

Q *That's because on January the 8th, 2004, you had no memory of those notes or those events, correct?*
A That's correct, sir . . .

Q *You told the FBI agents that, after the Novak article came out on July 14th, you had this discussion that [you] described to us with the Vice President and Mr. Libby about the dangers of exposing a CIA employee, right?*
A Yes, sir.

Q *You told the agents on January 8th, 2004, that this was the first time you discussed Valerie Wilson with either the Vice President or Mr. Libby, correct?*
A Yes, sir.

Q *So, to recap that interview, your best memory, six or seven months after these events that you've described today, was that the first time you discussed Valerie Wilson with the Vice President or Mr. Libby was after the Novak article came out on July 14th, correct?*
A That's correct.

JANUARY 25, 2007

CRAIG SCHMALL (continued)

ON THE MORNING OF JANUARY 25, the cross-examination of Schmall continues along the same lines as the afternoon before, and concludes with Schmall's confirmation that he turned down the defense attorney's request for an interview with him in advance of the trial.

After Schmall's testimony, and with the jury not present, the judge explores the defense's intention to mount a memory defense—the defense that, because of urgent and complex national security matters on his mind, any errors Libby made in his testimony resulted from mistake or faulty memory, not lying. The key issue was whether Libby's attorneys would be able to introduce the memory defense without their client taking the stand:

THE COURT: But I assume, based upon what counsel said during his opening statement, it would be suicide if he doesn't take the stand and testify because juries have good memories, and when you make promises about what somebody is going to say, especially when you are talking about a defendant, and then the defense doesn't bear out the obligation they have made a promise to the jury about, in my experience, that's devastating to the defense. So I don't have any real concerns about the fact that he is going to testify if he is going to present this memory defense because, otherwise, he can't present it.

AT ONE POINT, JUDGE WALTON SAYS, "There will be no memory defense if Mr. Libby doesn't testify," foreshadowing an issue that would arise again later in the trial. At this point, the defense gave no indication that Libby would not or might not testify. Prosecutor Fitzgerald pointed out the defense had in fact made no promises to the jury that Libby would testify, and Fitzgerald worried that the defense would be able to introduce material which they would not otherwise be allowed to do.

In the midst of this dispute, Walton praises Fitzgerald, calling him "one of the most scrupulous prosecutors I have had appear before me," and observing: "Well, just for the record, like I say, I don't think you have been hiding anything. I think, you know, you have been open and provided the type of discovery that you expect prosecutors to provide."

Before they move on to the testimony of Cathie Martin, Schmall is called back in and asked by the judge about his notes from June 14, 2003, and the fact that Schmall's note on Libby's question about the Wilsons was not a formal tasking (which Schmall would have noted with a "T"):

THE COURT: Did the fact that there was no "T" by that entry that you wrote on that document have any significance in reference to what you would or would not do in the future?

THE WITNESS: Well, it just means that that was not a formal tasking. It was a question that was asked, and there were a lot of questions that are asked that I don't put into a formal tasking.

THE COURT: And that entry that you put on that June 14th document—

THE WITNESS: Yes, sir.

THE COURT:—I think one of the jurors was asking, why did you put that there? What would have been the basis for having put that there, if you have a memory right now of that?

THE WITNESS: Well, I would have written a question down to something that I didn't know the answer to.

THE COURT: And would that have been based upon a question you had in your mind or what somebody else was asking you?

THE WITNESS: Well, if I am getting a question directly and I don't know the answer to it, I will write it down, whether it turns into a formal tasking or not. In that case, a question there without a "T" means that I wasn't able to answer it, but we didn't consider it a tasking.

THE COURT: You indicated in reference to Mr. Libby raising or having some concerns about CIA personnel revealing information about briefings—

THE WITNESS: Yes, sir.

THE COURT:—You said that he appeared to be irritated; I think that was the word you used.

THE WITNESS: "Annoyed." I think that was the word I used, yes, sir.

THE COURT: What's the basis for you saying that he appeared to be annoyed? Why are you saying that was the case?

THE WITNESS: Well, the tone of his voice and his mannerisms, having briefed him for a long time and understanding the difference between what his body language means.

Schmall was then dismissed, and Cathie Martin was called to the stand.

CATHIE MARTIN

IN THE SPRING AND SUMMER OF 2003, Cathie Martin was the Assistant to Vice President Cheney for Public Affairs—in essence, Cheney's Chief Press Aide. Because the response to the crisis of integrity in the Office of the Vice President and the White House over the sixteen words and Wilson's criticisms was to a great extent an issue of media strategy, Martin had a distinctive insight into the matter. From the prosecution's perspective, her unique insight into OVP's media strategy was as significant for what she saw (who learned what about Plame, and what they did with that information) as for what she didn't see—in particular, Cheney and Libby's compartmentalized strategizing with regard to Judith Miller.

Her testimony, both for the prosecution and under cross-examination from the defense of a former colleague with whom she appears to remain in sympathy, provides unprecedented insight into the operations of the office of the most secretive and powerful vice president in the history of the United States at a critical juncture. From her description of the initial role of an angry Eric Edelman (then Deputy National Security Advisor to Cheney and close advisor to Libby, and now Doug Feith's replacement as Undersecretary of Defense for Policy), in responding to Nicholas Kristof's May 6, 2003 piece mentioning OVP's involvement in the mission to Niger, through her account of the crucial week of July 6 up through her depiction of OVP's ongoing response in having conservative columnists over to Cheney's house on July 18—Martin gives us an inside look at a surprisingly beleaguered Office of the Vice President seeking to push back against one individual as well as the CIA, and faced with a press so accustomed to refusals to comment from OVP that it had stopped calling for their version. And because so much of the top White House staff were traveling with the President in Africa during the central week of July 6–13, Martin was more involved than she normally would have been in the White House's overall response to the sixteen words controversy, the contours of which are newly illuminated by her testimony. One of the most interesting aspects of her testimony was her description of how the Vice President overhauled the standard talking points the OVP was using on July 8. Fitzgerald would use the evidence of those changes to powerful effect in his rebuttal closing. It was one illustration of a more general point Fitzgerald brought out effectively through Martin's testimony: the unusual steps Cheney and Libby took during the week of July 6–13 to respond to Wilson, which he would argue show how focused they both were on the response to Wilson.

The prosecution called Martin not only to set the scene in OVP and the White House during the period of the response to Wilson and to show how focused both Libby and Cheney were on that response, but also, more specifically, to testify to two events. First, she was yet another government official who told Libby—and Cheney at the same time—that Wilson's wife worked at the CIA, a fact she learned, as her notes indicate, from the CIA's chief spokesman Bill Harlow. She placed the event some time on or before July 8, but the defense in cross-examining her did a persuasive job of suggesting that it took place in early- to mid-June, the same time frame in which Cheney told Libby, thus potentially defusing the testimony somewhat because Libby's original story was that he had forgotten the Cheney conversation by July when he heard about Wilson's wife again from Tim Russert. The second key event Martin testified about was her observation of Libby's side of his phone conversation with *TIME*'s Matt Cooper on July 12—one of the conversations Libby was specifically accused of lying about in the charges he faced. Martin had in fact e-mailed with Cooper and brokered the conversation between Libby and Cooper. She traveled with other members of OVP to and from Virginia on that Saturday on Air Force Two, and it was during that trip that Libby went and discussed media strategy separately with Cheney. Upon arrival back at . . . the air force base, Libby called Cooper, and Martin testified that she observed nothing that corresponded to the version of the conversation Libby gave to investigators and the Grand

Jury. (Somewhat ironically, it is significant for the prosecution that Martin did *not* hear Libby say anything explicitly about Wilson's wife.) However, the defense was able to get Martin to confirm that she was not fully attentive to the entire conversation, as she took another phone call in the midst of listening to Libby.

The defense used Martin's testimony for several other important purposes as well. They showed the OVP's official response to Wilson—manifest in talking points and in discussion—did not include Wilson's wife as part of the whole story that Cheney, in his refrain of that week, wanted to get out. The defense also used Martin's testimony that the OVP was shorthanded and that Libby took on a greater role in responding to the press to bolster its memory defense—that Libby was so busy with so many things that it is perfectly reasonable to think he forgot the Plame matter. The defense also went through the whole timeline with Martin in order to lay the groundwork for the argument that Libby was responding to Wilson on the merits, merely setting the record straight, rather than exacting revenge or any similar act.

Martin briefly recounts her educational and professional history leading up to her employment in the Office of the Vice President and then, after describing her subsequent employment, she is asked about her involvement in the response to the sixteen words controversy in spring-summer 2003:

A   I was recruited to work for the Vice President's office under Mary Matalin as the Deputy Assistant to the Vice President for Public Affairs and Mary Matalin's Deputy . . . That was in June of 2001, and I believe I stayed there until the winter of 2004. So the February-ish time frame . . .

Q   *Okay. Did there come a time when Ms. Matalin left the Office of Vice President?*
A   Yes. She left—I think she announced her resignation in December of 2002, and I took over at the beginning of 2003.

Q   *So can you tell us what your job title was in the beginning of 2003?*
A   Assistant to the Vice President for Public Affairs.

Q   *And where are you currently employed?*
A   At the White House, but I now work back in the communications world as Deputy Director of Communications for Policy and Planning for the president.

Q   *Now, going back to the period that we will focus on when you worked in the Office of Vice President . . . how much contact did you have with Scooter Libby?*
A   Scooter and I saw each other almost daily in a morning senior staff meeting when I took over as Assistant to the Vice President for Public Affairs. Prior to that, I saw him probably less.

And then, in addition—and while I was assistant to the Vice President for public affairs, I also participated in a number of . . . regularly scheduled meetings the president had throughout—almost every week. And Scooter was usually in those meetings.

And then in addition to that, I would have . . . my own scheduled meetings, as needed, . . . to talk to him . . . I had the political portfolio as well as both communications and press portfolio. So anything that came up in that world, I might have an additional meeting.

Q *Who else worked under your portfolio in public affairs?*

A There was a press secretary who was responsible for the daily press calls, and her name was Jennifer Millerwise. And I had two press assistants that worked in my office . . .

Q *And was there a policy or regular procedure in the Office of Vice President if some-one from the media, the press, wanted to speak to someone who worked in the Office of Vice President? What were the ground rules that you understood? . . .*

A Well, the general practice throughout the White House was if you got calls from the press, try to funnel them through the press office or through your communications office. And we generally followed the same practice.

Q *Can you tell us what you understood the ground rules were when you dealt with the press in terms of what "on the record" meant and what "off the record" meant and what "background" meant? . . .*

[Let's] use the example the car was red. If Cathie Martin spoke to the press on the record, they could put "the car was red" in quotes and then attribute it to Cathie Martin?

A Yes.

Q *If you said it on background, they could say the car was red according to a senior administration official, if that was the term that was agreed upon, correct?*

A Yes.

Q *And if it was on deep background, . . . the story might contain the information that the car was red, but it wouldn't contain a quote?*

A Right.

Q *And what did you understand "off the record" to mean?*

A "Off the record" meant that they couldn't use the information in their story, but it could help shape their thinking for the story. So if the car was green and I said the car was red, they might not write that the car was green, but they wouldn't put in the story that I said in any capacity the car really wasn't green.

Q *And in working with Mr. Libby, did he have any particular practices when deal-ing with the press above and beyond the usual ground rules?*

A No. My recollection . . . was Scooter's preference was to talk to the press off the record and then, if they wanted to use something either in his name or on back-ground, they would have to come back and clear quotes, which we would some-times have the press agree to do so that you could actually say, "Yes, you can use that quote, but you can't use this one." That kind of thing . . .

Q *Now, directing your attention to the spring of 2003, did there come a time when you read a column by a man by the name of Nicholas Kristof?*

A Yes, it was brought to my attention . . .

KRISTOF'S MAY 6, 2003 column is entered into evidence.

Q *Can you just briefly describe what your reaction was when you first read the Nicholas Kristof column[?] . . . I will read the fourth paragraph.*

"Let's fervently hope that tomorrow we find an Iraqi superdome filled with 500 tons of mustard gas and nerve gas, 25,000 liters of anthrax, 38,000 liters of botulinum toxin, 29,984 prohibited munitions capable of delivering chemical agents, several dozen Scud missiles, gas centrifuges to enrich uranium, 18 mobile biological warfare factories, long-range unmanned aerial vehicles to dispense anthrax, and proof of close ties with al Qaeda. Those are the things that President Bush or his aides suggested Iraq might have, and I don't want to believe that top administration officials tried to win support for the war with a campaign of wholesale deceit." . . .

[Without] commenting on the truthfulness of the article, is it fair to say that this was viewed in the White House as a negative article?

A Yes. It is fair to say that it would have been viewed as a negative article . . .

Q *And how much attention was paid to the Kristof article, as you recall, at the time it came out?*

A Not that much.

Q *If we can go to the second page: . . .*

"I'm told by a person involved in the Niger caper that more than a year ago, the Vice President's office asked for an investigation of the uranium deal, so a former U.S. Ambassador to Africa was dispatched to Niger. In February 2002, according to someone present at the meetings, that envoy reported to the CIA and State Department that the information was unequivocally wrong and that the documents had been forged."

Next paragraph:

"The envoy reported, for example, that a Niger minister whose signature was on one of the documents, had, in fact, been out of office for more than a decade. In addition, the Niger mining program was structured so that the uranium diversion had been impossible. The envoy's debunking of the forgery was passed around the administration and seemed to be accepted—except that President Bush and the State Department kept citing it anyway."

To your knowledge, was the issue of the Niger trip in the news at all prior to the May 6th Kristof piece?

A Not to my knowledge.

Q *Did it become more important in the news after—later on, after the May Kristof piece?*

A Yes . . .

Q *Did there come a time when you came to learn information about who the former ambassador referred to in connection with that trip was?*

A Yes.

Q *And who did you learn that former ambassador to be? ...*

A Joe Wilson.

Q *And who did you learn that information from?*

A My recollection is I learned it from Bill Harlow at the CIA.

Q *And can you tell the jury what Bill Harlow does at the CIA?*

A He [was] their equivalent of public affairs or communications director . . .

Q *As you sit here now, can you place an exact date on when it was that Mr. Harlow told you that this former ambassador was Mr. Wilson?*

A Not a precise date.

Q *Can you give us a time frame in which it must have happened?*

A I believe it happened between May 6th, this Kristof article, and the time that he appeared on *Meet the Press* and identified himself as Joe Wilson, which I believe occurred on July 6th.

Q *And why do you believe that it occurred before Mr. Wilson appeared on July 6th on* **Meet the Press?**

A Because I specifically remember not being surprised by who he was on *Meet the Press*.

Q *Okay.*

A I knew his name already . . .

Q *Now, is it fair to say that there are a number of conversations involving Mr. Harlow, Mr. Libby and the Vice President on the topic of Wilson or his wife and that you recall the conversations themselves?*

A I recall two—at least two—specific conversations . . . related to my conversations with Mr. Harlow that involved the Vice President and Scooter . . .

Q *And why don't you tell us, . . . were you directed to speak to Mr. Harlow by anyone else on either occasion?*

A . . . On both occasions . . . that I recall, I was told by somebody to call or talk to Bill Harlow. One occasion, I had spoken with a press aide in the National Security Council at the White House who suggested that I call Bill Harlow.

And on another occasion, I participated or was in a meeting in Scooter's office where he spoke to someone at the CIA in Bob McLaughlin's office, and from that conversation, I was told, "talk to Bill Harlow". . . .

MARTIN EXPLAINS THAT THE FACT that National Security press aide Michael Anton, and not the usual person, Anna Perez, was the one telling her suggests it may have happened while Perez was traveling with the President in Africa July 7–12:

Q *Your recollection is that the timing of [the first suggestion] that you call Mr. Harlow would have placed that conversation during the time frame when the president and other senior aides were traveling to Africa?*

A Right.

Q *Okay. And can you describe—when you were in the office of Mr. Libby and he was speaking to someone in Mr. McLaughlin's office at the CIA, can you tell us, in your experience, how common it was for you to be present when someone was talking to someone from the CIA?*

A It was rare.

Q *Describe what happened when Mr. Libby is in his office.*

A I remember standing in Scooter's office. He was on the phone with someone at the CIA that I thought was Bob McLaughlin or someone in his office. And at the end of the conversation, they—he and this person he was talking to—agreed that I would talk with Bill Harlow.

And from there, . . . that led to a conversation that I had with Bill Harlow. I don't recall whether I picked up the phone and called him or he called me, but we got on the phone together . . .

Q *Okay. So why don't you describe the conversations you had with Mr. Harlow that you recall.*

A Okay. The first conversation that I recall having with Mr. Harlow was a pleasant conversation. I had never spoken to him before. I remember him being very helpful.

And I remember talking to him about the press reports of a former ambassador who had been sent to Niger, and the press reports were saying because of an inquiry by the Vice President or sent by the Vice President—and I was asking him, who—we didn't send him, because I had spoken with my office, and everyone had said, we didn't send him.

So I was saying to him, ["W]e didn't send him. What are you saying? I mean, if we didn't send him, you must have sent him. Who sent him? Who is the guy? And, what are you saying to this press? Because it keeps getting reported that we sent him. They are not taking my word for it.["]

And he was helpful and . . . I remember him being like, "you know, I didn't really know who he was either when they first called. They knew more about this guy than I did."

And I remember him ultimately saying, ["Y]ou know, but apparently . . . his name is Joe Wilson. He was a chargé in Baghdad, and his wife works over here."

Q *Could you explain to the jury what you understand "a chargé" to be?*

A A diplomat that works in an embassy overseas . . .

Q *And did you take any notes during this conversation that you had with Mr. Harlow?*

A I did.

Q *Did you date the notes?*

A No . . .

Q *What did you do after you learned this information from Mr. Harlow on whatever day it was?*

A I asked to see the Vice President, and shortly, sometime thereafter, got in to see the Vice President to tell the Vice President—and Scooter [who] was there as well—what I had learned . . .

Q *And tell us what happened when you went to the Vice President's office.*

A I remember going into the Vice President's office. Scooter was in his office, which was pretty normal. And I said I had spoken with Bill Harlow at the CIA, and . . . he told me the former ambassador's name; his name is Joe Wilson. And apparently he was a chargé in Baghdad, and apparently his wife works at the CIA.

Q *And did either of them say anything in response as far as you can recall?*

A I don't remember any specific response.

Q *Okay. And can you describe the other conversation with Harlow that you recall?*

A I recall a second conversation, fairly specifically, of calling Bill Harlow to find out who was continuing to call on this story, because the story was continuing to be written and . . . the Vice President's office, . . . was still in the story as having sent him or him having traveled at the behest of.

So I was calling—I guess I should back up. Often press stopped calling our office. So at this point they weren't calling me asking me for comment. This had just become sort of . . . you know, true in the press. Just everyone that wrote the story just picked up on it, kept writing it; they didn't call and ask me for comment.

So I think I called . . . NSC, and this is how this led to this conversation . . . but I remember my conversation with Bill Harlow. In my conversation with Bill Harlow, he was a little less friendly and a little more reluctant, but he told me who was calling him and what reporters were working on stories. And he told me that Andrea Mitchell was working on a story and David Martin was working on a story.

Q *And do you know what time frame this was that Andrea Mitchell and David Martin were working on a story?*

A It was the week of July 7th . . .

Q *Okay. Now, moving to a specific date, July 6th, when the Wilson op-ed appeared in* The New York Times *and on* Meet the Press, *did you have . . . the same amount of contact with Mr. Libby thereafter or did that change during that week? . . .*

A The week of July 7th, in my memory, was a busy week, and I think I had more contact with Scooter that week. It was particularly busy because nobody was around and there was a lot going on in the press.

Q *And can you tell us what the ordinary practice was in the Office of Vice President to keep track of news stories? How would you come in in the morning and know what was being said in the press?*

A My staff would do a search every morning for stories that referenced the Vice President or the Vice President's office. And they would cut and paste these stories into a Word document . . . and they would bold the section that referenced our office so that it was easy for folks to just flip through a Word document and see what the media was saying about this, and we would usually put a cover page on it that . . . said "This story was in *The New York Times;*" "this story was in *The Washington Post*". . .

Q *And would you ordinarily see in the Office of the Vice President newspaper articles cut out of actual newspapers?*

A Not very often.

Q *And during the week of July 7th, 2003, did anything change . . . about the practice of keeping people up-to-date on what was being said in the media?*

A Sometime during that week we began monitoring the television commentators, because most of the time we were looking at print . . .

Normally we just looked in the morning for print . . . but that week, we started looking—watching the television and . . . keeping track of what people were saying, and [we] would pull the transcripts as they became available.

Q *When and why did that change?*

A At some point during that week, I had a conversation in the Vice President's office and recall the Vice President telling me to keep track of this story and who was continuing to comment—the commentators that were continuing to write on this story, talk about this story and talk about us as . . . having sent this person.

Q *And who was present when this conversation took place?*

A I believe it was just myself, the Vice President and Scooter . . .

Q *Do you recall the date it took place? . . .*

A This conversation occurred on or before July 9.

Q *Was there a particular program on MSNBC that you were keeping track of?*

A Well, we were paying attention to *Hardball* with Chris Matthews because he had been talking about it a lot.

THE QUESTIONING ABOUT the OVP's attention to *Hardball* that follows is designed both to bring out just how focused the Vice President and Libby were on responding to criticisms derived from Wilson's disclosures and to set up Libby's phone call with Tim Russert on July 10 or 11, since Libby was calling Russert to complain about Matthews' performance:

Q *And did you do anything to try to get more up-to-date information than what Mr. Matthews was saying faster than waiting for MSNBC to generate a transcript?*

A My press assistants were the ones that were really doing the work. I had come back from the Vice President's office and said, we need to keep track now, guys, of the TV stuff . . .

And there is a service in the White House press office that, if you want to see something that you can put a time frame on on a particular network, they can send you—it's called a shadow TV clip, which is basically a clip on your computer that they can send to you. They can pull it down, and you can watch it on your computer.

So a couple—I know that on a couple of occasions, Hannah Siemers, who was our press assistant, would pull those shadow TV clips . . . and she would transcribe it herself . . .

Q *And then what would you do with those when they were done?*
A Send them on.

Q *And were you receiving requests during this time for, you know, updates on transcripts? Was your staff or you?*
A . . . I know my staff continued to get... requests for more information. And it was for a period of time after the July 6th appearance of Joe Wilson.

Q *And who did the request come from?*
A Often from Jenny Mayfield . . .

Mayfield was Libby's assistant at the time.

Q *What topics were you following that week?*
A . . . That week, I was following the topic of the sixteen words in the State of the Union and the general story of whether or not those sixteen words should have been in the State of the Union—the whole big story.

FITZGERALD OPENS A LENGTHY LINE of questioning focused on Martin's role in preparing talking points for OVP that week. Part of the point is to show OVP's role in shaping the White House's first public response to Wilson on July 7. But the larger significance is to lay the groundwork for Fitzgerald's closing argument that Cheney overhauled OVP's talking points in light of his reading of Wilson's op-ed, and made the new primary talking point raising the question of who authorized Wilson's trip. Fitzgerald would argue that the notes Cheney took on Wilson's op-ed showed that he believed the answer to that question was "Wilson's wife"—and that Cheney was not only prompting the press to look into that question but was simultaneously involved in directing Libby to talk to Judith Miller on July 8, when Libby told the reporter that Wilson's wife worked at the CIA:

Q *Did there come a time that week when you prepared talking points to use in dealing with the press?*
A There did.

Q *And did you share the talking points with anyone else in the White House?*
A Well, yes. On Monday, after Mr. Wilson appeared on *Meet the Press*, I typed some talking points and sent them to Ari Fleischer, the then press secretary, for him to use in his morning briefing which I think that day was gaggle; that's what they would call the morning briefing.

And I sent them on to Ari so that he would have at least the points about the Vice President's office and us not having sent this man . . .

Q . . . *You mentioned a gaggle. So could you explain to the jury what a gaggle is in press terms?*

A In the morning, the press secretary usually meets with the press and gives them sort of an overview of the day and gets their initial feedback on kind of the questions— what they are thinking about for the day. And then mid-day he will do a briefing, which is . . . where he will often get back to them on some of the questions from the morning . . .

Q *With regard to the outside world, the gaggles are not televised, but the briefing in the afternoon is?*

A Right . . .

Q *I ask you to take a look at Government Exhibit 540 and tell us if you recognize what it is . . .*

A It's the e-mail that I sent to Ari Fleischer the morning of July 7th to give him the points responding to Joe Wilson's claims about the Vice President sending him to Niger . . .

Q *Ms. Martin, could you just read aloud the four bullet points you had on those talking points?*

A "The Vice President's office did not request the mission to Niger. The Vice President's office was not informed of Joe Wilson's mission. The Vice President's office did not receive a briefing about Mr. Wilson's mission after he returned. The Vice President's office was not aware of Mr. Wilson's mission until recent press reports accounted for it."

Q *And do you know who came up with these four talking points?*

A Well, my recollection is I had had conversations with Scooter and the Vice President at some point before this. These are talking points I was using even before . . . Joe Wilson . . . revealed himself. I was referring to him as a former ambassador previously, but now we know who he is, so it uses his name.

Q *And is there a reason why you felt you needed to send these talking points to Mr. Fleischer who is the White House Press Secretary?*

A Yes, because on that Sunday, Mr. Wilson had been on *Meet the Press* and had again said that he thought he had been sent by the Vice President's office and that his mission was because of inquiries by the Vice President's office that I was being told was not true and we did not believe was true. And he wrote that as well in a *New York Times* op-ed.

. . . It went to the credibility of the sixteen words that ended up in the State of the Union and the President's credibility of making the case for war.

I knew that Ari would get asked about him, and I wanted to make sure that he would get on the record this piece about how he was sent, that it wasn't because of us. Because the implication—and all of his media had been, "Well, they asked. They sent me. I assume they got a report back that I said this was not true."

Q *Okay. Did there come a later point in time when you created additional talking points to use with for the media?*

A There did . . .

Q *And do you recognize Government Exhibit 523? [See appendix.]*

A It is a set of talking points that I typed up that are more expansive than the ones I sent to Ari Fleischer . . .

Q *And looking at Government's Exhibit 522 first, do you recognize what that is?*

A Yes. It's my handwritten notes of talking points.

Q *Can you tell us when and how you created Government Exhibit 522?*

A That week, the week of July 7th, . . . I had a meeting with the Vice President up on the Hill . . . and I took the opportunity to talk to the Vice President about the press inquiries and press reports related to the Joe Wilson matter and his travel to Niger as it related to us. And he dictated to me what he wanted me to say. This is my dictation—my notes, my handwritten notes . . .

Q *Could you just read your handwriting to the jury[?] . . .*

A "Not clear who authorized his travel." 2. "He did not travel at my request. Don't know him." 3. "He was apparently unpaid." 4. "Never saw the document he was allegedly trying to verify.". . . [5.] "Said he was convinced Niger could not have provided uranium to Iraq, but, in fact, they did in 1980s, 200 tons, currently under IAEA seal." 6. "No written report." 7. "V.P. was unaware of Joe Wilson, his trip or any conclusions he may have reached until spring of '03 when reported." 8. "As late as last October, the considered judgment of the intel community"—'comm,' which was my 'community'—"was that s.h."—'Saddam Hussein'—"Had indeed undertaken a vigorous effort to acquire uranium from Africa . . . according to NIE."

Q *And what did you understand NIE to refer to?*

A National Intelligence Estimate.

Q *And 1 through 8 is what the Vice President dictated to you as you wrote it down that day?*

A Correct.

Q *And did he dictate the question mark to you to the left of the 8?*

A No.

Q *And why did you put it there?*

A I wasn't sure if I could use that point because it referred to the NIE, which was classified . . .

Q *And if you can look at government exhibit 524, which is the third document in front of you that I think we did not discuss.*

A Okay.

Q *And what is that?*

A It's a version of my typed-up talking points with some handwritten edits on it.

Q *And do you know whose handwriting it is that made the edits?*

A It looks like part of it's mine on the editing of the talking point, and then there is some handwriting in the column—in the margins that looks like it might be Scooter's . . .

Q *Ms. Martin, can you tell us what is different about the text, forgetting the handwriting for the moment—what's different about the text in this document versus the handwritten talking points that you have?*

A Well, first, I completed the sentences from my handwritten talking points and sort of just cleaned them up. And, second, under the second bullet, you see four additional bullets. Those are the bullets that I had—the basic bullets that I had sent to Ari Fleischer the day before. That was our talking points. So I just fleshed out that point and added those four points . . .

Q *And whose handwriting is on the lower left side, as best you can tell?*

A It looks like Scooter's.

Q *And can you read what it says?*

A "Wilson. Three points." I think that's what it says. And a colon, then "3–1999."

THE QUESTIONING SHIFTS to Martin having witnessed Cheney directing Libby on July 8, 2003 to get OVP's story out to two reporters, David Martin of CBS and Andrea Mitchell of NBC, and Libby calling Mitchell. The next day Cathie Martin would get in trouble with Steven Hadley for Mitchell's report the previous evening, which reported the White House was blaming the CIA for the sixteen words; Libby failed to take responsibility for talking to Mitchell.

Q *Okay. Now, during this time period, you mentioned earlier that you had a phone call with Mr. Harlow at one point where Mr. Harlow told you that a reporter named Andrea Mitchell had been calling him?*

A Yes.

Q *Can you describe what you did following that telephone call?*

A I remember going to the Vice President's office to give him an update on what I was hearing . . . it was an unscheduled visit—to get in and see him and talk to the Vice President and Scooter and told them that I wasn't getting any calls directly, but that I had spoken to Harlow and that I knew that Andrea Mitchell and David Martin were doing pieces for the evening news.

Q *And do you recall any further discussion during this meeting as to what should be done?*

A I remember discussing with them, you know, should we get in the story? Should we try to talk to them and make sure that they don't repeat the stuff that we think was false and it was continuing to be reported a lot of different places? And should we . . . just make sure that we are a part of the story, because they are not even calling?

And I think the general consensus was yes. And ultimately it was decided that Scooter would call them back.

Q *And . . . who was Mr. Libby to call?*
A The two reporters.

Q *And whose decision was it for Mr. Libby to make that call?*
A The Vice President's.

Q *And then were you present for either of those calls?*
A I recall leaving the Vice President's office and going into his outer office where Scooter had a little ante—like an ante-office, and going in there with Scooter, and him calling one of the reporters—I am not sure which one. But I was there for— at a portion of one of the phone calls.

The trial breaks for lunch.

*

AFTER THE LUNCH BREAK, Walton gives the jury an instruction, repeated throughout the trial, that there is no dispute that by July 8, 2003, certain portions of the October 2002 National Intelligence Estimate had been declassified. The only people who knew about this secret declassification by the President were Bush, Cheney and Libby. Fitzgerald resumes questioning Martin, first bringing out press aide Martin's ignorance of Libby's key July 8, 2003 meeting with Judith Miller, which Fitzgerald would argue showed the compartmentalized character of Libby's dealings with *The New York Times* reporter who was specially targeted with information about Wilson's wife, before turning to how the rest of the week unfolded:

By Mr. Fitzgerald:
Q *Turning to July 8th, . . . were you aware on July 8, 2003, of a meeting between Mr. Libby and reporter Judith Miller of* **The New York Times***?*
A I was not.

Q *Now, you mentioned earlier a telephone call with Ms. Mitchell. Did there come a time when there was discussion within the White House as to a news report or a news broadcast by Andrea Mitchell during that week?*
A There did.

Q *Can you tell us what happened and when?*
A The next day, which I believe was Wednesday, we have our morning senior staff meetings with the President's staff. And as typical, part of that meeting we talk about what was in the press the night before or was on breaking news or things that happened since the previous day.

At some point during that meeting, Steve Hadley, who was then the Deputy National Security Advisor to the President, raised the evening news report by Andrea Mitchell, . . . and said that there had been suggestions that . . . the White House was pushing blame towards the CIA.

And that that was not helpful and that was not what we should be doing. He suggested that George Tenet was not happy with it and sort of told us all we shouldn't be saying that.

Q *How many people were in the room approximately at this time?*

A There's typically about 20-some-odd people in the room. But my recollection is not everybody was there because a lot of people were on this trip to Africa and there were a lot of substitutes . . .

Q *Did you see any indication from Mr. Hadley as to who Mr. Hadley believed may have been the person who spoke to Andrea Mitchell?*

A While Mr. Hadley was saying this, he looked around the room and I sat behind him. He turned around and looked at me. So I felt like he was suggesting I had been involved in talking to the reporter and making this point.

Q *Had you actually yourself spoken with Ms. Mitchell?*

A No.

Q *Where was Mr. Libby when this conversation took place?*

A Seated directly in front of me.

Q *Did you notice what he was doing?*

A He looked down.

Q *What happened after this meeting where Mr. Hadley made these remarks?*

A Mr. Hadley asked me and others from the press office that were in that meeting and I think Michael Anton, who was his press person that I mentioned earlier . . . to come to his office to talk about the story.

And told us again we should not be pointing fingers. This was not helpful to the President. It wasn't helpful to the story. We shouldn't be making any suggestions that this was the CIA's fault in any way, shape or form.

Q *What, if anything, did you do as a response, in response to Mr. Hadley's comments to you . . . [?]*

A Well afterwards, at some point, I went to see the Vice President because I thought the Vice President should know that I believed Mr. Hadley thought that I or the Office of the Vice President had something to do with these reports.

So I went to see him at . . . some time in that morning, as soon as I could get in to see him after my communications meeting in the morning. Because I went from senior staff meeting to communications meeting. And then after that, I tried to find the Vice President, spoke to the Vice President, was able to see him.

Scooter was there. I told him what had happened at the meeting. And that he had kept us afterwards, and that I believed he thought that I, in particular, but that we had something to do with this.

Q *Then what happened the rest of the week in terms of your access to decisions about communication strategy?*

A . . . I was not involved from about that point on in any further discussions about how to deal with this story with senior people. I still continued to talk to my press colleagues in the White House about what we were hearing and trying to keep track of it.

Q *Were you the only press person who was excluded from the conversations at that point?*

A No, my understanding, in talking to my colleagues, was that everybody was sort of in the dark about what other conversations were going on in the White House amongst the senior staff.

Q *Did there come a time when you spoke to Mr. Libby about communications strategy later that week?*

A There did.

Q *Can you tell us when and where?*

A On Thursday evening about, of that week, which I believe was July 10th, I had been monitoring . . . what was going on in the media and letting them know whatever I heard . . . But I hadn't really talked to Scooter. And I wanted to make sure, before I left for the evening, that he didn't need anything.

So I either stopped by his office or called and suggested, you know, if you need me, I'm here. But if not, I'm going to leave. And Scooter said, you know what, actually, can you hang on a second. I'd actually like to talk to you. So he brought me into his office. We talked a little bit about that I hadn't been involved in the discussions that were going on.

He told me that there had been a decision not to have communicators involved in these discussions. But that he would feel more comfortable getting the judgment of someone that was in communications about what was going on . . . [H]e said what's going on is George Tenet is going to, we think, give a statement to the press about the sixteen words, how they got into the State of the Union . . .

And there have been discussions back and forth about what that statement will say. And we have a sense of what it will say. And I believe, maybe his assistant was in the room, Jenny Mayfield. And I believe she kind of had this paper that had notes that seemed to reflect conversations back and forth between the White House and George Tenet.

That, . . . it's my understanding, had been occurring through Steve Hadley, and Steve Hadley had been relaying it back to us. At some point during that conversation, Steve Hadley calls and Scooter asks me to leave the room since I was not supposed to be involved in this.

So periodically, I'm going in and out of his office . . . I sat in his outer office. While I was there, I took some notes thinking about how I could best advise them on the communications strategy about this statement that might be happening. And when I returned to his office and he got off the phone, we continued talking.

Q *Do you recall if anyone else besides Mr. Hadley was calling in at that time?*

A I don't recall whether the Vice President called Scooter or Scooter had to call the Vice President. But I think, during that same conversation, there were conversations between Scooter and Steve Hadley and Scooter and the Vice President. And I left for both conversations with either one of them.

Q *And when you went outside in the hallway or outside the office, wherever you were, what were you doing?*

A Writing some notes to myself, . . . and also thinking about the Vice Presidential piece of this, wanting to make sure that our little piece of that was in there as well . . . I was also trying to figure out what are the options for things we can do, communications tactics and press strategy around this... Like, what if [the statement] doesn't answer all the questions the press have about this story. And there are still more questions.

Q *Could you explain to us what you mean by "the Vice Presidential piece of this?"*

A Just, the talking points that we had been using. We didn't know who Joe Wilson was. We didn't request his mission. The Vice President didn't receive a report about his mission, that line of reasoning.

Q *And then what did you do when you eventually returned to Mr. Libby's office after you wrote these notes out?*

A . . . I talked with him, you know, what I thought about the statement, what my concerns were, that what was being conveyed about how strong the statement would be.

And said, you know, it doesn't end the story. It doesn't end there, then there are other things we can do. Tomorrow is Friday. I think I told him that there were, we could go on the Sunday shows, which is one way to really clean up something that's happened during the week because the Sunday news talk shows always talk about what happened that week.

So we would for sure talk about the story, so we could put someone in, and I suggested we could put the Vice President on *Meet the Press*, just a tactic we use when there is a big sort of comprehensive discussion of it, the Vice President would be the one to do that.

I told them there were a couple of reporters that were currently working on stories that I thought we could try to get in their stories. One of the tactics that you use in the press world is to let's give an exclusive to a reporter. I believe I wrote the word leak to a reporter in my notes, which I meant as, it's a term of art to give it . . . exclusively to that person.

I believe I suggested an [op-ed]. We could have somebody write an [op-ed] or we could . . . give it to . . . a columnist . . . Columnists tend to write the whole story, whereas the reporter, they might just write the news for the day.

Q *When you say you'd give an exclusive, would you explain to the jury why, if you wanted to get press attention to something, you would just give it to one reporter rather than all the reporters?*

A Reporters would like to have the story. And each reporter, they're competing against each other. So if you give it to one reporter, they're more likely to write the story if they think it's news and if they think it has just been given to them.

In addition, you can give it to them and do it as a senior Administration official. You don't have to say this is coming directly from the White House. You can say I'll tell you the full story but here is how we're going to do it.

Q *Let me approach you with what's been pre-marked for identification as Government Exhibit 541 . . . [See appendix.]*

Q *What is it?*

A . . .[I]t looks like the typed document that I think Jenny Mayfield gave me when I was in Scooter's office that night summarizing the conversation that went on between the White House and George Tenet about possibilities his statement would say. And then my notes that I wrote on it on the back of each page about the statement and about this press strategy . . .

Q *If you could show the other side of that page, Government's Exhibit 541, with the Bates stamp in the lower corner 2878. Can you tell us what that page is, both the blue and the black?*

A . . . The blue at the top is my notes about the statement and what I had hoped we might be able to get into the statement, the beginnings of my notes about it. About what I hoped George Tenet's statement would include. And the black is what I was writing down about what the press strategy options were.

Q *Focusing on the language in the black where it says options, can you run down the four options and describe what they refer to in these notes and what you discussed with Mr. Libby?*

A Sure. First note M.T.P., which is *Meet the Press*, dash VP. So this was my discussion about possibly putting the Vice President on *Meet the Press* that Sunday to give a fuller discussion of the whole picture.

Q *On the right you have another reference to M.T.P. Can you describe what that is?*

A I think I walked, this is me walking through the pros and cons of putting the Vice President on *Meet the Press*. And I wrote underneath pros, "best." This is our best format, and he's our best person on *Meet the Press*. Two, we control the message a little bit more. It was good for our—for us to be able to tell our story.

On the cons, it's too weedy, means the Vice President is going to get pulled into the weeds and specifics. We generally like to keep him at a pretty high level.

Too defensive. Looks defensive to rush him out on *Meet the Press*. It signals things to the media when we put a Vice President on *Meet the Press*, we feel.

And the third thing is it raises the bar. It just meant that I thought that it raises the bar on the story . . .

Q . . .[C]an you read the next line and explain what it means?

A After *Meet the Press*, on the left side then it says leak to Sanger, dash, Pincus, dash, news mags, dash, sit down and give to them.

Q *Can you explain what that means?*

A So, when I said we could give it to someone who was writing, I think that Sanger was, at that time, was working on, what I believe he thought at the time was a definitive piece about how the sixteen words got in the State of the Union. So he started writing the story. We could go to Sanger and say, okay, let me sit down with you and tell you our version of how this all happened.

Q *Can you just tell us who Sanger is?*

A I'm sorry. David Sanger is a reporter with *The New York Times*.

Q *Okay.*

A And then Pincus refers to Walter Pincus, who writes for *The Washington Post*. He must have been writing the story at the same time. I don't have a specific recollection of his particular story.

And then news mags was because it was the end of the week. News magazines are *TIME* and *Newsweek* and *U.S. News* . . . Generally . . . their deadlines are on Saturday. Then they go to print for the next Monday. So at the end of the week, a news magazine is doing again, the big picture of the week. And you can, typically they'll be writing a story that you would be able to sit down with one of them.

Q *Okay. And then the next, the third tick?*

A It says press conference, dash, Condi/Rumsfeld. And by this I was referring to, we could have a press conference and two of our potential people that could hold a press conference were Condoleezza Rice or Secretary Rumsfeld in my view.

And then the last line said OP/ED. By that, I meant an opinion piece. My recollection and my vernacular when I write OP/ED, OP/ED means not just we could write one, but a third party could write one. And it also would include opinion pages so you could go to a columnist that already writes.

Q *Okay. After you discussed this option, what did you do with your notes that day, or those notes in front of you, if you recall?*

A What did I do with my notes that day?

Q *Yes.*

A I believe that Jenny Mayfield asked me for a copy of them at some point to take them back. Before I gave them back, I just made a copy for myself . . .

FITZGERALD TURNS TO QUESTIONING Martin about her preparations for and observation of Libby's phone conversation with *TIME*'s Matt Cooper on July 12, 2003, one of the conversation about which Libby is accused of lying under oath:

Q *Directing your attention to July 11th, did there come a time when you had contact with a reporter from* TIME *magazine?*

A Yes, ... Matt Cooper from *TIME* magazine.

Q *And how did he contact you, if you recall?*

A . . . I'm not sure if he called or e-mailed me first. But he called and e-mailed me toward the end of that week.

Q *Do you know what general topic he was writing about?*

A He was writing about the story of the week, which was the sixteen words in the State of the Union, and how they got in the State of the Union. At this point, on Friday, I think we had said that they shouldn't have been in the State of the Union. So he was writing on the whole big picture.

Q *Did you get back to him with sufficient answers on Friday, July 11th?*

A No, I told him I didn't have a chance to get to anybody. He said he e-mailed me some questions, and I didn't have a chance to get to them. But that I would try to get to him the answers, but I couldn't get anybody on Friday.

Q *Did the statement you referred to by George Tenet come out that week?*

A It did. It came out Friday evening.

Q *What's the significance in terms of communications of the timing of the statement being released on Friday evening?*

A Fewer people pay attention to it later on Friday, much less late on Friday. And in our view, fewer people are paying attention on Saturday, when it's reported.

Q *Did you have any reaction or anyone in the Office of the Vice President express any reaction to the content of Mr. Tenet's statement when it came out?*

A My reaction was that it was helpful but probably didn't end the discussion . . . So my initial reaction was it was sort of mixed and some helpful but it probably wasn't going to [be] enough to end the story.

The next day was a Saturday. The Vice President had a trip that I was going to staff him on. So I saw my colleagues the next day, and I believe, at some point, during those conversations we talked about the statement.

Q *Did the Vice President express any opinion as to whether the statement was good enough?*

A To my recollection, I didn't talk to the Vice President that Saturday.

Q *How about Mr. Libby? Did you speak to him about whether he viewed the statement as good enough?*

A I'm pretty sure I did. I don't have a specific recollection of the words he used, but I'm pretty sure I expressed, at least expressed my opinion to him.

Q *Why don't you tell us about this trip you took on July 12th, this Saturday?*

A So on Saturday, July 12th, the Vice President was going to a . . . christening of the USS *Ronald Reagan*. We were basically going to send the ship off . . .

Mrs. Reagan was going to be there. It was very ceremonious. So we were traveling there because he was going to give remarks on the ship before they launched it.

Q *Who was on the trip from the people who worked in the Office of the Vice President?*

A Scooter was on the trip. I believe David Addington was on the trip, who at the time was the Vice President's counsel, lawyer. Claire O'Donnell, who was the Deputy Chief of Staff and for Operations, was kind of like the office manager . . .

Some people that were old Reagan staffers were on the trip . . .

Q *Did Mr. Libby go on the trip?*
A Oh, yes.

Q *Was he accompanied by family?*
A He was.

Q *Did you have any conversation relevant to the media strategy on the way down to the ceremony?*
A No, just, I reminded Scooter that I needed to get back to some reporters and we needed to talk some time today.

Q *Describe what happened on the return trip from the commissioning ceremony or christening ceremony to D.C.*
A On the return trip, I was sitting in the back of the plane. As was mentioned, Scooter's family was traveling with him. So, I would normally be sitting up front with the staff. But his family was traveling. There were additional people on the plane. So, I was in the back of the plane.

Scooter came back to see me and sat down next to me. And he said, . . . "What do you need to talk to me about?" And I told him that I had a couple of press calls. I had this call and e-mailed questions from *TIME* magazine from Matt Cooper. And I had . . . a call and a couple questions from Glenn Kessler at *The Washington Post.*

We talked about the Matt Cooper questions first because they were very specific and I had an e-mail. I showed him the e-mail. We talked about what his story was going to be, what Matt had given me generally about the story . . .

Q *Let me approach you with what's been pre-marked as Government Exhibit 527. I ask if you recognize what that exhibit is?*
A Yes, it's the e-mail that Matt Cooper sent me with his questions for his story.

Q *Is that the e-mail you discussed with Mr. Libby on July 12th?*
A It is . . .

Q *[W]hy don't we read the questions below, "Thanks so much for your help. Here are some questions."*
A "Who in the Vice President's office communicated to the CIA their interest in the Niger allegation? How and when was that communication performed?

"Did the V.P. or a member of his staff discuss the Niger allegation in any of his personal visits to Langley?

"Did the V.P. or a member of his staff play any role in the inclusion of the allegation in the President's State of the Union? . . .

"How many persons are employed by the V.P.'s national security staff?

"In previous V.P. stories *TIME* has done (before my time), we've been told that the V.P. has a voracious appetite for raw intelligence. Still true?". . .

Q *After your conversation with Mr. Libby about this e-mail, what happened next?*

A . . . Scooter and I kind of ran through these questions and talked about the questions themselves. And Scooter, I believe, took the questions and said, okay, well let me go talk to the boss and I'll be back. So he went up to the front of the plane to see the Vice President.

Q *What did you do?*

A Stayed seated where I was.

Q *Did there come a time when he came back?*

A There did. Right before we landed, he came back.

Q *Can you tell us what happened then?*

A He came back and he said, he had a card in his hand with some notes on it. He said, he wants us to give a statement on the record. And here is the statement. He had the statement written out, and he wants me to do it.

Q *When you say "he wants me to do it," can you explain who the "he" and who the "me" are?*

A The "he" is the Vice President, and the "me" is Scooter Libby.

Q *Let me approach you with what's been pre-marked as Government's Exhibit 528-A . . . [D]o you recognize what it is?*

A It looks like the card that had the notes on it about what we should say to *TIME* magazine.

Q *Just to jump ahead for a moment, did you later, following that day, do something with that card yourself?*

A Later in the day, I actually am not sure whether it was later in the day or maybe that Monday after this trip occurred. But at some point, I asked for this card so I could try to type up the quote because we were giving, Scooter was giving a quote on the record. And I wanted to be able to make sure that the reporter reports the quote exactly as Scooter gave it to him . . .

Q *Can we briefly display Government Exhibit 528-A? And can you describe to the jury what they're seeing on the screen?*

A The notes that I believe Scooter took at the front of the plane when he was talking to the Vice President about what to say to the reporter of *TIME* magazine.

Q *Whose handwriting is that?*

A Scooter's.

Q *If we could display Government Exhibit 528-B [see appendix]. Can you describe to the jury what they're seeing in 528-B?*

A This is the typed up, cleaned up version of what the card said.

Q *Okay. And the top says "on the record"?*

A Yes.

Q *And then there is a "deep background as administration official" section?*

A Yes.

Q *And there is a "notes" section?*
A Yes.

Q *And what happened after Mr. Libby told you that the Vice President wanted him to make a statement?*
A I think we were landing . . . [W]e talked about when we were going to call. It's hard getting people to call from the plane . . .

So we thought maybe it would be better just to try to take a few minutes and do it when we landed at Andrews Air Force Base inside from a regular phone so we weren't worried about reception, and getting cut off.

Q *Did you find a phone inside Andrews Air Force Base?*
A We did. There's a lounge area and we asked if we could use the phone. Scooter, Jenny Mayfield and I went back in the back office and borrowed a phone.

Q *And was there just the three of you in the room, you, Mr. Libby and Ms. Mayfield?*
A Yes.

Q *What type of phone did you use? Was it a speakerphone or a regular phone?*
A A regular phone.

Q *Could you hear Mr. Libby's side of the conversation?*
A Yes.

Q *Could you hear the other side of the conversation?*
A No.

Q *Describe what you recall about the telephone call between Mr. Libby and Mr. Cooper?*
A I recall, to my recollection, he hadn't spoken with Mr. Cooper before. In fact, I had never spoken with Mr. Cooper before this because Mr. Cooper was new. He was with *TIME* but he hadn't been on the White House beat . . .

Scooter called him directly. Then I remember seeing Scooter hold the card and saying, I have a quote for you, reading from the card.

Q *Did you hear any discussion during the telephone call about Ambassador Wilson's wife?*
A No.

Q *Did you hear any discussion during the phone call about what other reporters were saying at that time?*
A No.

Q *What happened after Mr. Libby spoke to Mr. Cooper? . . .*
A [A]t some point before we spoke to Mr. Cooper, . . . I think Scooter said, well, if we're calling *TIME*, should we call *Newsweek* to be fair because we don't normally give these quotes on the record. And I said, well, they haven't called, but maybe we could . . . And we were scrambling for a number for a reporter that we know there named Evan Thomas . . . So we talked about . . . call[ing] Evan.

And oh, we had this Glenn Kessler call from *The Post*. We need to get back to him too, but it had gotten a little bit late. And it was Scooter's son's birthday, so we were hopeful to move it on. Then so we said, Scooter was anxious to get home. So we said we'll ride home with you in the van that took you to the Andrews Air Force Base, and you can make these phone calls in the car. And then we'll go with the van back to the White House. That way you can get home sooner and be with your child.

Q *Did you at any point hear Mr. Libby reach out to Mr. Thomas from* Newsweek?
A Yes. We eventually got the number, and Scooter called and left a message, I believe. We just left a voice-mail message.

Q *You mentioned there was a call from Mr. Kessler as well?*
A I also had a call from Mr. Kessler who was working on a story. So Scooter called Mr. Kessler back because he was also waiting for an answer from me, and gave him the answers to his questions, which weren't specifically related to this sixteen words is my recollection. But it may have been related to some of the evidence around the sixteen words, just the evidence about the war.

Q *Any discussion about Mr. Wilson's wife during the conversation that you heard with Mr. Kessler?*
A No.

Q *Directing your attention to the date July 14th, the date that a column appeared under the name of Robert Novak concerning Mr. Wilson's wife, prior to that news-paper article, had any reporters contacted you as the public affairs person in the Office of the Vice President and told you that they had heard that Wilson's wife worked at the CIA?*
A No, not that I recall . . .

FITZGERALD ASKS MARTIN about the publication of the *TIME* article:

Q *What did you notice about Scooter's quote when you read* TIME *magazine?*
A They had substantially shortened it and taken, what I believed, taken it out of context . . . There was some discussion about how we should go about fixing this. And at some point I had conversations with Matt Cooper about my displeasure at the fact that I put Scooter on the phone with him, which we didn't do very often on the record with a quote, and he took just a piece of it, not the whole quote. That I thought it was done, taken way out of context and wasn't helpful. And I wanted them to correct it, print the whole quote.

Q *Did Mr. Cooper offer any solution to you?*
A . . . We had a lot of back and forth, but at some point he came back to me. They couldn't fix the magazine that had already been printed . . .

So he came back and said we're going to put the quote in a web story. *TIME* magazine has a Web site. They do Web stories, which is not the same . . . People don't read the Web site the same way they read the magazine.

FITZGERALD TURNS TO QUESTIONING Martin about the July 18 luncheon Cheney held with conservative columnists, to amplify the White House's briefing that day of the officially declassified NIE:

Q *Okay. Did there come a time the following week when there was a luncheon held for conservative columnists?*
A There did.

Q *Where was it held?*
A At the Vice President's residence.

Q *Who attended from the Office of the Vice President that you recall?*
A Myself and Scooter.

Q *How about the Vice President?*
A Yes, the Vice President. The Vice President was holding a luncheon with conservative columnists at his house.

Q *In your experience in the Office of the Vice President, did that occur frequently or infrequently?*
A Not real frequently. I think I recall four or five.

Q *Do you know the reason that that particular luncheon was set up?*
A So it's now . . . the end of the week. It's the 18th, and we're still having lots of questions about this story and the State of the Union and the words and how they got in and were we wrong. Did we know and all this sort of, it's part of the background that's going on.

   And the White House decides that we needed to do a briefing. Dan Bartlett, who was the President's Communications Director, and his counselor now, and Steve Hadley are going to do a briefing to walk the report, White House press corps through what happened, how the State of the Union was put together, how the sixteen words got in there. Our clearance process for getting things in the State of the Union, and how that whole process works.

   As part of that, there was a discussion about, as a tactic, a communications tactic, should we also do one of these . . . conservative columnist luncheons to the Vice President. It has been effective doing it in the past to tell the larger story to that audience . . . It was to amplify this press briefing that we were going to do . . .

Q *Who invited the various journalists to the conservative columnists luncheon the following week, the week following the Novak column?*
A We put together a list, and Scooter invited most of them. I invited a couple.

MARTIN IS QUESTIONED ABOUT the context of the beginning of the investigation in fall 2003:

Q *Did there come a time when you learned that people were asking the White House Press Secretary about Karl Rove's involvement or not in the conduct that was being investigated?*

A Yes . . .

Q *Did you ever discuss the investigation and any public statements to be issued with Mr. Libby?*

A Yes . . . [T]he press was asking specific names about specific people working at the White House, whether they were the ones that had spoken with Novak or they were the ones that had given this information about Mr. Wilson's wife.

And they specifically asked about Karl. They specifically asked about Scooter. They specifically asked about Elliott Abrams, if I recall.

Q *Can you describe what you recall about your conversations about this with Mr. Libby?*

A At some point, I had a conversation with Scooter. The White House Press Secretary, Mr. Scott McClellan, had made a statement to the press about Karl and hadn't made a statement about Scooter or Elliott Abrams. And Scooter had said to me, they said something about Karl. Why don't they say something about me. And I said, well, this is a White House story, and you need to talk to Scott . . .

FITZGERALD FINISHES his direct examination, and Wells begins his cross-examination of Martin by bringing out the fact that Martin took a phone call in the middle of Libby's July 12, 2003 conversation with Matt Cooper:

Q *And you testified to the jury how you were in the room while Mr. Libby was having a conversation with Mr. Cooper, right?*

A Yes . . .

Q *Mr. Fitzgerald asked you a question whether or not, during the Cooper conversation, you heard Mr. Libby say anything about what other reporters were saying, right?*

A Correct.

Q *Then you told the jury you heard no such words, right?*

A I did not hear anything.

Q *Okay. But there was something very critical left out, and that was you were not there for the whole conversation, were you?*

A I received a phone call during the conversation from my press secretary, who I had called prior to the conversation, to ask if she had Evan Thomas's number. She called me back and said she did have it. She was on the beach. She was on vacation. And if I wanted her to do, she would go back to the house and get it . . .

Q *So you were not present to overhear the entire conversation Mr. Libby had with Mr. Cooper because Ms. Jennifer Millerwise called you during the call. . . .*

A I was physically present, but I was on the phone for part of it.

Q *You've been very clear about the fact that you did not hear the entire conversation that Mr. Libby had with Mr. Cooper . . . , right?*

A Because of this phone call . . .

Q *And it was just pure happenstance that Ms. Millerwise happened to call at the very moment that you were listening to Mr. Libby have his conversation with Mr. Cooper, right?*

A Correct.

Q *And but for that happenstance, that Ms. Millerwise had called, you would have been able to tell the jury exactly what you heard during the entire phone conversation, right?*

A Yes . . .

Q *You knew that Mr. Libby was trying to get home because it was his son's birthday, right?*

A Correct.

Q *And while you were in the room making the calls, Mrs. Libby and the two kids were in the next room, right?*

A They were in the lounge waiting for us.

Q *Mr. Libby made it very clear he was not happy about having to make any calls. He wanted to get home because it was his son's birthday party, right?*

A Correct.

Q *The only reason the calls got made to the reporters that day was because you were nagging both Mr. Libby and the Vice President of the United States to return Mr. Cooper's call because Mr. Cooper had sent you an e-mail with various questions. And you thought the best thing for the reputation of the Vice President's office was to respond to Mr. Cooper or else a story might get written with incorrect information?*

A I think I nagged Scooter that we needed to decide affirmatively whether we wanted to be in the story or not, rather than just let the time go by and miss our window. If we decided affirmatively not to be in the story, then great. My recollection is my recommendation was we should be in the story. But I also didn't talk to the Vice President that day. So I wasn't nagging both of them, only Scooter . .

AFTER BRINGING OUT THE FACT that Martin's only discussion with Cheney or Libby about Wilson's wife was the conversation in which she told them she had heard about Wilson's wife's role from the CIA spokesman, the defense questions Martin about Cheney's refrain that week about getting the whole story out:

Q *Now, is it correct, that you have absolutely no knowledge of Scooter Libby ever discussing with any reporter, any information concerning Mrs. Wilson or her employment status?*

A I have no knowledge of that . . .

THE DEFENSE BRINGS OUT SEVERAL PIECES of evidence indicating that Martin's first conversation with Harlow, after which she told Cheney and Libby about Wilson's wife, happened on June 11 or so, 2003, not in July. Martin then confirms that during June-July 2003 the Vice President's office was operating shorthanded, and she herself was relatively new to her job as top press aide to Cheney. In this context, Martin observes that Eric Edelman, then Deputy National Security Advisor to Cheney, took initial responsibility for the internal response to Kristof's May 6, 2003 column noting the Niger mission and OVP's role. Wells then has Martin read through the Kristof column and offer the Vice President's talking points to some of the allegations it contained, and she testifies that the talking points were accurate to the best of her knowledge.

A   My understanding is Jennifer, my press secretary, came to me and said Eric had pointed this out to her, this Kristof article, and was upset about it and thought this wasn't right. This didn't make sense to him. He wasn't aware of us causing any former ambassador go on any fact-finding mission on Niger.

So Jennifer and I talked about it. Eric, I assumed, was going to be the one to figure out if there would be anything specific we could say. But, because this was a columnist who we didn't have a relationship with, and who frankly attacked us— our Administration—fairly regularly, . . . it rose in our . . . priority list for the day of, you know, we've got to back to Kristof and set him straight.

It was brought to my attention by Jennifer that Eric was concerned about it and was looking at it. So, we were just waiting to see what Eric had to say. We didn't feel any urgency to get to Kristof.

MARTIN GOES ON TO CONFIRM that the issue of the Niger documents and the sixteen words was sharpened when NSA Rice was asked about it on one of the Sunday talk shows on June 8th and then with the publication of Walter Pincus' *Washington Post* story on June 12 and another column by Kristof the following day. Martin explains the frustration within the OVP:

A   [T]he media was not reporting what we were saying. And if they were, in this case, they weren't believing us.

Q   *And that continues right through July 14th when Mr. Novak writes that article, right?*
A   Some journalists are getting it.

Q   *Right.*
A   Others continue to report other stories, which include this, so they just continue saying the same thing about the Vice President being involved in sending Mr. Wilson on this mission.

THE NEXT MAJOR EVENT is Wilson's appearance in his own name on July 6, 2003, and Wells walks through the timeline for the subsequent week with Martin, focusing first on the fact that many of the top White House people were with the President in Africa that week, before getting Martin to confirm that Libby worked closely with her for the most part, including on the OVP's talking points, and that Chris Matthews was being particularly critical of the OVP. The questioning returns to the construction of George Tenet's public statement for the 11th:

Q *Now, on July 10th, you learned that a decision had been made by the senior Communications team and by the President of the United States that George Tenet, the Director of the CIA, is going to publish a statement whereby Mr. Tenet would explain how the sixteen words came to be in the State of the Union?*

A I learned from Scooter that Scooter, the Vice President and Steve Hadley—well Steve Hadley more directly and George Tenet—were talking through Steve Hadley about the statement. I have no knowledge of what was going on in Africa with the team in Africa but assumed they were in the loop.

Q *Mr. Fitzgerald asked you some questions about you and other communicators being taken out of the loop with respect to the Tenet statement. Do you recall that?*

A Yes.

Q *And it was Mr. Hadley who made the decision to take the communicators out of the loop, correct?*

A That was my understanding.

Q *Wasn't Mr. Libby, it was Mr. Hadley, right?*

A That's what Scooter told me.

Q *And when you went to the Vice President and had a discussion with the Vice President about your concern that Mr. Hadley was blaming you for a possible conversation with Andrea Mitchell, the Vice President told you, looked you right in the eye and told you don't worry about it, right?*

A Correct . . .

Q *Now, even though Mr. Hadley had said he did not want any other communicators involved in working out the details of the Tenet statement, Mr. Libby came to you, correct?*

A I went to Mr. Libby and he said [*"*]please come in[*"*] and he brought me in . . . [and] invited me into the discussion.

Q *Mr. Libby said to you that Mr. Hadley had made the decision to keep the communicators out. That he thought they should have some communicators involved. He didn't agree with the decision. He asked you, because he told you he wanted your judgment and help, to work with him. But you have to do it in a way that Mr. Hadley wouldn't know about it, right?*

A Correct, except that last part, but that was the implication why he kicked me out of the room.

Q *Right and that you understood that's why you were being asked to step out of the room?*

A Right.

Q *When Ms. Jenny Mayfield asked you for the notes back, you had written the notes on the copy of the draft of the Tenet statement, right?*

A Correct.

Q *So, since you weren't supposed to be involved with the Tenet statement, they asked you for the notes back, right?*

A Presumably, yes . . .

Q *You recall that drafting the statement in a way that would be satisfactory to George Tenet, the head of the CIA, was turning out to be a fairly contentious issue?*

A It seemed like a delicate matter is the way I would put it. And a little contentious that it seemed rather delicate, like there was some delicate discussions going on and Steve Hadley was basically coming in between.

Q *Right, because Mr. Tenet didn't want to do anything that would embarrass him, right?*

A And we didn't want to do anything that would embarrass him. I mean I think there was a mutual understanding . . .

TENET'S JULY 11 STATEMENT is entered into evidence and parts of it are published to the jury before Martin explains why OVP was not fully satisfied with it, including that Tenet's statement made no reference to a January 24, 2003 fax from the intelligence community to the White House—just four days before President Bush's State of the Union address—that repeated the October 2002 NIE's claim about Iraq's vigorous pursuit of uranium from abroad:

Q *Okay. Now, it was your personal position that the Tenet statement, while it was being drafted, didn't go far enough, right?*

A That the detail of it didn't go far enough. That there was more detail he could have put into it to really show how much the CIA was telling the White House about this intelligence and how close in time to the State of the Union itself, they had told the White House . . .

Q *And Mr. Libby, based on discussions you were having with him at that time, he had the same view as you, correct?*

A Agreed.

Q *And when you just referred to the CIA telling things to the White House close in time, were you referring to the fact that, on January 24, only four days before the State of the Union Address in 2003, a document had been given to the White House setting forth certain information?*

A Yes.

Q *Okay. You thought that January 24 document should have been referenced and included in the Tenet statement, correct?*

A Correct.

Q *During the period that the Tenet statement was being drafted, you were aware of*

Q *the January 24 document that had been given to the White House?*
A Yes.

Q *Had you been permitted to review it?*
A I believe so.

Q *I'd like to approach. I'm going to show you, because of the classified nature of the document, there are a number of redactions. But this is the statement that has been unclassified for purposes of the trial.*
A Okay....

Q *This document, where the cover sheet is dated January 24, 2003, shows that the White House was told on that date the following: That "Iraq has about 550 metric tons of yellowcake (a refined form of natural uranium) and low enriched uranium at"—I can't pronounce it—"Tuwaitha, which is inspected annually by the IAEA. Iraq also began vigorously trying to procure uranium ore and yellowcake. Acquiring either would shorten the time Baghdad needs to produce nuclear weapons."*

So, only four days before the State of the Union Address, the CIA had said to the White House that Iraq had an intent to expand its nuclear program, make nuclear weapons and try to buy uranium, right?
A Correct.

Q *Neither you nor Mr. Libby were successful in persuading Mr. Hadley or Mr. Tenet to include the January 24 memo in the Tenet statement, right?*
A I don't believe it appears in the statement, so we weren't successful . . .

Q *Ms. Martin, what's on the screen and what was put into evidence by the Government are your notes that you made on July 10 while you were working with Mr. Libby with respect to the drafting of the Tenet statement, correct?*
A Correct.

Q *As you said, you're going in and out of the room. Is it right that these are notes that you're making out in the hall to yourself?*
A Yes, I think I'm looking at the statement, looking at the timeline and making these minutes to myself.

Q *I want to take the jury through your notes that you made in real time on July 10th. Now, at the top, and I can't read your writing, can you read for the jurors the top paragraph?*
A The top says the NIE, the highest consensus document in the U.S. intelligence community, said that Iraq was vigorously trying to, I wrote, I think, pursue, crossed it out, acquire uranium and cited intel via Iraq contacts with Niger and two other African countries as evidence, it says as evidence. I'm sorry. That was the end of the sentence. As an intelligence community we did not state express doubts about Niger and the NIE. It said the intelligence community did not state any expressed doubts about the Niger claims in the NIE.

Then 50 pages later, which is a reference to a footnote, 50 pages later in the NIE, of an intelligence division at the State Department that expressed some concern about this intelligence. But I comment that it's 50 pages later in a very thick report is what I was trying to say.

Q *Just stay on that paragraph. During the week of July 7, is it correct that you were personally taking the position that the N.I.E should be . . . declassified and given to the media.*

A Yes.

Q *It says January 4 document. Could you read [under] that and explain what that would be?*

A January 24. January 24 document. It says we reiterated our statement in the NIE that Iraq was vigorously pursuing. So this is referencing this January 24 intelligence memo that we received through the NSC chain. And it's ripe for the State of the Union. That restates the language that was used in the NIE back in October that Iraq was vigorously pursuing yellowcake from—actually it didn't say from but that they were vigorously pursuing.

Q *That reflects the fact that you, personally, and Mr. Libby were taking a position on July 10th that the January 24 document should be in the Tenet statement but you were not successful, right?*

A Correct . . .

MARTIN GOES ON TO CONFIRM that her views were shared by Libby, and at that point the jury and the witness are excused for the weekend.

Once the jury is out, the legal teams and the judge wrangle over how they will handle the fact that Ari Fleischer received immunity for his testimony and newspaper articles about the investigation and Plame's outing from the fall of 2003 that were involved in prompting Fleischer to seek legal counsel in the first place. The defense also raises questions about the nature of the interactions between the prosecution and Fleischer's lawyers and whether the defense has gotten full disclosure on it.

At one point, Fitzgerald explains the situation he faced with Fleischer:

MR. FITZGERALD: Your Honor, let me just give you three hypotheticals. Someone says, "Look, we're not going to give you any information without immunity. I can tell you my person knows relevant stuff. It may be helpful to you. And if I were you, I'd give immunity." That, to me, is not Giglio or Jencks for the defendant.

On the other side, if Mr. Fleischer sits down and says, "Here's a proffer. Here's the story I'm going to tell you under a queen-for-a-day protection,"—which did not happen—"but here's our statement." We don't even get to Giglio. It gets turned over to Jencks.

And in between, if a lawyer sits down and says, "Mr. Fleischer will say that on this day he told Mr. Libby or Mr. Libby told him 'hush hush QT,' and basically parrots what the person's going to say but takes him out of the loop, that's debatable. That did-n't happen. Did I know that he had relevant information? Sure I did. Were the lawyers wanting immunity? Sure they did. Did I want to give immunity? No, I didn't want to give immunity. I put him in the Grand Jury and asked him the questions. And because of good faith, I didn't know whether he would have asserted the Fifth. When he asserted the Fifth, I stopped. We understood he knew information. We understood he had learned information. We understood he had given it out to someone, but we didn't know it was a reporter. I had the sense that he had something important. But what are we supposed to do with that? That's not a statement of witness.

SHORTLY THEREAFTER, court is recessed for the weekend.

*

CATHIE MARTIN (continued)

WELLS WALKS CATHIE MARTIN through events to establish a timeline:

Q *It is correct that on Sunday, July 6th . . . Ambassador Wilson published his op-ed piece in* The New York Times *and also went on* Meet the Press?
A Correct.

Q *And then on Monday, July 7th, you developed certain talking points for Mr. Ari Fleischer which are now in evidence as . . . Government Exhibit 540, right? . . .*
A Sir, I didn't develop them for him. I already had them. I just sent them to him.

Q *Okay. And you had developed them some weeks prior?*
A Sometime prior to that, but I already had them. I was using them.

Q *Okay. And also on Monday, July 7, the White House admitted for the first time that the sixteen words were a mistake?*
A I believe sometime that evening there was something to the effect of they shouldn't have been in the State of the Union.

WELLS ENTERS a July 8, 2003 AP article that Martin forwarded to Libby's assistant at the time to refresh her recollection about the precise date.

THE COURT: In reference to this information, just like before, you can only consider it in your assessment of what her state of mind was. You can't consider it for the truth of what was contained in the article.

By Mr. Wells:
Q *And the article on page 2 states that, "White House spokesman Ari Fleischer set off a furor Monday when, under questioning by reporters, he acknowledged that Bush was incorrect in his State of the Union speech when he said 'The British government has learned that Saddam Hussein recently sought significant quantities of uranium from Africa.'" . . .*
On Tuesday, July 8th, you meet with Vice President Cheney and other staffers at Vice President Cheney's office up on the Hill, correct?
A Correct.

Q *And it is at that time that Vice President Cheney personally dictates to you the talking points that he wants you to deliver with respect to the Office of the Vice President's responses to the Wilson allegations, correct?*
A Correct.

Q *And also on Tuesday, July 8th, Andrea Mitchell goes on TV and reports that certain people at the White House are saying that the CIA is at fault, correct?*

A Some suggestion of that, yes.

Q *Okay. Now, if we go to Wednesday, July 9, that is the day . . . Chris Matthews goes on* Hardball *and continues to severely criticize Vice President Cheney with respect to the Wilson allegations, correct? . . .*

A Yes . . .

Q *Okay. Now, if we go to July 10, that is the day . . . you work with Mr. Libby on the draft of the Tenet statement, correct?*

A That evening.

Q *Yes. You started working with him that evening, and you worked late into the night, right?*

A Correct . . .

Q *Now, if we go to Friday, July 11th, that is when you drafted certain talking points that would possibly be used by Condoleezza Rice on the Sunday shows; is that correct?*

A I assisted the press office in the development of talking points to prepare Secretary Rice, who, at the time, was the National Security Advisor to the President, for her appearance on the Sunday shows . . .

Q *Now, also on Friday, July 11, there was a press gaggle that was issued from Africa containing comments by both Mr. Fleischer and Dr. Rice, and I want to show you that document.*

. . . I show you what has been marked as Defendant's Exhibit 1644 for identification and ask, can you identify that document?

A It's the press gaggle that occurred on Air Force One on July 11th . . .

Q *Would you start at the top—[Condoleezza Rice] is saying, "the CIA cleared on it"—and that refers to the State of the Union address, correct?*

A I believe so . . .

Q *And she goes on to say, "There was even some discussion on that specific sentence so that it reflected better what the CIA thought. And the speech was cleared." And you understand the reference to the "specific sentence" is to the sixteen words, correct?*

A Yes.

Q *Now she goes on to say, "Now, I can tell you, if . . . the Director of Central Intelligence had said, "take this out of the speech," it would have been gone, without question. What we've said subsequently is, knowing what we now know, that some of the Niger documents were apparently forged, we wouldn't have put this in the president's speech. But that's knowing what we know now."*

And then one of the reporters says, "Dr. Rice, it sounds as if you're blaming the CIA here."

Dr. Rice responds, "No. This is a clearance process."

And then the next question is, "Dr. Rice, given that, does the President—given that the CIA cleared the speech, does the President remain confident in the CIA's director?"

So at this point, at least from the press perspective, the press is asking questions about whether or not the White House and Dr. Rice are attacking the CIA and are putting blame on the CIA for the sixteen words, correct?

A It appears that way, yes.

Q And at the time that this gaggle is put out, the Tenet statement has not yet been put out, correct?

A Correct.

Q The Tenet statement is put out late on Friday, July 11th, correct?

A Correct.

Q And there was some questioning, I think on direct [examination], about the fact that, by putting it out on Friday, it would not get as much coverage. Do you recall that?

A Yes.

Q Now, you wanted to see the Tenet statement get out as early as possible and get as much coverage as possible, correct?

A Correct.

Q And the reason it was put out late on Friday was that the CIA was slow in approving the final draft of the statement, correct?

A I don't know that, but I assumed that.

Q Okay. But you wanted it out earlier and you wanted maximum press coverage, correct?

A Yes.

Q Now, if we go to Saturday, July 12, that's the day that you and Mr. Libby and the Vice President and Mr. Libby's family travel on Air Force Two to Norfolk, correct?

A Yes.

Q And you remember that the plane left very early?

A Early in the morning, yes.

Q And that was the birthday of Mr. Libby's son, right?

A Correct.

Q And also his daughter was on the trip, right?

A Yes.

Q So the kids had to be on the plane very early in order to go to Norfolk, right?

A Right.

Q And do you recall testifying how Mr. Libby, at the end of the day, was anxious to get home? Do you recall that?

A Yes.

Q *And you understood that was, in part, because the kids had gotten up very early, had been on an airplane all day, had attended a celebration involving the commencement of the* Ronald Reagan *ship, and now it was time to get the kids home, right?*

A I understood it was because it was his son's birthday, and his son shouldn't have to wait on his birthday.

Q *Right . . . The Saturday trip, it was basically a celebration for everybody on the plane, right?*

A Right. It was a fun trip.

Q *Okay. And . . . part of the reason for bringing the kids was so they could enjoy the celebration?*

A It was kind of a treat.

Q *Right. But by the time you got back and you were required to make certain phone calls, the day had been a pretty long day at that point, right?*

A Yes.

Q *All right. And it is also on July 12 that Mr. Libby made a telephone call to* TIME *reporter Matthew Cooper, correct?*

A Correct.

Q *And Mr. Libby made a telephone call to Glenn Kessler of* The Washington Post, *correct?*

A Yes.

Q *And Mr. Libby made a call to Evan Thomas of* Newsweek, *correct?*

A And left a message, yes.

Q *. . . . Then on Sunday, July 13th, Dr. Rice appears on the Sunday talk shows, correct?*

A Yes.

Q *Okay. And going back to the 12th, remember I asked you a question concerning whether you were, "nagging" Mr. Libby about sitting down with you to make a decision about what to do?*

A Yes.

Q *Just so the record is clear, the word "nagging," that is your word that you have used in the past to describe what you were doing, correct?*

A Yes. Nagging, bugging. I was bugging him . . .

Q *Okay. Then on Monday, July 14th, that is the date that one of Mr. Cooper's articles in* TIME *magazine comes out, correct?*

A Yes. The print magazine appears on the Monday . . .

Q *And the article starts off, "The State of the Union message is one of America's greatest inventions, conceived by the founders to force a powerful Chief Executive to report to a public suspicious of kings. Delivered to a joint session of Congress in democracy's biggest cathedral, it is the most important speech a president gives each year, written and rewritten and then polished again. Yet the address George W.*

Bush gave on January 28 was more consequential than most because he was making a revolutionary case: Why a nation that traditionally didn't start fights should wage a preemptive war . . ."

. . . [W]hen you said last week that your involvement in addressing the criticism of how the sixteen words got into the State of the Union was much bigger than the more narrow allegations of Ambassador Wilson, what did you mean?

A   Well, the story grew . . . [F]rom the Vice President's perspective, [the story] started as the Joe Wilson piece, the suggestion that this former ambassador had been sent by the Vice President's office . . . but as the story grew, as Mr. Wilson comes forward and identifies himself, and as the press begins asking questions about . . . Joe Wilson's article and what he is saying to the media . . . with respect to the sixteen words, it becomes a larger story about the State of the Union and about whether the sixteen words should have been in the State of the Union and whether we should have known not to put [in] that information . . .

Q   *Now, if we can turn to page 1645.3, that is the page that contains a portion of the quotation that Mr. Libby gave to Mr. Cooper on Saturday, July 12th?*

A   Correct.

Q   *And you indicated last week that you were upset with how Mr. Cooper had portrayed Mr. Libby's quote?*

A   Yes.

Q   *Could you explain that to the jurors?*

A   The quote that is included in the article says the Vice President asked a question about the implication of the report. That's all it says. And it's referring to the implication of this report about Niger and Iraq talking about uranium.

Joe Wilson's article and what he is saying to the media . . . with respect to the sixteen words, it becomes a larger story about the State of the Union and about whether the sixteen words should have been in the State of the Union.

And the implication, in my view, the way the article continued, was that it had been sort of a seed to lead to Joe Wilson's trip because he had asked about the implication of this . . . piece of intelligence . . . We had given a much broader . . . quote that explained that while we had asked a question about a piece of intelligence, we got an answer back; that was the end of the story as far as we knew. And we had no knowledge of anybody being sent to Niger to check this out because we had asked a question.

Q   *Now, did you express your upsetness to Mr. Cooper?*

A   I believe I did.

Q   *What did you say to Mr. Cooper?*

A   That I thought it was unfair and taken out of context and that we gave him a whole quote that explained the story, and this wasn't an explanation of what we gave him.

Q *And did Mr. Cooper offer a response?*

A …I don't recall that. I wouldn't say that Matt agreed with me, but he understood why I was upset, and at least was helpful in saying he would talk to his editors about it, and got back to me at some point and told me that they would publish the quote in a web story.

Q *Okay. So Mr. Cooper said it was too late to correct the way the quote was used in the print article because all the TIME magazines had been printed, right?*

A Right. We both understood that . . .

THEIR SUGGESTION WAS that they would include the full quote in another article that would be published in their online magazine.

Q *In the on-line article, Mr. Cooper wrote, "In an exclusive interview, Lewis Libby, the Vice President's Chief of Staff, told TIME: 'The Vice President heard about the possibility of Iraq trying to acquire uranium from Niger in February 2002. As part of his regular intelligence briefing, the Vice President asked a question about the implication of the report. During the course of a year, the Vice President asked many such questions, and the agency responded within a day or two, saying that they had reporting suggesting the possibility of such a transaction. But the agency noted that the reporting lacked detail. The agency pointed out that Iraq already had 500 tons of uranium, portions of which came from Niger, according to the International Atomic Energy Administration. [sic] The Vice President was unaware of the trip by Ambassador Wilson and didn't know about it until this year when it became public in the last month or so.' Other senior Administration officials, including National Security Adviser Condoleezza Rice, have also claimed that they had not heard of Wilson's report until recently" . . .*

Now, I would like to go to page 1 . . . of the article . . . dated at the top Thursday, July 17, 2003.

And the article opens up, "Has the Bush Administration declared war on a former ambassador who conducted a fact-finding mission to probe possible Iraqi interest in African uranium? Perhaps."

And you understood that the former ambassador being referred to was Joseph Wilson, correct?

A Correct.

Q *And then in the second full paragraph, . . . it states . . . "and some government officials have noted to TIME in interviews (as well as to syndicated columnist Robert Novak) that Wilson's wife, Valerie Plame, is a CIA official who monitors the proliferation of weapons of mass destruction."*

So this article specifically refers to the fact that Ambassador Wilson's wife is a CIA official, correct?

A Correct.

Q *And it also refers to the fact that a syndicated columnist by the name of Robert Novak had also written about the fact that Mrs. Wilson was employed by the CIA, correct?*

A It implies that, yes.

Q *And you recall that Mr. Novak's article came out in the press on Monday, July 14th?...*

A Yes.

Q *Now, after Mr. Novak disclosed in his article on July 14th that Mrs. Wilson worked at the CIA, is it correct that the talking points that you were using with respect to what the Office of the Vice President was saying about Ambassador Wilson did not change in any way?*

A Correct. They didn't change.

Q *At no time, even after the identity of Mrs. Wilson was disclosed and it was stated that she worked at the CIA, did the Office of the Vice President change its position that the talking points should be on the merits and that there was no need to mention that Mrs. Wilson worked at the CIA?*

A We did not change our talking points.

Q *Okay. So if you look at the talking points that the Office of the Vice President had before the Novak article or the talking points that the Office of the Vice President had after the Novak article, during both periods there is no mention of the fact that Mrs. Wilson worked at the CIA, correct?*

A Correct.

Q *And is it fair to say that when the Novak article came out and mentioned that Mrs. Wilson worked at the CIA, that at that time, from your personal perspective, that was not viewed as a big article that had some huge revelation, correct?*

A It wasn't a huge revelation to me because I knew, but I knew it was a huge revelation that he was putting it out there. So, I mean, I knew it was a big deal that he had disclosed it. I just didn't think it was that big a deal because I already knew . . .

> *It wasn't a huge revelation to me because I knew, but I knew it was a huge revelation that [Novak] was putting it out there. So, I mean, I knew it was a big deal that he had disclosed it. I just didn't think it was that big a deal because I already knew...*

Q *Now, if we continue on the timeline . . . President Bush, Colin Powell, Condoleeza Rice, Ari Fleischer and Dan Bartlett were . . . in Africa from July 7th until July 12th . . . [R]ight?*

A Yes.

Q *...[O]n July 15th, you draft certain talking points responding to Chris Matthews. Do you recall that?*

A I recall drafting them. I don't recall it being on July 15th . . .

Q *Now, is it correct that the talking points . . . were the first . . . that you drafted after the Novak article had been published?*

A I believe so.

Q *. . . Is it correct that the talking points you drafted to respond to Chris Matthews' criticism did not in any way, shape o[r] form make any reference to Mrs. Wilson?*

A I believe that's correct.

Q *Now, on Thursday, July 17, the second* TIME *article that we just discussed concerning a war on Wilson—that came out . . . And then you discussed on direct that on Friday, July 18th, there was a conservative columnist lunch, right?*

A Yes, at the Vice President's residence.

Q *Okay. And is it correct that, during that lunch, Vice President Cheney responded to certain of Ambassador Wilson's allegations?*

A Yes.

Q *And is it correct that during that lunch, at no time did Vice President Cheney use, as a talking point, the fact that Ambassador Wilson's wife worked at the CIA?*

A I believe so, yes. That's correct.

Q *That was just not something that Vice President Cheney, even after the disclosure that Mrs. Wilson worked at the CIA, was using as a talking point, right?*

A Correct.

MR. WELLS: Okay . . . Now, I want to develop another demonstrative very quickly. You have testified that you worked on four sets of talking points, correct, approximately?

A Four sets, yes.

Q *Okay. And the first set of talking points is government exhibit 540, which are the July 7th talking points that you gave to Mr. Fleischer, correct?*

A Right.

Q *And the second set of talking points is the July 8th set of talking points dictated by Vice President Cheney, which is government's exhibit 523, correct?*

A Right. Those are the typed version of the dictated—yes.

Q *Right. Because what you did, Vice President Cheney actually dictated the points to you. You took it down in longhand and then, later on, you typed up the points, right?*

A Yes.

Q *And the third set of talking points were, to your understanding, talking points dictated by Vice President Cheney to Mr. Libby on Air Force Two to be used with Mr. Cooper, right?*

A Yes.

Q *Okay. And they are in evidence as Government Exhibit 528b.*

And the fourth set of talking points were the . . . possible responses that you prepared for Chris Matthews on or around July 14th, which are now in evidence as defendant's exhibit 1609, right?

A Yes.

Q *Okay. And to the extent the jurors want to understand what were the actual talking points that you worked on with respect to responding to the allegations or challenges of Ambassador Wilson, those documents would set forth in real time . . . the talking points you were using . . . right?*

A Yes.

Q *And all those talking points respond to Joseph Wilson's claims, correct?*

A Yes.

Q *And none of those talking points mention Valerie Wilson, right?*

A Correct.

Q *And Mr. Libby reviewed these talking points with you, correct?*

A He reviewed the dictated version on July 8th, and those are the only ones I remember him reviewing with me . . .

Q *And with respect to the July 7th talking points, what you did, after the Vice President dictated his talking points on July 8th, you combined both the July 7th talking points and the July 8th talking points into one document, right?*

A Yes.

Q *And Mr. Libby did review that document?*

A Yes.

Q *And with respect to the Chris Matthews talking points, you do recall giving Mr. Libby a copy of those talking points?*

A Yes.

Q *So Mr. Libby saw all of the talking points, right?*

A Yes.

Q *And at no time did Mr. Libby suggest to you in any way, shape or form that the talking points should be expanded to include any reference to the fact that Valerie Wilson worked at the CIA?*

A No . . .

Q *In fact, during the entire period from July 6th through July—through the conservative columnist lunch, you never had any discussions with Mr. Libby about the fact that Valerie Wilson was employed at the CIA?*

A Not that I recall . . .

Q *And you have no evidence—you are not aware personally of any evidence that would show that the fact that Ms. Valerie Wilson worked at the CIA was an important point for Mr. Libby, correct? . . .*

A I am not aware of any specific evidence that would suggest that.

Q *Thank you. Now, I want to go back to July 8th. You said on direct that Mr. Bill Harlow was the press person for the CIA? . . . [Y]ou said you had two conversations with him. Do you recall that?*

A . . . [T]wo that I specifically remember.

Q *Right. And you said during the first conversation, he was a lot friendlier than he was during the second conversation, right?*

A Yes.

Q *And the second conversation was on July 8th, correct?*

A I believe so, yes.

Q *And at that time, Mr. Harlow told you that he . . . had had conversations with Andrea Mitchell of NBC News, right? . . .*

A It was my understanding, but I don't recall specifically whether he told me he had . . .

Q *And you understood that part of the piece involved information that the White House was criticizing the CIA?*

A . . . [W]hen it came out, yes.

Q *And also on July 8th, Mr. Hadley talked to you and other press persons about finger-pointing that was possibly being done whereby the White House was alleging that the CIA was at blame for the sixteen-words controversy?*

A I believe it was on July 9th. Andrea Mitchell's piece would have aired in the evening of the 8th. . . .

Q *. . . You said last week that in working on the Tenet statement . . . the discussions were, "delicate." Do you recall that?*

A Yes.

Q *. . . [W]hy did you use the term "delicate"?*

A It seemed delicate given the tight-knit group that was working on it. It seemed delicate because I understood that Steve Hadley asked, and people agreed, not to include press and communicators in those discussions of what they were doing. It seemed delicate because it appeared . . . from my conversation with Scooter, that Steve Hadley was talking to George Tenet and then relaying it back to Scooter, and they were sort of back and forth, but that multiple people weren't talking to George Tenet . . .

Q *Do you recall that during his July 9 conversation with you, Mr. Hadley had stated that Mr. Tenet was mad and upset that people were pointing a finger at the CIA?*

A He suggested . . . that that was the case, and that was what I took away from the conversation. I can't recall the specific words he used, but that was definitely my impression . . .

Q *Okay. And so what you understood was taking place in terms of drafting the Tenet statement on July 10 was that Mr. Hadley was in the middle, serving as a go-between for discussions with Mr. Tenet on one side and Vice President Cheney and Mr. Libby on the other, right?*

A Correct.

Q *Is it fair to say that . . . you and Mr. Libby thought [the final Tenet statement] was a good statement, but . . . it did not go far enough?*

A I think it's fair to say we thought it was pretty good, but we wished it had gone further....

Q *And is it correct that the Tenet statement makes only one reference to what Vice President Cheney knew about Ambassador Wilson's trip, right?*

A It makes clear that they didn't brief the Vice President, or the President, or other senior administration officials about Wilson's trip.

Q *Right. But except for that brief reference to the fact that Vice President Cheney was not briefed, the thrust of the Tenet statement is really to respond to the issue of whether or not President Bush was in error in using the sixteen words in his State of the Union speech?*

A Correct. But I remember somewhere in here it also makes clear, without referring to the Vice President, that the CIA sent him . . . on their own initiative . . .

Q *Right. But I just want to—*

A That was the only other piece for the V.P. part of this that was significant for me . . .

Q *The Tenet statement was not designed to be a response to Ambassador Wilson's specific allegations about Vice President Cheney?*

A No, only to the extent that it related to the sixteen words in the State of the Union.

Q *Okay. Thank you.*
I want to go to a different subject. You testified last week that Mr. Libby's primary job, in addition to being the Chief of Staff for Vice President Cheney, was to focus on national security issues, right?

A Correct.

Q *And is it correct that during the week of July 7th, when you were working with Mr. Libby in responding to the controversy concerning the sixteen words and also the controversy concerning Ambassador Wilson's allegations, that you observed that Mr. Libby still was attending to his regular national security responsibilities?*

A I observed that he was busy[,] . . . as he always was busy. But I don't know what— I never knew precisely what he was doing, but I, of course, knew he was busy in meetings with the Vice President. He spent a good deal of time with the Vice President . . .

Q *You remember you had to work around getting access to him because he was in various meetings?*

A Yes.

Q *. . . And those meetings would include both national security issues and also domestic policy issues?*

A Typically, they would, but I don't know that they did . . .

Q *Right. Now, you were asked questions last week about whether you had some discomfort with the fact that Mr. Libby was talking to Andrea Mitchell while he had the NIE open. Do you recall that?*

A Yes.

Q *...Is it correct that had you known that the NIE had been declassified at the time Mr. Libby was talking to Andrea Mitchell, you would not have had those feelings of discomfort?*

A Correct . . .

Q *Now, you testified that you would normally go to senior staff meetings every day, right?*

A Yes.

Q *And those senior staff meetings were still held even while the president and his staff was in Africa, correct?*

A Yes.

Q *And who were the persons who would be at those meetings?*

MARTIN IDENTIFIES SOME of the people there, but then Wells asks what he's after:

Q *Would Karl Rove be there?*

A Karl Rove would be there . . .

Q *Okay. And Karl Rove, in July of 2003, while he was attending the senior meetings, one of his primary jobs was political strategy?*

A Yes.

Q *Okay. And was Karl Rove viewed by you and others as being one of the persons most responsible for President Bush's election in 2000?*

MR. FITZGERALD: Objection.
THE COURT: Sustained.

By Mr. Wells:

Q *I asked you a question last week, and I just want to—I am almost finished. I just want to fix the transcript, if I can find it.*

Last week I asked you the following question: "So when you were on a mission to try to get the whole story out, you did not view the wife as part of that story, correct?" And you answered, "No."

Am I—I believe you meant "correct."

A Can you just repeat what you said?

Q *Okay. The question I put to you—why don't you let me put the question to you fresh because I think the transcript doesn't read properly.*

When you were on a mission to try to get the whole story out with respect to the

Vice President's response, to Ambassador Wilson, you did not view the wife as part of that story, correct?

A Correct.

Q *And I am just about finished. You were asked some questions last week concerning Government Exhibit 541, which are the notes that you took during the time you were working on the Tenet statement with Mr. Libby. Do you recall that?*

A Yes.

Q *And the exhibit is now contained in two plastic folders, but if you put the documents together, you can see that the documents were stapled together as one?*

A Yes.

Q *Okay. And what happened was that you were given by Mr. Libby or Ms. Jenny Mayfield a copy of the draft of the Tenet statement, right?*

A Correct.

Q *And also there were some notes concerning exactly what Steve Hadley was saying that the Vice President was saying, right?*

A Yes.

Q *And then, because you didn't have any paper, you wrote your notes on the back of the actual draft of the Tenet statement, right?*

A Right.

Q *And this is the document that Ms. Mayfield later came to you and said she wanted your notes back, right?*

A Correct.

Q *Okay. But what I have in my hand—these are the originals of your notes, right?*

A Yes.

Q *Nothing was destroyed, right?*

A No.

Q *They are right here?*

A Those are my notes.

Q *Ms. Martin, I want to show you defendant's exhibit 1639 for identification and ask, can you identify it?*

A It's e-mail traffic between Matt Cooper and myself on Friday, July 11th . . .

Q *So the top of this exhibit shows you writing to Mr. Cooper and you state, in your e-mail, "Matt, I got it, but have not gotten your answers."*

And you were referring to an e-mail that Mr. Cooper had sent you with certain questions he wanted answers to, right?

A Right.

Q *And then you said, "I am traveling with V.P. tomorrow morning and will likely be able to corner some folks," correct?*

A Yes.

Q *And your reference to cornering some folks was that you were going to try to get to Mr. Libby and hopefully the Vice President while they were on the plane traveling to Norfolk, right?*

A Yes . . .

Q *What did you understand the deadline was?*

A Well, I think he wanted me to get back to him on Friday, but I knew that magazines didn't close until sometime on Saturday afternoon. So if he could wait a little bit longer and was writing in the morning—he wasn't going to finish his story on Friday night—that then I could get him—might be able to give him answers to still be in the story because it wouldn't close for print until sometime on Saturday.

Q *Okay. And it was your recommendation that Mr. Libby should go ahead and talk to Mr. Cooper?*

A It was my recommendation that we . . . affirmatively decide whether we want to be in the story or not, and my view was we should be in the story telling our story. This was one more opportunity, and it was going to be a big picture story, and I thought we should be in it in some shape or form.

Q *Right. Mr. Libby followed your recommendation?*

A Yes.

Q *And as you said last week, Mr. Libby, to your understanding, had never talked to Matt Cooper in his life, right?*

A Correct.

MR. WELLS: I have no further questions.

Redirect examination by Mr. Fitzgerald:

Q *Good morning, Ms. Martin.*

A Good morning.

Q *I will try to direct your attention to the questions asked by Mr. Wells that I am following up on as best I can.*

A Okay.

Q *If you recall last week on Thursday, when you testified, the flip chart to your right was used. And Mr. Wells talked about a date of June 11th as a "makes sense" date. And he kindly noted "makes sense" in the left-hand corner. Do you recall that testimony?*

A Yes.

Q *And it made sense to you that the conversation that you had with Mr. Harlow could have occurred on June 11th; is that correct?*

A Correct.

Q *Prior to this trial, in any conversations you had with the government, did the government ever tell you what Mr. Grenier's testimony or recollection had been?*

A No.

Q *And prior to this trial, had the government or the FBI ever told you the recollection of a man named Marc Grossman?*

A No.

Q *And had the government ever told you the recollection of a man named Craig Schmall?*

A No.

Q *So your prior recollections were given without knowledge of what other people were saying?*

A Correct.

Q *Now, you have also testified that because the president and many others were on a trip to Africa during the week of July 7th, that that put an extra burden on you and others, including Mr. Libby, correct?*

A That I felt, yes.

Q *And that's because there weren't enough people to deal with this communications crisis when people were out of the country, correct?*

A Correct.

Q *Did the fact that people were out of the country on this trip to Africa—is that what caused the focus by the personnel in the Office of Vice President on the MSNBC show called* Hardball?

A No.

Q *What caused that?*

A Chris Matthews' focus on our office, the Vice President, and at some point mentioning Scooter by name as well, and his continued reference to Joe Wilson's trip having been at the behest or at the request of the Vice President, and I think he went further to say that we should have known what Mr. Wilson found on this trip since we asked for the trip. And so, therefore, the implication was that we should have known that, according to Joe Wilson, the information that we used in the State of the Union was false.

Q *And can you explain what the [OVP's] focus or part of the story was . . . that you were concerned about?*

A When I referenced OVP piece of the story or OVP focus, I was talking about our narrow piece of the story which is—which was that the Vice President didn't know Mr. Wilson, didn't know a former ambassador had been sent on any mission, and didn't know about his trip after it occurred until press reports revealed it.

Q *Now, you were asked whether or not any of your talking points before or after the Novak . . . ever made reference to Mr. Wilson's wife. Do you recall those questions?*

A Yes.

Q *Is it fair to say that if anyone in the office of Vice President talked to the press about Mr. Wilson's wife, it wasn't based on your talking points?*

A Is it fair to say—

Q *—that if anyone in the office of Vice President did talk to reporters about Wilson's wife, they didn't do it based on your talking points?*

MR. WELLS: Objection. How would she know?
THE COURT: I don't know how she would know that. Sustained.

By Mr. Fitzgerald:

Q *Now, you were asked questions by Mr. Wells last week as to whether or not the Vice President wanted to get the whole truth out, correct?*

A Correct.

Q *Did the Vice President ever specifically tell you whether or not the whole truth did or did not include the fact that Wilson's wife worked at the CIA?*

A No.

Q *And after the Wilson op-ed appeared on July 6th, did the Vice President ever show you a copy of the Wilson op-ed that he marked up personally?*

A No.

Q *And during June and July 2003, as far as you could tell, did the Vice President and Mr. Libby keep you current on anything they were doing with regard to the press or everything they were doing with regard to the press?*

A No.

Q *And when you had the conversation on the "makes sense" date of June 11th where you told the Vice President and Mr. Libby that you had learned that Mr. Wilson's wife worked at the CIA, did they tell you whether or not they had heard that before?*

A No.

Q *Did you know whether you were the first, the second, the third or the fourth person to tell them that?*

A No.

Q *After that, did they ever tell you . . . whether or not other people told them the same information?*

A No.

Q *Did the Vice President ever direct you to speak to Judith Miller?*

A No.

MR. WELLS: Objection. Leading.
THE COURT: Don't lead. Sustained.
MR. FITZGERALD: I asked whether something happened.
THE COURT: Don't lead.

By Mr. Fitzgerald:

Q *Were you aware of a meeting on June 23rd, 2003, between Mr. Libby and Ms. Miller?*

A No.

Q *Were you aware of a meeting on July 8th, 2003, between Mr. Libby and Ms. Miller?*

A No.

Q *You testified that [on July 12th] Mr. Libby was anxious to get home after you came back from this trip to go back to celebrate his son's birthday, correct?*

A Correct.

Q *Did Mr. Libby indicate to you at all whether or not he would be calling Judith Miller from home that evening?*

A No.

Q *Did he ever tell you afterward whether or not he called Judith Miller on the night of July 12th?*

A No.

Q *Did Mr. Libby ever tell you whether or not he ever discussed Mr. Wilson's wife with Judith Miller on any of the occasions, June 23rd, July 8th or July 12th?*

A No.

Q *And after the Wilson op-ed, you have testified that you urged that the NIE be declassified for use with the press, correct?*

A Correct.

Q *When you urged that, did anyone ever tell you that it had already been declassified? . . .*

A No. I continued to urge it.

Q *We went through some notes you wrote last week that were displayed where you handwrote notes while you were waiting in the hallway outside of Mr. Libby's office, correct?*

A Correct.

Q *And Mr. Wells took you through some of the references in the notes to things that we might want to say to the press concerning the NIE of January 24th. Do you remember that?*

A Yes.

Q *And you testified that you had a conversation with Mr. Libby about the possibility of giving a leak, which meant an exclusive story, to either* The New York Times, The Washington Post *or a news magazine, correct?*

A Correct.

Q *Did Mr. Libby indicate at any time on July 10th whether or not he had given any of that information already to any of those newspapers?*

A No.

Q *And you were asked earlier today whether or not Mr. Libby—you agree that Mr. Libby was in the loop on your talking points, correct?*

A Correct.

Q *Were you in the loop on what Mr. Libby and the Vice President were discussing as to what to say to the press?*

A No.

Q *Now, let me direct your attention to the July 12th telephone call that you heard. There was testimony about the fact that you took a telephone call [then].*

A Correct.

Q *Do you recall what Mr. Libby was doing when you took that telephone call?*

A I believe he was—still was reading from the card, talking to Matt Cooper.

Q *And when you say reading from the card, what do you mean he was doing?*

A Oh, reading the quote precisely. I mean, they have to go through word by word so that Matt could type exactly what Scooter was saying. So—it was a long quote. He was reading it slowly.

Q *And do you recall what Mr. Libby was doing when you finished [your] call...?*

A I think he was still reading from the card . . .

Q *Did you hear the end of the conversation, whatever happened after he finished reading the prepared statement?*

A I believe so.

Q *Now, you were asked questions about whether or not what you heard was memorable. I am going to ask you a question.*

I want you to listen to this. I am going to ask you two questions, but I will tell you the questions before I read it to you.

I am going to ask you whether or not this is something that you heard on July 12th and, secondly, if you had heard it on July 12th, whether or not it . . . would be memorable.

FITZGERALD READS FROM Libby's Grand Jury testimony:

"So I said, ['W]ell, I don't know why he said it. 'You know, I said, 'we are off the record,' and he agreed. And I said someone—I don't know why he said it, but I would have thought off the record—I would have thought that, that the CIA wouldn't tell somebody who is going on a mission who asked about it. And, you know, conversations the Vice President has, these things are supposed to be confidential. But if he did—if they did officially, they wouldn't officially tell such a thing. If they did officially tell someone, they would tell them the right thing, which was that the CIA decided to do it, which is what Director Tenet had said in his statement the day before.

"So I wouldn't have thought that officially he heard this . . . but, you know, he heard something unofficially. And if he heard something possibly unofficially, you know, maybe he knows somebody there, and somebody said something to him that was wrong because it was unofficial. And in that context I said, [']you know, off the record, reporters are telling us that Ambassador Wilson's wife works at the CIA, and I don't know if it's true. As I told you, we don't know Mr. Wilson. We didn't know anything about his mission, so I don't know that it's true. But if it's true, it may explain how he knows some people at the agency, and maybe he got some bad skinny—you know, some bad information.'"

Q *Did you hear that conversation on July 12th?*
A Not that I recall.

Q *And if you had heard Mr. Libby talking to Mr. Cooper about Ambassador Wilson's wife working at the CIA, would that have been memorable?*
A I think so.

Q *And, finally, . . . did you . . . hear Mr. Libby make a statement [on July 12th] that he did not know if Mr. Wilson had a wife. . .?*
A No.

Q *And, finally, . . . you agreed that you were aware of no evidence indicating that Mr. Libby thought that Mr. Wilson's wife was important, correct?*
A Correct.

Q *And as you sit here now, do you have a personal knowledge of what, if any, conversation Mr. Libby had with Marc Grossman in June 2003 about Mr. Wilson's wife?*
A No.

Q *As you sit here now, do you have personal knowledge of what, if any, conversation Mr. Libby had with Robert Grenier from the CIA in June 2003?*
A No . . .

Q *Do you have any personal knowledge of what, if any, conversation Mr. Libby and the Vice President had about Mr. Wilson's wife when you were not in the room?*
A No.

Q *. . . Do you have any personal knowledge of any conversation Mr. Libby had with Craig Schmall, a CIA briefer, on June 14, 2003?*
A No.

Q *At you sit here now, are you aware of any conversation that Mr. Libby had with Judith Miller on June 23rd, 2003, about Mr. Wilson's wife?*
A No.

Q *. . . Do you have personal knowledge of any conversation Mr. Libby had with Ms. Miller on July 8th about Mr. Wilson's wife?*
A No.

Q *And as you sit here now, do you have personal knowledge of any conversation Mr. Libby had with Ms. Miller on July 12th, 2003, about Mr. Wilson's wife?*

A No.

Q *And as you sit here now, are you aware—do you have personal knowledge of any conversation that Mr. Libby had with Ari Fleischer on Monday, July 7th, 2003?*

A No.

Q *Thank you.*

Recross examination by Mr. Wells:

Q *Ms. Martin, Mr. Fitzgerald asked you a question a minute ago, did you hear what occurred at the end of the conversation with respect to Mr. Libby and Mr. Cooper? And you said, "I believe so."*
Do you recall being asked that question and giving that answer?

A Yes.

Q *Now, you testified in the grand jury in April of 2004, right?*

A Yes.

Q *And at the time, you were sworn to tell the truth?*

A Yes.

Q *And in the grand jury, you were asked the following question and you gave the following answer.*
Question: "Okay. What happened at the end of the conversation with—between Scooter and Mr. Cooper?"
Answer: "I don't—it's not memorable to me. I don't—I don't remember. I think he finished the—they finished the quote, and then did whatever their back and forth was on verifying the pieces. And they hung up. He said, thanks. Done."
You gave that answer to that question in the Grand Jury under oath, correct?

A Correct.

Q *And you told the Grand Jury with respect to what happened at the end of the conversation that you did not remember, correct?*

A I don't have a specific recollection of the precise words they were using, correct.

Q *…[Y]ou accept that the court reporter got it down right?*

A Yes.

Q *Okay. And when you were asked that question in the Grand Jury, it was much closer in time to the events than we are now, correct?*

A Correct . . .

Q *So you have not been able to refresh yourself with any notes between the time of your Grand Jury and your testimony today, correct?*

A Correct.

MR. WELLS: No further questions.

THE COURT: Anything else from the government on that?

MR. FITZGERALD: Yes, Judge.

Further redirect examination by Mr. Fitzgerald:

Q *Is it still your testimony that you heard the end of the conversation?*
A Yes.

Q *Do you remember the precise words at the end of the conversation?*
A No.

Q *Has anything changed?*
A No.

Q *Thank you.*

THE COURT: Anything from the jury?

Walton poses questions from the jury:

THE COURT: In reference to the call between Mr. Libby and Andrea Mitchell —

THE WITNESS: Yes.

THE COURT:—You indicated some concerns that you had about information in the NIE being revealed.

THE WITNESS: Correct.

THE COURT: Tell us what your concerns were in that regard.

THE WITNESS: I thought the NIE was classified. And I thought we shouldn't be talking from the NIE.

THE COURT: Did you do anything after that to inform somebody of what you were concerned about?

THE WITNESS: No . . . I still understood it to be classified and was . . . urging them to disclose it to the media after declassifying it.

So it still hadn't been disclosed in a public way with, you know, a piece of paper handing them, here is what the NIE says.

So I was still concerned. I didn't understand what it meant.

THE COURT: But I guess the question is, if you had concerns, why didn't you take any further action to address those concerns after the conversation?

THE WITNESS: Because the Vice President of the United States had told me to say it, and I wasn't really sure what I was supposed to do with that. So I didn't know where I was going to go.

MR. WELLS: Your Honor, can you repeat the instruction?

THE COURT: Approach.

(At the bench.)

(In open court.)

THE COURT: In reference to the questions I was asking the witness based upon what you had asked me to ask, I am going to give you this instruction again, which I gave you before: there is no dispute between the parties that on July 8th, 2003, which was the date when the Vice President gave talking points to Ms. Martin and the date of the telephone call between Andrea Mitchell and Mr. Libby, that certain portions of the National Intelligence Estimate, or the NIE, had been declassified, although Ms. Martin had not been made aware of the declassification.

In reference to the discussion that Mr. Libby had with Mr. Cooper on the telephone out at Andrews Air Force Base—I think that was on July 12th.

THE WITNESS: Yes.

THE COURT: And you indicated that certain portions of that conversation you didn't hear because you were on another telephone call.

THE WITNESS: Correct.

THE COURT: Now, as I understand, you were in the same room where Mr. Libby was at that time?

THE WITNESS: Yes.

THE COURT: But you were on another call?

THE WITNESS: Correct.

THE COURT: Did you ever ask him what exactly he said to Mr. Cooper while you were on the other telephone?

THE WITNESS: No.

THE COURT: So you never received information from him as to what he said while you were on the other telephone?

THE WITNESS: No.

THE COURT: Okay. When you discussed your first telephone call with Mr. Harlow with Mr. Libby and the Vice President, how did you describe Ms. Wilson's employment?

THE WITNESS: I believe I said his wife—I was referring to Joe Wilson, and I believe I said his name —the former ambassador's name is Joe Wilson; he was apparently a charge in Baghdad, and his wife works over there, or at the CIA

THE COURT: Did you ever say that she worked at the CIA as a CIA agent?

THE WITNESS: I didn't say that, but I wrote it in my notes that I think were —

THE COURT: But you didn't say that to them?

THE WITNESS: No, I don't believe so.

THE COURT: Was it unusual, as you testified, not to involve the communicators in responses to issues by the press? Was it unusual for the communicators not to be involved when responses were being made to inquiries by the press?

THE WITNESS: Yes.

THE COURT: Did you have any concerns about the communicators not being included?

THE WITNESS: I was concerned from the perspective of here in Washington, D.C. I wasn't aware of what was going on, obviously, on the plane or on the trip in Africa. But from the perspective of Washington, D.C., I was concerned to the extent that we didn't know what was going on. We couldn't help advise them of how to address this with the press.

THE COURT: One of the jurors wants to know—I think it's about this exhibit. I think the juror may have the number wrong, but I think it's exhibit number 541. And in the middle there are some names that are crossed out. Could you look at that?

THE WITNESS: Yes.

THE COURT: Is there any significance to the fact that those names have been crossed out?

THE WITNESS: No . . . [T]hese are the notes that I was taking as I was sitting outside of Scooter's office during the . . . conversation between—I think it might have been Mr. Hadley and Scooter. And I was thinking about who could be—I think what I wrote first was [']actors,['] which I don't know why I wrote that. But then I crossed that out and wrote [']messengers[']: who would be our messengers from the administration? Who would we put, you know, out in a television appearance or on a press conference, et cetera.

And I wrote, V.P., Condi, I think Hadley and Scooter. And then I crossed out Hadley and Scooter. I think I thought that they weren't the appropriate administration folks to go out publicly, but that we needed to actually have, not the deputies, kind of the number 2's, but the number 1's.

THE COURT: And have there been other instances when you believe that reporters had failed to get the story right or omitted critical facts?

THE WITNESS: Yes.

THE COURT: And how did you deal with those situations?

THE WITNESS: It depends. It depended on the reporter and it depended on the facts. Reporters often get things incorrect. And I, in many cases, would . . . have to make a judgment call when . . . dealing with reporters to decide whether or not . . . to confront the reporter and say, I think this is so wrong and so egregious, we actually want you to correct it somehow.

So in a newspaper, you want them to actually put a correction, which you may or may not know is a small little blurb on the back of the front page which is after the story has already run, so it is often missed.

But we often have back and forth with reporters over whether or not they will ever do a correction. They don't tend to want to do corrections because they believe they were right. So there is a lot of back and forth. . .; you have to decide whether you want to go down that route and how productive it will be. And in some cases I felt like it would be productive and went down that route; . . . in some cases I won and in some cases I lost.

In other cases I particularly—I guess in reference, for instance, to the Kristof piece that we talked about in my testimony, if you don't have a relationship with someone—in my view, if I didn't have a relationship with this person and it was a columnist that tended to not agree with us and not—and be a little bit more aggressive towards us, you might aggravate and create another story by calling them.

So you have to make a judgment call about whether or not it's worth picking on this little piece of information, or big piece of information, depending on what it is.

THE COURT: Follow-up questions from counsel?

MR. FITZGERALD: No, Your Honor.

MR. WELLS: No, Your Honor.

THE COURT: Okay. Thank you.
THE WITNESS: Thank you.

Martin is excused, and the next witness, Ari Fleischer, is called.

ARI FLEISCHER

ARI FLEISCHER WAS the White House Press Secretary when the controversy over the sixteen words erupted, playing several key roles in the response to Joe Wilson. (Fleischer's last day on the job, interestingly enough, was July 14, 2003.) In fact, his testimony is an extraordinary portrait of the week of July 6–14, 2003 from the perspective of a White House under siege for its fundamental claims in justification of the war in Iraq. Fleischer publicly expressed the administration's first concession that it was no longer standing by the sixteen words in a dramatic press gaggle on July 7, and then subsequently dealt with the press as the issue dogged the administration on President Bush's trip to Africa that week, where Fleischer accompanied him, and as the tension between the White House and the CIA became acute.

But Fleischer's central importance as a witness was his testimony about his lunch with Libby on July 7, shortly after the press gaggle, in which Fleischer also publicly relayed talking points he'd received that morning from the Office of the Vice President clearing the Vice President of a role in Wilson's trip. At that lunch with Libby, according to Fleischer's testimony, Libby told the Press Secretary that Wilson's wife worked in the Counterproliferation Division of the CIA. Fleischer testified that Libby also may have identified her by name, "Valerie Plame." Libby told Fleischer, who characterized the whole lunch as weird, that the information was "hush-hush" and "on the QT." This event was just two or three days before Libby's conversation with Tim Russert in which, Libby later claimed to investigators, he was surprised to hear about Wilson's wife's affiliation with the CIA, since he was learning it as though it were new information.

Fleischer also testified that while he was on the Africa trip, he told reporters John Dickerson of *TIME* and David Gregory of NBC that Wilson's wife worked at the CIA. He denied, however, telling Walter Pincus of *The Washington Post*, although Pincus' subsequent testimony and other evidence would show convincingly that Fleischer had leaked to him on July 12, 2003. This was one of the strangest aspects of the trial. (Neither Dickerson nor Gregory was called by the defense, and Dickerson has publicly denied receiving a leak about Wilson's wife from Fleischer, although Fleischer did hint about it seemingly to encourage Dickerson to discover the information elsewhere.) Because he had leaked the information and feared prosecution, Fleischer initially refused to cooperate with the investigation, and received an immunity deal from Fitzgerald in early 2004 in exchange for his testimony—a deal that meant that Fleischer was immune from all charges except perjury if he lied under oath.

The defense sought to capitalize on Fleischer's immunity deal to suggest he was an unreliable witness. The defense also highlighted the fact that Fleischer had another source of information on Wilson's wife altogether—White House communications director Dan Bartlett, who mentioned it while reading the INR report on July 11, shortly before Fleischer revealed it to reporters for the first time. The defense thus sought to cast doubt on Fleischer's testimony that he received the information from Libby at all. It also highlighted Fleischer's account of leaking to Gregory and Cooper, seeking to suggest that Gregory learned the information early enough to share it with Tim Russert in time for Russert in turn to share it with Libby; and to suggest that Dickerson's knowledge meant that Libby need not have been a source on Plame for *TIME*'s Matt Cooper at all.

After Fleischer identifies himself and his current employment, prosecutor Peter Zeidenberg asks Fleischer about his role in the White House as well as his immunity deal, before moving on to Fleischer's account of the controversy that erupted over the State of the Union in 2003 and his own role in it:

A I was the White House Press Secretary from 2001 to 2003. . . . [M]y job as Press Secretary was to speak for the President, to answer questions on his behalf. It was to explain what the President is doing and why he was doing it, and to defend the White House, if there was a controversy or if allegations were made . . .

Q *Now, did you have, as Press Secretary, your own sources of information?*
A Yes, sir.

Q *And can you tell us what you mean by that?*
A The principal person I would get my information from was the President. The only way to be the Press Secretary and to speak for the President is to listen to him.

But you also get information from a large number of people at the White House, and that could include the Vice President; it could include members of the cabinet; it could include the President's senior staff, the Chief of Staff, the National Security Advisor, and the Deputy National Security Advisor.

All of these are people who I would go to and I would obtain information from. Some of them would give me information. So you learn that you have to listen to a wide variety of people to actually figure out what's going on inside the White House so what you say is as accurate as it can be.

Q *Now, have you testified previously in the Grand Jury about this case?*
A Yes, sir.

Q *And can you tell us—do you recall the dates, approximately?*
A I recall testifying before the Grand Jury or going before the Grand Jury in January of 2004, February of 2004, and then I believe September of 2004.

Q *And did you put—did you answer all the questions put to you on all three of those occasions?*
A No, sir.

Q *Can you tell us about that?*

A The first time I was asked to go to the Grand Jury in January of 2004. I did not answer the questions. I said to the government that I would refuse to answer any questions, and that I would refuse to cooperate in this investigation unless I was given immunity as a result of what I had done with information that I had been provided.

Q *And did you subsequently obtain a grant of immunity from the government?*

A Yes, sir . . .

Q *I would like to direct your attention and ask you some questions now about the spring and summer of 2003, if I may.*

First of all, can you tell the ladies and gentlemen a little bit about the State of [the] Union address that was given by the President in January of 2003 in terms of just what it was—what the State of the Union was—and the particular significance, if any, of the speech that year?

A Well, the State of the Union has historically been a major address that the President gives to the congress and to the country. It's typically the address the President gives that the most American people ever will watch. And so, for the White House, it's a very important event for the President to define what he seeks to do in whatever era any President lives.

In January of 2003, this was in the period leading up to whether or not the United States would go to war with Iraq. And the January 2003 State of the Union was a very important event for the White House to talk to the American people from President Bush's point of view about why we might actually go to war with Iraq.

Q *And in the next couple of months after that State of the Union address in January of 2003, did a controversy arise over a particular sentence that was included in the State of the Union address?*

A Yes. There was one sentence that the President gave which, as I recall it, was that according to British—or we have information from the British—that . . . Iraq was seeking uranium in Africa. And—the President did not mention a country. He said "from Africa."

It subsequently came to light in March of 2003, as I recall, that a part of the reason that the President said that turned out to be wrong. A part of why he said that turned out to be based on some documents that were forgeries. And so I started to get asked at the press briefings, does the administration still stand by those sixteen words that the President said?

Q *And what was your response when you would be getting those inquiries whether the President still stood behind the sixteen words, notwithstanding the fact that some of the evidence on which it was based appeared to be relying on forged documents?*

A Through the spring of 2003, my answer was, "yes, the President continues to stand by those words" because there was other evidence that supported the President's statement in the State of the Union, even though part of it turned out to be wrong.

Q *Now, late spring, talking about the period of the beginning of May and the beginning of June, do you recall any press accounts which discussed an envoy who went to Africa and these accounts which seemed to call into further question the validity of the sixteen words?*

A Yes, sir. I recall sometime in the spring of 2003 that there was something in the air. There were a couple things that were written. It wasn't a lot, but a couple of things had been written that re-examined this issue about these sixteen words the President gave and said that there could be no evidence that the President said that because work had gone into going to one of the countries in Africa, and that the information the White House used was wrong in its entirety.

Q *Now, directing your attention to July 6th of 2003, do you recall an op-ed piece in* The New York Times *being written by an individual who identified himself as Joseph Wilson, a former ambassador?*

A Yes, sir.

Q *Can you tell us about that day and your reaction to that article?*

A An article came out in *The New York Times* in its op-ed section that day, and the article had the name of this envoy who had previously been raising the questions in the spring that the President was wrong. And this article now had his name attached to it, the op-ed. And it said that the President, if he was relying on what this envoy said, must have twisted the intelligence in order to come to the conclusion that he used in the State of the Union.

So the envoy was challenging the honesty and the accuracy of what President Bush had said, and now he had put his name on it, what was previously in these columns that I said were up in the air, that were just kind of out there.

Q *I would like to go to the next day, Monday, July 7th. Did you have a press gaggle that morning?*

A I did.

Q *And were you asked questions that morning regarding the charges that Ambassador Wilson made in his op-ed piece?*

A Yes, sir. I was asked questions about it.

Q *And can you tell us about that, both what you recall being asked about and how you responded?*

A In that gaggle, this on-the-record session with the press, a reporter asked me, "What's the White House's reaction to the charges made in this op-ed?" And, as I recall, my answer was "there's zero, nada, nothing new here, other than we now know the name of the person who was making these charges."

And then I said that—I added, the Vice President did not send Ambassador Wilson to Niger as this op-ed had suggested. I said the CIA sent him on their own volition.

Q *And were you asked any further questions about whether or not the President or the White House still stood behind the sixteen words?*

A Then, later, I was asked a question about, given this op-ed, does the White House still stand behind these sixteen words? And on that question, I had been previously told to be careful not to repeat the White House's "we are standing by the sixteen words," because I had been told earlier that the ground might be shifting on that question.

The worst place to stand, as the Press Secretary, is when the ground is shifting. Now you can't say yes; you can't say no. And so at that briefing, I basically punted on that question and I said, sort of yes and no. And I told the reporter who was asking me that I would have to get back to him because I didn't know the answer.

Q *Now, that afternoon, July 7th, on that Monday, did you have lunch plans?*

A Yes, sir.

Q *And with whom did you have lunch plans?*

A Mr. Scooter Libby.

Q *Can you tell us about how that was set up?*

A What I recall is I had announced to the President and then made public in—sometime early, or mid-May that I was going to be leaving the White House, and that I was going to spend time with family and go into the private sector. And shortly after that, Mr. Libby asked me to go to lunch with him. He just said we should get together and go to lunch before you leave just to hear what you are going to be doing when you leave.

> *I was asked a question about, given this op-ed, does the White House still stand behind these sixteen words? And on that question, I had been previously told to be careful not to repeat the White House's "we are standing by the sixteen words," because I had been told earlier that the ground might be shifting on that question.*

Q *Was it a routine for you to have lunch engagements when you were working as White House Press Secretary?*

A Not often. Typically, I would eat at my desk.

Q *And had you ever had lunch with Mr. Libby before?*

A No, sir.

Q *What was your relationship with Mr. Libby?*

A It was good. I always liked Mr. Libby. I did not consider Mr. Libby one of the people I would use as a source at the White House. He was not somebody who would typically provide information to me.

What I recall most is when I would ask Mr. Libby about something that would take place, his typical response would be, you should check with Dr. Rice, the National Security Advisor.

Q *Notwithstanding the fact that he wasn't a source for you, your relationship with him was good?*

A Yes, sir.

Q *And can you tell us just about where it is you had lunch with Mr. Libby on July 7th?*

A We had lunch in the White House mess . . .

Q *And who was present?*

A Just Mr. Libby and me.

Q *Now, can you tell us about what, if anything, was discussed during your lunch with Mr. Libby?*

A At the lunch, we talked about my plans, what I was going to do when I left the White House, what I was going to do in the private sector and how I was setting up my career from that point forward.

    We talked a little about sports. I remember that we talked a little football. We are both fans of the same football team, the Miami Dolphins. And then I remember—I don't remember if I brought it up or if Mr. Libby brought up the briefing and what transpired at the briefing that morning.

Q *What do you recall being discussed about the briefing, regardless of who brought it up?*

A What I remember of the briefing was that I said to Mr. Libby that I got asked about Ambassador Wilson and I said that—what I was asked to say by the Vice President's office [—that] he got sent by the CIA on their own volition.

    And what I recall Mr. Libby saying to me was he reiterated the point that the Vice President did not send Ambassador Wilson to Niger, which I had heard previously from his staff.

    And then he continued and he said that Ambassador Wilson was sent by his wife. His wife works at the CIA. He said to me, as I recall, that she works in the Counter Proliferation Division. And then I believe—I think that he told me her name.

    And I recall Mr. Libby continued on to say something along the lines of, "This is hush-hush. This is on the QT. Not very many people know about this."

Q *And the subject of the wife came up in which context?*

A The context that I recall it is when we were talking about the briefing because I had been asked the question about Ambassador Wilson.

Q *And what exactly do you recall—the words Mr. Libby used when he described Wilson's wife? How did he describe her to you?*

A I just remember him saying that she works at the CIA and that she works in the Counter Proliferation Division.

Q *Did you know what the Counter Proliferation Division meant? Did it have any significance to you?*

A Not specific[ally]. I understand the general word "counter proliferation," but I don't know enough about the CIA's inner structures to know what that division means.

Q *Now, you said you believe he mentioned her name.*

A Yes, sir.

Q *What do you recall him—how did he describe her name?*

A I just remember him saying—this is all very matter-of-fact—just that his wife works there; she works in Counterproliferation. I think he just said, "her name is Valerie Plame."

Q *And was this information that was news to you?*

A Yes, sir.

Q *Had you ever heard it before?*

A About his wife, that was news to me. The information that the Vice President did not send him was not news because his staff had previously told me that. The information about his wife was the first time I ever heard it.

Q *And what did you understand Mr. Libby to mean when he said that this was "hush-hush"?*

A I didn't really know. I mean, I thought it was just kind of odd. It was hush-hush, QT. My sense of it was that Mr. Libby is telling me this is kind of newsy. This is kind of something that nobody knows about, kind of good information. That was what I took from that.

Q *Did you understand from that comment that this meant that this information he was providing you was classified?*

A Absolutely not.

Q *And why is that?*

A Well, there is a very strict protocol that's followed when classified information is provided, and it's especially the case when somebody gives classified information to a press person. My job is to speak to the press.

And so my experience at the White House was whenever somebody, particularly from the national security world, would convey classified information to me which I was authorized to hear, it also began with the protocol, "The following is classified; you cannot use it."

If I ever received a document and it was stamped "top secret" or "secret," it's obvious you cannot use it. When it's oral, the people I worked with always said, "This is classified; you cannot use it."

Q *And did you take it from that—the comment about the wife—that there was a suggestion that there may have been some improper conduct in the CIA of some sort?*

A My thought was that what I was hearing was that there was nepotism at the CIA, that somebody got a job because of their family member's position. That was kind of what I thought I was hearing . . .

THE COURT: Okay. It's 12:30, so we will break for lunch and come back at 1:30. Please don't talk about the case and continue to avoid everybody associated with the case.

I assume we have provided them with papers that have been screened, so you can read the paper because anything about the case has been deleted. Have a nice lunch.

Whereupon the luncheon recess was taken.

THE COURT: Good afternoon. Okay.

MR. ZEIDENBERG: Thank you, Your Honor. May I resume?

THE COURT: Yes.

(Ari Fleischer, witness for the government, previously sworn.)

Direct examination (resumed) by Mr. Zeidenberg:

Q *Mr. Fleischer, before the lunch break, I was just finishing up asking you some questions about your lunch on July 7th with Mr. Libby.*

Now, did Mr. Libby say anything to you during this lunch to make you think that the information he was telling you about the wife was classified or protected?

A No, sir.

Q *Now, later that day, July 7th, were you going on an overseas trip?*

A Yes.

Q *Can you tell us about that?*

A I departed the United States out of Washington, D.C., on the night of July 7th for a trip to Africa . . . It was the typical traveling party, the Chief of Staff, Andy Card; Secretary of State, Colin Powell; National Security Advisor Condoleezza Rice; Dan Bartlett, top communications official for the President; some other support people from the White House. The press was aboard Air Force One, the standard traveling party for an international trip.

Q *During the course of the trip, was the decision made that the White House was going to walk away from, if you will, or to no longer claim that they were standing behind the sixteen words in the State of the Union Address?*

A Yes, sir. There were meetings taking place in the White House to decide whether or not we were going to stand by what the President said in the State of the Union. [It was] said to me that the White House is not going to stand by those remarks any longer. And our position was that we didn't know if what the President said was accurate or not . . . [I]t did not rise to the level of what should have been included in a Presidential Address.

Q *Was that new White House position conveyed to the press?*

A Yes.

Q *And did that make the controversy pretty much go away?*

A No, sir. That's basically what started the controversy and made it flare up and become a dominant part of the trip to Africa.

Q *Later . . . were you engaged . . . with Dr. Rice [in] a press briefing or press gaggle on Air Force One concerning these same subjects? . . .*

A Dr. Rice came to the back of the plane on July 11th on a flight that left South Africa on the way to Uganda . . . That was a very contentious briefing, and the press was really asking how could this have happened. How could this mistake have gotten into the State of the Union? Shouldn't somebody have known better? You're the White House. Mistakes like this shouldn't happen. It's the most important address the President can give.

Dr. Rice, in the course of this briefing, had said to the press, something that had not previously been said, which was, had the Director of the Central Intelligence Agency wanted those words out, the sixteen words, had the head of [the] CIA wanted those words out, they would have come out.

That itself was a very big development because now here, the White House seems to be blaming the CIA for the words not getting taken out of the President's address.

[T]he whole trip was mired in controversy about the sixteen words. . . . [T]his emerged as by far the dominant story of the trip.

Q *Now, while you were on Air Force One on July 11th, did you hear someone in the . . . Administration make another reference to Wilson's wife?*

A Yes, sir.

Q *Can you tell us about that, Mr. Fleischer?*

A Dan Bartlett, who was at that time the Communications Director for the White House . . . said, . . . "I can't believe he or they are saying that the Vice President sent Ambassador Wilson to Niger. His wife sent him. She works for the CIA." And he said this in front of me.

Q *When you say, he was saying in it in front of you, would you characterize this as a conversation he was having with you?*

A No. Dan was basically venting . . . So that became the second . . . reference to Mrs. Wilson . . .

Q *. . . [W]hen you heard the information from Mr. Bartlett, what was your reaction?*

A My first reaction is I've heard all this before. And again, it never seemed to me to be very, you know, newsy . . . [I]t did back up my statement that I made in the briefing room earlier, that the Vice President didn't send Ambassador Wilson to Niger. He was sent by the CIA on their own. That's what I had previously said.

Now, I had just one more little nugget to back up what I said that the CIA sent him, sent by his wife. Now, two people had just conveyed that to me.

Q *Just so it's clear, the two people being?*

A Mr. Libby and Mr. Bartlett. . . .

Q *Can you tell us if you had occasion to talk to some reporters by the side of the road in Uganda? . . .*

A There were a group of reporters standing on the side of the road. I kind of went up and just got next to them and started talking to them. And during that conversation, I recall that I said to these reporters that—we were talking about the whole controversy of the week, what a bad week it's been for the White House. I recall saying to them that, if you want to know who sent Ambassador Wilson to Niger, it was his wife. She works there.

. . . Tamara Lipper of *Newsweek* . . . had . . . walked away before I said what I said about Ambassador Wilson and Niger. The remaining two reporters, as I remember it, were David Gregory with NBC News and John Dickerson, then of *TIME* magazine.

. . . I took that moment to say what I said, thinking, maybe this will help make this controversy go away. Maybe this will address some of these issues about, well, how could this get into the State of the Union.

Then did the President, did the Vice President send Ambassador Wilson to Niger[?] If he didn't, then it seemed to me, as Press Secretary, it backs up the White House's statement. We didn't know about what was in Ambassador Wilson's report at that time.

Q *What part of it backs up the White House account?*

A . . . [T]he allegation was that Ambassador Wilson wrote he had filed a report, or a report would have been filed, stating that Iraq could not have gotten uranium from Niger. He said that report, because Vice President Cheney played a role in sending him to Niger, must be known by the Vice President because the Vice President played a role in sending him.

. . . What I had been told by two White House officials . . . to pass on, was the Vice President didn't send him. He was sent by his wife. The Vice President wasn't involved in it . . .

Q *Did your statement to the reporters on the side of the road in Uganda get much of a reaction while you were standing there?*

A No, sir. The press's reaction was, "so what." They didn't take out their notebooks. They didn't start writing anything. They didn't ask me any follow-up questions as I recall. It was a big "so what."

Q *When you say "so what," do you mean a metaphorically speaking or did they actually literally say "so what?"*

A They did not say so what. Like a lot of things I've said to the press, it had no impact . . .

Q *Did you have any hesitation about sharing this information with reporters?*

A No, sir.

Q *Why is that?*

A Because I never, in my wildest dreams, would have thought this information [to] be classified. I never, in my wildest dreams, would have thought that what I was saying would have involved . . . , as I read the papers, a covert agent in the Central Intelligence Agency.

MR. JEFFRESS: Objection.

(Bench conference is sealed and redacted.)

The objection evidently has to do with the possible introduction of evidence of Plame's status at the CIA, because Walton issues a caution to the jury:

(Open court.)

THE COURT: Ladies and gentlemen, in reference to the witness's testimony about what he read in the newspaper about Mrs. Wilson's status with the CIA, that testimony is only relevant as it relates to . . . what his state of mind was with reference to this situation. It has no relevance whatsoever to this case.

I don't know, based upon what's been presented to me throughout this trial, what her status was. But in any event, whatever her status was, that's totally irrelevant to this case. That's not an issue that you should concern yourself with. And you cannot, in any way, use that testimony in your assessment of Mr. Libby's guilt or innocence in this trial.

By Mr. Zeidenberg:

Q *Mr. Fleischer, your last day at the White House was when?*
A July 14, 2003 . . .

Q *Now, directing your attention to late September 2003, about two and a half months later, did you, at that point, learn some information that caused you some concern?*
A Yes, sir.

Q *Can you tell us about that?*
A I remember I was at my parents' home. . . . I saw a small article in *The New York Times* that said that the Central Intelligence Agency had requested the Justice Department begin a criminal investigation or an investigation into whether or not an identity of a covert CIA agent had been leaked by people at the White House.

I later went on line . . . and read a very big story in *The Washington Post* about the CIA asking for a criminal investigation . . .

Q *Was the person who was alleged to be employed by the CIA, was this person identified in any fashion?*
A As I recall the story, yes, I think she was.

Q *In what fashion? Was she related to someone? How was she described in the article?*
A As I recall, it was Ambassador Joseph Wilson's wife.

Q *What was your reaction when you saw this news?*
A I was absolutely horrified.

MR. JEFFRESS: Objection as to what his reaction was.
THE COURT: Overruled.

By Mr. Zeidenberg:

Q *You can finish your answer.*
A I thought, "Oh my God, did I play a role in somehow outing a CIA officer? Did I convey information to the press, which I had no idea whether she was classified or she was covert?" I thought, "Did I do something that I could be in big trouble for?"

Q *As a result of being concerned that you were in big trouble, what did you do?*
A I contacted counsel.

Q *Is that how you subsequently obtained immunity?*

A Yes, sir.

Q *Prior to obtaining that immunity, would you answer any questions put to you by the Government?*

A No, sir.

Q *Why is that?*

A Because I thought, even though I had no idea about Mrs. Wilson's status, that I could somehow be in trouble for doing something that I never thought that I did. So I met with counsel and accepted my counsel's advice on this matter.

Q *Once you obtained immunity from prosecution in connection with your testimony in this matter, did you answer all the questions put to you?*

A Yes, sir, I did.

THE COURT: I just want to emphasize again that this article that he read is only admitted in reference to what impact it had on him and his state of mind. It has no other relevance to this case.

MR. ZEIDENBERG: I have no further questions, Your Honor.

> *I thought, "Oh my God, did I play a role in somehow outing a CIA officer? Did I convey information to the press, which I had no idea whether she was classified or she was covert?" I thought, "Did I do something that I could be in big trouble for?"*

THE DEFENSE'S INITIAL LINE OF QUESTIONING aims to show that Fleischer's testimony is practiced and polished, before seeking to undermine the substance of his testimony with regard to Libby and to bring out other testimony favorable to the defendant:

By Mr. Jeffress:

Q *Good afternoon, Mr. Fleischer. You spent two and a half years, I believe it was, answering questions twice a day, right?*

A Yes, sir.

Q *In formal settings and informal settings?*

A Yes, sir.

Q *You were representing the President of the United States and advocating his policies and explaining his positions, correct?*

A Correct.

Q *You got a lot of questions and some of them weren't so friendly, I suppose?*

A Yes, sir.

Q *Some of them were even hostile?*

A Yes, sir.

Q *But you've had a lot of practice?*
A I took a lot of questions.

Q *Now, how many times have you met with the prosecution to discuss your testimony in this case?*
A I met with them prior to each of my meetings in the Grand Jury other than the first one. I met with them prior to the indictment, many weeks prior to the indictment being handed out. Then I've met with them, I believe, four times, three times, four times, prior to this trial.

Q *How many times have you met with any representative of the defense?*
A I have not, sir.

Q *You were aware that we requested you to do so?*
A Yes, sir.

Q *You were aware that it would have been completely lawful and proper for you to do so?*
A Yes.

Q *But you refused?*
A I declined to do so, yes.

Q *And by the way, when you said that you met with the prosecutors before the indictment, you were talking about the indictment of Scooter Libby, correct?*
A Yes, sir.

Q *Now, as I understand it, you recollect that Mr. Libby told you information about Ambassador Wilson's wife at a lunch on July 7th, the Monday, correct?*
A Yes.

Q *And you saw no reason why you couldn't share that information; is that correct?*
A Correct.

Q *And you left on the plane that evening for Africa, correct?*
A Correct.

Q *There were lots of reporters on the plane, right?*
A Correct.

Q *Reporters from NBC News?*
A I don't know if that one particular reporter was on there. On Air Force One there's usually a smaller press pool. There is usually about six or seven actual reporters, about six or seven technical, camera people et cetera. There is a smaller group on Air Force One.

Q *So there were reporters on Air Force One and there [were] a lot more reporters on the second plane; is that correct?*
A Correct . . .

Q *I'm focusing on the day before you left for Africa.*

A Right.

Q *On that day, there was an article in* The New York Times, *you've already testified about, an op-ed by Joseph Wilson, correct? Did you read that?*

A I think so, yes.

Q *Part of your duties were to read the press critical of the President, correct?*

A That's correct.

Q *There was an article in* The Washington Post *by Richard Leiby and Walter Pincus, correct?*

A I think so.

Q *And there was an appearance by Mr. Wilson on television that day, correct?*

A The appearance on television I only know by looking backwards.

Q *...[T]his was a topic, as you've testified, that was, reporters were giving you a hard time about all week, right?*

A Only after we got to Africa. When I left on July 7th, it was not that big an issue . . . It was really only after the White House indicated we would no longer stand by the sixteen words that it became a major issue . . .

Q *Let me go to the conversation that you had with Mr. Libby. You recall that, of course you were leaving. As you said, you were leaving. You were resigning. That was well known that you were leaving the middle of July?*

A Yes, sir.

Q *This lunch that Mr. Libby set up with you had been set up some time before?*

A That's correct . . .

Q *You had had a press gaggle that morning, which is where you used the talking points that had been sent to you by Cathie Martin in the Office of the Vice President concerning Wilson's trip, right?*

A The information that I [gave] to [the] gaggle was provided to me by the Vice President's staff. I don't remember if Cathie said [it] to me orally or if she gave it to me in writing, talking points, but what I said was what the Vice President's office wanted me to say what they told me the facts were.

Q *It would be customary, would it, for Cathie Martin or somebody else in her shop in the Office of the Vice President, to e-mail you talking points if something concerning the Vice President might come up in your morning briefing?*

A Sure . . . I would often get information from other people at the White House because you can't possibly stay on top of everything.

JEFFRIES WALKS THROUGH some of the questions and answers from the July 7, 2003 press gaggle with Fleischer:

Q *Okay, a reporter asked you a question. "Can you give us the White House account* *of Ambassador Wilson's account of what happened when he went to Niger and investigated the suggestions that Niger was passing yellowcake to Iraq? I'm sure you saw the piece yesterday in The New York Times." Right?*

A Yes, sir.

Q *Your response was, "Well, there is zero, nada, nothing new here. Ambassador Wilson, other than the fact that now people know his name, has said all this before." Right?*

A Yes, sir.

Q *You were referring to articles that had been written before July 7th in which Ambassador Wilson obviously had been a confidential source?*

A That's what I interpreted those articles to mean after I saw his op-ed.

Q *Okay. Then you said, "But the fact of the matter is, in his statements about the Vice President, the Vice President's office did not request the mission to Niger." That's what Cathie Martin had told you, right?*

A That's correct.

Q *As far as you know, it's accurate?*

A That's correct.

Q *"The Vice President's office was not informed of his mission, and he," meaning the Vice President, "was not aware of Mr. Wilson's mission until recent press accounts"... Correct?*

A Correct, sir.

Q *Again, those were both talking points that Ms. Martin had asked you to say on behalf of the Vice President?*

A That's what I recall . . .

Q *Aside from the Vice President's office and Cathie Martin, had you received other information related to this controversy from other sources within the White House?*

A . . . I received other information dealing with why . . . the President [said] what he said in the State of the Union Address . . .

I received information from other people on the National Security Council saying why he might have said it. There were other nations . . . three . . . principally in Africa which provided uranium. The President said [it] because Iraq had previously acquired uranium from Africa, had a history of it.

Then in March of 2003, a report came out from the International [Atomic Energy] Agency that said a piece of this information dealing with the yellowcake was based on a forgery. So I received that information from people at the National Security Council.

And that led to the issue, do we still stand by it or was there other information, other reporting that would allow us to stand by it or was this forgery story enough that we can no longer use it? So that was the state at the time.

Q *When you said up in your gaggle that morning that the information on yellowcake did indeed turn out to be incorrect, were you referring there to the fact that,*

. . . it had been discovered, after the State of the Union speech, that documents reviewed by the Intelligence [sic: International Atomic Energy] Agency turned out to be forgeries?

A Yes, sir. That's what I just said. That was the yellowcake piece.

Q *Did you consider that day, or any other day for that matter, that Mr. Wilson's report was the reason why the White House took back or said that the words turned out to be incorrect?*

A I didn't know exactly why. I thought there probably would be, as always at the White House, many reasons. That could have been one of them . . .

Q *Let me go back to the meeting that you had with Mr. Libby. In terms of any conversation about Wilson's wife, that took, what, 15 seconds, 30 seconds?*

A That was a short conversation about Ambassador Wilson's wife.

Q *He didn't appear to be agitated or upset or angry? He just was very matter-of-fact?*

A . . . He was very plain-spoken and matter-of-fact.

Q *Mr. Libby did not use the word nepotism, correct?*

A That's correct. He did not.

Q *You said you believe that Mr. Libby told you the name?*

A Yes, sir . . .

Q *Well, let me ask you this, did you testify to the Grand Jury [on] February 27, 2004, "And it struck me that it was not material. The press would not find it interesting one way or another if his wife sent him. The press was very interested in the substance of did President Bush knowingly deceive the country, because he surely would have known about what Ambassador Wilson reported. The press was very focused on the substantive piece." That was your testimony, correct?*

A Yes, sir . . .

Q *Okay. Did you have a gaggle on the airplane on the way from South Africa to Uganda on June 11th?*

A Dr. Rice came back and briefed the press that day.

Q *You were present, correct?*

A Yes, sir.

Q *Now, was that before or after you met with Mr. Bartlett . . . ?*

A I believe I might be wrong about this. But I believe that Dr. Rice went back to the airplane prior to the conversation, or Mr. Bartlett saying that information.

Q *Is it fair to say that, at this gaggle that morning, that is July the 11th, that the press was all over the Wilson story?*

A The story they were [all] over was how could the President have put this in the State of the Union and then how could the White House walk away from it . . .

Q *After the gaggle, you, this is when you were sitting in the staff cabin reading a document, correct?*

A Yes, sir.

Q *What was that document?*

A That document was a CIA summary of Ambassador Wilson's trip to Niger, what he found according to the CIA.

Q *Why were you reading it?*

A Because, after Dr. Rice had gone back, I remember she was asked one question at the back of the plane about can you declassify any of the information . . .

There was a meeting in the senior staff cabin and I was in it . . . [W]e were all talking about whether or not we could declassify and make public why the President said what he said. One of those documents was a CIA summary of Ambassador Wilson's trip, what he found. I wanted to see that document because Dr. Rice said this part backs up what the President said.

Q *Was it while you were reading this cable that you've identified that Dan Bartlett came to see you?*

A That's when Mr. Bartlett walked in the area of the staff cabin I was in and said what he said, yes.

Q *Did he have a document in his hands?*

A Yes, sir. As I recall, he did . . .

Q *Did you see the document that Mr. Bartlett had in his hand?*

A No, sir.

Q *Did he [wave] it at you or show you anything in that document?*

A No, sir.

Q *When Mr. Bartlett said, "I can't believe they're saying the Vice President sent him[;] his wife sent him, she works there," now, he seemed to be, unlike Mr. Libby's demeanor during your lunch, he seemed to be, what, upset?*

A Yes, sir.

Q *Annoyed that people were making this, kept making this allegation?*

A Yes, sir.

Q *...[Y]our testimony is that's the same thing that Mr. Libby had told you, or one of the things he had told you back on Monday, four days earlier, right?*

A That's correct.

Q *Did you say . . . , "Well, I know that, Scooter Libby told me that four days ago["]?*

A No, I didn't say anything.

Q *You didn't tell him that, "Gosh, everybody knows that. That's not news to me.["] You made no comments like that at all?*

A What I recollect is I wanted to read the document that Dr. Rice had given to me. I was interested in that document. I was sitting there reading it. When Mr. Bartlett came back and said what he said, and the document he was reading, my first reaction is "I've heard this before". . .

Q *So he came in and he said to you, ["]I can't believe they're saying the Vice President sent him, because his wife works there, she sent him." And you don't say a word?*

A I did not say anything, sir. One of the things that I found in the government . . . [was to] finish what you start because you get interrupted by so many things when you're at the White House. You never stop. You never finish what you're reading. I wanted to finish this document, it interested me.

Q *Dan Bartlett is your boss, correct, at this time in July of '03?*

A Mr. Bartlett was nominally my boss . . .

Q *Now, you say you didn't say anything to Dan Bartlett about having already heard this from Mr. Libby, as a matter of fact, you didn't say anything at all because you were trying to read a document, is that it?*

A Yes, sir.

Q *[When] you testif[ied] before the Grand Jury, were you asked the following question?*
Question: "And is there a reason you didn't advise Mr. Bartlett of your lunch?" Referring to the lunch with Mr. Libby.
And your answer was, "Because, again, it just didn't strike me as news about whether the CIA had nepotism, or in this case was incompetent, was relevant to whether or not the President's statement about Iraq seeking uranium from Africa was germane."
Is that the answer you gave to that question about why you hadn't told Mr. Bartlett of your lunch with Scooter Libby?

A Yes, sir. I think I also told the Grand Jury what we just discussed as well.

Q *Now, David Gregory is a White House correspondent for NBC News; is that correct?*

A That's correct.

Q *Mr. Gregory asked you a lot of questions while you were Press Secretary, did he not?*

A Yes, sir, he did . . .

Q *Do you recall that at the gaggle, the morning of July 11th, when Dr. Rice was being insistently peppered with questions about this issue, David Gregory was one of the questioners?*

A Yes, sir, I think that's right . . .

Q *Ambassador Wilson's claims were only one part of the problem, so to speak, that you were facing and the White House was facing about the credibility of the sixteen words?*

A Yes, sir, I think that's accurate.

Q *One of the questions consistently being raised was who cleared the speech?*

A Right.

Q *There was some finger pointing going on, frankly, right?*

A Yes, sir.

Q *The finger pointing was between the CIA and the National Security Council, correct?*

A That's correct.

Q *As a matter of fact, there was a man named Alan Foley at the CIA, and people were talking about him, and there were reports that he had objected to it?*

A That's correct.

Q *And fingers were being pointed by anonymous sources that Ambassador Joseph in the National Security Council as somebody who had put the words in the speech?*

A That's correct.

Q *Did that cause some tension that week between the CIA and the White House?*

A Yes.

Q *A tension that you, as the Press Secretary, had to get involved in trying to solve?*

A Yes.

Q *That didn't have anything to do with Ambassador Wilson, correct...?*

A I think in the context of the controversy of the week, it's hard to tell what was attributable to one problem we had or another problem that we had. We had multiple problems that week. Ambassador Wilson was one of them, I think, it's fair to say. The very fundamental issues of why did the President say it in the first place was the driving issue. And it all kind of, as it always does, melts together in one big controversy.

Q *But in any event, in this press gaggle on the plane that day, . . . I guess the first two pages of it anyway, all have to do with who cleared the speech and who was at fault, the CIA or the National Security Council?*

A Yes, sir. I was making a reference earlier that there was one other development that took place in this timeframe. And that was a report that aired on the CBS News. I had the transcript of it in South Africa when I woke up that morning. The report on CBS said the source at the Central Intelligence Agency said that the President did know the information was false. And he deliberately put it in the speech even though he knew it was false.

So, that was aired that night back in America, that the President did it knowing it was wrong, which, of course, was opposite to everything that I was told.

Q *...Now, what Dr. Rice told the press that day is, "Now, I can tell you if the CIA, the Director of Central Intelligence, had said take this out of the speech, it would have been gone without question. What we've said subsequently is, knowing what we know now, that some of the Niger documents apparently were forged, we wouldn't have put this in the President's speech, but that's knowing what we know now." Correct?*

A That's what she said in that part of the transcript.

Q *Then she goes and continues on that and there is a question. As a matter of fact, what is the question? "Dr. Rice, it sounds as if you're blaming the CIA here." That was David Gregory, wasn't it?*

A I don't remember who asked the questions.

Q *Look at the top of page 6. If you will look down a little bit further, you will see where Dr. Rice refers to David.*

A Okay.

Q *David. And then I think you'll see, two paragraphs later, it's David. Does that refresh your recollection that's who she was talking to? That's who was asking the question?*

A I think that's possible it was David Gregory if she continued on and said his name later, sure . . .

Q *Would you turn to 1644.10? And right there at the bottom, the last things that Dr. Rice says on that page. Dr. Rice is being asked when she found out that the documents were forged. Do you see that?*

A Yes, sir.

Q *All right. You say, actually, the IAEA reported it, correct?*

A Correct.

Q *That's the International Atomic Energy Agency?*

A Yes . . .

Q *But that's not a U.S. government agency, that's an international agency?*

A Correct.

Q *And one of the problems was that our United States intelligence agencies had not discovered these forgeries, but within weeks after the IAEA got them, they discovered they were forgeries, right?*

A Correct, yes.

Q *So, Dr. Rice was saying that the I.A.E.A. reported it, I believe, in March, which was two months after the State of the Union speech?*

A Yes, sir.

Q *And then she says, "I will tell you that, for instance, on Ambassador Wilson going out to Niger, I learned of that when I was sitting on whatever TV show it was because that mission was not known to anybody in the White House."*
Do you recall that she had been on a Meet the Press *show June 8 of 2003?*

A I recall she was on some Sunday show.

Q *That came up?*

A I do recall the conversation coming up, particularly afterwards, yes.

Q *Dr. Rice then was the National Security Advisor, correct?*

A Correct.

Q *When somebody in that high-up position is going on a Sunday talk show, do you have a responsibility to brief them or prepare them for the show?*

A Yes, sir, I do.

Q *She had not been prepared prior to that June 8th show on anything involving Ambassador Wilson; is that correct? . . .*

A Certainly not by me.

Q *At least that early, though, high officials were being asked question about that subject by the press?*

A Yes, sir. As I said, there was something in the air that spring about that topic . . .

THE DEFENSE TURNS to questioning Fleischer about just when he says he leaked to some reporters. The timing matters because the defense wants to suggest that Fleischer leaked to David Gregory in time for Gregory to tell Tim Russert back in D.C., who in turn could have told Libby, according to the defense's proposed timeline. No evidence is introduced that Gregory did tell Russert; and Russert would testify that he did not know that Wilson's wife worked at the time of his conversation with Libby that week.

Q *. . . Now, when you encountered Mr. Gregory and Mr. Dickerson, was there a third reporter in the vicinity?*

A Yes, sir.

Q *Who was that?*

A As I recall, Tamara Lipper of *Newsweek* magazine.

Q *Do you know one way or another whether she was close enough to have heard your statement about if you want to know who sent him, his wife sent him, she works for the CIA?*

A My recollection is that she had walked off prior to us talking about that.

Q *Let's just talk about Mr. Gregory and Mr. Dickerson. They were asking you questions. As a matter of fact, look back at 1675, President Museveni and President Bush gave some short remarks. What was the very last question asked in those short remarks?*

A How did the information get into your speech?

Q *If it was erroneous, right?*

A That is correct.

Q *Some reporter is asking the President, even in a joint appearance with President Museveni, something about the sixteen words, right?*

A Yes, sir.

Q *Then you walked over and you saw these two reporters. Now, were they asking you questions again about Ambassador Wilson's claims?*

A No, sir, I volunteered it . . .

Q *Do you think it might have been that question asked of the President right there that provoked you to do it?*

A As I recall, . . . we were talking about what a bad week it was for the White House. What's it like? It's your last week you're dealing with this gigantic controversy. Just talked about that in general. And how could these words get in there. There was also the issue of why are you going after Director Tenet. It was follow-up to what Dr. Rice said on the airplane.

As I recall, in large part because of the report on CBS that aired the night before, that's what led me to volunteer it. Plus the fact that I had heard now from two Administration officials. So I volunteered it.

Q *You have a clear memory of another exchange with David Gregory of NBC News in that conversation, correct? . . .*

A Yes, sir.

Q *Tell the jury about that?*

A What I remember is Mr. Gregory was saying something about, what a terrible last week it has been. How does it feel to make this your last week on the job with this gigantic controversy. I remember saying to Mr. Gregory, something along the lines of, well, if it wasn't this crap, it would be some other crap.

Q *So the conversation with David Gregory, the whole conversation, including the wife is very clear in your mind, correct?*

A Yes, sir.

Q *Did you have second thoughts about saying to David Gregory that thing about crap?*

A Yes, sir.

Q *Why is that?*

A I don't think Press Secretaries should go around using that word. I said to Mr. Gregory, if you're going to use anything I said, please don't use that word.

Q *But you had no second thoughts about mentioning to him the information about Ambassador Wilson's wife, correct?*

A That's correct, sir.

Q *What you told Mr. Gregory, you didn't put off the record?*

A No, sir, not that I recall.

Q *He was free to report it or tell his superiors about it?*

A I don't recall if the conversation was what they call on the record or on background, it could very well have been on background.

Q *But even on background, he could use it. He just couldn't refer to you as the source; is that right?*

A That's correct. If it was on background, correct.

Q *Okay. But he would be perfectly free to call back to NBC News and say I just picked up a piece of information you might be interested in?*

A That's correct, sir.

Q *And Gregory, at the time on July 11th, 2003, worked for whom?*

A NBC News.

Q *Okay. He works out of the Washington Bureau, correct?*

A Yeah, he works out of the Washington Bureau. He works out of the White House.

Q *And on July 11, 2003, who was the head of the Washington Bureau of NBC News?*

A I believe that would be Tim Russert.

Q *Was another reporter standing with David Gregory? You said a second reporter was standing there at the same time?*

A Yes, sir.

Q *And again, he heard the same conversation?*

A Yes, sir. That's my recollection, yes.

Q *Who was that?*

A Mr. John Dickerson, then of *TIME* magazine.

Q *Okay. You said these same words that you said to Mr. Gregory, you said it to both of them, together; is that right?*

A That's correct.

Q *Again, John Dickerson, he worked for what magazine at the time?*

A *TIME.*

Q TIME *magazine at the time. Okay . . . [D]o you know a reporter named Matt Cooper, Matthew Cooper?*

A Yes, sir.

Q *He worked for the same magazine . . . at that time?*

A Yes, sir.

THE DEFENSE IS LAYING GROUNDWORK for its suggestion that Cooper did not need to use Libby as a source on Plame at all, since he would have had the information from Rove and from Fleischer via Dickerson.

Q *Did these reporters have telephones, cell phones and telephones back on the plane that they could call back to the states and file their stories?*

A . . .[Y]es, they did . . .

Q *So, at least a little bit after 8:00 in the morning, Eastern Daylight Time, both of these reporters, one from* TIME *magazine and one from the Washington Bureau of NBC News knew from you that Wilson's wife worked at the CIA and sent him on the trip?*

A Yes, sir.

Q *Is this, Mr. Fleischer, an article on Time.com dated July 17, 2003, entitled "A War on Wilson?"*

A Yes, sir.

Q *If we look at the second paragraph of that at the bottom, . . . it says, "And some government officials have noted to* TIME *in interviews, as well as to syndicated columnist Robert Novak, that Wilson's wife, Valerie Plame, is a CIA official who monitors the proliferation of weapons of mass destruction."*

Number one, you didn't tell these reporters that she, her name was Valerie Plame, correct?

A That's correct, sir.

Q *You didn't tell them that she monitors proliferation of weapons of mass destruction, correct?*

A That's correct, sir

Q *You did tell them, however, that she worked at the CIA?*

A That's correct, sir.

Q *The next sentence says, "These officials have suggested that she was involved in her husband's being dispatched to Niger." Now that's one you did say, right?*

A Correct.

Q *...[D]id you see the article when it appeared? . . .*

A I didn't know the existence of this article until after the stories broke of the investigation in late September, I believe.

Q *Okay. Would you look at the top? Would you highlight the authors. It's Matthew Cooper, Massimo—I hope I'm pronouncing that right—Calabresi, and John Dickerson. And John Dickerson is the one you talked to?*

A Right.

Q *Did you—the next day, July 12th, was the President and his group still in Africa?*

A Yes, sir.

Q *Again, there was a gaggle that morning, correct?*

A Correct.

Q *The questions about the sixteen words still hadn't stopped, right?*

A Correct.

Q *As a matter of fact, the night before—well, you've already said George Tenet issued a statement. Had that been issued by the time of the gaggle on the 12th?*

A Yes, sir, it had.

Q *That was the topic of some discussion, was it not?*

A Yes, sir. The other topic of discussion was did the President still have confidence in Director Tenet . . .

Q *As you say, a lot of questions were coming about, does the President still have confidence in Mr. Tenet. The CIA was kind of being blamed here for the mistake in the sixteen words, correct?*

A Correct.

Q *Did you have conversations with Bill Harlow that day?*

A I recall a conversation with Mr. Harlow, who is my counterpart at the CIA, the CIA spokesman. I recall on the day before, after Dr. Rice on the flight July 11th said if anybody at the CIA objected to those words, they would have come out, I called Mr. Harlow right after Dr. Rice's briefing to fill him in on what Dr. Rice just said knowing the press would right away start writing stories saying that the White House was blaming the CIA.

Part of my job was to deal with the tension between the White House and the CIA. I called my counterpart to let him know what Dr. Rice said, so he would not have any surprises . . .

Q *How many times did you talk to Bill Harlow that week while you were in Africa?*

A I remember talking to Mr. Harlow on, I believe it was, July 7th, could have been July 8th . . . I called him from Air Force One to say, "I'm being told by Ambassador Bob Joseph, the White House National Security Council, that the CIA did approve those words." [Harlow] said to me, "The CIA did not approve those words."

So the two of us, as spokespeople, were trying to figure out, we were getting different stories from the people we worked for. That's how we would try to coordinate what we would do as we approached our jobs . . .

Q *But . . . Mr. Harlow, who was the press spokesperson for the CIA, and the CIA generally felt the White House was blaming the CIA for the sixteen words being in the State of the Union, right?*

A Yes, sir. Mr. Harlow was not happy when I called him to tell him that Dr. Rice had just said that the if the CIA wanted those words out, they would have come out. He was not pleased to hear that.

Q *All right. Based on the Tenet statement, did you and . . . Dan Bartlett, have a conversation about reaching out to reporters about the Tenet statement?*

A Dr. Tenet's statement included . . . an official from Niger saying that they interpreted what Iraq was doing as an attempt to expand commercial relations between Iraq and Niger, and the official from Niger interpreted this as an overture to discuss uranium sales. So when I had this statement on July 12th, I wanted to let reporters know that the CIA summary actually supported what President Bush had said.

Q *Going back, did you and Dan Bartlett have a conversation about reaching out to reporters?*

A I recall we did. As I recall, on Air Force One flying back from Nigeria, we had talked about the CBS report that said the President had knowingly lied to the country, that he had the information that the report was false about Niger and he said it anyway. So I remembered talking to Mr. Bartlett saying we should call reporters and find out who else is writing this story . . .

I remember what I did. I called one reporter, Walter Pincus at *The Washington Post.* I think I believe that I tried to call another reporter at *The New York Times* but never reached anybody. And those are the calls that I made. I couldn't tell you what Mr. Bartlett did.

Q *Is it a fact, Mr. Fleischer, that you and Dan Bartlett, on July the 12th on the plane headed back from Africa, agreed to contact several, print and television media* *journalists?*

A That's my recollection, yes.

Q *And did you decide that you would contact* The New York Times *and* The Washington Post?

A That's my recollection.

Q *When you called, did you call somebody at* The Washington Post *as well—Walter Pincus?*

A Correct.

Q *Walter Pincus, can you say what area he writes in . . . ?*

A Walter Pincus covers intelligence matters for *The Washington Post . . .*

Q *[D]id you tell Walter Pincus, during that conversation on July 12th, that Wilson's wife worked at the CIA?*

A No, sir. I have no recollection of telling that to—

Q *No recollection of telling him that at all? You would remember if it happened—*

A Sure I would. I do not.

Q *And the immunity agreement that you're testifying under, by the way, is that something that your lawyer sought from the prosecutors, Mr. Fitzgerald and his team, back in February of 2004?*

A I couldn't tell you the exact date. I don't recall. It was right around that time frame . . .

Q *. . . I just asked you about Mr. Pincus and whether you told Mr. Pincus. You were asked about that at the Grand Jury, were you not?*

A That's correct.

Q *You testified under oath about that?*

A That's correct.

Q *You testified that you didn't tell Mr. Pincus anything about that?*

A Absolutely correct.

Q *You've not been prosecuted for perjury; is that correct?*

A That's absolutely correct . . .

Q *Mr. Fleischer, one thing that is memorable about your conversation with Mr. Libby is that you discussed the Miami Dolphins, right? You don't meet a whole lot of other people in Washington who are Miami Dolphins fans, right?*

A I do. I try to hang around them, but no objection—you don't often find them.

Q *But one thing you remember about that meeting was that Mr. Libby was a Miami Dolphins fan?*

A That is correct.

Q *As a matter of fact, let me show you what we've marked as Defendant's Exhibit 1647. Do you recognize this as the letter that you received?*

A Yes, sir.

Q *A letter you received from Scooter Libby?*
A Correct.

Q *It's dated July 10, '03, but you were in Africa at the time, correct?*
A That's correct. This was given to me on July 14th.

Q *The day after you returned?*
A Yes, sir.

Q *And your last day as Press Secretary?*
A Correct, sir . . .

Q *Would you read the letter?*
A Dated July 10, 2003. "Dear Ari. Without you, who will I turn to for solace on the Dolphins or Yankees? It will be lonely indeed. It will also be a lot less fun. But what a difference you have made for the President, Vice President and the country. You have been a one-man department of Homeland defense and occasional offense. Both are widely appreciated by your fans. We will still count on you to come to our rescue whenever the going gets tough. Best of luck. Scooter Libby."

MR. JEFFRESS: I pass the witness, Your Honor.
THE COURT: Redirect?

Redirect examination by Mr. Zeidenberg:

Q *I want to go back to a couple other questions that defense counsel asked you. Do you recall when he asked you if you thought that the information about the wife was significant and he asked you to read a portion of your Grand Jury [testimony] on page 40, Line 6. I'll show it to you. Can you see that from where you are?*
A Yes, sir.

Q *I believe Mr. Jeffress asked you to start at Line 6 where it says, "And it struck me that it was not material. The press would not find it interesting one way or the other if his wife sent him" . . . I'd ask you now if you could read the first part of that sentence?*
A "Other than one little piece that seemed to me to back up the CIA sent him or his wife sent him. Other than that, I thought it was a discussion about nepotism and I always, as Press Secretary, ask myself how would the press react to this information."

Q *The one little piece of information you're referring to in that answer is what?*
A That his wife sent him, which validated what I had said previously at the briefing, which documented as far as I was concerned that I was right when I said the CIA sent him on his own volition because I had that piece now to back it up . . .

Q *Now, when Mr. Jeffress was asking you some questions about your lunch conversation with Mr. Libby on July 7, 2003, at one point, in response to one of his questions, you indicated that you couldn't answer. Your memory wasn't clear to an absolute certainty. Do you recall giving that answer?*

A Yes.

Q *Can you explain to the ladies and gentlemen what portion of your testimony you were referring to when you said, you didn't have absolute certainty in your mind?*

A The only portion at lunch that I don't have certainty in my mind about was the piece about whether he indeed said the name. The rest I have certainty about.

Q *So the question about whether or not he discussed the wife. Is there any question in your mind about that?*

A No, sir. He told me that his wife sent him, that she worked at the CIA . . .

Q *To this day, do you have any animus or ill will towards Mr. Libby?*

A No, sir.

MR. ZEIDENBERG: I have no further questions, Your Honor.

THE COURT: Anything from the jury?

THE COURT: Some of the questions that you have submitted would call for this witness to speculate in order to respond to them. And witnesses can't speculate. They can only testify based on the actual knowledge that they have. So in reference to those questions, I'm not going to be able to ask him about that.

As I said in my preliminary instructions to you, if I've decided not to ask a question, I've concluded the question is not appropriate. Therefore the person who asked that question has to disregard the fact that they did ask it and cannot speculate as to what the answer would have been.

Mr. Fleischer, . . . at the gaggle that Dr. Rice had on Air Force One, why didn't you say anything about Valerie Wilson at that time?

THE WITNESS: My reason was I never really thought much about the information that I had been provided at that lunch. Really it kind of became something, I thought, maybe I should say it because I heard it from two people. After I saw that CBS report that said the President knowingly deceived the country, what struck me was that could be because if people believed what Ambassador Wilson had said, the Vice President sent him, the Vice President saw the report. If the Vice President knew it is wrong, the President must know it's wrong.

So that's when I thought my job was to explain why the President did what he did. So it was the combination of hearing it from two people. And that CBS report made me think maybe I'll try it. I'll say it and see if these reporters are thinking it means anything to them . . .

THE COURT: As the Press Secretary, did you think it was proper to ask Mr. Libby if what he told you about Mr. Wilson's wife was classified given that Mr. Libby said "this is hush hush" during the lunch?

THE WITNESS: No. I had never heard those words before, "hush hush, QT," in association with anything involving national security. The fact also that Mr. Libby had never previously been somebody who gave me information, was someone that never raised an alarm bell in my head that I should do that extra level of due diligence. Looking back, I wish I had. But at the time, at that moment, absolutely not. Didn't fit that category of classified.

THE COURT: You previously had testified about the procedure that was used when classified information was verbally communicated to you. What was that?

THE WITNESS: The procedure is very strict. And in my time at the White House, any time anybody from the National Security Council would orally say to me something that was classified, it always began "the following is classified, you cannot use it."

I think the reason for that, in my case especially as I'm the Press Secretary, by definition, I talk to the press. So I think there is a extra level of care that when somebody says something to me, the procedure is strict.

They need to preface it that way. So no, it did not occur to me that "hush hush, QT," would be the indication of something that was classified.

Mr. Zeidenberg asks yet another, brief round:

Q *Finally, Mr. Fleischer, you testified that you believed that the name Valerie Plame or Plame was used. The question is what makes you think that the name was used during that lunch?*

MR. JEFFRESS: Objection.

THE COURT: Overruled.

THE WITNESS: My memory. I just recall, I recall the lunch that Mr. Libby said that name.

MR. ZEIDENBERG: Nothing further, Your Honor.

Mr. Fleischer is dismissed and the next witness, David Addington, is brought in.

DAVID ADDINGTON

DAVID ADDINGTON REPLACED Libby as Chief of Staff to Vice President Cheney when Libby was forced to resign upon his indictment in October 2005. Before that, he was Counsel to the Vice President, and one of the key figures in the Bush administration's efforts to expand the power of the executive branch. Addington testified about a key conversation with Libby during the week of July 6–12 in which Libby asked him about what paperwork would exist at the CIA if the spouse of an employee was sent on a mission for the Agency, and about the president's powers to declassify classified material just on his own say so. (Not surprisingly, Addington took an unequivocal stance in favor of such presidential power.) In his closing argument, Fitzgerald would seek to pinpoint this conversation as taking place shortly before Libby's July 8 meeting with Judith Miller, and therefore another instance where Libby was discussing Wilson's wife shortly before the conversation with Russert during which Libby claimed to have been surprised to learn that Wilson's wife worked at the CIA.

Libby had testified before the grand jury that the conversation with Addington covered the declassification power of the president and only whether there was a contractual obligation for Wilson with respect to his mission, not specifically anything about a spouse. Libby also testified that he was in effect asking Addington about the power of the president to declassify the October 2002 NIE by fiat, which he and Cheney were involved in. It is noteworthy, therefore, that both Libby (in the grand jury) and Addington (at trial) testify that Libby did not specify what classified documentation or information he was interested in getting the president to declassify. On cross-examination, the defense confronts Addington with his initial testimony to the FBI and the grand jury, in which he described Libby's question about CIA contracts in vaguer terms, leaving out the issue of a spouse at the Agency. Addington was firm in his recollection that Libby had asked him a question specifically about documentation regarding a spouse, and he inferred that Libby was talking about Joe Wilson.

Addington introduces substantial evidence about the nature of the investigation itself, since he was deeply involved in the production of documents from the Office of the Vice President in response to requests and subpoenas from the FBI and subsequently from the grand jury. As such, his testimony is used to head off a challenge to the materiality of Libby's false statements, a requirement to prove the offenses with which Libby was charged. Finally, Addington testifies about a conversation with Libby during the early stages of the investigation in which Libby asked Addington, who had been General Counsel at the CIA, how one would know if a CIA employee were covert. Addington followed up his initial, oral response by giving Libby a copy of the Intelligence Identities Protection Act.

Q *Did there come a time in the summer of 2003 when you had a conversation with Mr. Libby about declassification authority?*
A Yes.

Q *Can you tell us about that conversation and where it took place?*
A Well, it took place in the Chief of Staff's office to the Vice President, which is in the West Wing of the White House. Chief of Staff has a small office in the West Wing of the White House, then a larger office over with the rest of the White House staff in the Old Executive Office Building across the street. That's a very small office. Probably about the size of the table that your government attorneys are sitting at. They're not very big, maybe six by ten feet, big enough for a desk and a chair.

The question was asked of me during our conversation by Scooter Libby, did the President have authority to declassify information. And the answer I gave was, of course, yes . . . [I]t's clear that the President has the authority to determine what constitutes a national security secret and who can have access to it.

I cited a specific case as authority for that proposition, which is *Department of the Navy vs. Egan*, decided by the U.S. Supreme Court back in the 1980s. In that case, the Court specifically said that the President, by virtue of his constitutional authority as President and Commander in Chief, had the authority to determine what constitutes a national security secret and who has access to it. And it says that that authority of the President flows directly from the Constitution and is not dependent upon a legislative grant of power from the Congress.

…[T]herefore, I said the President does have the authority, even though there is a separate provision in Executive Order 21958 that requires the President is to govern national security information. Although there are procedures in there for how you go about declassifying, that would not prevent the President himself directly from doing it correctly, as specified procedures in that Executive Order.

Q *Just a couple of quick follow-up questions on that. In your mind, when he asks you this question, was this a gray area or was this open and shut?*
A It was open and shut.

Q *When you cited the* Department of Navy vs. Egan, *was that a case that you had in your fingertips or did you need to go do some research and get back to him?*
A That's a case that I had dealt with regularly and was familiar with.

Q *What, if any, context did Mr. Libby give you as to why he asked the question?*
A He didn't give me any. He just asked the question about the President's power.

Q *Did Mr. Libby indicate whether or not he had in mind what he was going to do with any of the information that was declassified?*
A No, he just asked the question about the President's power to declassify.

Q *During this same time frame, did you have a conversation with Mr. Libby about CIA paperwork?*
A Yes.

Q *Can you tell us that conversation?*
A He asked me the question whether, if somebody worked out at the CIA and the CIA sent the person's spouse on a trip to do something for the CIA, would there be records out at the CIA of that. That was a normal question for him to ask me because [he] knew I [had] worked at the CIA.

What I said was it depended, the kind of paperwork would depend on whether you were on the operational side of the CIA, the folks that run spies overseas if you will, or it was on the analytical side, the folks at CIA that write reports for policymakers and so forth about what is going on in the world.

He asked me the question whether, if somebody worked out at the CIA and the CIA sent the person's spouse on a trip to do something for the CIA, would there be records out at the CIA of that.

I told him on the operational side, the CIA officers are not just free to go out and use whoever they want in their operations. They have to get permission known as operational approval from their higher-ups within the Director[ate] of Operations at the CIA. The course of requesting permission to go recruit or use somebody in an operation would generate paperwork approval within a Directorate of Operations at the CIA of that.

I said on the analytical side it would be likely that you would have a letter of instruction or contract or something evidencing that somebody was being asked to go and do something. And that, in any case, this is the government. When you spend money, there's almost always a money trail or receipt or something for the use of money. So there would be likely that there would be record out there.

I did tell him also that it had been 20 years since I worked at CIA so my knowledge was old. But I was pretty confident that was the way the Agency would still run.

Q *During this conversation, did Mr. Libby indicate to you why he was asking the question?*
A No.

Q *Did he give you a name of any particular person that he was inquiring about?*
A No.

Q *Where did this conversation about the CIA paperwork take place?*
A In that little office I described, the Chief of Staff of the Vice President in the West Wing of the White House.

Q *You described a conversation about declassification and you described a conversation about CIA paperwork. Were they the same conversation?*
A I believe so, yes.

Q *Do you know if the doors were opened or closed during this conversation?*
A Closed.

Q *Was there any reaction given to you about the level of your voice during the conversation?*
A At one point, he extended his hands out and pushed them down a little like that, that would indicate hold your voice down.

Q *Do you recall any further conversation besides any discussion about declassification and the paperwork?*
A No, not in that conversation.

Q *Okay. How did the conversation end?*
A I remember him getting up and going out the door.

Q *Do you know where he went?*
A He hooked a left around the executive secretary's desk and into the Vice President's office, following somebody. I think it was Steve Hadley. It looked like they were going in for a meeting with the Vice President.

Q *Can you date this conversation as best you can as to what had occurred?*
A It would have been after Mr. Wilson, Ambassador Wilson was on television. He

did Mr. Russert's *Meet the Press* Sunday talk show. It would have been after that because that's, I remember that in my mind is sort of, once I knew that, you knew the Wilson thing was going on. I think it was appearing in the papers at the time.

It would have been before we went on the *Reagan* aircraft carrier trip. . . . The number of the folks on the staff who had worked for Ronald Reagan, like I had, had gotten invited to go with the Vice President on that trip, which was a Saturday, mid-July roughly.

Q *Why is it that you're certain that the conversation took place after Mr. Wilson's appearance on* **Meet the Press?**

A Well, that's when Wilson came into my awareness as a sort of a hot topic, if you will, to be aware of. I remember thinking at the time of the conversation with Mr. Libby, . . ."I wonder if he's asking me about [the] CIA . . . if it's about Wilson." He didn't use the name Wilson. It was in my head thinking that that might be Wilson.

Q *Prior to that conversation, had you been aware from anyone that Mr. Wilson's wife worked at the CIA or was believed to work there?*

A No, and I wasn't aware of it from that conversation either. That was just me sort of thinking, this may be about Wilson, but he didn't use the name. And I don't remember being aware of the, gee, Wilson had a wife in the CIA unless later I read the column that Mr. Novak wrote in *The Washington Post* . . .

MR. FITZGERALD QUESTIONS Mr. Addington about document production in the context of the investigation:

Q *Mr. Addington, was it your understanding that the document production requests were limited to documents only concerning conversations with Mr. Novak, Royce or Phelps at this time?*

A No.

Q *The document that was in between the two dates, February 1, 2002 and September 30, 2003, that fell in any of these three categories would have been responsive to the instruction I sent out? Just so it's clear, if a person had a document concerning any conversation with Mr. Novak about any topic, did you understand that to be responsive?*

A Yes, if it fell within those two dates. The category C does not limit it to subject matter. It simply says if it occurred between the two dates and it was a contact with any of those three people, or with anybody acting for them, it would be responsive.

Q *If it was in the relevant timeframe and it was contact with a reporter other than those three named, but had concerned Mr. Wilson, his trip to Niger or his wife's purported relationship to the CIA, would that be responsive?*

A Yes, it would fall under category A or B.

ADDINGTON IS EXCUSED for the day, and his testimony continued the next morning.

JANUARY 30, 2007

DAVID ADDINGTON (continued)

DAVID ADDINGTON RESUMES TESTIFYING on January 30 and continues to confirm the details of the investigation before finishing his direct testimony by recounting a conversation he had with Libby in the fall of 2003 during the early stages of the leak investigation:

Q *Now, yesterday, you described a conversation with Mr. Libby in the summer of 2003 where he asked you about the paperwork that would be done at the CIA if an employee sent a spouse on a trip. Did you ever have a later occasion to discuss [this] with Mr. Libby . . . ?*

A Yes. Not specific employees, but in general—right before, when the investigation started. It would be the end of September of 2003.

Q *And why don't you describe what you recall about that conversation.*

A It was in the larger office of the Chief of Staff to the Vice President that's over in the Old Executive Office Building. It started—I don't remember exactly how he opened it, but it was clear to me from that that the subject of the conversation was going to be this case. And so I did something which is very standard that I did with him, and also with other employees, reminding them that I was an attorney for the government, not their private attorney. So they needed to remember that if they communicate things to me in the context of a criminal investigation under the case here in the District of Columbia that wouldn't necessarily be privileged.

He responded with a sort of "Thank you for the professional warning[.] I just want to tell you, I didn't do it." I didn't inquire what the "it" was.

Q *And what else was said during the conversation?*

A He asked me . . . how you would know, if you met somebody from the CIA, whether they were undercover . . .

. . .[A]s I mentioned earlier in my testimony, he knew I had worked at the CIA, so that's a reasonable question to ask me. [A]nd I said, . . . when I worked out there . . . I either made a point of not remembering the name or, if somebody introduced themselves, you would ask them if they were undercover so you'd . . . know to be careful with their names.

[H]e said, "Yeah, you used to work there, but just, you know, regular people, meeting somebody who is undercover in the CIA, how would you know if they introduced themselves, 'Hi, I'm so-and-so from the CIA?'"

And the answer, of course, is you wouldn't know whether they were undercover from a normal introduction like that. And that's what I told him, that you wouldn't know unless you ask or they tell you or you read it on a piece of paper where it's classified.

Q *And did you have any further conversation that day in relation to the investigation?*

A Yes. It may have been the tail end of that or maybe I called him afterwards, but I volunteered to him I could get him a copy of the Intelligence Identities Protection Act, which is the statute that, under very technical circumstances, makes it a crime to reveal the identity of a covert agent. And I took a copy of that, highlighted the parts that are relevant to government employees and took it down to his office and gave it to him.

Q *Did you have any further conversation with him about that following that?*

A No.

MR. FITZGERALD: Nothing further, Judge.

THE DEFENSE BEGINS ITS CROSS-EXAMINATION by asking Addington about that fall 2003 conversation:

By Mr. Wells:

Q *Good morning, Mr. Addington.*

A Good morning, sir.

Q *Let's start with the last conversation you referred to, during which Mr. Libby came to you right at the beginning of the investigation and indicated to you that he did not do it. Okay?*

A Yes, sir. Except it wasn't him coming to me. I went to his office.

Q *Okay. And he told you, "I did not do it," right?*

A Yes.

Q *You were the lawyer for the Office of Vice President, correct?*

A Yes, sir.

Q *And you told Mr. Libby during that conversation that anything he said to you would not be privileged and that you were not his personal lawyer, right?*

A Not privileged in the context of a criminal investigation.

Q *Okay. So you made it clear to him any question he asked you or anything he said to you was not privileged and could be revealed, if requested, to the government, right?*

A In the context of a criminal investigation . . .

Q *Okay. And it was in that conversation where you made clear there was no privilege and nothing would be secret, that Mr. Libby asked you a fairly simple question, in essence, how would you know if somebody was undercover, right?*

A Yes.

Q *Okay. And you understood that Mr. Libby knew that you used to work in the general counsel's office of the CIA, right?*

A I know he knew that I worked at the CIA. I don't know whether he knew I worked in that particular office.

WELLS THEN QUESTIONS ADDINGTON about the document production Addington ran for OVP. A number of intriguing, though unexplained features come up, such as the fact that there was an envelope full of documents from OVP that for some unexplained reason even Addington did not review. Apart from that, however, Addington reviewed all the documents from OVP and all its members. Another new revelation is that Addington was present for the interviews of witnesses from the OVP, including Libby's then-assistant Jenny Mayfield and Assistants to the Vice President Dean McGrath and Debra Heiden. The defense is making the point that Addington had more than personal knowledge of the case, which ultimately leads to a very intriguing disclosure:

Q *Okay. And you knew fairly early on that you were likely to be a witness in the case based on your personal knowledge, right?*
A The point at which I knew I was likely to be a witness in the case was when the government went to interview the Vice President and indicated they would prefer I didn't come and that only his private attorney came.

Q *Okay.*
A I don't remember when that interview occurred, but I am guessing in 2004 at some point.

THE DEFENSE REPEATEDLY QUESTIONS Addington about the fact that he testified after gaining more than personal knowledge, presumably to throw some doubt on his testimony. The defense then introduces Government Exhibit 104 (and GX 104T, the transcription of it; see appendix), which is Libby's note from his conversation with Cheney in early-to-mid June 2003 during which Cheney evidently told Libby that Wilson's wife worked in the Counterproliferation Division of the CIA. The point the defense is making, it appears, is that Libby was forthcoming with the investigation and responsive to the government's requests.

Q *And the way you got—and the way you received the document was you advised Mr. Libby that there was a request for documents by the government in connection with the investigation in this case, and he gave you that document in response to the request for documents, correct?*
A That's correct, the same way the other employees would have received the same memo and sent back their responsive documents.

Q *Okay. But Mr. Libby gave you the document?*
A Mr. Libby did, yes, sir. He produced it. I should say either he produced it or had his staff produce it, but it came to me.

Q *And you had made clear at the time you requested the documents that you were requesting the documents to give the documents to the government, right?*

A Yes, that's correct. Everybody understood that . . .

Q *Sure. Okay. Now, the document has a date in the top left-hand corner of 6/12/03, right?*

A Yes, it does, with a mark over the 12 . . .

Q *The document that you got either from Mr. Libby or Mr. Libby's staff for you to produce to the government shows the phrase "CP/—his wife works in that division." Do you see that?*

A Yes, sir.

Q *And if we go to the transliteration—q. I want to read that. It says—6/12/03 is the date. Then it says, "telephone—Vice President re: uranium in Iraq - Kristof New York Times article." Then it has a sign. Do you know what that sign means, the dot and the open paren?*

A . . . No, I don't know what that means.

Q *Okay. Then it says, "took place at our behest. functional office." Then it says, "CP —his wife works in that division."*

Now, did you come to understand, based on your review of all of his documents, that at least based on your analysis of the documents, that that exhibit showed that Mr. Libby had been told on June 12th, 2003, by the Vice President of the United States, that Mrs. Wilson worked in the CP section of the CIA? Did you understand that?

A No, I didn't draw that conclusion from this document. I didn't do analysis. I just went through these things and—

Q *Sure.*

A —sent them to the government. And you said something about it says that the V.P. told him this. And I didn't get that from the document either at the time I reviewed it or now, reading it.

Q *Okay. But it says, "telephone—V.P.," right?*

A Well, again, if I could see the original.

I can't testify as to what the symbol before the dash means. If that's a "t" and it means telephone, somebody else can testify to that. I really couldn't say that.

I am familiar with the sort of "y" looking letter with the slash over it. That appears enough in his records that I figured out that was his symbol for Vice President. So—

Q *And you do see right there it says, "CP/—his wife works in that division"?*

A Yes, sir.

Q *Based on your having worked at the CIA, what do the initials "CP" stand for? What could they stand for?*

A Based on my having worked at the CIA, I would have had no idea. I know today, just because of what I have read and so forth, I think that "CP" stands for Counterproliferation. The initials "CP" will appear a lot in Mr. Libby's documents.

A lot of times it's a reference to Colin Powell, who was the Secretary of State.

Here, I don't think it refers at all to that CP, and so it strikes me that this probably could mean Counterproliferation.

Q *Okay. Now, it states quite clearly his wife works in that division, right?*
A Yes, sir.

Q *You took the document that Mr. Libby or his staff gave to you and you produced it to the government?*
A Yes, sir, in the normal course of the document production.

WELLS NEXT INTRODUCES Libby's notes of his conversation with Addington in July 2003:

Q *Now, you testified yesterday that you recall having a meeting with Mr. Libby in Mr. Libby's anteroom in the West Wing, correct?*
A Yes, sir. He has a little office there.

Q *Okay. And it's a very small office. It's almost like a big closet, right?*
A Yes, sir.

Q *Is it your office today?*
A Yes, sir.

Q *Okay. And I don't think you testified yesterday as to how long that meeting was. Is it correct that the meeting was approximately two minutes?*
A Maybe that long. Very short meeting.

> *I am not sure he worded it exactly like that, but the substance is correct, that part of the conversation on declassification was me pointing out that there is an executive order that has a procedure for declassifying, but because the originating authority for all of that, the source authority, if you will, is the constitutional authority of the President, he could choose to exercise it himself without going through that procedure.*

Q *Okay. And during the approximately two-minute meeting, you and Mr. Libby discussed two subjects, right?*
A During the meeting, we discussed the paperwork—would there be paperwork at the CIA, and we discussed whether the President had authority to declassify.

Q *Okay. And with respect to whether the President had authority to declassify, Mr. Libby was asking you if the President of the United States could declassify a document on his own without going through the normal declassification process that exists in the federal regulations, right?*
A I am not sure he worded it exactly like that, but the substance is correct, that part of the conversation on declassification was me pointing out that there is an execu-

tive order that has a procedure for declassifying, but because the originating authority for all of that, the source authority, if you will, is the constitutional authority of the President, he could choose to exercise it himself without going through that procedure.

Q *Right. Okay. So you understood that the thrust of his question was whether the President could do it on his own?*

A I don't know about the word "thrust." He simply asked the question, could the President do it on his own? And my answer was yes.

Q *Okay. And you told him that the President did have the power, if he wanted to, to declassify any document or any portion of a document that he decided was appropriate?*

A I told him the President had the power to declassify any U.S. national security secret, yes; it would include portions or a whole document, if—

Q *Right. And the President would have the power not only to declassify a particular document; he would have the power to declassify that document and restrict its disclosure to a small group of people if he so decided, correct?*

MR. FITZGERALD: Objection, your Honor.
THE COURT: Approach.
(Sealed bench conference.)

THE BENCH CONFERENCE evidently deals with the issue of the declassification of the October 2002 NIE, and the court takes a recess for the parties to write out the instruction Walton goes on to give. Wells resumes his cross-examination concerning a note of Libby's that referred to a key conversation with Addington, but first Judge Walton addresses the jury:

THE COURT: Let me give you a further instruction at this time regarding the national intelligence estimate, also known as the NIE.

You have heard evidence regarding discussions Mr. Libby had with reporters about material contained in the October 2002 National Intelligence Estimate, also known as the NIE. There is no dispute that the President has the power to declassify previously classified information and to authorize its disclosure to the press, nor is there any dispute that at least as of July 8th, 2003, the President had exercised that power with respect to portions of the NIE in question in this case.

In other words, the government does not contend that Mr. Libby did anything improper during those parts of the conversations he had with reporters on or after July 8th, 2003, when he discussed portions of the NIE that had been declassified by the President.

MR. WELLS: Thank you, Your Honor. I will move on.

Q *Prior to your interview with the FBI, you had reviewed the document that is now in evidence as 178A, correct? [See appendix.]*

A I am not certain whether I had or not. It wouldn't surprise me at all; I just can't be sure of the timing. I certainly had seen it before I went to the Grand Jury.

Q *Okay. And that particular document makes reference to you by name, and it has the word "Addington" on it, correct?*

A Yes.

Q *And it says, "Addington on 1) declass; 2) Wilson contract," right?*

A The handwritten part says, "Wilson k." The symbol "k" is often used by lawyers to refer to a contract . . .

Q *And in your testimony yesterday, you said that Mr. Libby, in the discussion with you, used the term "spouse" with respect to the portion of the conversation dealing with the CIA, right?*

A Yes, sir.

Q *Okay. And at least in that section of the note, there is no reference to spouse, correct?*

A Correct.

WELLS SHOWS ADDINGTON NOTES from his FBI interview indicating that he had indeed discussed it, and then questions Addington about the notation further down on Libby's notes indicating that Addington had told Libby about the relevant case on Presidential powers of declassification, *Navy v. Egan.* Wells's point seems to be twofold: to suggest that Addington, having reviewed these notes before handing them over to investigators, may have gotten false memories from the notes; and to point out that there is no evidence in Libby's note of Libby talking about a spouse at the CIA.

Wells moves on to more from the same page of Libby's notes, a passage evidently taken down during a senior staff meeting. The point here seems to be to elicit some evidence about Rove for Libby's defense that he was sacrificed for Rove's sake.

Q *Okay. Now, just to finish going through the note, there is a section that says, "senior staff." . . . And the transliteration states, "senior staff: uranium story is becoming question of President's trustworthiness and leads all news. Turning to process: Rove: now they have accepted Joe Wilson as credible expert. We're 1 day late with getting CIA right response."*

In terms of the reference to senior staff, what do you understand that to refer to?

A Because it refers to Mr. Rove, that indicates that it would be the President's senior staff meeting rather than the Vice President's senior staff meeting. Each day at the White House there is a—on most days there is a meeting of the assistants to the President in the morning to discuss what happened yesterday, what might happen tomorrow and today, and that sort of thing.

Q *And Karl Rove would attend those meetings?*

A All the assistants to the President normally do, which would include him.

Q *Okay. And so the note at least suggests that Mr. Rove has . . . said, now they have accepted Joe Wilson as a credible expert, right?*

A That's what the transliteration said, and I think I can read that pretty much in the handwritten part, too. The transliteration seems to be an accurate reflection of what's written there that's readable about Rove commenting.

Q *Do you have any personal information concerning the actions of Karl Rove with respect to disclosing information about Ms. Wilson's employment to reporters?*

A No, I do not.

Q *Now, you have indicated that Mr. Libby's note does not use the word "spouse" or "wife," correct?*

A Yes, sir.

Q *And the note I am referring to now is defendant's 178A.*

A Yes, sir.

Q *Okay. There is another note that does have the word "wife," right, the first note that I showed you? That's 104-T where it said, "CP/—his wife works in that division". . .*

A Yes. It says CP, in capital letters, slash. There is a line drawn down. It says, "his wife works in that div'n," which I think means division.

Q *Okay. So the note that appears to refer to the discussion in the ante-room does not contain either the word "spouse" or "wife," right?*

A Correct.

Q *Okay. Now, you testified yesterday that when Mr. Libby was asking you a question about what type of CIA paperwork would be involved with respect to a trip, that Mr. Libby said, what would be involved if a spouse had been sent on a trip by a CIA employee? Right?*

A That's my recollection.

Q *Okay. And—now, you indicated already you were interviewed by the FBI on February 12, 2004, right?*

A The government stipulated to that, yes, sir.

Q *Right. And during that interview, you were asked to describe your conversations with Mr. Libby in the anteroom, correct?*

A I am not sure I have an independent memory of that, but that's what the paragraph said in this FBI report you showed me. It seems reasonable . . .

Q *Mr. Addington, is it correct that, as you sit there now, you do not have a specific recollection one way or the other as to whether, in your February 2004 interview, you used the term "spouse" or "wife" in connection with your describing a conversation in the anteroom?*

A I don't remember the contents of what they asked me and what I answered with the FBI.

WELLS MOVES NEXT TO QUESTION Addington about his interactions with Alberto Gonzales, then White House Counsel, in turning over documents to investigators. Addington's responses reveal an interesting fact: Gonzalez was able to review just about all the document production coming out of the OVP, which meant he had access to substantial evidence not from the White House proper. The defense's point seems to be to note that the White House became aware of Cheney's provocative note about the "meat grinder." But in the course of testifying, Addington recounts an extraordinary story about a contentious discussion he had with White House Communications Director Dan Bartlett:

Q *Now, in connection with your review of the documents in this case, is it also correct that you had a practice of having discussions with White House Counsel Alberto Gonzales with respect to the documents—with respect to certain of the documents that you were collecting?*

A I am not certain all of them. What I would do is when I got a package ready to produce to the government, I would let him look at those.

Occasionally that involved discussion. Most times, probably not, just flipping through and looking at them.

Q *And Alberto Gonzales is now the Attorney General?*

A That's correct.

Q *And at that time, Alberto Gonzales was White House Counsel?*

A He was counsel to the President.

Q *And as counsel to the President, Mr. Gonzales's job was to protect the interests of the Office of the President?*

A As counsel to the President, his job would be, first and foremost, to support and defend the constitution; second, to protect the legal interests of the institution of the Presidency, and third, protect the official interests of the incumbent President.

Q *Okay. And your job as Counsel to the Vice President was the same, only with respect to the Office of the Vice President?*

A That's correct.

Q *Okay. And the procedure that was set up was that after you reviewed the documents, you would then go and meet with Mr. Gonzales and either permit him to personally review the documents or to describe to him what you had found in the documents, right?*

A I would take the package over that I had prepared and signed out and ready to go, and take it over to him and he could go through it.

Q *Okay. And with respect to witness interviews that you attended, you would report to him about the nature of the witness interviews?*

A I don't recall doing that. I don't have a hard recollection that I didn't, either, but I don't recall doing that.

Q *Okay.*

A Frankly, the witness interviews I got to sit in didn't strike me as terribly big or important.

Q *Do you recall having discussions with Alberto Gonzales, the counsel to the President, about a document in the handwriting of the Vice President that indicated that one staffer should not be protected while another staffer was sacrificed?*

A I don't recall whether I discussed it with him or not. I am sure I either discussed it with him or showed it to him—

Q *Okay.*

A — you know, as part of production. I mean, I didn't hold anything back from him. It was in the stacks. He could look at all of it.

Q *I would like to show you a copy of that document. Now, you recall reviewing Government Exhibit 532 in evidence, correct? [See appendix.]*

A I am not really sure I understand the question, but I produced document number 009502 to the government in the course of this investigation.

Q *Okay. And in addition to producing it to the government, you personally reviewed it, right?*

A Yes, sir.

Q *Okay. And it's your recollection that you may have, in fact, had conversations with Alberto Gonzales, Counsel to the President, about the document, right?*

A I think it's likely I showed it to him. I may have talked about it.

Q *And, in fact, when you saw that particular document, you picked up the telephone and called Terry O'Donnell, counsel to the Vice President and told him about that document?*

A He and I may have communicated about it. Whether it was a telephone call or not, I can't say. I might have phoned him. I might have shown it to him. I think probably a phone call.

Q *Right. And you told Mr. O'Donnell you thought this was a very important document, didn't you?*

A I can't recall telling him anything like that.

MR. FITZGERALD: Objection as to relevance.
THE COURT: Sustained.

By Mr. Wells:

Q *Now, the top half of the document is in Mr. Libby's handwriting, correct?*

A I think so, particularly where I see the last line of the top half where it says, "classified information," the word "classified" there looks like his handwriting to me.

Q *And the bottom half of the document is in Vice President Cheney's handwriting, right?*

A Correct.

Q *And Vice President Cheney writes, "has to happen today. call out to key press say-ing same thing about Scooter as Karl. Not going to protect one staffer and sacrifice the guy"—and then something is crossed out. Can you make out what's crossed out, Mr. Addington?*

So "this pres." is crossed out by the Vice President. And the note goes on to read—well, let me just start again: "not going to protect one staffer and sacrifice the guy that was asked to stick his neck in the meat grinder because of the incom-petence of others."

Now, did you come to have any understanding of what was meant by those words, based on your discussion with Mr. Gonzales or Terry O'Donnell?

MR. FITZGERALD: Objection, your Honor.
THE COURT: Sustained.

by Mr. Wells:

Q *As you sit there, you don't have any personal understanding of what was meant by those words, correct?*
A All the knowledge I have about the content of this document is the document itself.

Q *Okay. So you don't know one way or the other, right?*
A No, sir.

Q *Okay. Let's read the top half of the document. And this top half you believe is in Mr. Libby's handwriting, correct?*
A Yes. Except over there in the left-hand corner where it says, "Tenet Wilson memo," I am not quite sure about that.

Q *Okay. In fact, "Tenet Wilson memo," that's in the Vice President's handwriting, isn't it?*
A I think it may be.

Q *Okay. And the top half—before I get there, it says, "the Vice President has seen," and that's in red?*
A Yes, sir.

Q *What does that mean?*
A That's a standard practice in the Vice President's office when he has looked at doc-uments and they come out of his out-box, his executive assistant will take a stamp and mark that the Vice President has seen, and send the documents back to the staff secretary.

Q *So that's done in the normal course of business, right?*
A Yes, sir.

Q *You did not put that on there; it was there when you got it, right?*
A Correct. Yes, sir.

Q *And the note reads, as a block, "people have made too much of the difference in how I described Karl and Libby." Close block. "I've talked to Libby. I said it was ridiculous about Karl, and it is ridiculous about Libby. Libby was not the source of the Novak story. And he did not leak classified information."*

And it's fair to say you have no personal knowledge with respect to what was meant by the words I just read to you, right?

A When you put it that way, yes. I have no idea how these words came to be written or why they were written and so forth. But I can recall that the White House press office—I think it might have been Scott McClellan himself who was then the President's press secretary—had made some statement about Karl, which is what I assume this refers to.

And I know this just because . . . when they make statements out of the press office, transcripts are made and then the staff gets them, and that's how I got it.

And I don't remember exactly what they said, but something that would lead the hearer to assume, oh, they decided, whatever it was that was bad here, Karl Rove didn't do it.

Q *Say it again. Whatever what?*

A Whatever was bad here, Karl Rove didn't do it. In other words, there's some kind of reference to Karl Rove.

Q *They exonerated Karl Rove publicly, right?*

A Yes . . . I don't remember the exact words used, but, yes, that's the purport of it—

Q *But the thrust of—*

A — that was exoneration of Karl Rove.

Q *The thrust of what you recall is that Scott McClellan, the Press Secretary for the President of the United States, had gone out and made a statement exonerating Karl Rove of any misconduct in connection with the controversy surrounding the disclosure of the fact that Mrs. Wilson worked at the CIA, correct?*

A Yes. And essentially—the reason this sticks in my mind is I had a conversation not too many days later with Dan Bartlett, who was then the assistant to the President for communications. And by this point, something had been said—I frankly don't remember what—again, by the press office, and it included Mr. Libby this time. And I made the comment to Mr. Bartlett, you know, I don't know why you are making these statements about, you know, this case—and I will explain why in a second.

But his reaction was, "Well, your boss is the one that wanted us to do it." And then I shut up.

But my reaction to that was, you know, I'm in my 20th year in government, and there are three things press offices generally shouldn't do in the government. One is don't talk about intelligence sources and methods because if you say no, no, no, no, no, denying, you set up a pattern that if somebody ever picks a particular intelligence source and says, "Is that the intelligence source?"—and you say, "Well, I can't confirm or deny it," you've said no. So you basically just can't talk about intelligence sources and methods because your patterns of answers are going to reveal things.

The second thing you shouldn't talk about are rules of engagement for the armed forces, because if you tell people when troops are allowed to shoot and not allowed to shoot and what they're doing out there, you're putting their lives more at risk.

And the third thing you don't talk about is what's going on in a criminal investigation because, frankly, you don't know. And to go out and say somebody did or didn't do something—you have no way of knowing that. You haven't conducted any investigation. That's what the government gets to do.

So my general attitude is those three subjects are not fit subjects generally for a press office to be talking about, and that's why I said that to Mr. Bartlett and got that response.

Q *And when Mr. Bartlett said your boss wanted him to do that, your boss is Vice President Cheney, right?*

A Yes, sir.

Q *What happened initially, as you said, is that the White House went out and exonerated Karl Rove—just Karl Rove, right?*

A The word "exonerated"—you know, they said what they said. You know, the purport[ed] meaning in the way a hearer would have heard it when they heard what they said about Rove is, "Oh, the White House is saying he didn't do it."

Q *Right. And when they exonerated Rove, they did not exonerate Libby, right?*

A My recollection is that—he did just Rove.

Q *Right. And by exonerating Karl Rove in the media and to the public, it created a clear impression that Scooter Libby had done something, correct?*

A I can't reach that conclusion.

Q *Did it create an impression by not exonerating Scooter Libby that he was being hung out as the scapegoat in public?*

A Not to me. What bothered me was the general policy that, in my view, press offices should not be discussing what's going on in criminal investigations, particularly where they don't know.

Q *So when you said to Mr. Bartlett, who is the head of communications at the White House, "Why are you doing this?" he said to you that your boss, the Vice President, in essence instructed him to go out and clear Libby in the same way that the White House had cleared Rove, right?*

A Well, let me just repeat what actually occurred. We were sitting at the White House at the staff table for lunch, which is one table in the mess room where we eat lunch, and anybody can just come in and take a seat; you don't need reservations. And he happened to be at the table that day, and so was I.

. . . I didn't ask him the question, "why did you?" What I just said is, "You know, we ought not to be out there saying people did or didn't do something in a criminal investigation. Why did you do this thing today . . . ?"

And his response was, "Well, your boss is the one who wanted us to."

Q *Wanted them to do it with respect to Mr. Libby, right?*

A Yes, sir.

Q *Okay. Just so that Mr. Libby would be treated by the White House the same way the White House was protecting Karl Rove by exonerating him, correct?*

MR. FITZGERALD: Objection.
THE COURT: Sustained.

AT THAT POINT, WELLS FINISHES UP his cross-examination by questioning Addington extensively about the document requests he got in the context of the investigation, seeking to show that Libby could have believed the investigation was focused solely on leaks to Novak and a pair of *Newsday* reporters, not leaks to reporters concerning Valerie Plame Wilson. After lunch, Fitzgerald takes up the redirect questioning of Addington, and begins with a line of questioning about the correspondence concerning the investigation. Fitzgerald's point is to show that from an early point the scope of the investigation clearly involved leaks to more than just Novak and Royce and Phelps, and Libby was in a position to know that.

Fitzgerald then opens up an intriguing line of questioning concerning the document (GX 104) of Libby's notes from his June 2003 conversation with Cheney about Plame, focusing on the fact that, uniquely among the documents Addington produced on behalf of the Office of the Vice President, the original of this document had been stamped "Treated as TOP SECRET/SCI." The Court evidently holds a closed hearing of the kind used to deal with potentially classified information (a CIPA hearing) which results in the government having the opportunity to try and show that Libby had some involvement in putting that stamp on the document. However, the government did not exercise that opportunity during its case, and the parties agreed later to have the government resubmit that exhibit with the stamp itself redacted, accompanied by a cautionary instruction from the judge.

By Mr. Fitzgerald:

Q *Now, I wanted to . . . focus on the stamp above it that says "treated as crossed out, declassified" . . . I want to come back to "treated as," but do you know what it says underneath "treated as"?*
A It says "treated as TOP SECRET/S.C.I." all in caps and then there's a line through it.

Q *Would the line have been through it when you produced it?*
A No, sir.

Q *Would the word "declassified" have been there when you produced it?*
A No, sir.

Q *What does S.C.I. stand for?*
A Sensitive Compartment Information is information that deals with intelligence sources and methods in the President's executive or classification. Executive Order

12958 authorizes the Director of National Intelligence to put specially sensitive information in a Sensitive Compartment Information. It has entire controls for dealing with that type of information. Fewer people have access to it.

Q *Now, the words "top secret" or "S.C.I."—are those classifications that are assigned to classified documents?*

A Top secret is a classification, and the Sensitive Compartment Information is special access rule. It is not technically a clearance.

Q *...[H]ave you seen documents . . . properly classified as "treated as TOP SECRET/S.C.I."?*

A I had never seen a stamp "treated as TOP SECRET/S.C.I." before documents were produced to me with that stamp on it.

Q *Is that in fact a proper classification?*

A The present Executive Order on classified national security information doesn't use that phrase . . .

Q *Just a question, yes or no, did you put that marking in there?*

A No, sir.

Q *Do you know when, how and who did, from personal knowledge?*

A On this particular page, no. But I can say that, in the course of production, there were situations in which I received in production copies of handwritten notes of Mr. Libby's that were marked treated as TOP SECRET/S.C.I. or treated as SECRET/S.C.I., various stamps saying treated as some particular classification.

That one, the government came back later and said give us the originals and the originals were produced. They would not have that marking on it. From that I would conclude that the documents were taken from his file, provided by his staff, Xeroxed and stamped. However, this one looks like it was stamped right on the original by someone.

Q *Let me move to a different exhibit, Government's Exhibit 532. If we could display that. And you were asked by Mr. Wells whether or not you discussed this document with Mr. Gonzalez when he was White House Counsel, correct?*

A Yes.

Q *You were also asked whether or not you discussed this document with Mr. Terry O'Donnell, correct?*

A Yes, sir.

Q *Could you tell the jury who Terry O'Donnell is?*

A Mr. O'Donnell is a partner in the law firm of Williams & Connolly in Washington, D.C., and has been for many years, the private attorney of Vice President Cheney.

Q *In your capacity at the time as Counsel to Vice President, would you explain the difference between your role and Mr. O'Donnell's role?*

ADDINGTON GIVES a long explanation of the relevant case law, the upshot of which is:

A The criminal context. Having said all that, the reason it's important in this case, not just for Vice President but others involved in the case, is if you want to communicate to an attorney and be represented in this case, you have to talk to your private attorney so that you have the same attorney-client privileges that you would have or Mr. Libby would have or anybody else would have in hiring an attorney.

But if you choose instead, a government employee, to go talk about a case with your government attorney, that government attorney, if . . . summoned to the Grand Jury, like I was, [he] has to answer the question. So, it's important to be careful what you're asking and which attorney is answering it. It's kind of an artificial complexity on representing people that was created by the D.C. Circuit about I guess ten years ago or so.

THE QUESTIONING THEN TURNS to Libby's notes from July 2003 (DX 178) and Fitzgerald focuses on Libby's notes about the senior staff meeting:

Q *First of all, is that a page of Mr. Libby's notes?*
A It's his handwriting, yes, sir.

Q *And the entry about what was said at the senior staff meeting by Mr. Rove, whose handwriting is that?*
A That's in his handwriting.

Q *And at senior staff meetings, do they cover many topics?*
A Oh, yes, sir. I just wanted to add. It's Libby's handwriting on the sliver I'm working on. I'm not working on [the whole] document, but the Rove is all his handwriting.

Q *Now, I'm going to show you . . . 178-AT. I'll ask you to look at that, but I'll tell you the question before you read it. I want you to see if, on Mr. Libby's notes, if there's anything else that he indicates happened at the senior staff meeting that he chose to note in this document or note as happening at the senior staff meeting?*

A The line you referred to where it says senior staff. Then there is a colon and [an] entry references Rove and so forth. Next is dash, dash, 9-11 Commission. Then you see, dash, house labor H.H.S. overtime and disclose, D-I-S-C-L-O-S, then a dash, and then veto threat. And I should add I'm reading from DX-178-AT.1, not the original document.

The next line says, "9-11 commission wants internal e-mails, mark ups of drafts of the President's speech, materials for President's discussion, where, et cetera." At least that far, I suspect that those are notes of what went on in senior staff that day, just because of the variety of information presented there . . . Other than a general staff meeting, you wouldn't be dealing with all those different subjects in one meeting . . .

Q *Is it fair to say, as you sit here now, you can't tell from the documents whether those next three entries were senior staff. . .?*

A No, I cannot tell for sure. It just strikes me that that variety of information in a meeting would be a general kind of staff meeting. But you're right, I can't tell just from looking.

Q *If all four were discussed at senior staff, the first item listed was the comments on the uranium story and Mr. Rove's comments of Joe Wilson before the 9-11 commission?*

A Right. Assuming the notes were taken down in sequence, yes . . .

Q *And the last area, Mr. Wells asked you questions about whether or not you recalled, you told the FBI about a spouse or a wife being discussed with Mr. Libby in that meeting in the anteroom. . . . [D]o you recall whether or not in that conversation with Mr. Libby in the anteroom outside the Vice President's office, you discussed a spouse of a person working at the CIA?*

A Yes, that's my recollection.

MR. FITZGERALD: Thank you.
THE COURT: Anything from the jury? . . .

THE COURT: Mr. Addington, several jurors have a couple of questions. One is a request that you provide clarification as to why, on some occasions, requests for documentation were sent to Mr. Libby, whereas on other occasions, it was not.

THE WITNESS: Yes. As Counsel to the Vice President, when a request comes in from the Department of Justice or from the Grand Jury, I have to make a determination who within the office could reasonably be expected to have responsive documents.

In many cases, as with the first request for example on October 3, 2003 from the Justice Department, it was very broad. So I sent it out to every employee in the place. . .

For some of the later requests, for example, requests for the originals of Scooter Libby's documents, or requests for the originals of Cathie Martin's documents, I only need to send those to Scooter Libby and Cathie Martin.

AFTER A FEW ADDITIONAL QUESTIONS from the jury for Addington, he is excused, and Judith Miller is called.

JUDITH MILLER

I N JUNE 2003, JUDITH MILLER, then a *New York Times* reporter, had just returned from Iraq, where she had been embedded with a military unit searching for—and failing to find—weapons of mass destruction. Miller had a deep interest in that futile search, as she had written (and, with Michael Gordon, co-written) some of the most aggressive and prominent pre-war reports on Iraq's purported WMD and WMD programs. Her longstanding interest in WMD threats and her hawkish reporting on Iraq for the most reputable newspaper in the United States made her a natural ally for Libby, with whom she became acquainted shortly before the war began.

The heart of Miller's testimony was that, on at least two, and possibly three, occasions in June and July 2003, Libby disclosed to her that Joe Wilson's wife worked at the CIA. The most significant of those occasions was on the morning of July 8, when, as Miller testifies, she met Libby for a two-hour breakfast at the St. Regis hotel. She planned to interview him for a story she was working on with a team of reporters about the failure to find WMD, but Libby came with his own agenda. He wanted to focus on the sixteen words controversy. Stipulating that when he spoke about Joe Wilson she must identify him in print as a "former Hill staffer" (though he had not worked in Congress for many years), Libby told Miller that Wilson's wife worked at the CIA.

Following her breakfast meeting with Libby, Miller claims she recommended to a *New York Times* editor that the paper pursue a story on the Wilsons. The story suggestion, if made at all, would not likely have been taken up anyway, because Miller—unbeknownst to Libby—had been restricted in her reporting by the *Times* as a result of her problematic earlier reporting on Iraqi WMD. Despite Libby's determined cultivation of Miller, she never wrote a story for The New York Times about Joe Wilson and Valerie Plame.

ACCORDING TO MILLER'S TESTIMONY, that breakfast meeting was not the first occasion she'd heard about Plame from Libby. She tells the court that Libby first mentioned Plame on June 23, 2003. However, when Miller first testified to the Grand Jury on September 30, 2005—after spending 85 days in jail defying Fitzgerald's subpoena—she overlooked that earlier meeting with Libby. After testifying, she subsequently found below the desk in her office a notebook of the June 23 interview with Libby, which, she claims, spurred her memory of the event. She testifies that, on that day, Libby had told her Wilson's wife worked at the "bureau," that Miller understood to be a nonproliferation unit within the CIA. (Miller returned to the grand jury on October 12, 2005 and testified to her June 23 meeting with Libby.)

Miller is questioned at the beginning of her testimony here about her note-taking practices. Her responses bolster her testimony, which would have otherwise been based on an admittedly shaky memory. Miller also testifies to a follow-up telephone conversation she had with Libby on July 12, 2003 that touched on the subject of Plame. However, Miller's recollection of that discussion is very fuzzy. In fact, the defense successfully got the piece of the obstruction count involving Libby's account of this conversation struck later during the trial.

During the cross-examination, the defense questions Miller aggressively on her lapses in memory. In particular, they target her inability to recall who else she talked to about Wilson's wife after speaking with Libby, even as she acknowledged that she had in fact talked to multiple government officials about the Wilsons. The defense also highlights the fact that Miller required an agreement from Fitzgerald to limit his questioning in order to submit to the subpoena, not just an explicit personal waiver of confidentiality from Libby. In so doing, the defense tries to underline how cooperative Libby had been with regard to Miller.

FITZGERALD BEGINS HIS SUBSTANTIVE questioning by asking Miller about the first time she met Libby:

A He said that he had liked my reporting on weapons of mass destruction and terrorism, the threat of terrorism to the United States. And I expressed a desire to interview him and talk to him on a regular basis, when I was working on something that, in which he might be helpful.

Q *What if anything did he say in response?*

A He said that that would be fine, but that he would prefer not to see his name in print. And that we could continue meeting as long as I agreed to identify him as an Administration official or a senior Administration official.

Q *Did you give any response?*

A I said that would be fine.

Q *First of all, why don't we take a moment, if you could explain the ground rules when you're a journalist and you speak to someone as to what "on the record" means, in your understanding, "off the record," "background," "deep background?"*

A To me, . . . "on the record" meant that one could use the material that the person being interviewed would give you. And that you could cite, you could attribute that information to the individual.

"Background," to me, meant I could use the information, but I could not name the individual but could identify the agency for which he worked or come as close as I could to naming him.

"Deep background" meant that . . . I could use the information, but I could not identify the agent, the agency or the part of the government in which the individual worked.

"Off the record," to me, meant that I could not use the information unless I confirmed it elsewhere. And [I] was able to attribute it elsewhere and not to the source who was providing it.

Q *After this first meeting with Mr. Libby, did you stay in touch with him?*

A I did . . . Usually through his assistant.

Q *Do you remember the name of the assistant?*

A Yes, Jenny.

Q *Did you ever have direct contact with Mr. Libby himself following your first meeting? Did you ever speak to him directly?*

A I believe we talked on the phone a couple of times, a few times.

Q *Did you ever contact Mr. Libby by e-mail?*

A No, I did not.

Q *Why not?*

A I don't believe I had Mr. Libby's e-mail because I don't believe he ever gave it to me.

Q *Let me have you briefly describe to the jury your process of keeping notes when you interview sources.*

A I normally take notes as I'm interviewing someone in a Steno notebook. As I'm interviewing somebody, I try and write down what he or she says, and then I go back after the interview, if it's an important interview, and I will underline or add things. Sometimes I do that . . . contemporaneously with the interview, and sometimes I do it after the fact.

Then, when a notebook is full, I go back and I do an index on the front page of what the notebook contains, who was interviewed, the timing of the interviews and sometimes the subject matter.

Q *Why don't we start with the first piece you described, which is just a particular interview. How much of the writing in your notes would be writing that you wrote down while the interview is actually taking place versus something you went back and checked and added to later?*

A Almost all of it is done contemporaneously with the interview.

Q *If you go back over the interview later, when do you do that in relation to the interview?*

A It depends on whom I'm interviewing. It can be immediately or it can be a day or two afterwards if it's very busy or I'm on deadline.

Q *Would you have any conventions as to what pen or pencil you would use if you went back to make any sort of highlights or changes?*

A Yes, I tend to use a different pen or pencil when I'm going back and adding anything or underlining something so that I know which notes are contemporaneous and which are added from memory after the fact.

Q *What conventions do you use in terms of highlighting in your notes what you believe to be important?*

A That can take several forms. I underline important things. I put an asterisk by them sometimes. I'll put a box around an important subject or topic. When I think that there's something I need to remember to ask or something that I know, I tend to put that either on the back of the preceding page of the notebook so that it's separate from the interview notes, or sometimes in brackets within the actual interview notes.

Q *If, when you're talking to a person and they change topics, do you have any convention that you ordinarily follow when they change topics?*

A Yes, I draw a line across the page.

Q *What do you do if they change ground rules during an interview?*

A I note that in the margin . . .

MILLER THEN EXPLAINS that she had been embedded as a reporter with WMD hunters in Iraq in spring 2003, returning on June 8, then working as part of a team of reporters at the *Times* on the prewar intelligence failures and the hunt for WMD. She was specifically working on the actual hunt for WMD in Iraq, and was supposed to pass on other useful information to other reporters. It was in that context that she met and interviewed Libby, and that he gave her information about Plame:

Q *Did you have a particular piece of that assignment?*

A Yes. I was supposed to write about the actual hunt for weapons of mass destruction on the ground in Iraq and how and why it was flawed. And I was also supposed to provide information for the other part of the project.

Q *So if I understand you correctly, you were focused on the hunt for weapons of mass destruction, but any information you had on other topics you would provide to fellow reporters?*

A Yes.

Q *Can you tell us the state of the public debate over weapons of mass destruction in Iraq when you returned to the United States in June 2003?*

A When I returned, I was surprised to see that there was a great debate building in the United States, a very angry one over whether or not the information about weapons of mass destruction had been distorted or whether or not the White House had actually lied about this information.

Q *Where [was] the [anger] directed at that point?*

A It was directed everywhere, but especially at the Administration, at the media in particular, and me, because I had written several of these stories.

Q *Now, did there come a time, during the month of June 2003, when you met with Mr. Libby?*

A Yes.

Q *Can you tell us where you met with him?*

A I met with Mr. Libby in the Old Executive Office Building.

Q *Do you know the date of that meeting?*

A Yes.

Q *When was that?*

A June 23rd.

Q *Can you describe Mr. Libby's demeanor during that meeting?*

A Yes. Mr. Libby appeared to me to be agitated and frustrated and angry.

Q *How could you tell that?*

A Well, he's a very low key and controlled guy, but he seemed annoyed. And what he said made me think that I was correct in that assumption.

Q *Did he indicate to you what he was annoyed at?*

A Yes. He was concerned that the CIA was beginning to back [pedal] to try and distance itself from the unequivocal intelligence estimates it had provided before the war through what he called a perverted war of leaks.

Q *Did the topic of Mr. Joseph Wilson come up during that meeting?*
A Yes, it did.

Q *What do you recall was said about Mr. Wilson?*
A He said that . . . his office had learned that Mr. Wilson had been sent overseas. I think he was initially referred to as a clandestine guy.

    And that the Vice President's office had actually asked a question about a report in winter of 2002 that Iraq was trying to purchase uranium in Africa. And that the CIA had sent Mr. Wilson out to investigate that claim.

Q *Just so I can make sure I understand it, was Mr. Libby indicating to you that the Vice President's office had sent Mr. Wilson on the trip?*
A No, it was the contrary. He said that he learned that Mr. Wilson had been sent out, but he said that the Vice President did not know that Mr. Wilson had been sent out on this trip . . . Mr. Libby said that the Vice President did not know of Mr. Wilson and that they never got a read out on what Mr. Wilson had or had not found on his trip . . .

Q *Can you describe what Mr. Libby said happened in the winter of '02 and how that related to this trip?*
A He said that there had been reports. A report had gone up to the Hill in, I believe it was, February of 2002 indicating that Iraq was hunting for uranium in Niger. And that the Vice President's office had asked about the implications of that report. And that the Agency had taken it upon itself to send out Mr. Wilson to find out more about that.

Q *Do you know if he used the word "Mr. Wilson" to describe Wilson at that point?*
A In the beginning, he referred to Mr. Wilson as a "clandestine guy."

Q *During your conversation on June 23rd, was there any discussion about Mr. Wilson's wife?*
A Yes.

Q *What was said about Mr. Wilson's wife?*
A …[W]hen Mr. Libby was discussing the intelligence reporting from the CIA, he said that his wife, referring to Wilson, worked in the bureau.

Q *What did you understand bureau to mean?*
A Well, I was a little unsure of what he meant by that because, in the beginning, my understanding of the word bureau is that it applied to the FBI. But in the context of our discussion, . . . I quickly understood that he was referring to the CIA.

Q *Did you understand that to mean any particular bureau in the CIA?*
A I thought he was using the word bureau to mean non-proliferation bureau, but I wasn't sure.

Q *Did you write anything about his reference to the wife working in the bureau in your notes?*
A Yes, I did.

Q *How did you write it in your notes?*

A I wrote it in parentheses.

Q *Why did you put it in parentheses?*

A Because he had mentioned it as an aside, or because I was puzzled by it, I put a question mark after the statement, after the word "bureau."

Q *Why did you put a question mark in your notes?*

A I can't really be sure. I have possible explanations, but I can't be sure.

Q *Was there any other discussion during June 23rd, about the relationship between the White House and the President, on the one hand, and the CIA on the other that you recall?*

A Yes . . .

Q *What do you recall?*

A Mr. Libby seemed really unhappy and irritated . . . [H]e accused the CIA of leaking information that would cast, that would attempt to distance the Agency from its earlier estimates.

And he said that nobody had ever come to the White House from the CIA and said, "Mr. President, this is not correct. This is not right." He felt that, if the CIA had had such doubts, they should have shared them with the President.

Q *Did Mr. Libby discuss with you at all the relevance of Mr. Joe Wilson to this controversy?*

A Yes, he said that people were beginning to focus on Mr. Wilson but that Mr. Wilson was a [ruse]. That was the word he used, "an irrelevancy," he said.

Q *During the course of this meeting, did you cover the area that you were assigned to for your report, concerning the efforts to hunt for weapons of mass destruction on the ground in Iraq?*

A No.

THE COURT: So was he using Wilson's name at that time or was he still referring to him in the terms that you indicated previously?

THE WITNESS: Yes, Your Honor. He referred to him first as a clandestine guy. Then he began talking about Mr. Wilson by name, Joe Wilson.

By Mr. Fitzgerald:

Q *Returning to your . . . discussion about the wife working in the bureau, did Mr. Libby indicate whether or not he had heard that information from other reporters?*

A No.

Q *Now, let me direct your attention forward to the month of July 2003 and to July 6. Did there come a time when you saw an op-ed piece in* The New York Times, *your newspaper then, by Mr. Wilson?*

A Yes.

Q *What was your reaction to that?*

A I was very surprised by it.

Q *Why?*

A Because it was the first time that someone who purported to have been part of the collection mechanism that people had actually investigated weapons of mass destruction, this was the first time that someone was publicly alleging that the Administration had lied or distorted information about WMD in order to go to war. It was a very serious charge. That was the first thing that surprised me.

And the second thing that surprised me was that, since Mr. Wilson wrote that he had gone out on this mission for the CIA, I wondered how the CIA would have permitted him to write such an article attacking the President. So I was curious about both things, the veracity of the allegation and how it was that an agency like the CIA would approve of such an article.

Q *Did there come a time following the publication of Mr. Wilson's op-ed that you met with Mr. Libby again?*

A Yes.

Q *When was that?*

A July 8th.

Q *Where did you meet?*

A We met at the St. Regis Hotel in Washington.

Q *Where in the hotel?*

A In the dining room.

Q *Whose choice was the location?*

A It was Mr. Libby's.

Q *How long did you spend meeting in the dining room?*

A About two hours.

Q *Do you recall if Mr. Libby had any papers or documents with him when you met?*

A I believe he just had a piece of paper in his pocket.

Q *Do you know if it was a single piece of paper or more than one?*

A I don't remember.

Q *What was Mr. Libby's demeanor during the meeting?*

A ...[F]rustrated and somewhat quietly agitated.

Q *What topics did you discuss during the meeting?*

A This was a more wide-ranging discussion about the intelligence that the Administration had collected before the issuing of the National Intelligence Estimate and the presentation by Secretary of State Colin Powell of its case that Iraq had WMD.

Q *By the way, I should have asked this about the June 23rd meeting. Do you recall what the ground rules were on June 23rd?*

A Yes, on June 23rd, Mr. Libby said he wanted this session to be off the record.

Q *Do you know how the meeting, what the understanding was at the beginning of the July 8th meeting?*

A There was no discussion at the beginning of any specific set of attributions.

Q *Did there come a time when, during this meeting, Mr. Wilson was discussed?*

A Yes.

Q *Can you tell us whether the ground rules remained the same or changed?*

A The ground rules changed.

Q *Tell us how that happened?*

A Mr. Libby said that, for, when we shifted into the topic of the alleged Iraqi efforts to acquire uranium, Mr. Libby said, for the purposes of this part of the conversation, he wanted to be identified not as a senior Administration official but on deeper background. I think that he said something like "former Hill staffer."

Q *Had you ever been asked by Mr. Libby before to treat him as a "former Hill staffer?"*

A No.

Q *What was Mr. Libby's demeanor when talking about the controversy concerning Iraq and efforts to obtain uranium from Niger?*

A It was equally frustrated and unhappy.

Q *Can you tell us what, if anything, was discussed about Mr. Wilson on this occasion?*

A Yes. Mr. Libby said that there had been plenty of information, before the NIE was issued and the Powell presentation was given, supporting the notion that Iraq had been hunting for weapons of mass—had been hunting for uranium in Africa.

> *He said that ... there were two reports, one ... [claiming] that Iraq was seeking a long-term arrangement for larger quantities of uranium [and one claiming that] there was a shorter-term effort to acquire a smaller amount of uranium.*

. . . [T]hat in fact it had been shown that Iraq had acquired uranium in Africa prior to the first Gulf War that, in the eighties, the International Atomic Energy Agency had stated in its reports that Iraq had acquired . . . [H]e said that, after that and more recently, there were several different reports that Iraq was in the market again for uranium.

He said that . . . there were two reports, one . . . [claiming] that Iraq was seeking a long-term arrangement for larger quantities of uranium [and one claiming that] there was a shorter-term effort to acquire a smaller amount of uranium.

He then referred to another report[;] I thought it was a third report. He said this was involved the arrival in Niger of a delegation of Iraqi officials in 1999. And that this Iraqi delegation was seeking a broader trade relationship with Niger.

Since Niger basically had only one thing to export, which was uranium, that officials in Niger had concluded that Iraq was interested in acquiring uranium. He said that the author of this report, which had gone up to the Hill, which was credited by the CIA, was Joe Wilson.

Q *When you say that the report "had gone up to the Hill," what are you referring to?*
A He was talking about information that had been provided to the Hill, which he said had prompted his questions, the Vice President's office's questions to the Agency about the ramifications of these alleged purchases.

Q *Did Mr. Libby indicate who it was that provided the reports to the Hill?*
A No, he did not.

Q *Did he indicate even the agency or department?*
A Yes, the CIA.

Q *Was there discussion at any time about Mr. Wilson's wife on this occasion?*
A Yes.

Q *Can you tell us what you recall about that?*
A Yes. Mr. Libby was discussing what he called two streams of reporting on uranium and on efforts by Iraq to acquire sensitive materials and components. He said the first stream was reports like that of Joe Wilson. Then he said the second stream, and at that point he said, once again, as an aside, that Mr. Wilson's wife worked at WINPAC.

Q *Can you tell us what WINPAC is?*
A Yes, WINPAC is, stands for Weapons Intelligence Non-Proliferation and Arms Control. It's a part of the CIA, which is specifically focused on weapons of mass destruction.

Q *Let me ask you this. On June 23rd when you met with Mr. Libby and discussed the fact that Mr. Wilson's wife worked in the bureau, had you ever heard before June 23rd, do you recall anyone ever telling you any indication that Mr. Wilson's wife worked at the CIA?*
A Not before that meeting.

Q *On July 8th, at this time, had you ever heard anyone indicate before that Mr. Wilson's wife worked at WINPAC?*
A WINPAC was new to me.

Q *Was there any discussion where Mr. Libby indicated . . . whether Mr. Wilson's wife was covert or not covert?*
A Not that I recall, no.

Q *Was there any discussion where he indicated whether she was classified or not classified, her status?*
A No.

Q *During this discussion, did Mr. Libby indicate whether or not he had learned this information from other newspaper reporters?*

A He did not.

Q *Was there discussion on this occasion about the National Intelligence Estimate or the NIE?*

A Yes.

Q *What do you recall about that discussion?*

A Mr. Libby defended the NIE, . . . portions of which had been published in October of 2002. And he said that it was based on reporting from many different sources.

And he said, because I asked him, that the classified version was even stronger and less—it was not at all equivocal, because I wanted to know whether or not doubts or information that was contrary, that might contradict the findings, had been contained in the classified version. He said, if anything, the classified version was stronger.

Q *Did he indicate whether or not there was any qualification in the classified version of the NIE?*

A I don't know.

Q *Did he indicate any place in the document where a doubt would be expressed?*

A Yes. He complained about the fact, and I didn't know whether or not it was in the classified or the unclassified version, that the Department of INR, Intelligence and Research Bureau, had expressed some doubts about the uranium hunting activities, alleged hunting activities of Iraq.

But that these doubts had been contained in the appendix of a section on . . . aluminum tubes for a nuclear program. In other words, what he was saying was that these doubts were not prominently featured and policymakers, he said, had not seen them.

Q *I'm not going to ask you the content of your notes, but first, did you take notes that day?*

A I did.

Q *Do you recall anything particular about the process of taking notes that day?*

MR. JEFFRESS: Objection, Your Honor.

THE COURT: Sustained.

Q *Do you know if you used a pen or a pencil?*

A Yes, I used a pen.

Q *Do you remember anything about the pen?*

A Yes, it didn't work.

Q *. . . Did you talk to other people during this time frame about Mr. Wilson's wife?*

A I think I did, yes.

Q *When did you begin talking to other people about Mr. Wilson's wife?*

A As soon as I remember learning that she may have worked at the CIA.

Q *As you sit here now, do you recall who else you talked to about Wilson's wife prior to publication of Mr. Novak's column?*

A No, Mr. Fitzgerald, I don't. I consulted my notes and there are references to her by initial and by various names, but they are not tied to any particular interview that I did in either notebook. And I just can't remember who it was that I talked to or the timing of it, whether or not it was before or after that information became public.

Q *Did you speak to Mr. Libby again following that week, following your meeting on July 8th?*

A Yes.

Q *Can you tell us the circumstances under which you spoke to him again?*

A I had indicated . . . , as I usually do in interviews, that I would want to follow up and be in a position to ask other questions. And that we would undoubtedly have more questions for him, and could we discuss them again in a separate interview.

Q *What happened then?*

A Well, Mr. Libby was traveling and I was traveling. So we agreed to speak on the phone.

Q *Did that happen?*

A It did.

Q *Tell us what you recall about that.*

A I recall less about that meeting. I do recall that the first time Mr. Libby called me I was getting into a taxi to go home. And I couldn't really take notes in a taxi or I didn't want to talk in a taxi about these matters. So I asked if we could talk when I got to my home in Sag Harbor, New York.

Q *Did you then speak from your home in Sag Harbor, New York?*

A Yes, we did.

Q *Without telling us what they say, did you take notes of the meeting?*

A Yes, I did . . .

Q *Have you reviewed those notes prior to testifying?*

A Yes.

Q *And reviewing those notes, does a clear memory of the conversation come back to you?*

A Not very clearly. There are a couple of things I remember, but not very much about it.

Q *What do you remember? Don't tell us what's in the notes. Just tell us what you remember in your head having reviewed the notes?*

A In my head, I remember a discussion of Valerie Plame Wilson, because I remember telling him that I didn't think that I was going to write a story about it. And I didn't think *The New York Times* was interested in pursuing it.

Q *Do you recall anything else, or is that the level of your memory?*

A No, I vaguely remember that we had discussed the retraction of the sixteen words and the fact that the White House had now walked back on the sixteen words and said they shouldn't have been in the President's speech.

But it was more, it was more kind of following up on the other two conversations. I don't remember. I don't have the specific memory of other things that were said other than the notes.

Q *Let's move forward. Did there come a time when you saw Mr. Libby in person again during the summer of 2003?*

A Yes.

Q *Can you tell the jury where that was and how that happened?*

A It was in Jackson Hole, Wyoming . . . We were at a rodeo.

Q *Who did you go to the rodeo with?*

A I went with my husband.

Q *Then what happened?*

A This figure approached me and began talking to me, and came time to introduce my husband, and it became clear to the person who was talking to me that I didn't know who it was.

Q *What happened then?*

A Mr. Libby took off his glasses and said, . . . "Judy, you don't know who this is. It's Scooter Libby."

Q *Can you describe what he looked like when you first met him?*

A Yes. At the rodeo, he was wearing sunglasses and a black T-shirt and blue jeans and a cowboy hat and cowboy boots. And I had never seen Mr. Libby in anything other than a suit.

Q *After realizing who he was, do you recall what, if anything, you discussed?*

A Just some banter about the meeting in Aspen that I had just come from.

Q *Just briefly describe what the meeting in Aspen was.*

A It was a meeting of the Aspen Strategy Group, which is a bipartisan group of experts on the national security, and the topic of the meeting had been weapons of mass destruction and the lack of such in Iraq.

Q *Now, did there come a time when you received a subpoena in connection with the investigation of this matter?*

A Yes.

Q *What did you do in response to the subpoena?*

A I decided to fight the subpoena.

Q *Where did you fight it?*

A In Federal District Court, this building.

Q *Do you know who the judge was?*
A Yes. Judge Hogan.

Q *What happened in the District Court?*
A We lost our effort to quash the subpoena.

Q *What did you do after the effort failed in the District Court?*
A We appealed.

Q *And who did you appeal to?*
A The Federal Appellate Court.

Q *What happened there?*
A Our appeal was rejected.

Q *And what did you do then?*
A We appealed to the Supreme Court.

Q *What happened there?*
A The Supreme Court declined to hear the case.

Q *Then what happened after that?*
A I returned to the District and to Judge Hogan's chambers, and he ordered me to comply with the subpoena.

Q *Did you comply with the subpoena at that time?*
A I told him I could not do so, because I did not have a waiver from my source that I believed was voluntary and personal. So I could not comply.

Q *Were you held in contempt?*
A Yes, I was.

Q *Is it fair to say that you violated an order of the Court? When the judge ordered you to testify, you did not testify?*
A I did not testify . . . [and] I was sent to jail . . . at the Alexandria Detention Center [for] eighty-five days.

Q *Then what happened?*
A Shortly before I was released, I received a personal written waiver from Mr. Libby and an opportunity to question him on the phone about that waiver. And, Mr. Fitzgerald, you agreed to narrow the focus of your questioning of me to Mr. Libby and to the subject matter of the Valerie Plame Wilson, the leak of her name.

Q *After you were released from jail, what did you do then?*
A I testified before the Grand Jury.

Q *And how long between when you got out of jail and you testified before the Grand Jury?*
A The next day.

Q *When you testified in front of the Grand Jury, did you tell them about the meeting on July 8, 2003 with Mr. Libby?*

A I did.

Q *Did you discuss the phone conversations from July, well, phone conversations later that week from your Sag Harbor home?*

A I did.

Q *Did you describe the June 23rd meeting at the Old Executive Office Building?*

A I did not.

Q *Why not?*

A Because I didn't remember it.

Q *When you left the Grand Jury, were you asked to do anything?*

A Yes.

Q *What were you asked to [do]?*

A You asked me, because I couldn't identify, I couldn't pinpoint the time of the second conversation meeting in Sag Harbor, I couldn't remember exactly when that had occurred, if I would check my notebooks and see if there was anything in them that would help me place the time of that conversation.

Q *Did you do that?*

A I did.

Q *What did you find?*

A That night, when I returned to my office in New York, I looked under my desk and there was a shopping bag full of my notebooks. And I looked through the notebook of July and I didn't see anything relevant. Then I picked up a notebook from June and I discovered the entire conversation with Mr. Libby that I had not testified about, and that I had forgotten.

Q *What did you do?*

A Well, I happened to be on the phone with my lawyer, and I immediately told Mr. Bennett what I had discovered. And I urged him to call you to tell you that there was more information than I had initially recalled.

Q *Did you return to the Grand Jury?*

A I did.

Q *Did you then describe that conversation?*

A I did . . .

Q *Ms. Miller, just one last question: without telling us the content of your notes, you mentioned that your pen wasn't working on July 8th?*

A Yes.

Q *Did you take notes on July 8th?*

A I did.

MR. FITZGERALD: Thank you, nothing further.

JEFFRESS BEGINS HIS CROSS-EXAMINATION of Miller by bringing out that Miller did not initially remember the June 23 meeting when she testified before the grand jury in fall 2005, before getting Miller to confirm that she told Philip Taubman, then Washington Bureau Chief of the *Times,* in fall 2003 that she did not think she was a target of a deliberate leak campaign by the administration. Miller also confirms that she did not write about Plame in 2003. Miller testifies that she recommended to Jill Abramson, then–D.C. Bureau Chief, that the *Times* pursue a story about the Wilsons. The defense would later bring in Abramson to testify that she had no recollection of such a recommendation from Miller in order to impeach Miller's testimony; although the prosecution would also get Abramson to acknowledge that she sometimes tuned out Miller.

Q *You never wrote anything [at] any time about Wilson's wife, did you?*
A No, I did not.

Q *Did you ever recommend doing so?*
A Yes, I did.

Q *Who did you make that recommendation to?*
A To the Washington Bureau Chief . . . Jill Abramson at that time . . .

Q *What is your recollection exactly of your conversation with Jill Abramson?*
A I remember that it was a very short time after my second meeting with Mr. Libby, and I was about to go back to my home in New York . . . I was in the Washington Bureau, and I went into her office and I closed the door. And I outlined some of the highlights of what I thought we knew so far about the hunt for weapons of mass destruction and the intelligence. Then I said that there was something I thought we ought to follow up on, a tip.

Q *What did you say to her?*
A I said I think that you should have someone pursue this, whether or not Joe Wilson's wife works at the Agency and, if so, what she does.

Q *Her response was what?*
A She seemed very distracted that day. It was a tumultuous period at the paper. The executive editor and the managing editor had just been fired, and she seemed distracted.

Q *What was her response?*
A She didn't have a response. She just said "uh-huh." Then we went on to talk about other things.

TURNING BACK TO THE EVENTS of fall 2003, Jeffress seeks to hurt Miller's credibility by noting her failure to remember the June 23 meeting. Jeffress asks:

Q *Put aside notes. Did you remember that conversation at any time between the time you received the subpoena and the time you were held in contempt?*

A Yes, I had a vague memory that I knew of Ms. Plame prior to my July 8th meeting with Mr. Libby, but I couldn't remember when and where I had heard it, and it bothered me. I just couldn't remember when and where I heard it.

Q *Is the answer to my question that you did not remember meeting with Mr. Libby on June 23rd?*

MR. FITZGERALD: Objection, Your Honor.
THE COURT: I don't think she said that. Rephrase.

By Mr. Jeffress:

Q *Ms. Miller, did you remember . . . the meeting with Mr. Libby on June 23, 2003, at any time between the time you got subpoenaed and the time you got held in contempt?*
A I don't believe I did or I would have mentioned it.

Q *You didn't remember it any time after you were held in contempt, while you were fighting the subpoena on appeal?*
A No, I did not.

Q *You didn't remember it when you were down in the, back down in the District Court and the judge, you were having to decide whether you were going to go to jail rather than testify?*
A I didn't remember specifics.

Q *You spent 85 days in jail, right?*
A Yes.

Q *I'm sure that wasn't pleasant.*
A No.

Q *Did you think about this matter while you were there in the Alexandria jail?*
A I thought about the need to protect the confidentiality of Mr. Libby until such a time that I got from him a personal and voluntary waiver, and I thought about should such a waiver ever materialize, how I would be sure that the prosecutor would not conduct a fishing expedition into other sources. That was what was on my mind at the time that I was in jail.

Q *The answer to my question is that you didn't remember the meeting while you were in jail?*
A I did not remember the meeting while I was in jail . . .

Q *After you appeared the first time before the Grand Jury and didn't remember this June 23rd meeting at all, you went back a second time after finding some notes, correct? Which obviously showed that there had been a meeting with Mr. Libby on June 23rd . . .*

After you found that notebook, you gave it to your lawyer, [who] informed Mr. Fitzgerald. Mr. Fitzgerald had you come back to the Grand Jury and testify a second time. Correct?

A Correct . . .

Q *Do you remember that you told the Grand Jury on that occasion that, with respect to the notes, that you had now produced all of your notes of June 23rd, July 8th and July 12? . . .*

And do you remember telling him that you have to be explicit about this? That your memory is really note-driven because you don't have an independent memory of much of this, apart from what is sparked by me reading my notes. Did you tell that to the Grand Jury?

A I think in certain context when asked specific questions I said something like that, yes.

Q *Well, that wasn't in a specific context, was it? That was a general question.*

A Generally, I am note-driven. And notes bring to mind a memory or they don't. Sometimes they did, sometimes they didn't . . .

JEFFRESS SEEKS TO CAST DOUBT on whether Miller had heard about Plame from Libby or rather from another source:

Q *Well, did you have in your notes before ever meeting with Mr. Libby on June 23rd, the name Joe Wilson?*

A Yes, I did.

Q *You had, not only his name, you had his telephone number; is that correct?*

A I did.

Q *You had not only his telephone number, you had his extension at that time; is that correct?*

A Yes.

Q *So who did you talk to about Joe Wilson?*

A I don't remember who I talked to about Joe Wilson.

Q *You don't remember?*

A No, I don't remember.

Q *Do you remember talking to Joe Wilson?*

A I don't believe I did . . .

Q *Did you tell the Grand Jury that you remembered Joe Wilson was in your notes before that "but so someone may have told me but I don't remember"? . . .*

A Yes.

Q *Tell me, how many people did you talk to during the period June and July of 2003 with respect to Joe Wilson or Valerie Wilson or Valerie Plame?*

A Sir, I have no idea.

Q *You have no idea?*

A No.

Q *It was lots, wasn't it?*

A There were many people that I talked to about weapons intelligence, and I have a vague memory of discussing it with many people. But I can't remember who . . .

Q *There were several people you talked to about Joe Wilson and Valerie Wilson or Valerie Plame before Mr. Novak's column ever came out, correct?*

A Correct.

Q *And you may have talked to somebody about that topic before you met with Mr. Libby, correct?*

A I don't have any memory of talking about his wife before my meetings with Mr. Libby.

Q *Might have happened but you have no memory?*

A I have no memory of that. I have no memory of that.

AFTER A LINE OF QUESTIONING about Miller's knowledge of the June 13 Nicholas Kristof column in the *Times* that used Joe Wilson as an anonymous source peters out without results, the questioning turns to Miller's efforts to resist the subpoena issued to her and the affidavit she filed with the court as part of those efforts, in which she acknowledged speaking with multiple sources about the issues raised in Wilson's July 6 op-ed:

Q *Is it true that you told the Court in August of 2004 that you have never written an article about Valerie Plame or Joe Wilson? You did, however, contemplate writing one or more articles in July 2003 about issues related to Ambassador Wilson's op-ed piece. Did you write that in your affidavit?*

A Yes.

Q *So that must have been true that you contemplated writing them; is that correct?*

A Not about Mr. Wilson and Ms. Plame. There were other things in that article that I wanted to pursue.

Q *That's fair. And then you also said, "In preparation for those articles, I spoke and/or met with several potential sources?" Right?*

A Correct.

Q *One of those would be Mr. Libby, correct?*

A Correct.

Q *Who are the others?*

A I don't remember who they were.

Q *Well just, can you name me just one of them?*

MR. FITZGERALD: Objection, Your Honor, may we approach?

AT THIS POINT, there is a bench conference and then the judge brings Bob Bennett, Miller's lawyer, into the discussion about whether he should allow the defense to ask Miller about other sources on Joe Wilson or on topics related to Wilson's op-ed. The defense wants to undermine Miller's credibility by her own assertion in her affidavit that she spoke with several sources about the subject of Wilson's op-ed, but could only remember Libby. The discussion continues until the judge recesses the trial until the following day.

*

JANUARY 31, 2007

JUDITH MILLER (continued)

BEFORE THE JURY IS BROUGHT IN at the start of the day, Judge Walton rules that the defense could not question Judith Miller about her sources other than Libby on topics in Joe Wilson's op-ed that went beyond Plame and Wilson himself. But the defense is able to question Miller about her other sources on the more immediate subject of the Wilsons, and in this connection the defense plays a video clip of an interview in which Miller talked about senior and "not-so-senior" government officials who talked with her about the Wilsons and the general issues raised in the former ambassador's column:

By Mr. Jeffress:

Q   *Ms. Miller, I don't want to ask you about the broader issues. Okay?*

A   All right.

Q   *... [Y]ou said that you told Mr. Goodale on television on the clip that we just played that you had conversations with senior government officials and not-so-senior government officials about Ms. Plame and Joe Wilson and this issue. Now—*

A   Yes, but I didn't say that I remembered their names.

Q   *No. I realize that.*

A   Okay. That's all I am saying. I don't remember their names. I don't know what you want me to say beyond that.

Q   *... [I]t's not what I want you to say. I want you to tell the jury whether it is true, as you told Mr. Goodale, that you talked to senior government officials, other than Mr. Libby, about Mr. Wilson and Valerie Plame?*

A   I don't remember whether the people I talked to about Mr. Wilson and Ms. Plame were senior or not so senior. I know I had several conversations, but, unfortunately there is no reference to them in my notebooks, and there is no independent memory of them.

Q   *All right. Not a single one of them, correct?*

A   No. The only one I remember, and because I was, in part, able to refresh my memory with my notebooks, was Mr. Libby. And there is no reference to any conversation about Mr. Wilson or his wife—that specific issue—before my discussion with Mr. Libby ...

Q   *There is a reference in your notes before your very first conversation with Mr. Libby to Joe Wilson, his telephone number—not just that, but his extension, right?*

A   Yes, there is, sir.

Q *All right. So you were talking to somebody about Joe Wilson before that?*

A Right. About Joe Wilson.

Q *Was that a senior government official or a "not-so-senior" government official?*

A I don't remember. And I went over my notes when I was preparing my Grand Jury testimony, and the interview that I had above it was unrelated to Mr. Wilson. So I cannot remember who told me that Joe Wilson might be helpful in terms of my quest to understand what had happened to the intelligence . . .

RETURNING TO THE SUBJECT of Miller's fight against her subpoena, under questioning Miller explains her decision to go to jail instead of testifying and how she eventually got a new lawyer (Bennett) to negotiate with Libby's attorney and with Fitzgerald to secure her release. The defense emphasizes how cooperative Libby was, and the fact that Miller also needed an agreement from Fitzgerald to limit his questioning of her to one source, Libby, and one subject, the Wilsons. The defense then returns to Miller's June 23, 2003 interview with Libby in the Old Executive Office Building:

Q *You have some five pages of notes, is that correct, from what was discussed in that meeting?*

A I don't remember without looking at the notes how many pages I had.

Q *You had several pages of notes.*

A Several pages, yes.

Q *And in those notes, as you testified yesterday, Mr. Libby was discussing the Niger uranium issue, correct?*

A Correct.

Q *And what the White House or the Vice President had or had not been told by the CIA about intelligence?*

A Correct.

Q *And he talked about two streams of reporting that the intelligence agencies had concerning the issue of Iraq seeking to obtain uranium from Niger, correct?*

A I don't remember if the term "two streams" was from the first or the second meeting, but that was the thrust of our discussion that day . . .

Q *Is it a fact that your notes say "first stream"—and then there's some notes having to do with Mr. Wilson's trip and what he did and did not report, right?*

A Yes.

Q *And then you have "second stream," and then you have something in parentheses under that; is that right?*

A Correct.

Q *And what that parentheses says was, "wife works in bureau?" Right?*

A Correct.

Q *Now, you said—is your memory fuzzy about that entry and where it came from and why it was said or what was meant by it?*

A The thing that's fuzzy is whether or not he used the word "may work in bureau" or whether or not I put the question mark there to say, that's odd; why is he saying this? Or how is this related to our conversation? Because that was the only reference to her.

Q *It's true, is it not, Ms. Miller, that you cannot be certain that you didn't already know about Wilson's wife working at the CIA prior to June 23rd?*

A Sir, I have no recollection of knowing that Valerie Plame Wilson worked at the CIA before my conversation with Mr. Libby that day.

Q *But you might have; you can't be certain about that.*

A I just have no recollection. I am confident that I didn't know that before. I had never heard that. I had heard about Joe Wilson, but I don't—I have no memory of hearing that before that conversation, and my notes reflect that.

Q *In your Grand Jury appearance where you talked—this is your second Grand Jury appearance where you talked about this meeting of June 23rd, at Page 50, Line 11, were you asked the following question and did you give following answer:*

[Q]uestion: 'And when you heard that, was that the first time—we may have covered this, but was that the first time you associated Mr. Wilson's wife with the bureau at the CIA?'

[A]nswer: 'I don't remember if that was absolutely the first time, but it was among the first times I had ever heard that. I don't—I can't recall for sure.'

Was that your testimony?

A Yes.

Q *Was it true?*

A Yes, I believe that's right. It was the—the use of the term "bureau." That she worked at the CIA—the use of the term "bureau" was new to me. That's what I am saying.

And, you know, that's what I was trying to say there. It's only the word "bureau" that leaps out at me in retrospect because I was confused by it and I had never heard that before. And it took me a while to figure out what it meant by that—what he meant by that.

Q *So you might have heard that she worked at the CIA, just not in a bureau; is that what you're saying?*

A I just don't have any recollection of knowing that—even hearing about his wife before Mr. Libby . . .

THE DEFENSE CONTINUES to press Miller on her Grand Jury testimony:

Q *And so it was true then and true now that you are not absolutely certain that you first heard that Wilson's wife worked at the CIA from Mr. Libby, correct?*

A   I believe it is the first time. I can't be absolutely, absolutely certain, but I have no recollection of an earlier discussion of it with anyone else, and there is nothing in my notes that reflects a discussion with anyone else about her . . .

JEFFRESS SEEKS TO CALL into question whether the reference to "bureau" in her notes for the June 23 meeting really had to do with the CIA:

Q   *You have actually never heard of any component of the CIA referred to as a bureau; is that correct?*
A   Some people refer to the Nonproliferation Bureau within the CIA.

Q   *This Nonproliferation Bureau within the CIA, where could we—you say some people refer to it. Who are those people?*
A   In my conversations with the sources about those broader issues, people refer to different components of the CIA in different ways. Occasionally, somebody says the Nonproliferation "Bureau." I don't remember who specifically said that or when they said it. It's sometimes called a division. It's sometimes called a unit. But normally, in Washington, when people use the word "bureau," they are talking about the FBI, and that's what struck me that day about the mention of Mrs. Wilson working for the bureau. I was confused for a moment, and I—I still am.

Q   *Okay. And it's not just the Federal Bureau of Investigation, but the State Department has many, many bureaus; is that right?*
A   There are many bureaus in Washington.

Q   *No. At the State Department?*
A   I don't know if they are called "bureau." I&R—Intelligence and Research. I mean, bureau—yes, you can use that word loosely. It is used loosely. I don't know how other people use it . . .

THE DEFENSE ASKS MILLER about her reaction to reading Wilson's op-ed:

Q   *And what was the way in which you found it interesting?*
A   I said I found it surprising because—in two respects. One, it was the first time that someone who had actually participated in the collection of WMD intelligence was saying that the White House and the President had distorted that information and disregarded it.

And the second thing that occurred to me is that if he had gone—if Mr. Wilson had been sent on this trip for the CIA, and usually such trips—one signs a waiver or one signs a pledge that one won't discuss these trips—that the CIA had permitted him to write this article in *The New York Times* attacking the President.

I found both of those significant, and they raised questions for me: Was this right? Had this happened? You know—

Q   *On that second point you mentioned, you would have thought, as somebody who has written about some aspects of national security over the years, that someone who went on a mission for the CIA would have some sort of contract that would prevent that person from publicly disclosing his mission?*

A   Yes. I assumed that when I read it.

Q   *And is it true that you decided, after reading the article, to ask as many people as you could think of about how Mr. Wilson could come to write such an article?*

A   I knew I was going to explore it in my questions, definitely.

Q   *I will come back to that, but you did begin talking to a number of people about how Mr. Wilson could come to write such an article, correct?*

A   I spoke to a number of people about that aspect of it, yes . . .

Q   *There is an entry [in your notes] with the name "Valerie Flame," beginning with an "f," right?*

A   Yes.

Q   *And that's not even her maiden name. You know that her maiden name was Plame, correct?*

A   Correct.

Q   *And that she goes by Valerie Wilson, correct?*

A   I don't know that.

Q   *But that entry, that information—where did you get that information?*

A   I don't remember.

Q   *It did not come from Mr. Libby, correct?*

A   I don't remember. I don't think so.

Q   *. . . [I]n fact, you do not believe that that name came from Mr. Libby, correct?*

A   I don't believe it did.

Q   *And is there another entry in your notes to a "V.F."?*

A   I believe so.

Q   *And another entry, "Valery" spelled v-a-l-e-r-y?*

A   I know there are several references to her by initials and with misspellings. I believe so. If you want me to say exactly where and when, I would need to see my notes.

Q   *Okay. But do you know where any of those—any of the information, any of the references to Valerie Plame, Valerie Flame, V.F.—where any of those came from?*

A   No, sir.

Q   *And you do not believe, correct, that any of those entries came from Mr. Libby?*

A   No, sir. I don't. I don't believe they came from Mr. Libby.

Q   *Okay. And you don't remember—do you remember anyone else that you talked to about Mr. Wilson's wife that might have given you that name or that information? . . .*

A   I have searched my memory, and I just can't remember specific discussions with people about her.

Q *Okay. And do you remember that the more people you talked to about her, you learned to spell the name semi-correctly?*

A I believe I did.

Q *Is it true that neither Mr. Libby nor anyone else you talked to about Wilson's wife said anything to lead you to believe that she had any kind of covert position with the CIA?*

A That is correct.

Q *When you—*

A Excuse me. Did you say—

Q *Any kind of covert—*

A —with respect to Mr. Libby?

Q *Or anyone else.*

A I don't remember what anyone else told me. I just remember that Mr. Libby—I don't recall any discussion with Mr. Libby about her status . . .

Q *Did you receive any information, before Robert Novak's article appeared, to indicate to you that Ms. Wilson had any kind of covert position at the CIA?*

A Mr. Jeffress, the only thing I remember is that there was a debate about that, that people were all over the fence on that. I can't remember who told me what about her, but I remember that there was some ambiguity about her role, and it was unclear to me what her status was . . .

Q *Let me go back and ask this: did Mr. Libby ever indicate to you any information that made you believe she was an undercover operative as opposed to an analyst?*

A No, sir . . .

JEFFRESS ASKS MILLER questions designed to show that when Miller met Libby on July 8, it was at her request, as far as she can remember, and it concerned WMD issues beyond the issue of uranium from Niger. He then asks Miller about her notes from that conversation:

Q *In the course of those pages, there is an entry, again, in parentheses, "wife works in WINPAC," correct?*

A Correct.

Q *And you know WINPAC to be—you knew at that time WINPAC to be a unit, I guess I would call it, of the CIA, right?*

A Correct.

Q *It's publicly known, correct?*

A I believe it's on their Web site now.

Q *Okay. And did you check into this? Have you ever found any information that, in fact, she does work in WINPAC?*

A I did not check into it.

Q *Okay. Would it surprise you if she had never worked in WINPAC?*

A At this stage, Mr. Jeffress, almost nothing would surprise me . . .

Q *Do you remember whether you talked to somebody prior to this July 8 meeting about Mr. Wilson's wife?*

A Well, we—Mr. Libby and I discussed it at the June 23rd meeting, "wife works in bureau."

Q *. . . Putting that aside, . . . you can't be certain, as you sit here today, that you hadn't already talked to somebody besides Mr. Libby about Wilson's wife before the July 8 meeting, correct?*

A I can't be absolutely certain, no.

Q *I asked you a little while ago about whether, after reading Mr. Wilson's article on the 6th, you decided to ask as many people as you could think of why Mr. Wilson would have been able to write such an article. Now, what's your testimony? Is that true or is that not true?*

A About both aspects of Mr. Wilson's article. I was interested in both aspects: the veracity of his charge, and how he could have come to write such an article.

Q *And among the people you decided to ask was Mr. Libby, correct?*

A Yes . . .

Q *Is it fair to say you might have talked to other officials about Wilson's wife during that time frame; that is, after July 6th? . . .*

A After July 6th, . . . I certainly would have asked people about that article and about Mrs.—no. No, wait a minute. I am not sure I knew—I can't remember exactly when I began discussing it with people.

I was focused on Mr. Wilson's charges and the CIA issue. I can't remember precisely when I started telephoning widely. I do remember that after the July 6th article, one of the first people I talked to about it was Mr. Libby because he was the first major interview I had scheduled after that article appeared.

Q *. . . When you testified before the Grand Jury, were you asked the following questions and did you give the following answers:*

[Question:] 'Is it fair to say that as you sit here today, you have no specific recollection of talking to any specific government official other than Mr. Libby about Wilson's wife working at the CIA during that time frame?'

And your answer was: "That is correct. I have no specific recollection of another conversation" . . .

Go back to the previous page and look up at—start at line 10:

Question: 'Is it fair to say from the time—moment that the op-ed appeared in The New York Times *on July 6th, until the time that Mr. Novak published his column on July 14th, in that eight-day window, that Joe Wilson was a topic of interest to you?'*

[Answer:] 'Yes.'

Question: 'Is it fair to say you were calling lots of people, including government officials, to find out what you could about Wilson and his op-ed and the background to it during that week?'

And you said, "yes."

Okay? So now—that's the time period, correct? Right?

A Correct.

Q *Okay. Now, let me go back to page 43 and finish up. Okay. So the question—the next question you were asked:*

[Question:] 'Is it also fair to say that you—you know, that you may well have talked to other officials about—official or officials—about Wilson's wife during that time frame?'

And your answer was, "I know that I did."

[Question:] 'Okay.'

[Answer:] 'But I—I can't remember who they are.'

That was your testimony, correct?

A That's correct.

Q *And that's true?*

A That's true . . .

JEFFRESS CONCLUDES his cross-examination and the prosecution takes up its redirect examination:

Q *Let me ask you this. Is there any reference in that notebook that includes the June 23rd conversation to Mr. Wilson's wife, either by reference to wife, spouse, name or initials, other than the one you described concerning your conversation with Mr. Libby?*

A No, sir.

Q *And turning to the notebook that reflects the July 8th conversation with Mr. Libby, . . . can you tell us is there any reference in the notebook to Mr. Wilson's wife, either by reference to wife, spouse, name, initials, or even an incorrect spelling of her name, prior to the reference in your notes to your July 8th conversation with Mr. Libby?*

A No, sir.

Q *And the references that Mr. Jeffress asked you about to "Ms. Flame," or to "V.F.," or the others, do they all occur later in the notebook?*

A Yes, sir.

Q *And are any of them tied to specific conversations with identified people?*

A No . . .

FITZGERALD ALSO ELICITS testimony that Libby used "bureau" in the June 23 meeting and that Miller understood him to be using it to refer to the Nonproliferation bureau of the CIA.

Q *By the way, there have been a number of references to an entry in your notes of Joe Wilson and a phone number. Did you ever speak to Joe Wilson?*

A No.

Q *Do you know if you tried? Or do you remember?*

A I think I might have called that number and gotten no answer. I remember having made an effort, but I remember not succeeding . . .

Q *And the question I am going to ask you … is whether or not you recall the discussion of two streams of reporting occurring on July 8th or June 23rd? …*

A Yes. July 8th.

FITZGERALD THEN GETS MILLER TO EXPLAIN that, though she had forgotten the June 23 meeting, she had never forgotten the July 8th meeting in which Libby had told her about Wilson's wife, and that even during her first Grand Jury appearance, she had a vague memory of talking with someone about Wilson's wife before the July 8 meeting with Libby—and it turned out that she had talked with Libby himself on the earlier occasion. Miller also underlines the fact that at their meetings, though she was trying to focus on the failure to find WMD in Iraq, Libby himself was focused on the sixteen words controversy and Wilson:

Q *On June 23rd, at that meeting, can you explain what your focus was and what Mr. Libby's focus was?*

A Yes. I remember that my focus was on those issues that had been plaguing me as I wandered around Iraq looking for weapons of mass destruction with the soldiers and watching them being frustrated: What had happened? Were they there? Was the intelligence slanted? Was the intelligence wrong? How had this gotten so screwed up? The big picture.

And Mr. Libby, being in Washington, seemed much more focused on the growing controversy over the—what the President had said in his state of the union and who said what to whom, what I call inside baseball in Washington.

And so, from my standpoint, it wasn't a very productive meeting.

Q *And how about your focus and Mr. Libby's focus on July 8th?*

A Once again, I was seeking to contribute to a broader story on what had happened to the intelligence and also to figure out how the hunt itself had been so mismanaged and so badly carried out and what had happened to the underlying intelligence.

And while we spoke somewhat about those topics, Mr. Libby seemed to want to focus on, once again, uranium and Niger and the sixteen words, and that just didn't—that wasn't my lane; it wasn't my focus. I was responsible mostly for biological and chemical weapons. That's what we had been searching for. And this other he said/she said, it's your fault, it's their fault—that struck me as Washington politics. That wasn't particularly relevant to the issues that I was concerned about at that point . . .

MILLER AND THE JURY ARE EXCUSED so that the parties can argue over whether Fitzgerald would get to question Miller about the letter Libby sent to Miller while she was in jail to assure her that his waiver of confidentiality was genuine and voluntary and, according to Fitzgerald, to outline to Miller what other witnesses had said and how he expected her testimony to help him. Walton is skeptical, and at one point his skepticism prompts Fitzgerald to indicate his belief that Libby was trying, but failed, to shape Miller's testimony:

THE COURT: If you were somehow suggesting that there was collusion between Mr. Libby and Ms. Miller and that this letter was designed to affect what she would say and, in fact, did so, then I guess I could see how, conceivably, it would be relevant. But I don't understand that to be the situation. I mean, she did not, as I understand, testify in a way before the Grand Jury that was, in fact, helpful to Mr. Libby. So the letter would not seem to have caused her to alter her testimony.

MR. FITZGERALD: And we don't think the letter worked . . .

WALTON REJECTS THE EFFORT to enter Libby's letter into evidence at this point, and then, having brought the witness and the jury back in, poses questions from the jury to Miller, which prompts Miller first to explain that she needed an agreement from Fitzgerald to limit the sources and subject matter about which she would be questioned before she would agree to testify, and then:

THE COURT: One of the jurors wants to know, why did you make the decision to go to jail?

THE WITNESS: Because everything that I do and I have done in Washington—all of my reporting depended on people coming to me and being able to trust ... that I would protect them. And it wasn't until I was absolutely certain that I had a voluntary and personal waiver—written waiver from Mr. Libby—not something his boss had asked him to sign, but something that he had given me and I was able to talk to him about, and knowing that I could protect the other sources—I really felt that, as a professional and ethical matter, I had no choice. It was all my conscience would allow.

I wasn't trying to be a martyr or make a stand. I was just trying to do the right thing vis-à-vis my sources, knowing that without that kind of trust, you can't operate in Washington when people can go to jail for even talking to you.

It was too important in national security reporting. So I felt I had no choice.

THE COURT: Okay. A juror also wants to know: Have you ever had instances in your professional career when you had memory losses of events like the memory loss that you say you had regarding the meeting with Mr. Libby?

THE WITNESS: Yes. Sometimes when I was preparing—yes. When I was preparing my last book, I remembered an incident in Beirut that I thought had happened when I was caught in a crossfire one way. I went back. I checked the notes, and I found out the actual story was very different. And even though the—I thought I had remembered it, I had actually misremembered it. And from that time on, I became very careful about notes and keeping notes and trying to be careful . . . .

THE COURT: The notes that you found after you were asked by Mr. Fitzgerald to look for notes, where did you say you located those?

THE WITNESS: Right underneath my desk at *The New York Times* in a shopping bag.

THE COURT: And is that where you kept your notes?

THE WITNESS: That's where I kept the notes for a relevant period of time that I had been working on before I went to jail.

THE COURT: Was this the standard method that you used for archiving your notes?

THE WITNESS: No. I was actually intending to take them home because when I came down to Washington to appear in Judge Hogan's court that day, I assumed that I would be given time to go home, and take those notebooks home for safekeeping. But, instead, I was surrounded by marshals and just taken off to jail immediately, so that's why they were there in that.

THE COURT: How many other notebooks were with this particular notebook that you made reference to, if you know?

THE WITNESS: There were about 15 or 20.

THE COURT: Thank you, Ms. Miller.

With that, Miller is excused, and the next witness, Matt Cooper, is brought in.

MATT COOPER

MATT COOPER WAS A *TIME* MAGAZINE reporter in 2003 when it published a piece in July 2003 entitled "A War on Wilson?" that reported that "some government officials have noted to *TIME* in interviews (as well as to syndicated columnist Robert Novak) that Wilson's wife, Valerie Plame, is a CIA official who monitors the proliferation of weapons of mass destruction." Cooper's first source on Plame was Karl Rove—who volunteered information about her as part of his criticism of Joe Wilson on July 11, 2003. (It was Rove's failure to acknowledge, over a long period of time, having given information on Plame to Cooper that nearly got Rove indicted.) According to his testimony, Cooper's confirming source was Libby, with whom he talked the next day, and it was that conversation that is the main subject of his testimony.

The defense raises several doubts about Cooper's testimony, principally that Cooper had nothing clear in his notes from his interview with Libby backing up his memory of what Libby said to him; and that Cooper's colleague John Dickerson also got disparaging information about Wilson from White House officials hinting at—or even, according to Fleischer's own testimony, outright disclosing—Plame's CIA affiliation and supposed connection to Wilson's mission to Niger. The cross-examination of Cooper is of particular interest because the false statement charge in the five-count indictment, based entirely on Libby's testimony about his conversation with Cooper, was the one charge on which the jury would acquit Libby.

After Cooper identifies himself and his position at *TIME* in 2003, and explains the basics of how newsmagazines like *TIME* work, he is asked about summer 2003:

Q *Directing your attention to the summer of 2003, did there come a time when you became aware of a controversy involving Joseph Wilson?*

A Yes.

Q *Can you tell us how you became aware of the controversy?*

A Well, I believe I watched the former ambassador appear on *Meet the Press* on July 6th, 2003, and read his op-ed in *The New York Times* that day as well.

Q *Okay. And did there come a time when you began to do something in connection with* TIME *magazine as a result of this controversy?*

A Yes. It became a big story, well, as soon as Mr. Wilson wrote his op-ed, but also as soon as the White House—I believe that was Monday, the day after his op-ed, or maybe it was Tuesday—said that the sixteen words about uranium and Africa should not have been in the State of the Union address. That made it a very, very big story.

Q *And what, in particular, did you do that week?*

A Well, I had recently become a White House correspondent for *TIME*, so I set about to find out as much as I could about the background of this controversy: How did the sixteen words that the White House had now taken back wind up in a speech that is so thoroughly checked and vetted? And I made a number of phone calls and such.

Q *And did there come a time when you discussed with anyone Mr. Wilson's wife?*

A Yes.

Q *And can you tell us when you first discussed Mr. Wilson's wife that week and with whom?*

A Sure. It was on Friday, July 11th, 2003. And it was with Karl Rove, a member of the White House staff.

Q *And can you tell us how that conversation came about?*

A Sure. Well, I put in a call to Mr. Rove's office. I believe I called through the White House switchboard, and I was routed to his office. At first they said he wasn't there or that he was busy, and then they put me through to him, and we talked.

And then he said, you know, it would turn out who was involved in sending him. And I had to draw it out of him a bit. I said, who? And he said, like his wife.

Q *And tell us what you recall about the conversation with Mr. Rove on that day.*

A Sure. Well, these aren't the exact words, but the gist of it was I said, you know, we are interested in this Wilson story and the sixteen words. By this time, it had become a very big story. And he immediately said, well, don't get too far out on Wilson, which I took to mean, don't lionize Ambassador Wilson or don't idolize him.

And he went on to say—and, again, I am paraphrasing—that a number of things were going to be coming out about Ambassador Wilson that would cast him in a different light. He said that the director of the CIA had not sent him. I believe he said the Vice President's office had not been involved in sending him.

And then he said, you know, it would turn out who was involved in sending him.

And I had to draw it out of him a bit. I said, who? And he said, like his wife.

And I guess I, until that point, didn't know Wilson had a wife; I hadn't even thought about it. And then I said, "The wife?" And he went on to say that she worked on WMD at the agency, and by that I took to mean the Central Intelligence Agency, not, say, the Environmental Protection Agency.

And we talked a bit more. And then, at the end of the conversation, he said words to the effect of, "I have already said too much. I have got to go." And that was it.

Q *About how long was that conversation, if you recall?*
A A couple of minutes.

Q *Were you familiar with a statement issued that week by George Tenet?*
A Yes.

Q *Did you pay attention to it when it came out at the time?*
A Yes. It was an important part of that week's events.

Q *And did there come a time that week when you came to speak to Mr. Libby?*
A Yes.

Q *Can you tell the jury how that happened?*
A Sure. Well, throughout the week, there had been a lot of interest in the Vice President's office because Ambassador Wilson had said in his op-ed that the CIA asked him to undertake the trip at the behest of an inquiry that came from the Vice President's office. So, obviously, there was a lot of interest in the Vice President's office[:] Was he aware of the Wilson trip? Did he know about the sixteen words? Did he fight to get them in? What was the behind-the-scenes story? And so I made great efforts to try to reach people in the Vice President's office.

And there came a point during the week where the Vice President's then–Communications Director, Cathie Martin, said that she was going to hook me up to speak with Mr. Libby.

Q *And did you communicate any of the questions in advance, if you recall?*
A I did send some questions to her in advance via e-mail, yes.

Q *And when did you actually speak to Mr. Libby?*
A I spoke to him on Saturday, July 12th.

Q *And do you recall the circumstances of what you were doing that day before you spoke to Mr. Libby?*

A Quite well. It was—it was an unusual day. I mean, we were very close to deadline, so I was, you know, very eager to get to Mr. Libby because ... the magazine goes to press on Saturday nights, and they like to have these stories more or less, you know, done on Friday nights as much as they can, and going into Saturdays is exceptional. So there was a sheer crunch of time.

Then, secondly, some friends of my family had invited us to the Chevy Chase Country Club where they were members to go swimming. It was a beautiful afternoon in July.

Now, this club prohibits the use of cell phones and BlackBerries on the premises. So—and I remember this quite well—I had to keep running out to the parking lot to, you know, check my BlackBerry, to make cell phone calls and try to figure out when I was going to speak with Mr. Libby, who was himself down at the christening of the USS *Ronald Reagan* in Norfolk, Virginia, another event I remember quite well because my now-late father-in-law was Ronald Reagan's ambassador to Austria, and he was at the ceremony. So the events of the day are quite vivid in my mind.

Q *And how did you finally speak with Mr. Libby?*
A We spoke by telephone that afternoon. I was in my home in Washington.

Q *And describe what you recall about how the conversation unfolded.*
A Sure. Well, he called me. It was on my cell phone. I don't know what phone he was on, obviously. He called me and then said he had a statement to read that was on the record. And he gave it to me.

And the gist of it—I am not quoting word for word, but the gist of it was that the Vice President didn't know about the Wilson trip, that he had made an inquiry, as he often does, about things, and that this trip had gone on without his knowledge and he had only recently heard about it. And that was the on-the-record part of the statement.

Q *...Did you take notes of this statement?*
A I did.

Q *And how?*
A I took them on my laptop computer.

Q *And what happened at the end of his on-the-record statement?*
A Well, then I posed some questions to him on varying degrees of confidentiality.

Q *And describe what you recall happened.*
A Sure. Well, I asked him some questions. I think I first said "on background." And one of the questions had to do with, you know, ... was your office involved in getting this now controversial sixteen words into the State of the Union address? And he said, no, that his office was more focused on another aspect of the President's State of the Union address, the—I believe it was called Project Bioshield, an antiterrorism thing.

And then I asked if it had come up—if Wilson or Niger uranium had come up on the visits that he and the Vice President had taken to CIA headquarters in Langley, Virginia, which had been written about. And he said that he didn't recall that.

And towards the very end of the conversation, I asked what he had heard about Wilson's wife being involved in sending him to Niger.

Q *And what, if anything, did he say?*
A Mr. Libby said words to the effect of, "yes, I have heard that, too," or, "yes, I have heard something like that, too."

Q *And anything further that you recall from the conversation after that?*
A That was pretty much it. There were a couple pleasantries at the end. I said, how could I get in touch with you? He said to call his assistant, Jennifer Mayfield. And I think that was about it. There was maybe another question or two in there.

Q *And do you recall what the ground rules were when you had that conversation?*
A Well, they varied. I said "on background" when I asked about the sixteen words and [then] going out to Langley. I believe just before the question about Wilson's wife, I said "off the record."

Q *And during the conversation, did either you or he ever indicate that Ms. Wilson or Mr. Wilson's wife's work at the CIA involved a covert status?*
A No.

Q *And did either you or he indicate in any way that her job affiliation with the CIA was believed to be classified?*
A No.

Q *And did Mr. Libby indicate to you how he had—who he had heard the information from?*
A Not in any way, no.

Q *And did he at any time indicate that he had heard the information from reporters?*
A No.

Q *And did you type notes of Mr. Libby's conversation with you when he said words to the effect of that he had heard that, too?*
A No, I didn't.

Q *And following that conversation, was there a column in the magazine that next Monday?*
A There was a cover story, yes, with the cover headline "Untruth and Consequences."

Q *And was there any discussion in that story about Ms. Wilson's or Mr. Wilson's wife's employment?*
A No.

Q *And the on-the-record statement that Mr. Libby gave you, did that appear at all in the magazine?*

A Only a very truncated version of it appeared in the magazine.

Q *And did anything happen as a result of the fact that the quote from Mr. Libby in the magazine was truncated?*

A Yes. I got a call from Mr. Libby that following week—I believe it was Tuesday, July 15th—complaining that the full context—full statement had not appeared in the magazine.

Q *And what, if anything, did you do in response to that phone call?*

A Well, I told him I would look into it, and I understood his concerns. I would talk about it with my editors. And I sent them e-mails and talked about it with them.

Q *You said you talked about it with them. Who is "them"?*

A I'm sorry. Various editors and bosses of mine about what we should do in response to this complaint.

Q *And did you end up doing something?*

A We did a couple of things. One is in the on-line version of that cover story, "Untruth and Consequences," we inserted the full statement. And I think there was a little notation at the top that the full statement had not appeared in the original print edition, and it noted the complaint from the Vice President's office.

Then I subsequently wrote a—co-authored, excuse me—a piece for *TIME*'s web site called "A War on Wilson?" the following week in which we included the whole on-the-record statement that Mr. Libby had given me.

MR. FITZGERALD: Your Honor, I was about to head into a different area.

THE COURT: It's 12:30, so we will recess for lunch. Come back at 1:30. Have a nice lunch . . .

COOPER AND THE JURY are excused for lunch, and the parties then address the government's intention of entering into evidence, after Cooper is done testifying, several videos from fall 2003 of Scott McClellan, the White House Press Secretary. McClellan initially cleared Karl Rove publicly, while notably not doing the same for Libby; he subsequently cleared Libby. Fitzgerald wants to use the videos in connection with other evidence that Libby first tried to get the White House to clear him and then, when that failed, prevailed on Cheney to intervene on his behalf. Fitzgerald explains that the evidence is relevant because it suggests Libby's motive to lie when he was first interviewed by the FBI on October 14, 2003:

FITZGERALD: When he sits down on October 14th, 2003, when he faces the FBI in an interview, he has basically gone to the Vice President of the United States, who has then had the White House Press Secretary tell the world that this man did not leak classified information, did not leak to Novak, and the Press Secretary said was not involved in this—and that goes to his state of mind when he's sitting there in the interview.

It couldn't be more probative to rebut the notion that he had no motive to lie than to say, I have had the White House, under a press storm, say that I have nothing to do with this—that he would then have every reason to do what we allege he did, which is to switch the source of his information from the Vice President and other officials to reporters spreading rumors.

THE COURT: So you're saying that because he went through these efforts and that the White House did exonerate him would provide a motive for him to say what he did to show that he wasn't guilty of what was being suggested, consistent with what the White House had said.

MR. FITZGERALD: Exactly.

MR. WELLS: Your Honor, in terms of the core story, there is no dispute. I think the facts show exactly the opposite, and I opened on it.

What I am objecting to is not the story, because that's laid out in the Grand Jury. The jurors are going to hear that. What I am objecting to is the playing of clips or transcripts that Mr. Libby did not see . . .

THE COURT: I will have to look at the testimony and, you know, try and assess whether this would suggest that he was aware of what Mr. McClellan was saying . . .

THE DEFENSE ARGUES that the video clips would be highly prejudicial, and that it isn't clear that Libby had seen them all. Fitzgerald notes that the statements in two of the videos, of McClellan clearing Libby, occurred because of actions taken by Libby.

The parties also discuss the government's intention to introduce, through FBI agent Deborah Bond, Libby's notes from a July 10, 2003 conversation with Mary Matalin, Cathie Martin's predecessor as press aide to the Vice President, where Libby sought Matalin's advice in dealing with Wilson. Matalin recommended that Libby call Tim Russert, that Wilson's purported partisan motivation be addressed, and that the President should declassify relevant material, among other things. She also complained about Wilson in colorful and partisan terms. The defense wants Matalin's nastiest comments about Wilson kept from the jury:

MR. WELLS: The government has advised me that they want to introduce a note that Mr. Libby took while he was having a telephone conversation with Mary Matalin, who used to be the public affairs person at the White House, and she was the person who Ms. Martin replaced.

And during the telephone conversation, Ms. Matalin stated—and Mr. Libby wrote it down in a note—that "Wilson is a snake." There is no dispute [that] Ms. Matalin said it and that Mr. Libby wrote it down. It has no evidentiary value.

THE COURT: Does the government seek to use that? The government is going to seek to use that?

MR. ZEIDENBERG: Yes, Your Honor. These are from Mr. Libby's notes dated July 10th. It's a conversation—

THE COURT: Is that something Mr. Libby was saying?

MR. ZEIDENBERG: Mr. Libby wrote down in his notes—

THE COURT: Based upon what Ms. Matalin said?

MR. ZEIDENBERG: That's correct, Your Honor.

THE COURT: Can he be held accountable for what she said?

MR. ZEIDENBERG: Well, Your Honor, if I could show Government Exhibit 115. What the testimony will be, Your Honor, is that Mr. Libby called Ms. Matalin for advice on how to deal with Wilson—the Wilson issue.

THE COURT: Right.

MR. ZEIDENBERG: Now, you will remember, on July 8th, Mr. Libby wrote down notes from a senior staff meeting in which Karl Rove said, "now people are taking Joe Wilson as a credible expert; we are one day late in getting a response."

THE COURT: Right.

MR. ZEIDENBERG: Two days go by. It's now July 10th. He calls Mary Matalin for advice. She tells him—among other things, she gives him strategy on how to deal with it. She tells him that "we need someone who can sum it up, Tenet-like." Then she tells him that "this is fitting into the Democratic story on the Hill and that the story has legs. It's fitting the Democratic theory . . . The story is not going away."

And she tells him, "We need to address the Wilson motivation. We need to be able to get the cable out, declassified. The President should wave his wand."

Mary Matalin then says, "call Tim—Tim Russert." At the top of the page is Tim Russert's phone number. Obviously, this is, in the government's view, because Mr. Libby is extremely upset with Chris Matthews.

Mary Matalin: Call Tim. He hates Chris. He needs to know it all.

And underneath that is Mr. Libby's notes: "Wilson is a snake."

So as a result of this note on July 10th, he calls Tim Russert. Now, the fact that he would write that down goes to his state of mind. All we have heard from the defense all along is that Mr. Libby was only interested in responding on the merits. On the merits. That's what we've heard, constant refrain.

THE COURT: But do you agree that that was a statement that Ms. Matalin made and not a statement that Libby made?

MR. ZEIDENBERG: That's correct, Your Honor, and there is not going to be a suggestion otherwise.

THE COURT: It's kind of a stretch. I mean, obviously, that's extremely prejudicial in that if the jury were to buy in on the proposition that that was Mr. Libby's state of mind in reference to Wilson, as compared to him just writing down that this is what Matalin said in reference to Wilson, then obviously that would buy in on the government's theory that the defendant had a motive to try and harm Wilson, and that one of the ways he tried to do that was by outing his wife.

JUDGE WALTON INDICATES that the marginal probative value of the comment is outweighed by its potential unfair prejudice to Libby. When the prosecution eventually enters the note into evidence, Matalin's snake comment would be redacted. The trial recesses for lunch, and after the break Fitzgerald concludes his direct examination of Cooper, eliciting testimony about Cooper's interaction with Libby when Cooper and *TIME* received the subpoena for his testimony in summer 2004:

By Mr. Fitzgerald:

Q *. . . [W]hat did you do in response to the subpoena [you received a subpoena in connection with this matter]?*

A Along with my company, Time, Incorporated, we fought the subpoena vigorously in court.

Q *Did there come a time during the course of the litigation when you spoke to Mr. Libby?*

A Yes, there did.

Q *When did that happen?*

A I believe it was on August 4, 2004. And I think we had decided at Time, Inc., along with my attorneys, that we would seek the personal permission of Mr. Libby for me to speak about the confidential portions of our conversation. We did not want to rely on the written waiver ... many people in this investigation had been asked to sign. We wanted more personal assurances. We decided that we would seek them from Mr. Libby. So, that day late in the afternoon I called him and we spoke.

Q *Describe the conversation.*

A It was fairly brief. It was amicable. I called him. It took several phone calls via his staff to track him down. Eventually we did speak . . . I was scheduled to be put in contempt of Court in Federal District Court for refusing to comply with the subpoena from your office.

So I called Mr. Libby and said, "You may have been reading about my court case. I wanted to seek your permission to talk about those parts of our conversation from last year that were confidential." I think I said, my words, well, you know, "I plan to tell the truth but maybe my words will probably be exculpatory." I believe I used that word.

Then he said, "Well, let me stop you there. And you know, it's okay by me." I'm not quoting directly, but the gist of it was "it's okay by me, if it's okay. So why don't you have your lawyer call my lawyer." So I told him I would have my lawyer, Floyd Abrams speak to his lawyer, Joseph Tate. Then we chatted amicably for a couple of minutes after that. And that was the end of it.

Q *You said something about "Mr. Libby said it was okay, if it's okay." What do you mean by that?*

A I think he said "it's okay by me. I want to grant you this permission to go testify that you're seeking. But I would like the lawyers, I would like to run it by my lawyer. I would like the lawyers to speak." So that's what happened.

Q *Thereafter, did the lawyers speak[?]*

A They did, over the next couple weeks, my attorney (then my attorney), Floyd Abrams, spoke with Mr. Libby's attorney, Joseph Tate. We were satisfied that Mr. Libby was offering a voluntary permission for me to go ahead and testify. That's what I did.

MR. FITZGERALD: Nothing further.

ON CROSS-EXAMINATION, the defense immediately raises the other sources for the article in *TIME*, which had multiple authors, bringing up not just Rove, who leaked information about Plame to Cooper the day before he spoke with Libby, but also John Dickerson, one of Cooper's coauthors, who had been on the trip to Africa with the President during that week in July. Ari Fleischer had testified that he had leaked to Dickerson. (Unknown to the jury during the trial, Dickerson had denied it publicly.) A close reading of Cooper's careful responses suggests that he used information Dickerson gleaned from White House sources, including Fleischer, to support the *TIME* article's assertion of a White House war on Wilson, but that information did not include Fleischer outright identifying Wilson's wife as a CIA employee to Dickerson.

Q *Okay. Now, in fact, when you wrote that article, you had one other government official you already testified to, Karl Rove, correct?*
A That's correct, sir.

Q *And did you have also some information from John Dickerson of* TIME *Magazine?*
A Yes, sir, I did.

Q *Did that information concern a government official?*
A Yes.

Q *Okay. That information was also a source for what you wrote in this magazine, correct?*
A Yes . . .

Q *July 11th is the date that you talked to John Dickerson?*
A I believe that's correct, sir, yes.

Q *It was some time shortly after noon. Is that your recollection?*
A Roughly, yeah.

THE DEFENSE ASKS COOPER about an e-mail he sent on July 11, 2003 asking Dickerson to call him:

Q *Why did you send this e-mail?*
A I wanted to discuss the story we were working on together with him.

Q *Had you talked to Karl Rove by the time you sent this e-mail?*
A Yes.

Q *And did the question that you were putting to Mr. Dickerson involve the information you learned from Karl Rove?*
A Yes, sir.

Q *So, you believe that you told another reporter the information that you had heard from Mr. Rove that morning?*
A I'm sure I did.

Q *And it was a reporter in Africa, correct?*

A Yes.

Q *Aside from Mr. Dickerson on the 11th, what other reporters, as far as you know, knew, prior to the time you talked to Mr. Libby, about Mr. Wilson's wife having worked at the CIA or sending him on the trip?*

A Well, as I sit here today, Mr. Jeffress, I certainly recall I know I sent an e-mail [see exhibit in appendix] to the Washington Bureau Chief of *TIME* magazine at the time, Michael Duffy, and his Deputy Bureau Chief James Carney alerting them to the conversation I had with Mr. Rove. As for others, I'm not so sure.

Q *Now, did Mr. Rove indicate to you, when you talked to him that, I believe you said—did he say something to you to the effect that it's going to come out who sent Wilson on the trip?*

A Yes, he did.

Q *Did he tell you how he knew that that was coming out?*

A I don't believe he did, no.

Q *You did see later, maybe not the same day it appeared, but you saw later that it came out in an article, a column written by Robert Novak, right?*

A I certainly saw the Novak column.

Q *That happened the 14th before you wrote anything about this issue?*

A The column came out before I wrote this piece, which we have in evidence here, yes.

Q *Okay. You didn't see that piece, that Novak piece? Do you see columns that go out on the A.P. wire?*

A No.

Q *You don't see those?*

A I may have access to them but I don't see them.

Q *So you didn't know that Mr. Novak was reporting about Wilson's wife until you actually saw the column whenever you happened to read it?*

A That's correct.

Q *Now, when Mr. Rove made his comment about Mr. Wilson's wife, you wrote that down in your notes, didn't you? You made a note of it?*

A I did indeed.

Q *It was news to you, correct?*

A That is correct.

Q *And it was something that you thought should be reported, correct?*

A I thought it was something that we should do further reporting on, yeah . . .

JEFFRESS' QUESTION ABOUT Cooper's notes on Rove foreshadowed the defense's efforts to highlight the fact that Cooper's notes from his interview with Libby did not include information about Plame.

Q *Let me go back to the e-mail. It says, "He says, 'Don't get too far out on Wilson,'"* *says that the—you got DCIA meaning the Director of the CIA?*

A That's correct.

Q *"Didn't authorize the trip" and that "Cheney didn't authorize the trip." That's the* *first thing you said, correct?*

A Uh-huh.

Q *"'It was,' Mr. Rove said, 'Wilson's wife who apparently works at the agency on* *WMD issues who authorized the trip. Not only the genesis of the trip is flawed and* *suspect but so is the report.' He implied strongly there is still plenty to implicate* *Iraqi interest in acquiring uranium from Niger. Some of this is going to be declas-* *sified in the coming days". . .*

So, the article that you wrote, that Wilson's wife—he, Karl Rove, didn't name the *wife either?*

A No, he did not.

Q *Where did you get that name, by the way?*

A I got it the week of the 14th, and I either got it, I've testified to this before, I either got it from seeing Novak's article during the week of the 14th, not that day, or from Googling Wilson's name [in] an Internet search engine.

Q *Apparently, if you Googled Wilson's name, you would pull up that his wife's name* *is Valerie Plame, correct?*

A Plame, yes.

Q *. . . Anyway, you did get from Mr. Rove that she was a CIA official?*

A Yes.

Q *And you say "monitors proliferation of weapons of mass destruction"—that's how* *you interpreted "works at the Agency on WMD issues" that Mr. Rove gave you?*

A Yes.

Q *All right. Now, when you said "some government officials," you were also thinking* *of the information that you had received from John Dickerson, correct?*

A That's correct.

Q *That information, did that also corroborate each of the things that you said in this* *article?*

A . . . I took it to be confirming as well, yes.

Q *All right. Now, Mr. Cooper, you and Mr. Dickerson, obviously, and perhaps other* *reporters, knew by the time you talked to Mr. Libby that, or at least you had heard* *before you talked to Mr. Libby, that Wilson's wife worked for the CIA. Correct?*

A Sure.

THE DEFENSE MOVES INTO QUESTIONING Cooper about his interview with Libby, seeking to cast doubt on whether Cooper's recollection of what Libby said was accurate and whether Cooper really could have used Libby as a confirming source. Briefly questioning Cooper about his interaction with Libby as Cooper sought to avoid contempt charges and underlining the fact that Libby encouraged Cooper to testify, the defense then returns to Cooper and *TIME*'s reporting in July 2003, bringing out the fact that what Dickerson heard from White House officials in Africa criticizing Wilson was used as a basis for claims in *TIME*'s reporting. This is intended to suggest that Libby had not in fact been disparaging Wilson to Cooper, but merely responding to Wilson on the merits. Cooper is asked to go through his typed notes.

After acknowledging that there were two distinct calls between Libby and Cooper, Cooper recalls that the mention of Wilson's wife came at the very end of their conversation. At this point, the defense focuses in on the fact that Cooper's notes from his conversation with Libby have no indication specifically that Libby discussed Wilson's wife:

Q *Do you remember that this question that you asked Mr. Libby about Mr. Wilson's wife came in the second part of that call, that is the five minutes?*

A Yeah, I recall it coming at the very end of our conversation.

Q *Now, I would like to show you your notes again of that conversation, which I believe are 816, Defendant's Exhibit 816. [See appendix.] Would you blow up the next-to-the-last paragraph?*

You testified on direct examination, Mr. Cooper, that this conversation you had with Mr. Libby is not in your notes. Do you remember that?

A Yes, I did.

Q *These were the notes that you typed sprawled on your bed on your laptop while you were talking to Mr. Libby?*

A Yes, these are those notes.

Q *Looking at this particular entry, first of all, the first word is, "had something and about the Wilson thing and not sure if it's ever." That's the way it reads just looking at it, is that right?*

A Yeah, that's correct.

Q *We noticed, in looking at some of the others, that you are typing quickly, and trying to get down what's happening. You make a lot of mistakes and you leave a lot of things out. Both of those are true?*

A I think in the course of typing, sure, that happens.

Q *It said, "had something." If you had asked Mr. Libby a question, you probably wouldn't have typed up your question—You probably would have typed up what he said; is that right?*

A Yes. That's right.

Q *If you said "off the record, have you heard anything about Wilson's wife being involved in sending him on the trip," you probably wouldn't have written that down, right?*

A Yeah.

Q *But if he said he had heard . . . you might have tried to type that down, right?*
A Sure.

Q *Now, you have the word "had." Is it possible, Mr. Cooper, that in typing, you would have typed down the word "heard" and, just typing quickly, you put "had"?*
A That's certainly possible.

Q *You might have said "had heard" for that matter, correct?*
A That's not my recollection of what he said, but—

Q *Okay. But anyway "had something." And it says "and about the Wilson thing." Now, looking at your notes, you typed that word "and" [when] lots and lots of times when people aren't saying it, right?*
A Well, I'm not sure I accept that characterization that people aren't using the word "and." I would have to look at what you're referring to.

THE DEFENSE CONTINUES in this vein, showing that Cooper often didn't finish a particular line of his notes, to emphasize that his notes are not complete or entirely accurate records of what the person being interviewed said. At one point, the defense draws attention to a line that might be interpreted as a mistyping for something along the lines of what Libby had testified he told Cooper. The defense also notes a small change between drafts of Cooper's published account of what he told the grand jury that Libby told him:

Q *Each time that you've been asked that, you said Mr. Libby replied to you, "I've heard that, too"?*
A I think, yeah, "I've heard that too." I've always qualified that by saying . . . "words to the effect."

Q *Let me ask, did you write an article actually about what you told the Grand Jury?*
A Yeah, I wrote a couple.

Q *Did you discuss in that article what you told the Grand Jury about Mr. Libby?*
A Yes.

Q *I show you what's been marked for identification as Defendant's Exhibit 713. Do you recognize this as being a draft actually of the article that you wrote?*
A Yes, I do.

Q *If you look at Page 7, you are discussing your testimony with respect to Mr. Libby. And you wrote, at least in this draft you wrote, "Libby replied, 'Yeah, I've heard something like that' or words to that effect." Do you remember putting that in your draft article?*
A I'm sure I did. I don't remember literally typing it sitting here today but I'm sure I did if it's in the draft.

Q *Okay. Then did you cause* TIME *magazine to change that?*

A I believe I did change it, yeah.

Q *Let me show you what is Defendant's Exhibit 850. Is that your e-mail?*

A Yes, it is.

Q *Does it concern this article and your reference to Mr. Libby's words?*

A Uh-huh . . .

Q *So, did you tell—now Bambi Wulf, was she copy editor or what?*

A She was, I forget her exact title. But she would have been the person to take a correction to on a Saturday.

Q *All right. Now, you said, "Change the Libby quote on Line 262 to 'Libby replied, "yeah, I've heard that too" or words to that effect.'" Correct?*

A Yes.

Q *What you had written in the draft was "Libby replied, 'yeah, I've heard something like that' or words to that effect." Is that correct?*

A Yeah.

Q *Did your memory of the conversation change between these two or you were just improving the quote, shortening the article or what?*

A Well, my memory of the precise words has been cloudy to the extent I've always thought he said words to that effect of "yeah, I've heard that too" or "I've heard something like that." I've used both phrases in my testimony. I think the slightly shorter "yeah, I've heard that too" is the one that remains a little more prominent in my mind. That's the one that went into the final article that was published for readers to read.

THE DEFENSE NEXT HAS COOPER TESTIFY about an entry he made in the *TIME* magazine computer filing system for his editor right after his conversation with Libby, which similarly had nothing about Libby telling Cooper about Wilson's wife. The way Cooper framed the story for his editor prompts him to explain the context of that week in July 2003:

A I was struck all week, the week of July 6, by what stuck in my mind as a contradiction. On one hand, after Mr. Wilson wrote his op-ed in *The New York Times* and appeared on NBC's *Meet the Press* to say that he had taken this trip to Niger and that he had not found evidence of Iraqi procurement of uranium, the Administration did something that it rarely does, that many a[n] Administration rarely does, which is to acknowledge a big error. They said that the sixteen words should not have been in the State of the Union. That was a big deal.

So I was very struck by that. That's what made it an even bigger story after the op-ed. But then I was struck all week by statements that were both public and private that seemed to be disparaging Mr. Wilson. So, on one hand, they were saying "you were right, the sixteen words shouldn't have been in the State of the Union." Then on the other hand, they were saying the methodology is bad: "He's kind of a mama's boy. His wife sent him." There seemed to be a contradiction. (That's obviously a paraphrase. Nobody used the word mama's boy.)

Q *Who told you he was a mama's boy?*
A I just said, that is my interpretation of the implication of the remarks about the wife or that it was somehow untrue. So, I was struck all week by a seeming contradiction there.

Q *Let me ask you about that testimony. The White House did say late in the day on Monday, July 7th, as a matter of fact, Condoleezza Rice said it, to be specific, that, "while the Administration sticks by the accuracy of the sixteen words, the confidence in its truth did not rise to the level where it should be in the State of the Union speech." Do you recall that?*
A Yes.

Q *That was her point, right?*
A Yeah.

Q *Did you have the impression that that statement by Dr. Rice was made because of something in Wilson's report or something Wilson was saying?*
A Do I think that they would have taken back the sixteen words had Wilson not written the op-ed on Sunday and appeared on *Meet the Press* and made the case about those words? I find it implausible.

JEFFRESS HAS COOPER CONFIRM that there were other relevant events calling into question the sixteen words aside from Wilson's op-ed:

Q *Do you remember that, after the State of the Union speech, the IAEA—the International Atomic Energy Agency—discovered that documents reporting to show a deal between Iraq and Niger had been forged?*
A I remember them.

Q *That was some time after the State of the Union speech, correct?*
A That was after.

Q *Do you remember Mr. Tenet, George Tenet, released a statement on July 11th, about the same time as the day before you talked to Mr. Libby?*
A Sure, I remember that.

Q *Do you remember Mr. Tenet said the CIA had not known those documents were forged beforehand?*
A Right, I remember that.

Q *That the CIA essentially took responsibility for not having corrected that line in the State of the Union speech?*

A Yeah, that's an accurate characterization . . .

JEFFRESS GOES BACK through Cooper's original notes from his conversation with Libby, and gets Cooper to acknowledge that he understands what almost all of the notes refer to except the section dealing with Wilson, and there is clearly nothing about Wilson's wife. Jeffress goes on to contrast Cooper's failure to include anything about Wilson's wife from Libby in his note to his editors with the importance Cooper attributed to Karl Rove's initial revelation about Wilson's wife to Cooper the day before the reporter spoke with Libby:

Q *Isn't [it a] fact that, in the rather lengthy memorandum …you sent to your editor immediately after the conversation, everything that you've described that Mr. Libby said to you that day is in this memorandum except anything about Wilson's wife?*

A Yeah, the Wilson's wife thing is certainly not in the memorandum. I don't know if there is anything else.

Q *That is consistent, Mr. Cooper, with the fact that whatever Mr. Libby said to you in that conversation was not confirmation of anything. Isn't it?*

A What I remember, Mr. Jeffress, distinctively over these past three and a half years—

Q *Are you answering my question or some other question?*

MR. FITZGERALD: Objection, Your Honor.
THE WITNESS: I think I'm answering yours.
THE COURT: Overruled.
THE WITNESS: What I remember is his saying, "yeah, I've heard that too" or words to that effect, but I took it as confirmation.

Q *Why didn't you put it in your memo to your editor?*

A I don't know. I can't explain that. I've certainly had occasion to reflect on it over the past few years. The only thing I can possibly attribute it to is the late day in the magazine and I just didn't write it down . . .

THE DEFENSE HAS COOPER consult Exhibit 845, which is an e-mail thread with an editor at *TIME*:

Q *This confirms your conversation with Karl Rove?*

A Yeah, and others, yeah. It's another one of these files that are a synopsis of my reporting.

Q *This is . . . sort of like what you typed … after your conversation with Mr. Libby?*

A Yeah, exactly . . .

Q *Go down to where it says "a startling charge." Okay. Now, after you talked to Mr. Rove, you wrote to your editors that [you'd heard] "a startling charge from a senior administration official that we need to handle with some caution." Right?*

A Yes, I wrote that.

Q *And if we go down further, we find that, what that charge is that, "don't get too far out on Wilson, Wilson was not sent by the Director of the CIA . . . Or Dick Cheney, and when it comes out who sent him, it will be embarrassing." Is that right?*

A Yes.

Q *You're telling Adi Ignatius, your editor, what Mr. Rove told you?*

A Came across in the computer system and then sent it back to me with this note, interesting.

Q *You say "when I pressed the official, he said it was somebody at the agency involved in WMD, Wilson's wife. This guy was not an emissary, the source claimed. His report is nowhere near the truth. The official added in fact it may be totally wrong et cetera."*

So you did, immediately after talking to Mr. Rove, write to your editor and tell him what he said about Wilson's wife?

A Yeah, I sent this later in the day but yeah, it's a few hours after I spoke to Mr. Rove.

Q *...Adi Ignatius replied to you and said "interesting," right?*

A He sure did.

Q *You replied to him and said Rove himself, right?*

A I did say that.

Q *It was not a name you used in the first e-mail?*

A That's true.

A BENCH CONFERENCE called by the judge puts an end to this specific line of questioning, for reasons that are not clear, and the defense concludes its cross-examination with another line of questioning designed to cast doubt on whether Cooper really could have used Libby as a confirming source at all:

Q *Do you remember, Mr. Cooper, when I was asking you about definitions, and I particularly asked you about "off the record," and you said you couldn't use it, right?*

A I said that, unless perhaps in a confirming way, yes.

Q *You asked Mr. Libby off the record?*

A I said "off the record," yeah.

Q *So, he wouldn't have been any source for anything you wrote then, right?*

A Again, as I said, I took it to be confirmation of something I had heard from Mr. Rove.

Q *So if somebody tells you something off the record, you can use it as confirmation of something?*

A I've taken it to be that, yeah.

Q *You have taken it to be that?*

A I took it to be that in this case.

Q *You say "in this case[.]" Is that something that you take when you talk to Administration officials or police or private citizens for that matter, and they say "I'm telling you something off the record." Do you think you can use that if somebody else has told you about it?*

A You can't use it, you can't quote it, or you can't put it directly in the story. But could one use that information that you now have to go ask other people about it and try to elicit more fulsome explanation from others. Sure, in that sense you can. I did take it to be a confirmation of what I heard from Mr. Rove.

Q *What Mr. Rove told you was not off the record, correct?*

A That's correct.

Q *What you heard from John Dickerson, whatever you heard from John Dickerson in Africa, that wasn't off the record, correct?*

A That is correct.

FITZGERALD'S BRIEF REDIRECT examination focuses on the issue of Cooper getting confirmation from Libby, and on Cooper's testimony that the discussion of Wilson's wife occurred at the very end of their July 12 conversation:

Q *Now, on July 12th, on the day you spoke to Mr. Libby, would you have taken it as confirmation if Mr. Libby had told you that he didn't know if the information were true and he didn't even know if Mr. Wilson had a wife?*

A No, quite the opposite . . .

Q *Would you take it as confirmation if Mr. Libby had told you that reporters were telling him that Wilson's wife worked at the CIA or sent him on the trip?*

A I would not have taken it as confirmation. Quite the contrary, it would have stirred my competitive juices that other reporters were onto this.

Q *In fact, when did you learn that Mr. Novak had written a story on July 14th?*

A It was not July 14th. I'm somewhat embarrassed to say . . . Again, because of the weekend schedule at *TIME*, I didn't look at the paper that morning. So I think it was Tuesday or Wednesday I finally came around and saw the Novak column.

Q *What was your reaction?*

A My reaction was: "Oh, this thing about the wife is out there. Do we want to write a story? Do we want to write something more generally about the, you know, whether there is a war on Wilson?"

Q *But you didn't know the Novak column was coming before it was printed?*
A Oh, no.

Q *Did you ask follow-up questions with Mr. Libby after he told you that he had "heard this too" or words to that effect?*
A I should have but I didn't.

Q *Do you recall why?*
A He seemed very eager to get off the phone. This was at the very end of the conversation. Again, I think he only wanted to give me the on-the-record comment. I had the sense, you know, he was reluctant to say on the phone. So I just, you know, bid adieu and said goodbye . . .

Q *What did you tell the Grand Jury about the timing during the phone call of the conversation of Mr. Wilson's wife?*
A I believe I told them that it came at the very end.

MR. FITZGERALD: Thank you, nothing further.

OF THE QUESTIONS the jury poses to Cooper via the judge, two are of particular substantive interest:

THE COURT: Okay. This question you have to answer with a yes or no. During the conversation you had with Mr. Dickerson on July 11th, during the phone call when he was in Africa, did he relay any information to you that he had received over there?
THE WITNESS: Yes.
THE COURT: Did you think, in reference to your conversation that you had with Mr. Libby, did you think about the substance of that conversation before you received a subpoena or was it only after you received the subpoena that you started to focus on what that conversation had been about?
THE WITNESS: No, I focused on it well before the subpoena . . . [F]irst in the week of July 14th, to write the "War on Wilson?" piece. And then as the story of the disclosure of the CIA agent became a big deal during the summer of 2003 and then really a big deal in the fall, I certainly had many occasions to reflect about my conversation with Mr. Libby and as well as others.

COOPER IS EXCUSED, and the judge also excuses the jury in order take up with the lawyers again the prosecution's desire to enter into evidence the videos of White House spokesperson Scott McClellan's press conferences. Fitzgerald argues that, because of Libby's efforts (and Cheney's efforts on his behalf) to get the White House to issue a statement clearing Libby of leaking to Novak and of leaking classified information, McClellan was essentially acting as Libby's agent, which would mean the Press Secretary's statements could be entered as evidence. Wells gives an intriguing response about the chain of decision-makers, bringing President Bush into it:

MR. WELLS: I don't think the transcript is going to answer it because I don't think anybody knows. I think you would have to talk to President Bush because he's probably somewhere in that chain.

MR. FITZGERALD: Your Honor, I think the transcript both in the Grand Jury and in Mr. Wells' opening says that the Vice President did this for Mr. Libby. And the note, it just says it right—

THE COURT: The opening statement is not evidence.

MR. FITZGERALD: But it is uncomfortable when someone takes an evidentiary position inconsistent with how they opened. As far as the White House, the White House was throwing Mr. Libby under the bus. Mr. Libby is trying to save himself through the Vice President. Now we're getting an implication that it must have been the President involved in this.

The testimony in the Grand Jury is that Mr. Libby went to people to get the clearing statement. Then he went to the Vice President. And that he understood the Vice President interceded for him.

We've heard evidence, not from [the] opening statement but from Mr. Addington, that when he went to Mr. Bartlett and said you people shouldn't basically be making these statements, Mr. Bartlett says, that decision was your boss . . . meaning the Vice President. That was yesterday.

We have the note—that's Government's Exhibit 532—in evidence, from the Vice President: "Has to happen today; call out the key press, saying same thing about Scooter as Karl. This is not—"

THE COURT: What date is that?

MR. FITZGERALD: It's not dated but it's prior to the statement. So it's probably around October 4. This is what Mr. Cheney, the Vice President, wrote. It's not a request to the President. It's a direction, and my understanding is the Vice President spoke to Mr. McClellan.

THE COURT: Who's that to? Does it say who he gave those to?

MR. FITZGERALD: No, but Mr. Libby testified in the Grand Jury that these are the words he wanted Mr. McClellan to issue, and Mr. McClellan then made a statement. We have evidence from Mr. Addington on cross examination yesterday, that when he made a comment to Mr. Bartlett about why this statement was made, Mr. Bartlett responded "That was your boss."

I think there is no dispute here that the decision to issue that statement did not come from the President. It came from the Vice President. There is no dispute that Mr. Libby asked the Vice President to intercede.

Mr. Libby also asked Mr. McClellan to intercede. It got done. I think that's right down smack down the middle of a statement by a person authorized by a party to make it.

MR. WELLS: I do not believe those are the facts. I do not believe the evidence will show that Vice President Cheney went to Andrew Card. I think maybe we ought to wait until the Vice President gets here to find out what happened. But I do not believe his recitation is based on the facts or is factual.

MR. FITZGERALD: Your Honor, I think the Grand Jury transcript will speak for itself. I also think the document speaks for itself. We have in evidence already. If Mr. Wells ever calls the Vice President, we can ask about that. But that shouldn't stop the Government's case when we've had testimony elicited through the defense's questions yesterday that the statement issued to clear Mr. Libby came at the direction of the Vice President. We have Grand Jury testimony by the defendant.

THE DEFENSE ALSO NOTES that it has a Rule 29 motion for immediate acquittal with regard to the part of the obstruction count based on Libby's testimony about his July 12 conversation with Miller. (The motion proves successful subsequently.) With that, court recesses for the day.

*

FEBRUARY 1, 2007

DEBORAH BOND

FOLLOWING THE TESTIMONY from journalists Judith Miller and Matt Cooper, FBI agent Deborah Bond would be the next witness. However, before she could begin her testimony about interviews that the FBI conducted with Scooter Libby on October 14, and November 26, 2003, there is a lengthy discussion among the prosecution, defense, and Judge Walton on the admissibility of certain pieces of evidence.

Among these pieces of evidence is the Classified Information Non-Disclosure Agreement (NDA) that Libby had signed when he joined the Bush administration in 2001. Another involves Bush press secretary Scott McClellan's statement from the White House podium that he had personally questioned administration officials, including Scooter Libby, about the leak of Valerie Plame's CIA employment. He said on October 10, 2003, that he had been personally assured by Libby that he'd had nothing to do with it. The prosecution wants a videotape of this statement to be played for the jury, while the defense insists that this would be unduly prejudicial to their client. The prosecution asserts that, in effect, Libby had appointed McClellan as his agent, who told the press and the public, that Libby's hands were clean on this matter. Fitzgerald says that Libby "hid behind Mr. McClellan to do it."

Deborah Bond is brought in. Currently the lead FBI agent on the case, she had been involved in the investigation since its inception, and her testimony serves to introduce the nature of the investigation, as well as the nature of Libby's statement to the FBI. Zeidenberg does the prosecution's questioning.

By Mr. Zeidenberg:

Q *Now, can you tell the ladies and gentlemen of the jury what this investigation was about?*

A It was about the possible unauthorized disclosure of classified information regarding Valerie Wilson's identity and her employment at the CIA to the media.

Q *What was it you were trying to determine in this investigation?*

A We were trying to determine how it happened that her name and her employment at the CIA got to the media.

Q *In trying to find out how her name and employment got to the media, what were the underlying facts you were trying to [uncover]?*

A We were trying to find out the identities of those who participated in disclosing Valerie Wilson's name, and her employment with the CIA to the media, whether they knew that the information was classified and what their intent was on disclosing the information.

Q *In determining the identity of those involved, as well as their intent, can you tell the ladies and gentlemen what underlying facts you were trying to determine so you could find out the intent and the identities of those involved?*

A We were trying to find out the source of the information. I can give you two examples. If they learned the information from a government source, like they were in a meeting where classified information was discussed, and they went out, they left the meeting, and they went out and they just told somebody, we would think that there was more likelihood that they knew, if they knew the information was classified they were disclosing and that they had intent to do so.

But for another extreme, if they were just out talking to somebody and they gave them the information and they went and told somebody, then it would be less likely that they knew the information was classified, and therefore less likely that they intentionally disclosed this classified information.

Q *... What were some of the other facts underlying this case that you were trying to undercover?*

A We were trying to find out the names of the people who knew about her employment at the CIA and her identity, as well as where they learned the information, who they told, ... if they told, somebody told them to disclose it to the media.

If they told reporters, we wanted to know who the reporters were and what they told them. And we wanted to know if they understood the information to be classified.

Q *Now, were you present for an interview with Mr. Libby on October 14, 2003?*
A Yes, I was.

Q *Can you tell the ladies and gentlemen who else was present for that interview?*
A Inspector Eckenrode with the FBI, Special Agent Kirk Armfield and myself, along with Mr. Libby and his attorney, Joseph Tate.

Q *Where did the interview take place?*
A It took place in Mr. Libby's office at the Old Executive Office Building adjacent to the White House.

Q *Approximately how long was the interview?*
A About an hour and a half.

Q *Now, did you drop in on Mr. Libby unexpectedly or was that interview set up in advance?*
A It was set up in advance.

Q *What was he told about what you were there to talk to him about?*
A He was told that we were there for an investigation being conducted about the possible unauthorized disclosure of classified information regarding Valerie Wilson's name and her employment at the CIA.

Q *Was Mr. Libby's attorney present during the interview?*

A Yes, for the entire time.

Q *Now, during the interview, did Mr. Libby . . . give you any documents?*
A Yes.

Q *Can you tell us about that?*
A He told us that he, in preparation for the interview, he had prepared a document and had it typed, entitled "Ambassador Wilson's Claims." On this document, there were four bullet points of what Ambassador Wilson had been saying in the press . . .

Q *Is this the document that is being shown on the screen? Is this the document that Mr. Libby was talking to you about?*
A It's a copy, yes.

Q *Can you tell us what Mr. Libby told you and the other agents during the course of the interview about Government Exhibit 10?*
A That, well, he prepared it for the interview and it was allegations that Joe Wilson was making against the Office of the Vice President.

Q *And what did he tell you about these bullet points?*
A That they weren't true. He didn't believe that they were true.

Q *Can you tell us how many times, if you know, Mr. Libby referred to Government Exhibit 10 during the course of your interview?*
A I believe three or four times.

Q *Now, did you talk with Mr. Libby about how it was he learned about Mr. Wilson's wife's employment with the CIA?*
A Yes, I did.

Q *Can you tell us what he told you?*
A Mr. Libby claimed that he first learned about Joe Wilson's wife from the Vice President during a telephone conversation with the Vice President on or about June 12, 2003.

Q *Did he give you a description of what happened during that telephone call?*
A Yes, he did.

Q *Did he have any documents with him in regards to that?*
A Yes, he showed us a handwritten note that he claimed that he had written during this conversation with the Vice President.

Q *What did he tell you about his conversation with the Vice President? First of all, why don't we start in talking about when he believed, the precise date of when he believed that conversation took place?*
A Well, on the note it's written "6-12-03," with a line on top, which he told us meant approximately. Mr. Libby told us, the conversation with the Vice President was in regard to an upcoming article being written with questions posed to the Vice President's office from Walter Pincus from *The Washington Post.*

Mr. Libby told us that he was aware that the articles being written for the newspaper for June 12th. So he believed that he talked to the Vice President about this, this note prior to then. That he had written the date earlier, after he had written the body of the document, within a couple days. But he couldn't remember precisely what date he put on the document.

Q *So it's clear, he dated the document some time after he wrote it. Is that what you're saying?*

A Yes.

Q *And just so it's clear, …he told you what about when he thought that telephone conversation most likely occurred?*

A A day or two before June 12th.

Q *What did he tell you the Vice President told him during that telephone conversation?*

A Mr. Libby told us that, during the telephone conversation . . . the Vice President told him that the former ambassador's wife worked in the CP division of the CIA. Mr. Libby explained to us that the CP stood for "Counter Proliferation".

Q *Did Mr. Libby tell you where he thought the Vice President had learned this information? …*

A Mr. Libby told us that the Vice President told him that he had received this information from someone at the CIA. Mr. Libby told us that he believed the Vice President had learned this information from the Director of Central Intelligence, George Tenet. However, he was not certain if it was Mr. Tenet or someone else at the CIA that the Vice President was referring to.

Q *Did Mr. Libby tell you what happened to his memory regarding this telephone conversation with the Vice President?*

A Yes. Mr. Libby claimed that he forgot about this conversation with the Vice President and the note. And when he learned it later in July from Mr. Russert of NBC News, that it was as if he had learned it for the first time. It was not until early October 2003 when he was searching through his documents for this investigation that he realized that he had actually learned about [the] former ambassador's wife working at the CIA in June of 2003.

> *Mr. Libby claimed that he forgot about this conversation with the Vice President and the note. And when he learned it later in July from Mr. Russert of NBC News, that it was as if he had learned it for the first time. It was not until early October 2003. . . that he realized that had actually learned about [the] former ambassador's wife working at the CIA in June of 2003.*

Q *Did he tell you when he actually learned the name of the former ambassador?*

A Yes, he did. . . . Mr. Libby claimed that he learned the name of the former ambassador . . . when he read Joe Wilson's op-ed in *The New York Times* on July 6.

Q *So, prior to July 6, he didn't know the name; is that correct?*

A That's what he told us.

Q *What about just the existence of an envoy that went to Niger? When did he learn about that?*

A Mr. Libby told us that he knew of an envoy after reading an article written by Nicholas Kristof on May 6, 2003 in, I believe, *The New York Times.*

Q *Now, did you ask him about any other reporters that he had talked to in the June/July 2003 time frame?*

A Yes, we did.

Q *Did the name David Sanger come up?*

A Yes, it did.

Q *Who brought up the name David Sanger?*

A Mr. Libby . . .

Q *Did he tell you where Mr. Sanger worked?*

A At *The New York Times* . . .

Q *Did he indicate the date on which he spoke with Mr. Sanger?*

A Yes, Mr. Libby told us it was July 2, 2003.

Q *Was that a date that you knew or that he provided?*

A . . . We did not know that date. Mr. Libby told us.

Q *Did he tell you about a conversation he had with Judith Miller?*

A Yes, he did.

Q *When did he tell you that he met with Judith Miller?*

A Mr. Libby told us that he met with Judith Miller on July 8, 2003, at the St. Regis Hotel dining room.

Q *What did he tell you about his meeting with Judith Miller on July 8, 2003?*

A Mr. Libby told us that, prior to meeting with Judith Miller, he had had a discussion with the Vice President regarding the October 2002 National Intelligence Estimate or NIE, in which Mr. Libby said that the Vice President wanted him to get it to the public.

However, Mr. Libby knew that this information was classified and went to David Addington, the General Counsel to the Vice President, and discussed with him whether the President had the authority to declassify a document. After Mr. Addington told him that the President did have the authority, he felt he was able to go out and talk about it.

Q *Now, after he spoke with Mr. Addington and Mr. Addington said the President had the authority, what did Mr. Libby say that he did?*

A Mr. Libby told us that, during his meeting with Judy Miller, that he discussed the NIE with her.

Q *Did he tell you what else he discussed with Judith Miller?*

A Yes, he did. Mr. Libby told us that they discussed a book that she had coauthored entitled *Germs* and that he had answered questions that she had about weapons of mass destruction in Iraq and, in general, the Joe Wilson matter.

Q *... Was Mr. Libby asked whether the subject of Wilson's wife, if it ever came up during his meeting with Judith Miller?*

A Yes, he was.

Q *What did he say?*

A Mr. Libby told us he had no recollection of discussing Joe Wilson's wife with Ms. Miller . . .

Q *Now, did the subject of Chris Matthews and his show* Hardball *come up during the course of your interview?*

A Yes it did.

Q *Can you tell us about that?*

A Mr. Libby told us that he had heard reports on July 8th or 9th about Chris Matthews, who was the host of MSNBC's news program, *Hardball*. Mr. Matthews was making, was criticizing the Office of the Vice President and, in particular, Mr. Libby and the Vice President. Mr. Libby believed that Chris Matthews ... was misleading the public and decided to call Tim Russert.

Q *Did he tell you why he decided to call Tim Russert?*

A Mr. Libby told us that he believed that, since MSNBC was under the umbrella of NBC, that possibly Mr. Russert could help him in convincing Mr. Matthews to straighten out the story and tell both sides of it . . . Mr. Libby told us that he contacted Mr. Russert and vented his complaint to [him] about Chris Matthews.

Q *Did he tell you when he spoke with Mr. Russert?*

A Yes, he did. Mr. Libby told us he . . . spoke to Mr. Russert on July 10th or July 11, 2003.

Q *Now, can you tell the ladies and gentlemen what Mr. Libby told you about what happened during that conversation with Mr. Russert?*

A Well, Mr. Libby told us that, after he told Mr. Russert about what he felt about Mr. Matthews, Mr. Russert told him that he didn't believe that there was anything he could do, because he wasn't the direct supervisor of Chris Matthews, but suggested he could call the producer of the show, *Hardball*.

Q *Was that the end of the conversation?*

A No, it wasn't . . . Mr. Libby claimed that Mr. Russert asked him whether or not Mr. Libby knew that Joe Wilson's wife worked at the CIA.

Q *Did Mr. Libby tell you how he responded?*

A Mr. Libby claimed that he said that, no, he did not know that.

Q *What did Mr. Libby say happened next?*
A Mr. Libby said that Mr. Russert told him that all the reporters knew that.

Q *What did Mr. Libby say happened then?*
A Mr. Libby told us that [he] told Mr. Russert that he didn't know that either.

Q *Did Mr. Libby tell you what he understood Mr. Russert to mean when he said all the reporters know that?*
A Yes, Mr. Libby told us that he believed it was the reporters in the Washington, D.C., area.

Q *Did Mr. Libby tell you what his reaction was when he heard this news from Mr. Russert?*
A Mr. Libby told us that he was surprised because … it was [as if]the first time that he had heard it.

Q *Now, did Mr. Libby tell you about a conversation he had with Karl Rove at about this time frame?*
A Yes, he did.

Q *Tell us, did he date the conversation?*
A Yes, Mr. Libby told us that he believed he spoke to Mr. Rove on July 11th.

Q *Can you tell us about what Mr. Libby said happened during that conversation with Mr. Rove?*
A Yeah. Mr. Libby told us that he spoke to Mr. Rove with regard to an upcoming statement being prepared by George Tenet that was going to be put out that evening as well [on] the Joe Wilson matter.

Q *And what did Mr. Libby tell you was said during that conversation?*
A Mr. Libby told us … Mr. Rove related to him that Mr. Rove had had a conversation with Bob Novak of the *Chicago Sun-Times* in which Mr. Novak told Mr. Rove that he had seen Mr. Wilson in a green room prior to the telephone program. And that Mr. Novak wasn't very impressed with Mr. Wilson. And he was planning on writing an article about him.

Q *What did Mr. Libby tell you about the rest of the conversation?*
A Mr. Libby told us that Mr. Rove had the understanding that Mr. Novak already knew that Joe Wilson's wife worked at the CIA.

Q *What did Mr. Libby tell you he understood from that conversation with Mr. Rove?*
A Mr. Libby told us that he was aware that Mr. Rove learned from Mr. Novak that Joe Wilson's wife worked at the CIA.

Q *Now, did Mr. Libby indicate to you whether or not he told Mr. Rove anything during that conversation?*
A Yes. Mr. Libby told us that, after hearing this from Mr. Rove, he told Mr. Rove about his conversation with Mr. Russert.

Q *Now, did you discuss with Mr. Libby a July 12th trip to Norfolk, Virginia?*

A Mr. Libby told us that the Office of the Vice President and many of the staff, including the Vice President, some of his family, Mr. Libby and his family, traveled on Air Force Two, to Norfolk, Virginia, to attend the commissioning of the USS *Ronald Reagan*.

Q *What did Mr. Libby say happened on the return portion of that trip?*

A Mr. Libby told us that, on the return trip, he went to sit with the Vice President to discuss matters that the Vice President wanted him to tell on the record to the press in regard to the Joe Wilson matter.

Q *What did Mr. Libby say that he did?*

A Mr. Libby told us that he wrote ... verbatim [notes] of what the Vice President told him to write and make statements to the press.

Q *...Did he tell you what happened once they landed?*

A Yes. Mr. Libby and his assistant, Jenny Mayfield, and Cathie Martin, the Assistant Vice President for Public Affairs, went to an office adjacent to the lobby at Andrews Air Force Base airport where they made calls to the press.

Q *Can you tell us who he said that they called?*

A Mr. Libby said that they spoke, they called, or attempted to call Matt Cooper of *TIME* magazine, Glenn Kessler of *The Washington Post* and Evan Thomas of *Newsweek*.

Q *Did Mr. Libby tell you whether or not he, in fact, was able to get in touch with Matt Cooper of* TIME *magazine?*

A Yes, they were.

Q *Can you tell us what he told you about his conversation with Mr. Cooper?*

A Mr. Libby told us that he called Mr. Cooper and read verbatim what he had written in his notes while he was on Air Force Two, and read them to Mr. Cooper.

Q *Did he tell you what happened after he read the verbatim statement to Mr. Cooper?*

A Yes. Mr. Libby told us that Matt Cooper then asked him why Mr. Wilson continued to blame the Office of the Vice President or say that the Office of the Vice President sent him to Niger.

Q *What did Mr. Libby say—how did Mr. Libby say he responded?*

A Mr. Libby claimed that he went off the record and told Matt Cooper that reporters were telling the Administration that Joe Wilson's wife worked at the CIA, but he did not know if it were true.

Q *Did Mr. Libby tell you about any conversations he had with anyone else from the media from Andrews Air Force Base that day?*

A Yes. Mr. Libby had left a message for Evan Thomas. He did not think that he spoke to him that day but maybe later. He told us that he got in touch with Glenn Kessler, but Glenn Kessler was at the zoo and told him he would call him back at a later time.

Q *Now, during the course of the interview, did you speak with Mr. Libby about a conversation he had with Andrea Mitchell of NBC?*

A Yes.

Q *Can you tell us about what he said about that, starting with when he thinks he spoke with her?*

A Yes. Mr. Libby told us that he believed that he had contacted Andrea Mitchell, who is with NBC News, after July 10th, but more likely after July 14th, because they had been playing telephone tag. And according to Mr. Libby, Andrea Mitchell made some negative comments about the Office of the Vice President. And he wanted to discuss them with her.

Q *Did he in fact speak with her? Did he tell you?*

A Yes, Mr. Libby said he spoke to her.

Q *Can you describe how Mr. Libby told you the conversation went?*

A Mr. Libby told us that . . . she asked him a question about why Joe Wilson continued to claim that the Vice President's office had sent him to Niger. He may have told her what the reporters were telling him, that Joe Wilson's wife worked at the CIA.

However, he claimed that he would have said it in a way in which she wouldn't have asked him how he found out because he didn't want her to know that he had learned this information from her boss, Tim Russert.

Q *Did he indicate why he didn't want Andrea Mitchell to know why he had learned, how he had learned the information from Tim Russert?*

A Mr. Libby told us that he thought it might be a little bit awkward if he knew, had learned this information from Tim Russert and she might not have known it.

Q *Now, did Mr. Libby tell you, during the course of the interview, how often he spoke to the press?*

A Yes, Mr. Libby told us he did not speak to the press very often.

Q *Was Robert Novak's name brought up at any point in the interview?*

A Yes, it was.

Q *When was that in the interview?*

A Toward the end of the interview.

Q *What was asked and what did Mr. Libby say?*

A Mr. Libby told us that he did not speak to Robert Novak during the week of July 7th through 14th. However, later in the month, he had gotten calls from Mr. Novak. And he returned the calls on about July 25, 2003.

Q *Can you tell us, Agent Bond, how the interview was concluded?*

A We asked Mr. Libby whether or not he would be available to talk with us again. We only had an hour and a half with him. He and his attorney said that they would meet with us, but they would like to review documents prior to another interview being set up.

Q *Again, this interview that you've just talked about, was on which date? ...*
A October 14, 2003 . . .

Q *What was the date of the second interview?*
A It was November 26, 2003 . . . The Wednesday before Thanksgiving.

Q *Were you present for this interview as well?*
A Yes, I was.

Q *In fact was it the same participants in this interview?*
A Yes and the same seating arrangements.

Q *Same office?*
A Same office.

Q *I'm going to ask you some questions about that interview. But let me just ask you, generally, did Mr. Libby basically tell you the same information in the second interview as he did in the first?*
A Just about. There were some documents that he had been able to review that refreshed his memory.

Q *Did his story change in any material respects?*
A No, it did not.

Q *And again, did you ask him again, how it was he learned about Wilson's wife?*
A Yes.

Q *What did he tell you in the second interview regarding that?*
A Well, as he had told us before, he told us that he had had this conversation, a conversation with the Vice President about June 12, 2003.

Q *Did Mr. Libby, during this November 26th interview, five weeks after your first one, did he tell you, during the course of that interview again, about his memory and what happened to it, of this June 12th conversation over the telephone with the Vice President?*
A Yes. Again, Mr. Libby told us that he had forgotten about this completely until he looked for it in October. His first memory of it, of Joe Wilson's wife working at the CIA, came from Mr. Russert on July 10th or 11th.

Q *During the course of that interview, did you ask him about his interactions with someone from the CIA by the name of Robert Grenier?*
A Yes, we did.

Q *Can you tell us what Mr. Libby told you about his interactions with Mr. Grenier?*
A Yes. Mr. Libby told us that he had been trying to get a hold of the Deputy Director of Central Intelligence, John McLaughlin, during the June 9th time frame. And when he was unable to get through to Mr. McLaughlin, he contacted Bob Grenier.

Q *Did he say whether or not he had had any difficulty getting in touch with Mr. Grenier?*

A He said he had played telephone tag with him for a few exchanges and may have talked to him once or twice.

Q *What did he say he wanted to speak with Mr. Grenier about?*
A Mr. Libby couldn't, told us he couldn't recall specifically what their conversation was about. But it could have been about the Nicholas Kristof piece from May 6, 2003.

Q *Did he say when it was he was trying to get in touch with Mr. Grenier?*
A Around June 9th, give or take a day.

Q *Did Mr. Libby tell you if the subject of Wilson's wife came up in his conversation with Mr. Grenier?*
A No, he did not.

Q *Did you ask Mr. Libby about a lunch he had with Ari Fleischer on July 7, 2003?*
A Yes, we did.

Q *And can you tell us what he told you about that?*
A Mr. Libby told us that he had wanted to go to lunch with Mr. Fleischer since Mr. Fleischer was leaving the White House the next week. He set it up to go to lunch. They had lunch around or on July 7th at the White House mess.

Q *Did Mr. Libby tell you what it was that he and Mr. Fleischer spoke about during their lunch?*
A Yes, Mr. Libby told us that they had discussed Mr. Fleischer's future plans in general. The Joe Wilson issue that had just come out into the press the day before and … the Miami Dolphins football team.

Q *Okay. Other than Mr. Fleischer's future plans, the Wilson matter that had just come out in the press the day before and the Miami Dolphins, did Mr. Libby say anything else came up during his lunch with Mr. Fleischer?*
A Not that I recall . . .

Q *Did you ask him if the subject of Wilson's wife came up at any point during their lunch?*
A Yes, we asked him. But he adamantly denied knowing about Joe Wilson's wife or discussing it with Mr. Fleischer.

Q *Did he say how it was he could be so sure?*
A He didn't remember it until, he didn't know that Joe Wilson's wife worked at the agency until he spoke to Tim Russert on July 10th or 11th . . .

Q *Did you ask him, once again, whether or not the subject of Wilson's wife came up during his meeting with Judith Miller on July 8th?*
A We did. And again, Mr. Libby told us that he did not recall having that discussion with Judy Miller.

Q *Did the subject of the July 10th or 11th Tim Russert conversation come up again on November 26, 2003?*
A Yes, it did.

Q *Can you take us through what Mr. Libby told you about that conversation on November 26th?*

A Like he had told us in October, he had called Mr. Russert because he was upset with what Mr. Matthews was reporting about the Office of the Vice President. After Mr. Russert told him that there was nothing he could do, Mr. Russert gave him the name of the producer of the show *Hardball* [and] told him to call him . . .

Q *What did Mr. Libby say Mr. Russert said after they complained to him about* **Hardball?**

A Mr. Libby told us that Mr. Russert asked him whether or not he knew if Joe Wilson's wife worked at the CIA. Again, Mr. Libby told us that he told Mr. Russert that he did not know that.

Q *. . . Did he tell you, once again, what Mr. Russert's response was when Mr. Libby said he did not know that?*

A Yes, Mr. Libby claimed that Mr. Russert told him that all the reporters knew that.

Q *Did Mr. Libby tell you what the ground rules were, if any, for the conversation with Mr. Russert?*

A Yes. Mr. Libby told us that he went off the record when he had this discussion with Mr. Russert.

Q *Did you ask Mr. Libby how sure he was that he learned this information, or that he at least thought he was learning this information from Mr. Russert on July 10th or July 11th?*

A Yes, Mr. Libby told us he was sure he spoke to Mr. Russert, not any other reporter, about Joe Wilson's wife working at the CIA.

Q *. . . Did the subject of Andrea Mitchell come up again?*

A Yes, it did.

Q *And did Mr. Libby tell you the same thing about the conversation with Andrea Mitchell that he told you on October 14th?*

A Basically the same, yes.

Q *During the course of that conversation, did you have an opportunity to show him a draft of the July 11th Tenet statement that we've heard about from the CIA Director, George Tenet?*

A Yes, we did.

Q *Was that a document that you had obtained during the preceding five weeks?*

A Yes, we received a lot of documents from the Office of the Vice President during the five weeks before.

MR. ZEIDENBERG: If there is no objection, I would like to show the witness Government Exhibit 542?

MR. WELLS: No objection.

THE COURT: Very well.

By Mr. Zeidenberg:

Q *Can you tell us what the front is of 542?*

A It's a fax cover sheet to Steve Hadley, Deputy National Security from John McLaughlin, the Deputy Director of Central Intelligence.

Q *Attached to 542, if we could go to the next page, can you read that for the record?*

A It's dated July 11, 2003. It's from the Deputy Director of Central Intelligence. And it states, "Steve, here is our draft we plan to release at 13:15 hours," which is 1:15 P.M. Signed John McLaughlin.

Q *If you just go to the first page, I'm sorry, the next page of this document. It's fair to say that this was a draft of the George Tenet statement that was ultimately released late in the day on July 11, 2003?*

A It is. But I know it came out later in the day. So, if it came out at 1:15, it might have been a draft. I can't tell from reading this that it was a draft.

Q *But this is at least a version—*

A A version, yes.

Q *—of the Tenet statement, fair to say?*

A Yes.

Q *If we could just go to the very first page of 542. Can you read for us the handwritten comment?*

A It says "unsatisfactory" and it's underlined.

Q *And did you ask Mr. Libby whose handwriting he thought that was?*

A Yes, we asked Mr. Libby. And he told us that it looked like it could have been that of the Vice President. But it also could have been that of Steve Hadley.

> *Mr. Libby said that they were not happy with the statement. It didn't quite explain . . . that the Office of the Vice President did not send Joe Wilson to Niger.*

Q *Do you know, from looking at the Bates number on this production, whose production this came from?*

A Yes. I've reviewed thousands of documents. I recognize this as coming from the production of Debra Heiden, who is the Executive Assistant to the Vice President.

Q *Did Mr. Libby tell you what the Vice President's reaction was to the Tenet statement?*

A Yes, he did. Mr. Libby said that they were not happy with the statement. It didn't quite explain . . . that the Office of the Vice President did not send Joe Wilson to Niger.

Q *During the November 26th meeting with Mr. Libby, did the subject of . . . the July 11th conversation that Mr. Libby said he had with Karl Rove . . . come up again?*

A It did. He said the same thing as before. However, Mr. Libby told us that . . . he may have brought up his conversation with Mr. Russert first before Mr. Rove explained to him his conversation with Mr. Novak.

Q *Did you speak with Mr. Libby in the second interview as well about the July 12th trip to Norfolk?*

A Yes, we did.

Q *Did he tell you any more about the Vice President's feelings towards the Wilson matter at that point in time?*

A Yes. Mr. Libby told us that, again, that they weren't satisfied with the Tenet statement. And they wanted to get out to the press, make it clear to the public, that the Office of the Vice President did not know about and did not send Mr. Wilson to Niger.

Q *Did he tell you about the Vice President's mood in regards to this matter?*

A He was frustrated and upset that the press was still claiming that the Vice President's office sent Joe Wilson … when they claimed they didn't send him.

Q *Did Mr. Libby tell you about a meeting that he had with the Vice President on Air Force Two on the return trip from Norfolk?*

A Yes, like he had told us before, Mr. Libby said that he went to the Vice President's cabin and got the statement. In addition, there was some discussion about whether or not they should report to the press that Ambassador Wilson's wife worked at the CIA. However, Mr. Libby was not sure of that.

Q *Just to go back over that … If you could just explain what Mr. Libby told you about his conversation, any conversation he may have had with the Vice President about Wilson's wife while they were on Air Force Two?*

A Yes. Mr. Libby told us that, after he spoke with Mr. Russert and learned that Ambassador Wilson's wife worked at the CIA, he discussed it with the Vice President. He's not certain exactly when they discussed it.

Q *… Did you ask Mr. Libby whether or not he and the Vice President discussed whether the information about the wife should be made public to the press?*

A Mr. Libby told us he believed that they may have talked about it but he was not sure.

Q *Did Mr. Libby, once again, talk to you and tell you about what he said transpired once he landed at Andrews Air Force Base and called members of the media?*

A Yes, he did.

Q *Specifically, did he tell you, once again, about his telephone conversation with Matthew Cooper of* TIME *magazine?*

A He [said], like he had told us previously, that he had, along with Jenny Mayfield and Cathie Martin, made the calls to the press . . . He said he contacted Matt Cooper and read the statement to Matt Cooper.

And when Mr. Libby claimed, after Mr. Cooper asked him about Joe Wilson, he went off the record and told him that the information that was being spread around about Mr. Wilson might not be true.

Q *Now, who said the information being spread around might not be true?*

A I'm sorry. Mr. Libby.

Q *And what did Mr. Libby say happened next in that conversation?*

A Mr. Libby then told us that he had told Matt Cooper that the reporters were telling the Administration that Joe Wilson's wife worked at the CIA. And again, he told us that he told Matt Cooper that he didn't know if that information was true.

Q *Now, at the end of the interview, did you ask Mr. Libby if he was willing to sign a waiver?*

A Yes, we did.

Q *Can you just tell us briefly what that waiver was?*

A It was a waiver that we were showing to people and asking them to sign that would have released their confidentiality with reporters, so that they could, so the reporters would want to talk to us . . .

Q *Now, in January 2004, did a Grand Jury here in the District of Columbia begin investigating this case?*

A Yes, it did.

Q *Can you tell us what your understanding was of the purpose of that Grand Jury investigation?*

A It was basically the same as the previous investigation, gathering all the facts and circumstances surrounding how the disclosure of Valerie Wilson's name and employment at the CIA got to the media. In addition, we wanted to make sure that the information we were receiving was truthful and accurate.

MR. ZEIDENBERG: Your Honor, I don't have any further questions.

THE CROSS-EXAMINATION BY TED WELLS quickly becomes contentious with the defense attorney questioning Agent Bond on her memory of the FBI's first interview with Scooter Libby. Wells is intent on establishing that his client had not had the opportunity to review certain contemporaneous notes, and that Joseph Tate, the attorney then representing Libby, states this at the beginning of the October 14 interview. Bond admits that her notes of the meeting don't reflect certain statements by Tate. Wells later questions Bond on what the FBI told Libby was the scope of their investigation. He also elicits from Bond the admission that her very first day on the case was the day of the Libby interview, October 14. Despite Wells's insistence that Libby had little opportunity to review relevant notes prior to Libby's first meeting with the FBI, he quickly bores in on what he believes is exculpatory conduct by his client, concerning one document that Libby did bring to the interview.

By Mr. Wells:

Q *Is it correct that, in the October 14 interview, that Government Exhibit 104 was discussed?*

A Mr. Libby brought it to us.

Q *He brought a copy of the document to the meeting?*

A Yes.

Q *Now, so the document that Mr. Libby brought to his first FBI interview reflects that, on June 12, 2003, Mr. Libby had a telephone call with Vice President Cheney during which Vice President Cheney disclosed to Mr. Libby that Ambassador Wilson's wife worked in that division. And that division was the Counter Proliferation Division, correct?*

A Yes.

Q *Mr. Libby, at the very outset of the interview on October 14, said to you, that he had reviewed Government Exhibit 104 and that that exhibit had refreshed his recollection and that he now recollected, as of October 14, that he first learned about Mrs. Wilson's employment at the CIA from the Vice President of the United States, correct?*

A That's what he claimed.

Q *That's what he said. He didn't use the word claim. That's what he stated at the interview?*

A That's what he claimed.

Q *That's what he said?*

MR. ZEIDENBERG: Objection, Your Honor.

THE COURT: It is a matter of semantics. Did he say that?

THE WITNESS: He told us that, yes.

Q *He told you his name was Scooter Libby, right?*

A Yes. It took us a long time to get him to tell us what his first initial stood for.

Q *He still won't tell me. He also said he was the Chief of Staff to the Vice President of the United States?*

A Yes.

Q *Now, Mr. Libby made clear, at the outset of the interview, that he did not first learn that Mrs. Wilson worked at the CIA from Tim Russert but rather he learned it from Vice President Cheney on or about June 12, 2003. Right?*

A He told us he had forgotten about the note and the Vice President telling him until he reviewed his documents in October. But his first memory of it, he told us, was his conversation with Tim Russert.

Q *His first memory after the criminal investigation started, that's what he told you, correct?*

A I'm not sure what words he said. He told us that his first memory at the time we talked to him on the 14th.

Q *Agent Bond, I'm going to show you a copy of your written memo of Mr. Libby's first interview. It's marked as DX-1509 for identification. Can you identify it?*

A Yes, it is a 302 of Mr. Libby dated October 14th.

Q *You prepared that document?*

A Yes, I did.

Q *I'm going to show you a copy of your handwritten notes that you took during that interview. That's identified as Defendant's Exhibit 1508; is that correct?*

A That's correct.

Q *Then I'll leave them here and you can refer to them.*

Do you have a recollection, as you sit there now, that Mr. Libby told you early on, during the October 14 FBI interview, that earlier…, when Mr. Libby was reviewing documents to turn over in response to this investigation, he found notes reflecting a telephone conversation he had with Vice President Cheney on or about June 12, 2003. Did he tell you that? …

A Yes.

Q *And Mr. Libby also told you that those notes refreshed his recollection of that conversation with Vice President Cheney, correct?*

A That's what it says.

Q *And Mr. Libby also told you that his notes reflect that the Vice President mentioned … that the individual who went to Niger was married to a woman who worked at the CIA in the CP Division, which meant "Counter Proliferation", correct?*

A He was interpreting, reading his note to us.

Q *He told you, based on reading his note, that his recollection was refreshed, that he had been told by the Vice President during a telephone call that Mrs. Wilson worked at the CIA in the Counter Proliferation Division, correct?*

A Yes, but that he had forgotten about it.

Q *Right. Okay. He said, in terms of what he recollected, he was telling you his recollection as of October 14, when he was sitting in the interview room with you, right?*

A Yeah, with the note.

Q *With the note. Now, just stay with the note for a minute. Is it correct that the note refers to CP and then has the word division, right?*

A At the end.

Q *Yes. And Mr. Libby told you, during the interview, that he understood, based on his refreshed recollection from reviewing the note, that Mrs. Wilson worked in the Counter Proliferation Division at the CIA, correct?*

A Based on his note, yes.

AS SEEN IN THE EARLIER TESTIMONY of Judith Miller, the notion that Valerie Plame worked in "the bureau" was raised in her notes. Miller testifies that for a time she thought this meant that Joe Wilson's wife worked for the FBI, though she soon realized that it was the CIA. In the section that follows, Wells brings up the word "bureau," and points out that it was not in Agent Bond's notes. Thus, he is perhaps hoping to show that Scooter Libby did not use the word in his FBI interview, and thus raise doubts about Miller's credibility.

Q *And the note does not refer in any place to Mrs. Wilson working at a bureau, correct?*
A That's correct.

Q *The word bureau is not on the note anywhere, correct?*
A No.

Q *And the note does not reflect that Mr. Libby said that Mrs. Wilson worked at a place called WINPAC, correct?*
A Correct . . .

IN THE BALANCE OF TESTIMONY on Friday, February 1, Wells is intent on pointing out that in Scooter Libby's taped interviews with the FBI, he was a willing participant, and that he shared his recollections in good faith, though he continues to emphasize that his client's memory was aided by little consultation of his notes and other documentary materials. Bond is dismissed for the day, and Judge Walton takes up whether the recordings of Libby's grand jury testimony should be released to the press.

THE COURT: I have concerns about it. I try to be as open as I can and make the proceedings open, but, you know, it's tough when you have a case with the level of publicity that this case has engendered.

And obviously to put those tapes out in the public domain while this case is being tried, even I think makes it more difficult, obviously, to ensure that the defendant receives a fair trial, which is the principal obligation I have. I respect the press's right to have information. They obviously will be here.

They'll have a chance to hear what he says and they can obviously report that to the extent that they want. But to put those tapes out there in the public domain, I think compromises my ability, even to a greater extent, to be sure that the defendant receives a fair trial because of the sensationalism of having his voice, I think, is just going to enhance the amount of media coverage that would be regarding the case.

And I'm struggling all I can to make sure that I don't have a problem with my jury. I'll continue to do that. But at some point, I guess I'll have to hear from, I understand, there is somebody from the A.P. who wants to represent the press position. I'll hear that at some point. But as I understand, the defense is opposing that, right?

MR. JEFFRESS: That's correct, Your Honor.

THE COURT: Okay . . . We'll address that issue next week before we actually get to the playing of the tapes.

Anything else?

MR. FITZGERALD: No, Your Honor.

MR. WELLS: No, Your Honor.

THE COURT: Have a good one.

(Whereupon, at 5:10 p.m. the trial recessed.)

FEBRUARY 5, 2007

DEBORAH BOND (continued)

AS ANTICIPATED, before the jury is brought into the courtroom, and before Agent Bond can begin her second day of testimony, Judge Walton and the attorneys resume their debate on the release of the tapes of Scooter Libby's testimony to the Grand Jury. Following lengthy discussion, which includes an appearance by Mr. Nathan Siegel, an attorney representing the Associated Press, Judge Walton weighs several options, including the possible limited release of redacted transcripts. Ultimately, however, Judge Walton's rules to release all of the tapes in audio form.

THE COURT: So with that said, I just think that legally, even though I have concerns, that those concerns are not sufficient for me to conclude that the right of access should be denied. So once the tapes have been played to the jury in their entirety, just like all other exhibits, I will have to make them available. And I will even emphasize to a greater degree to the jury—and I think we have a very conscientious, intelligent jury, and I think they appreciate what their role is—and I can only hope that, with appreciation, that they will continue to do what they need to do to isolate themselves from media coverage about this case . . .

THE LAWYERS AND JUDGE WALTON next have a discussion about whether copies of certain newspaper articles published prior to Scooter Libby's first interview with the FBI that were in Scooter Libby's office files will be seen by the jury. Like his boss, Vice President Cheney, Libby clipped articles and sometimes wrote notes on them. The first article the lawyers discuss was published in *The Washington Post* on September 28, 2003, shortly after the leak case exploded into public view, when the CIA requested that the Justice Department begin a criminal investigation. Reporters Dana Priest and Mike Allen, wrote "Yesterday, a senior administration official said that before Novak's column ran, two top White House officials called at least six Washington journalists and disclosed the identity and occupation of Wilson's wife. The second article, from *The Washington Post* on October 4, 2003, was headlined, "Leak of Agent's Name ".

The defense argues that if these articles are deemed admissible it may prejudice the jury against their client, since it will indicate the harm that the disclosure of Plame's employment may have done to her, her network of contacts, and the country. Fitzgerald argues that this shows potential motive on the part of their client, who may have had reason to dissemble about his role in this activity. Judge Walton insists, despite the defense team's vehement protests, that the articles will not be cited as fact by the prosecution. Indeed, Valerie Plame's covert status would not be considered in the trial. He pledges that the prosecution may only use the articles as an attempt to show what may have been the state of mind of the defendant, and thus, what his motive may have been. Despite Judge Walton's assurances, Defense Attorney Jeffress tries strenuously one more time to explain why he believes the judge's reasoning is flawed:

MR. JEFFRESS: Your Honor, that doesn't tend to prove anything the government is arguing is relevant, and I would ask that that paragraph be redacted from "that same week" through the end of the paragraph.

MR. FITZGERALD: Your Honor, first of all, they are talking about the paragraph that was underlined.

THE COURT: Right.

MR. FITZGERALD: And he is asked about it in the Grand Jury. I think it's highly probative because he is sitting there trying to figure out—if the allegations are that two people may be calling six journalists, doesn't that go directly against his notion that he thinks this is only about Novak; it's about a single journalist; he had no motive to lie; he had nothing to fear; and he had no reason to lose his job? And he is underlining the day of the interview or the days before the interview that they are looking at people calling six journalists, and he is someone who has talked to multiple journalists about this—I think it's directly on point.

THE COURT: Why wouldn't that suggest that the reader would appreciate that the scope of the investigation went beyond the communications that would have been made to Mr. Novak, and whether this information is true or not, it would put the reader on notice that the investigation conceivably would involve individuals actually in the White House who disclosed the information, and since he worked in that capacity, that, conceivably, the focus might be on him?

MR. JEFFRESS: Your Honor, if you go back to the top of this—that's what's said in the first and second paragraphs of this article. That's what the article is all about, the scope of the investigation. They don't need this accusation which we think is totally untrue, based on Mr. Fitzgerald's investigation, that two top officials told six Washington journalists—if that's true, we can't figure out who they are. We know about Mr. Armitage and the State Department, but we certainly don't know about two White House officials doing anything.

As far as we can tell, after Mr. Fitzgerald's investigation, this is untrue. It's prejudicial. It's suggested it was done to get back at Wilson. And it's certainly not necessary to show the scope of the investigation. That's in the first and second paragraphs of the article.

MR. FITZGERALD: Your Honor, besides Mr. Armitage, I think we have heard about Mr. Rove from the defense, and we have heard about Mr. Libby calling journalists. We've even heard about Mr. Fleischer talking to journalists. So the notion that suddenly we forget all that the defense has been bringing out—but it's what Mr. Libby underlined so we're going to—

THE COURT: Are you saying that there is a semblance of truth regarding what is said in that paragraph?

MR. FITZGERALD: There is. We're not going to be arguing that, but we're arguing—whether it's true or false, it's what's in Mr. Libby's mind at the interview that he underlined it.

THE COURT: Do you agree with Mr. Jeffress that at least part of that is not accurate?

MR. FITZGERALD: The two top officials is correct. Mr. Rove made disclosures. Mr. Libby made disclosures. The "at least six Washington journalists"— we know about Mr. Rove. We know about Mr. Cooper being told. We know about Ms. Miller. That's three already.

THE COURT: You said Mr. Rove.

MR. FITZGERALD: Mr. Rove made disclosures, the defense has brought out.

THE COURT: But I thought we were talking about reporters.

MR. FITZGERALD: Right. And I was counting the two—oh, I'm sorry. I may have misspoke[n]. In terms of journalists, we have Novak, Cooper, Miller, and then there is testimony from Mr. Fleischer saying that he told two journalists at the side of the road in Uganda. So we are at five. And I believe the defense may be calling a witness, Mr. Pincus, to claim that he was told. So we are talking about at least six.

And we also—the defense is going to be calling Mr. Woodward, so that's seven. So we have more than two officials, and we have more than six journalists.

My point is we are not going to be arguing that as fact. This is not offered for the truth of the matter asserted. But to act as if this has been disproved is to go the other way in a way that is not accurate.

THE COURT: Okay. The next matter.

MR. JEFFRESS: 423, Your Honor, is the more serious. This is the one that no amount of a limiting instruction could possibly remove the unfair prejudice.

If the court please, this entire article, 423, is about—the headline is, "Leak of Agent's Name Causes Exposure of CIA Front Firm."

Your Honor understands, I think, from prior pleadings that the defense very much disputes that the CIA was engaged in any active efforts to keep her [Plame's] identity secret and very much disputes that she was in any role at this time that was covert.

. . . From published newspaper articles, it appears that she was listing her employment as this Brewster-Jennings firm. And this entire article by Walter Pincus and Mike Allen has to do with the fact that she did list her employment as this Brewster-Jennings, and that that was a CIA front firm. And down in a part of it, it says, "the document establishes"— the document, which is a Federal Election Commission filing about a political contribution that Ms. Wilson made and listed her employment as an analyst with Brewster-Jennings—the article says, "The document established that Plame has worked undercover within the past five years. The time frame is one of the standards used in making determinations about whether a disclosure is a criminal violation of the intelligence identities protection act."

Now, you know, under the guise of putting this in for Mr. Libby's state of mind, the government is putting in proof of something which they have fiercely resisted discovery about the truth of that, and they are expecting that if Your Honor tells the jury, "Oh, by the way, don't take this for the truth of the matter asserted"— this is such a highly prejudicial newspaper article that that kind of limiting instruction could never be followed.

. . . The courts say that when there is a document or evidence that is so prejudicial that a limiting instruction is not sufficient to allow it in—and if the court please, I am trying to find that case, but I think Your Honor did receive our memorandum.

THE COURT: Yes.

MR. JEFFRESS: Okay. So that article—there is simply no way that anything can be redacted from that article. It's the entire article as well as the headline.

THE COURT: And as I understand it, there was questioning of Mr. Libby regarding this article?

MR. JEFFRESS: No. I am sorry.

THE COURT: Was there, before the Grand Jury?

MR. JEFFRESS: No. I don't believe so.

And, Your Honor, the other thing about this one is, as I said before, there are thousands—it may not be thousands. There were hundreds, at least, and maybe thousands of newspaper articles that are in Mr. Libby's file. This one, 423, does not have any underlining by Mr. Libby.

There is nothing, other than the fact that Ms. Mayfield found that article in the file at the time the Grand Jury proceedings started, to prove that Mr. Libby read it at all.

THE COURT: …Generally I think, … people don't put things in their files that they haven't read. So I mean, obviously, he could bring out the fact that there are a lot of other articles, and that may suggest that, conceivably, because of the volume of articles, the jury can infer that he read it. But I think the fact that it was in his file is sufficient for the jury to at least infer that he read it.

But the concern I guess I have is that it does contain relevant information, but I would also agree that it contains information that is significantly more prejudicial than the information in exhibit 422. And it seems to me, conceivably, one could argue that it's cumulative in considering the significant prejudice because it does talk about a lot of speculation about, conceivably, the harm that could have been done by disclosing her information, and that even with a cautionary instruction, it may be difficult for the jury to overlook that.

But why does the government believe that it needs this in addition to 422?

MR. FITZGERALD: Your Honor, for the precise reason why Mr. Jeffress argued, this would show what impact it would have on Mr. Libby before he is interviewed. Mr. Libby is the Chief of Staff, the National Security Advisor. He has these nondisclosure agreements. And the most charitable view of the evidence is that if Mr. Libby did not know anything about Ms. Wilson's status at the time he had whatever conversations he had, he then, in the fall of '03 is asking Mr. Addington, how would you know?

And to show the impact this article would have on his motive to lie—to switch any information he gave away from the Vice President and other government-official sources to a newspaper reporter where he is saying, I just passed on something that wasn't known to me, and I did not believe it's true, would be the impact he would have if he is reading this with no idea or personal knowledge of her status before then, in the most charitable view, and then reads that this may be a real problem. Somebody screwed up. Whoever gave out information about her may have compromised other people.

That gives a strong motive to lie. And I think it's entirely—the prejudice is not unfair prejudice. It goes to his state of mind when they opened and said, ["]This is all about—you know, this theory is stupid. He had no motive to lie. He had no fear to lose his job.["] And that's what they are going to be arguing again to the jury. And then to tie our hands behind our back and say, you can't prove that he actually read something that gave him the greatest motive to lie—and where they're arguing that he has all these other national security duties on his plate, and that this is sort of a trivial matter—this is the sort of thing that's going to grab his attention and say, ["]If I screwed up and I told someone official information, I caused a real problem, and I could lose my job. I could be fired. I could be in trouble.["] It gave him the powerful motive to create the story that fell apart. And we can't have our hands tied behind our back and say, you can't try your case, proving he had a motive to lie, and then watch them argue to the jury, where is the motive? This goes directly to that point.

MR. JEFFRESS: If the court please, Your Honor asked the government early on in this litigation what newspaper articles it intended to offer. This wasn't one of them.

Had the court known that the government, under the guise of presenting cumulative evidence that Mr. Libby had reason to believe that [Plame's] employment might be covert—if the court had known that they were going to put in hearsay evidence saying that not only was she covert, the leak of her name caused exposure of a front firm, giving all of these details, I respectfully suggest that the court's decision on whether Mr. Libby should have discovery of the truth about that matter would have been different.

THE COURT: But if he had discovery about the truth, and even assuming he was able to establish that this information is not correct, how would that make it relevant? Because, as I have said all along, whether she was covert or not—whether what was revealed would cause damage or not is not germane to this case.

What's relevant is whether he thought that, conceivably, she was covert and had revealed that and whether he thought that, conceivably, having revealed that would cause damage. And if that's so and he thought that, regardless of whether it's true or not, that would still provide an incentive, if he thought that, conceivably, he had done something wrong, to provide false information.

Even if you had discovery, I don't see how you would be able to present evidence showing that this isn't true unless you were also able to show that he knew it wasn't true.

MR. JEFFRESS: Your Honor, you watch. They are going to put this article up on the screen and they are going to say she worked for Brewster-Jennings, and this exposed a CIA front firm and put people in danger—

THE COURT: They can't do that.

MR. JEFFRESS: Well, you are going to admit it in evidence, Your Honor.

THE COURT: They can't do that. The only thing they would be able to do is to say, "we found this evidence in Mr. Libby's files. We submit that you can infer from the fact that it was in his files, that he saw fit to save it, and that he read it. And if he read it, we believe that that would have given him reason to believe that, conceivably, he had done something that was wrong and, therefore, when he talked to the FBI and when he went before the Grand Jury with the fear that he had done something wrong, he said what he said to protect himself." That's the only way that they can argue it. They can't argue anything beyond that.

MR. JEFFRESS: But, Your Honor, they are going to put it up on the screen. I am not talking about what they are going to argue. They are going to put it up on the screen and they are going to read—

MR. WELLS: But—

MR. JEFFRESS: And Your Honor is going to say, "Oh don't assume that's true." But, you know, jurors—look, they are ordinary people. You can't totally put out of your mind this kind of information. I mean, it indicates to them that it's true, and we have been deprived of the ability to show it's not true.

THE COURT: But, it's not being given to them. Even if you were able to definitively show it wasn't true, you couldn't present that to the jury because it would be irrelevant. Just because it was determined after the fact that it wasn't true doesn't bear any fruit on the issue of whether Mr. Libby, at the time he provided the information that's the subject of this case, thought it might be true.

So I don't see how you would be able to refute that. I mean, I will give the strongest instruction possible to make it clear that they cannot consider this information for its truth. Whether it's true or not is totally irrelevant to this case, and for them to, in fact, use it that way would be unfair, and they can't, therefore, do that, and they can only use it for the limited purpose I have been telling them all along.

If I am wrong, again, the court of appeals will tell me I am wrong. But it seems to me that, you know, when the government has an obligation to show that the statements were, in fact, made willful with the knowledge that they were false, it seems to me they have got to be able to show that there was a motive to do that.

And I don't see how it's not relevant when they find documents in Mr. Libby's files that would suggest that he saw these articles to be sufficiently important to download them from the computer and keep them—I think the jury could infer that he read them.

And whether the information was true or not, if he read them, conceivably, it caused him to have concerns about whether he had done something wrong and, therefore, would have an incentive to say what he said in order to protect himself.

MR. JEFFRESS: Number one, there is not and will never be any proof that he did, in fact, read this article.

Number two, this entire motion in limine we went through on Ms. Plame's, you know, identity and so forth, it's all undermined by now the government proving by a newspaper article—even though I understand Your Honor is going to give an instruction, there's no way in the world that a human being could follow that instruction and not use this evidence improperly.

And number three, under 403, it's cumulative—it's cumulative of what's in Mr. Libby's own Grand Jury testimony.

So we respectfully submit, Your Honor, that for those reasons, this denies Mr. Libby a fair trial.

THE COURT: I think the government has already indicated that it would hold off on introducing this until after the tapes are read—or played to the jury. I understand your position, but I just don't see—I mean, some of the information, it seems to me, may not go to the issue of his state of mind from the government's perspective, and I would take that information out, if that's the case.

But it just seems to me that to the extent that the articles are suggesting or indicating that there was wrongdoing that was done, as I say, the fact that it's in his files—maybe he didn't read it, and maybe the jury will reach the conclusion that there is not sufficient evidence that he read it. But I think they could reasonably infer that he did read it because I think it's reasonable to infer that people don't download from the computer and keep things in their personal files unless they actually read the information.

Now, that, I think, becomes a factual question for the jury. But I think from the standpoint of admissibility, there is a sufficient quantum of evidence from which the jury could make that reasonable inference. As these articles relate to claims of wrongdoing, I will permit them to come in, as I say, just for the state-of-mind question. And I will give the strongest possible instruction to let the jury understand that they can only consider it for that purpose.

And, again, I would ask the government to read the articles and see if you can agree that there is, in fact, misinformation in the articles. If that's true, and I were able to say that to the jury, I think that would enhance my instruction to them that they cannot consider these articles for the truth because the government is conceding that the articles do, in fact, contain information that is not accurate.

Okay. I guess that's it for now. I know there are some issues, I guess, in reference to Mr. Russert. I guess we can address that issue later, right before his—well, I don't know. The defense may feel they need that information now.

As I understand, the defense is requesting all information regarding Mr. Russert, including an affidavit that would have been filed to quash the subpoena that was served on him.

MR. FITZGERALD: And, Your Honor, I believe, as we have represented to the defense, we would be filing something today. We had two typos this morning, and our computer system went down. So I am expecting that we will be filing something maybe within the hour. So it might make sense to discuss it after we serve papers . . .

THE COURT: Let's proceed, then. I hate to keep the jury waiting.

(Deborah Bond, government's witness, previously sworn.)
(Jury in.)

THE COURT: Good morning.
THE JURORS: Good morning.

THE COURT: I apologize again for the delay, but there were a number of legal issues that were raised that I had to resolve before we could proceed. I try to avoid those delays, but sometimes it's just inevitable.

Let me just make sure that all of you have stayed away from all media coverage about this case. Is that correct?

THE JURORS: Yes, Your Honor.

THE COURT: And it's going to be particularly important that you continue to do that because I suspect there may be media coverage even to a greater degree about this case, and it's going to be particularly important that you make an extraordinary effort to make sure you don't have such contact. Okay.

MR. WELLS: May I begin, Your Honor?

THE COURT: Yes.

MR. WELLS: Thank you.

(Cross-examination continued)

By Mr. Wells:

Q *Good day, agent Bond.*

A Good morning.

Q *Last week you testified with respect to Mr. Libby's description and comments about his lunch with Ari Fleischer on July 8, 2003, correct?*

A I think you have the date incorrect. It was July 7th.

Q *On July 7th, 2003. I apologize. And you were asked this question and you gave this answer . . .*

> *Question: "Did you ask him if the subject of Wilson's wife came up at any point during their lunch?"*
> *And you answered, "Yes, we asked him. But he adamantly denied knowing about Joe Wilson's wife or discussing it with Mr. Fleischer."*
> *Do you recall that?*

A Yes.

Q *And the 302 report that was done in connection with the November interview of Mr. Libby reflects also that Mr. Libby adamantly denied discussing Mr. Wilson's wife at the lunch, correct?*

A Yes.

Q *Now, I want to turn to the notes that were taken during the November interview of Mr. Libby, and I want to ask you some questions about those notes. And I want you to go to the notes which are identified as DX-1511, and I want you to go to page 4.*

MR. WELLS: Can we put that up on the screen, please? And could you yellow from July 7th down?

MR. ZEIDENBERG: Your Honor, I object to these being published at this time.

MR. WELLS: This is impeachment.

THE COURT: I think she should—is it clear those are her notes?

THE WITNESS: They are not my notes.

THE COURT: Approach.

(Sealed bench conference.)

THE COURT: I will sustain the objection.

Q *Agent Bond, the notes that underlie the November 302 were taken by whom?*
A Kirk Armfield.

Q *And before the 302 was prepared, did you review the notes?*
A No, I did not.

Q *Who dictated the 302?*
A I don't believe it was dictated. I think it was just typed. And Mr.— Agent Armfield would have typed it.

Q *And after it was typed, did you review it?*
A Yes, I did.

Q *Could you look at the bottom of the 302 for November, and it says, "Deborah S. Bond." Then it has, "colon, D. S. B." what does that mean?*
A That's the first interview.

Q *I am sorry. That's the October one?*
A Yes.

Q *Okay. Now, in preparation for your testimony, did you review the notes of the November interview?*
A I did.

Q *And did you find the notes to be fair and accurate?*
A To the best of my recollection, they are.

Q *And the notes were consistent with your recollection of what took place at the interview?*
A Not everything that was said in the interview is in the notes. But it's—you know, it appears that—you can't—when we take notes, at least on my part, I can't take a verbatim statement. So it's—you take notes as you—quickly as you can and as accurately as you can.

So—accurate? I would say yes.

Q *Thank you.*

MR. WELLS: May I now impeach, Your Honor?

THE COURT: Does the government have any position?

MR. ZEIDENBERG: I would like to know the question. It's hard, without knowing the question.

THE COURT: Okay. Let me hear the question. Okay.

Q *Ms. Bond, you've just stated that you believe the notes are accurate. Now, is it correct that the notes do not reflect that Mr. Libby denied discussing Mrs. Wilson at his lunch with Mr. Fleischer?*

A I believe it says that he didn't recall, but I recall, being in this interview, where he was asked on several occasions—more than once; I am not sure how many times—about whether or not he may have spoken to Mr. Fleischer about Joe Wilson's wife, and he said "no" each time.

So the way it was written up in the 302, to me is accurate.

MR. WELLS: May I publish the notes, Your Honor? She has adopted the notes as accurate.

MR. ZEIDENBERG: I would object to that, Your Honor.

THE COURT: Approach.

(Sealed bench conference.)

THE COURT: The objection is overruled.

MR. WELLS: Please display the notes.

Q *Agent Bond, I want to read with you from Defendant's Exhibit 1511, page 4. And the notes taken by the FBI agent concerning questions put to Mr. Libby at the November interview about his lunch with Mr. Fleischer read, "July 7th. Ari Fleischer lunch prior to Africa trip. Libby recalls having lunch before he left. This seems to be the date. It was mostly a going-away lunch. Libby probably talked about the Wilson matter, but he cannot recall. Libby does not recall discussing with Ari if Wilson's wife worked at C.I.A. Libby"—arrow—"it is possible he could of [sic] talked about Wilson. They talked about Miami Dolphins football, et cetera."*

And my first question: is it correct that that paragraph is a paragraph that describes what Libby said about his discussion with Mr. Fleischer during the November FBI interview?

A It's what the agent wrote down.

Q *And in terms of what the agent wrote down with respect to the issue of the wife, it states, "Libby does not recall discussing with Ari if Wilson's wife worked at the CIA," correct?*

A That's correct.

Q *The notes clearly and unambiguously use the phrase "Libby does not recall," right?*

A That's what it reads.

Q *And then what happened, when the agent wrote up the report, the agent wrote something different from the notes, correct?*

A I think—could you tell me what page it was? I am pretty sure that it is not the exact words that were in the notes, but if I could read it.

Q *Well, if you go to the 302 report, page 4, you will see the phrase "adamantly denied."*

A Okay.

Q *And what the agent wrote was that he, meaning Libby, "adamantly denied there was any discussion during the lunch about Wilson's wife." That's what the agent wrote, right?*

A Correct.

Q *And that's what you testified to in this courtroom under oath, correct?*

A Yes, because we asked him more than once. It may not be reflected in the notes, but we asked him—and I can't tell you how many times.

Q *So is it your testimony that you recollect now, as you sit there on the stand years later, that even though the notes say that he said he did not recall, that he later changed that to adamant denial? Is that your testimony?*

A No. We asked him, and he—I am not sure—"adamantly" might not be the perfect word. I didn't write this 302.

Q *Well, you testified to "adamantly"—*

A But "adamantly denied"—

Q *—under oath last week.*

A Right.

THE COURT: One at a time.

Q *You testified under oath last week to the word "adamantly." That was your word that you adopted and you used under oath to this jury, correct?*

A Correct.

Q *So now is it your testimony that it might not be the right word?*

A It—yes, it is—to me, it is the correct word.

Q *But it is a word that is not reflected in the notes, correct?*

A Correct.

Q *And the word "denial" is not reflected in the notes, correct?*

A Correct.

Q *And you know that Mr. Libby produced hundreds and hundreds of pages of notes to the government in response to the government's document request, correct?*

A Yes.

Q *And is it correct that the only reference that you know of in any of Mr. Libby's notes that makes any reference to Ambassador Wilson's wife or to Ambassador Wilson's wife working at the CIA is Government Exhibit 104, which is now on the screen?*

[This is the note Libby brought to the FBI interview in October 2003] . . .

A Yes, it is.

Q *Okay. Now, I was asking you some questions about the July 12 conversation between Mr. Libby and Ms. Judy Miller—do you recall that last week? Right?*

A I do.

Q *And the July 12th conversation between Mr. Libby and Ms. Miller—that conversation is part of the obstruction of justice count for which Mr. Libby has been charged, right?*

A I believe so.

Q *Okay. It's a very important conversation, correct?*

A It has been a while since I have read the indictment, but, yes.

Q *And during the first interview of Mr. Libby in October, after the interview, a 302 was prepared, correct?*

A Yes.

Q *And the 302 makes no reference at all to any discussion of the July 12 conversation between Mr. Libby and Ms. Miller, correct?*

A That's correct.

Q *And we discussed last week that in the notes with respect to the October interview, that there is a reference to the conversation in the notes, right? And if you go to 1508, page 9—*

A Yes.

Q *Okay. And what's set forth in the notes concerning—I am sorry—concerning the July 12 conversation is, "Judy Miller, re: research weapons in Iraq, 7/13/03," then a dash—and that means probable, right?*

A Yes.

Q *And you said last week that 7/13 probably relates to the 7/12 conversation, right?*

A Correct.

Q *And then it says in your notes, . . . "ambassador Wilson's wife—may have mentioned indirect," and then it says question mark, right?*

A Right.

Q *And you said indirect meant indirectly, correct?*

A Well, indirectly, and then I have a question mark because I don't think I finished the sentence that I was writing and I never had a chance to go back and ask the question again so I could fix my notes. So—

Q *I mean, there were no restrictions on you in that October interview—*

A No, but I think I forgot. And I wasn't conducting the interview. So I had a question mark for me to go back. And it was my fault. I didn't go back and ask the question again.

Q *Okay. So the only information that Mr. Libby stated at the October interview concerning the July conversation with respect to the wife was, "Ambassador Wilson's wife—may have mentioned indirectly," right?*

A Right, but the line beneath it, "why did they send this guy?"— would have been a question that Judy Miller posed to him.

Q *Okay. And then you had a question mark, and you didn't go back, right?*

A Right.

Q *And you have taken—you take responsibility for that, right?*

A I do.

Q *Okay. And then you had a second interview, and the second interview was in November, correct?*

A Correct.

Q *Okay. And is it correct that the second interview, the November interview, makes no reference at all to the July 12 Judy Miller conversation between—makes no reference at all to the conversation between Mr. Libby and Ms. Miller on July 12th?*

A That's correct.

Q *Okay. There is not one reference to it in the final 302 report, correct?*

A Not by her name, no.

Q *And there is not one reference to it in the notes that were taken during the November FBI interview, correct?*

A Yes. Right.

Q *So it looks like not only did you fail to follow up on that conversation in October, but you didn't ask one question about it—at least as reflected by the report and the notes—about it in the November interview, right?*

A It looks that way, yes.

Q *Okay. Now, the next time that Mr. Libby was questioned by either prosecutors working with you or anybody on your team was when he appeared in the Grand Jury in March of 2004, right?*

A Yes.

Q *Okay. And you can point to no discussion between Mr. Libby and either the FBI or the prosecutors about the July 12th conversation that occurred prior to the March 2004 Grand Jury appearance, right? …*

A Right. Correct.

Q *Okay. So it's clear that the first time Mr. Libby was asked to describe the substance of the conversation between he and Ms. Miller on July 12, 2003, was nine months after the conversation had occurred in the Grand Jury, correct?*

A Yes.

Q *Okay. Now, I want to go to a different subject. I want to ask you about some questions and answers you gave last week concerning what took place at the second FBI interview in November 2003 in connection with Mr. Libby's description of his conversations with Vice President Cheney on Air Force Two . . .*

You testified last week as follows:

Question: "Did Mr. Libby tell you about a meeting that he had with the Vice President on Air Force Two on the return trip from Norfolk?"

Answer: "Yes, like he had told us before, Mr. Libby said that he went to the Vice President's cabin and got the statement. In addition, there was some discussion about whether or not they should report to the press that Ambassador Wilson's wife worked at the C.I.A. however, Mr. Libby was not sure of that."

Question: "Just to go back over that, did you say the subject—if you could just explain what Mr. Libby told you about his conversation, any conversation he may have had with the Vice President about Wilson's wife while they were on Air Force Two."

Answer: "Yes. Mr. Libby told us that, after he spoke with Mr. Russert and learned that Ambassador Wilson's wife worked at the CIA, he discussed it with the Vice President. He's not certain exactly when they discussed it."

Question: "Did they discuss—did you ask Mr. Libby whether or not he and the Vice President discussed whether the information about the wife should be made public to the press?"

Answer: "Mr. Libby told us he believed that they may have talked about it, but he was not sure."

Now, I want to review with you the notes taken during Mr. Libby's November interview in connection with what he said—or what the notes reflect about what was said concerning discussions that occurred on Air Force Two . . .

Now, the notes reflect, with respect to what occurred on Air Force Two—and I am just going to read the section—"on plane in cabinet. Libby thinks they talked on the way back. Talking points. The V.P. was frustrated and wanted to get the story out."

Now, I am going to stop right there. Do you remember testifying to the jury last week that "the V.P. was frustrated and upset?"

A   Yes.

Q   *Okay. Do you see the word "upset" anywhere in the notes?*
A   No.

Q   *That was your word, right?*
A   Yes.

Q   *It goes on to read, "they wanted to get tenet's statement out. The V.P. dictated points he wanted out." So in terms of what the V.P. wanted out, the notes reflect that the V.P. dictated what he wanted out, correct?*
A   In that sentence, yes.

Q   *Then is the word "TIME"? Right after "wanted out," it says, "TIME, Newsweek," arrow, correct?*
A   Yes.

Q   *Then it says, "deny Wilson V.P."—and what's the word after V.P.?*
A   I think it's "link."

Q —*"V.P. link on the record. Libby did this at V.P.'s request. Libby does not recall anything about Wilson's wife. Libby knew at some point he talked with V.P. about wife."*

But with respect to what Libby said during the interview concerning what was discussed on Air Force Two, Libby said he did not recollect anything about Wilson's wife. Is that what is reflected in the notes?

A At that point in the notes, yes.

Q *Okay. And I want to focus on what occurred on Air Force Two, okay, Agent Bond? . . .*

A Okay.

Q *Then it goes on to say, "Libby knew at some point he talked with V.P. about wife. This was probably on July 11th or 12th."*

So now, Mr. Libby, according to the notes, is talking about in general what he may have talked to the Vice President about concerning the wife on July 11th or 12th as opposed to being on Air Force Two, correct?

A Well, they were on Air Force Two on the 12th, but yes.

Q *Then it goes on to read, "If there was an opportunity, Libby would have told V.P. Libby does not recall V.P. discussing that Wilson's wife should be part of the story."*

So the notes reflect that Libby has said he does not recall V.P. discussing that Wilson's wife should be part of the story, correct?

A At that point, yes.

Q *And then it goes on to state, "Libby would have raised the wife topic"— what's the word after "topic"?*

A *"Based."*

Q *"Based on discussions with Rove, Russert."*

MR. WELLS: If we can move up.

Q *"The notes on Bates 1734 is what the V.P. wants out in the press."*

So Mr. Libby stated in the interview that what the Vice President of the United States wanted out in the press [is] . . . the document that's on the screen now, correct?

A Yes.

Q *And you know, from your review of that document, that there is absolutely no mention of the wife in that document, correct?*

A That's true.

Q *Okay. And just so the jury can read it . . . if we go to DX-803.1, which is the transliteration of that handwritten document, that document talks about what the Vice President wanted to be said on the record and then as deep background and as notes, correct, Agent Bond?*

A That's what it says.

Q *And as you indicated a minute ago, there is no reference to the wife on that piece of paper, correct?*

A That's true.

Q *Now, if we go to the next page of the notes . . . Mr. Libby has left his discussion about what took place on Air Force Two. He has commented at the bottom of the previous page about some conversations with Mr. Cooper. And then he makes another comment about conversations with Vice President Cheney, right?*

A You are right, but I think this is still what he was discussing with the Vice President on Air Force Two.

Q *Well, if you just read the first sentence, the first sentence says, "Libby had conversations with Vice President about the wife after July 10th," right?*

A Yes.

Q *Okay. So there is no reference to Air Force Two in that portion of the notes, correct?*

A Correct.

Q *And Mr. Libby and you and the other agents had been discussing, just before this note was taken, what had taken place on Air Force Two on July 12th, correct?*

A Correct.

Q *So Mr. Libby certainly knew that the Air Force Two flight to Norfolk, Virginia, occurred on July 12th, right?*

A Yes.

Q *Okay. So the notes read, "Libby had conversations with V.P. about the wife after July 10th. The issue remained around awhile." And that's without any time frame, correct?*

A I don't really know what that means.

Q *Then it says, "Libby thinks that he may have mentioned to the V.P., do you want me to get something out on Wilson's wife?" Right?*

A Yes.

Q *And "Libby does not recall"—and you understood that to mean that Libby did not recall that conversation, correct?*

A He didn't recall if he actually had that conversation.

Q *Right. Right. Okay. So he told you in the interview he did not recall if he had that conversation and what he said was that it's possible, right?*

A Right.

Q *Okay. Because what happened in the interview was that Mr. Libby stated clearly to you and the other agents that he had no recollection of discussing with Vice President Cheney whether the wife should be part of the information that would be given to the press, and you and other agents kept asking him, well, "is it possible, is it possible, is it possible?" And at some point he said, "yes, anything is possible." Correct?*

A No. He said he may have mentioned it.

Q *Then he said, but he didn't recall it, and the "may have mentioned" came about when you were pressing him about, well, is it possible, is it possible? That's what happened.*

A I don't remember pressing him on it.

Q *If I take away the word "press," you kept asking the question, "is it possible, is it possible?" And he said, "yes, it's possible."*

A Well, it's only written down here once, so I don't know.

Q *Well, if you look at Mr. Tate's notes—withdrawn.*
You know Mr. Tate was Mr. Libby's lawyer, right?

A Yes.

Q *He was at the interview, correct?*

A Yes.

Q *You had an opportunity to review Mr. Tate's notes, right?*

A No.

Q *You didn't review his notes?*

A No, I did not.

Q *You know we gave his notes to the government?*

A Yes, I do.

Q *And they didn't give them to you to review?*

A No, they did not.

Q *Okay. Let's move on. Now, you were asked last week the following question and you gave the following answer . . .*
Question: "What did Mr. Libby tell you or, if he did, did he tell you whether he had any memory of Wilson's wife during the time frame of June 12, 2003, when he learned it from the Vice President, and … July 11th when he talked to Tim Russert?"
And you answered, "Mr. Libby claimed that he had no knowledge of Joe Wilson's wife during that time period."
Do you recall being asked that question and giving that answer?

A Yes.

Q *Now, is it correct that there is no statement in the October 302 report where Mr. Libby states that he had no knowledge of Joe Wilson's wife during that time period?*

A It says that he had no memory of it until he heard it from Tim Russert on—his earliest memory of it was from July 12th—10th or 11th when he talked to Mr. Russert. But after he found his notes for this investigation in October, he found the note dated about June 12th. And then he sort of recalled that he had had a conversation with the Vice President.

Q *Okay. But in terms of what you told the jury last week about what he claimed, "that he had no knowledge of Joe Wilson's wife during that time period," Mr. Libby* *did not make that statement during the interview; you inferred that from other things Mr. Libby said, correct?*

A He said he forgot about it.

Q *I want to be very specific. Is it true or false: did Mr. Libby make a statement in the interview, as you testified last week, "that he had no knowledge of Joe Wilson's wife during that time period"?*

A Does it say a time period?

Q *These are your words.*

A I know they are, but I can't remember what the words before the words—

Q *Oh, do you want me to—*

A No. Give me the time frame.

Q *This is on direct. You and Mr. Zeidenberg, you practiced your testimony, didn't you?*

A He told us that he saw the note, he forgot about it, and he learned it like he had never heard it before when he talked to Mr. Russert in July.

Q *I accept all of that. But he did not tell you, as you said to this jury last week, during that interview that he had no knowledge of Joe Wilson's wife during that time period, yes or no?*

A Not in those exact words.

Q *Okay. What you did, you took from something Mr. Libby said during the interview and then you inferred what the position should be, and then last week you testified under oath that Mr. Libby claimed that he had no knowledge of Joe Wilson's wife during that time period, fair?*

A He forgot about it.

Q *Okay. There is no such statement in the interview with respect to what you testified to last week in those words, right?*

MR. ZEIDENBERG: Objection.
THE COURT: Overruled.
THE WITNESS: Not in those exact words, no.

By Mr. Wells:

Q *Isn't it true that Mr. Libby repeatedly stated in the October interview that he had no recollection of discussing Wilson's wife before his discussion with Tim Russert?*

A Can I look at this?

Q *Yes.*

A Like I said before, he told us that after he found the note in October, then he realized that he learned it in June, but he forgot about it until July when he heard it from Mr. Russert.

Q *Is it correct that he told—you were asking him questions in the interview about—*

A No, I wasn't asking the questions, actually.

Q *Okay.*

A I was a participant, though, yes.

Q *An FBI agent with 19 years experience, you are sitting there, you're listening, and you're part of the team, right?*

A I am sitting there listening, yes, but I am not asking the actual questions.

Q *Okay. Were you forbidden from asking questions?*

A No, I was not forbidden, no.

Q *Now, you were asking Mr. Libby questions—if he had conversations with other government officials concerning the wife before he had his conversation with Mr. Russert on July 10 or 11, right?*

A I am not sure if we asked him about government officials.

Q *Okay.*

A I don't want to—

Q *No, no, no. That's fine. I think that came in November. Those are in November. We're going to get to November in a minute.*
Do you recall, for example—if you go to the 302 for October and if you go to page 3—that Mr. Libby said he did not recall discussing Mr. Wilson's wife with Judy Miller on July 8th?

A That's correct.

Q *Okay. Mr. Libby did not deny that he may have had such discussions. He said he did not recall having discussions concerning the wife prior to his conversation with Tim Russert on July 10 or 11, correct?*

A I just want to make sure that—that's correct.

Q *Now, if we go to the November interview, Mr. Libby was asked a number of questions about whether he had conversations with various government officials concerning Mrs. Wilson prior to the time he talked to Tim Russert on July 10 or 11, right?*

A Yes.

Q *And what Mr. Libby said was that he had no recollection of having such discussions, correct?*

A Correct.

Q *Mr. Libby did not deny that such discussions did not take place, right?*

A I think—like we discussed earlier with Mr. Fleischer, I think he answered our questions several times that he didn't know, that he didn't do it. So I think he denied that.

Q *Well, the notes say nothing about denial; the notes clearly read, he does not recall, right?*

A That's true.

Q *And with respect to the other government officials that he was asked about in November of 2003, Mr. Libby did not deny having such discussions but said he did not recall such discussions, correct?*

A Correct.

Q *And, in fact, during the November FBI interview, Mr. Libby said that he would have discussed Mrs. Wilson with Cathie Martin, but he could not recall the specifics, correct?*

A I think you are right.

Q *Let's get it right. Let's go to page 10.*

A It says he would have only had discussions with the Vice President or Cathie Martin.

Q *Let's read the first sentence. The first sentence reads, "Libby does not recall any conversations with any other administration officials concerning the exposure of Wilson's wife's identity or employment in the public domain," correct?*

A Correct.

Q *Okay. "And other than the aforementioned conversations with Karl Rove, Libby said he would have only had discussions with the Vice President or Cathie Martin concerning Wilson's wife, but he does not recall the specifics of those conversations," right?*

A Yes.

Q *And what's happening at page 10, that is the general conclusion after you have asked him specific questions concerning conversations with people like Mr. Fleischer or Mr. Grenier, correct?*

A Correct.

Q *And we saw that when you were ... asking him specific questions about conversations with, say, Mr. Fleischer, that the notes reflect that he said he did not recall, right?*

A Yes.

Q *And last week when I questioned you about what Mr. Tate, Mr. Libby's lawyer, said at the outset of the October FBI interview, and whether he said that Mr. Libby had not had time to refresh his recollection and gave you other information, you said you did not recall everything that I asked you about in terms of what Mr. Tate said, right?*

A That's true.

Q *And you said—then I asked you, "Are you denying that Mr. Tate said it?" and you said, "No, I am not denying it; I just don't recall it."*

I am going to ask you some questions about comments Mr. Libby made during the October interview. And then, after I walk through those comments, I want to turn to some comments that he made during the November interview. Okay?

A Okay.

Q *And I want to start with page 3 of the October interview and if you go to the last paragraph.*

What I want to do first, to put this in context—I think it would be better to … review with you some of the questions and answers you were asked last week about Mr. Libby's conversation with Karl Rove following the Russert conversation. Okay?

A Okay . . .

Q *Do you recall last week saying that in the October interview, Mr. Libby said that after his conversation with Tim Russert on July 10 or 11, he then had a conversation with Karl Rove on July 11, correct?*

A That's what he told us.

Q *And on direct, you were asked these questions and gave these answers last week.*
    Question: "Now, did Mr. Libby tell you about a conversation he had with Karl Rove at about this time frame?"
    Answer: "Yes, he did."
    Question: "Tell us, did he date the conversation?"
    Answer: "Yes. Mr. Libby told us that he believed he spoke to Mr. Rove on July 11th."
    Question: "Can you tell us about what Mr. Libby said happened during that conversation with Mr. Rove?"
    Answer: "Yes. Mr. Libby told us that he spoke to Mr. Rove with regard to an upcoming statement being prepared by George Tenet that was going to be put out that evening as well as the Joe Wilson matter."
    Question: "And what did Mr. Libby tell you was said during that conversation?"
    Answer: "Mr. Libby told us that Mr. Rove related to him that Mr. Rove had had a conversation with bob Novak of the Chicago Sun-Times *in which Mr. Novak told Mr. Rove that he had seen Mr. Wilson in a green room prior to the telephone program. And that Mr. Novak wasn't very impressed with Mr. Wilson, and he was planning on writing an article about him."*
    Question: "What did Mr. Libby tell you about the rest of the conversation?"
    Answer: "Mr. Libby told us that Mr. Rove had the understanding that Mr. Novak already knew that Joe Wilson's wife worked at the CIA."
    Question: "Did Mr. Libby tell you about—what else did Mr. Libby tell you about Mr. Novak's—Mr. Rove's reaction to that? Let me ask you again. What did Mr. Libby tell you he understood from that conversation with Mr. Rove?"
    Answer: "Mr. Libby told us that he was aware that Mr. Rove learned from Mr. Novak that Joe Wilson's wife worked at the CIA."
    Question: "Now, did Mr. Libby indicate to you whether or not he told Mr. Rove anything during that conversation?"
    Answer: "Yes. Mr. Libby told us that, after hearing this from Mr. Rove, he told Mr. Rove about his conversation with Mr. Russert."
    So what Mr. Libby said in the October interview was … that Joe Wilson's wife worked at the CIA, right?

A I believe I misspoke, but—that's not what's in—exactly the way it's in the 302.

Q *Well, that's what you testified to last week under oath, correct?*

A It is.

Q *Do you want to correct it?*

A I think I stumbled over my words. When it says "he was aware that Mr. Rove learned from Mr. Novak." . . . Mr. Rove had the understanding that Mr. Novak already knew about the wife.

Q *Okay. So when you said last week that Rove learned from Novak, is it—that testimony was incorrect?*

A It's what I said, but I think, in being up here on the stand and being a little bit nervous—that's what I said. And when I read that, it's like I can't believe I said that, but that's what I said.

Q *Sometimes people make mistakes, right?*

A Yes, that's true.

Q *And only if you have an opportunity to review documents or notes do you realize you made a mistake, right?*

A Sometimes, yes.

Q *And as you sit there now, you just can't believe you made that statement, right?*

A I believe—I can see it here that I said it.

Q *Okay. And you said it in good faith, correct?*

A I think—yes, I did.

Q *So—okay. How do you want to change it?*

A Like I said a few minutes ago, that Mr. Libby told us that he believed that Mr. Rove had the understanding from his conversation with Mr. Novak, that Joe Wilson's wife worked at the CIA that Mr. Novak already knew that.

Q *Okay. And there is nothing in the FBI 302 to the effect that Karl Rove disclosed to Scooter Libby that Karl Rove had leaked information to Robert Novak, correct?*

A Correct.

Q *So at least as of July 11, Mr. Libby is saying that he knew, based on his discussions with Karl Rove, that Robert Novak was saying that Mrs. Wilson worked at the CIA, right?*

A Mr. Libby said that he—that Mr. Rove—he believed that Mr. Rove had that understanding.

Q *Okay. And that Mr. Rove had passed that understanding on to Mr. Libby on July 11, right?*

A That's what he told us.

Q *Okay. So at least as of July 11, Mr. Libby is saying to you that he, Scooter Libby, understands that Robert Novak is saying that ... Robert Novak is saying that Ms. Wilson works at the CIA, right?*

A Through Mr. Rove.

Q *Right. So by July 11th, Mr. Libby has communicated to you that he has the belief that two reporters are saying that Ms. Wilson works at the CIA—that Tim Russert* *has said it to him on July 10 or 11, and that he has learned, by talking to Karl Rove, that Robert Novak is saying that Mrs. Wilson works at the CIA, correct?*

A That's what he told us . . .

Q *Assume the Tim Russert conversation never took place. Okay? Mr. Libby still stated to you and the other agents at the interview in October of 2003 that he, Scooter Libby, understood, as of July 11th, that Robert Novak was saying that the wife worked at the CIA, correct?*

A That's what he told us . . .

Q *Did Mr. Libby also emphasize ... during the conversation with Karl Rove, that Libby's primary concern was focused on what D.C.I. Tenet was going to report in his statement regarding the President's State of the Union address and, consequently, Libby did not put much importance on the discussion regarding Wilson's wife?*

A Yes.

Q *Okay. Did Mr. Libby also state in the October interview that he was not aware that Mrs. Wilson was employed in a covert capacity or that her employment status was classified?*

A That's what he told us, yes.

Q *Did Mr. Libby also state in the October interview that on September 30, 2003, during a principals meeting in the Situation Room at the White House, Secretary of State Colin Powell made a comment about how "everyone knows" that Wilson's wife works at the CIA?*

A That's what he said.

Q *Did he also say that Colin Powell also stated that there was a meeting in which officials from the State Department and the CIA were present, including Wilson's wife? Do you recall that?*

A Yes.

Q *And ... Secretary Powell said that that meeting had occurred in February of 2002, correct?*

A Yes.

Q *And Secretary Powell also said that, allegedly, during this meeting, Wilson's wife suggested that they send her husband to Niger, correct?*

A Correct.

Q *And Mr. Libby said he had learned all of that information from Secretary Powell on September 30th, 2003, only about two weeks before the FBI interview, correct?*

A Correct.

Q *Mr. Libby also stated during the October interview that since the Kristof article was published on May 6, 2003, Libby has seen the CIA report of debriefing of Wilson from March 2002, correct?*

A Yes.

Q *Mr. Libby also said that he had read general CIA reports regarding Niger and other countries in Africa as pertaining to information from the NIE, correct?*
A Yes.

Q *And Mr. Libby told you that there was no mention of Wilson's wife in any of the reports that Libby had read, correct?*
A That's correct.

Q *I want to go to the November 302.*

MR. WELLS: Your Honor, this would be a good time—
THE COURT: Very well. We will break at this time for lunch and come back at 1:30. Please continue to comply with all of the instructions I have previously given. Have a nice lunch.

*

IN THE CONCLUDING SEGMENT of Agent Bond's testimony, a primary issue is the question of whether Scooter Libby did have sufficient time and opportunity to review relevant notes before the October 14 interview. The defense produces Mr. Libby's schedule for the week prior to meeting with the FBI, indicating the narrow window of time their client would have had to prepare; the prosecution indicates that, although the time frame was limited by such events as the defendant's travel schedule, and other duties, his schedules nonetheless do show time reserved for reviewing documents and for consultation with his then-attorney, Joseph Tate. The prosecution also points out that between Libby's first and second interviews with the FBI, the defendant had approximately five weeks to review materials, refresh his recollections, and revise any statements that were inaccurate.

The defense also draws an admission from the witness that Mr. Libby willingly, without evident reluctance, signed the waiver that would release journalists with whom he had confidentiality agreements. Agent Bond also admits as correct this statement by Defense Attorney Wells: "At the time you started on the investigation on October 14, 2003, your team had already discovered that Richard Armitage had provided the information to Robert Novak concerning Ms. Plame's employment at the CIA."

The attorneys and Judge Walton also discuss that following Agent Bond's testimony the Court would begin playing the tapes of Scooter Libby's Grand Jury testimony.

By Mr. Zeidenberg:
Q *What do those notes read?*
A "No conversations with Rove/Ari."

Q *What's your understanding of what that reflects?*
A That Mr. Libby told us that he had had no conversations with Karl Rove or Ari Fleischer.

Q *Regarding?*
A Regarding Wilson's wife.

FEBRUARY 6, 2007

GRAND JURY TAPES

FITZGERALD ANNOUNCES THAT, following Deborah Bond's dismissal, he is ready to begin playing audio tapes of Libby's Grand Jury testimony, which took place over two days—March 5 and March 24—in the fall of 2004. Before the tapes—totaling just over eight hours—can be admitted as evidence, there are a few objections by the defense. The government's position is that all evidence shown to Libby during his testimony should be admissible in court, whereas the defense objects to certain pieces. The main objection centers around the Andrea Mitchell broadcast (which Cathie Martin testified about) about the 16 words controversy and inaction on the part of the CIA.

The government then reads a stipulation agreed to by the defense stating that the transcripts of Libby's testimony are "true and accurate to the best of [the court reporter's] ability." Then Kedian speaks:

KEDIAN: Your Honor, at this time, we would like to begin the audio recording of Mr. Libby's Grand Jury testimony from March 5, 2004.
THE COURT: Very well. The tape is in evidence, so you may consider what is being played to you as evidence in this case.

With that, the tapes begin.

By Mr. Fitzgerald:
Q *And Mr. Libby, if you could state your name for the record and spell your name?*
A I. Lewis, L-e-w-i-s; Libby, L-i-b-b-y.

Q *And do you have a nickname?*
A I do.

Q *Okay. And that is—*
A Scooter.

Q *Okay. And can you give us a brief description of how you got the name "Scooter" so no one spends their time thinking about that?*
A Are we classified in here? It's—my family is from the South and it's less, it's less uncommon than it is up here.

Q *Okay. Good morning. There's a glass of water in front of you. That's not from a prior witness, so feel free to use it.*
A Thank you.

Q *Let me just introduce myself again. My name is Pat Fitzgerald. I'm a Special*

Counsel in this matter, joined by other attorneys with the Special Counsel's Office seated at the table. And this Grand Jury is investigating possible offenses of different laws that include Title 50 of the United States Code, Section 421, which concerns the disclosure of the identity of a covert agent; Title 18 of the United States Code, Section 793, which is the illegal transmission of national defense information; or Title 18, Section 641, theft of government property; or Title 18 United States Code, Section 1001, false statements. That means that this Grand Jury is investigating those offenses. It doesn't mean there's any determination been made whether or not those offenses have been committed . . . Do you understand the general nature of the investigation?

A I do, sir.

Q *I should tell you that you have a constitutional right to refuse to answer any question if a truthful answer would tend to incriminate you. Do you understand that you have that right?*

A I do, sir.

Q *And you should understand that if you choose to answer questions, any answer that you do give can be used against you by the Grand Jury or in any other legal proceeding. Do you understand that?*

A I do . . .

Q *And you have a right to consult with an attorney, and if you could not afford an attorney one could be appointed by the Court for you. Do you understand that?*

Q *And in fact, you are represented by an attorney. Is that correct?*

A That is correct . . .

Q *And you also understand that we may ask questions about state of mind, which is what people thought, believed or understood, and that may be important to the Grand Jury in order to determine motivation?*

A Yes, sir.

Q *And if, if someone does commit a false statement or commit perjury, they could be prosecuted by up to five years in jail for each such false statement. Do you understand that?*

A Yes, sir . . .

Q *As you were advised prior to coming in, in the presence of your attorney, …you, among others, are a subject of the investigation. And that does not mean that anyone has decided to charge you with any crimes, but just is to advise you of the serious nature of the proceeding. Do you understand that?*

A I do . . .

Q *Why don't you tell the Grand Jury what your job titles are and then give us a brief explanation of what your duties are?*

A I have three job titles at the moment. One is Assistant to the President; one is Chief of Staff to the Vice President; and the last is National Security Advisor to the Vice President.

And as National Security Advisor to the Vice President, it's my job to advise him on issues of national security, to meet with and represent him in inter-agency meetings or occasionally meetings with outside parties to describe his views or to learn from them, to gather information to repeat back to him. It's part of my job to listen to what other people in the White House are saying, . . . to meet with foreign leaders on occasion and to report those things back to him. It's my job to work with the White House staff . . . to develop policy and to implement policy, and to take that information and go back and explain that to the Vice President. Occasionally it's part of my job on his behalf to talk with the press and to relay his positions to the press if he so wishes or to other issues what the White House is doing.

Q *Okay. And so in effect, you're an assistant both to the President himself directly and to the Vice President himself?*

A That is correct, sir.

Q *And can you tell the Grand Jury what security clearance level you have?*

A I have a TS, Top Secret, and a secure compartmentalized intelligence clearance, and clearances in numbers of boxes along the way, numbers of compartmented intelligence.

Q *Okay. And can you tell us in the course of your daily work how much contact you have with the intelligence community and how much access you have to classified documents?*

A Oh, I have a lot of access to classified documents. I meet every morning—my day usually starts at 7 o'clock in the morning, or sometimes a little earlier, and I'll get an intelligence briefing. I'll sit down with someone from the Agency, usually with the Vice President, and we have a book of intelligence that they provide with this, and he is there to answer questions from us and to take questions that we ask back to the Agency and get us further information. That meeting usually goes 30, 45 minutes.

Then during the day I attend meetings and frequently the Deputy or one of the top officials from the Intelligence Agency will be at that meeting and will discuss policy issues, Liberia, Haiti, Iraq, those sorts of things.

I also will occasionally be part of a principals meeting where the Director of Central Intelligence is present. And during the day I will receive other written products from the Agency and go through those.

Q *And just so we're crystal clear, I think it's obvious, but when you refer to the Agency, you're referring to the CIA?*

A I'm sorry. Central Intelligence Agency.

Q *...And do you, yourself, at times read the raw intelligence reports to see what's behind some of the summaries that you're given?*

A Yes.

Q *And does the Vice President do that as well?*

A Yes . . .

Q *With what frequency do you have contact with the press in your . . . job?*

A It, it goes in spurts . . . I have an assistant who is charged with being in charge of relations with the press, and so we try and funnel most of those types of requests.

. . . I'll get calls from reporters about things that they're hearing. You know, we hear the President's going to make a trip or something. And they'll call me and usually I'll defer that to somebody else. And then sometimes I am charged to go talk to the press about an issue along the way.

Q *. . . You mentioned there is someone on your staff who is charged with dealing with the press. And what is that person's name?*

A Currently it's a person named Kevin Kellums. Before Kevin Kellums it was someone named Cathie Martin. And before that, it was Mary Matalin.

Q *And you mentioned that sometimes you're charged with dealing with the press directly rather than through your press people. And who would tell you to do that?*

A Well, Cathie would recommend it usually and then I would talk to them . . .

Q *And in your understanding, did you need to check with the Vice President in order to talk to the press and get authorization to talk—*

A I don't need to. Sometimes I do.

Q *And have there been occasions when the Vice President has told you that you are to speak to the press rather than other people?*

A Yes.

Q *And when you deal with the press, what is your understanding of the ground rules of what they can do with the information you share with them?*

A Well, there are different ground rules. There's "on-the-record," which means they can quote me by name in the piece. So they can say, "Lewis Libby said such-and-such."

And then there are other gradations after that. One of them is "background" in which I think they—this varies by reporter actually, but it usually means, I think, that they can say—sometimes they call me a senior administration official, because they want to make their piece look important—so they'll say "senior administration official said such-and-such."

There's something called deep background, which usually, I think, means they just get to say it as if somebody said it but they don't really tag it . . .

And then there's something called "off-the-record."

When you talk off-the-record it is supposed to not ever be repeated by the reporter to anybody, including their editors . . . It's something you tell them so they can get it in their head and it informs them as to what they can say, what they can ask about, but they're not supposed to go and repeat it to anybody, and they're not—certainly not supposed to write about it . . .

Q *Okay. So "off-the-record" is . . . more stringently controlled than deep background?*

A Yes, sir. That's how I understand the terms.

Q *Okay. And do you have ground rules when you talk to reporters about how they* *would verify any quotes they might attribute to you either as by name or by senior administration official?*

A Yes. The ground rules may be set in the beginning of the conversation or as the conversation goes along sometimes you say to them, "okay, this you can say on-the-record, and this you can't. This is for off-the-record or something else." ...

Q *And in this case, one of the matters being focused on in this investigation is a column written by Robert Novak in July 14, 2003. I take it you're familiar with that column as we sit here today?*

A Yes, sir, I am.

Q *And there's some information contained in that article concerning the employment—the alleged employment—of former Ambassador Wilson's wife at the CIA Do you know that fact that it's contained in the article?*

A Yes, sir, I know it's contained in the article.

Q *And were you a source for Mr. Novak ... in that article about the employment of Mr. Wilson's wife at the CIA?*

A No, sir.

Q *Were you a source for any information for Mr. Novak in that article?*

A No, sir.

Q *Do you know if you spoke to Mr. Novak at or about the time the article was prepared?*

A ...I have a recollection that I did speak to Mr. Novak once in that general time frame, but my notes indicate, notes that you have, indicate to me that in fact that was a week and a half or so after the article appeared . . .

Q *And to the extent that the Grand Jury is familiar with the "sixteen words" that have caused controversy since then, were you involved in either the drafting or vetting of those sixteen words?*

A No, sir, I don't think I was. It may have been in a draft that I saw, but I don't think so.

Q *And there's a document known as the NIE, the National Intelligence Estimate, that concerned in part efforts by Iraq to obtain uranium. Did you review the NIE at some point in 2002 or 2003 concerning Iraq and efforts to get uranium?*

A Yes, sir.

Q *And do you recall whether or not there were any doubts expressed . . . in the NIE about the allegation that Iraq had tried to get uranium from Niger?*

A The NIE has a fairly clear declarative sentence in the section on uranium and Iraq, and it says something like, "Iran [sic] began vigorously trying to procure uranium,"—something like pretty close to that. And that is unqualified in the section on uranium ... There are some sections towards the back in which State Department expresses some doubts about uranium. I think it had to do with whether or not someone could actually procure, actually get the uranium as opposed to trying to get uranium, if you follow what I mean. And I think they had some doubts ... about the centrifuge tubes, whatever they proved to be. So that's my recollection. I could look at the document and tell you. But I recall that there was something in the back of the document, not in the section itself but way in the back.

Q *Okay. And do you know if that was—just going from memory, whether the part in the back was in text or in a footnote, do you remember?*

A It's not a footnote in the sense that you or I use the term where there's a . . . small . . . number six, and you go to the six at the bottom. I think it was in a blue box, if I recall, but I haven't looked at this in awhile. It might an appendix actually. I'm not sure if it was in the text or an appendix . . .

Q *Let me direct your attention then forward to May, 2003, and in particular to an article that appeared in* The New York Times *on May 6, 2003 written by an author named Kristof. . . Do you recall that article being published in or about that time?*

A I do, sir . . .

Q *And is it fair to say . . . the article is critical of the administration in terms of stating that, for example, one quote[:] "It's disingenuous for the State Department people to say they were bamboozled because they knew about this for a year"?*

A That sounds critical . . . There is a not very nice statement in there . . .

Q *And do you recall they're criticizing, according to the article, and I'm not saying this is true or false, but the premise of the article was that the White House and the State Department had actual knowledge that documents that had been forged and kept citing them to the public, and that this was disingenuous on the part of the administration?*

A I don't actually recall whether this article ... said that, but I don't dispute it. I just don't recall it; I haven't read it recently.

Q *Do you recall any reaction that you had to the article when you read it at the time? . . .*

A [M]y major reaction to this article had to do with this passage about being told that a person involved in the Niger caper more than a year ago ... said that the Vice President's Office asked for an investigation of the uranium deal. That, ... either at the time or subsequently, caught my eye.

Q *And the article contends, for example, at a certain point, "There are indications that the U.S. government souped up intelligence, leaned on spooks to change their conclusions and concealed contrary information to deceive people at home and around the world." . . .*

A [T]hat's not good stuff.

Q *And then the sixth paragraph, is that a reference to what you were recalling, "I'm told by a person involved in the Niger caper that more than a year ago the Vice President's Office asked for an investigation of the uranium deal, so a former U.S. ambassador to Africa was dispatched to Niger. In February 2002, according to someone present at the meetings that envoy reported to the CIA and State*

Department that the information was unequivocally wrong and that the documents had been forged." Is that, is that what stuck in your mind about an allegation that the Office of Vice President had—

A Right, because that had to do basically with us . . .

Q *And who did you discuss this article with once you read it and saw that there were allegations that attacked the credibility of the President, the Vice President, State Department and basically the administration?*

A I discussed it with my Deputy, probably discussed it with the Vice President . . . The article was a little bit of a sleeper from my point of view . . . I didn't pay much attention to it for a while, and then it sort of built momentum as it went along . . .

Q *And as you sit here today, you don't recall whether or not you talked to the Vice President within a couple of days after the article came out?*

A I, I don't recall . . .

Q *And did the Kristof article, as you say, gain momentum over time?*

A Yes.

Q *Okay. And can you tell us what happened as it gained momentum over time in terms of who you spoke to?*

A Well, the, the content of it sort of kept coming up. It didn't go away readily. At some point in June Walter Pincus was thinking—was doing—was calling our office, calling probably Cathie Martin at that point, and wanted . . . to ask questions about the article . . . Cathie talked to me about it at that point, and at some point around then I talked to the Vice President about how we would respond to this. I also talked to . . . our Central Intelligence Agency briefer, to ask him if in fact we—he had any record of us asking about this, and I talked to the Vice President about that . . .

Q *And what's the name of your briefer?*

A Craig Schmall, at that point . . .

Q *And do you know if during this time between the Kristof article in early May, and the Pincus article, which will eventually come out on June 12th, if you spoke to Marc Grossman from the State Department about the events described in the Kristof article?*

A . . . I don't recall it. . .

Q *Do you recall if you ever asked Secretary Grossman whether or not the State Department had sent the former ambassador in response to a request from the Vice President? . . .*

A No, I don't recall that . . .

Q *And do you . . . recall any conversation with Secretary Grossman about who was responsible for sending Wilson on this trip to Niger?*

A . . . I don't recall a conversation with him about it.

Q *And do you know if you ever discussed with Secretary Grossman whether Wilson's wife worked at the CIA?*

A No, I don't recall ever discussing that . . .

Q *You mentioned that there came a time when you talked to the Vice President about the Walter Pincus article. And can you tell us who was present when you talked to him and what was said?*

A I talked to him on the phone. I don't think it was anyone present . . . He was relaying to me some information that he had learned, in the first part of the conversation. And in the second part . . . he gave me instructions as to what I should, what I should say to reporters, and from the time frame I'm pretty sure we were talking about—specifically about the Pincus article.

Q *And why don't you tell us, first, what information the Vice President told you he had learned, and then what he told you to do with it?*

A Okay. Well, I had some notes that I took down at that point. But my best recollection sitting here is that he had been speaking to someone who was either from the CIA or it was someone who had spoken to someone from the CIA, and he was relaying to me what the CIA had said about how this came about. And it says something like—my notes about it say something like, he was sent at our request, our behest or something, and then it says something about it being a functional office. So he told me that, that they had said that the person was debriefed in the region, . . . if I recall correctly, and . . . hadn't made a written report, made an oral report, but there was a report, something along those lines. There are notes of this which I think you all have . . .

And in the course of describing this he also said to me in sort of an off-hand manner, as a curiosity, that his wife worked at the CIA, the person who—whoever this person was. There were no names at that stage so I didn't know Ambassador Wilson's name at that point, or the wife's name. And I made a note of that also.

He then went on to say, here's what we'd like you to say to the reporters, I think it was Pincus, as I said before, and he gave me three points. The first point was that we did not request a mission to Niger. The second point, as I recall, was that we had not gotten a report back from the mission to Niger until—or we hadn't seen any such report until after the State of the Union, when these newspaper articles started. And there was a third point which is that—I think, was that he had seen the National Intelligence Estimate and that that's what he took to be authoritative. I think those were the points. I remember this from my notes more than actual recollection but I looked at the notes in connection with this inquiry. He then said to make these several points and I asked him if he also wanted me to make an earlier point which he had made in the first half of the conversation, which I think I omitted to tell you, which was that the Office of the Vice President, the State Department and . . . some other bureaucracy, maybe Defense Department, had asked questions about this—about an earlier report about Niger, that it wasn't just the Office of the Vice President asking questions . . . I sort of numbered these as he was talking to me, and I remember numbering that one the fourth point and saying, do you want me to . . . say, when I talk to the press, that we were not the only office asking this question? And he quite rightly said, no, we shouldn't say that, that should be said by the Agency because we didn't know that.

Q *...You referenced that you recall the Vice President told you something about a functional office. Can you explain what you understood a functional office to mean?*

A The State Department and the agency, to my understanding, have regional offices, that is an office which focuses in a given region of the world such as the Middle East or Europe. They also have some offices which look globally at a type of problem like proliferation ... There might be a terrorism office, for example, that would look at terrorism globally. It would not be limited to Middle East or Southeast Asia, or Northeast Asia.

Q *And did you understand, when he told you that this former ambassador's wife worked at the CIA, do you have an understanding of whether or not she worked in that functional office?*

A ...The note indicates I knew she worked at the functional office.

Q *And we'll come back to the note in a minute. Before we look at your actual notes, how certain are you from memory that the information about the wife working in the functional office at the CIA, the wife of this former ambassador, was information that Vice President Cheney imparted to you as opposed to information that you imparted to Vice President Cheney?*

A Oh, I'm pretty certain of that.

Q *And what makes you certain?*

A I sort of remember him saying it, you know, in an off sort of curiosity sort of fashion. That's my recollection of it anyway ... And also since I wrote it down like that, it would indicate to me it was something I was taking down as he was speaking. Sometimes I make my notes as he speaks. Sometimes it turns out I didn't need to write it down, but ... you know, he is the Vice President. I don't want to make him take time to repeat himself, ... and then if I figure it's not important, I can get rid of it later.

Q *And what was it about the way he discussed that fact with you that sticks in your mind or lets you know it was a curiosity or off-hand?*

A It came out of order. You know, he was going through the order, and as I recall, it came in later. And tone of voice, as I recall it. I think I'm recalling accurately.

Q *And what, what was different about the tone of voice?*

A Sort of the way—it wasn't like the other tone of voices which was much more matter of fact and straight. It was just a little bit of a curiosity sort of thing.

Q *And not to mince words, but when he was curious, was he curious about it in a sort of a negative way? Did he think that was sort of odd that a former ambassador's wife worked in the functional office at the CIA?*

A I wouldn't say negative, but I would say ... not everybody's wife works there ...

Q *Did you . . . have any understanding whether or not Vice President Cheney thought that that fact might have played into his selection as the envoy for this trip?*

A No, we didn't, we didn't discuss that . . .

Q *. . . [Was there] any indication in that conversation that the Vice President thought this might be sort of nepotism that she worked at the Counter Proliferation Division and the envoy went on this trip?*

A I don't recall that.

Q *. . . Let me go back in time to a conversation you said you had with [Schmall] . . . Do you recall whether that took place before or after the conversation you just described with the Vice President?*

A . . . I don't recall.

Q *Okay. And was that an in-person meeting with the briefer, your daily meeting?*

A I meet daily with him. Whether I passed this question to him in the briefing or over the phone, I'm not sure.

Q *Okay. And do you know if the Vice President participated in this conversation or not?*

A I would think not . . . I don't usually ask the briefer questions and make [the Vice President] sit there while I ask a question. So my recollection of it would be that normally I don't do it that way . . .

Q *I'll ask you to look at that Exhibit, 51, and ask you if that's a note reflecting your conversation with the briefer, Craig Schmall, about your inquiry, your question?*

A Yes, sir.

Q *And is that your handwriting?*

A Yes, sir.

Q *. . . Is it fair to say that you have your own little shorthand?*

A Yes, sir, my apologies.

Q *And yourself, you refer to yourself as SL?*

A Yes.

Q *And you refer to the Vice President in your notes with a Y with a line on the top of it?*

A Yes, sir.

Q *And some of your notes have a date. Can you tell the Grand Jury what the date is of these notes?*

A It looks like 6–9, June 9.

Q *And this is a note that you kept from June 9th, 2003. Anything about the topic that made you want to keep the note for your file?*

A Well, it was in the press at this point that we had purportedly made a request for this mission, and so I checked with my CIA briefer and he told me there was no OVP request about this, so I wrote down what he told me so I'd have a record of it in case I forgot and wanted to check . . .

Q *Okay. And just transliterating this note, it says, Craig—and that would be a reference to Craig Schmall?*

A Correct.

Q *It says, "No OVP request re uranium procurement." Is that your handwriting?*

A Correct.

Q *Is that what it says?*

A Yes, sir . . .

Q *Okay. And looking at June 9, '03, the first check on that item on that page, does that indicate the President was interested in the State of the Union and the Kristof article?*

A Yes.

Q *And do you recall what the occasion was that, that you came to learn that the President was interested in the Kristof article?*

A . . . I don't . . .

Q *Any recollection of discussing with the Vice President the interest of the President in the Kristof article?*

A I don't, I don't have a recollection of it.

Q *Did you ever recall talking to the President himself about the Kristof article?*

A No, I don't, I don't think so . . .

Q *Now, …have you come to learn that there was a report prepared by the Bureau of Intelligence and Research at the State Department commonly known as INR on about June 10th of 2003?*

A Yes, sir. The FBI told me about it.

Q *Okay. And when you say the FBI told you about that, that would be some time after October 1st of 2003 when the investigation began?*

A Yes, sir.

Q *Prior to that time had you ever heard of the existence of an INR report concerning the trip to Niger and the role played by former ambassador Wilson?*

A Yes, sir.

Q *Okay. And tell us how you learned of it.*

A At the end of September there was a meeting in the Situation Room underneath the White House, [the] Classified Meeting Room, and it was a very long meeting that covered several subjects. Towards the end of the meeting, we were in a very small group which included the Secretary of State, and the Secretary of State in that meeting alluded to the fact that there was a memo from the State Department— so this was like September, late September of '03, that there was a memo from the State Department written much, much earlier which talked about a meeting in which this assignment came about, I guess the origins of the assignment, Ambassador Wilson's assignment.

Q *. . . Did that meeting in the Situation Room occur at a time after the investigation had become public in* **The Washington Post?**

A *. . .* If I recall, it became public in the *Post* on September 28 or so?

Q *Yes.*

A Is that correct? So it was a couple days after that.

Q *Prior to Secretary Powell mentioning that document, had you ever heard of the existence of the INR report prior to that date?*

A I don't have any recollection of an INR document prior to that date . . .

Q *. . . Do you recall during the time period prior to June 10th ever asking Secretary Grossman questions about what role, if any, the Office of Vice President had played in causing this mission, this trip to Niger by the former ambassador?*

A *. . .* I really don't recall a discussion with Secretary Grossman . . .

Q *. . . But you did understand the person who went was a former ambassador?*

A Yes, sir.

Q *And in the Kristof article, there was a claim that the former ambassador reported to the State Department what his findings were. Correct?*

A Actually, I had forgotten that . . .

Q *Do you know if you spoke to anyone else at the State Department about ... who was responsible for sending Ambassador Wilson to Niger?*

A I don't recall a discussion with people from the State Department about it.

Q *And do you recall discussing it with anyone else at that time, any other agency?*

A Well, the discussion with Craig Schmall, and . . . I may have tried to speak to . . . John McLaughlin who is the Deputy at the Central Intelligence Agency which would have been the people to send him. Again, during an interview with the FBI agents they raised an incident which I spoke to Bob Grenier who works for McLaughlin, or is a Deputy for McLaughlin . . . I recall talking to Bob Grenier about something and it could have been this inquiry, but I don't ... really recall the discussion in detail.

Q *And do you recall ever having a discussion with Marc Grossman before, during or after a Deputy's Committee Meeting where Marc Grossman told you that he had learned the former ambassador's wife had worked at the CIA in the Counter Proliferation Division?*

A No, I don't.

Q *Do you recall any conversation at any time when Secretary Grossman told you that the former ambassador's wife worked at the CIA?*

A I, I don't recall.

Q *You have no memory of that whatsoever?*

A Sorry, sir, I don't . . . And at some point, as I recall, I went and—from the spacing, esoteric, . . . I recall that I went back and wrote in, because at some point, I think after he initially said it, he told me, I guess Counter Proliferation, which I think the CP is, and then his wife works in that division.

Q *Okay.*

A And then he switched from debriefing me about what someone had told him to giving me the points that he thought I should make in talking to the press . . . And he said, didn't know about the mission, didn't get a report back, oh, and didn't have any indication of a forgery . . . I guess I . . . should say [it] didn't have any indication of a forgery until the IAEA, or the first indication of a forgery was from the IAEA, but I just mixed it up when I was writing it . . .

Q *Okay. And then the arrow . . . attributes something to the Vice President. If you could tell us what that says?*

A It says, hold, get the Agency to answer that. So as he went through his points I made these notes, one, two and three to clarify in my mind what it was I was doing, and then I wrote down point four and suggested should I also—or said, should I also say OVP, and Defense and State—it wasn't just us, it was several offices asking about this? And he quite rightly said, no, you should get the Agency to say that . . .

Q *. . . As you sit here today, is it possible that you're the person who had learned that the former ambassador's wife had worked in the functional office in Counter Proliferation and that you had told Vice President Cheney that on this date?*

A I don't think so, sir.

Q *And is that . . . based upon your memory?*

A Yes, sir.

Q *And anything about the document that would indicate that it was Vice President Cheney who told you the information rather than the other way around?*

A Well, the way the, the way the line is drawn, and then it doesn't say SL saying this, it looks like him saying it. I wouldn't normally write down something I said because I said it . . . So I think in this case, usually when I wrote something down that I say, I put SL colon, and then the statement. So I was hurried here because I was trying to not hold him up and get down everything that he said accurately, and I think that's what he said. And I . . . have this recollection of him saying it . . .

Q *And did you respond in any way to that, to that fact?*

A I don't think so.

Q *What did you think of that fact at the time?*

A Curiosity. Doesn't—might mean nothing, might mean something, I don't know.

Q *And do you know if on or about June 12th Marc Grossman from the State Department had had a conversation with you about Wilson's wife working at the CIA?*

A I don't recall anything about a Grossman conversation, sir.

Q *And do you recall if you ever had a conversation with Mr. Grenier in which you discussed Wilson's wife's employment?*

A I don't think I discussed Wilson's wife's employment with, with Mr. Grenier. I think if I discussed something it was what they knew about the request . . . about Mr. Wilson. I don't recall the content of the discussion.

Q *And do you recall if there was an urgency to the conversation when you spoke to Mr. Grenier?*

A I recall that I was reaching Mr. Grenier—I was trying to reach Mr. McLaughlin and couldn't, and spoke instead to Mr. Grenier. And so if I did that instead of just waiting for Mr. McLaughlin, it was probably something that was urgent in the sense that my boss, the Vice President, wanted, wanted to find something out. Not, not necessarily in the real world, but he wanted an answer and usually we try and get him the answer when we can.

Q *So it is fair to say in looking at the document that the three points the Vice President wanted you to make were that—he didn't know about the mission, there wasn't a report given back, you need to look at the—*

A Thank you. Sorry.

Q *That he didn't know, the Vice President didn't know about the mission, that the Vice President's Office didn't receive a report back, and that there wasn't an indication that the documents were a forgery until the IAEA so indicated?*

A Yes, sir.

Q *And that your suggestion that you pointed out the trip took place at the behest of other agencies as well was, was rebuffed by the Vice President who thought the better course was to have the Agency, CIA, come out and say that themselves?*

A Yes, sir.

Q *Now, did you talk to Mr. Pincus at* The Washington Post?

A Yes, sir, I did.

Q *And did you talk to him prior to the article on June 12th?*

A Yes, sir, I did.

Q *And do you recall what you told him?*

A I told him that . . . the Vice President didn't request the mission. I think I told him that we did not get a report back from the mission. And I assume from this note that I also told him about the IAEA . . .

Q *. . . In your conversations with Mr. Pincus prior to the June 12th article, did you understand from, from your conversation with Vice President Cheney whether or not there was any problem with you telling Mr. Pincus that Wilson's wife worked at the CIA?*

A No, he was not telling me to mention that part and I didn't understand that to be part of what I was supposed to talk to Mr. Pincus about.

Q *And did you think there was a reason you couldn't tell Mr. Pincus that Wilson's wife worked at the CIA?*

A   No, it just wasn't a particularly powerful point compared to the other points. I didn't understand it to be a point worth mentioning in that context.

Q   *The Vice President obviously thought it was important enough to share with you, or interesting enough to color the background. Fair enough?*

A   Yes, sir.

Q   *And you thought it interesting enough to write in your notes. Correct?*

A   Just a slight emendation of that. I—as I said, often take my notes as he's speaking because I don't know what is going to later be important. So I took the note because he was saying it. But it was not a point that I even considered as something that I was going to be discussing with Mr. Pincus . . .

Q   *Did you consider there to be any sort of prohibition when you're just discussing the fact that the ambassador's wife worked at the CIA when you spoke to Mr. Pincus?*

A   No, sir.

Q   *And in terms of telling the story to you in context, the Vice President referenced that fact in telling you. Did you see any reason why you shouldn't reference that fact in giving the context to Mr. Pincus?*

A   No, sir.

Q   *Do you know if you talked to Mr. Pincus about Wilson's wife?*

A   No, I, I believe I did not, sir.

Q   *Can you rule out the possibility that you told Mr. Pincus about Wilson's wife during that conversation?*

A   I have no recollection of having discussed it with Mr. Pincus and I don't think I did.

Q   *Can you rule out the possibility that you did, in your mind?*

A   I don't think I did.

Q   *And I understand that it's very clear that you don't think you did. I'm just saying, can you rule out that you didn't do that when you spoke to Mr. Pincus?*

A   I don't quite know what to say, sir. I don't think I did. I have no recollection of doing it. It's not what I set out to do. I don't believe I did. Just "rule out the possibility" is an odd phrasing to me. I'm, I'm reasonably certain I did not.

Q   *Let me give you an example. The President of the United States called you in and said, this is super-super secret that we can't even tell you the clearance level this is at, and this involves the most sensitive intelligence gathering matters ever to be conducted by the United States. And you went and had a meeting with a reporter afterwards, and we said, do you recall telling that person that information. You could say, not only do I not remember, there's no way I could have done that. And I guess, now I'm asking you here, you indicate that the information about Wilson's wife you didn't understand to be a prohibition on it. So I'm simply asking that, even though you think you didn't talk with Pincus about it, is it possible that you did?*

A Well, I didn't think it was under the super-super secret categorization. So in that part of the analogy, it was nothing like that about what he said. But as I say, I don't think I talked to Mr. Pincus about it.

Q *Is it possible you did?*

A Best of my recollection of the conversation, no. I did not talk to him about it.

Q *Now, this conversation you had with the Vice President was prior to your speaking to Mr. Pincus. Correct? . . .*

A Yes. Yes, sir.

Q *And you spoke to Mr. Pincus before he printed the June 12th article?*

A Yes, sir.

Q *So the conversation with the Vice President was some time before June 12th. Correct?*

A Yes, sir.

Q *And was that the first time you had heard from anyone, as far as you can recall, that Wilson's wife worked at the CIA?*

A Yes, sir.

Q *And you have a recollection of this being a new fact as you heard it?*

A Yes, sir.

Q *And so that based upon your recollection, not your notes, that you recall that that's the first time that you heard about the former ambassador's wife working at the CIA?*

A Yes, sir, although my recollection is not perfect. That was my recollection . . .

Q *. . .Are those notes that you made?*

A Yes, sir.

Q *And are they dated June 3rd, at least in the upper left corner of the page?*

A Yes, sir . . .

Q *It says on there, talk to VP about Walter Pincus article.*

A Yes, sir . . .

Q *In [an] article [by David Sanger of The New York Times] the relevant sentence I wanted to—sentences I wanted to call to your attention. Let me pull out a copy. One indicated that Wilson had said that he reported back, that the intelligence was likely fraudulent, indicating that the intelligence by Iraq trying to get uranium, and it said, White House officials say his warning never reached them. Do you know if you would have provided information to David Sanger indicating that the warning by Wilson never reached the White House?*

A I, I actually—I don't know that Ambassador Wilson actually warned that the documents were fraudulent. There is, to my knowledge, all I had seen was one memorandum which may or may not still be classified in which is a report about Ambassador Wilson's trip. In that report there are denials from the Niger government—this is actually in Director Tenet's July 11th statement about it, there are—public statement so it's not classified—there are denials in the first part of the report from the Niger government that they ever provided uranium. But there is also an assertion from a former Nigerian, I think prime minister, that in fact an Iraqi delegation had come to Niger seeking to open relations and the Niger government, the prime minister, interpreted that to mean they were interested in purchasing uranium. So in fact, within Ambassador Wilson's—within the report of Ambassador Wilson's trip and his finding was evidence that Iraq was trying to acquire uranium and that's what the CIA eventually puts into the NIE which is also unclassified now.

As to the fraudulence of the documents, I don't think Ambassador Wilson as I have seen later, had ever actually seen the documents. I don't know if he opined on whether they were fraudulent or not.

Q *Let me draw your attention ahead to July 6th—*
A Yes, sir.

Q *—when three things happen. First, there is the op-ed in* The New York Times *by Joseph Wilson. Secondly, he appears on* Meet the Press *with Andrea Mitchell as the host. And third, there's a piece in* The Washington Post *talking about his op-ed in* The New York Times *and giving some further information. Do you recall which of those two articles you read that day and whether or not you saw Wilson on* Meet the Press?
A I don't think I saw Wilson on *Meet the Press* . . . I don't know if I read the articles that day. It was Sunday and often I take the day off, but I think I read them—I read them subsequently.

Q *And what was your reaction when you read the op-ed piece by Joseph Wilson?*
A I recall that … here was this guy saying it was him who had done it . . . He was saying that … he thought that he had sort of definitively proven in his trip that there was no attempt by the Iraqis to purchase uranium in Niger. And that's not what his report actually proved. He was saying that we had asked for the trip, or he said that the next day on television, I've forgotten which, and that was not the case. He was saying that because we had asked about the trip, the Vice President must have gotten a report back about his trip and that was not the case. He was saying, because his report was definitive, which it wasn't, and because the Vice President had asked, which he hadn't, the Vice President must have gotten a response, which would have convinced the Vice President that, that Iraq had not tried to buy uranium, and therefore the Vice President must have twisted the facts, or other people must have twisted the facts. And as I was indicating, the premises were wrong, we didn't get his report. What we did get was intelligence from the CIA, not that one piece but the considered judgment of the CIA that in fact Iraq had tried to buy uranium. The Vice President had not asked for someone to go on a mission to Niger, so therefore he didn't get that, report back. So there were a lot of things in there that were wrong . . .

Q *Now, is it fair to say that the article was viewed as an accusation by many, including the administration?*

A Yes, sir.

Q *If you accepted the premises of his article, his op-ed, as being true, it would indicate that the Vice President knowingly allowed the President to lie to the American public and the world about what the United States government believed about Iraq's activities with regard to uranium. Fair to say?*

A Not quite. Because he, he is straightforward in saying, all I know about is my report. And if they have other, other evidence then there's other evidence . . .

Q *But it's fair to say that most people took away from that article as reported was an assertion by Wilson that the government misled the American people, not as an "I'm not sure what happened and I want an answer"? Is that fair to say?*

A . . . If you look at his article, I think he does say in there . . . if there's other information, there's other information, he was pretty careful about that. Maybe people read it too quickly, as you say, and took away a different interpretation of it . . .

Q *Doesn't the second paragraph say, "Based on my experience with the administration in the months leading up to the war I have little choice but to conclude that some of the intelligence related to Iraq's nuclear weapons program was twisted to exaggerate the Iraqi threat."*

A Right, some, "some of the intelligence," yeah.

Q *Was it fair to say you were upset when you read the article?*

A There were a lot of articles to come out that … say bad things about the administration and I guess I've gotten a little bit inured … to them. But I didn't like—I did not like the article.

Q *Were you upset?*

A I guess I was upset. I was disturbed by the article, didn't like the article. Upset's a fair word, I guess.

Q *And did you discuss it with the Vice President?*

A Yes . . . I'm just trying to think about when . . . He was in Wyoming, I think, over the July 4 weekend. So I probably didn't see him until, you know, Monday or Tuesday, I've forgotten when it was, after that, and I would have discussed it shortly thereafter . . . I did not see him on Sunday.

Q *Do you know if you discussed it by telephone with Vice President Cheney?*

A I don't think I spoke to him by phone that weekend.

Q *And can you tell us about the first time you discussed the article with Vice President Cheney?*

A You know, I don't remember it in any detail. It was the same claim that we had had around since May. It's just now it had a name of it. Now we knew it was Ambassador Wilson. And there was this, you know, accusation of twisting the facts directly by somebody by name. So it was a concern.

Q *Do you recall any reaction, whether he was upset?*

A I'm sure he was upset. I don't recall the conversation all that clearly, but I'm sure he was upset.

Q *And in terms of accusations against the administration, putting aside the truth or falsity of it . . . this . . . was a direct accusation that the Vice President was dishonest, if you followed the inferences that Mr. Wilson made, that the President was dishonest and that the country was misled into war. Is it fair to say that that was the—perhaps the most serious attack on the administration's credibility thus far in the Presidential term?*

A It was a serious accusation . . . I'd have to go back . . . over the administration to evaluate it compared to other attacks, but it was, it was a very serious attack.

Q *Well, as you sit here now, can you think of any other time in the administration where someone directly came out by name and accused the administration of deliberately exaggerating and twisting intelligence with regard to specific facts?*

A . . . This . . . comes to mind, as a very serious attack . . . I don't recall sitting here whether there was anything in tax policy or any other policy that quite amounts to this.

Q *And given that the sixteen words were believed to have been part of a speech setting up the administration's case for war against Iraq, is it fair to say that this was a very, very serious matter during the week of July 7th through the 14th at the White House?*

A Yes, sir.

Q *And was it a discussion of—that was—was it a topic that was discussed on a daily basis?*

A Yes, sir.

Q *And it was discussed on multiple occasions each day in fact?*

A Yes, sir.

Q *And during that time did the Vice President indicate that he was upset that this article was out there which falsely in his view attacked his own credibility?*

A Yes, sir.

Q *And do you recall what it is that the Vice President said?*

A I recall that he was very keen to get the truth out. He wanted to get all the facts out about what he had or hadn't done, what the facts were or were not. He was very keen on that and said it repeatedly. Let's get everything out. He wanted to get it all out. That, that I recall.

Q *Do you recall if you ever discussed a copy of the article with Vice President Cheney—in front of you when he talked about [it]?*

A Physical copy in front of him? I don't recall that. He often cuts out an article and keeps it on his desk somewhere and thinks about it and I subsequently learned that he had such an article from the FBI agents who talked to me.

Q *And had you seen that copy of the article before the FBI showed it to you during the course of the investigation?*

A I, I don't recall it. It's possible if it was sitting on his desk that, you know, my eye went across it. I don't, I don't recall him pulling it out and saying something to him, but we talked about the article a fair amount . . .

Q *And in looking at Grand Jury Exhibit 8 [see appendix], can you tell us if you recognize the handwriting at the top, top of both pages?*

A Yes, sir. It looks like the Vice President's handwriting . . .

Q *Okay. And is it fair to say that there's various items underlined in this copy?*

A Yes, sir.

Q *Does that include the sentence, "I have little choice but to conclude that some of the intelligence related to Iraq's nuclear weapons program was twisted to exaggerate the Iraqi threat?"*

A Yes, sir.

Q *And does it also include handwriting at the top of the page that says, that reads, "have they done this sort of thing before?". . .*

A Yes, sir, it does.

Q *And does it say beneath that, . . . "send an ambassador to answer a question?"*

A Yes, sir.

Q *And does it say below that, "do ordinary send people out pro bono to work for us?"*

A It does, sir.

Q *And does the top of the page have a note that continues over to the second page, "or did his wife send him on a junket?"*

A Yes, sir.

Q *And do you recall ever discussing those issues with Vice President Cheney?*

A Yes, sir.

Q *And tell us what you recall about those conversations.*

A I recall that along the way he asked, is this normal for them to just send somebody out like this uncompensated, as it says. He was interested in how did this person come to be selected for this mission. And at some point after we learned that his wife worked at the Agency, . . . that was part of the question.

Q *Okay. And is it fair to say that he had told you back in June, June 12th or before, prior to the Pincus article, that his wife worked in the functional office of Counter Proliferation of the CIA. Correct?*

A Yes, sir.

Q *So when you say that after we learned that his wife worked at the Agency, that became a question. Isn't it fair to say that you already knew it from June 12th or earlier?*

A I believe by, by this week I no longer remembered that. I had forgotten it. And I believe that because when it was told to me on July 10, a few days after this article, it seemed to me as if I was learning it for the first time. When I heard it, I did not think I knew it when I heard . . .

Q *And so your recollection is that . . . you discussed with the Vice President, did his wife send him on a junket? As a response to the July 14th Novak column that said, he was sent because his wife sent him and she works at the CIA?*

A I don't recall discussing it—yes, I don't recall discussing it in connection with when this article first appeared. I recall it later.

Q *And are you telling us under oath that from July 6th to July 14th you never discussed with Vice President Cheney whether Mr. Wilson's wife worked at the CIA?*

A No, no, I'm not saying that. On July 10 or 11 I learned, I thought anew, that the wife—that, that reporters were telling us that the wife worked at the CIA.

And I may have had a conversation then with the Vice President either late on the 11th or on the 12th in which I relayed that reporters were saying that. When I had that conversation I had forgotten about the earlier conversations in which he told me about—reflected in my notes that we went over this morning, in early June, before the Pincus article, when he had told me about that the wife worked at the CIA. I had just forgotten it.

Q *. . . Who did you speak to on July 10th or 11th that you recalled learning again, thinking it was for the first time, that Wilson's wife worked at the CIA?*

A Tim Russert of NBC News, Washington Bureau Chief for NBC News . . .

Q *Is it your testimony under oath that you don't recall discussing Wilson's wife working at the CIA between the July 6th date when the Wilson's op-ed appeared and your conversation with Tim Russert?*

A That's correct, sir, but my—I don't really—I don't recall discussing it. What I do recall is being surprised when I talked to Mr. Russert on the 10th or the 11th, and I am inferring from that surprise that I hadn't talked about it earlier in the week. I simply do not recall any discussion early in the week about Mrs. Wilson. What I do recall is that I was surprised when I heard it from Mr. Russert.

Q *Let me ask you this. Do you recall going to lunch on July 7th with Ari Fleischer?*

A I do, sir.

Q *Okay. And do you recall what you discussed over lunch with Ari Fleischer?*

A Yes, it had been scheduled for some time. Ari was leaving the White House. He was a friend, is a friend. And we had decided we would get together for lunch before he left as sort of a good-bye lunch. And we discussed the Miami Dolphins, because we're both Miami Dolphins fans; we discussed his plans for the future, what he was going to do, work in New York, I think it was, or start a consulting-type firm if I recall; and you know, it had been fun to work together; and we probably also discussed the uranium business because it was a very hot topic at that point. I don't recall it as clearly as I do the Miami Dolphins and his plans for the future because that was the point of the lunch.

Q *And in the discussion, discussing the uranium issue, do you know if you discussed Mr. Wilson?*

A I don't recall it, but I suspect we did because it was a very—you know, that was just—now, but I don't recall it.

Q *And on July 7th, do you recall if at the 6:45 briefing in the morning [with] you and the Vice President asking Craig Schmall about Mr. Wilson and the circumstances of his trip?*

A I don't, but it makes sense because the article had come out the day before.

Q *And do you recall if at the senior staff meeting at 8:45 that day whether or not Karl Rove and others discussed that we needed to get a message out about Mr. Wilson, which is that the administration and the Vice President in particular, did not send him to Niger and that his report did not resolve the issue?*

A That sounds right. There was a day—I recall a day or maybe two when Karl spoke about it at the senior staff meeting. In one of them, I made some notes about it. I don't recall the date, but . . . it was within a day of that, if it wasn't that day.

Q *And are you aware that at 9:22 that day Cathie Martin, the Press Secretary, e-mailed Ari Fleischer with four talking points to get out—the talking points concerning the Vice President's position which included the fact that the Vice President didn't send Wilson to Niger? We can show you that e-mail, I believe, as an exhibit, and see if that refreshes your recollection that the Vice President's press person was addressing this issue to Mr. Fleischer that day . . . And I'll just read into the record, July 7th, 9:22, response to Joe Wilson. Four bullets.*
> *The Vice President's Office did not request the mission to Niger.*
> *The next bullet: The Vice President's Office was not informed of Joe Wilson's mission.*
> *Next bullet: The Vice President's Office did not receive a briefing about Mr. Wilson's mission after he returned.*
> *Final bullet: The Vice President's Office was not aware of Mr. Wilson's mission until recent press reports accounted for it.*

A Yes.

Q *Do you, do you recall if you were aware of those talking points at the time, on July 7th?*

A I don't know that I saw this e-mail, but those were our basic talking points that we tried to get out, and I recall that Ari some time that day, it might have been at the 1 o'clock, made a statement which covered these types of points. And so therefore, it's quite likely I talked to him about it at the lunch as well.

Q *And I believe if we checked, it might be at 9:36 that morning that Ari Fleischer, in a press gaggle, made the points that the Vice President did not request the trip, or know about it, or get briefed on the results.*

A That actually sounds right, sir.

Q *And thereafter, after the 6:45 briefing with the CIA briefer, and the senior staff meeting, and then Cathie Martin's e-mail, and Ari Fleischer's press gaggle, you then went to lunch with Mr. Fleischer about noon?*

A Yes, sir. Yes, sir.

Q *And do you have any recollection as you sit here now discussing Mr. Wilson with Ari Fleischer?*

A I don't, I don't recall it, but . . . it makes sense and it's pretty likely. I just don't recall that, that part of the discussion with, with Ari. I think, if we were . . . discussing uranium in that period what I would be particularly concerned about was the NIE and what the . . . NIE had actually said because we were still in a stage before, as I recall, before Ari Fleischer came out and said it was a mistake to have the claim about uranium in the State of the Union . . . This was a much bigger issue than the Wilson trip as to whether or not it was a mistake to have it in the State of the Union. And there was this NIE which had this assertion about the uranium. So I suspect that would have also been my focus . . .

Q *Do you recall if you discussed Mr. Wilson's wife during the lunch with Ari Fleischer?*

A I don't recall discussing the wife. Because I was surprised at the discussion a few days later with, with Tim Russert, I would think that we did not discuss the wife . . .

Q *And as you sit here today, you do recall that that was the day that Ari Fleischer addressed some questions about Mr. Wilson's article at the press gaggle. Correct?*

A I've seen the transcript since then, so that's what I recall really.

Q *And you recall that some time that day, but not by lunchtime, Mr. Fleischer, or some time after lunch either that day or the next, Mr. Fleischer issued a statement indicating in effect that the President didn't stand behind the sixteen words. Is that correct?*

A I recall from looking at the record that it was the 7th that he made that statement, and that was the day I had the lunch.

Q *And you recall that you had lunch with Mr. Fleischer?*

A Yes, sir.

Q *And you recall discussing Mr. Fleischer's future. Correct?*

A Yes, sir.

Q *And you recall discussing the Miami Dolphins. Correct?*

A Yes, sir. I recall all that quite clearly. I had a lot of conversations during this period about this other stuff and I just don't recall it as distinctly as I only had one conversation about the Miami Dolphins in that period, so—

Q *Do you recall telling Mr. Fleischer that Wilson's wife worked at the CIA in the Counterproliferation Division?*

A No, I don't.

Q *And is it possible that you told Mr. Fleischer during that lunch that Wilson's wife worked at the CIA in the Counter Proliferation Division?*

A It's possible—well, I don't recall it and I recall being surprised by Russert. So I tend to think I didn't know it then, but that's all I actually recall.

Q *Isn't it a fact, sir, that you told Mr. Fleischer over lunch that this was "hush-hush" or "on the QT" that Wilson's wife worked at the CIA?*
A I don't recall that.

Q *Do you recall discussing Mr. Wilson's wife's name with Mr. Fleischer?*
A No, I don't think I knew it until the Novak article.

Q *And what do you recall Mr. Wilson's wife's name to be?*
A From the Novak article, Plame. Valerie Plame.

Q *And how would you pronounce it, in a hard A or in a French way?*
A I guess just what I said, Plame, like blame, I guess.

Q *And as you sit here today do you recall whether or not you discussed whether or not Mr. Wilson's wife worked in the Counter Proliferation Division?*
A I do not recall discussing Mr. Wilson's wife at all with Ari. All I recall is—from that week is the Tim Russert conversation.

Q *So as you sit here today, it's your testimony that prior to your conversation with Tim Russert you neither discussed Wilson's wife's employment with either the Vice President or with Ari Fleischer, following the July 6th article?*
A I'm sorry, my mind wandered. You're asking about—could you repeat it? I'm sorry.

Q *Sure. From July 6th up until the point when you spoke to Tim Russert, but not after, is it your testimony that you have no recollection of discussing Wilson's wife's employment at the CIA with either Vice President Cheney or Ari Fleischer?*
A Yes, sir. In that period I have no recollection, that's correct.

Q *And do you recall discussing with Cathie Martin between July 6th and July 10th the fact that Wilson's wife worked at the CIA?*
A No. As I say, when I heard it from Tim Russert, which was on the 10th or the 11th, I was surprised by what I heard, and that's all I really recall from that week. So, I don't recall any other discussion earlier in that week about it.

Q *Prior to your conversation with Tim Russert on July 10 or 11, do you ever recall a conversation where Cathie Martin told you that Wilson's wife worked at the CIA?*
A No, sir.

Q *And do you recall an occasion on or about July 8th where Cathie Martin came into the Vice President's Office with you present, and the Vice President, and indicated that Wilson's wife worked at the CIA, that she had learned that?*
A I—again, sir, I don't, I don't recall. What I recall—all my recollection on this point is hinged on my surprise when I heard it from Tim Russert and I'm inferring the rest from that. I don't recall much about . . . anything about that subject in the week. What I recall from that week is being concerned to get a clear statement out

from the CIA, the Agency, from Director Tenet, and there was a lot of discussion during that week, as you've probably seen, in my notes, and I was very much focused on getting the main part of the case out about what the CIA had told us in October and subsequently about uranium, and I don't recall these discussions that you're referring to.

Q *And is it fair to say that th[e] reason this became such a hot issue that week was the sort of the firestorm that came as a result of the July 6th Wilson op-ed piece? Correct?*

A Yes, sir.

Q *And just so we're clear, I understand what you recall about your conversation with Russert, but the time period before that, are you telling this Grand Jury you have no recollection of having the conversation on any day that week in which Cathie Martin told you in the, in the presence of the Vice President that Wilson's wife worked at the CIA?*

A I have no recollection of that conversation. My first recollection is Tim Russert telling me that.

Q *Now, do you recall a conversation in which Cathie Martin told you and the Vice President that Bill Harlow, the public affairs person at the CIA, had been receiving calls from Andrea Mitchell and David Martin about the controversy about the State of the Union address?*

A I recall that the CIA was receiving calls. Yes, I recall something about that. I don't recall the Cathie Martin part, but it makes sense that it was Cathie that told us.

Q *And do you recall being instructed by the Vice President that you should call Andrea Mitchell and David Martin?*

A It sounds right, sir, yes.

Q *Do you recall calling Andrea Mitchell?*

A Yes, I recall calling Andrea Mitchell and I recall calling David Martin.

Q *And do you know how many times that week you spoke to Andrea Mitchell?*

A My recollection is that I talked to her once about an incorrect report, and then after my phone call with Tim Russert I spoke to her again . . .

Q *So you have two conversations with Andrea Mitchell. One before your Russert conversation and one after your Russert conversation?*

A That's my general recollection, sir.

Q *And do you recall the subject matter of the conversation you had with Andrea Mitchell before you spoke to Tim Russert?*

A Yes. She had said something incorrect in one of her television appearances, and I was trying to correct that.

Q *Do you know what it was that she said that had been incorrect?*

A There were two things in that period that people were saying incorrectly that touched on the Vice President's Office. One had to do with Halliburton. I think this had to do with the Wilson claim that we had sent him, but I'm not sure. I'd have to see what—if I looked at what she said that week I might be able to figure it out.

Q *Okay. And why don't we show you the July 8th transcript of Andrea Mitchell speaking at 6:40 p.m. Are you finished reading the article?*

A Yes, it says towards the bottom of the page here it says, "The White House blamed an October CIA report for ignoring Wilson's information and not requesting the original documents in which the charge was based for more than a year." Two things—it was not right. I don't think anybody blamed the CIA for ignoring his information. In fact, I think he—the CIA had looked at his information, had found that it, as reported in the NIE in October, . . . in fact, far from ignoring it, they looked at it and found that it did not contradict the claim, and in fact supported the claim that Iraq was trying to buy uranium from Niger. But phrased this way, that we blamed—that the White House blamed an October CIA report for ignoring the information, quite to the contrary. I think it was argued that the CIA had properly taken everything into consideration and it still concluded, as they said in the October NIE, which was six months after Ambassador Wilson's report, . . . that there was good grounds, and in fact had concluded flat out that Iraq had begun vigorously trying to procure uranium. So there wasn't a criticism of the CIA for ignoring Ambassador Wilson as she said. I thought the CIA was right in how they evaluated it. But phrased like this, it would likely be a subject that got the CIA upset.

Q *And is it fair to say that earlier in the transcript that Ms. Mitchell, who had been the person to interview Mr. Wilson on* Meet the Press *just two days before, had discussed Joseph Wilson in that brief TV segment, and also played a news clip from his Sunday TV appearance?*

A Yes, it shows that here.

Q *In your conversation with Andrea Mitchell, the first conversation that week which you recall happened before you spoke to Mr. Russert, do you know if you spoke to Ms. Mitchell about Ambassador Wilson?*

A I think if I, if I spoke to her earlier that week this probably was the subject that I was speaking to her about. . .

Q *Well, her appearance on TV was the 8th. And I believe if we look at some notes ... there's an indication that the Vice President told you to speak to Andrea Mitchell on the 8th.*

A Well, that would have been before this broadcast then most likely. And this is a 6:30—am I reading this right, it's a—

Q *Yes, it's a 6:30 broadcast.*

A So if it was during the day that day, maybe he was referring to an earlier thing, that's all I'm saying. I don't know.

Q *And do you know, do you have a recollection of whether or not you discussed Ambassador Wilson's wife when you spoke to Andrea Mitchell during the conversa-*

tion that week that occurred prior to your speaking to Russert?

A I, I do not believe that I spoke to her about, about Ambassador Wilson's wife prior to my conversation with Tim Russert.

Q *Do you remember Bob Novak calling you on July 8th?*

A No, sir.

Q *Do you know if you spoke to him at all prior to the July 14th column appearing under Novak's byline?*

A No. I remember I had one conversation with Bob Novak in this period. My recollection of it is that when I spoke to him he had all of the basic facts that we have in our case, by which I mean the type of facts that Cathie Martin gave to Ari Fleischer that morning that the Vice President didn't request the mission, etc. . . I have a note . . . which is dated in late July, that I spoke to Novak or something about Mr. Novak regarding uranium, and so I tend to believe that was when I had my conversation with Mr. Novak. But I don't recall—other than that, I can't fix the time of my conversation with Mr. Novak other than to think I had only one. That's all I recall, and I have no recollection of talking to him about Ambassador Wilson's wife.

Q *In reading this column, could you look to see if you believe you're the source for anything in the column which would indicate that you spoke to Mr. Novak before July 14th.*

A I was not the source for Mr. Novak . . .

Q *Do you have any recollection of speaking to Mr. Novak prior to July 14th about the substance of the State of the Union address, Mr. Wilson or his trip to Niger?*

A I don't.

Q *Have you ever provided information to [Novak] knowing that it would appear in a column?*

A I don't think I've ever intentionally provided information for a column.

Q *Let me show you what has been marked as Grand Jury Exhibit 7. First, I'll ask you if you recognize the handwriting on those notes?*

A It's not my handwriting. It, it might be Cathie Martin's handwriting . . .

Q *You can assume for purposes of this that it is Cathie Martin's handwriting.*

A Yes, sir, I will.

Q *And assuming that these are notes prior to July 14th, do you see the reference to Bill Harlow?*

A Yes, sir.

Q *And assuming there are notes from July 8th or prior, "CIA and DCI talked to VP about it today." And then down below, "Harlow, don't know anything on ambassador. We had stuff sensitive source," an arrow, and then what appears to be "chargé in Baghdad." You'll agree with me that chargé is a French word for State Department-type person, ambassador—official.*

A Yes. That's a fair description, sir.

Q *And then beneath that, "married to a CIA agent"? And I asked you—looking at this, does this refresh your recollection as to whether or not Cathie Martin was discussing with you in periods prior to your conversation with Tim Russert the fact that the person who was involved in Iraq in this trip to Niger is married to a CIA person and whether or not it refreshes your recollection on whether or not that was brought to the Vice President's attention during that week prior to your conversation with Mr. Russert?*

A "Goes out in a report." Quite right. It doesn't. I don't know about the "chargé in Baghdad" line if that's what that is.

Q *Is it fair to say that Ambassador Wilson had been a chargé in Baghdad back in the first Gulf War and had attained some fame for [that] fact?*

A Yes, sir, that's right, yeah, that's correct.

Q *And looking at a "sensitive source" who reported that Niger official had nothing to do with the report, arrow, chargé in Baghdad, married to a CIA agent?*

A . . . I don't recall any discussion with Cathie prior to when I heard it from Russert, and my recollection that I was surprised when I heard it from Russert. This doesn't change my recollection on that.

Q *Do you remember speaking with a reporter named Judith Miller on July 8th?*

A Yes, sir, I do.

Q *And is she a reporter who had been embedded with the forces over in Iraq?*

A She was in Iraq. I don't recall if she was embedded or not, but she was doing reporting in Iraq.

Q *And at the time in June of 2003 there was some controversy in the press about whether or not her journalistic credentials had been compromised by some people criticizing that she was a mouthpiece of the administration, to put a blunt word on it? I'm not saying that's true or not, but was that criticism being made?*

A I don't recall that but I'll take your word for it.

Q *Do you know if she did columns with her byline that stopped appearing in June, July of 2003 for some time?*

A I don't really. I did not notice that.

Q *Do you know what occasioned your meeting with Judith Miller on July 8th?*

A Yes, I believe I had met with Judith Miller once before, or this was the first meeting, but I think she may have come to my office once before. She's a very—from my point of view, responsible reporter who has had a long interest in the biological warfare issue. She wrote a book about it called *Germs* with another fellow, Steve Engleberg, who I know. They had actually talked about me a little bit in that book, but I had never met her . . . I wanted to meet her because I think she cares about the issue and really tries to understand . . . the threat that someone would use a biological agent to attack America or other places. And so I had wanted to meet her.

In—as we started to go through the week of July 7, after the Wilson report, the Vice President thought it was very important that what was in the NIE become known publicly because the National Intelligence Estimate, the NIE, came out in October of '02, as I mentioned earlier, six months after Ambassador Wilson's trip and had concluded that Iraq had tried to buy uranium from Niger. . . . And so we thought it was important that the NIE come out. There was also another document, and I guess I need your guidance as to whether I can talk about that document.

Q *Is it dated January 24th?*
A That's correct, yes.

Q *Just describe the January 24 document generically.*
A Okay. The January 24 document had the exact same content as the NIE, word-for-word as the NIE, and also saying that Iraq had vigorously begun trying to procure uranium from Niger. And it listed a couple of examples, not just Niger but two other examples. And one of the examples, as I recall, is the 1999 delegation, or seems to be the 1999 delegation that went to Iraq that Ambassador Wilson himself told the CIA about, according to this cable.

So both in October of 2002, and January 24, three days before the State of the Union, the CIA in writing sent to the White House this consensus language which said Iraq had tried to buy uranium from Niger, the exact point that the President was making in the State of the Union. That's what the Vice President had seen. It's the only thing the Vice President had seen after Wilson went out on his trip . . . And that at least was the primary thing he had seen. I don't know of anything else. And it was pretty definitive against what Ambassador Wilson was saying, and that's the way Director Tenet reports it on July 11 when he issues his public statement. So we thought it was important that Judy Miller, or somebody, report this. Now, I was unaware that she was actually not writing in this period and the Vice President instructed me to go talk to Judy Miller, to lay this out for her. And I said, "That's a problem," Mr. Vice President, because the NIE is a classified document. And the Vice President said that he would talk to the President and get the President's approval for us to use the document. I had previously spoken to our General Counsel, David Addington, [asked], does the President have the ability if he wants to take any document and say it's declassified, go talk about it? And Mr. Addington had told me, as our Counsel, that if the President says to talk about a document to the press, or publicly, it is declassified as of that moment . . . But I made a note and talked to the Vice President before July 8 and told him about this—that I could talk to her about the NIE, but he would have to get the President to declassify it . . . before I could talk about it . . . The President came back to the Vice President and said, yes, it would be okay, or I should go talk to somebody, and I selected Judy Miller because I know her to be a responsible reporter. It was, I guess, a poor choice if she wasn't actually writing in that period. But that was . . . who I went to talk to.

And so I called Judy Miller up and went and had a discussion with her.

Q *There [were] efforts at times to declassify the January 24th report as well?*

A ... The Vice President was of the view, and I was of the view, that ... the public should have all of the documents basically because they were all useful for the public to have.

Q *And was there also an effort to declassify the reports concerning the Wilson trip?*

A There's only one report that I knew ... that the CIA had issued, and yes, we also wanted that to be declassified. And I was told that that was declassified by the CIA although I don't know ... they've ever actually issued it.

Q *And when you had this conversation with Mr. Addington, do you recall where that conversation took place about the law of declassification?*

A I think actually it was in the corridor outside my office the first time, although I'm not sure. I went back, ... and he gave me the case name and I wrote that down in my notes also. *Navy versus Egan,* I think it is.

Q *And can you recall what—in your conversation with Mr. Addington about declassification, do you recall if you discussed any other topics with Mr. Addington at the time?*

A Yes. I also discussed in that conversation or close to that conversation, the question of whether there was a contractual obligation for Mr. Wilson. You know, whether it was normal for ... someone going out on a mission for the Agency to be able to just talk about the mission, which he had done, or whether there was some—you had to sign some agreement of some sort that you wouldn't be talking about it. And he told me that it takes all sorts of different forms.

Q *And did you have concerns during the week of July 7th as to whether or not the statement that Director Tenet would ultimately issue, which came out on July 11th, would be adequate to serve the interests of explaining the administration's position?*

A Yes, sir.

Q *Now, getting back to your conversation with Judith Miller, did you talk about Mr. Wilson with Judith Miller, and his trip?*

A I don't recall specifically discussing with Judith Miller about Mr. Wilson, but I do recall specifically discussing the NIE and as it relates to uranium, and therefore I'm pretty certain that I did discuss Mr. Wilson's trip at the same time because of how it fits in. I just don't recall the details of it in that way.

Q *And do you know if you discussed Mr. Wilson's wife and her employment with Ms. Miller?*

A I do not believe I discussed Mrs. Wilson—Ambassador Wilson's wife in this conversation with Ms. Miller.

Q *And is it also your testimony that your belief was at the time of the Judith Miller conversation you did not recall what you had learned about Wilson's wife working at the CIA.*

A It is, sir. But I recall this was, this was a couple days before I talked to Tim Russert and I recall being surprised by what Tim Russert told me.

Q *And do you recall on July 9th which would be the Wednesday following the . . . Wilson op-ed . . . morning meeting that was chaired by Stephen Hadley at the White House?*

A . . . Could you give me more about the meeting?

Q *Do you recall a circumstance in which Mr. Hadley was angry that some White House officials had evidently spoken to Andrea Mitchell and to David Martin and he indicated that George Tenet was very upset by what had appeared on the TV the night before in terms of David Martin's broadcast and Andrea Mitchell's broadcast?*

A Yes, sir, I do recall that.

Q *And do you recall him looking at Claire Buchan and Cathie Martin during that conversation as if . . . they might be responsible?*

A I don't recall that, but it's possible.

Q *And do you recall—was that the day following your conversation with Andrea Mitchell? Had you spoken to Andrea Mitchell and David Martin the day before Mr. Hadley expressed his concern about their press coverage?*

A It could be. I don't know the dates. I did speak to them. . .

Q *Do you remember when Mr. Hadley was angry about people speaking to those reporters, if you recall sitting there at the time thinking, I just spoke to those reporters?*

A That could be. Yes, sir. I do recall a conversation like that.

Q *Do you know if you told Stephen Hadley, the Deputy National Security Advisor, that you had spoken to Andrea Mitchell or David Martin?*

A I don't know that I told him.

Q *And do you recall whether or not Cathie Martin came to the Vice President's Office and told him in your presence that Stephen Hadley was angry and thought that she had been the one speaking to the reporters, Mitchell and Martin?*

A I think I do recall that. Yes, sir.

Q *Okay. What do you remember about that?*

A . . . Hadley was upset, reporting . . . that Director Tenet was upset. This rings a bell with me.

Q *And do you recall having to take any action as a result of the fact that Hadley was upset with Claire Buchan or with Cathie Martin?*

A No.

Q *Were either Claire Buchan or Cathie Martin excluded from any contacts with the Agency that week?*

A Cathie Martin . . . was restricted from it—I don't recall it being for that reason. The Tenet statement became very close hold as it was being worked, and the boss kept it very small.

Q *And do you recall on July 9th Steve Hadley indicating at a meeting that we need to do something about Wilson now, we need to discredit him?*

A To discredit him?

Q *Yes.*
A I don't recall that particular phrase. . .

Q *Forgetting whether the word "discredit" was used—*
A Uh-hum.

Q *—do you recall the concept coming across from Stephen Hadley that we need to do something about Wilson now, or we need to discredit him, forgetting what words he used?*
A Yes, we definitely were interested in getting the Tenet statement out to refute what Ambassador Wilson was saying. So if you had said "discredit what he is saying," there was lots of effort to get a statement out to discredit what he was saying. I just don't recall whether Steve Hadley used words about discrediting him personally as opposed to what he was saying. We were definitely trying to get out a statement. As I say, there was a debate whether it would be from Dr. Rice or from Director Tenet to discredit what he was saying because the record was actually quite good that what he was saying was not accurate, so we wanted to get that out.

Q *Do you, do you see what appears—is this your handwriting?*
A Yes, sir, it is.

Q *Why don't you just read that line across?*
A "Uranium story is becoming a question of the President's truthworthiness [sic]. Lead all new." Probably, "leads all the news" is what I was saying. It's turning to a process story is what the thought was, I believe. And then it has Mr. Rove at the senior staff meeting saying, "now they have accepted Joe Wilson as credible expert?" "We're one day late with getting CIA write response," I think that's what it—

Q *Okay. Fair to say at the senior staff meeting, there was concern expressed that this is a question going to the trustworthiness of the President at this point?*
A Yes, sir.

Q *And there's a question here that's leading all the news, and Rove is complaining that Mr. Wilson is being taken as a credible expert?*
A Yes, sir.

Q *Fair to say that there was an effort to undermine his credibility as an expert?*
A I don't know about that. My view was that we could get the facts out about what he had done, that would be more than sufficient because the record was very clear about what he had done and hadn't done, and that the CIA had not accepted what he had done as, as refuting the point. So I don't know that there was an effort to undermine him as a credible expert for what he did. . .

Q *Well, in the effort to undermine the story were people going around saying, let's undermine his story but let's be very careful not to hurt him?*
A I never heard that.

Q *And is it fair to say that there was a considerable degree of frustration at this point?*
A Yes, sir.

Q *. . . This is going right to the President's trustworthiness and people want to set the President's record straight.*
A Yes, sir.

Q *Now, do you recall an effort being made to push back against Wilson's credibility that week?*
A Yes, I recall the effort being made to get—we made a lot of effort that week to get the CIA Director or Dr. Rice . . . to issue a statement which would set the record straight about what Ambassador Wilson had said, and what he had found and not found, and the Agency had not found it to disprove the President's statement, and in fact found it to support the President's statement. The irony to all this was that if you . . . read Ambassador Wilson's cable, they thought the first part of it, as Director Tenet made clear at the end of the week, didn't disprove much at all . . .

Ambassador Wilson had gone to the government of Niger and said, I'm going to tell the United States government what you tell me. Did you in effect sell uranium to the number one enemy of America in the world which might use it to make an atomic bomb that might be used to threaten America? And a Nigerian official said, why no, we didn't do that. And I think the CIA found, as Director Tenet said on the 11th, that there's only so much credibility you can add to that because it would be amazing if they said, yes, we did do that.

The second part of what Ambassador Wilson's report said was that in fact a delegation had come from Iraq to talk to the Nigerians, to see if they would sell uranium to Iraq or that's how the Niger official interpreted it. So, in fact, his cable was not taken by the CIA to disprove that Iraq had gone, as Director Tenet himself says on July 11th when he finally issues his statement. And in fact, there was evidence in the cable, which was directly contrary to what Ambassador Wilson was saying . . . telling America what he had found which was there was no attempt to procure uranium. And so if you could just get that story out, maybe said better than I just said it, it would be pretty clear what Ambassador Wilson was saying didn't hold water . . . So there was a strong attempt by us to get those facts out.

Q *Is it fair to say though that the sound bite you I took away from Karl Rove is they're now accepting Joe Wilson as a credible expert? Correct?*
A Yes, sir.

Q *And is it fair to say that many would think that if Joe Wilson were hired because of nepotism, because of a contact he had at the Agency, that might undermine his credibility as an expert?*
A Some people may have taken it that way. That was never—what I took out of it . . . because what he did he was perfectly competent to do. What he did was he went and he sat down with the people from Niger and said, hi, I'm here, I'm going to talk to the United States government, as he says in an article, he sat down and had tea with them and asked them what they had done or hadn't done, and ambassadors do that

all the time. So I thought he was very competent to do that mission.

Q *Sir, are you telling us under oath that you never thought that Mr. Wilson was hired because of nepotism?*

A I didn't know why he was hired and I did not know at this point, I think I had forgotten exactly how he came . . . to be hired at this point. I think that came out with the Rove report. What I had known but forgotten at that point was that his wife worked at the division, but I didn't know at that point that his wife had anything to do with hiring him as far as I can recall. And on this day, July 8, as I've tried to make clear, the best of my recollection is that I was surprised when I learned from Russert that his wife worked there. So I think I had forgotten it.

Q *And you're clear in your mind that you weren't telling Ari Fleischer over lunch the day or two before that look, here's some information that's hush-hush or on the QT, Wilson's wife works at the CIA?*

A I don't recall discussing that with, with Ari Fleischer at lunch. I'm sorry, I just don't recall it. Sorry to keep saying this. But all I recall is that I, I recall being surprised on the 10th when I spoke to Tim Russert.

Q *Okay. Now, it says, "Wilson is declassified"?*

A Yes, sir.

Q *Is that to you an indication that the report on Wilson was declassified?*

A Yes, sir.

Q *And then what does the next sentence say?*

A "We haven't started to declassify NIE." And then Steve Hadley started to say something which I didn't have time to write down.

Q *And the next attribution, is that Hadley quoting Condi Rice?*

A Yes, sir.

Q *Okay. And what does that say?*

A "Spoke to President, he's comfortable."

Q *And does that indicate despite the stress of the time that the President is okay with—so far with how things are going?*

A It's not clear to me what. There's a space missing there—

Q *Okay.*

A —and I probably didn't write something down. I left a space to go back and I probably never got—I never got back to it. So—these things look sort of like a transcript but they're not really because there could be long moments when I don't write anything down. So she was saying the President was comfortable about something, but I don't know what the antecedent was to—

Q *And the next line?*

A Steve Hadley [is] saying, no question, it's better if we leak the NIE.

Q *What does that mean?*

A Steve Hadley is saying that it would be better if we got the NIE out, and "leak" means telling it to—giving it to a reporter to say, you know, here's something you can write about. It's like an exclusive or something like that.

Q *And had the NIE been declassified at that point?*

A It had in the sense that the President had told me to go out and use it with Judith Miller. I don't, I don't know that Mr. Hadley knew that at that point.

Q *Okay. And did anyone decide to leak the NIE that week?*

A Well, the President had told me to use it and declassified it for me to use with Judith Miller. I don't think Mr. Hadley was told to go out and talk about it.

Q *—so prior to July 10th you had talked to Judith Miller about the NIE?*

A Correct, sir.

Q *And your understanding is that even though it was a classified document the President had authorized you to talk to her about it?*

A Definitely, sir.

Q *. . . Did you tell Mr. Hadley at the time that you had already in effect leaked the NIE—with the President's approval by telling—Judith Miller?*

A I don't know if it's leaking once it's declassified and you're told to do it. I had talked to Judith Miller about the NIE at the President's approval relayed to me through the Vice President, and I did not tell Mr. Hadley at that time.

Q *And was there any reason why you didn't tell Mr. Hadley that you had told Ms. Miller about the NIE?*

A I was sitting with the Vice President. The Vice President knew it and chose not to tell Mr. Hadley and so I didn't change what he had done.

Q *Now—*

A And then there's a comment below it from the, from the Vice President.

Q *Yes?*

A Should I read that for you?

Q *Sure.*

A He says, "anything less than full and complete disclosure is a serious mistake." And Steve Hadley says, "I will—I told that to George Tenet." So the Vice President is pushing it. He does on a number of these things, get all of this stuff out. Let's have every—it's a good story, tell it all, get all these documents out to the public.

Q *And the Vice President, to be blunt, was frustrated that it wasn't all getting out there and it wasn't sort of putting the story to rest, and he was sort of getting ticked off that we needed to resolve this issue?*

A I'm not sure I would use the word "ticked off," but he was frustrated. Yes, sir, that's a fair, fair statement. And this—the statement from Director Tenet was supposed to come out—first it was going to be, I think, Tuesday night, and then it was going to be Wednesday night. It took a long time to get this statement out. It was useful when it did come out, but it took too long to get it out. People were saying, you know, "get it out".

Q *Now, tell me about the circumstances of your conversation with Mr. Russert.*

A Chris Matthews, who is an NBC correspondent, has a TV show at night, and he is a rather outspoken fellow. He was saying on this television show that the Vice President sent Joe Wilson out on this mission, that the Vice President got a report back from Joe Wilson on this mission, that the Vice President therefore knew that the uranium report was false and should have stopped the President from putting it in the State of the Union. And I believe he said it both on the night of the 8th, the night of the 9th, and he was saying this even though the White House Spokesman had come out, the Office of the Vice President had come out and the CIA spokesman had come out, all of them had come out on the public record and said, the Vice President did not ask for this mission, he did not get a report back, the report wasn't definitive and the intelligence was actually the other effect. So Mr. Matthews was saying these things on national television, ignoring the public record, and not even referring to the public record. It would be one thing if he says, now, the White House has denied this, and the CIA has denied it, and the Office of the Vice President has denied it, but I'm telling you nonetheless that the Vice President asked for this report, but he wasn't doing it. He was just saying flat out that the Vice President had known this, and should have told the President. Otherwise—and me also, me by name. And so this was frustrating to us and we wanted to get him to acknowledge that the public record was other than he was saying. This wasn't the first time Chris Matthews had said something negative about the White House, and I had prior discussions about this with Mary Matalin who was for the first two years . . . the Vice President['s] communications person. And so I called Mary to find out what she thought we could effectively do to try and get Mr. Matthews to acknowledge the public record and to stop saying these things in such an unqualified and incorrect fashion. I reached Mary by phone and she had her own view of where we were and relayed to me in depth her view of where we were. And—but also in the course of it said, look, the thing for you to do is to call Tim Russert and she gave me his phone number which I wrote on my notes which I turned over to you guys. [Exhibit GJ-60; see appendix.] And so I called Tim Russert. Want me to continue?

Q *Yes.*

A So I called Tim Russert. I can't recall whether I got him on the phone right away or whether he had to call me back. When I eventually spoke to him—this note with Mary Matalin is dated on the 10th, and I think I called Mr. Russert sort of lateish on the 10th, either late afternoon or early evening and went through—I, I got him on the phone, we had some—we have mutual friends in common, I'd known him a little bit over the years, and then I, I didn't want to take up much of his time, and I turned to our issues. And I said, I had two things that were bothering me. One is that some things that Andrea Mitchell was saying, and I think that may have been the comment on the 8th that we referred to before, but it might have been something earlier, but I said that, I'm not really calling you tonight about what Andrea Mitchell is saying. I'm calling you about what Chris Matthews is saying. And then I ran through for him what it was that Chris Matthews was saying and why it was wrong and on the public record wrong. That it seemed to me good reporting, he at least had to say that the White House has denied this, the CIA has denied this, the Vice President's office has denied this. And Mr. Russert said—after he got the facts about it, I am unclear, I apologize but I'm unclear as to whether he then said, I'll have to call you back, but I think he said, I'll have to call you back. And I think then there was a delay and then a second phone call with Mr. Russert. What I'm about to tell you is either in the second phone call, or if there was one phone call it was in the first phone call, I just don't recall. My sense of it is that there was a delay, a sort of longish delay which I was uncomfortable with. I think the second phone call was on the—that there was a second phone call and it was on the 11th because it was a long delay. In any case, it was longer than I anticipated it would be for him to get back to me is my recollection. In any case, one of these two times we had a fuller conversation in which he told me, you know, he understood what I was saying, that there wasn't much he could do about what Chris Matthews was saying. He understood that it was not [a] complete given that the public record was the other way. And then he said, you know, did you know that this—excuse me, did you know that Ambassador Wilson's wife works at the CIA? And I was a little taken aback by that. I remember being taken aback by it. And I said—he may have said a little more but that was—he said that. And I said, no, I don't know that. And I said, no, I don't know that intentionally, because I didn't want him to take anything I was saying as in any way confirming what he had said, because at that point in time I did not recall that I had ever known this, and I thought this is something that he was telling me that I was first learning. And so I said, no, I don't know that because I want to be very careful not to confirm it for him, so that he didn't take my statement as confirmation for him.

Now, I had said earlier in the conversation, which I omitted to tell you, that this—you know, as always, Tim, our discussion is off-the-record if that's okay with you, and he said, that's fine.

So then he said—I said—he said, sorry—he, Mr. Russert said to me, did you know that Ambassador Wilson's wife, or his wife, works at the CIA? And I said, no, I don't know that. And then he said, yeah—yes, all the reporters know it. And I said, again, I don't know that. I just wanted to be clear that I wasn't confirming anything for him on this. And you know, I was struck by what he was saying in that he thought it was an important fact, but I didn't ask him anymore about it because I didn't want to be digging in on him, and he then moved on and we finished the conversation, something like that.

Q *Is that—are those are your notes from July 10th and a telephone conversation you had with Mary Matalin?*

A They are indeed, sir.

Q *Okay. And you mentioned earlier that she had given you Russert's telephone number. Would that be listed at the top of the page?*

A Yes, sir.

Q *And what's under MM, is that the time of the call?*

A No, I think that says not, 6:15 to 7:15. And I think what she's telling me—she's telling me not to call somebody between 6:15 and 7:15. I think it's actually probably Russert that she's telling me not to call in that period. And if that's the case, I wrote it in the wrong place, but that's what I think it is. It might be her but—

Q *Okay. And below that does it say, re Niger, Niger—*

A Yes.

Q *—and go broad?*

A Yes.

Q *Does it say something—well, why don't you just read that sentence?*

A Yes. It says, "go broad, there were other countries, Saddam Hussein is a bad guy, this is feeding into the Democrats' case that Bush's credible—credibility something, keep saying our story." And she says, we need someone who can sum it up, "Tenet-like." If I can editorialize for a second?

Q *Sure.*

A She, she did not know at this point that we were working on the Tenet statement very hard trying to get a Tenet statement out, and I don't tell her in this conversation, I don't believe. So she's saying, we've got to get somebody out there and while she's saying that we're struggling mightily to get this statement out, but I didn't tell her that because I didn't know if I was supposed to, as I recall.

Q *If you could skip to the first box—*

A Yes, sir.

Q *—and just transliterate what's there?*

A She says—this is Mary Matalin again saying, "get *The New York Times,* Sanger or someone, to expose Wilson's story, give it to them."

Q *And the next box?*

A "Story has legs. Fits the Democrats' theory for the campaign," similar to what she said above, "will not go away," the Democrats and then something that doesn't I didn't finish.

Q *And then the next sentence?*

A "Need to address Wilson motivation."

Q *And the next sentence?*

A "We need to get cable out declassified, President should wave his wand." This is referring to the notion that he could declassify anything he wants, if he says so, that's what she means by wave—he should wave his wand, meaning he should use his power to declassify anything.

Q *And the next sentence?*

A "Call Tim. He hates Chris." That refers to Chris Matthews. "He needs to know it all. He needs to know the whole story and that Chris Matthews is not getting it right.". . . It [also] says, "eventually it will come out." . . .

Q *When you met with [Walter] Pincus before the June 12th article, you were going to him as a reporter to give him the administration's point of view. Correct?*

A Yes, sir.

Q *When you met with Judith Miller on July 8th you went to her as an administration official talking to a reporter to give her the background of the full story?*

A Correct, sir.

Q *When you called Russert, were you calling him as manager or as a reporter?*

A I was not trying to get him to write a story. I was trying to get him to exercise influence on Chris Matthews. I don't know technically whether he is the manager of Chris Matthews, but he's got a lot of—he's a respected figure in the news industry and I thought moral persuasion from Tim Russert would have some influence but he chose not to exercise it as far as I can tell.

Q *And why were you so concerned that you didn't confirm anything to Mr. Russert about something you weren't providing him?*

A I just—because sometimes reporters will call you with something that you don't know and try and get you to confirm it. Sometimes reporters will call you and try to get you to confirm something. You may or may not know what they're calling you with is true or not.

Q *And at the time did you think there was anything sensitive about whether his wife worked at the CIA that you wanted to make sure that you weren't a confirming source for that fact?*

A Not sensitive in the sense of a classified factor or anything. I didn't know it. I didn't—I had forgotten what I knew, and I didn't know if it was true or false or anything. I didn't want to be a confirmation of that.

Q *And as you sit here today, do you have a specific recollection of remembering that you had forgotten that you knew that Wilson's wife worked at the CIA?*

A As I sit here today I have a specific recollection that I was surprised when Tim Russert said it, and I thought during that conversation—when I said, "I don't know," I thought I was actually being truthful. I was being truthful, I didn't know as I sat there.

Q *If Cathie Martin had told you about Wilson's wife working at the CIA prior to July 10th, it's your testimony that you had forgotten that fact when you spoke to Tim Russert on July 10th?*

A My testimony is I don't remember Cathie doing that, and I was surprised on July 10. I don't mean to say that if she told me, that I forgot it in those two days, I just don't recall her telling me that at all.

Q *And it's your testimony that if you had discussed Wilson's wife with Ari Fleischer over lunch that Monday, July 7th that you did not recall it at the time that you spoke to Tim Russert on July 10th or 11th?*

A My recollection is that I was surprised when Tim Russert told me this fact, and told me that all the reporters knew that. And from that I think I wasn't knowledgeable about it earlier in the week, just because I didn't remember it when he told me on July 10th and those were only a few days earlier.

Q *... Did Russert tell you who the reporters were, who were saying that Wilson's wife worked at the CIA?*

A No. No, sir.

Q *And did you check with the Press Office to tell people, hey, have you guys heard what all the press are saying, that Wilson's wife works at the CIA?*

A No, sir.

Q *Had anyone told you from the Press Office that we've been getting calls from the press calling up to find out if Wilson's wife works at the CIA?*

A I don't recall any discussion with the Press Office about that.

Q *And what did you do as a result of the fact that Russert told you something that you believed, you believed at the time was new to you, the fact that Wilson's wife worked at the CIA?*

A I don't believe I really did much of anything, but there were subsequent events that I can describe for you if you wish.

Q *Did you tell the Vice President about Russert informing you this curious fact that Wilson's wife worked at the CIA?*

A I don't recall if I told the Vice President at that time what had been told to me. I'm not sure if I saw him at that time and had a chance to tell him. I don't recall telling him at that time.

Q *What's the next conversation you recall where you discussed Wilson's wife's employment with anyone?*

A On what I believe to be the 11th so I think later the same day I heard from Tim Russert. We were still waiting for Director Tenet's statement to come out and that was holding us up from getting our story out because once, once Director Tenet's statement came out we would have on the record that the Vice President hadn't asked for the mission, and didn't get the reports . . .

Towards the end of the day I went to see Karl Rove to tell him where I thought we were on getting Director Tenet's statement out which would be a very useful thing that we were all waiting to get out. And I went up to Karl Rove's office and told him about where we were on Director Tenet's statement, that I thought we were going to get some useful stuff out of Director Tenet's statement, I wasn't sure that we were going to get everything that we would have wanted out of Director Tenet's statement.

And during this conversation Karl Rove said to me that he had had a conversation with Bob Novak. And I thought that—my sense was that it was recent, although I didn't—I don't know what gave me quite that sense. And he told me that Bob Novak had told him that. Karl Rove told me that Bob Novak had told [him] that he was going to be writing about Ambassador Wilson, my sense was that weekend. And that he had run into Ambassador Wilson in [a] Green Room. Novak had run into Ambassador Wilson in a Green Room at some point and, you know, had a bad taste in his mouth after running into Ambassador Wilson. I've forgotten exactly what it was, but somehow Ambassador Wilson sort of turned him off. And that Bob Novak had concerns as to how Ambassador Wilson came to be chosen for this mission because Ambassador Wilson, in Novak's view, as related to me from what Karl had taken away from his phone call, Ambassador Wilson had—might not be a fair and impartial reporter of all this, might have an axe to grind. And then the third thing that Karl told me was that Novak had told Karl that Ambassador Wilson's wife worked at the CIA. So this was confirmation of a sort, from what I had heard from Tim Russert that all the reporters know that Ambassador Wilson's wife works at the CIA. This was on the 11th, as I understand it.

I told Karl that I had heard from Tim Russert the same thing, that the ambassador's wife works at the CIA and that Tim Russert had told me that all the reporters know this. I don't remember the exact order of this conversation, but that's the sum and substance of what, of what we talked about with regard to that.

Q   *First of all, do you know where the conversation took place?*
A   Karl Rove's office.

Q   *Do you know which day of the week it was, which day or date?*
A   It was after my conversation with Tim Russert, so I believe it was on the 11th, but I'm not—it was certainly after my conversation with Russert on the 10th. I believe it was on the 11th.

Q   *And whatever day it was, you recall it being in the evening?*
A   I tend to believe it was late in the day but, you know, in the West Wing everything feels like evening. There are not a lot of windows.

Q   *You had been sort of beaten up all week, the administration, both the President and the Vice President, about all the allegations stemming from the Wilson story. Was there a sense of relief that finally somebody is going to write something that will sort of respond to this?*
A   He didn't use any words about that. He didn't seem distressed that he was writing about it. I think he thought it was a good thing that somebody was writing about it. But it was more body language and the tone in which he said things rather than any words he used, as I recall. And the more important thing to me was that the Tenet statement was about to come out, and the Tenet statement was going to have directly on the facts rebut the things that Ambassador Wilson had been saying.

Q *Putting the Tenet statement aside, were you happy that Mr. Novak was going to write a column responding to Mr. Wilson's allegations?*

A Well, I didn't know what Mr. Novak was going to say in his column, so if he said the right things, I'd be happy about it. I was glad somebody would be out there saying—if he was going to address the merits. There were plenty of merits at this point including that we had all denied that the Vice President had sent him out. If that was in the column, that would be good.

Q *But sir, if people are saying the Vice President sent Wilson to Niger, and he didn't, isn't it fair to say the logical common man on the street question is, well, if the Vice President didn't send him, who did?*

A Yes.

Q *And if the story comes out, it's his wife who sent him, doesn't that make it more powerful an argument to say see, we told you Mr. Cheney had nothing to do with it?*

A If it came out that way, but I don't think I knew at that point that it was his wife who sent him. All I knew is his wife worked at the CIA. Thousands of people work at the CIA. The point about it was his wife who suggested it, I don't think I knew until the 14th when the column appeared.

If you had told me that, if somebody said, yes, it was going to be clear in the column that it wasn't us, that it was the CIA who sent him, that would have been a good fact. Yes, sir.

Q *What occasioned you and Mr. Rove to talk about the fact that the two reporters knew that Wilson's wife worked at the CIA?*

A Well, as I say, I came up to his office to tell him about the Tenet statement. That the Tenet statement was about to come out, you know, it was something we were waiting for.

Q *When you did speak to Andrea Mitchell, do you recall discussing Wilson's wife with her?*

A What I recall for sure is an awkward moment in that I was talking to her about all this, and I remember sort of being concerned about talking to her about the wife because Tim Russert had told me about it, and he had said all the reporters know. And as I was talking to her, I realized that I didn't know if Andrea Mitchell knew, and if Andrea Mitchell didn't know and I told her that, that I had heard this, and she asked me where it was, I didn't want to lie to her and I didn't want to tell her—it's a little bit convoluted—I didn't want to tell her that Tim Russert had told me it if in fact Tim Russert had not told her because I didn't want to get her mad at Tim Russert for not having shared something with her that he had shared it with me, and that's what I most recall about it. I may have gone on to talk to her about—that part I don't really recall—but I recall this sort of dilemma about, about—

Q *So—and let me make sure I understand this. So either you talked about it with her and you were worried as you talked about with her that you may reveal to her that*

Tim Russert had told you, or you didn't discuss it but you had the concern as the conversation was going that if it came up you might reveal that Tim Russert had told you?

A   Correct. I had the concern, yes, that's correct.

No, I don't, I don't know when it was. It was some time after Russert, I'm sure of that. It may have been, it may have been before the 14th. The only thing that fixes is the NBC statement that Andrea Mitchell didn't talk about this until after the 14th. But I don't, I don't know.

Q   *Well, if Novak had already published in the newspaper that Wilson's wife worked at the CIA, why would you be concerned that you might tip her hand that you knew something?*

A   I was afraid that she might ask me, you know, is this true, or when did you learn this, or something like that, that's all.

Q   *And why couldn't you just tell her, I can't comment?*

A   I could, but I don't usually like to obfuscate in that way, but I, I could. I just was concerned about—

Q   *And you don't recall any conversation with either Grossman, or Fleischer, or Cathie Martin concerning Wilson's wife. Correct?*

A   Correct.

Q   *Now, did there come a time when you took a trip on Air Force Two on July 12th?*

A   Yes, sir.

Q   *And was that for the purpose of going down to the christening of the USS* Ronald Reagan?

A   Yes, sir.

Q   *And were you accompanied on that trip by your family?*

A   Yes, sir.

Q   *And was it your son's birthday?*

A   Right, sir.

Q   *And at that time were there—reporters [who] had been calling about various stories during those few days?*

A   Yes.

Q   *And was there an outstanding request by a reporter named Matthew Cooper?*

A   Yes, sir.

Q   *And is he with TIME magazine?*

A   Yes, sir.

Q   *And were there other reporters who had made outstanding requests at that time?*

A   Yes, sir. Most of these go to Cathie Martin, but there were a number of calls in during this period that she would know about.

Q   *And you recall that the 12th was a Saturday. Correct?*

A   Correct.

Q *And is it fair to say that on Air Force Two flying down that you sat up front with the Vice President and your family on the trip down to the USS* Reagan?

A No, sir. I sat with my family on the flight.

Q *Okay. And did you do any work on the way down?*

A My recollection is no, we did not do work on the way down.

Q *And you didn't do any work other than being there at the christening of the* Reagan?

A Correct, sir.

Q *On the way back did you address—on the return flight on Air Force Two, begin to address how to respond to Mr. Cooper and others?*

A Yes, sir. Either on the return flight or actually when we had landed at the return, but it was in that period.

Q *And did you have a conversation with Cathie Martin about what it was that Cooper wanted to know?*

A Yes, sir.

Q *Okay. Do you recall reviewing an e-mail that came from Mr. Cooper raising certain questions?*

A I recall that there was an e-mail. Yes, sir.

Q *And did you—and when you, when you discussed this with Cathie Martin is it fair to say that you were in a part of the plane away from the Vice President?*

A Yes, I, I think so, sir.

Q *Did there come a time you went forward to talk to the Vice President about how to respond to Mr. Cooper?*

A Yes, sir.

Q *Okay. And did you go forward with Cathie Martin or alone?*

A I don't recall. I think I was alone but I don't recall. She may have been with me.

Q *And did you discuss with the Vice President what it was that you were to say to the press?*

A Yes, sir . . . I went forward to talk to the Vice President about what we were going to do about getting the Tenet statement out, answering the questions from time. But it was . . . broader than just the *TIME* magazine questions. It was the whole issue of now the Tenet statement was out, what would we do?

Q *And did you have a discussion with the Vice President about what would be said to the press, in what language, and who would be the person to say it?*

A Yes, sir.

Q *And what do you recall the Vice President telling you?*

A Vice President was dictated to me what he wanted me to say to the press. He specifically said he wanted me to make the statement on-the-record to *TIME* magazine because he wanted it to get some attention. And he felt if I put my name on it, it would get more attention than just a senior administration official. So he dictated things for me to say and he instructed me to say it—with *TIME* magazine, to give it basically word-for-word quote that he dictated, some background material that he wanted me to use.

Q *And did you actually write down word-for-word what it is that he wanted you to say?*

A I did, sir, on a card that I turned over to you all.

Q *And before we get to the text of it, did the Vice President indicate who should actually speak to the reporters, as between you and the press people?*

A Yes, he wanted me to do it.

Q *And why did he want you to speak to the reporters as opposed to Cathie Martin using your name?*

A Well . . . you could give a statement from Cathie Martin to me, but he wanted me to give the statement. He wanted to make sure it was done exactly correctly and he wanted me to give it in name, and so I was the one who called.

Q *And is it fair to say that sometimes you would have a press person give an exact statement, a quote, in your name if you write it out and say, call a reporter, here's what I have to say, and attribute it to my name?*

A Yes, they could, but in this case he wanted to not just a direct on-the-record statement but also some points on deep background and background, as we discussed earlier today, and those there was no direct text for. That was something you would have to talk your way through and he wanted me to do that.

Q *Okay. And do you recall what he told you to say on background and deep background?*

A It's in the notes. But my recollection was that he wanted me to say—first, he had a long direct quote. On background, deep background, he wanted me to talk about what was in the, that Director Tenet had now talked about on the record.

The top part of this page are notes that I had made to talk about with him when I got some time with him, which would—on the way back or on the ground, and I had written down the magazines as a reference to *TIME* and *Newsweek*. *TIME*—both *TIME* and *Newsweek* had calls in to us. And the question that I was writing down, does he want us to deny the VP/Wilson link on the record. Does he want me to, you know, do you want to do it on the record either in his name, my name or Cathie's name or somebody's name? And we covered that point and I crossed out the line. And then he dictated what he wanted us to say.

Q *Okay. And then the dictation on the first page of this card has on the record on the left column?*

A Yes, that's correct.

Q *And if we could turn to the other side of the column—card, if you could transliterate what this card says?*

A Under deep background, sir, or the whole thing?

Q *The whole thing.*

A VP was maybe unaware of Joe Wilson trip and didn't know about it until this year when it became public after the State of the Union.

Q *And what was the part that was crossed out? You said, did not know anything?*

A Did not know anything, right. He got more specific.

Q *And then if you could read what it says under deep background?*

A Only written record of Wilson trip included a statement that the former Prime Minister of Niger was saying that he had been approached by the Iraqi officials in what he believed to be an official . . . effort to acquire uranium in 1999. That's the point from the second part of the Wilson cable, and he thought on deep background I should make sure that people understood that.

Q *Okay. And the next bullet point?*

A He didn't see this until recently. That he saw the NIE last fall, which I, meaning the Vice President, took to be authoritative. This is all stuff to say on deep background.

Q *And then the next reference?*

A Deep background, as an administration official as opposed to, I guess, deep background, a senior administration official. That I should give a straight report on the NIE which was also covered in Tenet's statement . . . that said that Iraq had begun to vigorously pursue trying to procure uranium. . . . He wanted it very clear that it was the NIE six months after Wilson's trip where the CIA and the intelligence community was saying affirmatively that they had tried to procure uranium, and that's what he had taken to be authoritative.

Q *Okay. And at this point do you know if you talked to Vice President Cheney about the 12th about the conversation you believe you had on the 11th, perhaps the 10th, with Mr. Russert, and then later with Mr. Rove where reporters were indicating that Wilson's wife worked for the CIA?*

A I don't recall. It's not on my list here of things to raise with him that day. I don't recall if I talked about it to him the previous night.

Q *And you recall discussing with Rove, but you don't recall whether you discussed it with the Vice President?*

A Correct. I recall with Rove in part because of the Novak bit that he had done. I don't recall whether I discussed it with the Vice President. I'm not sure if I—I don't know that I saw him in, in that sort of a setting after my discussion with Rove because my discussion with Rove may have been later in the day, and I had no private time with him in the morning, and then I went into this. So I don't recall.

Q *And to the extent that it was written out pretty much verbatim what your statement would be on the record.*

A Yes, sir.

Q *And it's written out verbatim what your statement would be on deep background. Correct? Tell us about the calls you made to the, to the press.*

A We went into a lounge at—we were on the airplane and we needed a land line phone or, you know, a phone where we could have a good connection. So we went into the lounge at Andrews Air Force Base, and we found a phone that we could use. And we sat down to make the phone calls, we being Jenny Mayfield, my assistant; Cathie Martin; and I. And we tried to call three or four reporters at that point. Matthew Cooper from *TIME* magazine; Evan Thomas, who had calls into us from *Newsweek* magazine; Glenn Kessler from *The Washington Post*; and later I talked to Judith Miller. I think we tried her then but I'm not sure if we didn't try her later. And I wanted to—you know, it was a Saturday, everybody had spent the whole day doing this commissioning ceremony and I wanted to get everybody out of there, so we tried to place all the calls right there from Andrews while we were all together. We were unable to reach Glen Kessler at first. Well, we did reach him shortly thereafter. We were unable to reach Evan Thomas at all for a while but we did reach him later. But we did reach Matthew Cooper while we were sitting in the lounge and so I had a conversation with Matthew Cooper in the lounge.

Q *And what did you tell Matthew Cooper?*

A I had not met Matthew Cooper before, so Cathie introduced us. She said that, you know, we wanted to have this phone call in response in part to his questions, that some of the conversation would be on-the-record, some of it would be on deep background, some of it might be off-the-record, but we would have different layers of, of press conversations.

So I—after she finished that preliminary, I talked to him about the Tenet statement and I gave him this quotation on-the-record that we had here, and I think I also covered some of these background points with him in the phone call.

Q *Did you have a discussion with Mr. Cooper about Wilson's wife?*

A Yes, sir.

Q *Okay. Tell us about that conversation.*

A I went through—just a little bit of preliminary. I went through these points and I went through what Tenet had said that, you know, the day before in his statement, you know, I hope you noticed Director Tenet's statement the day before, which is why we were making these calls. I said, you know, off-the-record, reporters are telling us that Ambassador Wilson's wife works at the CIA and I don't know if it's true. As I told you, we don't know Mr. Wilson, we didn't know anything about his mission, so I don't know that it's true. But if it's true, it may explain how he knows some people at the Agency and maybe he got some bad skinny, you know, some bad information. So that was the discussion about Ambassador Wilson's wife.

Q *And his response?*

A I don't recall specifically what he said about that. I recall the response, "why does he say it," because that's what led into this conversation.

Q *And it's your specific recollection that when you told Cooper about Wilson's wife working at the CIA, you attributed that fact to what reporters—*

A Yes.

Q —*plural, were saying. Correct?*

A I was very clear to say reporters are telling us that because in my mind I still didn't know it as a fact. All I had was this information that was coming in from the reporters.

Q *And at the same time you have a specific recollection of telling him, you don't know whether it's true or not, you're just telling him what reporters are saying?*

A Yes, that's correct, sir. And I said, reporters are telling us that, I don't know if it's true. I was careful about that because among other things, I wanted to be clear I didn't know Mr. Wilson. I don't know—I think I said, I don't know if he has a wife, but this is what we're hearing.

Q *Did you have any further conversation about Wilson and his wife with Cooper during this phone call?*

A I don't think so and I don't think I had a subsequent phone call with him. That was it for Mr. Cooper.

Q *And any other reporters that you discussed Wilson's wife with on that day, July 12th?*

A Yes, sir. I talked to three other reporters that day. Towards the end of the day I believe I talked to Judith Miller, and I know that I discussed it with Judith Miller, *New York Times,* and the discussion was pretty much as I just described with Ambassador—excuse me, with Matthew Cooper.

Q *Why don't you describe the conversation for us?*

A I said, that—I went through all about the Tenet statement, that the Tenet statement had just come out, you know, please pay attention to the Tenet statement which said that we didn't know about the trip, that we didn't get the report, that the report was not definitive, that the NIE actually comes out and says that Iraq had begun to vigorously pursue acquiring uranium, and that—and I did not use this text, as an exact quote, I did not use it exactly again, but I went through some of the same points with her. And I don't remember exactly how it came up, but I said to her . . . that I didn't know if it was true, but that reporters had told us that the ambassador's wife works at the CIA, that I didn't know anything about it.

Q *To finish the Judith Miller conversation. Was there something that triggered it, your conversation with Judith Miller, to discuss Wilson's wife's employment in the way that Cooper had asked you, "Why is Mr. Wilson saying this?"*

A I think there was. I don't recall exactly what it was. Something that she said—I thought something that she said, I think, triggered it. That's my, my vague recollection about it. You know, it had been something that was important to Tim Russert. It was something that, you know, Cooper still wanted to know at this point and I think partly by the time I talked to Judith Miller I was thinking, you know, the reporters seem to have this unopen—unanswered question, and the question was, Wilson had said that someone had told him that the Vice President requested the mission. He said that on national television earlier in the week. And even with the explanation from George Tenet, it leaves unanswered this question well, how did he happen to hear it? And so, you know, I was pretty ready to explain that I didn't think he would have heard it officially, but he might have heard it unofficially, but I think there was something that she said that led me into it.

Q *Okay.*
A Evan Thomas?

Q *Yes.*
A I, I recall, recall that I did reach Evan Thomas eventually. I drew his attention to the Tenet statement that had come out the day before. Evan was calling me in part because we were going to meet about something else. And he said, "I got it," my recollection. In other words, when I, when I laid out what, what Tenet had said . . . that the CIA had not taken Wilson's report to be definitive, he said he got it, and he wanted to move on and I just moved on. So I did not discuss it with Evan Thomas.

Q *And are you sure you did not discuss it with Evan Thomas?*
A Pretty sure.

Q *And did you talk to Glenn Kessler that day?*
A I did. We didn't get Glenn Kessler while we were in the—at Andrews, but we got him on a cell phone while we were in the car driving back from Andrews to my house. Kessler was, Kessler was, was contacting me primarily about Colin Powell's February 5th presentation. He was interested in the origins of the presentation that Colin Powell had made back on February 5th. And what I recall about this conversation was that Glenn Kessler was at the zoo with his kids, and yet he was able to have this lucid conversation, something that I could never do with my kids at the zoo on a sunny day with, you know, hundreds of people milling around.

Q *Did you talk about Wilson's wife working at the CIA with Glenn Kessler?*
A I don't know for sure. What I—I believe I did have a conversation with Glen Kessler about, about Ambassador Wilson's wife. I tend to think it was later, not in this conversation, but it was possibly in this conversation. I'm not sure.

Q *We'll wrap—we're going a little bit late. I'll just take a minute to wrap something up. When the Novak column came out on July 14th, did you—you knew it was coming from your conversation with Rove. Had you ever heard or seen an advance copy of the Novak column?*
A No, sir.

Q *Did anybody indicate to you whether or not anyone had received a draft column either by fax or by e-mail?*
A I've never heard that, sir.

Q *And do you have any recollection of when it is that you discussed with Vice President Cheney, his comments about whether or not Ambassador Wilson had been sent on this trip by his wife as a junket?*

A I know that there—that Vice President Cheney asked—made some comments like that. I think of them in my mind as later, you know, later in July or August or later, asking not so much in me, but just sort of how did he come to be sent on this? I don't know if he also made them earlier. That sort of runs together for me.

MR. FITZGERALD: Why don't we adjourn—

WITNESS: Can I just make one other comment about this stuff? I get a lot of information during the course of a day. I probably get—you know, after this all came up I sort of for a few days tried to take a census of how many pages of stuff I get in a day, and I tend to get between 100 and 200 pages of material a day that I'm supposed to read and understand and I—you know, I start at 6:00 in the morning and I go until 8:00 or 8:30 at night, and most of that is meetings. So a lot of information comes through to me, and I can't possibly recall all the stuff that I think is important, let alone other stuff that I don't think is as important.

And so when a lot of this—a lot of stuff that comes to me, what I will normally do is I'll gather my staff together and say, hey, what happened here? You know, there was some meeting we had on, let's say, Iraq. What did, what did people say, or what happened last week when we had that meeting? Did State agree to do something, or was the Defense Department supposed to do something? And we'll sort of pool our recollections of it and that almost always bring me a fuller recollection of what's happened. I haven't done that here because as I understand it, you don't want me to do that here. I'm happy to do it at some point, but I haven't. So I apologize if my recollection of this stuff is not perfect, but it's not in a way that I would normally do these things. I would normally—in the normal course of what we do in a day, I would bring the staff together or ask the Vice President and go through all this, and I haven't done that here, and I apologize if there's some stuff that I remember and some I don't, but it's—I'm just trying to tell you what I do, in fact remember.

GRAND JUROR: Thank you, Mr. Libby.

WITNESS: Thank you.

(Whereupon the witness was excused at 4:38 p.m.)

WITH THAT, THE MARCH 5, 2004, GRAND JURY recording concludes. Because there is additional time left in the afternoon session, Kedian moves to enter the March 24 Grand Jury tapes into evidence. Walton accepts, and the recording begins:

MARCH 24, 2004, GRAND JURY TESTIMONY

By Mr. Fitzgerald:

Q *I'd just like to briefly re-advise you of all your constitutional rights, which is that, again, you have the right to refuse to answer any question to which a truthful answer would tend to incriminate you. Do you understand that . . . ? You just have to say yes or no.*

A Oh, yes, sir . . . Yes, sir.

Q *And secondly, obviously even though you answered questions the last time, you still have the right to refuse to answer questions this time or change your mind at any time. Do you understand that?*

A Yes, sir.

Q *And obviously, you still have a right to counsel . . . Correct?*

A Correct, sir . . .

Q *And as we confirmed prior to you appearing . . . you remain the same status as a subject. You understand that?*

A Yes, sir . . .

Q *You have no recollection of ever telling Mr. Fleischer that this is either "hush-hush," or "QT" or words to that effect, that Wilson's wife works out at the CIA?*

A No, sir, I don't.

Q *And no discussion that you recall where either one of you implied with Wilson had obtained the assignment to go to Niger as a result of perceived nepotism?*

A No, sir, not that I recall . . .

Q *. . . Do you recall in the June time frame ever receiving a document from the White House Situation Room, a fax that was to be hand-delivered to you and to John Hannah which contained a document that the CIA had prepared in earlier 2003? Does that ring a bell with you at all?*

A . . . I did receive documents from the CIA, you know, that came through the SIT room, and . . . I retained them . . .

Q *Why don't I show you some documents? . . . Without getting into the contents it's . . . from John Hannah to the Vice President and concerning a CIA paper on the Iraq/Niger/uranium deal. Do you recognize that?*

A I do, sir.

Q *Okay. And do you recall receiving it on or about June 9th?*

A Yes, sir.

Q *And do you recall what it was that occasioned Mr. Hannah to prepare this?*

A We had gotten a paper from the CIA. It was a very long paper. I think it's attached here, eight single-spaced pages with a lot of data in it, and a lot of dates and meetings and discussions, and he . . . summarize[d] some of the things that were in the CIA paper . . .

Q *Then the document that Mr. Hannah prepared is a summary of what was contained in the transmission from CIA to Congress which included the eight page single-spaced statement?*

A Yes, sir . . .

Q *To Jenny Mayfield. And does it say, "Please pass to Mr. Hannah and Mr. Libby ASAP?"*

A Yes.

Q *And does that appear to include the CIA transmittal sheet to Congress from earlier that year, and then that eight page document you referenced?*

A Yes, sir.

Q *And do you know if you discussed this with the Vice President on or about June 9th when this was prepared?*

A I did discuss points in that memorandum with the Vice President . . .

Q *Okay. And do you know if you discussed the identity of the envoy who had . . . been sent . . . to Niger in 2002 to investigate the yellowcake claims with Vice President?*

A Yes . . .

Q *And do you know whose handwriting that is?*

A . . . It might be the Vice President's, but I'm not sure . . . It is around the time that we were doing the Pincus article, you know, preparing to talk to Pincus, so it could be in relation to that, or it could just be an inquiry, but I don't know. ASAP is not a particularly, you know, hair-on-fire type marking, but I don't, I don't know.

Q *You understand ASAP stands for "as soon as possible"?*

A Yes . . .

Q *And that was during the time frame when you were talking with the Vice President and others about how to respond to Mr. Pincus's inquiries for an article he would eventually publish on June 12th. Correct?*

A Yes, sir.

Q *And at the time did you know the name of the envoy who had gone to Niger as being Mr. Wilson?*

A No, sir. Not the best I recall . . .

Q *Is that a CIA cable concerning the trip that Ambassador Wilson took to Niger—*

A Yes, sir.

Q *—in 2002? And is there handwriting on the first page?*

A Yes, sir.

Q *And does it say the word "Wilson"?*

A Yes, sir.

Q *And do you know whose handwriting that is?*

A Again, it looks to me like it might be the Vice President's.

Q *And do you recall ever discussing this cable with the Vice President where he would have written down the name Wilson?*

A I recall discussing the cable with the Vice President. I don't recall him having written the name Wilson on the cable while we talked about it . . .

Q *And what were the circumstances under which you discussed the Wilson cable with the Vice President?*

A . . . It came up multiple times . . .

Q *So is it fair to say when the allegations came out in the Kristof column and later in the Wilson piece, that Wilson's trip had sort of debunked the sixteen words contained in the State of the Union that one of the points the Vice President and yourself wanted to make was that you believed that Wilson's trip had sort of corroborated the sixteen words to the extent that he had reported back that there had been prior efforts to open commercial—or establish commercial relations between Iraq and Niger?*

A Yes, sir. That's what we understood the Agency took . . . that to mean, and from this it looks that way to us too . . .

Q *The last time we showed you a document that you had dated as approximately June 12th which indicated a discussion at that time with the Vice President where you noted that he had indicated to you that the ambassador's wife had worked at the functional office at the CIA, referred to as CPD, the Counter Proliferation Division. Do you recall that?*

A Yes, sir.

Q *And do you know if you had reviewed some—any of these documents, the Wilson cable or the June 9th report, with Vice President Cheney at or about the time of the conversation where he told you that the ambassador's wife worked at the functional office in Counter Proliferation?*

A Did I review the CIA document that's dated June 9 and the cover memo?

Q *Yes . . . There was conversation during the early June time frame between yourself and the Vice President where you were discussing this envoy's trip to Niger. Correct?*

A Yes.

Q *And during that—those conversations you learned from the Vice President that the envoy's wife worked at the functional office concerning Counter Proliferation at the CIA. Correct?*

A I think I only . . . had one conversation about that point with the Vice President. It was not a fuller discussion of the substance like this cable. It was a very short discussion which was relating to me something he had learned . . .

Q *And is it fair to say that during the time frame you were having discussions with the Vice President in preparation for your speaking to Mr. Pincus who was going to write an article for* The Washington Post?

A I think that was the discussion prior to my talking to Pincus.

Q *Okay. And when you say that was the discussion, the discussion—*

A The one, the one where I wrote the notes that you're referring to.

Q *Okay. So the conversation reflected in the notes where the Vice President advised you that the envoy's wife worked at the CIA in Counter Proliferation was a discussion you had with the Vice President in preparation for your speaking to Mr. Pincus?*

A Yes. There were two parts to that conversation. There was a background session and then there were the points that I was supposed to raise with Pincus. The point about the wife was in the first part, physically on the paper anyway. And the points for the—to raise with Pincus were at the bottom of the page.

Q *And do you recall if your notes distinguished between background and what to raise with Mr. Pincus when you wrote them down?*

A Yes, they do to me.

Q *And did you ever have a discussion with . . . the Vice President [who] told you either that you should or should not tell Mr. Pincus about the envoy's wife's employment at the CIA?*

A No.

Q *Did you ask the Vice President whether it was appropriate if you could tell Mr. Pincus this fact?*

A No.

Q *And is it possible that you told Mr. Pincus that fact?*

A No, I don't think I did . . .

Q *And did you understand at the time that you were legally prohibited from doing so?*

A No.

Q *And the last time we spoke you indicated that you had a conversation with Judith Miller on July 8th. Is that fair to say?*

A Correct, sir.

Q *About how long was that conversation?*

A An hour perhaps, maybe, maybe a little over.

Q *And you mentioned that prior to having that conversation you had a discussion with Vice President Cheney as to what you could discuss with Judith Miller?*

A Correct, sir.

Q *And can you tell us when you had the conversation with the Vice President and what concerns you raised, and what he told you in response?*

A The Vice President and I discussed the need to get into the public domain that the CIA National Intelligence Estimate made it clear to recipients of the National Intelligence Estimate that Iraq had been attempting to procure uranium. This was similar to the point that the President raised in the State of the Union in the famous sixteen words. And despite the fact that there had been a lot of talk about particular documents having been forged, the Vice President's point was that the policymakers, he, had seen and had relied upon the National Intelligence Estimate . . . The portion about uranium is short and there's some key judgments at the front that were short, which are short compared to the length of the document.

And the problem in letting people know what the National Intelligence Estimate said on that was that it's a classified document. So we could not talk to the press about it until it was declassified, and I discussed that with the Vice President . . . I was informed by the General Counsel to the Vice President's office that the National Intelligence Estimate, or any other document that's classified, can be declassified by the President if he wishes. And so the Vice President thought we should get some of these facts out to the press, but before it could be done, the document had to be declassified. I had had a conversation with David Addington that we talked about in our last session when he relayed that. He had mentioned to me a legal case. I had written down the name of the legal case. I'd forgotten it the first time. I came back to him, had a second conversation, wrote it down in my notes, reported to the Vice President . . . And he then undertook to get . . . permission from the President to talk about this to a reporter. He got the permission. Told me to go off and talk to the reporter. My recollection is that I did not accomplish it right away, and he told me at one point to hold up, and then he came back and said to go ahead. And so at that point I went ahead and scheduled the meeting and had the discussion.

Q *Now, can you fix the date when you first spoke to the Vice President about trying to get the facts out from the NIE, the National Intelligence Estimate, and then you in that conversation expressed your reservations because it was a classified document?*

A No. I think there were several over a period of time, none of them being long. It was not a long debate. But there was several times it was talked about that, you know, the NIE was clear, this cable was actually not persuasive even to Director Tenet or the CIA as Director Tenet made clear in his July 11th statement. When the entire NIE was declassified, these portions of the NIE were declassified by the Agency and then provided to the press on July 18, it was clear from that text that it was all declassified . . . There were discussions about getting the Agency to declassify it separately. There were discussions with the Vice President . . .

Q *And when you say the President had already declassified it, you're referring to what you had been told by Vice President Cheney as to the fact that the President gave you permission to talk about parts of the NIE with Judith Miller?*

A Yes, sir. I don't think the President knew Judith Miller, but…with the press. Yes, sir.

Q *And did the Vice President know Judith Miller at the time he authorized you to discuss it?*

A Yes, . . . before I actually went and talked to Judith Miller I think he knew it was Judith Miller I was going to talk to . . .

Q *Was Judith Miller the first reporter you, you discussed the NIE with?*

A The first reporter that I discussed the text of the NIE with . . . In terms of the first discussion I ever had about, you know, the language of the text, yes . . .

Q *Okay. And . . . was it your understanding that you would show the text of the relevant portions of the NIE to Judith Miller when you discussed it with the Vice President?*

A Yes, sir.

Q *And did you in fact show those relevant portions of the text?*

A Talked it through with her and I think I gave it to her, showed it to her, an excerpt.

Q *Okay. And when you showed it to her did you let her read the relevant portions of the whole document or did you have a redacted version?*

A Oh, no, redacted . . .

Q *Okay. Who created that document?*

A I did.

Q *Personally?*

A Yes . . . I didn't type it . . . but I directed it to be done . . .

Q *So what was your understanding? What did the Vice President tell you the limits were on what you could share with Judith Miller from what was contained in the NIE?*

A I could talk to her about the uranium section of the NIE and about some of the key judgments from the NIE which made it clear that Iraq was seeking weapons of mass destruction.

Q *And what was it that you understood was not in what you could share with Judith Miller that hadn't been in the public domain yet, hadn't been discussed by other government officials?*

A The language of the NIE . . . that Iraq had begun to vigorously pursue . . . the acquisition of uranium or the procurement of uranium, something like that.

Q *So the phrase including, . . . the word "vigorously" trying to obtain or procure uranium was what the Vice President wanted you to get into the public domain through Judith Miller?*

A Yes. Flat declarative statement that it was so. And that there were other instances, I guess. There were several countries mentioned. There were countries mentioned in addition to Niger . . .

Q *Okay. Was there any—was the fact that you were meeting with her and sharing* *information with her exclusively one of the factors that wanted you to meet with her outside of the building?*

A It could have been. It was also consistent with that . . .

Q *In your career had you ever been authorized before to talk about a document that you knew to be classified with the press and therefore understood that the direction to talk about the document with the press had in effect declassified it?*

A I think this may be the first time I've ever talked about a classified document in this fashion, getting it declassified first . . .

Q *And do you know if the Vice President and the President talked about [the NIE] in person or by telephone?*

A I don't know . . .

Q *And who else in the administration was told, as far as you know, that you were authorized to discuss the relevant portions of the NIE with Judith Miller?*

A Nobody as far as I know.

Q *So as far you know, the only three people who knew about this would be the President, the Vice President and yourself?*

A Correct, sir . . .

Q *And during those conversations did you ever tell any of the other people that in fact the President had already declassified the NIE in your mind?*

A No, sir.

Q *And in your presence did the Vice President ever tell these other people that you understood that the NIE had already been declassified?*

A No, sir.

Q *And as far as you know, was the CIA or Director Tenet ever notified that the NIE had been declassified in your mind as of July 8th with regard to those portions concerning uranium?*

A No, sir.

Q *And were there conversations in which Mr. Hadley discussed declassification of the NIE?*

A Yes, sir.

Q *Were there conversations where Dr. Rice discussed declassification of the NIE?*

A Yes, sir.

Q *Were there conversations in which Andrew Card, the Chief of Staff, discussed declassification of the NIE?*

A Yes, sir.

Q *And during all those conversations it remained unknown to them that in fact you understood that the NIE had already been declassified?*

A By the President. Yes, sir.

Q *And is it fair to say that on July 10th the Vice President, according to your notes, indicated that he would recommend to the President declassification of the relevant parts of the NIE?*

A My recollection is that's what he was telling Steve Hadley should pass on to Director Tenet, that they wanted to get those portions declassified and then they were declassified.

Q *And so in your mind, the Vice President was telling Steve Hadley to tell George Tenet that we, the Office of Vice President, would recommend declassification even though at the time, according to your account, both he and you knew that the NIE had already been declassified?*

A Yes, sir . . .

Q *Was that unusual for you to have the National Security Advisor, Director of Central Intelligence and the White House Chief of Staff, among others, in the dark as to something that you had done regarding declassification?*

A It is not unusual for the Vice President to tell me something which I am not allowed to share with others. And it's so —it doesn't happen very often—well, it happens often that the Vice President will tell me something that I cannot share with other people and I will sit in the room with them while they talk about something. I think that many times when they know something and I know something, but neither of us know that the other person knows it or is supposed to know and we don't talk about it, that happens quite frequently actually . . .

Q *And did Judith Miller ever write a piece as a result of your meeting with her?*
A No.

Q *Why not?*
A I don't know. It was a totally failed effort to get the NIE out as far as I could tell.

Q *. . . The last time you told us about a conversation you had with Judith Miller, you believe on a Saturday where you discussed Wilson's wife working at the CIA. Do you recall that testimony?*
A It was on the weekend of the aircraft carrier trip, July 12th, 13th. Yes, sir.

Q *And how certain are you that you had a conversation with Judith Miller about Wilson's wife working at the CIA on the weekend as opposed to being part of the July 8th meeting?*
A I'm certain I talked to her about it from my home because I remember where I was.

Q *And where were you?*
A In my little office, cluttered . . .

Q *Clarifying two points on the conversation with Judith Miller. Do you recall whether or not you discussed Mr. Wilson's wife at all during your conversation on July 8th with Ms. Miller?*
A I don't recall. I don't recall any discussion—

Q *And do you recall if you discussed Mr. Wilson at all during your conversation with Judith Miller on July 8th?*

A I don't recall any discussion of it . . .

Q *And do you know if you ever discussed with either the Vice President or whether he discussed with anyone else whether you could share with Judith Miller the fact that Wilson's wife worked at the CIA?*

A I don't recall any discussion with the Vice President about Wilson's wife working at the CIA, about sharing that with the press. Now, after July 14, after the Novak article came out, in that time frame I may have asked him, you know, "Do you want me to refer to that?" And it's possible I may have asked him that after even Russert—although I don't . . . recall anything about it . . .

Q *You say that it's possible that you talked to the Vice President after you spoke to Mr. Russert to ask him whether you could share with other reporters what you had learned about Wilson's wife from Russert. And do you have a recollection of, of having that conversation?*

A No, sir. No recollection.

Q *And you say it's possible that you may have talked to the Vice President after the Novak column appeared, asking him whether it was appropriate for you to share with other reporters, call their attention to Novak's column. Do you have a recollection of that conversation happening?*

A I have recollections of talking to the Vice President at times about does he want me to share some point of fact with reporters . . . About, you know, many things over three years. I don't recall specifically having a conversation with him . . . about Wilson's wife. But it's possible. I just don't recall it.

Q *And is it fair to say you had, in a prior FBI interview . . . indicated it was possible that you may have talked to the Vice President on Air Force Two coming back from the ceremony involving the USS* **Reagan** *about whether you should share the information with the press about Wilson's wife?*

A It's possible that would have been one of the times I could have talked to him about what I had learned from Russert and what Karl Rove had told me about . . . Mr. Novak.

Q *And as you sit here today, do you recall whether you had such a conversation with the Vice President on Air Force Two on July 12th?*

A No, sir. My, my best recollection of that conversation was what I had on my note card which we have produced which doesn't reflect anything about that . . .

FEBRUARY 7, 2007

GRAND JURY TAPES (continued)

THE NEXT MORNING BEGINS with a motion to quash filed Charles Leeper, the lawyer for *New York Times* Washington correspondent David Sanger. Leeper outlines his reasoning why Sanger should not be called to testify:

LEEPER: He is a reporter in this town. He makes his living by persuading people to disclose to him information . . . on condition of confidentiality, and often on a condition of anonymity . . . [I]f he is required to testify up here later this week, Your Honor, he has a well-rounded fear that his sources—his existing sources and his future sources—are going to hear that David Sanger testified in federal court today.

JUDGE WALTON BRISTLES at the suggestion that "just because somebody works for the press and has sources of this nature, that puts them above the law," and Leeper quickly corrects himself, basing his objection on the fact that all sides agree Wilson's wife was not mentioned during his July 2nd interview with Libby. Ultimately, Walton rules that Sanger will indeed be called to testify the next week.

The jury is then called in, for the recommencement of the Grand Jury tape from where it had left off the evening before. Walton is aware of how taxing this might be on the jury, telling them at one point, "If you find yourself getting a little sleepy, just raise your hand."

Q *Do you know if you spoke to* **The Wall Street Journal** *prior to July 18th about the NIE contents before the July 18th date came around and made the NIE publicly available?*
A I did not . . . Secretary Wolfowitz did.

Q *Okay. And how do you know that?*
A Because I discussed [that] with the Vice President . . .

Q *And do you know when that week, when you spoke to Secretary Wolfowitz, and if you know, when Secretary Wolfowitz spoke to* **The Wall Street Journal***?*
A I don't . . .

Q *Did you think [Wilson] was qualified to have gone on the mission that he went on back in 2002?*
A Yes, sir . . . [H]e went and he talked to a former Nigerian Prime Minister and a former Nigerian Economic Minister, maybe some others . . . [A]s an ambassador he was perfectly capable to conduct those missions.

Q *And did you think that—putting aside what was characterized about the trip— that it was appropriate for him to go on that mission back in 2002?*

A It's not really for me to say . . . what type of mission is appropriate and who is the appropriate person to do it. That's a Central Intelligence Agency matter. I thought that he was qualified to go talk to foreign government ministers. That's something he had done as an ambassador presumably many times . . .

Q *In your opinion, did you think at that time in . . . July, that he had gone as a result of nepotism?*

A I didn't know why he had gone, sir.

Q *But do you have an opinion one way or the other as to whether or not Ambassador Wilson had been selected because of nepotism?*

A I didn't know whether he had been selected because of nepotism . . . I thought he was fully qualified to do the mission that . . . I understood he had performed. There was a suggestion in the Novak column that his wife had been the one who suggested him to go, but I thought he was qualified to do what he went to do.

Q *. . . [I]n your state of mind, were you thinking that he went on this mission because of nepotism?*

A Nepotism has two meanings to me. One is of a person who is unqualified to do something but he gets the job because he's somebody's nephew. I didn't think he was unqualified to do the job that he was given. I suspected, having seen the Novak column, that if he had not been her husband they may not have picked him for this mission or they might not have done this mission, but I thought he was qualified to do the mission . . .

Q *And did the Vice President ever indicate his belief that Ambassador Wilson was selected to go on this mission because of his marital relationship with someone who worked at the CIA.*

A I think he, at times, had suspicions about . . . why [Wilson] was selected for this mission . . . I think he made comments about it[:] . . . "You know, his wife works there." It wasn't a full sentence, I don't think, but that's the sort of notion I took from it.

Q *An implication that if his wife hadn't worked there, he wouldn't have been the one sent to do the job?*

A Something like that. Yes, sir.

Q *And when did the Vice President say that?*

A Oh, these were in discussions, July, maybe—late July, maybe September, things like that . . .

Q *Do you recall if the Vice President had questions about the credibility of Wilson in light of the fact that he was not on the payroll of the U.S. government when he took the trip?*

A It's possible . . .

Q *And did the Vice President at any time express to you that he thought this trip was handled in an unusual or other than normal fashion by the CIA?*

A Yes.

Q *When did he express that? . . .*

A I think back in June when he was asking about . . . how did this trip come about, this trip being in the May Kristof column, an ambassador was sent, he went on this mission, and then he was talking about this mission which we had only in a classified cable. He was sort of, you know, asking about, oh, how did this mission come about that this fellow went out and talked about it? And so there was some unease at that point. And then I, as I say, I think I recall, . . . after the Wilson column came out, he may have also wondered about it . . .

Q *And have you ever seen the Vice President with a paper copy of the Wilson column? And by paper copy I mean one not printed off the Internet, not printed off a computer, but the actual physical newspaper column?*

A I don't recall.

Q *Did you often see him with . . . actual physical columns from newspapers?*

A Yes, he often will cut out from a newspaper an article using a little pen knife that he has, and put it on the edge of his desk or put it in his desk and then pull it out and look at it, think about it. That will often happen.

Q *Okay. And do you recall if he did that on this occasion on July 6th?*

A Evidently he did, but I don't recall . . .

Q *And the handwriting at the top, is it fair to say that that appears to be the Vice President's handwriting?*

A Yes, sir. As I told you last time . . .

Q *And does one of the questions indicate at the top here say, "Have they done this sort of thing before?"*

A Yes, sir.

Q *And do you recall the Vice President ever asking you whether or not the CIA had ever done this sort of thing before?*

A I think he did at one point.

Q *And do you know when that would have been?*

A No, sir.

Q *And it says here, underneath that, says, "send an ambassador to answer a question". Did . . . he ever express to you his disbelief that they would send an ambassador to answer a question?*

A I don't recall him asking that specific question.

Q *Knowing the Vice President the way you do, . . . would the question, "send an ambassador to answer a question," indicate some sort of belief on his part that this seems sort of silly to send an ambassador overseas to answer a question?*

A It certainly seems like he thought it was an issue, yes.

Q *And the next question written is, "do we ordinarily send people out pro bono to work for us?" Do you recall the Vice President asking you a question to the effect of, do we, the United States government, send people unpaid to go work for us?*

A Yes, sir. I think he asked something like that.

Q *And do you recall when he asked about that?*

A I don't.

Q *And lastly, it says, "or did his wife send him on a junket?" Do you recall the Vice President indicating or asking you or anyone in your presence whether or not Ambassador Wilson's wife had arranged to have him sent on a junket?*

A . . . I don't recall him asking me that particular question, but I think I recall him musing.

Q *Okay. And do you recall when it was that he mused about that? . . .*

A I think it was after the Novak column.

Q *Okay. And you mentioned last time that you thought that the questions written, handwritten here, may have been discussed at a later date, like August or September by the Vice President?*

A Yes, sir . . . I don't know when, but yes.

Q *Okay. And can you tell us why it would be that the Vice President . . . had questions, some of which apparently seem to be answered by the Novak column, he would go back and pull out an original July 6th op-ed piece and write on that? . . .*

A [H]e often kept these columns for a while and keeps columns and will think on them. And I think what may have happened here is he may have . . . pulled out the column to think about the problem and written on it, but I don't know. You'll have to ask him.

Q *All right. As you sit here today are you telling us that his concerns about Ambassador Wilson, his concerns that he's working pro bono, his concerns that he's an ambassador being sent to answer a single question, his concerns that his wife may have sent him on a junket, would not have occurred between July 6th and July 12th when you were focusing on responding to the Wilson column but instead would have occurred much later?*

A Only the part about the wife, sir, I think might not have occurred in that week. The rest of it, I think, could have occurred in that week because, you know, it's all there. You say it's all in the column. The part about the wife I don't recall discussing with him. It might have occurred to him but I don't recall discussing it with him prior to learning again, about the wife.

Q *And when you say "learning again," you mean your conversation with Mr. Russert . . . where he told you about the wife? And your recollection is that you did not remember you knew about the wife, even though your notes show that you discussed that with Vice President Cheney in June?*

A Yes, sir, that's right . . . [M]y recollection is that I had forgotten it by the time I heard it again from Tim Russert . . .

Q *Now, getting back to your conversation with Mr. Russert, you said that when you spoke to Mr. Russert in July . . . that you thought you were hearing for the first time about Wilson's wife working at the CIA. Correct? . . .*

A Yes, sir, that's my recollection . . .

Q *Is there any reason why you wouldn't have shared that with the Vice President after you learned that from Mr. Russert?*

A No, sir.

Q *And do you have any recollection of letting the Vice President know what you had learned from Russert at that time?*

A No. But if I can explain and maybe amend the previous one. There's no reason that I would not share that content with him . . . [T]he only question is, did I have a time with him when I had the time to go into that with him. Remember, I think I learned this on the 11th; . . . I had the discussion with Rove on the 11th . . . I don't know if I saw him that night. The next morning I didn't have any private time with him until the airplane at which point he was giving me discussion about . . . the talking points that he wanted me to use with the press. So there's no reason I wouldn't have talked with him about it. I do not know if in fact I did talk with him about it right then.

Q *So you're trying to recall in your mind whether or not, one, you had the opportunity to talk to him about it; and two, whether during the opportunity on Air Force Two that you discussed it?*

A That's correct . . .

Q *And when you told Mr. Cooper, as you say, that "reporters are saying that Wilson's wife worked at the CIA," who were the reporters, in plural, that you were referring to?*

A I think what I said was "reporters are telling us." And I knew from Mr. Russert. He had told me, "All the reporters . . . know it about the wife." . . . When I said "the reporters are telling us," I was referring to Russert having told me, and Mr. Rove having told me that . . . Mr. Novak had said it to him . . .

Q *And when you spoke to Ms. Miller over that weekend and you told her that reporters were saying that Wilson's wife worked at the CIA, did she indicate to you that she had heard that already?*

A No, she did not . . .

Q *Did any reporter that you told about reporters were saying that Wilson's wife worked at the CIA indicate to you that they had already heard that account?*

A No . . .

Q *And let me show you . . . a column from October 12th from* The Washington Post *. . . "FBI Agents Tracing Linkage on Envoy CIA Operative." [Exhibit GX-422; see* *appendix.] Do you see that it's underlined at various portions in the article? . . . Does that underlining appear to be your underlining?*

A I don't usually underline like this, but it could be my underlining. But I don't . . . usually do it this way.

Q *This is an article written October 12th describing the leak investigation. [The] last paragraph . . . says, "Novak reported that Wilson's wife worked at the CIA on weapons of mass destruction, that she was the person who suggested Wilson for the job. Officials have said Wilson, a former ambassador to Gabon and National Security Council senior director for African Affairs was not chosen because of his wife. On July 12th, two days before Novak's column, a* Post *reporter was told by an administration official that the White House had not paid attention to the former ambassador's CIA sponsored trip to Niger because it was set up as a boondoggle by his wife, an analyst for the Agency working on weapons of mass destruction. Plame's name was never mentioned and the purpose of this disclosure did not appear . . . to be to generate an article, but rather to undermine Wilson's report."*
   Do you recall reading that in . . . The Washington Post?

A I recall reading it, probably on October 12th . . .

Q *And you had spoken to Mr. Cooper about Wilson's wife before July 14th. Correct?*
A Yes, sir.

Q *You had spoken to Ms. Miller about Wilson's wife before July 14th. Correct?*
A Correct.

Q *And you had perhaps spoken to Mr. Kessler . . . about Wilson's wife either on the 12th or after the 14th?*
A Yes, sir.

Q *And you had spoken with Mr. Russert for which you believe hearing from him about Wilson's wife. Correct?*
A I believe I had heard from him, yes, sir.

Q *And you had spoken to Mr. Rove, who said he had spoken to Mr. Novak who talked about Wilson's wife. Correct?*
A Correct, sir.

Q *And at that time, there was also a public statement that came out where Scott McClellan indicated to the press at a gaggle, I believe, that Karl Rove has nothing to do with this leak, and that there is no White House involvement and no involvement from Karl Rove. Correct?*
A Correct.

Q *. . . [H]e was then asked questions, I believe, turning to you and to Mr. Abrams about whether you were involved, and he sort of drew the line and said, "I'm stopping at Mr. Rove. I'm not going to go down that road." Correct?*
A Yes, sir.

Q *And you were not happy with him drawing the line where he did. Correct?*

A Correct, sir.

Q *And where were you when you heard about Karl Rove, or how did you learn that Scott McClellan had cleared Karl Rove and then declined to clear anyone else including you?*

A If memory serves . . . I was . . . at the White House . . . I went to talk to Andy Card and Scott McClellan about the time it came out . . . And Scott said, "Well, we don't want to go down the whole list." And Andy said something about the same. And I said . . . I didn't feel that was quite right since I didn't talk to Novak and I didn't think it was fair that they were saying Karl Rove didn't speak to Novak but not saying I wasn't the one who spoke to Novak. But I accepted that. Then, as time went on, it became clear that there was no list to go down. The only people they were really talking about was me, and I guess you reminded me, Elliott Abrams, but I don't think he got discussed as much as I did . . . I felt it was unfair that they were saying that about Karl and not about me when there was no long list . . . [A]s far as I was concerned, there were only two of us that were getting a lot of attention in part because of this . . . So then I called back to say, "Hey, look, there is no list. There's not a long list, there's just two of us and I think you ought to be saying something about me too."

Q *Where did that conversation take place as you best recall?*

A I think the conversation with Andy Card took place in Andy Card's office. I think the conversation with McClellan took place on the margins of a senior staff meeting or in the corridor near the Roosevelt Room . . .

Q *And when you spoke about the fact that Mr. Rove had been cleared, did you indicate to either one of them that in fact Mr. Rove had spoken to Mr. Novak some time prior to July 14th?*

A No, I don't think I did.

Q *Was there a reason you didn't share that fact with them?*

A It wasn't what I was most concerned about. What I was most concerned about was getting them to say something about that I had not been the one that spoke to Novak.

Q *But when you heard about the investigation and heard about the Rove clearing did you think to yourself, "It's a little odd that they're saying that Mr. Rove had nothing to do with this when in fact I know that Mr. Rove spoke to Mr. Novak and told me what was coming in the column before it ran?"*

A You know, I didn't in those terms. What Mr. Rove had told me was that Novak had told him about the wife and had already knew it by the time he spoke to Karl Rove. So I didn't . . . raise that argument. I didn't think that Mr. Rove had spoken to Novak and I knew that I hadn't spoken to Novak.

Q *In your conversations with Card and McClellan . . . as far as you know, did anyone else in the White House know that Mr. Rove and Mr. Novak had spoken before July 14th?*

A Not that I know of.

Q *As you sit here today do you know if anyone in the White House besides you and Mr. Rove is aware of the conversation that took place between Mr. Rove and Novak prior to July 14th?*

A I don't think so.

Q *And where were you when you called back to say, "Hey, wait a minute, the list is a lot shorter than they thought and I'd like to become number two on the list?"*

A I was in Wyoming.

Q *Were you with the Vice President?*

A Not with him physically. He was at his home, I was in the condo that we rent.

Q *And did you talk this issue through with the Vice President before you called back to revisit the question of whether you should be cleared?*

A . . . I assume I talked to him about it before or after.

Q *Did you seek the Vice President's help to make sure that Andy Card got the message that this is something you'd really like to have happen?*

A At some point I did . . . [I] told him that I thought it was unfair that . . . Scott McClellan had said something about Karl Rove and not something about me since I didn't talk to Novak either . . . I was not the source of the leak to Novak, and told him that I thought it should be fixed. What I can't remember is whether I had this conversation with him the first time I got rejected or the second time.

Q *Do you recall if the Vice President ever picked up the phone and called back to Card or McClellan and let them know that this was something he wanted to see happen?*

A I hope he did.

Q *But at this point in early October, it's front-page stories, it's going crazy about who the leak is. Correct?*

A Yeah.

Q *And everyone saw Rove get cleared. Correct?*

A Correct.

Q *And "Scooter" Libby is sitting out there alone as someone who's named but not cleared. Correct?*

A Correct.

Q *So it was very important for you to have someone come out and say "it's not him." Correct?*

A Correct.

Q *Did you tell the Vice President that you had actually spoken to* TIME *magazine and Mr. Cooper and had discussed Wilson's wife's work with Mr. Cooper?*

A . . . I don't know that I discussed that with the Vice President. I did tell him, of course, that we had spoken to the people who he had told us to speak to on the weekend.

Q *Did you tell him in July 14th or afterwards that when you had spoke[n] to the people on the telephone, you had relayed to them this conversation about Wilson's wife working at the CIA?*

A I don't recall.

Q *So as far as when October came around and the front page headlines are saying that two officials may have called six reporters, did you have any idea whether or not the Vice President understood that you had contacted those reporters and actually discussed with them Wilson's wife's employment?*

A I don't recall whether he knew that or whether I said something to him at the time. What I was clear with him about was I was not the person who talked to Mr. Novak and . . . leaked this bit about the wife.

Q *But it's fair to say, that as was clear in the open press, they were looking into not just who the leak was to Novak but who was calling out to reporters in the period prior to Novak's column. Correct?*

A Yes. And, and he knew that I was calling out to reporters in the weekend before-hand because of the George Tenet statement . . .

Q *But did he know that you had talked to those reporters about Wilson's wife when you talked to them?*

A That's an interesting question. I don't know.

Q *In late September and early October did you [say] to Vice President Cheney, "By the way, you should know that I did speak to Cooper, the author of the* TIME *magazine article, and we discussed Wilson's wife. And I spoke to a* Washington Post *reporter and discussed Wilson's wife. And I talked to Judith Miller and discussed Wilson's wife." Did you have any conversation where you relayed that information to the Vice President?*

A . . . I think I did in that there was a conversation I had with the Vice President when all this started coming out and it was this issue as to . . . who spoke to Novak . . . I went to the Vice President and said, "You know, I was not the person who talked to Novak." And he something like, "I know that." And I said, "I learned this from Tim Russert. And he sort of tilted his head to the side a little bit and then I may have in that conversation said, ". . . I talked to people about it on the weekend." . . . I don't remember whether I did that or not at that point, but I may have.

Q *Are you saying you're not sure whether you told Vice President Cheney in the fall about your conversation in July, or did you tell him in the fall that you weren't sure what you had said in July?*

A The former, if I got it right.

Q *Okay . . . [S]o you're not sure whether you told the Vice President in the fall about the fact that you had conversations in July with reporters about Wilson's wife?*

A Well, I told him about Russert, that I had learned it from Russert. And I think at that point I may have told him . . . that I had talked about the wife to Cooper. I just don't recall that. But what was important to me was to let him know I wasn't the person who leaked the information to Mr. Novak, and that in fact I had heard it from Russert, at which point Mr. Russert told me it was well-known, known to all the reporters.

Q *And was this a conversation you had in person or on telephone with the Vice President?*

A In person . . . I think . . . at his desk in the White House.

Q *And you said he . . . tilted his head. What did you understand from his gesture or reaction in tilting his head?*

A That the Tim Russert part caught his attention . . . [H]e reacted as if he didn't know about the Tim Russert thing or he was rehearing it, or reconsidering it or something like that . . . new sort of information. Not something he had been thinking about.

Q *And did he at any time tell you, "Well, you didn't learn it from Tim Russert; you learned it from me?"*

A No.

Q *I'll hand you a copy of what we'll mark as Grand Jury Exhibit 72 [exhibit GX-532 in this trial], and ask you to look at that and tell us first whether you've ever seen it before? . . .*

A Certainly the top half. It's my writing, I think.

Q *Sure. You were smiling. What was it that made you laugh?*

A I was just smiling that my boss was—it looks like my boss's handwriting and I was smiling. It looks like he's trying to protect me a little bit, which is nice.

Q *Looking at the top of the document, is that your handwriting? Let's break it into three portions. There is some print above the line, there's some script below a line, and then there's three words written in script by a hole punch.*

A Correct, sir.

Q *Focusing on the print above the line . . . is that all your print?*

A I'm ashamed to say it is, sir. Ashamed because of the handwriting.

Q *I've seen worse. My own. Let me read to you, make sure I have it transliterated correctly. "People have made too much of the difference in how I described Karl and Libby," in brackets. What is that referring to?*

A These were points that I was hoping that Scott McClellan would make, I guess.

Q *And then underneath it, it says, "I've talked to Libby," period, and is that a suggested talking point for Scott McClellan?*

A Yes.

Q *And then it says, "I said it was ridiculous about Karl and it's ridiculous about Libby."*

A Yes, sir.

Q *And that was, again, what you hoped that Scott McClellan . . . would say?*

A Yes.

Q *And then it said, "Libby was not the source for the Novak story," period. "And he did not leak classified information," period.*

A Yes, sir.

Q *And what you were hoping was at the end of the day, as a result of the intercession of the Vice President or others, that that statement would be made by Scott McClellan to put you in the footing that you're not involved in this leak?*

A Yes, sir.

Q *And you wrote this out. And do you recall sharing this with the Vice President?*

A I think I wrote this out to say, "This is what I think Scott McClellan should say." And I think the Vice President then said, "Well, let me, let me take it." I am recalling that he then came back to me and said that he had made the calls.

Q *Now, wasn't it fair to say, what was swirling around in the press was people were saying, "Who outed Wilson's wife? Who told the press that Wilson's wife worked at the CIA?" And you could have, you could have in the abstract asserted, "I had nothing to do with telling people that Wilson's wife worked at the CIA." But the statement here says, "And he did not leak classified information." Were you deliberately drawing that language because of the fact that you had told reporters what was being said about Wilson's wife's employment?*

A It could be.

Q *Did you tell Mr. McClellan during your conversation with him, "By the way, just so you're not surprised, I did talk to Mr. Cooper of TIME magazine, and I did talk to a Washington Post reporter, and I did talk to Judith Miller, I did talk about Wilson's wife. But what I didn't do was I didn't tell Novak, and when I did tell the reporters I qualified it by saying that other reporters were saying the story"?*

A No, I did not tell him all that.

Q *Didn't the President indicate to the entire staff that anyone who had relevant information should come forward?*

A And I did. I came forward to the Vice President and told him I would tell him anything that he wanted me to talk to him or anybody else about, and that I was not the source of the leak for Novak.

Q *But did you think that prevented you from sharing with people that you had spoken to reporters? Where did you get the sense from the President's direction that people should come forward with all information the notion that you shouldn't share any details with others?*

A I didn't get it from that. I got the sense generally that the FBI doesn't like you talking to everybody else about . . . what you think your story is.

Q *Did you think it was something that the Vice President and the President would want to know that if an official in the White House had spoken to those reporters,* *which are now being discussed as leaks, that they learned who the person was that spoke with them prior, prior to July 14th?*

A I would have been happy to unburden myself of it, about all of this, and I went to the Vice President and offered to tell him everything I knew, and he didn't want to hear it, and I assumed that I should not go into it, and that if he wanted to hear it, I would be happy to tell him. I'd be happy to tell him today if you like. I have no problem telling him what happened.

Q *I'm trying to fix the mind-set before the FBI interviewed you on October 6th. Did you tell the Vice President you'd be happy to tell him everything he wants to know?*

A Yes.

Q *In those words?*

A Yeah.

Q *And what did he say?*

A He said, "You don't have to. I know you didn't do it. I know you weren't the source of the leak." [S]omething like that.

Q *. . . [W]hen you offered to tell him everything you knew, did that include things other than the contacts that you didn't have with Novak?*

A I haven't told him anything.

Q *And when he said, "I know you're not the leak," did you say, "Well, slow down a minute, sir, I want to tell you one thing, which is I spoke to some of these reporters before July 14th, and they're now saying that they learned this, and so I don't want you to be in any way misled that I didn't have contact with them"?*

A I may have. I don't recall.

Q *Isn't that something . . . I mean, how often do you report to the Vice President to let him know that you didn't commit a crime?*

A Well, the talking to the other reporters about it, I don't see as a crime. What I said to the other reporters is what, you know—I told a couple reporters what other reporters had told us, and I don't see that as a crime. But set aside it was a crime, I don't—I did not mean to do anything wrong or don't think I did anything wrong with it. But I was happy to tell him absolutely everything he wanted to know.

Q *And when was this conversation with, with Vice President Cheney when he told you, you didn't need to tell him anything?*

A There are actually two, and I don't recall exactly.

Q *And what was it that led you to go back a second time, that made you want to make sure that he knew that you were willing to tell him everything?*

A It was still out there, and there was still talk about it. I had a second conversation with him, or maybe it's a third. In my first conversation with him I told him, "Look, I wasn't the source of the leak of this. In fact, I learned it from Tim Russert."

In the course of the document production, the FBI sent us a request for documents, or Justice Department, I'm not sure technically. In the course of that document production, I came across the note that is dated on or about June 12th . . . [that] shows that I hadn't first learned it from Russert. And so I went back to see him and said, "You know, I told you something wrong before. It turns out that I have a note that I had heard about this earlier from you and I . . . didn't want to leave you with the wrong statement that I heard about it from Tim Russert. In fact, I had heard about it earlier, but I had forgotten it."

Q *And what did he say?*
A He didn't say much . . . [H]e said something about, "From me?", something like that, and tilted his head, something he does commonly, and that was that.

Q *And did you have any discussion with him at that time about your conversations with Cooper, Kessler and Miller?*
A No, I don't think so. Not in that conversation.

Q *And what's the third conversation with the Vice President?*
A I think I went back to him a second time, as I told you before . . . to . . . volunteer again to tell him if he wanted to know anything. I shouldn't say, I think. I did go back second time to tell him, . . . offering to tell him if he wanted to know everything I did, I'd be happy to tell him everything I did.

Q *The third conversation, the one where you pointed out that you had seen a document indicating that you had learned this the first time from Mr. Cheney himself, the Vice President?*
A Yes.

Q *And the conversation where you told the Vice President, which is at least the second conversation when you said, in effect, let me correct myself because I saw a document indicating that I learned it from you, not from Mr. Russert, the first time, was that before you had been interviewed by the FBI?*
A Yes.

Q *And the third conversation, do you know if that was before you were interviewed by the FBI?*
A I think they were all before I was interviewed by the FBI.

Q *Now, continue on the document, and I'll just finish off the shortest piece. There's handwriting on the left that . . . appears to say, "Tenet, Wilson and memo," above the three hole punch.*
A Yes, sir.

Q *And do you know whose handwriting that is?*
A Looks like the Vice President's.

Q *And then below the line: . . . "Has to happen today, call out to key press saying same thing about "Scooter" as Karl. Not going to protect—" Why don't you read it since you know his handwriting better than me?*
A "Not going to protect one staffer and sacrifice the guy that was asked to stick his neck in the meat grinder because of the incompetence of others."

Q *And if you look at the crossed-out words, what do they appear to say?*

A "This has."

Q *And any chance that it says, "the Pres"?*

A I think it says "this," not the "the."

Q *Okay.*

A I don't know. Maybe it is "the Pres".

Q *And what does the word "meat grinder" refer to as far as you understand it?*

A I think it refers to the fact that the press, as you say, was beginning to talk about me since . . . I was not exonerated, if you will, whatever the word is, by McClellan.

Q *And when it says, "because of the incompetence of others," who did you understand "others" to refer to?*

A I think this refers to . . . the uranium claim getting into the State of the Union in the first place with this uncertainty that eventually develops about it. And then it may refer to the decision . . . to treat it the way they had treated it in early July where they said that . . . it shouldn't have been in the State of the Union at all . . . [I]t could be either or both of those two things.

Q *Right, as to sticking his neck in the meat grinder because of the incompetence of others. And you've testified, I think at least the last time and today, that Vice President Cheney on Air Force Two had wanted you in particular to be the one to deal with the press on July 12th.*

A That's correct.

Q *And so you're in the sights of the press and in* The Washington Post *as being a person who had dealt with* TIME *magazine because you had talked to* TIME *magazine on July 12th at the express direction of the Vice President?*

A That's correct, yeah.

Q *And looking back on that, does that refresh your recollection in any way as to whether or not on July 12th, flying back on Air Force Two from the* Ronald Reagan *ceremony whether you discussed with Vice President Cheney the fact that Tim Russert or anyone else had told you that Wilson's wife worked for the CIA?*

A No, it doesn't; it doesn't draw that for me at the moment.

Q *It still remains that it is possible that the Vice President could have told you to talk to people about Wilson's wife working at the CIA, but you do not remember that?*

A It's, it's not what I had on my card from that meeting, and I don't recall him telling me to talk . . . to anybody about the wife working at the CIA on the airplane that day.

Q *But you do recall him telling you, back in June, from your notes dated June 12th, and you recall that that stuck in his mind then in June as a curious fact the way he observed to you that his wife worked there. Correct?*

A Yes, sir.

Q *And you do know that Vice President Cheney was quite frustrated during the week of July 6th through July 12th at how the media was treating this issue, and the fact that he was being unfairly maligned in the media. Correct?*

A Yes, sir.

Q *And you had gotten an e-mail, I believe, from Jay Carney of* TIME *magazine the day before saying "people are pointing fingers at OVP." Correct?*

A That sounds right, sir. I haven't looked at it recently, but that sounds right.

Q *And so, on July 12th, Vice President Cheney was still determined to get the full story out. Correct?*

A That's correct, sir.

Q *And Vice President Cheney talked about it with you for the first time that your notes reflect, he brought up that Wilson's wife worked at the CIA in the functional Office of Counter Proliferation. Correct?*

A Back in June . . .

Q *And the column July 6th written by Mr. Wilson with the Vice President's annotations asked "did his wife send him on a junket." Correct?*

A Whenever he made that note. Yes, sir.

Q *And so you told the FBI in your first interview, or one of your two interviews, that it's possible that the Vice President could have told you on Air Force Two that you should tell the press about Wilson's wife, but you do not recall that happening. Correct?*

A Correct.

Q *And does that remain true?*

A It remains true that it was possible.

Q *Now you mentioned before that you do not think that you committed a crime by talking to these reporters and telling them what other reporters said. Correct?*

A I certainly hope not. Yes, sir.

Q *And it's your understanding of the law that you can commit a crime by telling someone classified information that comes from a classified source. Correct?*

A I suppose you can . . . yes, under the proper circumstances, you could commit a crime.

Q *And also is it your understanding that if you tell someone classified information that's been published in a newspaper already or is learned from a non-classified source and merely repeated, that you're not committing a crime?*

A It's sort of a complicated question. If you're telling somebody something that's from public sources, I don't think it's classified. I don't think that's wrong. My understanding is that if something has been cleared for use in the press and has been used in the press, that it's been in effect unclassified and is okay to refer to. My understanding is that, technically, if something has appeared in the press through a leak but has not been unclassified, you're not supposed to talk about it. I don't know whether it's a crime or not, but I think you're not supposed to talk about it.

Q *So that if you knew a fact that was classified in your current position that you learn today from a classified document or a classified briefing, and tomorrow without you playing any role in it whatsoever it ran on the front page of a newspaper, those facts are reported by a columnist that, you know, "here is what the government plans to do regarding a certain crisis in the world," and that's a classified fact that appears in the newspaper, do you understand that you're entitled by law to direct other columnists to that article in the newspaper, not saying, "here's what I know is a classified fact," or not saying, "here's what I got from a classified briefing," but you might want to pick up* The New York Times *and read the story on page one?*

A I'm sort of uncomfortable because I don't know—I mean, there are a lot of variations of these things and I haven't looked at the law for it, so I'm not totally—

Q *I'm, I'm asking for your state of mind. I'm not asking you to explain the law to the Grand Jury. I'm glad you mentioned that so I can tell them. I'm not asking Mr. Libby as an attorney to tell you what the law is. I'm trying to understand in your mind-set what you think the law is, right or wrong.*

A My understanding is, if something is on the front page of the paper because in effect the President has directed that it be put out, that those things are commonly done.

Q *And when you were interviewed by the FBI, the first interview in this case, did you understand that if you had told reporters that Wilson's wife had worked at the CIA, based upon knowledge you had learned from the government or from conversations with Vice President Cheney, that you could have committed a crime?*

A My understanding, when I heard it from Vice President Cheney, was that it wasn't classified information. So my understanding would be, if I didn't think it was classified information, if it wasn't presented to me as classified information, if I wasn't intending to release classified information, that it wouldn't be a crime. But I'm not—this is not my area of the law.

Q *Is it fair to say, though, that as a National Security Advisor and Chief of Staff to the Vice President, and Advisor to the President on national security matters, that if the Vice President learned something from the CIA during a brief or from reviewing CIA material, that one can assume much of that material is classified?*

A He's usually very clear . . . I usually have an understanding of what is classified or not classified. The thing that he presented to me about the wife, if that's what you're referring to, on or about June 12, I did not understand to be classified.

Q *Did you have any sense that if you revealed the person's identity out at the CIA you may be compromising the identity of a covert person?*

A Any person? No, sir. I mean, . . . my understanding is that most the people at the CIA are not covert and . . . their employment there is open and above board.

Q *Your understanding is that most of the people at the CIA their employment is above board? They go around telling people, "I work at the CIA"?*

A Yeah.

Q *And you didn't consider that there might be a risk that a person working at the CIA might be overt to other CIA employees and even sometimes to the government, but may be operating undercover?*

A In general [or] in this instance?

Q *The general first and then this instance.*

A In general, there are a lot of people I know who work at the CIA who, you know, I play softball with or football with, and they tell everybody in the game they work at the CIA. I mean, a lot of people work at the CIA and it's not a secret that they work at the CIA. In this instance, I had no sense when I learned it and then forgot it that it was classified.

And when Tim Russert told it to me, I had no sense that what he was telling me was something classified. And when I heard from Karl Rove that Bob Novak had told him, I had no sense that it was something classified. And when I talked to the reporters about it, I explicitly said, . . . "I don't know if this is true, I don't know the man, I don't know if he has a wife, but reporters are telling us that." So I didn't think I was saying anything that was classified.

*

TIM RUSSERT

IN A SCANDAL THAT WOULD EVENTUALLY draw more than two dozen journalists and broadcasters into its vortex, Tim Russert—with his dual appointment as host of *Meet the Press* and as Washington Bureau Chief for NBC News—was arguably the most high-profile of all these media figures. He had become a player in the CIA leak case when Scooter Libby claimed early in the investigation that he effectively learned of Valerie Plame's CIA employment during a telephone call with the broadcaster. Libby contended that Russert also added that, "All the reporters are saying this."

Like nearly all the other journalists involved in the case, Russert did not want to give testimony and, with NBC lawyers, fought a 2004 subpoena from the Grand Jury. This professed reluctance would later prove embarrassing for Russert as his testimony in the criminal trial reveals the fact that, when an FBI agent called to ask him about Libby's claims in fall 2003—rather than refusing to discuss this, as a matter of journalistic principle—he instead freely offered his recollections of the phone call.

After Russert identifies himself and his multiple roles at NBC, Patrick Fitzgerald asks him about the July 6, 2003 broadcast of *Meet the Press*, when Andrea Mitchell filled in for him, with a line-up of guest interviews that, remarkably, included Ambassador Joseph Wilson and Robert Novak. Fitzgerald then inquires about the events of the rest of that turbulent week following Wilson's *New York Times* op-ed, including Russert's phone conversation with Libby later in the week:

Q *When did you learn that Ambassador Joseph Wilson would be appearing on* Meet the Press *on Sunday, July 6, 2003?*

A Not until Saturday night, the night before, because there was a late booking. The producer called me on vacation and said, "Just a heads up—a fellow named Joseph Wilson has written an op-ed piece for *The New York Times*. We've called him at home and he's agreed to come on *Meet the Press* tomorrow." I said, "Good, thank you."

Q *Did you watch the show that day?*
A Yes.

Q *When did you return to Washington, D.C. from your vacation?*
A Tuesday, [July 8] . . .

Q *Did there come a time when you had a conversation with Scooter Libby that week?*
A Yes.

Q *Can you tell us . . . what you recall about when it happened?*
A It was later that same week. I don't know exactly the day, but I do remember the conversation.

Q *Tell us what you recall about the conversation. Where were you when you received the call?*
A I believe I was in my office. And the call came through. It was Mr. Libby. And he was agitated. He wanted to complain about something he had seen on *Hardball*. I was at a disadvantage because I had not seen the program or programs that he was talking about.

Q *Do you know what programs, which days they were that he was complaining about?*
A Well, I was able to ascertain later it was July 8th and 9th.

Q *Had you received many calls before from Mr. Libby?*
A No.

Q *How did you know he was agitated?*
A Well, you could tell agitation in a voice, his use of words. He was very firm and very direct that he did not like some of the things he had heard.

Q *Do you recall any of the words that you heard that indicated to you that he was agitated?*
A "What the hell is going on with *Hardball*?" And "Damn it, I'm tired of hearing my name over and over again." And "what's being said is not true."

Q *Had you ever received a call like that from a Vice President's Chief of Staff?*
A No.

Q *Tell us what else you recall about what unfolded during the phone call?*
A . . . [H]e asked me . . . what [I] would do about this situation. I said, "I don't have management responsibilities for MSNBC or for *Hardball*." . . . I recommend[ed]

he call Chris [Matthews] directly. Or he could talk to Erik Sorenson, who was at that time head of MSNBC, or Neal Shapiro, who is the president of all of NBC News. And Neal's responsibility is not only to broadcast but also to cable. And I offered to give him Neal Shapiro's direct line to facilitate his getting through the bureaucracy.

Q *Did you give him the direct line?*
A Yes.

Q *During this phone conversation, did [you] at any time . . . discuss with Mr. Libby the wife of Ambassador Joseph Wilson, whether referred to as the wife of Ambassador Wilson or by the name Valerie Wilson or Valerie Plame?*
A No, that would be impossible because I didn't know who that person was until several days later.

Q *And did you ever tell Mr. Libby that Wilson's wife worked at the CIA during that phone call?*
A No.

Q *Did you ever tell Mr. Libby that all the reporters were saying that Wilson's wife worked at the CIA?*
A No, I wouldn't do that. I didn't know that.

Q *Did Mr. Libby ever tell you during the phone call that Wilson's wife worked at the CIA?*
A No.

Q *What would you have done if he had told you that? . . .*
A I would have asked him how he knew that, why he knew that, what's the relevance of it. And then, with that kind of information involving a national security issue, I would have called my superiors and began to talk about it, to vet it, to try to pursue it, and then to make a judgment as to whether or not it was something we could broadcast because that would be a significant story.

Q *. . . [D]o you recall if you had any explicit ground rules with Mr. Libby for the conversation you had with him that day? . . .*
A No. But when I talk to senior government officials on the phone, it's my own policy that our conversations are confidential. If I . . . want to use something on the record, then I will ask that, not to blindside or to try to trick anybody.

This call began as a confidential call and then evolved into a viewer complaint in effect once I heard why he was calling. But I still respected the confidentiality by not going on the air and saying, "I just got a complaint call." Rather, I honored that as is my policy.

. . . I did call Neal Shapiro, the President of NBC News, to say I had just received a phone call from the Vice President's Chief of Staff who was quite upset by some program he had watched on MSNBC. And I advised Neal I had given [Libby] his direct line and that he may be hearing from him.

Q *Now, did there come a time when you heard a claim that . . . Ambassador Wilson's wife worked at the CIA? . . .*

A The following Monday I was home . . . I read *The Washington Post*; . . . there was a column by Robert Novak.

As I read down it, I got to the part which talked about Joseph Wilson's wife, Valerie Plame, CIA agent or operative, whatever, involved in the trip. And I said, "Wow, look at this. This is really significant. This is big." And I went to work and began to ask people I was working with what we knew about that. Why we didn't have the story. Because to me it was a significant development in the story.

Q *Did anyone indicate to you that they knew the story?*

A No, quite the contrary.

Q *Now, did there come a time when you received a subpoena in connection with the investigation concerning this matter?*

A Yes.

Q *And what did you do in response to the subpoena?*

A We went to court and tried to fight it.

Q *What happened when you tried to fight it?*

A We lost. But we felt very strongly as journalists about the First Amendment, about forcing journalists to go into court and talk about conversation[s], any kind of conversation[s], with any kind of source or . . . high government officials. But Judge Hogan felt otherwise.

Q *What happened when Judge Hogan ruled otherwise?*

A I was forced to testify.

Q *And where did you testify?*

A I testified in the office of the NBC lawyers, a lawyer who we retained.

Q *Were you sworn to an oath?*

A Absolutely.

MR. FITZGERALD: Thank you, I have nothing further.

AFTER THIS VERY BRIEF direct examination, Wells begins what will turn out to be a cross-examination of many hours' duration, extending well into the following day. The defense initially highlights the fact that Libby's telephone call was really a complaint call (and not a call from a source). The defense also brings out the fact that Russert had no particular connection to Libby—the implication being that Libby would have no reason to expect that Russert would treat the call as confidential. Thus, Wells implies, his client would not have been able to count on Russert to resist testifying about it; hence, Libby would not have lied about it.

Noting Russert's value to NBC, the defense goes on to question Russert about the competitive importance in the news business of aggressive reporting and getting a story as soon as possible. Wells asks Russert to recount how the program had booked Wilson.

Russert confirms that when he got back from vacation on July 8, Wilson was a hot topic at NBC News, following his op-ed and his *Meet the Press* appearance. This leads into questions about Russert's contact with Libby that week as the defense seeks to cast doubt on the plausibility that Russert, given the opportunity, would have failed to ask Libby about Wilson's mission to Niger:

Q *How was it that* **Meet the Press** *was able to book Mr. Wilson to be on that show?*

A Well, as I recall, our producer saw the opinion piece moving on the wires because the early edition [of] the Sunday . . . *New York Times* sometimes comes out on Saturday night. And it was just through initiative that she called him at home and said, "Would you come on and talk about your op-ed piece?"

Q *Would that be a normal approach in the newsroom, for people to watch the wires to see which stories would come out in advance on the wires?*

A Not always . . . I don't know the specifics of this because I wasn't there.

Q *How about yourself? I mean do you try to keep abreast of stories that are coming out on the wires even before they get out on the news?*

A Not particularly. I track the wires, I read papers and magazines, but I don't have much time or ability to foresee what's coming . . .

Q *Now, as I understand, it is your testimony that you have no recollection of asking Mr. Libby any questions concerning the Wilson trip during your telephone call with him during the week of July 6. Is that right?*

A That's correct.

Q *. . . [Y]ou find yourself on the telephone during the week of July 6 with the Chief of Staff to the Vice President of the United States. There is a story of great national import going on where the Office of the Vice President is involved. And you are Tim Russert, the person who takes every opportunity he can to uncover the news . . . [I]t's your testimony you . . . have the Chief of Staff of the Vice President of the United States on the telephone and you didn't ask him one question about the Wilson issue?*

A It was very much a listening mode. He was very agitated, and very quick with his words, wanted action taken about MSNBC. And frankly was not in the mood to talk.

Q *Well, as a good news person, even though he wasn't in the mood to talk, you would certainly, would you not, at least try to take the opportunity to see if you could get some information that might further your news-gathering efforts. Isn't that true?*

A I was listening because he was making the case that the Vice President was not involved in the trip. And that had already been said publicly. There was no new information being offered. I very much took his call in the spirit he was offering it.

THE DEFENSE CONTINUES PRESSING Russert in this vein, and seeks to ascertain whether Russert specifically recalls that he did not tell Libby anything about Wilson's wife, or whether he was reconstructing that notion in light of the professed impossibility of having told him anything about Wilson's wife, because he supposedly did not know anything about her at the time. This typifies a major defense strategy: to call into question Russert's memory. The defense goes on to ask Russert about his FBI interview several months after the event, trying to get Russert to acknowledge areas of uncertainty he exhibited with the FBI agent, after confirming that Russert had no contemporaneous notes of any kind from his phone conversation with Libby. The defense presses Russert on whether he told the FBI in November 2003 that there might have been not one, but two conversations with Libby the previous July. This leads the defense into an extensive line of questioning about Russert's interview with the FBI, but first the witness is asked about different aspects of his memory of the conversation with Libby:

Q *Am I correct that you cannot recall on what date the conversation occurred?*
A Correct.

Q *And is it correct that you recall that the shows that Mr. Libby were complaining about, the Chris Matthews show[s], had run on July 8th and July 9th?*
A Those were the dates of the shows, yes.

Q *Do you recall that you indicated that the call to Mr. Libby could have been the next day or two or three days?*
A Yes. It was during that week. I don't know the exact date.

Q *Am I correct that you have no memory of what time of day the conversation occurred?*
A I'm not sure, no.

Q *You have no memory of how long the conversation with Mr. Libby lasted?*
A Correct.

Q *You have no calendars or diaries that might refresh your recollection about when the conversation took place?*
A No.

AFTER ASKING A FEW QUESTIONS underlining the fact that the November 2003 FBI interview was much closer in time to the events he was asked about than Russert's subsequent testimony to the Grand Jury and at trial, the defense presses Russert on statements he made to the FBI in November 2003:

Q *[D]o you recall saying to the FBI in November of 2003 that you did not recall stating to Libby anything about the wife of former Ambassador Joe Wilson?...*
A I did not raise her name, no.

Q *Do you recall stating to the FBI in November 2003 that you could not completely rule out the possibility that you and Mr. Libby had such a conversation?*
A No.

Q *You do not recall saying that to the FBI?*

A No . . .

Q *Is it your testimony that you did not say in words or substance to the FBI that you could not rule out the possibility of having such an exchange with Mr. Libby in July 2003, although you were at a loss to remember it at that time?*

A That's correct. I did not know it and did not talk about it.

THE DEFENSE ASKS RUSSERT about the buzz regarding the Wilsons in July and NBC's pursuit of the story:

Q *Did you tell the FBI, in November 2003, that the observation that Joe Wilson's wife worked at the CIA seemed to [you] in retrospect to be a fact that [you] learned only after the Novak column appeared in the public media on July 14, 2003?*

A I don't know what that means. What I do know is what I said. And that is, if I had known about Valerie Wilson, if I had been told by anybody, I would have remembered it. It's a very serious and significant fact. And I did not know that until I read Robert Novak's column. I wish I had known it before then, but I did not . . .

Q *After Mr. Novak's column appeared in July of 2003, when was the first time, Mr. Russert, that you reported on that disclosure?*

A That I reported?

Q *I'll start with you, yes, sir.*

A I didn't report on that. But we worked very diligently on that story. And when Mr. Novak's column broke, we had long and serious and extended discussions about whether or not it was appropriate to broadcast that fact, that identity, the whole relationship with the CIA. It took several days, perhaps a week before we decided, as a news division, to go forward.

Q *So, it's clear, even though you said this was a big story and you wished you had it, that after the Novak article was published, NBC News in Washington did not go out and publicize the issue, right?*

A We worked very diligently to vet it. We also undertake very serious national security consideration when it comes to revealing the identity of someone who works at the CIA. That's our policy.

Q *Sure. But at that point in time, it had been divulged in Robert Novak's column and really it was public information at that point, correct?*

A Well, that was very much debated as to what her role was and what her exact status was.

THE DEFENSE IS PERHAPS SUGGESTING that NBC could have known about Plame before the Novak column even though it didn't broadcast the information. The defense immediately moves to question Russert about the statement NBC issued after he gave his deposition to Fitzgerald in August 2004. The defense highlights the fact that while the NBC statement denied that Russert knew Plame's name or that she was a CIA operative at the time of his conversation with their client, Libby himself had testified to something importantly different: that Russert told him simply that Wilson's wife worked at the CIA. As the defense puts it:

Q *[T]he statement focuses on the fact that you did not know Mrs. Plame's name and her role. It does not say anyplace that you did not know that she worked at the CIA. Is that correct?*

A I did not know that she worked at the CIA.

Q *But the statement does not say that, correct?*

A Well, as I read it, that I did not know Mrs. Plame's name or that she was a CIA operative included the fact that I did not know the fact that she worked at the CIA. That's the simple fact.

Q *Did you review the statement before it was released?*

A Sure, I read it.

Q *And did you point out to anybody that the question Mr. Fitzgerald asked . . . was whether you knew that the wife worked at the CIA? Did you make that comment that the statement doesn't address that issue?*

A I believe it does, sir.

Q *You believe it does because you focus on, she was a CIA operative, right?*

A Well, and because I did not know she worked at the CIA.

Q *I'm just questioning you now about the statement that NBC News issued. And in terms of simple English, there is no statement in the second paragraph that you did not know that she worked at the CIA period, correct?*

A I did not know who she was, what her name was or where she worked.

THE COURT TAKES A BRIEF BREAK and when the cross-examination resumes, the defense opens a new line of questioning about an unrelated episode from June 2004 in which Russert, a native of Buffalo, New York, wrote a letter to the *Buffalo News* admitting and expressing regret that, during a May 2004 interview with Howard Kurtz of *The Washington Post,* he failed to recall a telephone conversation he had had with Mark Sommer, a reporter for the *Buffalo News.* Sommer had written a critical commentary on Russert's performance as moderator of a debate in the 2000 New York Senate race. Russert denied to Kurtz that he had placed a call to Sommer to complain about his negative article, which he had in fact done. The defense is seeking to undermine the credibility of Russert's testimony and raise the probability that Russert likewise is misremembering his conversation with Libby:

Q *[Y]ou were interviewed by* The Washington Post *magazine, [by] a person by the name of Howard Kurtz . . . [H]e asked you during the interview, which took place in May of 2004, only a few months before your deposition by Mr. Fitzgerald, . . . if you had placed a call to Mark Sommer of the* Buffalo News *with respect to the dispute between the two of you. And you said no, you had not placed that call. Do you recall that?*

A I'm trying to recall it. I know there was an exchange of letters. The specifics, I don't recall.

Q *Do you accept that you did write a letter of regret to the Buffalo News?*

A Yes.

Q *Okay. And the regret related to the fact that you had failed to recollect that you had made a telephone call to Mark Sommer during the time there was a dispute concerning your conduct as a moderator of a debate with Hillary Clinton?*

A Yes. But there was a much larger issue at stake here.

RUSSERT PROVES TO BE A DIFFICULT WITNESS over this matter and it takes quite a long time to establish the basic facts of the episode and the fact that Russert recalls them at all. The defense highlights the fact that this episode took place just a few months before Russert testified in the Grand Jury, and drives home the point of this line of questioning: Russert had misremembered a complaint call (one in which he was the complainant, presumably a more memorable scenario because of his personal involvement in the situation). The defense wants the jury to note that Russert's memory was refreshed by contemporaneous documents—which are lacking in the present instance involving his phone conversation with Scooter Libby:

Q *When you told Howard Kurtz of The Washington Post that you had not called Sommer, is it correct that you believed, in good faith, that you were giving an accurate recollection of the events at that time?*

A Yes. I remembered I had written him a letter, which was in essence what I had said on the phone call, but I did not remember the phone call.

Q *When you denied making the phone call to Mr. Kurtz, you weren't trying to lie, you were giving your best good-faith recollection at the time, right?*

A Sure.

Q *When you said to Mr. Kurtz, "I didn't make that call," you said it with a degree of confidence in its accuracy, correct?*

A I'm not sure those are my exact words to Mr. Kurtz.

Q *When you denied making the phone call, in words or substance, you made that denial with a degree of confidence?*

A I don't think I made a phone call. I don't know. I'd like to know what I said. But I did recall sending a letter to Mr. Sommer. You saw the result of it.

Q *Now, when you published your letter in the Buffalo News admitting to a faulty recollection regarding the telephone call, you admitted your error based on your subsequent review of certain written materials in your files that showed you had in fact called Mr. Sommer, right?*

A Yes.

Q *What caused you to change your recollection of what took place was that you had some documents in your file that showed that your earlier recollection was incorrect?*

A Yes, I had the written letter and obviously a notation that I had made a call to tell him the letter was coming.

Q *But for the existence of the written notation in your file, you would have continued to have believed that you did not make the call, correct?*

A I did not recall.

Q *And with respect to the telephone conversation you had with Mr. Libby, you have no written notes or file memoranda, correct? . . .*

A I have nothing, no.

Q *Now, when Mr. Libby called you, he called you primarily to make a viewer complaint, not about you but about Chris Matthews, right?*

A About *Hardball* and MSNBC hosted by Chris, yes.

Q *So Mr. Libby's call wasn't one where he was voicing personal criticism of your conduct, correct?*

A Correct.

Q *Now, in contrast, the telephone call that you forgot concerning Mr. Sommer, that arose in the context of a situation where Mr. Sommer had made personal allegations about your conduct, correct?*

A Well, I wouldn't say they were personal. And it was a debate in 2000. So, it was some [four] years ago at that time. He was suggesting that I had asked questions of Hillary Clinton that had been asked before. And in fact, they were not that at all. And the debate received an extraordinary amount of coverage. So, it was not personal.

THE DEFENSE THEN CITES the strong criticism of Russert's performance from the *Buffalo News* reporter, and asks about this in connection with Russert's faulty recollection:

Q *Even though Mr. Sommer's personal attack on you was of a personal nature, when you were interviewed by Mr. Kurtz in May of 2004, you just totally misrecollected how you had responded to Mr. Sommer's attack, correct?*

A I recalled that I sent a letter. I didn't recall calling him. But the essence of my call and the letter were the same. That he had gotten his facts wrong as a critic. But it's his right to have his own opinion but not his own facts.

THE DEFENSE MOVES INTO a new line of questioning, on Russert's November 14, 2003, interview with FBI agent Jack Eckenrode, at that time the lead investigator on the case, which did not then yet involve the special prosecutor. The defense brings out the fact that Russert did not invoke any journalistic privilege nor refuse to speak with the FBI, but instead offered a refutation of Libby's version of the conversation. The defense will use this to raise the specter of hypocrisy and worse on Russert's part for failing to admit to this when he fought the Grand Jury subpoena months later in June 2004.

Q *And is it your testimony that, when you got a telephone call . . . in November 2003, that you don't recollect, as you sit there now, that the FBI agent said he was part of the team involved in the CIA leak case?*

A He said that eventually.

Q *I'm sorry. He said it "eventually"? Tell me what he said.*

A He said, "Tim, this is Jack Eckenrode. Remember, we met when I was at *Meet the Press*. I brought a church crew with my son and father Mike. You were kind enough to talk to us afterward, take a picture and things like that."

　　. . . I vaguely remembered it, and said, "Yeah, now I do, yes." He said, "I'm working on this CIA leak case you may have read about." . . . [T]hen he said . . . Mr. Libby had said that I had told him about Valerie Wilson.

Q *Do you recall telling Mr. Eckenrode during the conversation that you recall at least one and possibly two telephone conversations that you believed you had with Lewis Libby?*

A As I said before, I remember one call. I don't recall a second call.

Q *Do you recall telling Mr. Eckenrode that the time frame of these conversations was very likely between July 6, 2003 and July 12, 2003, which is the week that you were vacationing with your family on Nantucket?*

A Well, I came back from vacation on July 8th. So it would have to be after July 8th, and it would have to be after the Chris Matthews programs of the 8th and 9th. So it would be later in the week. I believe I said a day or two or three after that.

Q *Do you recall telling the FBI agent that Mr. Libby contacted you to complain about the biased reporting of Chris Matthews of MSNBC's* Hardball *regarding Joe Wilson's accusations about the Vice President?*

A He called to complain about reports on *Hardball* that he thought were unfair to the Vice President. I don't recall the use of the word "bias." But his words to me were very strong; . . . he was upset by the reporting.

Q *But I want you to answer as to what you remember telling the FBI agent who called you on the telephone and asked you questions and to whom you gave answers. Do you recall giving that answer to Mr. Eckenrode?*

A I told him that the call was a call of complaint about what had been on *Hardball* regarding descriptions of the Vice President's office involvement in the Wilson trip.

Q *Do you recall telling the FBI agent that [you] told Libby that there wasn't much that could be done inasmuch as MSNBC was not in [your] portfolio?*

A What I recalled saying was that I did not have management responsibility for MSNBC or for *Hardball* [and] that Mr. Libby could call Chris Matthews directly or Eric Sorenson, who was the head then of MSNBC, or Neal Shapiro, the President of NBC News. I offered and gave him the direct phone number for Mr. Shapiro.

Q *Now, is it correct that, during your November 2003 FBI interview, you did not refuse to answer the questions of the FBI agent about your July 2003 telephone conversation with Mr. Libby? Yes or no? . . .*

A I did talk to him, yes.

Q *And during your November 2003 FBI interview, you did not state that there was an understanding that your July 2003 telephone conversation with Mr. Libby would be held in confidence, correct?*

A Correct, because [the FBI agent] was relaying to me things that Mr. Libby had said about what I had said. And I felt very comfortable talking about that.

Q *And you felt very comfortable when the FBI agent called you on your telephone, said he was involved in a criminal investigation, discussing a conversation that you had with Mr. Libby in July 2003 . . . ?*

A Comments that Mr. Libby had attributed to me, correct.

Q *. . . You talked about what Mr. Libby said to you and then you told the FBI agent . . . what you said to Mr. Libby?*

A In order to respond to what I had said, I had to say exactly what he had said, correct.

Q *So you described the conversation to the FBI agent in November of 2003 in a manner very similar to your Grand Jury testimony in August of 2004, right?*

A Yes, sir.

Q *At no time did you assert any privilege of confidentiality or pledge of confidentiality as a reason for refusing to answer Mr. Eckenrode's questions, correct?*

A I did treat that conversation in confidence. I did not report on it.

Q *. . . When you say you treated it in confidence, an FBI agent calls you on the telephone, makes a reference to having met you in connection with a prior social occasion, and then you freely discuss with the FBI agent your conversations with Mr. Libby that are being questioned about in connection with the CIA leak case, correct?*

A No, what I just said was that the conversation I had with Mr. Eckenrode I treated as a confidential call.

Q *Mr. Eckenrode's call was treated as confidential, right?*

A In the same way I did not report [on] Mr. Libby's call to me, I did not report this phone call because [that], as I explained earlier, [is] my policy.

Q *Well, you talked freely to the FBI agent when he telephoned you in November 2003 about Mr. Libby's call, correct?*

A This is after Mr. Libby had talked to him and he made allegations about something I had said. And my first reaction was, of course, that's just not true.

Q *How do you know Mr. Libby actually did that? All you knew is that somebody was on the other end of the phone who identified himself as Agent Eckenrode, and you didn't have any evidence or proof beyond what he said to you about what Mr. Libby had actually said, correct?*

A I didn't doubt who he was.

Q *Did you doubt perhaps what he was saying?*

A I made my best judgment at the time. I thought it was imperative that if someone was going to suggest that I had said something . . . [un]true, that I address it.

Q *Well, what did Mr. Eckenrode say of such great importance that you felt it necessary to address it immediately? What did he say Mr. Libby had said?*

A He talked about whether or not Mr. Libby had learned about Valerie Wilson from me.

Q *That representation by Mr. Eckenrode, without any consultation with Mr. Libby, made you feel it was appropriate to discuss your conversation with Mr. Libby in July of 2003. Is that your testimony?*

A Yes, sir.

WELLS TURNS TO RUSSERT'S FIGHT against the subpoena from Fitzgerald in 2004, leading up to his questioning Russert's truthfulness in failing to acknowledge his testimony to Eckenrode as he fought the subpoena in court:

Q *Okay. Now, in May of 2004, you were served a subpoena to appear before a Grand Jury to testify about your conversation or conversations with Mr. Libby during the week of July 6, correct?*

A Yes, sir.

Q *And a week or so later, on June 2, 2004, your lawyer, Lee Levine, received a letter from Mr. Fitzgerald describing the testimony he sought to elicit through the subpoena, correct?*

A I don't recall that specifically.

Q *I'll show you a copy of the letter. I['ll] show you what's been marked as DX-1696 for identification, which is a letter from Mr. Fitzgerald to your attorney, and ask to review it and tell me if you have seen it before.*

A (Peruses the document.) I don't recall seeing this specific letter. But certainly it was something that Mr. Levine would have described to me.

MR. WELLS: I don't want you to discuss conversations with your counsel.

THE JUNE 2 LETTER from Fitzgerald to Russert and NBC's lawyer, Lee Levine, is entered into evidence and Wells goes through it with Russert, who apparently didn't know specifically about the substance of the letter but who did know generally about how Fitzgerald had agreed to limit the questioning to what he had told Libby. Referring to NBC's public statement at the time, indicating that it was resisting the subpoena to avert a chilling effect on its newsgathering procedures, the defense homes in on its omission of Russert's November 2003 interview with the FBI, asking, for instance:

Q *The statement is silent about the fact that you had already freely discussed the con-*

tent of your conversation with Mr. Libby when the FBI agent called you in November 2003, right?

A It does not mention that meeting, no.

RUSSERT TESTIFIES THAT HE cannot recall discussing the fact that he had spoken with the FBI with NBC News President Neal Shapiro, to whom Russert had referred Libby; and that he did not say anything to NBC reporters Andrea Mitchell or David Gregory. Then Wells asks Russert about the affidavit he swore to in connection with his June 4, 2004, motion to quash the subpoena, raising the possibility that Russert made false statements in the affidavit. In the affidavit, Russert had explained that he treats all his conversations with government sources in confidence. Wells focuses on what Russert's affidavit had stated about the Libby conversation:

Q *Now, the official with the executive branch who you are referring to in paragraph 6 is Scooter Libby, correct?*

A Yes.

Q *And you are referring to the conversation you had with Scooter Libby on or about July 10, 2003, correct?*

A Yes.

Q *And the next sentence reads, "I cannot provide such testimony without violating the understanding that I share with my sources that our communications, including the fact that we have communicated at all, will be held in confidence."*
    So is it correct you are now saying to Judge Hogan, with respect to your July 10, 2003 conversation with Scooter Libby, that you cannot provide testimony concerning that conversation without violating the understanding that you share with [your] sources that . . . [what they] have communicated . . . will be held in confidence[?] That's what you said to Judge Hogan under oath, right?

A What I said very clear[ly] to the judge, yes, is I think it would have a chilling effect on my ability as a journalist.

Q *"As a result, I can neither confirm that I had any substantive communications with the public official at issue during the relevant time period, nor can I describe the nature of my discussions that we may have had." . . .*
    You are saying to Judge Hogan that it is your position under oath that you can't confirm that you even talked to Scooter Libby, nor can you disclose the substance of communications you had with him, correct?

A I was saying very clearly that, as a journalist, I did not want to do that because it could have an effect upon my ability as a journalist, correct.

Q *But you said to Judge Hogan, not just that you didn't want to do it, you said you can't do it because there is a shared understanding of confidentiality, correct?*

A When it comes to a confidential conversation, yes.

Q *And you don't say anything to Judge Hogan in paragraph 6 that you had disclosed the fact that you had a conversation with Mr. Libby in July of 2003 to FBI agent Eckenrode in November of 2003, correct?*

A There is no mention of that.

Q *And there is no mention of the fact that you discussed in November of 2003 the content of your conversation with Mr. Libby when Agent Eckenrode asked you to describe the content of the conversation, correct?*

A To me, there is a very clear distinction as to what I said in a conversation as to an open-ended questioning of what I say or sources say to me.

Q *But I have a very simple question. Did you disclose in paragraph 6 to Judge Hogan, when you swore to it under oath, that you had already disclosed both the fact that you had the conversation with Mr. Libby on July 10, 2003, and you had disclosed the contents of the conversation you had with Mr. Libby in July of 2003?*

A I did not.

Q *Thank you. Now, [there was an] affidavit you signed on June 4, 2004, correct?*

A Yes.

Q *So, was it your position, as of June 2004, that your July 10 conversation that you had had with Mr. Libby was pursuant to an understanding that you had neither disclosed the fact of the conversation nor the content of the conversation? Was that your position as of June 4, 2004?*

A My position was exactly as stated here.

Q *Is it correct that, when you disclosed to Agent Eckenrode on November of 2003 the fact that you had had a conversation with Mr. Libby and the content of that conversation, that you violated that understanding of confidentiality?*

A No, sir...The phone call I received from Mr. Eckenrode was... about what I said in a conversation, whether or not I had said anything to Mr. Libby about Valerie Wilson. The area of conversation from Mr. Libby was the complaint about Chris Matthews, which I have said repeatedly was a viewer complaint, not in any way confidential information from a confidential source.

Q *So, it's your testimony then that the conversation with Mr. Libby, in terms of what he said, was not one that was to be held in confidence?*

A It is my testimony that any suggestion that I talked to Mr. Libby about Valerie Plame Wilson was wrong and I felt compelled to correct the record.

Q *What I want to understand is whether the statements you made in paragraph 6 to Judge Hogan were true statements or false statements?*

A They're absolutely true.

Q *So, if they're true, then that means, does it not, that you violated your duty to hold, as confidential, your discussions with Mr. Libby with respect to the July 10, 2003 conversation when you disclosed both the facts of the conversation and the content to Agent Eckenrode in November 2003?*

A Again, when I discussed it with the agent, the focus was on my words—my words, not Mr. Libby's words. Mr. Libby's viewer complaint, as I have said over and over, was not in any way words from a confidential source or words that I had to keep in confidence. I did not report them as is my policy. But I did share them with Neal Shapiro because I felt an obligation to do that.

Q *Mr. Russert, you have testified that the only thing you recalled Mr. Libby saying in the conversation was his complaints about Chris Matthews. You said that's the only thing Mr. Libby talked about, correct?*

A That's correct.

Q *So what are you doing writing a sworn affidavit to a United States Federal District Court judge where you say you can't confirm that the conversation took place or the contents of the conversation?*

A Because in [the] subpoena that we had been served, we do not want to be involved in an open-ended fishing expedition to find out who I talked to, why I talked [about] a whole variety of issues. We tried very diligently to resist the subpoena.

THE DEFENSE CONTINUES TO PRESS Russert, seeking to pin him on one horn of a dilemma or the other: either Russert gave a false statement in his affidavit, or he violated its declared principles of confidentiality by talking to the FBI in fall 2003. Russert's self-defense is twofold: first, the resistance to the subpoena was in the name of the larger issue of avoiding a chilling effect on newsgathering; and he only told Eckenrode what he had said in his July 2003 conversation with Libby. The jury and Russert are then excused for the day, to return the following morning for more cross-examination of the witness. The parties briefly address some procedural matters and the court recesses for the day.

FEBRUARY 8, 2007

TIM RUSSERT (continued)

THROUGHOUT THE TRIAL, Judge Walton has firmly and repeatedly reminded jurors not to read or view any news coverage of the trial. For the duration, daily newspapers bound for the jury have been scanned by court employees who clip and dispose articles with trial coverage. However, on the morning of February 8, a potentially nightmarish scenario arises; a copy of *The Washington Post* with an article by media reporter Howard Kurtz about Russert's appearance in the trial had made its way to the jury. Fortunately, one or more alert jurors had noticed the headline before reading the article and Judge Walton was quickly notified of the problem. Once he establishes that it was a minimal and controlled breakdown, he cautions everyone again and defense attorney Wells resumes his tough cross-examination of Tim Russert.

Wells begins by questioning Russert about his June 2004 affidavit, and how it diverged from what he earlier told FBI agent Jack Eckenrode about the July 2003 conversation with Libby. Russert insists that he took the call from Libby thinking Libby was calling as a source but then realized Libby was calling to complain, while Wells seeks to emphasize that the entirety of the call was therefore a viewer complaint call. This is significant because the defense is seeking to cast doubt on Russert's credibility on the basis of the fact that his affidavit referred to protecting sources. But the defense is more concerned with pressing the idea that Russert was misleading in his affidavit because he had already discussed the Libby conversation with the FBI in some depth. Russert strains to explain the difference one more time:

A As I said, when I received the call from the FBI agent sharing that information with me—I was not volunteering that information; I was not sharing it. But I also could not leave a misstatement of fact about that conversation and not respond to it.

   When I wrote the affidavit regarding a subpoena, that's a much different situation where I would be asked to go before a court and volunteer information, and it could be very open-ended questioning. That is something, as a journalist, I did not want to do. There is a clear distinction between each situation.

THE DEFENSE CONFRONTS RUSSERT with the fact that at the time he signed the affidavit, he already knew that Fitzgerald would limit his questioning of Russert, and Russert eventually acknowledges this. Wells again presses Russert on the fact that his affidavit failed to acknowledge the conversation he had with Eckenrode in fall 2003. Fitzgerald repeatedly seeks to object and is overruled, while an uncomfortable Russert appears to evade the question, and is pressed for an answer by Wells, which he finally gives:

Q *I am sorry, sir. I am asking you a question. In the affidavit, do you disclose to the court that you had already communicated to the FBI the fact of your communication with Mr. Libby?*

A No.

Q *. . . Do you disclose in the affidavit to the court that you had already disclosed to the FBI the contents of your communication with Mr. Libby?*

MR. FITZGERALD: Objection. Asked and answered.

THE COURT: Overruled.

THE WITNESS: As I have said, sir—

Q *Yes or no, please, to the question.*

A I would like to answer it to the best of my ability.

Q *Sir, this is a very simple question. It's either in the affidavit or it's not in the affidavit.*

A But the communication from the FBI agent was to me; it was not me to him. It was not a voluntary attempt to share information.

He raised with me the content of the call from Mr. Libby, saying, one, he called you to complain about . . . *Hardball,* and two, that you shared with him information about Valerie Plame. That was very important for me to address, that misstatement. And that's exactly what I did.

Q *Okay. And after he raised it, you discussed with him your recollection of what Mr. Libby said to you and what you said to Mr. Libby, correct?*

A I responded that that did not happen, but I did confirm that he had called to complain about *Hardball.*

Q *Okay. Now, my question is, in the affidavit that you signed to Judge Hogan, do you state that in November you had already had discussions with the FBI during which you had disclosed the content of your communications with Mr. Libby?*

THE COURT: I think it's the way you are asking your question that's confusing him.

By Mr. Wells:

Q *Is there any statement in the affidavit that you had already had a conversation with Mr. Eckenrode about your conversation with Mr. Libby?*

A No.

Q *Thank you.*

THE DEFENSE SHIFTS ITS QUESTIONING slightly, pointing out that Fitzgerald did not himself raise Russert's interview with FBI agent Eckenrode during the fight over the subpoena in 2004, suggesting some impropriety on the part of the government, and that Russert got a deal, in essence, allowing him to save face. It becomes evident that Russert is unaware of the substance of the negotiations between his lawyer and Fitzgerald over his testifying:

Q *Let's go to a different area. Now, the government did not take the position in the litigation that your disclosure of your conversation to the FBI in November of 2003 constituted a waiver, correct?*
A I do not know that, sir.

Q *Do you know that the government and your lawyers cut a deal with Mr. Fitzgerald whereby they agreed that they would not take the position it was a waiver?*
A I am not aware of that.

Q *You have never heard that before?*
A No.

Q *Okay. Do you have any knowledge of what, if anything, was said to Judge Hogan in the ex parte affidavit filed by Mr. Fitzgerald with Judge Hogan concerning your discussion with the FBI?*
A No.

Q *Do you have any knowledge of what was set forth in the pleadings concerning your discussions with the FBI?*
A I have no recollection of that, no.

Q *Okay. Are you aware that your lawyers worked out various arrangements with the government regarding the scope of your testimony?*
A Yes.

Q *Okay. And I would like to show you a letter dated July 27.*

THE LETTER, WHICH SETS OUT the arrangements for Russert's testimony, is read aloud. Surprisingly, though it concerned him directly, Russert has never seen the letter, though he understood that he would be obliged to testify under oath, just not before the grand jury. The defense is seeking to suggest that this too constitutes a favorable or special deal for Russert. The defense then reads part of the agreement that Russert would give a deposition instead of being in a grand jury, and would get to have his attorney present, unlike in a grand jury. This leads to a question and answer that would give rise to much incredulity on the part of observers and embarrassment for Russert:

Q *So you understand that the normal procedure when someone goes into the Grand Jury, they are not permitted to have their lawyer in the room, correct?*
A I don't know that, but I accept your description.

Q *You have never, in the course of your years of reporting, come to know that lawyers are not permitted to be in the Grand Jury room?*
A No.

Q *You are an attorney, correct?*

A Non-practicing.

Q *But there was a period in your life when you served as counsel to—was it the Senate?*

A Yes, but not involving criminal matters whatsoever. The most important thing to me in this whole matter is that—

Q *Sir—I am sorry, sir. I am going to ask you questions, and I am going to ask you to answer to the best of your ability. Okay? But if I don't ask you a question—okay?*

RUSSERT CONFIRMS THAT while he spoke publicly about his testimony and his fight against the subpoena, he never publicly disclosed that he had previously spoken with the FBI agent; and the questioning returns again to the fact that Russert had disclosed the substance of his conversation with Libby to Eckenrode. Wells next uses the absence in an earlier letter of any mention of Russert's interview with Eckenrode to ask Russert about the deposition, getting Russert to confirm it was only 22 minutes long. The questioning is meant to suggest that Fitzgerald had not conducted a very thorough investigation, specifically with regard to whether Russert could have in fact known about Plame before he spoke with Libby, and focuses in particular on Russert's colleagues, David Gregory and Andrea Mitchell, whom the defense would like to suggest possibly and perhaps even probably learned about Plame and would have passed such information on to Russert, making it plausible and possible that he did in fact pass the information to Libby:

Q *[I]s it correct that during the 22-minute deposition, with respect to your conversations with your colleagues, you were asked one question, and the question was: "At that time, did you have any understanding from anyone else that Mr. Wilson's wife worked at the CIA?" and you answered, "No." One question, right?*

A I am not sure, but I remember being asked that question. There may have been another, but I would have to read it to refresh my recollection.

Q *And you were not asked any specific questions concerning what knowledge David Gregory may have had about Mrs. Wilson's employment at the CIA, correct?*

A I believe I referred to my colleagues in one of my answers that I did not have information from my colleagues.

Q *. . . Were you asked any specific questions that focused on what information David Gregory may have had with respect to Mrs. Wilson's employment at the CIA?*

A I don't believe his specific name came up.

Q *Okay. And it is also correct you were not asked any questions that specifically referred to what information Andrea Mitchell may have had about Mrs. Wilson's employment at the CIA, correct?*

A Not her specific name, no.

Q *Okay. Now, in terms of how the NBC News reporting [on] the Wilson matter worked, there were a number of reporters on the story, correct?*

A Yes, sir.

Q *And Andrea Mitchell—she was one of the reporters on that story, correct?*
A She was.

Q *And what is her title?*
A Chief Foreign Affairs Correspondent.

Q *And David Gregory was also one of the reporters on that story, correct?*
A He was.

Q *And what is his title?*
A White House Correspondent.

Q *. . . Mr. Wilson first appeared on* Meet the Press *with Andrea Mitchell serving as the host because you were on vacation that weekend, right?*
A Yes, sir.

Q *And during the week of July 6, Ms. Mitchell was on TV reporting on the Wilson issue and covering that story, right?*
A Yes, she was reporting on it. I am not sure how many times she was on TV, but she reported on it.

Q *And David Gregory—during the week of July 6th, he was in Africa with President Bush, correct?*
A Yes.

Q *David Gregory flew on Air Force One with President Bush?*
A I am not sure he flew on Air Force One or [on] the press plane.

Q *Okay. But you know he was in Africa during the week of July 7 forward, right?*
A Yes.

Q *During the deposition, did Mr. Fitzgerald put any questions to you about what information or discussions David Gregory may have had with Ari Fleischer in Africa? Were any such questions put to you in the deposition?*

MR. FITZGERALD: Objection.
THE COURT: Sustained. He would be asking him about hearsay statements . . .

Q *Now, in the deposition, you testified that if you had known that the wife worked at the CIA, what you would have done would be to have called your colleagues together; do you remember that?*
A Yes, sir.

Q *And you said how you had several reporters working on the story and, if you had gotten the information, you would have called the reporters together and you would have discussed what to do with it, right?*
A Yes, sir.

Q *And is it fair to say that if Andrea Mitchell had information that Mr. Wilson's wife worked at the CIA, she would have called the team together and discussed it with the team in terms of the practice of how the team worked?*

MR. FITZGERALD: Objection.
THE COURT: Sustained. About what somebody else would do . . .

Q *Well, based on pattern and practice that existed in terms of how news teams worked at NBC News, was the expected practice that if one of the key reporters on the team got important information, that they would come and report it to the group?*
A Yes.

Q *Okay. And Ms. Mitchell and Mr. Gregory—they were important members of the Wilson team, correct?*
A They were two of them.

Q *Right.*
A And they never came forward.

Q *Okay. And, in fact—*

MR. WELLS: I will move to strike that. I asked no such question. If I could—
THE COURT: Very well. Disregard the statement that they never came forward.

Q *Now, were you aware that the special prosecutor had asked to interview Andrea Mitchell and she refused to be interviewed?*

MR. FITZGERALD: Objection, Your Honor.
THE COURT: Sustained.

THE DEFENSE GOES ON to ask Russert about his conduct immediately after Libby's indictment at the end of October 2005; the emphasis, again, is on the fact that Russert made no mention of his discussion with Eckenrode in November 2003. After more questioning, the judge calls a brief recess to give the jury a break. Before the jury returns, the parties engage an issue that will consume considerable attention: the link between Russert and Andrea Mitchell and her purported knowledge of Plame before Novak's column. Mitchell had made some ambiguous and—she later claimed—mistaken statements in October 2003 suggesting she might have known about Plame's CIA employment before Novak's column. Libby's lawyers want to try to suggest that Mitchell knew, could have told Russert, and that when it became publicly relevant in 2005 that Mitchell had made the 2003 comments, Mitchell and Russert in essence decided to cover it up. Wells explains the defense's position to the judge:

WELLS: She says on TV that she discussed this issue with Mr. Russert, and he acknowledges knowledge of the issue. And what it shows, ultimately, Your Honor, is that after he has been out on TV following his deposition and going on right up until after the indictment saying to everybody, "Nobody knew, we all learned about it in *The Washington Post*"— that it comes about, unbeknownst to anybody, that Ms. Mitchell had made a statement in October of 2003 that she did know.

And now they are in a position where it looks like they have been giving inaccurate information this entire time about whether NBC knew about it and whether [Russert] knew about it—because he has admitted that if she knew, he would know; it would have been reported. And now everybody is in the box.

AFTER SOME MORE EXPLANATION and playing the videos, the judge expresses skepticism, suggesting this is a collateral issue, and the defense again responds with some revealing comments:

THE COURT: It's extremely collateral to Russert's testimony. I mean, this is nitpicking at the best. I really just don't see how this becomes relevant to Russert's credibility. To suggest that, somehow, because he said what he said in reference to what she had said would suggest bias is a stretch beyond, I think, reality.

MR. WELLS: Your Honor, Mr. Russert has gone out repeatedly since his deposition and said to the American public on TV show after TV show, "I know that Scooter Libby and I didn't discuss the wife," or "I didn't ask Scooter Libby a question about the wife because I didn't know about the wife." Okay? That's his core thing. He says "The reason I know it wasn't discussed is because I didn't know about the wife until the Novak column."

Now, his right-hand person, Andrea Mitchell, it turns out, after he has taken all these public positions—it turns out that, in October 2003, she has said something that totally blows up his core statement that he didn't know about the wife. He has admitted that if she knew, he knew, and the whole team would have known.

And there is nothing peripheral about this, Your Honor. And he has got now every motivation to stay where they are and to deny her statement in 2003 as being misspoken. And I should be able to confront him with it and her with it.

And, Your Honor, this goes—there is nothing nitpicking . . . [T]he core of his testimony is based on the fact that he says he knows it's impossible—that it didn't happen; that is, that he did not ask Libby a question about Mrs. Wilson because he did not know until after the Novak column.

His right-hand person has said on TV clearly and unambiguously that it was widely known by her and people covering the intelligence community that [Valerie Wilson] worked at the CIA, though they did not know her role.

THE JUDGE REMAINS SKEPTICAL, and in seeking to answer him, at one point Wells lays out what his point is:

WELLS: Evidence has been admitted based on what are inferences. It is certainly based on what he says was the practice, that if [Mitchell] knew or Gregory knew that the wife worked at the CIA, the practice would have been to tell [Russert]. [Russert] has said, if he knew, he would have gone and told them.

It is certainly a fair and powerful inference, and that's why it does go to questions of bias and motivation because I would expect, given the spot they are in now, having repeatedly gone on national television and said it didn't happen, this is a highly embarrassing and troubling disclosure because it looks like they have gone out and said to the world "nobody knew, we didn't know," and now it's discovered, when the tape comes out—and it comes out after the indictment—that she did, in fact, say it.

And to deprive me of the right to confront Mr. Russert with this bias and motivation, and later to confront Ms. Mitchell with it, is really to deprive us in the most fundamental respect of our right to present our case and to a fair trial. This goes right to the heart of what the justice system has to be about.

THE COURT: I don't try to undermine the justice system, and the suggestion that somehow I am trying to do that—

MR. WELLS: No, I didn't say that. I want you to—

THE COURT: Let me hear from government counsel.

MR. FITZGERALD: Your Honor, if we allow this line of examination, we might as well throw out Wigmore on evidence and replace it with Imus on evidence.

THE COURT: We can go to O.J. on evidence, I think, which is why O.J. took nine months to try, but go ahead.

FITZGERALD WEIGHS IN against this idea—at one point noting that there is no Imus exception to the hearsay rule—and the parties go back and forth again. Walton does not allow the evidence in, Russert and the jury are brought back in, and Russert is again grilled about having withheld from the public the fact that he spoke with Eckenrode in November 2003, before Wells turns to asking Russert about what he had previously testified to concerning the July 2003 conversation with Libby, noting a discrepancy between his deposition and what he had testified to the previous day at trial. Then Wells abruptly shifts to another major theme of the defense's cross-examination: that Russert and NBC News were biased against Libby, presumably giving Russert motive to lie:

Q   *In your grand jury [deposition] you were asked this question and gave this answer . . .*

    Question: "Okay. What do you recall about the substance of what Mr. Libby said when he vented about Mr. Matthews's coverage?"

    Answer: "He said that Chris Matthews keeps saying that the Vice President had to have been informed about the Wilson trip, and 'he keeps repeating my name: Scooter Libby, Scooter Libby, Scooter Libby. And, you know, he—he doesn't know what he is talking about.' And I said, 'Well, you should call him and tell him. I have no management responsibility over Chris Matthews or of Hardball.'

    So when you were asked to describe the conversation during the deposition, you made no reference to Mr. Libby using the words "hell" or "damn," correct?

A   Specifically, no. I would include that in "venting" . . .

Q   *Now, do you agree that there is a lot of bad blood between Mr. Libby and you and NBC News?*

A No, sir.

Q *Weren't you almost elated on the morning on which Mr. Libby was indicted?*
A No, sir.

MR. WELLS: Play T.R. 22.
(Playing videotape.)
MR. FITZGERALD: Objection.
THE COURT: There is an objection. Approach.

IN ORDER TO PREVIEW what the defense wants to play from the day of Libby's indictment and how they want to use it—to argue that Russert was elated at the news that Libby was going to be indicted not just because it was a newsworthy surprise but because he was simply happy that Libby had been indicted—the parties discuss it outside the presence of the jury and the witness. The judge says he is going to hear how Russert responds to the question of whether he had heard that morning that Libby was to be indicted and then he would address whether it was appropriate to play the recording. The court takes a break for lunch before proceeding.

*

WHEN THE TRIAL RESUMES AFTER LUNCH, before Russert and the jury are brought back in, the defense shows exhibits indicating that various news outlets, including NBC, were reporting that Libby would be or would likely be indicted. Fitzgerald argues that there is a significant difference between the frenzy over the news, and the defense's claim that people at NBC were taking pleasure in reports that Libby was going to be indicted; for the prosecution, showing the recording would be unduly prejudicial with the jury. Judge Walton rules, however, that the tape can be played. The cross-examination is resumed with Wells asking Russert if he recalls news reports before the indictment that Libby was going to be indicted, which Russert does not; neither does Russert recall appearing on the Imus show and the *Today* show that morning discussing the issue nor does Wells' effort to refresh Russert's recollection with the news reports succeed. At one point, Wells brings up the specific terms in which Russert discussed it with Katie Couric on the *Today* show:

Q *Do you remember saying to Ms. Couric, "It's huge, Katie. This is the first time in 130 years, as we mentioned the other day, that a sitting White House official would come under indictment." Do the words, "It's huge, Katie—the first time in 130 years." Does that refresh your recollection that it occurred?*
A No, I don't question I said it. But I just don't remember it.

Q *Do you have a bad memory?*
A No, sir.

Q *Are you able to remember some things better than others?*
A Yes, sir.

Q *Do you think you would remember a situation where you appeared on the* Today *show and made comments about the possible indictment of the Chief of Staff to the Vice President of the United States in a case where you were a potential witness? Do you think you would remember that?*

A Well, sir, I'm on television a lot, and I do a lot of interviews and a lot of programs for NBC. It's hard for me to remember all of them by the specific date. And this one, I just don't remember.

THE DEFENSE'S EFFORTS TO PROVOKE Russert's memory are unavailing, but it is allowed to play the tape of the broadcaster on the Imus show the morning of October 28, 2005, and question him about it.

Q *Do you have a recollection when you said, "This is like Christmas Eve"; do you recall what you meant?*

A I don't remember saying that. Many times when events are unfolding, Harriet Miers or I remember the Bush/Gore Supreme Court decision, there was a lot of anticipation in the newsroom. I don't specifically remember saying that . . .

RUSSERT FINALLY HAS SOME MEMORY, triggered by the term "surprises," which enables him to explain the atmosphere of anticipation at NBC. In the course of concluding his questioning, this enables Wells to make what appears to be oblique allusion to the fact that, among critics of the administration, the anticipated day of the grand jury's indictments was sometimes referred to as Fitzmas, a play on Christmas and Fitzgerald's name:

Q *Do you have a recollection of what you meant by, "it was like Christmas Eve?"*

A [I] Was referring to surprises.

Q *Do you have a recollection of what you meant by "Santa Claus was coming?"*

A In terms of [it] being a large news day, . . . a significant news day. Having given me days of the fact that Harriet Miers had stepped down the day before, that's the expectation.

Q *Do you have a recollection of what the presents were going to be under the tree?*

A No, sir . . .

Q *Is there any possibility that when you referred to Santa Claus, you were referring to Mr. Fitzgerald?*

A No, sir.

Q *Is there any possibility when you were referring to presents under the tree, that you were referring to the indictment of Scooter Libby?*

A No, sir.

Q *You looked very happy on the tape, did you not?*

A . . . I think that was a still photo.

Q *It was a great picture, though, wasn't it?*

MR. WELLS: No further questions.

FITZGERALD'S REDIRECT EXAMINATION immediately gives Russert an opportunity to rebut the notion that he took pleasure in Libby's indictment:

By Mr. Fitzgerald:

Q *Did you take joy in Mr. Libby's indictment?*
A No, not at all. And I don't take joy being here.

Q *Sir, which makes bigger news, the possible indictment or an actual indictment?*
A The actual indictment.

Q *You were asked about your memory that day. Tell us what you recall without look-ing at things on that day about the case involving the CIA leak investigation?*
A The news conference was announced in the afternoon. It was a special interrupt [on] the network, which is very significant. That doesn't happen very often. Not just cable but across the network. I remember sitting there and frankly hearing my name which was rather jolting. And then immediately after your presentation, Brian Williams asking me questions about what I had just witnessed and to talk again about my role, which I did.

But it was the first time I had ever heard a prosecutor utter my name. And that makes an impression.

Q *Two things. Do you have any belief that your discussion that morning about Christmas and surprises was your personal joy at the possibility that Mr. Libby would be indicted?*
A Absolutely not.

Q *And do you remember reading anything in particular that day? The date, October 28, 2005, that the indictment was announced?*
A Probably the newspaper but I don't remember the specific articles.

Q *Did you read the indictment that day?*
A As you read it, it was probably made available after your news conference. I did, yes.

Q *Do you recall anything about reading the indictment?*
A Yes. I remember reading some of the things that I allegedly had said.

Q *Did you have a reaction to them?*
A Yes. I didn't recognize many of the things.

MR. FITZGERALD: Thank you, nothing further.

BEFORE POSING THE QUESTIONS from the jury, Judge Walton rules one out which evidently bears on Valerie Plame's status at the CIA, because Walton issues a caution-ary instruction:

THE COURT: One of the questions that have [been] asked, I'm not sure exactly what is being said if anything in the question. But I want to make something perfectly clear, which I instructed you on several times already. What Mrs. Wilson's status was at the CIA, whether it was covert or not covert, is not something that you're going to have any evidence presented to you on in this trial. And whether she was or whether she was not covert is not relevant to the issues you have to decide in this case. And there will be no evidence presented to you on that issue.

Let me just ask, Mr. Russert, I'm going to ask this a little different than what the jurors asked:

Have there been any discussions at NBC News, that you're aware of, before the Novak article regarding Mrs. Wilson and her affiliation with the CIA?

THE WITNESS: No.

THE COURT: After his article was published, without telling us what the discussions were, were there discussions after his article was published about her situation with the CIA?

THE WITNESS: Yes.

THE COURT: During your deposition in Mr. Levine's office, were you presented with a list of questions ahead of time?

THE WITNESS: No.

THE COURT: Was there any script that you were required to stick to when you provided your testimony?

THE WITNESS: No.

THE COURT: Did you approve or decline to answer questions in advance?

THE WITNESS: I was not presented any questions whatsoever. I was told I was under oath with a penalty of perjury. I answered every question that was asked.

THE COURT: So you didn't present any questions that you needed to be asked?

THE WITNESS: No, sir.

THE COURT: In the telephone call to Mr. Neal Shapiro, did you relate to him the claims made by Mr. Libby regarding Mrs. Wilson's status with the CIA?

THE WITNESS: I don't remember that. I remember telling him about the complaint about Chris Matthews. But I didn't, I don't recall anything else I may have said.

THE COURT: That's the only thing you remember relating, this complaint that was made about *Hardball*?

THE WITNESS: Uh-huh.

RUSSERT IS THEN ASKED to recount the episode with the *Buffalo News,* and finally Wells asks one question on recross before Russert is excused:

Q *Mr. Russert, just one question I want to make clear, in light of the jurors' question, you have no recollection of Mr. Libby telling you any information about Mrs. Wilson, correct?*

A That's correct.

MR. WELLS: Thank you.

THE COURT: Anything else?

MR. FITZGERALD: No, Your Honor.

THE COURT: Thank you, sir.

(Witness excused.)

RUSSERT IS THE FINAL PROSECUTION WITNESS. The prosecution concludes its case by entering a number of additional documents and stipulations into evidence. The most significant are (exhibits GX-402,GX-403, GX-412, GX-413, and GX-5A; see appendix):

• The 2004 version of the Department of Justice guidelines for the issuance of subpoenas to members of the news media, which is intended to show the jury the constraints under which Fitzgerald was operating as he dealt with the media in the investigation.

• A stipulation of what an employee of the Office of the Vice President would testify to, in effect authenticating Government Exhibit 402—is the copy of Wilson's op-ed with underlining and notes that "appear to be in the Vice President's handwriting." The stipulation further specified that the handwritten notes on Government Exhibits 1552—a copy of the CIA report from Wilson's mission to Niger—and 1558—a copy of a virtually identical cable of the report appear to be in Cheney's handwriting. Those notes identify the source of the report, not named in the report itself, as "Wilson" and "Joe Wilson."

• An underlined copy of Wilson's original July 6, 2003 op-ed "produced from Mr. Libby's files under Mr. Libby's certification"—that is, Libby's copy.

• A copy of a July 13, 2003 column by Maureen Dowd from *The New York Times* also from Libby's files, with what are evidently Libby's detailed notes.

• "A collection of newspaper articles" dealing with the Niger issue "with a table of contents that the defense has stipulated was produced from Mr. Libby's files under Mr. Libby's certification."

• A copy of one of the classified information non-disclosure agreements that Libby signed in 2001, at the outset of the Bush administration.

A MEMBER OF the prosecution, Kathleen Kedian reads part of the NDA to the jury:

KEDIAN: This is reading from paragraph 1 of Government Exhibit 5-A from Mr. Libby's non-disclosure agreement:

"Intending to be legally bound, I hereby accept the obligations contained in this agreement in consideration of my being granted access to classified information."

Then at the end of that paragraph[:]. "I understand and accept that, by being granted access to classified information, special confidence and trust shall be placed in me by the United States government."

Then Paragraph 2: "I hereby acknowledge that I have received a security indoctrination concerning the nature and protection of classified information, including the procedures to be followed in ascertaining whether other persons to whom I contemplate discussing this information have been approved for access to it and that I understand these procedures."

Paragraph 3: "I have been advised that the unauthorized disclosure, unauthorized retention or negligent handling of classified information by me could cause damage or irreparable injury to the United States or could be used to advantage by a foreign nation. I hereby agree that I will never divulge classified information to anyone unless, A., I have officially verified that the recipient has been properly authorized by the United States government to receive it. Or B., I have been given prior written notice of authorization from the United States government department or agency herein after department or agency, responsible for the classification of the information or last granting me a security clearance that such disclosure is permitted.

I understand that, if I am uncertain about the classification status of information, I am required to confirm from an authorized official that the information is unclassified before I may disclose it, except to a person as provided in A. or B. above. I further understand that I'm obligated to comply with laws and regulations that prohibit the unauthorized disclosure of classified information."

Paragraph 4: "I have been advised that any breach of this agreement may result in the termination of any security clearances I hold, removal from any position of special confidence and trust requiring such clearances or the termination of my employment or other relationship with the departments or agencies that granted my security clearance or clearances.

In addition, I have been advised that any unauthorized disclosure of classified information by me may constitute a violation or violations of United States criminal laws, including the provisions of Sections 641, 793, 794, 798 and 952, Title 18, United States Code.

The provisions of Section 783(b), Title 50, United States Code, and the provisions of the Intelligence Identities Protection Act of 1982, I recognize that nothing in this agreement constitutes a waiver by the United States of the right to prosecute me for any statutory violation."

Paragraph 11: "I have read this agreement carefully and my questions, if any, have been answered. I acknowledge that the briefing officer has made available to me the executive order and statutes referenced in this agreement and its implementing regulation, 32 CFR Section 2009.20, so that I may read them at this time if I so choose." Then the signature, Lewis Libby, January 23, 2001.

THE COURT: Is that it?
MS. KEDIAN: Yes.

WALTON INSTRUCTS THE JURY that they may consider the NDA only for its impact on Libby's state of mind and thus whether Libby had a motive to lie under oath.

Exhibit 422 is an article from *The Washington Post* of October 12, 2003, again produced from Libby's files under his certification. Kedian again reads parts of the article to the jury. The first paragraph refers to Plame as a CIA officer. This article also contained a reiteration of a claim from an incendiary *Washington Post* story two weeks previously.

KEDIAN: "Two top White House officials disclosed Plame's identity to at least six Washington journalists, an Administration official told the *Post* for an article published September 28.

"The source elaborated on the conversations last week, saying that the officials brought up Plame as part of their broader case against Wilson. 'It was unsolicited,' the source said. 'They were pushing back. They used everything they had.'"

THE LAST PARAGRAPH alludes to the *TIME* story for which Libby had been a source.

KEDIAN: And then the last paragraph. "On July 17, the *TIME* magazine website reported that some government officials have noted to *TIME* in interviews, as well as to syndicated columnist Robert Novak, that Wilson's wife, Valerie Plame, is a CIA official who monitors the proliferation of weapons of mass destruction. On July 22, Wilson appeared on NBC's *Today* show and said that disclosing the name of a U.S. intelligence officer would be a breach of national security, could compromise that officer's entire network of contacts and could be a violation of federal law. Wilson said that brought an immediate halt to the reports he had been getting of anonymous attacks on him by White House officials. An Administration source said one of the greatest mysteries in all this is what was really the rationale for doing what they did in the first place."

GOVERNMENT EXHIBIT 423 is a *Washington Post* article from October 4, 2003, saved in Libby's files, on how the leak of Plame's identity also exposed the identity of a CIA front company for which she purportedly worked. The article refers to Plame as a "CIA operative." Once Kedian has read parts of the article to the jury, and the judge has given the jury another instruction, Fitzgerald says,

MR. FITZGERALD: Your Honor, at this time, the Government rests its case.
THE COURT: Very well. The Government has now completed the presentation of its case. I need to have some discussions with counsel before we can proceed further.

THE JUDGE EXCUSES THE JURY for the day so that he can deal with some issues between the parties. First, the defense wants to call Andrea Mitchell and question her about her knowledge of rumors about Plame before Novak's column, noting that she refused Fitzgerald's request to be interviewed under oath. The defense argues that they can call Mitchell to ask her whether she had heard even a rumor about Wilson's wife before Novak's column, even if they expect her to say no. Part of what is at issue is that on an October 3, 2003 talk show, Mitchell appeared to indicate that a number of reporters had picked up on the fact that Wilson's wife worked at the CIA before Novak's column came out. Mitchell retracted the statement publicly thereafter. Judge Walton is more skeptical that the defense should be allowed to introduce or question Mitchell about that past statement, since she had already retracted it (and there are issues with calling a witness just to impeach them). It is also complicated by the fact that Mitchell was not being brought on just to be an adverse witness; rather, the defense also expected her to testify, as Walton puts it,

THE COURT: She is going to say at the same time Mr. Libby was purportedly saying these things about the wife to other reporters, he had a conversation with her around that same time and did not say anything.

So you're going to be asking the jury on one hand to credit her testimony as it relates to that aspect of her testimony. But then on the other hand, you're going to be seeking to show that she's a liar in reference to not having previously heard about the wife's name and then, I mean, it's kind of a dichotomy that you're going to vouch for her credibility in one sense and then try to destroy her credibility in another sense.

AT ONE POINT, WELLS DISCLOSES Mitchell's response to the efforts of investigators to speak with her:

WELLS: I mean, she shut down the system at every point.

Mr. Fitzgerald wanted to talk to her. The first in the discovery, one of the first discovery letters we got, Andrea Mitchell declined to talk to us. I think that's wrong because my client may have been hurt by her exercise back then of a decision to refuse to talk. We might not even be here on these Russert counts if she had talked back then.

And the notion is she can continue just kind of to [game] the system by not talking to the FBI, telling her lawyers, just make a representation, this is what I'm going to say, there is something wrong with that.

WALTON CALLS ON MITCHELL'S LAWYER, who is present, and he makes a strong statement:

MR. LEVINE: Your Honor, very briefly, three points. I don't want to try your patience. Number one, I am representing to you as an officer of the Court that Ms. Mitchell, if called to testify on these matters, would testify that she heard no rumor, that she had no information and no knowledge about the wife of Ambassador Wilson prior to the Novak column. I'm representing that.

Number two, this business about the FBI interview, there has been a lot of discussion about the reporter's privilege. I'm not going into it. But one thing everybody in this courtroom has to agree to is that there are Attorney General guidelines that Mr. Fitzgerald had to follow and that Ms. Mitchell was entitled to take advantage of because she viewed it as important to her role as a journalist.

So to say that she was gaming the system by exercising the right that she had under the guidelines, to tell Mr. Fitzgerald what she didn't want to talk to him, frankly, is offensive.

LEVINE'S THIRD POINT HAS TO DO with the relevant legal cases.

The second overall issue Walton has to deal withis over allowing Jill Abramson, who had been Judith Miller's editor in the D.C. Bureau of *The New York Times,* to testify. The judge rules that she will be allowed. The third issue concerns one part of the obstruction of justice count which the defense moves to strike, since it concerns the July 12, 2003 conversation between Libby and Miller and the defense contends the prosecution entered no evidence that it did not occur as Libby originally claimed. The prosecution does not object.

Finally, at this point, the defense notes that the prosecution did not take an opportunity to show that the "TREATED AS TOP SECRET/SCI" stamp put on the original document of Libby's notes from his June 2003 conversation in which Cheney told Libby that Wilson's wife worked in the Counter Proliferation Division of the CIA was done by Libby or at his behest. Consequently, the defense argues, the judge should instruct the jury to disregard the stamp. The parties promise to try to work it out, and the trial recesses for the day and the weekend.

*

FEBRUARY 12, 2007

THE INTERLUDE BETWEEN the close of the prosecution's presentation of witnesses and the opening of the defense case occasions a lengthy court session with the jury out of the courtroom.

The first issue involves Andrea Mitchell's possible testimony.

The prosecution argues that the defense—while in part planning to call Mitchell because she will testify that she spoke with Libby during the week of July 6–13 and he said nothing about Wilson's wife—would chiefly be bringing her in to try and reveal to the jury her prior, since-redacted statement that she had, in fact, known about Plame before Novak publicly identified her.

Rebutting Fitzgerald's point, the defense raises a new argument: the intensity with which Mitchell, and NBC News generally, was working on the story of Wilson's criticism, and the fact that she was talking with CIA spokesman Bill Harlow, and the State Department's Richard Armitage, who knew that Wilson's wife worked at the CIA and in fact told this to other reporters, makes it more likely that Mitchell had somehow learned about Wilson's wife. The defense's point is that they have a reason, apart from Mitchell's repudiated statement, for asking her whether she knew about Wilson's wife before Novak's column was published. As part of this argument, the defense suggests it is going to call the FBI agent who interviewed Russert to testify that the broadcaster indicated he could not rule out the possibility that he had heard about Wilson's wife before his conversation with Libby in July 2003, contrary to his testimony. Wells also notes the disturbing fact that the original notes taken by the FBI agent from his discussion with Russert are lost, uniquely among the relevant notes in the case.

The parties mention that they've reached agreement on the contentious matter of the "TREATED AS TOP SECRET/SCI" stamp on Libby's note from the June 2003 conversation where Cheney told him about Wilson's wife: a new version of the document with the stamp redacted will be given to the jury, and the judge will give the jury an instruction on this. They then turn to the question of how the jury should be instructed on the fact that Libby's testimony about the July 12, 2003 conversation with Judith Miller is no longer a basis for convicting him. Fitzgerald's concern is that he does not want the jury to believe that Miller is removed from the case altogether. He says, "The Judith Miller conversations are still part—an important part of the evidence in this case."

After a brief recess, Judge Walton declares that the defense's only apparent purpose for bringing up Mitchell's testimony about her work on the Wilson case is to bring out her prior inconsistent statement to impeach her. Walton offers to have Mitchell testify for the record outside the presence of the jury, to see if she says something that would permit the defense to bring out its desired information.

WALTER PINCUS

THE DEFENSE THEN BEGINS its case with Walter Pincus, the venerable national security and intelligence reporter for *The Washington Post.* Winner of several journalism prizes—a fact the defense highlighted with Pincus and its other journalists witnesses (with the exception of Robert Novak) to boost their credibility—Pincus has been a reporter for fifty years. He wrote several articles key to the case: a June 12, 2003 article on the Niger uranium controversy that used both Wilson and Libby as anonymous sources; a July 6 profile of Wilson that coincided with the appearance of Wilson's op-ed; and an October 12, 2003 story on the investigation into the blowing of Plame's cover. The defense calls Pincus for two key reasons. He is the first of a succession of journalists who will testify that while they interviewed Libby in the relevant June-July 2003 period about the sixteen words controversy and even about Wilson, Libby did *not* disclose information about Wilson's wife to them. The point of this testimony is to bolster the defense's contention that Libby did not consider Plame's CIA employment a part of the case against Wilson, which they say he was making on the merits. Thus, the defense claims, Plame's CIA employment would have been eminently forgettable. The second reason is to undercut Miller's testimony that Libby did tell her about Plame by showing that Libby had many opportunities to blow Plame's cover with other reporters but did not take advantage of them. Another reason for calling Pincus was for his testimony that on July 12, 2003 he was told about Plame by Ari Fleischer—contrary to Fleischer's own trial testimony, thereby undercutting Fleischer's credibility which Libby's lawyers fear may prove particularly damaging to their client among the jurors.

After going through Pincus's credentials and the circumstances through which he came to testify about his conversations with Libby, the defense asks Pincus about his June 12, 2003, *Washington Post* article that heightened the profile of Wilson's criticism considerably. Jeffress goes through the parts of the piece that use Wilson as an anonymous source, and brings up a part of Pincus' piece that was later called into question before getting into the part that used Libby as an anonymous source:

Q *You reported in this article of June 12, 2003, "After returning to the United States, the envoy reported to the CIA that the uranium-purchase story was false, the sources said. Among the envoy's conclusions was that the documents may have been forged because 'the dates were wrong and the names were wrong,' the former U.S. government official said."*

   Now, the former U.S. government official, again, is Mr. Wilson; is that correct?

A That's correct.

Q *Did you come to learn whether he saw any documents or whether his report actually said anything about forgeries?*

A I came to learn later that, no, it didn't talk about forgeries.

Q *And then go down to "the CIA's decision"—it's a little below.*

Now, there are two paragraphs here, Mr. Pincus, I want to read you: "The CIA's decision to send an emissary to Niger was triggered by questions raised by an aide to Vice President Cheney during an agency briefing on intelligence circulating about the purported Iraqi efforts to acquire the uranium, according to the senior officials. Cheney's staff was not told at the time that its concerns had been the impetus for a CIA mission and did not learn it occurred or its specific results."

Then the next paragraph is: "Cheney and his staff continued to get intelligence on the matter, but the Vice President, unlike other senior administration officials, never mentioned it in a public speech. He and his staff did not learn of its role in spurring the mission [until] it was disclosed by New York Times *columnist Nicholas Kristof on May 6, according to an administration official."*

Now, Mr. Pincus, my question is, did you speak to Mr. Libby before writing this article?

A I did.

Q *And the two paragraphs I just read to you, were they based in part on information given to you by Mr. Libby?*

A Yes.

DEFENSE ATTORNEY JEFFRESS asks Pincus to describe the telephone call with Libby in preparation for the article:

Q *And were you asking him about the truth of this unnamed envoy's claims about his trip to Niger?*

A Yes.

Q *And, briefly, do you recall what Mr. Libby told you on that subject?*

A That his memory—he did not know that—how it had come about—how ambassador Wilson's trip had come about.

Q *That the V.P. did not?*

A Well, he didn't really talk about the Vice President. He talked about himself in terms of the staff.

Q *Now, Mr. Pincus, in this conversation before June 12, did Mr. Libby say anything about Joseph Wilson's wife?*

A No, he did not.

Q *He didn't mention her at all?*

A No.

Q *Are you sure about that?*

A I am sure.

Q *So this conversation was . . . prior to the 12th. We will put it June, say, 11. Would that be fair?*

A That's pretty tight, but it may have been that day or it may have been the day before that.

Q *Okay.*

JEFFRESS ASKS ABOUT Pincus' July 6, 2003 piece on Wilson, co-authored with *Post* reporter Richard Leiby. For the article, Wilson, knowing that his *New York Times* op-ed would appear that day, had permitted the two reporters to fully identify him in the story. He then turns to when Pincus read about the disclosure of Plame's CIA status:

Q *You interviewed him . . . at his home?*
A I talked to him on the telephone.

Q *At that time—that is, the time that you published the July 6th article in* **The Washington Post**—*were you aware that Mr. Wilson's wife worked at the CIA?*
A No.

Q *When did you first learn that fact?*
A On July 12th . . .

Q *Was that by phone or in person?*
A By phone.

Q *And where were you when you had this telephone conversation on July 12?*
A At my desk in the *The Washington Post.*

Q *Even though that's a Saturday?*
A Even though that's a Saturday.

Q *And what exactly were you told about Mr. Wilson's wife in that telephone conversation on July 12?*
A I was writing a story about another aspect of the Niger story . . . It was about weapons of mass destruction. And in the midst of a discussion about an answer to a question about the story I was writing, the person calling suddenly swerved off and said, in effect, "Why do you keep writing about Joe Wilson and Joe Wilson's trip? Don't you know,"—in effect—"his wife works for the CIA, is an analyst on WMD and arranged for the trip? And that's why people weren't paying attention to it."

Q *Was the person who told you this on July 12 by telephone a government official?*
A Yes, he was.

Q *Was it Mr. Libby?*
A No, it was not Mr. Libby.

Q *Who was it?*
A It was Ari Fleischer.

Q *Was he, at the time, just finishing his term as the White House Press Secretary?*
A Yes, he was.

Q *And are you certain it was Ari Fleischer?*

A Yes, I am.

JEFFRESS THEN ASKS about the October 12, 2003 *Post* article, on the suddenly burgeoning investigation into the leak, using it to establish several points:

Q *Going to the next paragraph, second part, "Wilson said…he told Kristof about his trip to Niger on the condition that Kristof must keep his name out of the column."*

   Now, that's an article . . . Nicholas Kristof had published in The New York Times *on May 6th. Do you recall that article?*

A Oh, yes.

Q *And that's the first one, as far as you know, that reported publicly on Mr. Wilson's trip to Niger?*

A Yes.

Q *And that column mentioned the alleged role of the Vice President's office for the first time, correct?*

A Yes.

BUT JEFFRESS IS MOST INTERESTED in the *Post* story's account of a leak to a *Washington Post* reporter on July 12—Pincus himself, though not identified in the October 2003 story:

Q *You report, Mr. Pincus, that, "On July 12, two days before Novak's column, a* Post *reporter was told by an administration official that the White House had not paid attention to the former ambassador's CIA-sponsored trip to Niger because it was set up as a boondoggle by his wife, an analyst with the agency working on weapons of mass destruction. Plame's name was never mentioned, and the purpose of the disclosure did not appear to be to generate an article, but rather to undermine Wilson's report."*

   Now, Mr. Pincus, the reporter who you say was called in that paragraph, who was that?

A That was myself.

Q *It was not Glenn Kessler of* The Washington Post?

A No, it was not.

Q *And the person that you refer to who made the call to* The Washington Post *reporter was who?*

A Ari Fleischer . . .

Q *Now, Mr. Pincus, I am going to ask you what the specific words were that Mr. Fleischer used in the conversation he had with you on July 12. Do you need to see your notes for that?*

A That would be helpful, yes . . .

Q *What were Mr. Fleischer's words in describing Mr. Wilson's wife and her role at the CIA?*

A I can't tell you the exact words. The notes I took were, "Wilson's wife," "an analyst" and "WMD." That's the way I sort of shorthand things.

Q *Analyst in WMD?*

A I don't know the exact phrasing, but clearly, handling WMD, and it may have been weapons of mass destruction.

Q *Okay. Now . . . do your notes reflect anything about her working in the Counterproliferation Division of the CIA?*

A No.

Q *Now, I notice, Mr. Pincus, . . . you use the word "boondoggle" in this paragraph that we just read. Was that Mr. Fleischer's word or was that your —*

A No, that was my shorthand way of describing.

Q *That was going to be your take on the message he was giving?*

A The inference that he was applying to the trip.

Q *And what were the rules, if any, under which Mr. Fleischer was giving you this information?*

A That I wouldn't associate his name with the information he gave me.

JEFFRESS AND PINCUS go through the circumstances of his conversation with Fleischer in September 2004, and Pincus has an opportunity to note that he did not name Fleischer in his testimony for the Grand Jury—though who he was talking about would have been perfectly clear to Fitzgerald and the members of the Grand Jury. Pincus explains,

A I feel very strongly about the identification of sources, and since the prosecutor knew who the source was, I wanted to be able to say that I did not disclose his name.

AFTER THE DEFENSE ENDS its examination of their first witness, Fitzgerald begins his cross-examination by getting Pincus to confirm that his testimony was under circumstances similar to those of Russert—in his lawyer's office under oath, instead of in front of a grand jury—to persuade the jury to discount the defense's contention that Russert received special treatment. The cross-examination covers a couple of other topics:

Q *Now, with regard to Mr. Fleischer, is it fair to say that, as you sit here now, it's clear in your mind that the person who first told you about Mr. Wilson's wife was Ari Fleischer on July 12th, correct?*

A Yes.

FITZGERALD UNDERTAKES a preemptive effort to discount Bob Woodward's anticipated testimony that he told Pincus about Plame back in June 2003, after learning
about her from Richard Armitage. (In published reports, Pincus was clear it did not
happen—or that if Woodward tried to tell him, he certainly heard no such thing.)

Q *Now, did Mr. Fleischer ever tell you where he first learned about Wilson's wife
   working at the CIA?*
A No, he didn't . . .

Q *Did you write articles on intelligence matters that touched upon the Office of Vice
   President in the last week of May 2003?*
A Yes, I did.

Q *And, finally, I would like to turn to the conversations that you had prior to June
   12th with Mr. Libby and the June 12th article that Mr. Jeffress asked about . . .
   Is it fair to say, Mr. Pincus, that Mr. Libby was a source for the information in
   these two paragraphs?*
A Some of it, yes.

Q *And I will read you a line here, one sentence, the first sentence . . . : "The CIA's deci-
   sion to send an emissary to Niger was triggered by questions raised by an aide to Vice
   President Cheney during an agency briefing on intelligence circulating about the
   purported Iraqi efforts to acquire the uranium, according to senior officials."*
   Was Mr. Libby a source for that statement?
A He was one of the sources, yes.

Q *And did Mr. Libby indicate to you that the person who actually asked the questions
   was the Vice President, not an aide to the Vice President?*
A No. He said "aide to the Vice President."

Q *So in Mr. Libby's account, it was not the Vice President who asked the questions,
   correct?*
A He told me it was an "aide to the Vice President."

Q *And that's clear in your mind that he did not say the Vice President?*
A Oh, no. I am certain about that.

MR. FITZGERALD: Thank you. Nothing further.

LIBBY'S STATEMENT IS CONTRADICTED by documentary evidence entered at trial
showing that in fact it was Cheney himself who raised the questions about the report
on the Niger story. This evidence is the basis for Fitzgerald's passing remark in his
rebuttal closing that Libby lied to Pincus at the time.

With no questions from the defense or the jury, Pincus is excused. The jury is also
excused briefly so that the prosecution could voice its objection to the defense playing

a tape recording that Bob Woodward, the next witness, made of his June 13, 2003 interview with Richard Armitage in which Armitage blew Plame's cover to him—the first known instance of a government official disclosing Plame's CIA identity to a reporter. Judge Walton rules the tape admissible.

BOB WOODWARD

SHORTLY THEREAFTER Bob Woodward is called. Bob Woodward is, of course, the legendary *Washington Post* reporter and author whose reporting on Watergate brought down Richard Nixon. His significance to the defense is somewhat different from that of the other reporters: Woodward was told by Richard Armitage, Colin Powell's deputy at the State Department, that Wilson's wife worked at the CIA on WMD on June 13, 2003, making this the first known leak of Plame's CIA identity to a reporter. Woodward, working on a book at the time, interviewed Libby two weeks later, and had with him a note (in fact, notes for an interview with Andy Card a few days earlier, though Woodward did not bring up Wilson's wife at that interview) that refers to Wilson's wife; Woodward cannot rule out the possibility that he asked Libby about Wilson's wife, though he has no recollection of doing so, and if he did, Libby said nothing about it, as Woodward's notes reflect.

Woodward states his credentials as a journalist, and confirms that in June 2003 he was writing the book that became *Plan of Attack*:

Q *How many current or former government officials did you interview in the course of your preparing to write that book?*
A Certainly several hundred. Seventy-five primary sources, though, people who were in positions to know.

Q *Was one of those people Mr. Scooter Libby?*
A Yes.

Q *When did you talk to Mr. Libby?*
A Lots of times.

Q *Do you remember speaking to him on one occasion on June 27, 2003?*
A I do.

Q *And how did that interview get arranged?*
A Well, it started with an interview with him on June 2nd.

I was trying to interview Vice President Cheney, and it looked like it had been arranged, and I prepared a detailed list of possible questions and topics I wanted to go over with the Vice President. And four days before that June 23rd interview, I sent—I think it was 18 pages or 16 pages of questions to Mr. Libby.

Q *Let me ask you one thing. You said the June 23rd interview. Did you misspeak about that?*

A Well—I am sorry. Maybe I did. We talked on the phone that day—

Q *On June 23rd?*

A —when I sent the questions over.

Q *But the interview itself took place what day?*

A On the 27th.

Q *Okay. And after you had sent over those questions and after you had spoken to Mr. Libby on the 23rd, what happened in terms of your planned interview of the Vice President?*

A Well, the interview with the Vice President was supposed to be at 1:00 on the 27th. That morning, Mr. Libby called me to tell me that, essentially, I had overplayed my hand, and sent in too many questions. There were dozens—really a hundred or more questions on this list with questions like "what was the reaction?", "what do you remember?", and so forth.

And so the interview with the Vice President was off, but Mr. Libby said he would see me at 5:10 that day . . .

Q *Before you met with Mr. Libby on June the 27th, had you received any information about Joseph Wilson's wife?*

A Yes . . . Two weeks before, on June 23rd, I was doing a lengthy interview with Richard Armitage, the Deputy Secretary of State, for the book—

Q *Can I just interrupt you a minute. You said two weeks before, on June 23rd.*

A Did I? I am sorry. June 13th.

Q *Okay.*

A And that was two weeks before the interview with Mr. Libby. I am sorry. It was June 13th I interviewed Mr. Armitage for the book.

Q *June—do you recall that there was an article in* **The Washington Post** *on June the 12th by Walter Pincus that discussed a former ambassador, without naming him, and a trip to Niger?*

A . . . I do. I had read the article.

Q *All right. So in the conversation you had with Richard Armitage, did you raise the subject or did he raise the subject of the ambassador?*

A I raised the subject—even though Wilson was not identified in the article, I knew it was Wilson. So I asked Armitage essentially why he had been sent.

Q *I am going to introduce and play for the jury about a one-minute excerpt from your interview with Mr. Armitage. Let me ask you first, was it tape-recorded?*

A Could I just say one thing?

Q *Yes.*

A This was also a background interview for the book. Since this controversy and investigation arose, Mr. Armitage has released me and said that I can testify about it and present any information I have. In fact, he has gone so far as to request that I testify and provide all information that I can.

Q *Thank you.*
A Thank you.

THE TRANSCRIPT OF THE TAPE is also admitted into evidence, and the defense plays the audio excerpt for the Court. [Exhibit DX-511T; see appendix.]

Q *Now, Mr. Armitage—at the time you interviewed him, what position did he hold?*
A He was the Deputy Secretary of State.

Q *He was not in the White House, correct?*
A That's correct.

Q *And after that interview with Mr. Armitage . . . you didn't write anything about this information, did you, about the wife?*
A No. I did not, for *The Washington Post*.

Q *. . . You continued doing interviews with persons after that other than Mr. Libby?*
A Yes.

Q *I am going to show you what's marked as Defense Exhibit 812.*

THIS IS THE REDACTED LIST of potential questions that Woodward took with him for an interview with then–White House Chief of Staff on Andy Card on June 20, 2003. All that is discernible is that it is is a sheet of questions for Card and, at the bottom are the words, "Joe Wilson's wife."

Q *And if we saw the rest of the page, there would be some other potential questions?*
A Correct.

Q *Do you recall whether, when you met with Mr. Card, you did ask this question about Joe Wilson's wife?*
A I did not. The interview with Mr. Card was tape-recorded, and I have gone through the tape and the transcript, as have my attorneys, and the subject did not come up.

Q *Now, this particular note—when you went to see Mr. Libby on the 27th, did you take this list of questions . . . with you to that interview?*
A I believe I did.

Q *And what time did the interview start with Mr. Libby?*
A On the 27th—so this was a week after the Card interview. I have it in my appointment book as 5:10.

Q *And how long did it last?*

A I don't know. It could have been 45 minutes. It could have been twice that long, or even longer. I know it was clearly the end of the day. We had the "q-Cheney" list of questions to go through, which, as best I recall, I did.

What I do is take questions from earlier interviews and bring them to interviews that I am doing, trying to focus in on subjects. And in my Cheney/Libby file, this full list of questions for Card a week earlier was there. And I believe I took this, along with the "q-Cheney," 18 pages, 16 pages, and maybe other lists of questions.

Q *Okay. During the interview, did the subject of the "sixteen words" controversy in the State of the Union come up, broadly speaking?*

A The subject of the National Intelligence Estimate came up. I don't recall specifically whether the sixteen words were discussed . . .

Q *Did the issue of uranium from Africa come up during the interview?*

A The issue of yellowcake, which is a form of uranium oxide, I believe, did come up.

Q *Okay. Now, did you ask Mr. Libby any questions about Joseph Wilson's wife?*

A Not that I recall.

Q *Is it possible you did?*

A Yes.

Q *Did you—did Mr. Libby say anything to you, if you did, about Mr. Wilson's wife?*

A Obviously, I have thought about this as best I can and reviewed the notes. And there is no doubt Mr. Libby did not say anything about Wilson's wife, because I would have had it in my notes.

I was taking notes. I then dictated a memo—I think you have it—of the subjects we did discuss where he said something in the affirmative. This is an interview where we're going through all of the list of questions on the Cheney list, and . . . I am seeing if he will try to get answers for me or information on those subjects.

So it's one where, hopefully, I am going to be able to talk to Cheney and go over these questions at some point, but I am also seeing what I can get from him.

Q *Going back one moment to the conversation that you had with Richard Armitage, when Mr. Armitage said "the CIA is not going to be hurt by this one" and "we are clean as a whistle," was he specifically referring to the "sixteen words" controversy?*

A What he was referring to is . . . a speech that President Bush gave October 7, 2002, in Cincinnati. And what he was telling me . . . is that the CIA Director, George Tenet, got the reference to uranium from Africa removed from that speech . . .

Q *. . . That was a point being raised by people about, if it was removed in Cincinnati, how did it get into the State of the Union?*

A That's exactly what I asked Armitage. How come, if it was removed in October of 2002, a version of it was in the State of the Union address the end of January 2003.

Q *All right. And so why did you get into the question about Ambassador Wilson's trip with Mr. Armitage? . . .*

A Well, I am not sure we were talking about Ambassador Wilson. We were talking about what happened in the Cincinnati speech, and we were talking about what was in the National Intelligence Estimate . . .

Q *. . . And what Mr. Armitage told you about Ms. Wilson, did that indicate to you that she had any covert or undercover capacity?*

A No, not at all. In fact, just the opposite. I think in that portion of the interview you played, where I didn't think the audio—the audio I had heard was a little better, and you redacted some words that are offensive—

Q *Just to be clear, those were expletives.*

A Yes, that's correct. In the raw, it has a little more fire. And what he said specifically is that Joe Wilson's wife was a WMD analyst at the CIA.

MR. JEFFRESS: I pass the witness, Your Honor.

THE CROSS-EXAMINATION BEGINS with Fitzgerald having Woodward confirm that his Grand Jury testimony was in his lawyer's office under oath, an accommodation similar to that made for Russert. Then Fitzgerald asks Woodward about his interview with Armitage:

Q *Now, turning to the tape that you were just discussing and the transcript, Defense Exhibit 511T, two questions. First, I think this is clear, but is it fair to say that all the redactions are the fiery, off-color words, but they don't involve any discussion of the classified or covert nature or alleged covert nature of anyone's employment, correct?*

A That's correct.

Q *And secondly, in Defense Exhibit 511T, there is a point where you say, "Why doesn't that come out? That [has] to be a big secret? Everyone knows."*
Do you recall that section?

A I do.

Q *What are you referring to as something that "everyone knows"?*

A What that's referring to is the article by Walter Pincus did not name the ambassador. I knew it was Joe Wilson. Mr. Armitage knew it was Joe Wilson. But that had not come out, and I was wondering why that was not being disclosed at that point.

Q *At that point in time—did you know before your conversation with Mr. Armitage that Mr. Wilson's wife was alleged to work at the CIA?*

A I did not.

Q *Okay. And were you referring to Mr. Wilson's wife's employment when you referred to "everyone knows it"?*

A No. I was referring to everyone knows—the "it" being that the unnamed ambassador in Walter Pincus' article or the references that others had made was Wilson.

WOODWARD CONFIRMS that his list of questions for White House Chief of Staff Andrew Card contained a number of other items besides the note about Wilson's wife, and that, while he is certain that he brought his list of questions for Cheney to the June 27, 2003 interview with Libby, he believes he also brought the list from the Card interview.

Q *Is it fair to say that in this list of questions that was brought to the interview, under "q-Cheney," there is no reference to Mr. Wilson's wife?*
A That's correct.

Q *Now, is it also fair to say that you recall that during the interview that was conducted on June 27th, 2003, that Mr. Libby was extremely defensive and protective of the Vice President during the course of the interview?*
A Well, in my notes, when we got to the issue of the National Intelligence Estimate—I mean, the context in June 2003, it was three . . . or four months after the invasion, and no weapons of mass destruction had been found. The President and the administration and many had said with great certainty that they believed there were weapons of mass destruction.

So the question became "What was the basis for that decision?" And part of [the] basis was the National Intelligence Estimate.

And as I went through that with Mr. Libby, he was taking the position, reasonably founded, that the CIA had insisted there were weapons of mass destruction. That's the first sentence in the National Intelligence Estimate. And he was defensive about things the Vice President had said publicly and—

Q *And did you note that he went on and on and on about defending the Vice President?*
A Yes . . . And it does say in those notes that when we dealt with the subject of the National Intelligence Estimate, Mr. Libby was very defensive of Cheney . . . I think one of the lines is—["][he] went on and on and on."

Q *And is it fair to say this interview was understood to be for a book? Correct?*
A Correct.

Q *And any articles that would appear in* The Washington Post *. . . usually would appear at the time that the book is about to be released, correct?*
A Yes.

Q *And is it fair to say that, as you sit here now, you have no actual specific recollection of talking to Mr. Libby about Wilson's wife on June 27, 2003?*
A That's correct. I do not.

Q *Thank you. One last thing. As of June 27th, was it your understanding that all the reporters in the United States understood that Wilson's wife worked at the CIA? June 27, 2003.*
A I had no idea.

MR. FITZGERALD: Thank you. Nothing further.

THE DEFENSE'S BRIEF redirect examination pushes back on the issue of Libby's defensiveness over Vice President Cheney, and seeks to raise the question of whether Armitage might have meant that everybody knew about Wilson's wife:

By Mr. Jeffress:

Q *Would you expect someone who works as Chief of Staff for the Vice President to defend his boss?*
A Yes.

Q *Now, concerning . . . this thing about "everybody knows it"? . . . [W]here Mr. Armitage first tells you, "His wife works in the agency"—you ask, "Why doesn't that come out? Why does—" and he interrupts you, and . . . says, "Everyone knows it," correct?*
A Yes.

Q *That's not you . . . saying "everyone knows it," right?*
A That's correct. But —

Q *And you are asking, "Why does that have to be a big secret?" And he says, again, "Everyone knows," correct?*
    So that's him speaking?
A That's correct.

MR. JEFFRESS: I pass the witness, Your Honor.

THE JURY HAS ONE LINE of questioning, posed by Judge Walton:

THE COURT: Question: As of June 27th, 2003, to your knowledge, did other reporters know anything about Ambassador Wilson's wife working at the CIA?
THE WITNESS: It's possible.
THE COURT: Do you have any specific knowledge of whether that was the case?
THE WITNESS: The reporter working on Wilson after I had interviewed Mr. Armitage—I told him about it.
THE COURT: So that would be the only other reporter that you have personal knowledge of who would have known about it?
THE WITNESS: Correct, Judge.

FITZGERALD HAS ONE FOLLOW-UP QUESTION, getting Woodward to identify the other reporter as Walter Pincus, who had provided contradictory testimony already:

Q *You just mentioned there was one reporter that you have personal knowledge might have known about Mr. Wilson's wife. Can you tell us who that was?*
A Walter Pincus.

MR. FITZGERALD: Thank you.

DAVID SANGER

THE DEFENSE NEXT CALLS David Sanger, then White House Correspondent for *The New York Times* who, in June–July 2003, was aggressively pursuing the controversies roiling the Bush administration: the failure to find WMDs in Iraq, and the upheaval over the disputed sixteen words uttered by the president in his 2003 State of the Union address.

After spelling out his journalistic bona fides and the conventional journalistic practice of talking to sources on a confidential basis—on background, on deep background and off-the-record—Sanger is asked by defense attorney Jeffress about a big story on the prewar intelligence he was working on in later June and early July 2003, which eventually came out on July 12, and about interviewing Libby for that story:

By Mr. Jeffress:

Q *By looking at that document, does that refresh your recollection as to the date and the time of your meeting with Mr. Libby?*

A This says Wednesday, July 2, at 10:00 a.m., and that sounds right to me.

Q *And how long did that interview last?*

A . . . Just under an hour, I believe.

Q *Was the interview at your request or his?*

A The interview was at my request.

Q *Who had you spoken to in setting up that interview?*

A I believe I had spoken with Cathie Martin who, at the time, was in the Vice President's press office.

Q *In the course of those discussions with Ms. Martin, did you give any indication of the subjects that you wanted to cover with her or with Mr. Libby?*

A Yes, in general terms.

Q *And did those subjects include the "sixteen words" controversy involving uranium from Africa?*

A Yes, it did.

Q *And when you met with Mr. Libby, did you cover that subject?*

A Yes, we did.

Q *What, if anything, did Mr. Libby say to you on July 2 in that hour-long interview about Joseph Wilson's wife?*

A Nothing. I don't believe her name came up.

Q *Are you certain of that?*

A Yes, I am.

SANGER IS ASKED ABOUT his July 12, 2003 story, which discussed the Vice President and Wilson again without mentioning Wilson's wife:

Q *Is that because you didn't know it at the time?*
A I believe I probably did not know it at the time, no.

Q *You can't be sure of that, though; is that correct?*
A Almost quite certain of that....

MR. JEFFRESS: I pass the witness.

FITZGERALD BEGINS HIS CROSS-EXAMINATION by having Sanger confirm that Judith Miller, like all the defense journalists thus far, has won Pulitzer Prizes, before turning to Sanger's July 2 interview with Libby to bring out that it was focused on Powell's presentation to the UN in February 2003, and did not involve allegations by Wilson. Fitzgerald asks several questions about the circumstances of the interview, designed to highlight that Judith Miller's interview with Libby on July 8 was unusual:

Q *And will you agree with me that this interview with Mr. Libby occurred in the Old Executive Office Building?*
A Yes, it did.

Q *And you walked in the front door and you went to Mr. Libby's office, correct? Or you walked in the building?*
A I walked in the building, yes.

Q *And during the entire interview, Cathie Martin was present?*
A I believe she was.

Q *So during an interview with a* New York Times *reporter in the presence of Cathie Martin on July 2, 2003, in the Old Executive Office Building, Mr. Wilson's wife was not mentioned, correct?*
A That's correct.

THE JURY WANTS TO KNOW how Sanger learned of Plame:

THE COURT: Sir, did there come a time when you found out about Ambassador Wilson's wife working at the CIA?
THE WITNESS: Yes.
THE COURT: Do you recall when that was?
THE WITNESS: Probably it would have been after . . . the publication of Mr. Novak's column.
THE COURT: So that would have been the source of your finding out about that, to your knowledge?

THE WITNESS: To the best of my knowledge, yes.

THE COURT: Okay. Anything else?

(No response from the jury.)

THE COURT: Thank you, sir.

THE WITNESS: Thank you.

THE JURY IS EXCUSED FOR LUNCH, and Judge Walton and the legal teams take up the issue of Libby's memory defense. In pre-trial discussions, the defense had indicated their intention to call the defendant to the stand when presenting their case, as part of an aggressive memory defense, which they said would show that their client's job was so intense he could not be expected to remember details about Valerie Plame. Although they had not promised with certainty that Libby would testify, much of their pre-trial wrangling had focused on the possibility that he would. From the outset of the trial, they had argued for the inclusion of evidence that would support the memory defense, and Judge Walton had agreed to consider this, while the prosecution, as might be expected, was less sanguine about it. Now, the subject is joined again, over what evidence the defense will be allowed to enter into the record if Libby does not testify, although they state that a final decision has not yet been made on whether Libby is going to testify. This lasts for the rest of the morning without clear resolution, and will be taken up again at the conclusion of the day's witness testimony. That testimony continues in the afternoon.

ROBERT NOVAK

OPENING THE AFTERNOON SESSION, the defense calls Robert Novak, the syndicated conservative opinion writer who blew Plame's cover with his infamous "Mission to Niger" column of July 14, 2003 (exhibit GX-414).

The two senior administration officials who were his sources on Plame, as Novak testifies below, were Richard Armitage and Karl Rove. Armitage told Novak that Wilson's wife worked at the CIA and had suggested him for his mission on the afternoon of July 8, 2003. Armitage evidently learned of Wilson's wife when his subordinate Marc Grossman had the INR report prepared in early June. By the time Armitage disclosed Plame's identity to Novak, Libby had already done so to Judith Miller twice according to her testimony, including earlier that day. But Armitage had leaked earlier still, as Bob Woodward testified, on June 13. Rove confirmed Plame's CIA employment to Novak on July 9, 2003, in the closing minutes of a phone call that also dealt with a different woman entirely. This was Frances Fragos Townsend, whom President Bush had recently named to be the administration's deputy national security adviser. Her record in government included a stint in the Clinton-era Justice Department, which had raised skepticism of her among Novak and other conservatives. The columnist had sought comment from Townsend and other members of the administration during that tumultuous week, and Rove was detailed to return his calls and shore up support for Townsend in her new assignment. Novak testifies below that when he talked with Rove, he was mainly interested in Joe Wilson's mission to Niger and asked him a number of questions about it.

Federal prosecutors later learned from Novak and Rove that the former brought up Plame's name. He had already spoken with Armitage and was prepared to report that "Wilson's wife" had sent her husband to Niger, but was seeking a second confirming source. "Oh, you know about it too," was Rove's reply, according to Novak, and he took that as clear confirmation. ("I heard that too" was Rove's response, according to some other accounts.)

Despite Rove's support for Townsend, Novak indicated that he would still be publishing a critical column about her. While Novak acknowledged that this would no doubt displease the administration, he also signaled that another column he was planning for that week would be about Wilson and Plame. "You are going to be unhappy with something that I write, and I think you are very much going to like something that I am about to write," Novak told Rove.

Indeed, on July 10, Novak published a column on Townsend that observed she could become an "enemy within." Novak suggested she might be disloyal to the administration because she was once "an intimate advisor of Janet Reno," and had earlier worked for a U.S. attorney with "liberal Democratic" leanings.

Four days later, the fateful column on Plame was published. Though it undoubtedly did please the administration at first, it is just as true that the firestorm it unleashed—the chief of staff to Vice President Cheney indicted on five felony counts, and the inner workings of the administration, including the ways they spin the media, exposed for all to see—punctured the pleasure they took in seeing Ambassador Wilson's credibility brought into question.

NOVAK DISCLOSES IN HIS TESTIMONY that he interviewed Libby on July 9, 2003, the day after Libby met with Judith Miller and, according to Miller's testimony, told her that Wilson's wife worked at the CIA. Libby, however, did not share that information with Novak, according to the columnist's testimony. (Libby professed no recollection of such a meeting in his grand jury testimony; it is clear from Fitzgerald's questioning of Libby that the prosecution already possessed Novak's account of that conversation, which Novak repeats here.) However, Novak did leave open the possibility that he had mentioned Wilson's wife to Libby. The timing of Novak's column has some significance: though it was published on July 14, 2003, Novak finished it and got it to his editor by early afternoon on July 11, the previous Friday, and by ordinary practice it would go out on the newswire shortly thereafter. This goes to the issue both of when the White House could and would have learned of Plame from Novak's column; and when other journalists, including Tim Russert, could and would have. An intriguing disclosure in this regard is Novak's testimony about the role of lobbyist and Republican activist Richard Hohlt, who acted as a go-between for Novak and Karl Rove. According to Novak, he gave Hohlt a copy of his column on July 11 and Hohlt conveyed it to the White House, meaning the White House knew by the afternoon of July 11 that Novak was going to publish Plame's identity.

After recounting his long career as a journalist, Novak is questioned about the week of July 7, 2003.

Q *Now, directing you to the week of July 7, 2003, what news stories were you working on that week?*

A I was working on the change of the counterterrorism aide, Ms. Townsend, at the White House. I was working on several small stories that ran in the weekend items column I wrote. I was working on . . . former Ambassador Joe Wilson's mission to Niger, which he had written about in an op-ed in *The New York Times* the previous Sunday.

Q *How did you come to be working on the column concerning Ambassador Wilson's trip to Niger?*

A The previous Sunday . . . he had his column . . . revealing his report on an alleged attempt by Iraq to buy yellowcake uranium from the country of Niger. He had written an op-ed in *The New York Times* that Sunday and was on *Meet the Press* that Sunday morning.

I happened to be on the roundtable on *Meet the Press* that day and came in contact with him. And became, I had been interested in the story but became more interested in the story of how—of his report and whether the President had ignored that report in opting for a military intervention in Iraq.

Q *Now, I want to display on the screen what has been admitted into evidence as DX-709-B. [I] ask—is that a copy of the column that you wrote concerning Ambassador Wilson's mission to Niger?*

A It appears to be.

Q *. . . In paragraph 6 of your article you wrote, "Wilson never worked for the CIA, but his wife, Valerie Plame, is an Agency operative on weapons of mass destruction. Two senior Administration officials told me his wife suggested sending Wilson to Niger to investigate the Italian report. The CIA says its Counterproliferation officials selected Wilson and asked his wife to contact him. 'I will not answer any questions about my wife,' Wilson told me."*

With respect to your statement that "two senior Administration officials" told you that his wife suggested sending Wilson to Niger, who were the two senior Administration officials?

A Both of those officials have signed waivers specifically involved in this case, so I am free to give their names. They were the then Deputy Secretary of State, Richard Armitage, and Senior White House Aide Karl Rove.

Q *Now, I would like to start first with how you came to speak with Mr. Armitage during which he gave you information concerning Ambassador Wilson's wife. Could you relate the background of that conversation to the jurors?*

A I had been trying to get an appointment to have a conversation with Secretary Armitage since the Bush Administration started, the year 2001. And he had not only declined to see me but indicated it wasn't because he was too busy. He just didn't want to see me. After 9-11, I tried again and again. I got rebuffed.

Then, at the end of June—the last week of June of 2003—his office contacted my office and said that he would see me. I had not pressed the case in a couple of years. And we made an appointment for July the 8th, a Tuesday afternoon in his office at the State Department.

Q *Tell us what you recall about your July 8, 2003 conversation with Mr. Armitage at his office at the State Department.*

A The only people in the room were Secretary Armitage and me. There were no aides. There was no tape recorders on either side. I did not take notes. It was . . . by stipulation, [in interview on] background, that is to say . . . I assumed I could write what was said. But that I wouldn't be able to quote him or identify him. And we discussed a broad range of subjects, far beyond the scope of this case.

. . . I had decided by then I was probably going to write a column about Ambassador Wilson's mission to Niger. And I asked him several questions about that.

Q *What, if anything, did he tell you with respect to Ambassador Wilson's wife?*

A At one point[,] . . . we had talked about Ambassador Wilson's mission. I asked him, I said, "How is it possible? Why in the world did they name Ambassador Wilson when he had been a staffer in the Clinton National Security Council?" He was believed to be critical of President Bush—that he had no experience in nuclear policy, [and] this was an alleged purchase of yellowcake uranium.

He had not been in Niger since he was a very junior foreign service officer in the 1970s. So it seemed an odd choice. At that time Secretary Armitage said, "Well, it was suggested by his wife Valerie, who was employed in the Counter Proliferation division at the CIA."

Q *. . . Do you specifically recall that Mr. Armitage referred to Ambassador Wilson's wife by name?*

A Yes, as Valerie, no last name.

Q *Did there come a time when you learned her last name?*

A Yes.

Q *How did you come to learn her last name?*

A I looked up by Ambassador Wilson's entry in *Who's Who in America,* and it was listed as Valerie Plame.

Q *So you just went to a book where Ambassador Wilson was listed and his wife was identified as Valerie Plame?*

A That's correct.

Q *Mr. Armitage did not give you the last name?*

A Correct.

Q *You used the term "agency operative" to describe Mrs. Wilson in your column. Did that come from Mr. Armitage?*

A No, it didn't. I refer to people probably too much as "operatives." I have politicians I refer to as "political operatives." It was, it didn't indicate that I had any knowledge of her being an intelligence operative but an employee of the CIA.

Q *At the time you wrote the article, did you have any knowledge that Mrs. Wilson was covert or classified?*

A No.

Q *So, it's fair to say Mr. Armitage was the primary source for the information in your article concerning the fact that Mrs. Wilson worked at the CIA?*

A That's correct.

Q *Did you have a confirming source?*

A Yes, I did.

Q *Who was that?*

A That was Karl Rove.

Q *Who was Karl Rove in the year 2003?*

A [In] 2003, he was the Senior Advisor to the President on a wide variety of subjects . . .

Q *Was he a personal friend of yours in 2003?*

A No, I wouldn't call him a personal friend. I would call him a very good source. And I talked to him about two or three times a week at that time.

Q *Now, when did you speak with Mr. Rove in connection with your story about Ambassador Wilson?*

A I called his office immediately after I got back to the office from the State Department. And I can never remember getting Mr. Rove on the first bounce, but he always called back.

I have no clear recollection whether it was that day or the next day. I think it was that day that he returned the call, the same Tuesday.

Q *Okay. Can you tell us what you recall about the conversation you had with Mr. Rove on the next day, which would have been July 9th?*

A When we had our full conversation, . . . it could have been the next day or might yet have been that day I have not been able to pin that down . . . So we went over a number of things. But mainly, I was interested in the Wilson mission to Niger.

I asked him several questions about that and about Administration policy, [he] usually gave terse answers. Then I also asked him about, near the end of the conversation, I believe, about Ambassador Wilson's wife. I asked him if he knew—I commented that I . . . had been told she was an employee of the Counterproliferation Division of the CIA and [she] suggested the mission for her husband.

Q *What did he say?*

A He said, "Oh, you know about that too?"

Q *Now, based on your prior relationship with Mr. Rove as a source, did you take that as confirmation?*

A I took that as confirmation. When I said something that he said was not true, he would say "no, that's not true." We didn't have very lengthy conversations. He usually gave me a quick answer one way or the other, and I took that as a clear affirmation.

Q *But that, it was an affirmation again based on a long-standing relationship of many conversations?*

MR. FITZGERALD: Objection, leading.

THE COURT: Sustained, leading.

By Mr. Wells:

Q *To what extent did your long-standing relationship factor in with respect to your decision to take that as confirmation?*

A I knew how—we had a, particularly since he came to the White House, we had a modus operandi, you might say, where I knew without him getting into a long dissertation, I knew when he was confirming something or rejecting something or at least I felt that way. And I was very confident of it, if he didn't know about it, he would say "I've never heard about that" or "I don't know anything about that." When he said, "Oh, you know that too," I took that as confirmation.

Q *I want to go now to your conversations, if any, with Mr. Libby during the week of July 7th. My first question[:] did you also speak with Mr. Libby during the week of July 7th?*

A Yes, sir.

Q *And what was your relationship at that time in July of 2003 with Mr. Libby?*

A I had never had any contact that I can remember with Mr. Libby until the election of Vice President Cheney in 2000. I then had some contacts with him and a couple of social events. I asked him out to lunch . . . one time . . . He wrote a novel; I went to his book party. I called him a couple or three times during that year about questions. That was about the extent of it.

WELLS SHOWS NOVAK a phone record of a one-minute call from Novak to Libby at 4:46 p.m. on July 8, 2003, and Novak explains he left a message and spoke with Libby the next day:

Q *Do you have a recollection of talking to Mr. Libby following your placing a call to him on July 8, 2003?*

A Yes. I believe I talked to him on the next day, July 9th. I believe he returned the call.

Q *Please describe to the jurors your recollection of your conversation with Mr. Libby the next day when he returned the call?*

A I was trying to find out some more information about Ambassador Wilson's mission to Niger and the Vice President's connection with it. And the thing that is most memorable about the call is that I asked Mr. Libby if he might be helpful to me in establishing a timeline on the sixteen words that appeared in the State of the Union Address as to when they came in, who proposed it—sort of a consecutive account of what happened that I could put in the column.

I interpreted him to say that he thought he could be helpful and he would try to find out what he could . . . That was the impression I received from him.

Q *In the context of talking to Mr. Libby about Mr. Wilson's trip to Niger, did the topic of where Ambassador Wilson's wife worked come up?*

A I don't remember exactly. I might have raised that question. What I am absolutely confident is I got no help and no confirmation from Mr. Libby on that issue. The reason I'm fuzzy as to whether I brought it up is that I talk to a lot of people in government and politics every day. And . . . usually, a lot of them are not very helpful to me.

I kind of discard unhelpful conversations in my memory bank. So I might have asked him about it, and he said no. Or I might not have asked him about it, I just don't remember.

Q *It's fair to say that you have a clear recollection, as you sit there today, that he gave you no information about her?*

A I'm sure he gave me no information about her.

Q *If you might have asked him about the wife, do you mean by that, you might have asked him if he had heard that the wife worked at the CIA?*

A I might have.

Q *I just want to put on the screen a timeline that reflects that, on July 8th, you talked to Mr. Armitage. Then, on July 9th, you talked to Mr. Rove. Also on July 9th, you talked to Mr. Libby. Are those dates, to the best of your recollection, correct?*

A I am not sure about the Rove conversation. It might have been on the 8th or the 9th. I'm not positive on that.

Q *Thank you.*

Now, could I have Mr. Novak's article back on the screen. Blow paragraph 6 up.

Now, paragraph 6 reads, "The CIA says its Counterproliferation officials selected Wilson and asked his wife to contact him."

Now, I'm not going to ask you the name of the person you talked to, but is it fair to say you wrote that statement—

MR. FITZGERALD: Objection, Your Honor. May we approach?
(Bench conference is sealed and redacted.)
(Open court.)

By Mr. Wells:
Q *Mr. Novak, I want to see the front of the article. Is there a date on it?*
A No, apparently there is no date.

Q *The article says,* Chicago Sun-Times, *Monday, July 14, 2003. Mr. Novak, when did you write your July 14th column?*

A I wrote it the morning of Friday, July 11th.

Q *After you wrote the column on the morning of Friday, July 11th, what did you do with it?*

A . . . [I]mmediately after I finished writing it, it was e-mailed to my syndicate in Los Angeles, Creators News Syndicate . . .

Q *What do they then do with your article?*

A An editor goes over it. After a while, calls me back and we discuss further changes I might want to make and a second reading, a final reading of the column, changes that the editor wants to make with my agreement, and then, in its final version, it is given to the Associated Press for distribution to the clients who buy my column.

Q *Approximately how many clients?*

A It's over a hundred newspapers.

WELLS ASKS NOVAK about the process of sending the piece over the wires, there are a series of objections from the prosecution, and eventually Wells asks Novak just about the process of how it is done:

A Usually, as soon as the column is cleared, the edited version is cleared between the editor and me. It is immediately given to the Associated Press, and it's on the wires quite soon, within an hour I would say . . .

Q *With respect to the usual practice, after you wrote an article, at what time of day would it have been distributed on the Associated Press wire?*

A It depends on when I wrote the column and got it to the syndicate. In this case, my recollection is that, since I had a really busy afternoon, I wanted to finish the column by noon. It was sent [at] noon, and the editing was done before 1:00 o'clock eastern time. So following usual practice, it would have gone out on the wires a little bit thereafter.

Q *Now, once the article is put on the A.P. wire, what is your understanding as to whether or not the news outlets that have received it can print it?*

A It is . . . called [in] the news business an embargo and it is not to be printed until, in this case, Monday morning's newspapers.

Q *To your understanding, are people in the newsrooms permitted to review it?*

A All they have to do is take a look at it . . . Anybody who subscribes to the column, that becomes general knowledge of the editors of that newspaper or anybody else in the paper that happens to see the column.

MR. WELLS: I have no further questions.

MR. JEFFRESS: One moment, Your Honor.

(There was a pause in the proceedings.)

By Mr. Wells:

Q *With respect to the conversations you had with Mr. Libby, Mr. Armitage and Mr. Rove, when did you first testify about those conversations to Mr. Fitzgerald?*

A I first testified to Mr. Fitzgerald as differentiated from the FBI.

Q *Let's start with the FBI.*

A I believe I haven't reviewed those dates and I don't have a terribly good memory for dates. But I would guess that I talked to the FBI, to Inspector Eckenrode, a couple of months after the investigation started, which would have been in October, starting October 1st of 2003.

I talked to him subsequent to that. At that time, I did not mention the names of any of my sources. I talked for the first time—some months later and into the new year, I can't give you an exact date—with Mr. Fitzgerald. And at that time, my attorneys were informed before we went into the inquiry that they would have waivers only in the case of Mr. Armitage and Mr. Rove.

> *So there was no point in dissembling since they already knew the sources and had found out one way or another on their own.*

In other words, they knew my sources. So there was no point in dissembling since they already knew the sources and had found out one way or another on their own. And that's when I, for the first time, discussed with federal authorities who my sources were in this case, discussed it with Mr. Fitzgerald.

Q *I show you a copy of your Grand Jury testimony, dated February 25—*

MR. FITZGERALD: We'll stipulate to the date, February 25, 2004.

THE COURT: Very well.

Q *The Government has stipulated that you testified before the Grand Jury on February 25, 2004. Is that the first time that you testified in the Grand Jury concerning Mr. Armitage and Mr. Rove?*

A Yes, sir.

Q *And you told the Grand Jurors that Mr. Armitage had been your primary source and Mr. Rove your secondary source?*

A Yes, sir.

Q *Did there come a time when you received a waiver with respect to Mr. Libby?*

A Yes, sir, at some time I did receive a waiver from Mr. Libby indeed.

Q *Do you recall when that was?*

A No, I don't.

Q *And did there come a time when you testified in the Grand Jury concerning Mr. Libby?*

A Yes, sir.

Q *And you told the Grand Jury that Mr. Libby had not given you any information—*

MR. FITZGERALD: Objection, Your Honor.

Q *—about the wife?*

(Bench conference is sealed and redacted.)
(Open court.)

MR. WELLS: We're going to work out a stipulation. I have no further questions.

UNDER CROSS-EXAMINATION by Fitzgerald, Novak clarifies his understanding that when his columns go out on the wire, they are not publicly available, and then Fitzgerald asks Novak about his reaction to his first encounter with Wilson in the green room of *Meet the Press* on July 6, 2003 and whether that and some other specific information was a part of his conversation that week with Rove:

Q *Did you have any feeling when you left the green room that you didn't like Mr. Wilson?*

A Well, what I—can I give my feeling of how I felt about him when I saw him?

Q *Sure.*

A He was, usually in the green room people are circumspect, reading papers, reading notes. He was giving his opinion at some length on how things had been done in the Clinton administration versus the Bush in a very loud voice. I thought that it was kind of an obnoxious performance even though I kept it to myself.

Q *Did you share that experience and your views with Mr. Rove when you spoke to him that week if you recall?*

A I think I might have. I'm not a hundred percent sure, but I believe I might have.

Q *Do you know if, during your conversation with Mr. Rove that week, you discussed anything about a 1999 trade delegation from Iraq to Niger with Mr. Rove?*

A I think I did because that was part of the whole issue of the question of whether there had been an attempt to buy yellowcake uranium, an Iraqi attempt to buy yellowcake uranium from Niger.

IT IS UNCLEAR WHY FITZGERALD asks Novak this last question, though it is intriguing because Novak had reported on the Iraqi delegation, in slightly garbled form, in his original July 14, 2003 column, explicitly noting that the report from Wilson's trip, which noted the delegation, remained classified. (In his Grand Jury testimony, Libby took note of the way Novak garbled this information.) It should be noted that, though Novak contends in his testimony that Wilson hadn't been in Niger since the 1970s, he had actually undertaken government work in Niger in the 1990s.

Finally, Fitzgerald gets Novak to acknowledge no specific recollection that he might have indeed told Libby about Plame, while underlining that Novak did speak with Libby on July 9—the jury had already heard Libby in the grand jury testify to no recollection of having spoken with Novak that week:

Q *As you sit here now, is it fair to say you have no specific recollection of discussing Ambassador Wilson's wife with Mr. Libby that week?*
A I don't have any specific recollection, as I said in testimony, I might have raised it, but I am not sure. I don't have a specific recollection.

Q *The one thing you are clear on though is that you did talk to Mr. Libby that week?*
A Yes, sir.

Q *So it would be accurate to say that you and Mr. Libby spoke that week?*
A Yes, sir.

Q *And inaccurate to say that you did not?*
A Yes, sir.

MR. FITZGERALD: Thank you.

THE DEFENSE'S VERY BRIEF REDIRECT simply brings out the fact that Novak's column would have been available in-house at some of the largest newspapers in the country on July 11.

The questions from the jury posed by the judge bring out Novak's contact with the CIA spokesman that week in July 2003, and the follow-ups from both sides raise the role of Richard Hohlt as a go-between for Novak and the White House:

THE COURT: Mr. Novak, without relating what somebody would have said in response to what you may have said, let me just ask you—did you, once you learned about Joe Wilson's wife and the fact that she worked for the CIA on July 8, 2003, did you discuss that information with anyone besides Karl Rove prior to your article being published on the 14th of July?
THE WITNESS: Yes, Your Honor.
THE COURT: And who were those individuals who you spoke to?
THE WITNESS: I spoke to Bill Harlow, who was the . . . spokesman for the CIA.
THE COURT: Anybody else?
THE WITNESS: I believe that was the only other one. Excuse me, Your Honor. I testified that I might have asked Mr. Libby about it, but I don't have a clear recollection because I didn't get a positive response from him.
THE COURT: Follow up?

By Mr. Wells:

Q *Do you recall talking to a Mr. Rick Hohlt?*
A Yes, sir.

Q *Who is Rick Hohlt?*
A Rick Hohlt is a lobbyist and a very close friend of mine and I talk to him about every day.

Q *After you learned that Mrs. Wilson worked at the CIA, did you have conversations with Mr. Hohlt about it?*
A About Mrs. Wilson?

Q *About your article? I'll rephrase the question. The article that you wrote on the 11th, did you give Mr. Hohlt a draft of the article on the 11th?*
A Yes, I did.

Q *So that's the article that referred to Mrs. Wilson working at the CIA, right?*
A Yes, sir.

Q *Mr. Hohlt had the article in his hand about 4 o'clock that day?*
A I would imagine about then, yes.

Q *Mr. Hohlt is a lobbyist about town?*
A Yes, sir.

Q *Have you described Mr. Hohlt before as a gossip?*
A I wouldn't be that critical. He talks to a lot of people about a lot of things, including me. He is a good news source.

Q *He is a good news source. He talks to a lot of newspaper reporters and media people?*
A Yes.

MR. WELLS: No further questions.
THE COURT: Anything else?

Recross examination.
By Mr. Fitzgerald:

Q *Did you have an understanding with Mr. Hohlt about what he could do with the draft or the copy of the article?*
A No, sir. I didn't have any understanding with him on that, no.

Q *Did you have an understanding with him that he was not supposed to share it with anyone else?*
A No, sir. I didn't have that understanding. If I could add, I had assumed he would not share it with anybody else. But I didn't, there was not an agreement made between us . . .

Q *As far as you know, did he ever tell you he had shared it with anyone or spoke to anyone about it as far as you know?*

A I have a vague recollection that he had indicated that he had told the White House, whoever the White House was, that there was an interesting piece coming out. That's my recollection of all he said.

Q *When did he tell you that he might have told the White House that an interesting piece was coming out?*

A I think the conversation that I had with him [was] on that Friday. That's my recollection. I'm not terribly confident of that, though.

Q *But your belief is that he told the White House on Friday that an interesting piece was coming out?*

A I believe, I think he indicated that to me, yes.

MR. FITZGERALD: Thank you.
THE COURT: Thank you, sir.
THE WITNESS: Thank you.

GLENN KESSLER

GLENN KESSLER IS a Pulitzer Prize–winning diplomatic correspondent for *The Washington Post*. Kessler is one of the reporters who spoke with Libby during July 2003 but with whom Libby did not bring up Wilson's wife. He interviewed Libby on July 12 (while he was at the Washington Zoo with three young children) and July 18th. Fitzgerald had pressed Libby fairly hard during his grand jury testimony on whether he had leaked information about Plame to Kessler.

After giving his journalistic credentials, Kessler recounts, under questioning by Brochin for the defense, his July 12, 2003 telephone interview with Libby. Touching on the ground rules, Kessler then explains the core of the conversation:

Q *What were the ground rules for your discussion with Mr. Libby?*

A Well, this is complicated as it always is in these matters. Scooter said to me, he was talking to me off the record. Now, this was for an article and I had previous conversations with both Cathie Martin and her predecessor, Mary Matalin, who explained to me that when Scooter said "off the record" he really meant "deep background."

Q *In your experience as a diplomatic correspondent, was it common for government officials to ask to speak to you either off the record or on background or some form, in seeking some form of confidentiality?*

A Almost every single conversation I have in Washington is on background or deep background . . .

Q *Speaking generally, did your conversation with Mr. Libby involve issues relating to Iraq and post-war planning and the role of the Office of the Vice President in those subjects?*

A Yes, uh-huh.

Q *Did Mr. Libby say anything to you about Ambassador Joseph Wilson's wife during that conversation?*

A No, he didn't.

Q *Did you say anything to him about Ambassador Joseph Wilson's wife during that interview?*

A No, I did not.

Q *Are you certain about that?*

A I'm certain.

BROCHIN THEN GETS KESSLER to confirm that Kessler was not the reporter referred to in *The Washington Post* report of October 12, 2003 as having received a leak about Wilson's wife on July 12, 2003. Walter Pincus had previously testified that it was, in fact, he who had received that leak, from Ari Fleischer.

Fitzgerald's cross-examination gets Kessler to confirm that he had an arrangement for being deposed similar to Tim Russert. Fitzgerald also asks Kessler about his memory and notes from his conversation with Libby, culminating in questions about his reaction to Novak's column that appear to be designed to set up an echo with Russert's similar testimony:

Q *Is it also . . . fair to say that one of the reasons you are certain you didn't discuss Mr. Wilson's wife with Mr. Libby on July 12th is you had a reaction to a later event when you learned about Mr. Wilson's wife. Is that correct?*

A Right.

Q *Can you tell us how you learned about Mr. Wilson's wife?*

A I read it in the newspaper on the 14th.

Q *And which newspaper and which column?*

A It was *The Washington Post*. It was the Robert Novak column on the 14th.

Q *What was your reaction when you read it?*

A I said, "Boy, this is interesting."

Q *Knowing that when you read Mr. Novak's column and said, "Boy, this is interesting," that reinforces to you that there is no way you had a conversation about Mr. Wilson's wife with Mr. Libby two days before?*

MR. BROCHIN: Objection.
THE COURT: Overruled.
THE WITNESS: I didn't say to myself, "Oh, that's what Scooter told me." I said, "Oh, this is news to me."

By Mr. Fitzgerald:

Q *So that reinforces to you that you had no such conversation with Mr. Libby, correct?*

A Correct.

MR. FITZGERALD: Thank you.

THE DEFENSE'S REDIRECT QUESTIONING briefly underlines the role of Kessler's notes in refreshing his recollection, and Kessler is excused.

The next witness is Evan Thomas, an editor and reporter at *Newsweek*, who is on the witness stand for mere moments. Thomas testifies that he has no recollection of having spoken with or gotten a message from Libby on July 12, 2003, although phone records show that Libby (or someone he was with) called Thomas for 35 seconds that day; and that Libby did not mention Wilson's wife to Thomas at any point during that week in July 2003. There is no cross-examination, and the next witness, Carl Ford, is called to be questioned by Bourelli for the defense.

CARL FORD

IN 2003 CARL FORD WAS the head of the State Department's intelligence unit, the Bureau of Intelligence and Research. He was tasked by Marc Grossman with coming up with information on Wilson's trip, and produced the so-called INR memo that identified Valerie Wilson as a CIA employee involved in her husband's mission. Ford was brought on by the defense to contradict certain key aspects of testimony Marc Grossman had given under cross-examination: Ford placed the whole episode in June 9–11, contradicting Grossman's testimony that his initial contact with Ford came at the end of May; Ford testified that Grossman never mentioned Libby to him, nor did Grossman specifically request a written response; and Ford testified that he had no contact with Walter Kansteiner on the matter.

After explaining his job and role heading INR, Ford is asked about Grossman's request to him and its timing:

By Mr. Bourelli:

Q *Let me direct your attention to approximately June of 2003. Did there come a point in time in June 2003 where Marc Grossman requested that you provide him information about issues relating to Iraq's attempt to acquire yellowcake from Niger?*

A Yes, that's my recollection.

Q *And can you tell us the precise date on which he made that request?*

A Well, it was the first week or so in June.

Q *What were the circumstances under which he made that request? Was that an in-person request?*

A Yes.

Q *And is there anything that you recall about that particular day that helps you fix the date?*

A It was an unusual request to begin with. I had a handful of requests from Secretary Grossman over the previous two years but never about weapons of mass destruction in Iraq and didn't receive any after that. So just the notion that he was asking for information about that particular issue was unusual.

Q *Was there a senior staff meeting that day?*

A There was.

THE DEFENSE SHOWS Ford Grossman's calendar from June 9, already entered into evidence by the defense when questioning Grossman, and Ford confirms that that was the date of Grossman's initial request to him. Bourelli asks Ford about that request:

Q *Did Mr. Grossman—do you recall Mr. Grossman ever asking you or telling you that the purpose of him asking that information was because Scooter Libby had requested the information?*

A No, he did not.

Q *Is that the type of information you would have recalled had he done that?*

A Yes, I would have recalled that.

Q *After Secretary Grossman asked you to find out that information for him, what next did you do?*

A Well, I came back to my office and I called the people in INR responsible for following the Iraq weapons of mass destruction issue. The director of that office, a gentleman named Neal Silver, came over. I gave him the assignment that I had just received from Secretary Grossman.

Q *At some point in time was a memo created to capture the information that Secretary Grossman had requested?*

A Yes, it was.

Q *Mr. Ford, I'm showing you what's been entered into evidence as DX-71 and ask if you recognize DX-71?*

A Yes, I do.

Q *What is DX-71?*

A This is the memo that INR prepared and submitted to Secretary Grossman . . .

Q *How long, to the best of your recollection, did it take for you and your staff to prepare DX-71.1 [see appendix] after Mr. Grossman requested information about Niger and yellowcake?*

A It took approximately less than a day.

THE DIRECT EXAMINATION concludes with Ford noting that he had no contact with Walter Kansteiner of the State Department about the matter:

Q *In connection with preparing the memo that's dated June 10, 2003, DX-71, . . . did you have any meetings or any relations with Walter Kansteiner in connection with creating that memo?*
A No, I did not.

Q *Was there ever a point that you can recall where Secretary Grossman indicated to you that the information you provided with respect to his request was somehow incomplete and needed, and he asked that you work with Walter Kansteiner or somebody else in the African Bureau to correct it?*
A I certainly don't recall anything of that nature. I don't recall him even saying anything to me about the memo after it went to his office.

THE PROSECUTION'S TWO QUESTIONS in cross-examination get Ford to confirm that he gave the INR memo with information about Wilson's wife to Grossman on June 10 or 11—the implication being it was in time for Grossman to share the information about Wilson's wife with Libby. Ford is excused and, with no more witnesses available at the moment, the jury is excused for the day as well.

The parties continue their dispute over just how the defense will be able to present the memory defense through witnesses other than Libby. One intriguing disclosure is Fitzgerald's suggestion that at this point not just John Hannah, who would ultimately testify, but also Eric Edelman might be a witness for the defense, though he would not ultimately be called. The prosecution also asks the judge to consider allowing them to enter evidence that Valerie Plame worked in the CIA's Counter Proliferation Division. The issue arises in part because of Judith Miller's testimony that her notes from her July 8 conversation with Libby refer to Wilson's wife working at WINPAC, and it appears that the defense is contemplating calling a CIA witness, perhaps Bill Harlow, who will give evidence that Plame did not work in WINPAC.

Shortly thereafter, the trial recesses for the day.

*

FEBRUARY 13, 2007

JILL ABRAMSON

BEFORE THE JURY and the witness are brought in for the day, the judge takes up the issue of whether the prosecution would be allowed to introduce evidence that Plame worked in the Counter Proliferation Division of the CIA, which remains undecided, as well as the issue of Andrea Mitchell's testimony. The judge rules in essence against the defense on the latter, though he permits them the opportunity to examine Mitchell outside the presence of the jury, which the defense opts not to do.

Jill Abramson, now managing editor of *The New York Times*, was in the summer of 2003 the paper's Washington Bureau Chief. She was the editor for the team of reporters working on prewar intelligence on Iraq and the failure to find WMD in Iraq of which Judith Miller was a part. Abramson was brought in for one reason—to contradict Miller's testimony that Miller had gone to Abramson to recommend the *Times* pursue a story on the Wilsons. The prosecution has an even briefer cross-examination that seeks to rehabilitate Miller's version of the story:

By Mr. Jeffress:

Q *Do you recall that on July 6th, 2003,* The New York Times *carried an op-ed column . . . by Joe Wilson . . . called, "What I Didn't Find in Africa"?*

A Yes.

Q *And did that article cause something of a stir?*

A It caused a stir, and in the ensuing week, we had reporters chasing that story.

Q *In the week that followed that article, did Judith Miller come to you to recommend that* The New York Times *pursue a story about whether Joe Wilson's wife works at the CIA and, if so, what she does there?*

A I have no recollection of such a conversation.

MR. JEFFRESS: I pass the witness.
THE COURT: Cross-examination?

By Ms. Bonamici:

Q *Good morning, Ms. Abramson.*

A Good morning.

Q *In your dealings with Ms. Miller, I wonder if you can tell me if you sometimes found yourself tuning out of conversations with her?*

A I don't remember a specific example of that, but it's possible that I occasionally tuned her out.

MS. BONAMICI: Thank you.

ABRAMSON IS EXCUSED and before the next witness is brought in, Jeffress reads a stipulation agreed to by both sides into the record; it addresses the issue of where Plame worked in the CIA:

MR. JEFFRESS: If the court please, I would like now to read a stipulation that has been signed by the defendant and the counsel for the government and defense.
THE COURT: Very well. You may consider what is going to be read to you as undisputed evidence.
MR. JEFFRESS: The stipulation is as follows: "The weapons intelligence nonproliferation and arms control center, otherwise known as WINPAC, is a center within the Central Intelligence Agency. The records of the CIA reflect that Valerie Wilson did not work for, nor was she detailed to WINPAC in 2003 or at any other time."

JOHN HANNAH

JOHN HANNAH REPLACED LIBBY as Vice President Cheney's National Security Advisor when Libby was indicted in 2005. In 2003 he was Libby's deputy for national security affairs to do with the Middle East, but because Libby's principal deputy Eric Edelman left in early June of that year, Hannah took on the duties of the principal deputy until a replacement was found. The key reason Hannah is brought in as a witness is to testify to how busy Libby was working on very sensitive and important matters areas during June and July 2003, as well as how busy he himself is in just one of the two jobs Libby had in the Vice President's office. Hannah also testified to Libby having an awful memory for certain things in order to bolster Libby's defense that he could have misremembered or forgotten how he received and handled the information about Plame.

The cross-examination by Fitzgerald brings out some information adverse to Libby, including Hannah's testimony that Libby's time was very precious and it was difficult to get time with him during the workday. This is to the prosecution's advantage in suggesting that Libby taking several hours to talk with Miller meant it was a particularly important meeting to him. In questioning, it also emerges that Libby was focused on Wilson in June and had learned about Wilson and the details of the report from his trip. The jury's questioning also elicits an answer from Hannah indicating that, though Libby was bad at remembering the source of information, he had an excellent grasp of facts and arguments—which could suggest that while Libby might possibly forget where he had learned information, it was less likely that he would be surprised by information from Tim Russert that he had already heard on multiple occasions.

The substance of the defense's direct examination begins by highlighting the fact that Libby was both Cheney's National Security Advisor (NSA) and his Chief of Staff during the period the defense was asking about—May 2003 to March 2004, the bookends between when the events alleged by the prosecution began and when Libby finished his grand jury testimony.

By Mr. Cline:

Q *Is it fair to say, then, that during the period that we are talking about, May of 2003 through March of 2004, Mr. Libby had essentially two full-time jobs?*

A From my perspective, yes.

HANNAH HIGHLIGHTS all the factors that would have made Libby's day as Cheney's NSA extraordinarily busy. Then, questioned about the period that he worked closely with Libby, Hannah speaks to Libby's personal traits:

Q *I think you have said several times now, [you] worked closely with Mr. Libby for several years, correct?*

A Yes.

Q *Did you have an opportunity during those years to observe how well he remembered things?*

A I did. I had experience with that.

Q *And what did you observe?*

A On certain things, Scooter just had an awful memory.

Q *Can you give us an example from your experience?*

A Times too many to count, I would come in to Scooter in the morning, and we would discuss an issue. I would give my views on it, give a policy recommendation, give an analysis, and show up six, seven hours later that evening, and have Scooter in a very excited fashion repeat back to me the analysis, the recommendations, and have no idea that I had actually told him that the very same morning. It was very striking.

Q *Would you sometimes call that to his attention?*

A I think I did it on occasion, just in exasperation, but at some point in time—that was Mr. Libby.

HANNAH THEN WALKS THROUGH Libby's typical workday between May 2003 and March 2004:

Q *Is it fair to say that a lot of Mr. Libby's time during the day when he was in Washington was consumed with meetings of one kind or another?*

A Yes. Certainly at the time that you are talking about, we would . . . in any single week, have multiple meetings, interagency meetings of the deputies committees or the principal meetings of the National Security Council.

THE DEFENSE AGAIN, as it does repeatedly, recalls that what Hannah is describing is just one half of Libby's job in OVP, before turning to questioning Hannah about Deputies Committee and other meetings and other manifestations of how busy Libby was. In this connection, Hannah confirms that several exhibits entered into evidence are memos written by Hannah for Libby on various national security subjects. Libby typically ended his work day fairly late in the evening—8 or 9 p.m., if not later:

Q *Is it fair to say that, based on your experience, sometimes the only chance you got to see him in the course of his day was in the evening when the press of business had slowed down a little?*

A Absolutely. That was certainly the best time, if you wanted to get Scooter's attention, to go see him.

HAVING DEALT WITH a typical day for Libby, the defense turns, after a brief break for the court reporter, to the matters Libby was dealing with during the period that Plame was outed, before launching into a line of questioning about the details of what Libby was interested in:

Q *I want to go through this with you, but, as you know, when we get into this area, we begin to get into areas that might involve classified information. So with the permission of the government and the court, I am going to ask you a lot of leading questions that will just call for "yes" or "no" or "I don't know" answers from you. Okay?*

A Okay.

MR. FITZGERALD: We don't object, Judge.
THE COURT: Very well.

THE DEFENSE MOVES INTO asking Hannah about the many subject areas that he had to focus on in his job. In national security alone, these included multiple issues related to Iraq, Iran, Israel and Palestine, Al-Qaeda, Pakistan, Turkey and Liberia.

The defense asks questions designed to sum up its account of Libby's heavy responsibilities at the time of the outing of Plame:

Q *Now, we have, in the course of our time together this morning, discussed a number of national security and foreign policy issues, correct?*

A Correct.

Q *And some of the issues we have discussed were ones for which you had personal responsibility, and others other deputies were responsible for?*

A That's correct.

Q *Mr. Libby was responsible for all of these issues?*

A Yes.

Q *And is it fair to say that there were other national security and foreign policy issues beyond the ones that we have discussed this morning for which he had responsibility?*

A Absolutely.

Q *And is it fair to say that what we have been discussing this morning was part of his job as the national security advisor to the Vice President?*

A Yes.

Q *And that was half his job?*

A It was certainly part of his job, in addition to a full range of other responsibilities he had, yes.

Q *Including a full-time job as the Chief of Staff, correct?*

A Yes . . .

Q *One more question. We have been talking about national security and foreign policy issues. Mr. Libby also had responsibilities in the domestic arena, did he not?*

A Yes, he did.

Q *And those are areas that you didn't have any responsibility for, correct?*

A That's correct.

THE PROSECUTION CROSS-EXAMINES Hannah, beginning with questioning Hannah about whether Libby's role as Chief of Staff to Cheney meant protecting the Vice President and his office from public criticism, before cleverly using Hannah's testimony about how valuable Libby's time was to imply that the time Libby blocked out for Judith Miller on July 8 meant it was of unusual significance:

By Mr. Fitzgerald:

Q *If we could talk for a moment about the scope of Mr. Libby's job as Chief of Staff as you understood it. Is it fair to say that part of Mr. Libby's job as Chief of Staff during the relevant time frame was to protect the Office of Vice President and the Vice President from public criticism?*

A I guess it's not the formulation I would use, but they would need to go out and truthfully defend the office from unfair criticism.

Q *. . . [I]t would be important for Mr. Libby to respond to criticism, especially if viewed unfair and especially if the criticism was directed at the integrity of either the Vice President or the office of Vice President; is that fair to say?*

A That's probably fair, yes.

Q *And it would be especially important if the criticism went to the integrity of the administration, the Office of the Vice President or the Vice President himself in terms of the rationale for the war in Iraq, correct?*

A It would be important to push back on those kinds of issues, yes.

Q *. . . And you mentioned to Mr. Cline that the best time you found that you could see Mr. Libby would be in the evening, correct, because of everything else that was going on?*

A That's correct.

Q *And particularly if you focus on the week following July 6th, when, if you look at what was going on, there was a war in Iraq, there are terror threats from Al Qaeda and others in the post-9/11 environment, there is this crisis in Liberia, there is this crisis in Turkey—is it fair to say that if, during that week, you went to Mr. Libby and said, "Look, how about tomorrow morning we take an hour or two, go out for coffee and I download you on what your thinking is," that that just wasn't going to happen?*

A It would be harder, but I wouldn't want to say it wouldn't happen. Scooter was pretty good about, if I felt something was important, giving me time.

Q *And so if he gave someone an hour or two during that week, it was something that Mr. Libby thought would be important, correct?*

A Again, with regard to me, yes.

AFTER GETTING HANNAH TO CONFIRM that he has no recollection that Libby would have seen the memos on national security matters that Hannah had drawn up and that had been introduced as evidence, Fitzgerald focuses on Hannah and Libby's interaction over the memo Hannah drew up in June on Wilson's mission to Niger:

Q *. . . Around June 10th and 11th of 2003, do [you] recall that during the time frame following June 9th, 2003, that Mr. Libby asked you at that time to focus on researching what it was that the Office of the Vice President knew about a trip by a former ambassador to Niger?*

A Yes, he asked me about that.

Q *And is it fair to say that you went and canvassed people in the Office of Vice President to find out what they knew about the trip, and you learned that it didn't seem like people in the office knew about the trip prior to that time? Is that fair to say?*

A That's correct. Nobody has been aware of any envoy sent anywhere on behalf of the Vice President. Nobody had seen a report. Nobody was aware of a report....

Q *And is it fair to say that, as a result of the research that Mr. Libby asked you to do, you came across a report not written by Mr. Wilson, but a report about Ambassador Wilson's trip, correct?*

A Yes.

Q *And is it fair to say in this time frame following June 9th and the days after, you brought this report to Mr. Libby, correct?*

A Yes. The date is vague, but, yes, I would have brought it to him.

Q *Is it fair to say that when you brought the report to Mr. Libby, you are not sure you left him with the report, because when you went to describe the contents of the* *report, you came to understand that Mr. Libby already knew about what was described in the report about Wilson's trip, correct?*

A That's my recollection, yes.

Q *And it was your recollection and understanding at the time that, although Mr. Libby had asked you to find this out, by the time you got an answer back to him, he had found the answer out somewhere else, correct?*

A That was my impression, yes.

Q *...And what you also recall was that at the time you discussed the report about Ambassador Wilson's trip, one of the things that was foremost in Mr. Libby's mind at the time was the content of the report where it discussed a 1999 trip by a trade delegation from Iraq to Niger; is that correct?*

A Yes, that was something that definitely caught people's attention, yes.

Q *And I am focusing on Mr. Libby's attention at the time. Is it your recollection that when you went to discuss this report with Mr. Libby, one of the reasons you knew that he was familiar with it already was the fact that Mr. Libby was discussing with you the contents of the report which focused on the 1999 trip?*

A That's my recollection, yes.

Q *And this would be back in the early June time frame. [I]s [that] your understanding?*

A Yes, I think that second week in June.

Q *Is it fair to say that, in Mr. Libby's role, what was important to the Vice President was important to Mr. Libby?*

A Yes.

Q *Thank you.*

THE DEFENSE HAS ONE QUESTION in redirect and then Judge Walton poses questions from the jury, which are unusually revealing:

By Mr. Cline:

Q *Mr. Hannah, the report that Mr. Fitzgerald asked you about didn't say anything about Mr. Wilson's wife, did it?*

A It did not, no.

Q *Thank you.*

MR. CLINE: No further questions.

THE COURT: A couple questions, sir. Aside from Mr. Libby's difficulty with his memory, did his extensive involvement in Middle East affairs also lead you to have concerns about his effectiveness?

THE WITNESS: Never.

THE COURT: When Mr. Libby had memory lapses, what was said or done by you to trigger Mr. Libby's recall of the issues previously discussed but seemingly forgotten?

THE WITNESS: Again, it would often be the case that he was quite good at remembering ideas and concepts and arguments, and very bad at sort of figuring out where those arguments might have come from and how they may have come to him. So I think I would simply say, "Yes, that's a great idea because I told you this morning" . . .

THE COURT: Would Mr. Libby deny, acknowledge or debate that you had informed him of these particular matters earlier?

THE WITNESS: Never.

THE COURT: Based upon your observations, were there things that Mr. Libby had a good memory about?

THE WITNESS: Again, it's hard. This kind of thing that I just described was a fairly regular pattern with Scooter, but he was certainly very good at remembering his own arguments and key points—key factual points that he would want to be able to make in any kind of policy argument. He was very good at keeping those types of things in his head and keeping his arguments organized.

THE COURT: Were the national security issues being addressed during the period of May 2003 to March 2004 greater than or less than the usual amount or level of national security and foreign policy issues that are typically dealt with at the national security advisor level?

THE WITNESS: As I said, this period since September 11, 2001, has been, I think, particularly intense for any relative period of American foreign policy. I think that period in May and June was, again, particularly intense because of this initiative that the President had decided to take in Iraq, the invasion of Iraq, the liberation of Iraq and the aftermath of that, of having that many American forces in this country in such a major, major undertaking—it was a particularly fast-moving, intense period of time for high-level people in the United States government to try and manage American policy.

So I think it's fair to say it was a more intense period in an always intense environment.

AFTER A COUPLE OF QUESTIONS along similar lines, Hannah is excused and the jury leaves for lunch. The parties briefly address the defense's intention to put three CIA briefers on to discuss various specific intelligence matters they presented to Libby; the prosecution objects on the basis of the fact that Libby himself would not be testifying to the effect the briefings had on his state of mind. Court breaks for lunch.

Judge Walton declares his intention to let the jury go because the federal government has shut down because of bad winter weather. Wells for the defense makes a dramatic if not entirely unexpected announcement, and then Libby is heard from:

MR. WELLS: Prior to lunch, I indicated to the Court that I would be making certain recommendations to Mr. Libby with respect to the progress of his case. Then I hoped to be able to advise the Court after lunch about our intentions.

Over the lunch hour, Mr. Jeffress and I advised the lawyer for the Vice President that we did not intend to call the Vice President. We had told the Court if we had called, he would have been available to testify on Thursday. And we have released the Vice President as a potential witness and we advised him over lunch.

Mr. Jeffress and I also recommended to Mr. Libby that we believe, subject to putting on the briefers and certain documentary evidence, that we believe he should rest his case following the admission of that evidence.

Mr. Libby, after consulting with us and his wife, has indicated to us that it is his intention to follow our advice. That we will rest his case tomorrow following whatever Your Honor decides with respect to the briefers and certain other documentary evidence . . .

THE COURT: I believe I do have an obligation to inquire of Mr. Libby about him deciding not to testify.

Mr. Libby, I'm sure you understand, based upon your discussions with your lawyers and the fact that you are a lawyer yourself, that you fully appreciate that, under the United States Constitution, you have the absolute right to testify in your defense.

THE DEFENDANT: Yes, sir, I do.

THE COURT: Understanding that right, is it your decision, after consultation with counsel, to not testify in this trial?

THE DEFENDANT: Yes, sir. I thank you for the concern. I will follow the advice of my counsel.

THE COURT: Very well. Thank you.

WALTON HAS THE JURY BROUGHT IN just to excuse them and give them an update on the schedule. The parties then take up the issue of the CIA briefers' testimony about briefing Libby on specific terrorist threats, as well as the issue of a previously agreed-upon statement of relevant facts whose status has now been called into question because of Libby's decision not to testify. Walton reserves his rulings for the following day. The prosecution also objects to the defense's desire to introduce evidence to impeach Tim Russert's testimony, relating to benefits the defense wants to argue Russert received conditioning his testimony, including three videos from TV shows (and a transcript) where Russert appears to show he understands that witnesses must testify before a grand jury without a lawyer present, inconsistent with his testimony at trial. Walton again reserves his ruling. The defense also presents its desire to present the government's admission that NBC's Andrea Mitchell and David Gregory refused to be interviewed by the government and were not subpoenaed, in order to call into question the thoroughness of the government's investigation:

MR. WELLS: The final point relates to admissions by the Government where they provided counsel during discovery with admissions to the effect that, "We further advise you that reporters Andrea Mitchell, NBC, have declined to be interviewed and were not subpoenaed. And also we further advise you that David Gregory, NBC, has not been interviewed or subpoenaed."

I'll hand to your court clerk what has been marked as DX-1808, which is a redacted copy of the letter in which the Government makes those two statements.

THE COURT: You want this—

MR. WELLS: It can be either read or presented.

THE COURT: They refused to be interviewed by the Government also, right? Or they were interviewed by the Government?

MR. WELLS: No, sir. They were not interviewed.

THE COURT: So neither side had a chance to interview them?

MR. WELLS: No, no. What I want—I want it in to show that, during the investigation, Your Honor, when Mr. Russert was being interviewed in his deposition for 22 minutes, the Government already had been told in the Grand Jury that Ari Fleischer had told David Gregory. So they had that information in hand, that David Gregory, one of Mr. Russert's chief reporters, had been told that the wife worked at the CIA.

Mr. Fleischer testifie[d] in the Grand Jury in February of '04.

THE COURT: What inference are you asking to be drawn from this?

MR. WELLS: That the Government stood up in its opening statement and went on about the search for the truth and how they were trying to get to the bottom of things.

Wanted to understand the facts and what really happened. They then also admitted into the record the Department of Justice guidelines concerning the limitations on the Government and how they couldn't perhaps do everything that was necessary in the case because they had these guidelines to comply with.

So, they have talked, not only in the opening statement about their search for the truth, but they have also put in the record—

THE COURT: You're suggesting that the fact that they didn't subpoena these witnesses, that that fact should be construed adversely to the Government?

MR. WELLS: Absolutely, Your Honor.

IN THIS CONTEXT, there is some interesting discussion of the behind-the-scenes negotiations over opening statements:

THE COURT: I think they only presented that in reference to the witnesses who were actually called. And they only decided, as I understand, to do that because of some suggestions that were being made that somehow they had done something inappropriate as it related to the reporter who they called to testify.

MR. WELLS: Actually, it was in response, they said they wanted to put it in response to my opening, and I told them my opening remarks were in response to their opening remarks about telling this jury how they were on a search for the truth, and they were going to get to the bottom of it when they had in their possession evidence that David Gregory had been told about the wife.

WALTON IS SKEPTICAL of the argument on legal grounds having to do with the requirements to be met to argue about a missing witness. Wells insists:

MR. WELLS: They want to put the integrity of their search for the truth in play by making such comments, I should be permitted to say to the jury, they interviewed Tim Russert for 22 minutes at a time when they knew full well that David Gregory had been told, according to one of their main witnesses, that Mrs. Wilson worked at the CIA. Not only did they not propound any questions to Mr. Russert about it, what they did, they went out, asked Mr. Gregory to be interviewed. Mr. Gregory refused. They just let it go . . .

When they walk away from Gregory with full knowledge that Gregory had been told about the wife, and they go to Gregory and they don't— well, it says Gregory was never even interviewed. I don't even know if they asked Gregory for an interview. I know he was not interviewed.

But if they were going to pound their chests and say, we're on the search for the truth and we did a great job, I don't have any problem with it, okay, because we're on even playing field. But if they're going to stand—

THE COURT: David Gregory was allegedly told this by Ari Fleischer?

MR. WELLS: In Africa, yes.

THE COURT: How would that elucidate the transaction? That doesn't tell us anything really because, I mean, . . . how would that have in some way potentially exonerate Mr. Libby?

MR. WELLS: Because Mr. Russert has said, pattern and practice, if Gregory knew, Gregory would have told us. If he had known, he would have told Gregory. That's in the record.

. . . Uganda time is eight hours ahead of us. So Gregory is told about the wife on the 11th about 8:00 in the morning, Eastern Standard Time. Nobody knows what time the call is on the 11th. Gregory could have called Russert. They should have looked at it. They should have interviewed him.

They had the evidence in their possession. They decided, for whatever reason, not to. Now, look, Your Honor, I said if they're going to stand up and argue about they did this great truth finding mission, I don't need it.

IN PART BECAUSE the defense has the ability to subpoena Gregory themselves, Walton rules against the defense, and after the parties raise a few issues still to be addressed, the trial is recessed for the day.

*

FEBRUARY 14, 2007

LEGAL DISCUSSION

THE DAY BEGINS WITH the parties tussling over whether the prosecution should be allowed to enter a stipulation that Plame did in fact work in the Counterproliferation Division of the CIA. Most employees at the CPD are covert—something that Libby and Vice President Cheney would arguably have known. The heart of Fitzgerald's argument that it should is:

MR. FITZGERALD: But, Your Honor, we had a ruling that I think we were reasonably entitled to rely upon where Your Honor said, "If it comes out that the defense elicits that she worked at WINPAC, I will allow evidence that she worked at CPD." That is then, if the ruling changes, we should not be said to have waived our rights by relying upon the fact that, if that evidence were to come out, we could respond . . .

JEFFRESS'S COUNTERARGUMENT:

MR. JEFFRESS: Your Honor, I don't want to repeat my argument. I hear all these things about I'm saying they waived something or contradicted a prior ruling. All I'm saying is, I'm asking that the Rules of Evidence be applied on the government's rebuttal. Nothing unfair was done here. The government closed its case. We put on our case. We put on no evidence as to where she worked. And the government is simply precluded from going into it on their case . . .

WALTON RULES IN FAVOR of the prosecution:

THE COURT: I understand it may not fit . . . neatly within what is appropriate rebuttal. But I think, having indicated what I said at the prior hearing, I just think it would be unfair now to stop the government from doing what they otherwise could have done but didn't do because I didn't know that this would arise in the way that it did. So, over objection, I will permit, however it's done, whether by stipulation or otherwise, for that information to come in . . .

THE NEXT ISSUE JUDGE WALTON must deal with is Tim Russert. On the agreement for testimony that Fitzgerald reached with Russert's lawyer, Lee Levine, and the issue of Russert's statements to FBI agent Eckenrode in fall 2003, Fitzgerald recounts an interesting narrative:

MR. FITZGERALD: Your Honor, if I could make a factual proffer. First of all, in the brief filed this morning by the defense, they make it seem as if that accommodation was part of the deal that led to Mr. Russert testifying in a deposition. It was not.

I think we have to go back to the conversation we had last week. There were two phases of the proceeding. The first phase was the effort by NBC and Mr. Russert's counsel to talk us out of . . . subpoenaing either Mr. Russert or NBC. There were actually three phases.

Then there was the litigation before Judge Hogan, . . . and eventually Judge Hogan denied the motion to quash. Then there was negotiation of the deal, which basically said "you will testify at deposition with counsel present." That's been explored and that deal is in evidence . . . The discussion about not making the argument that the conversation between Mr. Russert and FBI agent Eckenrode in the fall of 2003 in a brief occurred in . . . the beginning of a motion to quash.

And what simply happened, Judge, is we never thought we would walk into court and argue in a case that was resolving the application of Branzburg versus Hayes and had First Amendment principles and attorney general guidelines. That when we make a technical argument that the conversation that happened between Mr. Russert and the FBI agent constituted a waiver, we were going on broader principles.

Mr. Levine asked two things to frame the motion. One, we had all discussions pursuant to the guidelines outlining what the scope of his testimony was. Mr. Levine didn't know how to frame that for Judge Hogan in terms of saying "how do I tell him what you're asking for." So, we sent him a letter outlining it so he could attach it as an exhibit so he had something to shoot at for his motion to quash.

Mr. Levine also told me that he was going to brief the issue as to why it was that Agent Eckenrode's conversation with Mr. Russert wasn't a waiver if we were to contend that. We said, "No, we're not contending that." So, we had an understanding, an oral understanding, that that wasn't going to be an issue that we would raise in our brief.

When it came time to file an ex parte affidavit or to explain the facts to Judge Hogan, we gave a complete factual record but didn't want to give the impression or have Mr. Levine think that we went ex parte and told the judge about this conversation. So we made an express notation in the footnote, I believe, that said "we're not claiming, we've agreed with the defense that we're not going to claim that this constitutes a waiver."

I believe I just took that one sentence and made sure I was on good paper with Mr. Levine because I didn't want to say something to Judge Hogan that was inaccurate. That was the circumstance of how this came up.

Then the motions were filed. They were argued. And Judge Hogan ruled . . . The motion is decided and NBC and Mr. Russert lose and decide "we'll go and give a deposition," then we put the terms of the agreement in that letter in July 2004.

It did not merit a letter from either Mr. Levine back or litigating a motion. It did not merit putting in writing except that I wanted to make sure that Judge Hogan wasn't misled. The notion that Mr. Levine would be telling Mr. Russert that there is a footnote in an affidavit in one of the filings in these extensive pleadings, Mr. Russert wasn't the lawyer in the case. He was the client.

I have every reason to believe that that level of detail was never broached to Mr. Russert . . . when the July letter came about that says "we'll do this in a deposition, we put the terms in that agreement."

The defense said, "We want know every possible agreement." We went through exhaustively and said, "Okay, let's look at everything," and we saw that footnote in a brief and said "I guess that could be construed as agreement." So out of abundance of caution, even though we don't think it's discoverable, we'll let them know that we did tell the court that we weren't arguing a waiver point.

To now lead a brief as this was the deal that Mr. Russert struck to testify outside the Grand Jury is complete fiction. Mr. Russert, I have no reason to believe, was aware of this level of detail. I don't believe Mr. Levine would say anything different.

To throw this before the jury as if there's some secret understanding of great import to me. This is beyond collateral, way beyond collateral, and I think should be excluded under 403 in addition to the fact that the Government's letter to defense counsel is hearsay . . .

THE DEFENSE ARGUES that the fact that a lawyer negotiated an agreement as an excuse to keep out information having to do with the accommodations or benefits a witness may have gotten for his or her testimony, and emphasizes the importance of the prosecution's agreement not to argue that the conversation with Eckenrode constituted a waiver on Russert's part, insofar as the information then did not become public (until the trial itself). As Wells sums it up:

WELLS: So in terms of value, I would rank this number one on the things that he got from the Government. [T]he fact that because they decided it was not, they won't say it was a waiver, it was totally kept out of the public record. Mr. Russert took great advantage of that . . .

AS FITZGERALD OBSERVES, the fact of that conversation was included in an affidavit filed ex parte. He also argues again that there's no indication that Russert was aware of this point of negotiations between his lawyer and Fitzgerald, and to that extent could not have played a role in his decision-making. Walton defers his decision until after lunch, and then addresses the statement admitting relevant facts previously agreed to but now thrown into doubt once again because of Libby's decision not to testify, and he disallows the statement. The next issue addressed is the testimony of the CIA briefers. Court breaks for lunch before the issue is resolved.

*

AFTER LUNCH, Judge Walton resolves several outstanding issues.

First, Tim Russert's lawyer Lee Levine is called on to confirm that Russert never learned of Levine's discussion in 2004 when Fitzgerald told the attorney he would not be raising the issue of Russert's conversation with FBI agent Eckenrode in the context of the prosecution's effort to enforce its subpoena for Russert's testimony in 2004. In part because of that, Judge Walton rules it may not be argued that Russert received a benefit that influenced his testimony in that regard.

Second, Walton rules that—despite Russert's startling testimony about being unaware that witnesses in the Grand Jury are not joined there by their attorneys—Russert cannot be called to the witness stand again.

Third, with regard to the defense's desire to put on CIA briefers as witnesses to introduce parts of Libby's memory defense, Walton distinguishes the amount and nature of the work Libby was involved in from the impact it had on him—the latter cannot be introduced through others such as the briefers. And Walton determines that much of this sort of detail cannot be introduced without Libby himself testifying.

The jury is brought in and something very unusual happens. Evidently responding to the fact that all the jurors but one are wearing red shirts, Judge Walton wishes the jurors a happy Valentine's Day. A representative from the jury speaks:

THE JUROR: Valentine's [Day] is certainly a unique opportunity for all of us to express our appreciation and thanks to you for your, for our comfort and safety, also to staff and Mattie and Brad and the Marshal Service.

However, while we're united in this, this is where our unity ends at this time. We're committed to our oath to evaluate the evidence, listen to it independently and succinctly and base our decision on the individual basis.

That being said, Valentine's wishes to you all as well.

(General applause.)

THE COURT: Thank you very much. You've been a very attentive jury and everybody appreciates it.

CLINE FOR THE DEFENSE then reads a stipulation agreed to by the parties which enumerates a total of 27 areas that Libby's morning intelligence briefing covered on June 14, 2003. They include such particulars as an attempted bombing in Yemen; tension between the Israeli government and Hamas; and housing shortages in Iraq. In the same meeting, Libby queried his briefers on a dozen topics, such as reports he had of possible surveillance by suspected terrorists of the U.S. Embassy in Beirut.

The defense enters another stipulation, effectively representing what the testimony of the FBI agent who interviewed David Addington in February 2004 would be, the heart of which is that his report of that interview states:

MR. WELLS: Mr. Addington did not remember the exact date of the conversation [between Addington and Libby], but placed it between July 6 and July 12, 2003. During the conversation, Mr. Libby asked Mr. Addington about two issues, the President's declassification authority and a CIA contract issue.

The February 26 report states that Addington advised, with respect to the contract issue, that Mr. Libby made "a general inquiry about the CIA's relationship with people who are not employees but perform assignments for them." The February 26 report does not reflect that Mr. Libby made any reference to a spouse or a wife, either when Mr. Libby asked this question or at any other point during the conversation in the anteroom office with Mr. Addington.

THE DEFENSE ALSO ENTERS into evidence three newspaper article from the fall of 2003 that were produced under Libby's certification for the purpose of illuminating Libby's state of mind at the time. One is an article by Clifford May which states that he was told that Wilson's wife worked at the CIA casually by a former government official and that he inferred that it was well-known among insiders. The second is a *Wall Street Journal* editorial from October 1, 2003 arguing that the outing of Plame was justified and that it is unclear that any law was violated. The third is a *National Review* editorial from the end of October, 2003 similarly suggesting that no law had been broken and that the CIA and Wilson himself bore considerable responsibility for his wife's outing.

The defense also enters, though it does not publish to the jury, a transcript of Condoleezza Rice's June 8, 2003 appearance on the *This Week* program on ABC.

The defense last enters a stipulation about FBI agent John Eckenrode bearing on his interviews of Tim Russert, and rests its case. Afterward, the prosecution enters the original of Cheney's copy of Wilson's July 6, 2003 op-ed, with Cheney's underlining and notes, into evidence and presents a rebuttal case consisting of one stipulation of its own.

> Stipulation regarding former FBI Inspector in 19 charge John Eckenrode.
> "The defendant, I. Lewis Libby, by his attorneys, William H. Jeffress, Jr. and Theodore V. Wells, Jr., and the United States of America by Patrick J. Fitzgerald, special counsel, hereby agree and stipulate as follows.
> 1. In 2003, John C. Eckenrode was a Special Agent in the Federal Bureau of Investigation. Mr. Eckenrode was the inspector in charge for the investigation concerning the possible unauthorized disclosure of Valerie Plame Wilson's affiliation with the CIA.
> 2. On November 14 and 24, 2003, Agent Eckenrode spoke by telephone with Tim Russert, Washington Bureau Chief for NBC News.
> 3. Agent Eckenrode prepared an FBI form FD-302 report dated November 24, 2003 (the November 24 report) that recorded the information that Mr. Russert provided. Agent Eckenrode intended the November 24 report to be an accurate report of his conversations with Mr. Russert.
> 4. The November 24 report states that "Russert was specifically requested to refrain from reporting on the FBI's interview questions and he thereafter acknowledged and agreed to the FBI's request."
> 5. The November 24 report describes Mr. Russert's account of what he said to I. Lewis Libby and what Mr. Libby said to him in discussions over the telephone in July 2003. Mr. Russert advised that he recalled at least one, and

possibly two, telephone conversations with Mr. Libby between July 6 and July 12, 2003.

6. The November 24 report states in part, "Russert does not recall stating to Libby in this conversation anything about the wife of former Ambassador Joe Wilson. Although he could not completely rule out the possibility that he had such an exchange, Russert was at a loss to remember it, and moreover, he believes that this would be the type of conversation that he would or should remember. Russert acknowledged that he speaks to many people on a daily basis and it is difficult to reconstruct some specific conversations, particularly one which occurred several months ago."

WITH THE READING of that stipulation concerning Mr. Russert's interview, the defense on behalf of Lewis Libby rests.

THE COURT: Very well, you can consider that stipulation, again, that was read to you as undisputed evidence. The defense has now completed the presentation of its evidence.

Anything from the Government?

MR. FITZGERALD: Yes, Your Honor. We'll be very brief. Ms. Kedian will read one stipulation into the record . . .

MS. KEDIAN: Your Honor, pursuant to agreement with defense counsel, we'd like to offer Government Exhibit 402, which is the original of a document that is already admitted in evidence.

MR. JEFFRESS: No objection.

MS. KEDIAN: Your Honor, in rebuttal, the Government would like to read a stipulation that has been signed by the parties.

The United States of America, by Patrick J. Fitzgerald, special counsel, and the defendant, I. Lewis Libby, by his attorneys, William H. Jeffress, Jr. and Theodore V. Wells, Jr., hereby agree and stipulate as follows.

The Counterproliferation Division, otherwise known as CPD, is a division within the Central Intelligence Agency, CIA. The record of the CIA reflects that Valerie Plame Wilson worked for the Counterproliferation Division throughout 2003. And it is signed by the parties."

And with that, Your Honor, the Government rests its rebuttal case.

THE COURT: Very well, all of the evidence that you will hear in this case has now been presented to you.

WALTON GIVES THE JURORS a number of cautionary instructions bearing on issues that have been hotly contested during the trial (or in pre-trial proceedings):

THE COURT: I do not know if you do, but you may recall seeing a stamp that began with the words "treated as" on Mr. Libby's June 2003 note of his conversation with the Vice President. That stamp has been removed from the exhibits in evidence. I instruct you that you should disregard the evidence concerning that stamp, including the testimony from Mr. Addington about it during his January 30, 2007, afternoon session . . .

Now, when this trial started, I described to you the charges against Mr. Libby. I told you that Count I, which charges obstruction of justice, alleges that Mr. Libby falsely testified to the Grand Jury concerning conversations with three reporters, Mr. Russert, Mr. Cooper, and Ms. Miller.

Now, however, this trial has progressed to the point where the Government has rested its case and one of those allegations, that being that Mr. Libby lied about his conversation with Judith Miller on June 12, 2003, has been dismissed.

MR. FITZGERALD: July 12th.

THE COURT: I'm sorry, July 12, 2003, has been dismissed. That aspect of the obstruction of justice charge must be of no further concern to you, and the fact that Mr. Libby was previously alleged to have obstructed justice by lying about his conversation with Ms. Miller on July 12, 2003, cannot in any way influence your verdict regarding the guilt or the innocence of Mr. Libby on the remaining charges in the indictment.

Count I, the obstruction of justice count, is now based solely on the allegation that Mr. Libby falsely testified to the Grand Jury concerning his conversations with two reporters: Mr. Russert and Mr. Cooper. You may, however, consider evidence presented at trial related to Mr. Libby's July 12, 2003, conversation with Ms. Miller in evaluating whether the Government has proven the remaining allegations against Mr. Libby beyond a reasonable doubt.

I also previously gave you this instruction but I'll give it to you again. You have heard evidence regarding discussions Mr. Libby had with reporters about material contained in the October 2002 National Intelligence Estimate, also known as the NIE. There is no dispute that the President has the power to declassify previously classified material and to authorize its disclosure to the press. Nor is there any dispute that, at least as of July 8, 2003, the President had exercised that power with respect to portions of the October 2002 NIE.

In other words, the Government does not contend that Mr. Libby did anything improper during those parts of the conversations he had with reporters on or after July 8, 2003, when he discussed portions of the NIE that had been declassified by the President. I would ask that you keep those instructions in mind.

You will be provided with written instructions and you will have these with you when you go back to deliberate. And that you adhere to these instructions and limit the evidence that these instructions relate to in the manner I've indicated.

Anything else at this point from counsel?

MR. FITZGERALD: No, Your Honor.

MR. WELLS: No, Your Honor.

THE COURT: Very well. You'll get a chance to go home a little early today.

WALTON INFORMS THE JURY of the upcoming schedule, warns them to not view any media coverage of the case, and excuses the jurors. Once the jury is out, Wells immediately addresses the good faith of the defense's prior professed intention to have Libby testify as well as the Vice President, which leads to an interesting exchange with Judge Walton. Wells explains the defense's evolving thinking over time and sums up:

MR. WELLS: I'm only saying, Your Honor, we've proceeded at all times with Your Honor in good faith. And to the extent there is any concern on Your Honor's part that in some way counsel during the CIPA hearings were in some way playing fast and loose, . . . that's not so, Your Honor.

We've prepared, we spent hours working on putting the Vice President on the stand. We've spent untold hours being ready if we decided it was the right thing to do, to put Mr. Libby on the stand. But we have to make these decisions based on our confidence as to whether or not the Government has proved its case beyond a reasonable doubt.

We will argue on Tuesday we don't think they have and we made that decision . . . I'm in the business of convincing the jury that the Government hasn't met its burden of proof. There is no box on the verdict sheet that says innocent or did you tell your full story. The box says guilty or not guilty, and I'm the one that makes the call.

It was my recommendation, along with Mr. Jeffress, that we not put him on the stand. The same decision was made with respect to the Vice President. I had the Vice President on hold right up until the last minute. Your Honor knows we had him scheduled to testify on Thursday. He had cleared his schedule. He was ready to testify.

He was never subpoenaed. He was always holding. He had his schedule open and we were ready to go forward. I just want to make clear, . . . we've been up front with Your Honor, I believe, at all times. But we've got to make decisions that are in our client's best interest. There is no question that, once we saw that Jencks material in late December, our view of how we might try this case radically changed and it continued to change based on what we felt was the performance of the Government's witnesses in this case.

I just want to make that clear, Your Honor.

THE COURT: Well, I assume your comments are precipitated by an article that had been issued by the Associated Press entitled "Judge, Defense Misled Court About Libby." I never said that. What I said was that I was under the impression, based upon what I had been told, that Mr. Libby would be testifying. And I did not intend to suggest that there had been any intentional misleading of the court on that matter.

It was indicated by Mr. Cline that there was a qualification. I may have not seen it as an absolute qualification that Mr. Libby wasn't going to testify. And I assumed, based upon what you're saying now, that in fact it was not an indication that he wasn't going to testify. And I accept that as an accurate statement.

So, to the extent that changes can be made in newspaper articles that are about to go out, it just should be noted that I have never suggested that there was any intentional attempt to deceive the court during the CIPA hearings.

MR. WELLS: Thank you, Your Honor.

THE DEFENSE TAKES THE UNUSUAL STEP at this point in the proceedings to move to have two news articles from the fall of 2003 that the prosecution had entered struck. This is rejected. The defense also moves to have portions of Libby's grand jury testimony bearing on the NIE struck, but Judge Walton, after being reminded by the prosecution of the pre-trial motion under which he earlier denied a similar request, refused to revise his ruling This offers interesting insight into what happened with regard to this important aspect of the case.

After hearing a few more issues from the defense, Judge Walton recesses the trial for the day.

*

FEBRUARY 20, 2007

CLOSING ARGUMENT ON BEHALF
OF THE GOVERNMENT

MR. ZEIDENBERG: Ladies and gentlemen, about a month ago, both sides in this case gave opening statements. Mr. Fitzgerald, on behalf of the government, stood before you...and told you what he expected the evidence in this case to show. And he told you that he expected that the government would prove beyond a reasonable doubt that this case was about lying and that the evidence would show that Mr. Libby, the defendant, lied to the FBI and the Grand Jury about how he learned about Joseph Wilson's wife, Valerie Wilson, who he talked to about Mr. Wilson's wife, and what he said when he discussed Mr. Wilson's wife with others.

Now, the defense didn't have to give an opening statement. The defense has no burden of proof in this or any other criminal case. But on behalf of the defense, Mr. Wells elected to give an opening, and he painted a very different picture. He told you about a White House conspiracy to scapegoat Mr. Libby, about an effort to make Mr. Libby into a sacrificial lamb, to hang him out to dry so that Karl Rove, the lifeblood of the Republican Party, would go free.

Now, you have heard the witnesses testify in this case, and you heard witness after witness after witness, take that witness stand, raise their hand, take an oath, and testify about one conversation after another that they each had with Mr. Libby about Valerie Wilson, Mr. Wilson's wife, during the time period Mr. Libby claimed to the FBI and the Grand Jury that he had no memory of Mr. Wilson's wife.

You heard Tim Russert testify, take an oath and say that he never spoke to Mr. Libby about Wilson's wife, in direct contrast to what Mr. Libby claimed to the FBI and the Grand Jury.

Now, did you hear any evidence about a conspiracy—a White House conspiracy to scapegoat Mr. Libby? If you think back and you draw a blank, I suggest to you, ladies and gentlemen, it's not because there is a problem with your memory. There was no such evidence.

And I bring that to your attention for one reason and one reason only: to remind you, ladies and gentlemen, that what is evidence in this case is what happens from that witness stand and what was introduced as an exhibit at trial. That is the evidence in the case. Unfulfilled promises from counsel do not constitute evidence.

Mr. Fitzgerald told you that this case was about lying, and I submit that's exactly right. It's not a case about scapegoating. It's not a case about conspiracies. It's not a case about bad memory or forgetting.

Mr. Libby does claim that he forgot nine separate conversations with eight individuals over a four-week period about Joseph Wilson's wife. But he also invents out of whole cloth—absolutely fabricates two conversations that never happened, his conversation with Matt Cooper and his conversation with Tim Russert. That, ladies and gentlemen, is not a matter of forgetting or misremembering. It's lying.

Now, I would like to talk to you about the evidence that you did hear in this case, and when I do that, I'm also going to discuss . . . the credibility of the witnesses because you are going to have to make the determination when you go back in the jury room—how do you judge their credibility? And you are going to get factors—instructions from the judge in his jury instructions, but I suggest to you they will be things that you know from your common sense and your common experience how to judge whether someone is telling the truth.

I am going to suggest to you some facts that you can consider and you should consider, but use your common sense. And when you are weighing the credibility of the witnesses, don't look at them in isolation. Look at them together, how their testimony fits together, whether it makes sense, and how well it fits together with the documentary evidence that's been introduced.

I want to start by talking a little bit about Marc Grossman, the first witness you heard from. Mr. Grossman—I remind you, the number-three person at the State Department, Under Secretary for Political Affairs—he told you how, on May 29th, outside a deputies committee meeting, he was approached by Mr. Libby, who wanted information about a trip by an ambassador to Niger. He wanted to know what Mr. Grossman knew about that trip.

Mr. Grossman didn't know anything about that trip. He had never heard of it, and it bothered him that he didn't now about it because here he was being asked by the Chief of Staff of the Vice President of the United States something which he should have been aware of in his own mind.

So he goes back to the State Department. He tells Mr. Libby he is going to look into it. He digs around and he finds out some information. He finds out that there was an ambassador who went. His name is Joseph Wilson. He went to Niger. He reported back. And Mr. Grossman calls and tells Mr. Libby that information that day.

Mr. Grossman is not satisfied that he has all the information and wants a report. He wants something on paper. He goes on foreign travel. He comes back. And July 10th or 11th, he is handed from Carl Ford, from the State Department's intelligence and research branch, what's been referred to as the INR memo, dated June 10th.

This memo contained a paragraph which referred to Valerie Wilson, Joseph Wilson's wife, and indicated that she worked at the CIA and that she had a role in sending her husband, Mr. Wilson, on the trip to Niger.

And as you will recall, Mr. Grossman told you that this fact leaped out at him. It was really remarkable to him. He thought it verged on the edge of impropriety. He thought it was somewhat bizarre.

He sees Mr. Libby again within a day or two—most likely June 12th—and he sees Mr. Libby outside, again, a deputies committee meeting, and he tells Mr. Libby, "I have some more information for you. I owe you this information. I have looked into it. I have looked into the question that you asked me. And I found out, yes, an ambassador went. It was Joseph Wilson, he did report back."

And then Mr. Grossman said another thing. He said, "There is something else that you should know. Wilson's wife works at the agency. She works at the CIA." Mr. Grossman thought that this was important that he tell this to Mr. Libby. And why wouldn't he? He had already been caught short, in his own mind . . . not knowing about the ambassador.

He looks into it. He is reporting back to the Vice President's Chief of Staff, and he is going to hold back this piece of information? No. He remembers telling this to Mr. Libby. And I suggest to you, ladies and gentlemen, when Mr. Grossman told this to Mr. Libby on June 12th, it was the fourth time in two days that Mr. Libby had been told about Ambassador Wilson's wife. The fourth time.

Now, I am going to go through with you in just a moment the first three. But before I do, I want to just touch on Mr. Grossman's testimony and why you can rely on it.

Remember, Mr. Grossman was the number-three person at the State Department. He was a former colleague of Mr. Libby's. He has a clear memory of this. There wasn't any confusion about this. It stood out in his mind. And I suggest to you there is no reason in the world that he would have to be biased against Mr. Libby.

Remember, his testimony is corroborated by the very fact that there is an INR report. Remember what Mr. Ford said? He was called by the defense. He said it was unusual for him to have gotten a request of this nature about this subject from Mr. Grossman. This wasn't his area. Mr. Grossman himself told you that this was a zero on his radar screen. He had no interest in the subject. The only reason he looked into it was because he was requested to by Mr. Libby.

So he was the fourth person. The first three? Well, the first you know, June 11th or thereabouts, was the Vice President of the United States. And you heard how the Vice President told Mr. Libby on what we believe to be—and the evidence shows—was about June 11th. And the way you can date this is you saw Mr. Libby's notes from June 11th, and this was where he wrote down "wife works at CP," Counterproliferation Division. This was as a result of a phone call with the Vice President.

And if you will recall, it was in anticipation for an article that was being written by Walter Pincus of *The Washington Post*. So even though the date has a squiggly line over it and it was an approximation, you can know that it was right about just prior to the publication of the June 12th Walter Pincus piece.

And, as I will explain in just a minute, the evidence can pretty much tie that down exactly to June 11. So Mr. Libby learns from the Vice President on June 11th.

What else happens on June 11th? Look at Government Exhibit 702—701. This was a call slip . . . of Mr. Libby's call to Robert Grenier at the CIA You will recall that this was an unusual event. Mr. Grenier had never received a phone call from Mr. Libby before.

June 11th, 1:15, he gets a call. He calls Mr. Libby back about 2:00, he thinks. Mr. Libby has got some specific questions. First of all, he is upset. He is upset with the CIA;

there is some fellow named Joseph Wilson talking to the press. According to Mr. Libby, this fellow Wilson is saying . . . that he has been told by the CIA that he was sent to Niger as a result of a request from the Office of the Vice President. And Mr. Libby wants a couple things from Mr. Grenier.

He wants to know if it's true that the CIA sent him, and he wants to know if it's true that he, Mr. Wilson, was sent solely as a result of interest from the Office of the Vice President.

Well, Mr. Grenier, like Mr. Grossman before him, when he gets a request from the Chief of Staff of the Vice President, he looks into it. He calls down to the Counterproliferation Division. He finds out information. He gets a call back, and he gets briefed on the trip. He finds out there was an ambassador. Mr. Libby is correct. Mr. Libby is using the name Joseph Wilson in this phone call. Mr. Libby is correct. There was an ambassador. He did get sent to Niger. He reported back.

He learned some other facts. He learns that there was interest not just from the Office of the Vice President, but from the Defense Department and the State Department. And Mr. Grenier learns another interesting fact when he is talking to the Counterproliferation Division. He learns that Valerie Wilson, Joseph Wilson's wife, worked in the unit that sent him. Now, the name is not used; Valerie Wilson is not used, but the description, "Wilson's wife."

SO MR. GRENIER HAS THIS INFORMATION that was requested by Mr. Libby. And if you will recall, he was in a dilemma at that point because by the time he got this information, it's in the afternoon. He has got a 4:15 meeting with the director of the CIA regarding Iraq. So he is caught between, "Do I call back Mr. Libby with this information he needs? Do I go to the meeting?" And if you recall, he remembers that quite clearly, being torn about what he should do.

And he decides, "I will go to the meeting. I will call Mr. Libby back after the meeting." Just a short time after he is in that meeting, there is a knock on the door and he is pulled out. The first time in his life Mr. Grenier is pulled out of a meeting with the director of the CIA. That, ladies and gentlemen, is something that you will remember.

And he is told that Mr. Libby wants him to call, and Mr. Grenier realizes, of course, at that time that he had made a mistake; he should have called Mr. Libby back right away. This is obviously something of some urgency. Remember, Mr. Grenier said he sees Mr. Libby two to three days a week. So unless there is an urgent matter, he is going to see him face-to-face. Clearly, this was a pressing matter.

He calls Mr. Libby outside the meeting and he gives him the download of what he had learned. He tells him about the trip . . . He told him that there was interest . . . not just from the Office of Vice President, but from the Defense Department and the State Department. And Mr. Grenier tells Mr. Libby another fact. He said Wilson's wife works in the unit that sent him.

So that is the second person that day Mr. Libby heard that information from. First from the Vice President, then from Mr. Grenier.

Mr. Libby wants to know whether the CIA will go public with this information. Will they confirm publicly that the interest was not just from the Office of Vice President, but from the Department of State and Defense.

As you will recall, Mr. Grenier says, "I don't know if that will be a problem. The person I've got to check with is in the meeting, Bill Harlow." And he described how he put the phone down. He believes he hung up the phone so he wouldn't keep the Vice President's Chief of Staff on hold.

He puts the phone down, goes in the meeting, pulls out Mr. Harlow, the press person for the CIA, and briefs Mr. Harlow, "This is what's going on." Mr. Harlow says, "I think we can do that. I think that won't be a problem."

Mr. Grenier calls Mr. Libby back. He says, "I have Mr. Harlow here. I don't think it will be a problem. The CIA will confirm this publicly." Mr. Libby says, "Great," and he says, "You should have Harlow talk to my press aide." And Mr. Grenier recalls her— it's a woman he believes with the first name of Cathie. And you all now know who that is. It's Cathie Martin. So Cathie Martin gets on the phone with Mr. Grenier.

. . . **BEFORE I FINISH** with Mr. Grenier, I want to talk a little bit about his credibility. You heard him cross-examined extensively by the defense in this case. And you heard him explain on direct that when he was first put in the Grand Jury and interviewed, he was not certain, in his own mind, whether he shared the information about Wilson's wife with Mr. Libby. He knew he was told that information when he talked to the Counterproliferation Division. He never had any doubt about that. What he was uncertain about was whether he shared it with Mr. Libby.

As he said, he thought—and he testified earlier that he might have, but he wasn't sure and he wanted to err on the side of caution. He didn't want to say he was sure if he wasn't. And now he testified at trial that he was sure that he shared that information.

And I want to just remind you of how he accounted for that. It wasn't so much the memory of the conversation that became clear in his mind as it was the memory of his feeling of discomfort and how uncomfortable he felt after that phone call, that he said too much to Mr. Libby, and that he shouldn't have shared this information about someone who worked in the Counterproliferation Division, someone who may well have been covert.

And he remembered feeling unease after he hung up the phone call, and that was the feeling that he remembered, and from that he could infer what happened and understand . . . And it became, when he thought about it, as he thought about it, quite clear in his own mind that he did, in fact, have this conversation.

Now, he didn't come forward right away as soon as he realized this. Why? As he told you, he didn't think this information was important. He didn't think it was relevant. As he understood it, this was a leak investigation into who leaked a particular name. And he knew he didn't tell Mr. Libby the name. So he figured, it's probably not important.

And as press accounts became public that there were questions raised about where people learned this information, where Mr. Libby may have learned this information, and speculation in the press that Mr. Libby may have learned this information from the press, then Mr. Grenier realized that the information . . . that he possessed was relevant and may be very important. And . . . he felt an obligation to come forward and share it, . . . and let you, ladies and gentlemen, sort it out.

. . . [T]he easiest thing in the world would have been for Mr. Grenier to keep his mouth shut and go about his business. He doesn't work for the CIA anymore. He doesn't have a dog in this fight.

He used to work with Mr. Libby. You heard no issues of any ill will or animosity between him and Mr. Libby. There is no reason for him to come in here and put up with a day of cross-examination when the easiest thing in the world would have been to stay home and keep his mouth shut, except that he felt he had information that was relevant and pertinent to the case, and for you to make the determination.

And I suggest there is no reason to think that Mr. Grenier would fabricate that, would make it up, or would say that he is confident and sure of that memory if he wasn't.

As I said, Mr. Grenier is the second person. The Vice President. Mr. Grenier. The third person Mr. Libby heard about Joseph Wilson's wife from on June 11th: Cathie Martin. As I told you, she is the one who is put on the phone—Mr. Grenier puts her on the phone. Mr. Grenier has Mr. Harlow get on the phone and talk to Cathie Martin.

And Cathie Martin told you that she remembers learning about Joseph Wilson's wife from Bill Harlow of the CIA . . . She told you that Mr. Harlow told her that Wilson's wife—that Joseph Wilson was a former charge in Baghdad, an ambassador, and that his wife works at the CIA.

Cathie Martin told you that as soon as she got this information, she went into the Office of the Vice President. The Vice President was there. Mr. Libby was there. And she told them both exactly what she had just learned. Wilson—the ambassador, former charge in Baghdad, wife works at the CIA. That is the third conversation he had on June 11th.

And, again, this is corroborated by the other witnesses. And I want to show you what else it's corroborated by, and that is the defendant's notes . . . This is a portion of Mr. Libby's notes that he took on that day . . .

If you could just look at the full page for a second.

In the upper-right corner, it says "CP his wife works in that division". . . . This is the note which Mr. Libby writes down from his conversation with the Vice President on June 11th.

Now, let me just show you that other portion of that same note. "OVP and defense and state expressed strong interest in issue." and then off to the left, that "y" with the line over it you have been told is Mr. Libby's—how he makes a symbol for the Vice President. The Vice President: "Hold. Get agency to answer that."

So it's clear from this note that Mr. Libby is told by the Vice President that . . . the OVP, Defense and State—that they all expressed a strong interest in the issue. He wants—the Vice President wants the CIA to say that.

And that, ladies and gentlemen, explains why Mr. Grenier got pulled out of that meeting with the Director of the CIA on June 11th. That is why this issue couldn't wait. That's why Mr. Libby called Mr. Grenier, when he had never called him ever prior to that, twice in one day and pulled him out of that meeting, because this was a matter of some urgency.

The Vice President wanted Mr. Libby to get the CIA to say this publicly. Remember, there is an article coming out the next day and they want to get this out before that article is published.

And I suggest this note corroborates the testimony of both Cathie Martin and Mr. Grenier because this is exactly what Mr. Grenier told you that Mr. Libby wanted. Mr. Grenier, obviously, didn't have access to Mr. Libby's notes. They weren't dated. Cathie Martin didn't have access to Mr. Libby's notes.

But despite the fact that Cathie Martin couldn't initially remember the date of her conversation with Mr. Libby and the Vice President about Wilson's wife, you know now it was, in fact, June 11th.

She always remembered the sequence of events. She always remembered that when she saw Joseph Wilson on *Meet the Press* on July 6th, she knew Wilson's name at that time. She already knew it . . . Obviously, she had learned it prior to that.

She also remembered she learned it from Bill Harlow, and she also remembered she got on the phone with Harlow after Mr. Libby had been talking to Deputy John McLaughlin at the CIA. Well, Bob Grenier is a deputy at the CIA, a deputy of John McLaughlin.

So from those facts, from the testimony of those witnesses, when you put it together, it's clear the conversation of Cathie Martin with Bill Harlow was June 11th. And as she told you, she immediately told Mr. Libby. So that's the third time on June 11th Mr. Libby gets that information about Wilson's wife.

The very next day, June 12th, . . . Mr. Grossman tells them . . . the same information, tells Mr. Libby about Wilson's wife. Four times in less than 48 hours.

What happens next? June 14th, Craig Schmall, the CIA briefer—you heard how Mr. Schmall briefs Mr. Libby alone on the weekends. June 14th was a Saturday. There's only two people in that room: Mr. Libby and his briefer.

Now, take a look at Mr. Schmall's notes from that day . . . Now, Mr. Schmall told you that he only writes down what the person he is briefing says. He doesn't write down his own questions, naturally enough. He writes down the questions of the person he is briefing. And what does he write down on that day? Why was the ambassador told this was a V.P. office question? Joe Wilson, Valerie Wilson.

Think about that question . . . because that is the question that Mr. Libby keeps trying to answer and to put to bed because the press keeps asking about the connection between the Vice President's office and this trip. And Mr. Libby asked Mr. Grenier why . . . Joseph Wilson is saying that he heard this from the CIA, that the CIA is telling him that he was sent because the Vice President wanted it done.

And here is the question: why was the Vice President told this was a V.P. office question? Joe Wilson, Valerie Wilson.

Mr. Schmall did not know the names Valerie Wilson and Joe Wilson on June 14th. The person he was briefing, Mr. Libby, knew more about the issue than did Mr. Schmall, the CIA briefer.

And Mr. Schmall's testimony corroborates the testimony of Mr. Grossman, Mr. Grenier, and Cathie Martin because they have told you, ladies and gentlemen, that they gave this information to Mr. Libby on June 11th, and here you have proof that on June 14th he had remembered it. And Mr. Schmall could write it down, took notes.

Now, you have heard some suggestion from the defense in this case as if to suggest to you that if you don't take notes of a conversation, it's not possible to remember it, or you couldn't expect to remember it. And we all know from our everyday lives that we can remember plenty of conversations that we have had in our lives with people, and we remember them quite well. Very few of us take notes during the day in the course of our lives, and yet we have no difficulty recalling conversations.

But in any event, in this case, there are notes, and they are irrefutable that Mr. Libby told Mr. Schmall that. And I suggest there is no reason to suggest that Mr. Schmall's memory or these notes should be questioned. So that is the fifth person that Mr. Libby discussed Wilson's wife with in a three-day period.

THE NEXT PERSON: JUDITH MILLER. June 23rd. This was a meeting at the Old Executive Office Building in Mr. Libby's office. Ms. Miller, you will recall, is a *New York Times* reporter. She is taking notes. She recalls that Mr. Libby was agitated, upset. He was angry with the CIA. He felt that they were . . . backtracking on what they had said publicly before the war.

He was very familiar with Joseph Wilson. He said that Wilson was a ruse, an irrelevancy, and should be ignored. He was very familiar with Wilson's trip. He had been sent to Niger in February 2002 to look into this question. He was familiar with Wilson's wife. He said that she worked in the bureau. From the context, Ms. Miller understood this to be a reference to the bureau in the CIA that deals with nonproliferation issues.

Ms. Miller was the sixth person that Mr. Libby talked to about Wilson's wife during that short span of time between June 11th and June 23rd, less than two weeks.

What's next? Ari Fleischer, July 7th. They are having lunch at the White House mess, just the two of them. Only two people present. It's an event that stands out in Mr. Fleischer's mind. Why? Because it was his last full day working. He was about to go on a trip for the week and then he was leaving. Even more significantly, it was the only time he had ever had lunch with Mr. Libby. It was a unique event, and Mr. Fleischer's memory of it was clear.

He remembered that they talked about Mr. Fleischer's future employment plans. Mr. Libby thanked him for what he had said earlier that day in the press gaggle that morning, . . . when he was addressing the "sixteen words" question. They talked about the Miami Dolphins. Mr. Fleischer remembered all that. And he remembered another thing that Mr. Libby told him.

Mr. Libby said that he had some information that was "hush-hush" and "on the QT." He said that Wilson wasn't sent because of interest from the Vice President's office. He was sent by the CIA, and that Wilson's wife works in the Counterproliferation section, the CP division, the same division . . . that Mr. Libby was told about and what you saw referred to in his note from the Vice President.

. . . Mr. Fleischer took this as gossip, as information that was passed on. And it was unusual to him because Mr. Libby was a tight-lipped individual who didn't share information normally. He was not someone that Mr. Fleischer could go to normally and get information about what was going on.

And you should ask yourselves, ladies and gentlemen, why did Mr. Libby choose to share this information with the Press Secretary of the White House on that date. And ask yourselves if you think it was because the conversation had just lagged at lunch and he had run out of things to say, or did he tell him that because he knew it was Ari Fleischer's job to talk to the press, and that by ceding it to Ari Fleischer, he could spread it around without it ever coming back to him, Mr. Libby.

And I suggest to you it's the latter . . . that he gave this information deliberately to Mr. Fleischer, hoping that Mr. Fleischer would talk about it with reporters. And, ladies and gentlemen, that's exactly what did happen.

Mr. Fleischer, you heard, went to Africa. He is at the side of the road. A couple of reporters are there: David Gregory and John Dickerson. And Mr. Fleischer talks to them and tells them about Wilson's wife in the context of why—who sent him and why. And he explains, the wife sent him; his wife works there.

No reaction from them. They don't take out their pens. They don't write it down in their notebooks. And you heard no evidence that they ever printed anything about this. There were no articles published. Nevertheless, in September—late September or early October, when Mr. Fleischer reads press accounts that there is a criminal investigation into the unauthorized disclosure of classified information and the possible outing of a covert agent, he is mortified. He is horrified because he sees that this information that he knows he talked about with reporters appears to have been classified, and it appears to have involved a covert agent.

And then, of course, he went and got a lawyer and got immunity from prosecution. And you should think about that because that immunity agreement protects him only if he tells the truth. The only thing he can be prosecuted for is lying.

He told the government about his conversations with Gregory and Dickerson on the side of the road in Africa. They never published. He told the government.

Now, he was cross-examined about his conversation with Walter Pincus, and he said he has no recollection of talking about Wilson's wife with Walter Pincus. And you heard Walter Pincus come in here and say he recalls Ari Fleischer telling him about Wilson's wife.

We don't dispute Mr. Pincus's testimony. I want to suggest to you, ladies and gentlemen, that the fact that Ari Fleischer doesn't remember which reporters or all the reporters he spoke to about Wilson's wife does not in any way, shape or form suggest a reason why Ari Fleischer would fabricate, make up, or invent a story about a lunchtime meeting with Mr. Libby in which Mr. Libby told him about Wilson's wife working at the Counterproliferation Division.

It is an irrefutable fact that Mr. Fleischer knew Valerie Wilson worked at the Counterproliferation Division of the CIA.

Ask yourselves, how did he learn it? What was his source of information? And why in the world would he lie about it? You saw the letter—the nice warm letter that Mr.

Libby wrote to Mr. Fleischer when Mr. Fleischer left. Mr. Fleischer had nothing but warm things or nice things to say about Mr. Libby. There is no ill will. They are former colleagues. They worked together at the White House. Why in the world would Mr. Fleischer lie about that conversation? There is no reason. And there is not a question about his memory. It was a unique event that he remembered clearly.

So Mr. Fleischer was the seventh person that Mr. Libby discussed Wilson's wife with during that period he claims to have had no conscious memory of her.

WHAT'S NEXT? David Addington, the Vice President's current Chief of Staff and former colleague of Mr. Libby's. He used to be the counsel to the Vice President.

Now, this conversation took place on July 8th . . . Mr. Addington didn't remember the precise date. All he could remember was it happened between the time Wilson went on *Meet the Press* and the time of the trip on the aircraft carrier to Norfolk, which you know was July 12th. I can explain to you why we can date this to be July 8th in just a minute.

Mr. Addington described an unusual . . . conversation with Mr. Libby where Mr. Libby buttonholed him outside of that tiny anteroom office, closed the doors and shushed him. And you remember Mr. Addington was a soft-spoken man. Several times he mentioned to keep your voice down. He wanted to know a couple things.

He wanted to know about declassification authority of the President. Does the President have authority to just declassify things on his own? And Mr. Addington said, "yes, he does." And he cited a case to him, *Navy v. Egan*. And you will recall, Mr. Libby mentioned that case, *Navy v. Egan,* in his . . . Grand Jury in his testimony. He recalled that.

And then Mr. Libby had another question: what paperwork would there be if someone at the CIA sent a spouse on a trip? Mr. Libby didn't mention Wilson by name. He didn't mention Valerie by name. But it's clear, isn't it, from the context, what he was referring to? Have you heard any other evidence about any other spouses being sent on trips that week?

Who in the world do you think Mr. Libby was referring to except for Joseph Wilson and his wife?

How do you date that conversation? Well, you can date it because you know the part about the declassification. The declassification, obviously, referred to the National Intelligence Estimate, the NIE that was the document that Mr. Libby was going to leak to a reporter. And he wanted to . . . make sure the President had the authority to do this. And he was going to leak it, as you will recall, to Judith Miller on July 8th.

So by virtue of that, we know that this conversation had to have happened prior to the meeting with Judith Miller on July 8th . . .

Now, there was some suggestion when Mr. Addington was cross-examined about the fact that Mr. Addington did not mention the word "spouse" when he was first interviewed by the FBI, and there may be a suggestion, ladies and gentlemen, that somehow he is making that up now. And I want to ask you to think about that and consider the fact that Mr. Addington right now, today, works for the Vice President. He used to work with Mr. Libby as a colleague.

If Mr. Addington had a bias in this case, in which direction do you think it would be: on behalf of the prosecution or on behalf of the defense? And I'd suggest to you there is no reason in this world that Mr. Addington would come in here and testify that he recalls Mr. Libby talking about a spouse being sent on a trip in the context of the CIA if that isn't his accurate memory. He is a careful, precise lawyer, and he was clear in his memory.

Mr. Addington was the eighth person that Mr. Libby talked to about Wilson's wife during that period.

The next, Judith Miller, again on July 8th. This was the meeting at the St. Regis Hotel, a two-hour breakfast meeting. This was an important meeting. This is where Mr. Libby was going to leak the NIE this was a highly unusual event. There's only three people, apparently, in the entire United States that was aware at this point that the NIE was declassified: the President, the Vice President, and Mr. Libby.

The director of the CIA, George Tenet, didn't know about it. Condoleezza Rice didn't know about it. Stephen Hadley didn't know about it. Just those three: the President, the Vice President, and Mr. Libby. And they are going to pick Judith Miller to give it to, an event that you would think would stand out in one's mind.

So he meets with Ms. Miller at the St. Regis Hotel. And you will recall Ms. Miller testified. She had her notes from that. She told you that Mr. Libby was agitated, that he was angry. He had a wide-ranging discussion with her, she told you, about the National Intelligence Estimate and its findings, what was in there.

She told you that they talked about the Powell presentation to the United Nations and the run-up to the Iraq war in February. She told you another thing. She told you that the ground rules of the interview changed in the middle.

First, he was to be referred to as a "senior administration official." Then the rules were to change. All of a sudden, he says, "I want to be referred to for this next portion as a 'former hill staffer.'"

Mr. Libby didn't work on Capitol Hill . . . He worked in the Office of the Vice President. He, obviously, didn't want this next part of the information to come back and be in any way linked to him or his office.

And the conversation then turns to Wilson and Wilson's wife. And he tells Ms. Miller that Wilson's wife works at WINPAC—the WINPAC section within the CIA.

Now, can you trust and corroborate and take as credible Ms. Miller's testimony? Remember, when she first testified in the Grand Jury about the July 8th meeting, she didn't remember the June 23rd meeting. Can you find her testimony about that credible?

Well, let me tell you a couple things to keep in mind when you are thinking about her testimony. First of all, who is Judith Miller? You heard she won a Pulitzer Prize. You heard someone testify about that. You also heard that Mr. Libby had some very nice things to say about her in the Grand Jury.

And think about this, ladies and gentlemen. The NIE gets declassified. Only three people in the United States know about it, as I told you. They could leak this to any reporter in the United States. This is an exclusive . . .

Remember, also, the circumstances when Ms. Miller first testified in the Grand Jury. They were hardly what you would call ordinary. She goes in the Grand Jury after spending the preceding 85 days in jail. She was in the Alexandria county jail for 85 days fighting a subpoena from the Office of Special Counsel. She didn't want to have to testify in this case.

So she has no access to her notes . . . She understands the interview in the Grand Jury to be about July 8th. And she is asked what happened on July 8th. And she testified, as she told you, that she remembers Mr. Libby talking about Wilson's wife working at the CIA on July 8th.

And she is asked in the Grand Jury, "Is this the first you ever heard this information?" She said, "You know, I have some memory of having heard this before, but I can't place it. I can't place the source. But I think I may have heard it before."

And she is asked then to go find her notes, to look for them. And you remember she went back to *The New York Times*. Her notes are in a shopping bag underneath her desk. She finds her notes from June 23rd and she finds, [them] there . . . And guess who her source was on June 23rd? It was Mr. Libby. And she looks at her notes, and it refreshes her recollection.

What's the other corroboration? Well, take a look at Mr. Libby's calendar for June 23rd. This is a portion of it. June 23rd, 3:00 p.m., 30-minute meeting, Mr. Libby's office. So you know that they did, in fact, meet on June 23rd.

Look at Mr. Libby's calendar entry for July 8th. 8:30 meeting. "Office time—private meeting at St. Regis." Next scheduled event is 11:45. That's the meeting that M[s]. Miller told you about that took place at the St. Regis.

NOW, A COUPLE THINGS I want you to think about . . . Remember how busy Mr. Libby was. Remember how he was doing the work of two men. Remember how much was on his plate and yet he can block off several hours to meet with Ms. Miller to deal with a political public-relations matter.

That tells you, ladies and gentlemen, how important and how pressing this issue was.

What's the other corroboration? Well, I want to show you a portion of Ms. Miller's testimony about June 23rd. I am going to show you a document that was introduced as a defense exhibit originally.

This is what she said in her testimony, a small segment of it. She is referring to Mr. Libby here, and she says, . . . "I think he was initially referred to as a clandestine guy, and that the Vice President's office had actually asked a question about a report in winter of 2002 that Iraq was trying to purchase uranium in Africa and that the CIA had sent Mr. Wilson out to investigate that claim."

So this is what Ms. Miller was explaining she took from what Mr. Libby told her on June 23rd.

This is a fax to Mr. Libby, sent June 9th, 2003. This is the time period that Mr. Hannah said Mr. Libby was doing his homework on Mr. Wilson.

. . . This is a memorandum dated February 14th, 2002, memorandum for the Vice President[:] "In response to your question on the possible sale of uranium from Niger to Iraq and its implications for Baghdad's nuclear program, we have tasked our clandestine source with ties to the Nigerian government." . . .

So Ms. Miller is able to accurately, in her notes, recount what Mr. Libby told her on June 23rd, 2003, and is able to come in here in January of 2007 and accurately tell you information that was in Mr. Libby's files from a fax that's sent to him from the CIA on June 9th.

And there's a couple things you should take away from that . . . Number one, you know Mr. Libby was doing his homework in June 2003 on Wilson, just like Mr. Hannah said.

Number two, Mr. Libby was able to remember those facts from June 9th to June 23rd, when he met with Ms. Miller.

Again, remember Mr. Hannah said Mr. Libby had a great memory when it came to remembering facts that supported his argument.

Number three, Ms. Miller was able to accurately get that information down in her notes and tell you about it from that stand in January 2007.

Ms. Miller was the ninth person who talked about Wilson's wife with Mr. Libby during that period between June 11th and the time he claims he was surprised and taken aback by the information he learned, as if for the first time, from Tim Russert.

The next conversation I want to talk about with you is the one with Tim Russert on July 10th or 11th.

Now, before I discuss Mr. Russert's testimony, I want to remind you first what Mr. Wells said about Mr. Russert in his opening. He said, "I do not contend that any of those reporters, Mr. Russert, Mr. Cooper or Ms. Miller, are going to come into this courtroom and give false testimony or lie. They are going to give, I believe or assume, their good-faith recollection, based on their oath. And they are going to do their best. I do not contend any of them are lying. They may, however, be mistaken, just like Mr. Libby may be mistaken.

"Mr. Libby, for example, in his Grand Jury, . . . talks about Tim Russert. He makes clear he thinks Tim Russert is one of the most respected reporters in the United States and that he deserves that respect. That's what he makes clear.

"So I want to make clear, when I cross-examine these reporters as the evidence comes in, I am not arguing now, nor will I argue later, that anybody is telling any intentional lies."

THAT'S WHAT HE TOLD YOU IN OPENING. And then on cross-examination for five-and-a-half hours, Mr. Wells tries to suggest to you that Mr. Russert is, in fact, lying, and that he is lying apparently because he wants so badly to avoid having to actually go into the Grand Jury. And the lure of going and being deposed in a lawyer's office under oath is so great that he would lie. And he is lying also, apparently, because of this feud—this bad blood between NBC News and the Office of Vice President.

Well, let's talk about that—but, first, I want you to recall what Mr. Libby said about the Russert conversation in the Grand Jury. He referred to that conversation between two-and-three-dozen times in the Grand Jury . . .

And his testimony . . . was not that he thought he probably or likely learned the information about Wilson's wife from Tim Russert, or he was pretty sure he learned it from Russert. He was unequivocal. He was certain. He remembers being struck by the news. He remembers what he was thinking when he was told this information by Tim

Russert. He remembers what he was feeling and how it struck him that Tim Russert thought this information was important . . .

Mr. Russert took the stand, and he recalled that conversation clearly. It was unique in his mind. He had never received a phone call like that from a high government official who was acting in the manner Mr. Libby did: swearing, angry, "what the hell is going on here? Damn it. I don't want my name to keep being mentioned on *Hardball*."

He is watching *Hardball*, . . . monitoring what's being said about him. With all that was going on in this world that was on his plate . . .

So Mr. Russert has a clear memory of this conversation. Mr. Russert never talked to Mr. Libby about Wilson's wife. He never said "all the reporters know about Wilson's wife." It never happened. Mr. Russert didn't know about Wilson's wife. He read about Joseph Wilson's wife in the newspaper. That conversation never happened.

Now, Mr. Wells wants to suggest to you that Mr. Russert is fabricating this . . . Well, let's just talk about those motives briefly that were suggested on cross-examination, that somehow not having to go to the Grand Jury would be some kind of a motive to fabricate testimony . . .

Why would Mr. Russert testify falsely under oath in a deposition? Because of a feud? Because of bad blood? Do you buy that? To buy that, ladies and gentlemen, you would have to believe that when Mr. Russert was home that morning getting his son ready for school and he got a call from Special Agent Jack Eckenrode asking him whether or not it's true that he told Scooter Libby that Joseph Wilson's wife works at the CIA and that all the reporters know it. Mr. Russert . . . right then and there, thought, "This is my chance; I am going to stick it to Scooter Libby. I am going to falsely deny that conversation took place because of this bad blood we have."

And then, of course, when he goes to the deposition and is placed under oath, he has to continue that lie, and, of course, he then has to continue that lie from the witness stand because of this feud, evidence of which is completely absent from the trial.

Wouldn't you think Mr. Libby, when he went in the Grand Jury in March of 2004, would have known about that bad blood? Instead, you hear the nice things he has to say about Mr. Russert. Wouldn't you think Cathie Martin, his press aide, who said that they always considered *Meet the Press* and Tim Russert to be a good venue for the Vice President, would have been aware of that bad blood?

It's a sign of how desperate the defense is to try and discredit Mr. Russert and his testimony that they would even suggest such a thing . . .

So let's add it up. Nine conversations about Wilson's wife with eight different people. Mr. Libby claims to remember none of them. The one conversation about Wilson's wife he says he has with Tim Russert, a conversation you now know never happened.

WHAT'S NEXT? MATT COOPER, JULY 12TH. You recall this was a conversation that took place when, at the end of that trip from the commissioning of the aircraft carrier, Mr. Libby is calling Mr. Cooper from Andrews Air Force Base. And you will remember Mr. Cooper and what he testified to about that conversation. He said that at the end of the conversation, Mr. Libby said to him, ["W]hat have you heard about

Wilson's wife sending him on the trip?" Libby's response: "Yes, I have heard about that." That's what Mr. Cooper said.

Now, in his opening, Mr. Wells suggested to you that the difference between what Mr. Libby said and what Mr. Cooper said is just the difference of a couple words because, according to Mr. Wells, Mr. Cooper, as he testified, said, I heard that too. And according to Mr. Wells, what Mr. Libby said was, I heard that too, but I don't know if it's true . . .

Mr. Libby never said to Matthew Cooper, "Reporters are telling the administration." He never told Matthew Cooper, "I don't know if it's true." He never told Matthew Cooper, "I don't even know if he has a wife." It's made up, made up out of whole cloth.

Ladies and gentlemen, Mr. Cooper could never have taken as confirmation the statement that Mr. Libby claims he made to him. Remember, Mr. Cooper took Mr. Libby's statement as confirmation for the tip he had gotten the day before from Karl Rove. How could he have taken as confirmation a statement that Mr. Libby claims he made: "I don't know if this is true; I don't even know if he has a wife?"

Mr. Cooper is corroborated by Cathie Martin. You remember Cathie Martin was present, . . . sitting next to Mr. Libby during the end of the call. She never heard Mr. Libby say any of what you just heard Mr. Libby claim he said in the Grand Jury. She never heard him say, "I don't know if it is true; reporters are telling the administration; I don't even know if he has a wife."

And if she had heard it, she would have said something because she knew that wasn't true. She had told Mr. Libby herself about Wilson's wife thirty days earlier.

Finally, ladies and gentlemen, you heard from Mr. Cooper that this was a conversation that kept playing through his mind. He has thought about it often, and beginning right away, because it was significant. It was the confirmation for a story that got a lot of attention.

Then there was the leak, the Robert Novak article. Then there was the litigation. Then he was subpoenaed. So he has had many occasions to think and reflect back, and he is sure about what he testified. And there is no reason in the world he would say it if he wasn't . . .

Mr. Libby has tried to obscure and hide from the FBI and the Grand Jury where he learned this information. Why? Because in doing an investigation into whether something is classified, obviously you need to know where you learned it because if you learned it in a classified briefing and you walked out and told the first person you know, there is a very high degree of likelihood that you knew that the information you are conveying is classified.

If you are passing along gossip, ladies and gentlemen, it's very hard to say that that was a knowing, intentional disclosure of classified information . . .

The other point I want to remind you is when you are considering the testimony and whether those statements have been proved false or not, don't consider just Tim Russert's testimony, for instance, on that first statement. Consider all the testimony of all the witnesses. So when Mr. Russert says—when Mr. Libby claims he was surprised by that information that Mr. Russert told him, you don't have to consider—and you shouldn't consider just Mr. Russert's testimony. Consider all the witnesses who testified, from Cathie Martin, Grenier, Grossman, Schmall, and Judith Miller—all the witnesses. All of it is relevant and all of it should be considered by you . . .

Now, ladies and gentlemen, thus far I have talked about the Government's case and what we think and we submit we have proved. I want to talk just a little bit about what the defendant's Grand Jury testimony reflects and whether you should accept it as credible.

If you will recall, . . . in his opening statement and in cross-examination of witnesses, the defense has tried to suggest that Mr. Libby was so busy, had so much on his plate, and had so many responsibilities that it's simply unreasonable to expect that, months later, he could remember what Mr. Wells likes to call a little snippet of conversation, just a little piece, gossip. Is it fair to expect him to remember? And if he doesn't, is it fair to call that a lie?

Well, I wanted to take you back to some testimony that Mr. Libby gave about another conversation he had on July 11th with Karl Rove. And before I play that tape, I just want to remind you what was going on on July 11th. This was the end of the week, that horrible week for the administration. July 6th was a Sunday. Joseph Wilson's op-ed appears. Joseph Wilson appears on *Meet the Press*. All the questions. The firestorm starts. What about the sixteen words? Did the President lie us into war?

The next day, July 7th, the administration says the sixteen words shouldn't have been in the State of Union address. It's like pouring gasoline on the fire. The questions are raging, the criticism.

Mr. Libby is back at the White House. The President and his entourage are in Africa, and he has got to deal with this issue. So it's a horrible week. And you will recall they are waiting for the Tenet statement to come out, which they are hoping will address some of these questions. So the 11th is a Friday.

And you will recall Mr. Libby talks about a conversation he had with Mr. Rove about a conversation Mr. Rove had with Bob Novak about Wilson's wife . . . I want you to think . . . carefully [of] all the details that Mr. Libby is able to recall eight months later when he is testifying in the Grand Jury, without the benefit of notes, about this conversation that occurred at the end of that week, July 11th, 2003 . . .

Now, consider how amazingly sharp and clear the details of that conversation are, . . . that Mr. Libby can recount for the Grand Jury, eight months after he has it, every detail of a conversation that Karl Rove has with Bob Novak and what Novak tells Karl Rove about Wilson's wife, but he can't remember one out of nine conversations that he himself has about Wilson's wife because it's a trivial detail? Isn't it the same trivial detail that he learned from Karl Rove in that conversation, and yet he can remember it with no difficulty and no notes?

When you consider Mr. Libby's testimony, you will find, ladies and gentlemen, that there is a pattern of always forgetting the piece about Wilson's wife.

Remember his testimony when he testified in the Grand Jury about his lunch with Ari Fleischer? He remembered meeting with Ari Fleischer. He remembered talking about Ari Fleischer's future plans, . . . thanking Mr. Fleischer for what he had said that morning at the gaggle. He remembered talking about the Miami Dolphins—talk about a trivial detail that he can recall months later. He remembers the Dolphins, but doesn't remember talking about the wife.

He remembers meeting with Judith Miller on July 8th and talking about the NIE, the Powell presentation and the Wilson story generally. Doesn't remember talking about Wilson's wife. Remembers meeting with David Addington and talking about declassification. Remembers Mr. Addington citing a case, *Navy v. Egan*. Doesn't remember talking about the wife.

Ask yourselves if that pattern is just a convenient way of avoiding the truth. Is that truthful testimony, ladies and gentlemen? Mr. Libby's memory is such that he can remember with specificity what he didn't talk about.

What do I mean? Look at Government Exhibit GX-402. This is the newspaper article, the Wilson op-ed . . . and these are the questions that the Vice President wrote in his own hand at the top of that op-ed, which was published on July 6th: "Have they done this sort of thing before, sent an ambassador to answer a question? Do we ordinarily send people out pro bono to work for us? Or did his wife send him on a junket?"

Those are the questions that the Vice President was asking on July 6th, 2003. Now, ask yourselves, the Vice President has those questions. Who is he going to discuss them with? Do you think he is just pondering this on his own, idly wondering these things? Or is he going to talk about them to his Chief of Staff? Isn't it obvious that he is going to be working on that with his right-hand man, Mr. Libby?

And when Mr. Fitzgerald asked those questions to Mr. Libby in the Grand Jury about didn't these issues come up that week of July 6th, Mr. Libby has a specific memory of talking about everything except the wife . . .

I want to talk to you for just a minute about Robert Novak. There was a suggestion in the opening that maybe all that's happened here is that Mr. Libby confused Mr. Novak with Mr. Russert, and that's the source of all this confusion. I don't know if the defense is going to argue that to you or not. But sitting right here and looking at the two, I would suggest it wouldn't be easy to confuse those two men.

But think about this, ladies and gentlemen. When Mr. Libby was asked about Mr. Novak in the Grand Jury—according to Mr. Wells in his opening—Mr. Libby thought the investigation was all about Novak. That's what Mr. Wells told you. And when Mr. Libby was in the Grand Jury, he said he hadn't talked to Mr. Novak for a year and a half prior to the publication of that article. And now there is a suggestion, well, maybe he just forgot that he learned it and he confused the two.

Well, ladies and gentlemen, I will just ask you this question: if you thought an investigation was all about who leaked to Robert Novak and you are called to the Grand Jury, and instead of leaking to Robert Novak, you learned that same information from Robert Novak, don't you think you would remember it?

Finally, ladies and gentlemen, in talking about the credibility, just consider Mr. Libby's story that he forgot the information the Vice President told him about Wilson's wife on June 11th. Just think about it in the isolation. Forget for a second about the testimony of those nine conversations you have heard about that I have gone through with you. Just imagine—and I want to suggest to you it's simply not credible to believe that he would have forgotten this information about Wilson's wife between June 11th and July. It's ludicrous.

Here is an issue that is front and center. Joseph Wilson is spurring headlines, accusing the government, the White House, of lying the country into war, and the Vice President's office is in the hot seat. Mr. Libby is the Vice President's right-hand man. They are asked a question over and over: why does Wilson say the Vice President sent him? Mr. Libby thinks he has got an answer: the wife. That's why he says it. He is getting this information—"bad skinny," as he calls it—from the wife. He writes it down in his notes.

Why would the Vice President have shared this with him if the Vice President didn't think it was important, and why would Libby have written it down if he didn't think it was important? And he wants you to believe, notwithstanding the fact that this question gets asked to them over and over, that he is doing his homework that John Hannah told you, . . . to school himself on what is going on with Joseph Wilson, and he so completely forgets the information about Wilson's wife that when Russert tells him about it, supposedly, on July 11th, it rings no bells, and it sparks no memory? Not a question of where did I hear this before, but struck anew as if hearing it the first time? Ladies and gentlemen, it's just not credible.

I want to talk, finally, ladies and gentlemen, about Mr. Libby and his motive to lie in this case. Mr. Wells told you something in his opening with which the government fully agrees. He said people don't lie for the heck of it; they have to have a reason.

That is absolutely true. And I want you to consider that when thinking about the testimony of all of the government witnesses and ask yourselves, what possible reason could they have to lie? And is it conceivable that . . . all of those witnesses would make the same mistake, the same error in their memory [so that] all happen to recall having this conversation with Mr. Libby?

Well, let's look at Mr. Libby and his motive to lie, because Mr. Wells told you there was no motive to lie. Well, think about what Mr. Libby was confronting when he went to the FBI on October 14th, 2003. Think about what was in his head. What did he know? He knew that there was a criminal investigation into the possible unauthorized disclosure of classified information. He knew that. He knew he had talked to at least three people about Wilson's wife. He knew he had talked to Judith Miller. He knew he had talked to Matthew Cooper. He knew he had talked to Ari Fleischer. So he knows those facts.

Now, what else do we know that he knows? Look at GX-422, a newspaper article taken from Mr. Libby's files. It's dated October 12th. And if you look at the bottom, it appears it was printed out on October 14th, 2003, the very day Mr. Libby was interviewed by the FBI.

"FBI agents tracing linkage of envoy to CIA operative. FBI agents investigating the disclosure of a CIA officer's identity have begun by examining events in the month before the leak, when the CIA, the White House and Vice President Cheney's office first were asked about former ambassador Joseph C. Wilson's CIA-sponsored trip to Niger, according to sources familiar with the probe.

"In their interviews, FBI agents are asking questions about events going back to at least early June, the sources said. That indicates investigators are examining not just who passed the information to Novak and other reporters, but also how Plame's name may have first become linked with Wilson and his mission, who did it and how the information made its way around the government.

"One reason investigators are looking back is that even before Novak's column appeared, government officials had been trying for more than a month to convince journalists that Wilson's mission was not as important as it was being portrayed.

"After the June story, a lot of people in government were scurrying around asking, who is this envoy and why is he saying these things, a senior administration official said.

"On July 17th, the *TIME* magazine web site reported that some government officials have noted to *TIME* in interviews, as well as to syndicated columnist Robert Novak, that Wilson's wife, Valerie Plame, is a CIA official who monitors the proliferation of weapons of mass destruction."

LADIES AND GENTLEMEN, reading that article would tell any intelligent man—and there is no question Mr. Libby is one—that the FBI is looking for him. They want to talk to the person in the Office of the Vice President that was, in the month before the Novak column—remember, Novak is published July 14th—the month prior to that, who was scurrying around trying to find out about Wilson. That was Mr. Libby. So that's on his mind.

Look at GX-423, published October 4th, taken from Mr. Libby's files. "Leak of agent's name causes exposure of CIA front firm. The leak of a CIA operative's name has also exposed the identity of a CIA front company, potentially expanding the damage caused by the original disclosure.

"After the name of the company was broadcast yesterday, administration officials confirmed that it was a CIA front."

Skipping down, "The justice department began a formal criminal investigation of the leak September 26th."

And this article goes on to talk about the damage inadvertent disclosure of the name of a business affiliated with the CIA could cause the agency and the government.

Remember the testimony of Craig Schmall, the CIA briefer. He told Mr. Libby when this story broke that the disclosure of a covert agent's name is serious business. People can be harassed. People can get arrested. People can get killed.

Remember the testimony of David Addington. He testified that Mr. Libby came to him and asked him, "How would you know if someone is covert?" Why would Mr. Libby be asking that question if he wasn't wondering exactly the questions that are being asked in these articles? Who did it? And remember Mr. Addington's answer: "You wouldn't know." Not much comfort, that answer.

Look at Mr. Libby's nondisclosure agreement that he signed with the government. He agreed, . . . "I have been advised that the unauthorized disclosure, unauthorized retention or negligent handling of classified information by me could cause damage or irreparable injury to the United States. I understand that if I am uncertain about the classification status of information, I am required to confirm from an authorized official that the information is unclassified before I may disclose it, except to a person provided."

And the fourth, "I have been advised that any breach of this agreement may result in the termination of my security clearances." . . .

Now,…knowing his nondisclosure agreement has been signed, and looking at those articles, there can be no question that Mr. Libby would have had reason to think he is going to be fired, at a minimum . . . And think about the political damage.

And remember, Mr. Libby early in October went to the Vice President and said he wanted to be cleared like Karl Rove had been cleared. And you remember Government Exhibit 532. This is a statement that he gave to the Vice President—the top half was identified as Mr. Libby's—saying that he wanted to be cleared and get a clearing statement and, in fact, he got one . . .

They were not involved in this. So he has had the White House stake its credibility that he was not involved. Now he is in a vice because if he admits—after asking the Vice President to get him cleared by the White House, he is going to have to retract his public statements made to the world. He knows what he did. And now the FBI comes knocking. He knows that there is a criminal investigation, and he knows from press accounts that it appears that this woman, Ms. Wilson, Valerie Wilson, was a covert agent.

Now he has a choice to make. He can tell the truth and take his chances with the investigation or he can lie. And ladies and gentlemen, he took the second choice. He decided to lie, and he made up a story that he thought would cover him.

He knew he had a note in his files from the Vice President which indicated that he had learned about Wilson's wife on June 11th. So he had to somehow account for that. This is an official source. The Vice President learned it from the director or a high official at the CIA.

So he had to come up with a story that was innocuous. So what he said that would account for that note was "I forgot; I forgot all about what the Vice President told me. And I learned this anew, as if for the first time, from a reporter, Tim Russert. And Tim Russert told me that all the reporters know it. Everyone knows this. And all I did was pass this information on as if it were gossip." And that's the description of what he was doing, because whenever he talked and described his conduct, he always said—"I said, reporters are telling us. I don't know if it's true. I don't know even know if he has a wife." Because that would make his conduct appear innocuous. Not criminal. Innocuous.

And that is the story that he came up with. And after he told the FBI that on October 14th, his feet were planted, and he had to maintain that story [in] a second FBI interview and his two appearances in the Grand Jury.

Ladies and gentlemen, as Mr. Fitzgerald told you in his opening, this is a case about lying. It's not a case about conspiracies. It's not a case about scapegoating. There is no

White House conspiracy here. There is no NBC conspiracy here. Mr. Libby is not here because of any bad deeds or misconduct by others. He is here because of his own choices and his own decisions. He decided to lie to the FBI and the Grand Jury.

Ladies and gentlemen, when you consider all the evidence, we suggest the government has met its burden of proof and has established the defendant lied under oath to the Grand Jury and committed perjury. He made false statements to the FBI and he obstructed justice.

We would ask you to convict Mr. Libby on each count in the indictment.

Thank you.

CLOSING ARGUMENT ON BEHALF
OF THE DEFENDANT

THE DEFENSE'S CLOSING ARGUMENT is done by both Wells and Jeffress. Wells begins, and he starts by addressing the prosecution's claim that he had made claims in his opening argument that he had failed to deliver on during the trial, particularly about the White House scapegoating Libby to save Rove. It should be noted that Wells periodically uses the third person to refer to himself.

MR. WELLS: Judge Walton, the prosecution team, and ladies and gentlemen of the jury: I was sitting there listening to the prosecutor talk about my opening statement and things I said. For a few minutes, I said, "Well, maybe I was drunk or something when I made my opening because he sure sounded like I said a lot of things that I could not deliver on."

The prosecutor said, "Mr. Wells said, with respect to the Cooper conversation, there were a very few words: 'I have heard that, too, but I don't know if it's even true.'"

The prosecutor said, "Mr. Wells said that, but then he played you the grand jury—the rest of the conversation."

Now, you are going to get instructions tomorrow from Judge Walton, and the instructions will set forth exactly what the charges are and what you are going to have to discuss and debate among yourselves in the deliberations room.

And let me show you what is in Judge Walton's instruction about the Cooper conversation in terms of count 3. That's Mr. Libby's statement to the FBI. Let's just put it on the screen and see if what is charged is just what I told you in my opening, and it is about a very few words. This is right from Judge Walton's instructions that you will have. He gave it to us over the weekend. We have it. I am going to quote from his instructions today.

Count 3 of the indictment alleges that Mr. Libby falsely told the FBI on October 14 or November 16, 2003, that during a conversation with Matthew Cooper of *TIME* magazine on July 12, 2003, Mr. Libby told Mr. Cooper that reporters were telling the administration that Mr. Wilson's wife worked for the CIA, but that Mr. Libby did not know if this was true.

That's what I told you in my opening statement. That's what the charge is.

Now, what Mr. Zeidenberg did was something that I am not going to characterize because I don't want it to be personal. But what he did, he read to you from count 5, which is a longer statement from a different count concerning the Cooper conversation. But it's kind of interesting how the longer statement came . . . about because count 3 is based on what Mr. Libby said when he went into the grand jury in October and November, and—when he went before the FBI in October and November. And that's what Mr. Libby said to the FBI, and that's the basis of that count.

THEN WHAT HAPPENED, months later, in March, they get Mr. Libby in the Grand Jury and they start beating on him . . . And as they are beating on him in the Grand Jury in that first day and that second day, Mr. Libby, because he is reconstructing . . . then says, for the first time, "Well, maybe I even said he didn't have a wife." The conversation expands as they are beating on him in the room . . .

What I said to you in my opening is just what you are going to get. You look at count 1, the obstruction count, that deals with the Cooper conversation—just what you will see in count 3. Only the longer conversation is in count 5, but that is the one after they get him in the grand jury and he starts expanding as they are beating on him.

Then Mr. Zeidenberg said to you I said in my opening statement that there was a White House conspiracy and that he didn't see any White House conspiracy. The scapegoat, Scooter Libby. He said there was no proof of it.

In this case, the issue is whether or not Scooter Libby intentionally made false statements. And one of the key questions is, what was Scooter Libby's state of mind right before he went and was interviewed by the FBI? That meat grinder note shows what was Scooter Libby's state of mind right before he was interviewed by the FBI; it is one of the most important . . . pieces of evidence in this case . . .

What I promised was that I would show you a note and introduce into evidence a note, which I did, that showed that the Vice President of this country wrote a note in his own hand, with his own pen, and he wrote that it was not fair to protect Karl Rove and to sacrifice Scooter Libby.

Now, Ted Wells did not make those words up . . . The Vice President wrote, "not fair to protect Rove and sacrifice Libby."

. . . [W]hat that note shows is that for Scooter Libby to get cleared by the White House, he had to go fight for it.

They went out and cleared Karl Rove on day one. Scooter Libby, you will see from that note, because it shows his state of mind, acted like an innocent person. He was mad . . .

After they cleared Rove, [Libby] went to Andy Card, the Chief of Staff to President Bush. He says, "it's not fair; you should clear me, too. I didn't do anything." Andy Card blew him off.

Scooter Libby . . . then went to Scott McClellan: "You cleared Rove; you should clear me. I didn't do anything."

Scott McClellan said, "No, I am not going down the list. Just Rove, not you."

And then Scooter Libby did what I suggest only an innocent person would do. He knew he didn't do anything. He is ticked off. He goes to the Vice President of the United States and says, "This is not fair. I didn't do anything. Why am I being left out there by myself?"

The clear suggestion, once they cleared Rove, was that Scooter Libby had done something. The clear suggestion was that he was going to be the public scapegoat.

And so he goes to the Vice President—only an innocent person would do this—and says, "It's not right; it's not fair." And the Vice President writes in his own handwriting: "It's not right to . . . protect Rove and sacrifice Libby."

As I said, Ted Wells doesn't write that. Scooter Libby didn't write it. It was written, and it exists.

Now, I want to start . . . the way I had intended to start before some of Mr. Zeidenberg's personalized comments. I opened to you about a month ago. And now that we have had a month of testimony, witnesses and documents, I submit to you that nothing has changed from what I said to you in my opening statement.

I told you that Scooter Libby was . . . totally innocent. I told you he did not commit perjury, did not commit obstruction of justice, and did not make any false statements. I said he was an innocent man and he had been wrongly charged.

And I also told you that this was a case about he said/she said. It's a case about different recollections between Mr. Libby and some reporters . . .

[I]n terms of what you have to decide as jurors, in terms of what the government has to prove beyond a reasonable doubt, it relates to Mr. Libby's conversations with the reporters. Those are the charges, and they are set forth in detail in the jury instructions . . .

Now, something has changed in a material way since I opened. When I opened, I told you the case was about three reporters, three telephone calls, and recollections about what took place three months previously. But Judge Walton last week dismissed the charges with respect to Ms. Miller's July 12th conversation.

Let me read to you again what will be in Judge Walton's instruction. Again, these are taken verbatim from what Judge Walton has given us.

. . .Count 1, the obstruction of justice count, is now based solely on the allegations that Mr. Libby falsely testified to the grand jury concerning his conversations with two reporters, Mr. Russert and Mr. Cooper . . .

Let me talk for a minute about Mr. Cooper. The facts are almost undisputed in terms of the background of the Cooper conversation. Mr. Libby gets up on the morning of July 12th. He takes his wife and his two children—it is the birthday of . . . the son, his tenth birthday. And the Libby family, on that Saturday—they go to Andrews Air Force Base, they get on Air Force Two, and it's a day of celebration because they are going to Norfolk to watch the commemoration of the *Ronald Reagan* ship, and it's like a holiday for the kids. That's the birthday present to the little boy. Great birthday present. Air Force Two in the front with the Vice President. Great birthday present.

And Ms. Martin told you that Mr. Libby—he really didn't have his mind on talking to any reporters that day. But Ms. Martin says to Mr. Libby, look, reporters have been calling, including Matt Cooper . . . Are we going to talk to them? Are we not going to talk to them? Mr. Libby: okay. He walks up to the front of the plane, Air Force Two, talks to the Vice President, and comes back with talking points: this is what I am supposed to say.

You don't have to guess about what he said or was supposed to say, because there are contemporaneous notes. See, nobody could have predicted on July 12th that one day there would be a criminal case in this courtroom. Those notes are contemporaneous notes. Nobody could ever have thought they would be in evidence in a criminal case. The notes speak the truth . . . And those notes don't say anything about Valerie Wilson.

And so the plane lands. Mr. Libby goes into a small room at Andrews Air Force Base with Ms. Martin there. Jenny Mayfield is in the room. And they call Matt Cooper. And while they are calling him, Ms. Libby and the two children are in the next room.

And Ms. Martin testified Mr. Libby wanted to get home. Those kids had been up since 6:00 in the morning. They wanted to get home to put those kids to bed. And Ms. Martin said Mr. Libby didn't want to be on the calls. He wanted to get his children home.

He had never talked to Matt Cooper in his life. And he gets on the phone and he has a conversation with Matt Cooper. And Matt Cooper testified, Scooter Libby didn't say anything about the wife. Scooter Libby wasn't running around trying to leak something. Matt Cooper said he was trying to keep Libby on the phone. So he throws out one: ["H]ey, have you heard that the wife sent him on the trip?"

Matt Cooper says Scooter Libby said, "I heard that, too." Scooter Libby says in his FBI interview that he said, "I heard that, too, but I don't know if it's true. Don't know if it's even true."

And it is just about a few words, regardless of what he says . . . And what did we learn? We saw what was, in essence, a Perry Mason moment in this courtroom when my partner, Bill Jeffress, one of the great lawyers in this country, questioned Mr. Cooper and put up on that screen the notes that clearly show—"I don't even know," and the guy stops. It shows what Mr. Libby said was accurate, and that's what happened.

And maybe when it happened, maybe some of you start to open your mind and say, maybe something else is going on in this courtroom. Because when that was up on that screen, it was clear. What Scooter Libby said he recalled, "I don't even know," and the guy stopped writing—that was up there, and that's the piece Mr. Cooper said, ["W]ell, I can't explain it." . . .

Scooter Libby is innocent. He didn't do anything. He didn't leak to anybody. I mean, think about the madness of this prosecution. He is being charged with a conversation on July 12th with a reporter he had never met in his life, never talked to in his life, trying to get home and get the kids home.

And . . . if you want to be fair-minded, the notes support Mr. Libby. Yet he has been indicted for perjury, false statements. There is a craziness to this case.

Let me talk for a minute about Mr. Russert. I am going to talk a lot about Mr. Russert. Mr. Russert took the stand and said, ["I]t was impossible for me to have asked Scooter Libby a question on July 11th. It was impossible because I did not know then that Mrs. Wilson worked at the CIA, so I could not have asked Mr. Libby the question," Mr. Russert said, "because I didn't read about it until July 14th in *The Washington Post*, and I read it in the *Post* and I said, 'Wow.'"

Well, I then introduced, as the last piece of my case, . . . a stipulation as to what case Agent Eckenrode, who is the head of the whole FBI investigative team [said] . . .

". . . Russert does not recall stating to Libby in this conversation anything about the wife of former ambassador Joe Wilson, although he could not completely rule out the possibility that he had such an exchange."

That's what Agent Eckenrode would have testified to. That's what Tim Russert said in November of 2003. He could not completely rule out the possibility that he had such an exchange. Russert was at a loss to remember it, and moreover, he believes that this would be the type of conversation that he would or should remember. Russert acknowledged that he speaks to many people on a daily basis, and it is difficult to reconstruct some specific conversations, particularly one which occurred several months ago.

That statement that he could not rule it out is totally contrary from what he told you on the witness stand. And with respect to the counts involving Tim Russert, those counts rely almost exclusively on Tim Russert's testimony. He is a one-man show. There is no corroboration. It's what I mean when I say he said/she said. It's what Russert said he recalls and Libby says he recalls. That's it.

They want you to make a choice, with no corroboration, between Mr. Russert and Mr. Libby where the choice—if you were to say, well, I believe Mr. Russert beyond a reasonable doubt, that my client's life would be destroyed; his reputation would be destroyed.

That stipulation in and of itself is reasonable doubt—in and of itself. I don't have to talk about what Mr. Russert didn't remember about the *Buffalo News*. I don't have to talk about Mr. Russert's misleading affidavit that he filed with the court. I don't have to talk about how forgetful he was up on the stand about the morning of Mr. Libby's indictment . . . That stipulation in and of itself is reasonable doubt. That he made a statement that was different than what he told you in this courtroom at an earlier period, back in November of 2003, is reasonable doubt. It is what is called an impeaching statement.

Some statements come into evidence for impeachment purposes. Others come in as impeachment and substantive evidence. This is not a substantive-evidence statement; it is an impeachment statement. But the mere fact that he made a different statement at an earlier point in time in a case where it's one-on-one, his word versus Libby's word, where the stakes are a man's reputation, a man's life. That's reasonable doubt in and of itself.

Now, Mr. Russert says, it was impossible for me to have asked the question because I didn't know until I read it in the newspaper. Well, what did we learn from Robert Novak? I am going to walk you through this because it's some of the most important testimony in the whole case. It says that the government's entire timeline is wrong.

The government says the Novak article doesn't come out until July 14th. But it came out on the A.P. wire by 2:00 on July 11th. If you lived in that world of the media, if you lived in that world of reporters, you could get access to it. You could read it. You could have it read to you. People could call you and talk about it.

Maybe for those of us who are non-reporters, we couldn't have seen the article until Monday. But if you lived in Tim Russert's world, if you lived in the world of the media, it was on the A.P. wire, even though it was what is called embargoed; that is, it couldn't be printed. But reporters could read it. They could talk about it . . .

Now, maybe all that happened in this case is that on July 11, Tim Russert read the column. Maybe somebody from *The Washington Post* called him and talked to him about the column, and the only thing perhaps is that Tim Russert has misrecollected the date on which he heard about the column. Maybe he is confused, like a lot of witnesses were, to think that he heard about it from the *Post* on Monday, the 14th, and the only thing that happened was that he heard about it on the 11th and he asked Scooter Libby a question: "Do you know anything about the wife working at the CIA?" And Mr. Libby said, "no," because that's Mr. Libby's style, not to confirm.

And Tim Russert says, "Well, all the reporters know." It would be a natural response, if Mr. Russert had known it was out on the wire, to say "all the reporters know." And maybe all that has happened in this case is that Tim Russert has forgotten that he heard about it on the 11th rather than the 14th. It may be as simple as that, a simple piece of misrecollection . . .

And think about the statement . . . "all the reporters know." By the 11th, it is a true statement. That article by the 11th, by 2:00, is in the newsrooms of over a hundred media outlets . . .

The sole question for an American jury in a criminal case . . . is whether the government has proved guilt beyond a reasonable doubt. Jurors are not, in their deliberations, to ask a question, well, is he innocent? Was innocence proven? That is a forbidden question because, under our system of justice, innocence is presumed . . . So the sole question is whether you have been given such a quality and quantity of evidence that the cloak of innocence has been ripped away from Mr. Libby and the government has established guilt.

So please, I urge you, follow the instructions . . . Don't get it backwards. Don't start, well, did he prove innocence, or did he prove he made an innocent mistake, or did he prove he was confused? The sole question for you is, did the government prove that he intentionally, deliberately made false statements? That is the principle . . .

Think about the phrase, "firmly convinced." You are only to check the guilty box if you are firmly convinced, based on the evidence they have given you, of Mr. Libby's guilt.

The instruction goes on to say, reasonable doubt is the kind of doubt that would cause a reasonable person, after careful and thoughtful reflection, to hesitate to act in the graver or more important matters in life.

It is an extraordinarily high standard of proof that the government must meet . . .

Now, let me talk about Mr. Libby's defense to each and every charge in the indictment. Let me first quickly talk about the charges. There are five counts. You are going to get a verdict sheet with five counts. In the instructions, each count will be discussed and the elements will be discussed, exactly what the alleged statements are.

Count 1, that's obstruction of justice based on two alleged false statements: Mr. Russert and Mr. Cooper.

Count 2, false statement, Tim Russert.

Count 3, false statement, Matthew Cooper.

Count 4, perjury, Tim Russert.

Count 5, perjury, Matthew Cooper.

I want to again note, Libby has not been charged with leaking classified information. There is no such charge in the indictment. There has never been any such charge. And with respect to the conversations with Mr. Russert and Mr. Cooper, they are—as I said, they are he said/she said. There are no recordings. There are hardly any notes.

There is nothing. Just two guys on one side, one guy on the other, with different recollections about something that happened months and months earlier.

Remember when I told you in my opening statement: it's like if you were young and 21 and had this great memory and you got out of school in June and you spent the summer on the beach and you're back in college in September and somebody said, tell me about a telephone conversation you had in June. I mean, if you were just laying on the beach all summer, you still couldn't do it, much less if you lived in the world of Scooter Libby.

He didn't get to lay on the beach. He hardly got to see his wife and family. He worked—as you heard, . . . 14 hours a day dealing with important issues.

So the notion of asking this man, well, what happened on the Russert call or what happened on the Cooper call three months earlier—again, there is a madness to even putting the question to people—the notion that somebody could be charged with something like this.

Now, what are Mr. Libby's defenses? The same defense to every count: the government hasn't established beyond a reasonable doubt that he made intentional false statements. They have got to prove intentional lying—deliberate lying. Libby acted in good faith, and the government has not proved beyond a reasonable doubt that Libby acted with criminal intent . . .

Now, there is one other instruction I want to talk to you about. It's called the "good faith" instruction. It will be in your book. It's one of the most important instructions, I submit, in the case, though all the instructions are important.

And the "good-faith" instruction reads, . . . "A person who makes a statement based on a belief or opinion which he honestly held when the statement was made has not violated the statutes the defendant is charged with violating in this case. Merely because the statement turns out to be inaccurate, incorrect or wrong—making an honest statement that turns out to be inaccurate, incorrect or wrong because of mistake, confusion or faulty memory, or even carelessness in one's recollection, does not rise to the level of criminal conduct." . . .

Mr. Libby, when he was being interviewed by the FBI and when he was in the grand jury, that he gave his best, good-faith recollection . . . [A]ny misstatements by Libby were innocent mistakes . . . Libby had no knowledge that Valerie Wilson's job status was classified. No one has testified that they told Scooter Libby that Mrs. Wilson's job status was covert or classified. It has not happened. It did not take place. You listened to the grand jury. He says it under oath: "I had no idea. I had no idea."

And . . . whether or not she was classified, Judge Walton has ruled, is out of bounds. We can't get into that, either side.

Libby did not push reporters to write about Valerie Wilson. I mean, we heard testimony about Armitage over at the State [Department]. He was out telling people about Ms. Wilson.

We heard about Karl Rove. He told Matt Cooper about Valerie Wilson. We heard about Ari Fleischer. He told David Gregory. He told Pincus about Valerie Wilson. But Mr. Libby, I submit to you, told no one. He didn't confirm it. He didn't tell anybody.

I mean, when Judy Miller testifies, oh, well, Mr. Libby said something to me on July 8th about WINPAC. Mrs. Wilson didn't work at WINPAC. I mean, Mr. Libby is not a nut. Is he going to go out and—oh, I am going to leak; let me give false information. She didn't work at WINPAC . . .

Libby did not leak to Robert Novak. Richard Armitage did. Mr. Fitzgerald candidly conceded to you in his opening statement that Mr. Libby was not the source for Robert Novak. There is no dispute among the parties about that.

Libby is innocent and he had no motive to lie. He had no motive . . .

. . . Russert said, "No, it would be impossible because I didn't know who that person was until several days later." And I want you to note that there is nothing but Russert's uncorroborated testimony that supports his version of the July 2003 telephone call with Libby. I mean, Russert has no notes. He has no recordings. It is a classic case of Russert, this is what I remember, and Libby, this is what I remember . . .

I will tell you right now what I said to you in my opening statement, that you do not have to find that Tim Russert is a liar, or I would not argue in my opening, as I said, that he is a liar—I am not arguing that now. You do not have to find that Tim Russert took the stand and intentionally lied. I stand by what I said in my opening statement. You don't have to make that finding.

But I am saying to you in the strongest, unambiguous terms that Tim Russert, based on the cross-examination and based on the evidence in the record—his testimony is not sufficiently reliable that any American jury can fairly convict a person beyond a reasonable doubt on the testimony in this case of Tim Russert.

You don't have to decide, did he lie? Because what Mr. Russert is saying basically is it's impossible, and I submit to you he just doesn't recall. It wasn't an important conversation to him, and he just doesn't recall.

NOW, THE FIRST QUESTION to ask yourself . . . just use your common sense: Why in the world would Scooter Libby make up a lie and use Tim Russert as his cover? Mr. Libby has no personal relationship with Tim Russert in the world. He has never been out to dinner with him . . . It's a purely professional relationship. You ought to stop right there and say, it doesn't make any sense that he would use Russert to cover . . .

Secondly, well, was the Russert conversation some kind of conversation that Mr. Libby could know with confidence would never be examined because it was protected by the reporter's privilege, protected by the First Amendment? It wasn't that kind of conversation. Mr. Libby says in the grand jury and Mr. Russert said from the stand, it was just a viewer complaint . . . Mr. Libby calls Russert in his capacity as manager. It had nothing to do with the First Amendment, reporter's privilege at all.

Third, NBC was not exactly the friendly network at that point in time with respect to the Wilson matter to Scooter Libby. NBC is where Chris Matthews was on the TV all the time bad-mouthing the Vice President. That was Tim Russert's network. And NBC was where Ambassador Wilson made his debut. When he first came public, he went on NBC. That was his network. That was his home spot on *Meet the Press*, sitting there with Andrea Mitchell . . .

Reasons to doubt Russert's trial testimony[:] . . . .

First, he has no notes of the conversation. Second, his trial testimony is inconsistent with his FBI interview. I have already reviewed that with you. Third, the evidence shows Russert could have known about Wilson's wife prior to July 14, even if he has forgotten that now, because you know from the evidence that David Gregory was told by Fleischer in Uganda that the wife worked for the CIA, and there is a stipulation in evidence that the time difference in Uganda—because they are ahead of us—is such that Gregory is told about 8:00 in the morning on the 11th. And that's stipulated. That is not even disputed in terms of the time difference . . .

Also, there are serious questions about Russert's credibility—again, not that you have to find him to be a liar, but in terms of his general credibility. [A]m I going to convict another human being on the basis of this man's testimony?

We know he filed a misleading affidavit with Judge Hogan when he said to Judge Hogan that I am protecting the First Amendment; I can't even talk about the fact that I had a conversation with Scooter Libby, when we know he already had the conversation with the FBI in November concerning his talk with Scooter Libby. Then he filed a misleading affidavit . . . You all read it. Ask yourselves, does that comport with what happened in November?

We also know Russert gave a misleading account of his involvement in this case to the public. Russert went out on TV and said, ["O]h, the story with me is very simple. I just got a subpoena. I fought it. I lost. And then I testified in a deposition." He never tells the public, ["O]h, and by the way, before I got the subpoena and fought it, I had been called by the FBI and I discussed the whole conversation freely."

Finally, Mr. Russert has memory problems. Okay? He forgot a very important telephone call that involved himself—a personal attack on his own credibility involving the *Buffalo News,* only a few months before he went into the Grand Jury in this case . . .

He may have forgotten a second call. You look at the Eckenrode affidavit. He told you there was only one call. He said to Eckenrode it was one, possibly two calls. And he said that the calls could have been out to the 12th . . .

I would ask you, do not . . . convict Scooter Libby or anybody else on the word of somebody who is suffering public memory lapses. That wouldn't be fair. That wouldn't be right . . .

Remember I was cross-examining him and I was asking him questions about, did he remember what happened on the day of Mr. Libby's indictment? And I showed him newspaper article after newspaper article. And—"I don't recall, I don't recall, I don't recall, I don't recall." He said he didn't remember being on the *Today* show. He was on the *Today* show that morning with Katie Couric talking about how "this is huge," Mr. Libby's indictment is "huge. It's the first time in 130 years." He had to do research to do that. He said, "I don't recall any of it. Any of it". . .

Then I played the Christmas Eve tape—and I call it the Christmas Eve tape, but he was on Imus that morning . . . [H]e didn't even remember that . . . He remembered none of that. He didn't remember the *Today* show, didn't remember talking about Santa Claus and surprises. He remembered none of it.

You cannot convict Mr. Libby solely on the word of this man. It would just be fundamentally unfair . . .

Maybe Russert is right and Libby is wrong. Remember, Robert Novak testified that he may have asked Mr. Libby right around the same time that Mr. Libby recollects being asked by Mr. Russert if he knew the wife worked at the CIA. Mr. Novak said he might have done it. He wasn't a hundred percent sure. He said it might have happened, though he had no present recollection. But it would have been natural, I submit to you, for a reporter with the information that he had already gotten from Mr. Rove, if he had Mr. Libby on the phone, to have asked that very same question. And the question may have been asked.

So maybe Mr. Libby has done nothing more than confuse Novak with Russert. That's what I mean. This is a case where perhaps Mr. Libby is confused. There is no question that he has gotten certain things wrong in the grand jury. No question about it. But you have got to ask, did he engage in intentional lying?

The same thing with Matt Cooper. What Matt Cooper asked Mr. Libby is similar in part to what he remembers Russert saying. Maybe three months later, he got Cooper confused with Russert or he got Novak confused with Russert. But all of these things exist, and what it shows is it's impossible to show with any degree of certainty in terms of being firmly convinced that Mr. Libby is engaged in intentional lying. That's the key point. And that's what you have got to decide. And that's where the government's proofs have fallen short . . .

The evidence has shown that the Russert story was unnecessary. That is a very important point. The government says Mr. Libby concocted the Tim Russert story because he wanted to have a reporter who he could say, ["W]ell, I learned this from a reporter. So I learned it from Russert. So I don't have to say I learned it from Cheney; I learned it from Russert."

But he wouldn't have to concoct a false story with Tim Russert because the testimony of Mr. Libby . . . that he gave to the FBI and in the grand jury is that on the same day he talked to Russert, Karl Rove told him that Robert Novak was writing the story and knew that the wife worked at the CIA.

So he didn't need to invent a phony story. If all he wanted to do was have a reporter to give him cover, all he had to say to Cooper or Miller or anybody else: "I heard Novak has it. I heard Novak knows it."

. . . It is a point that blows up entirely the government's entire theory . . . [A]ll they have is a theory as to why Mr. Libby would make up a phony story . . .

MR. FITZGERALD, in his opening statement, talk[ed] about the whole meat-grinder note. He just didn't show it to you the way I showed it to you. That's Mr. Fitzgerald's opening statement. What Mr. Fitzgerald said, as you can imagine, the defendant was not happy—that's Mr. Libby. The defendant did not like seeing his name in print. He certainly didn't like to see his name in the press concerning this.

So the defendant decided to go to someone to see if he could get help. That's the whole meat-grinder story.

To get the White House Press Secretary to clear him the way Rove had been cleared, the defendant went to his boss, the Vice President . . . [T]he defendant took out a piece of paper and wrote out a note—that's the meat-grinder note that I showed you . . . [H]e wrote out the words that he wanted the White House Press Secretary to tell the world to make clear that he was not involved.

You will also see that the Vice President wrote on that note, and the Vice President wanted to make sure that the White House Press Secretary did for the defendant what had been done for Karl Rove. You will also learn that the White House Press Secretary came through on more than one occasion . . .

The Vice President uses the word "sacrifice." I use the word "scapegoat." Mr. Fitzgerald uses the words "sitting out there alone." I don't care what words you use. Karl Rove had been cleared. Scooter Libby didn't think he had done anything wrong. He wanted to be cleared. And he had to go all the way to the Vice President to get cleared. And that's a person that's innocent.

Next slide. Okay. This is Libby describing to the Vice President what he's testifying to in the grand jury. He told the Vice President, "I thought it was unfair that McClellan had said something about Rove and not something about me, since I didn't talk to Novak either."

See, Rove had lied. Rove did talk to Novak. Rove lied. Scooter Libby didn't lie. Okay? Scooter Libby was saying, ["T]his is not fair." Scooter Libby didn't know anything about what Novak did . . . That's how the note was written. The note is in evidence. Look at it.

"Has to happen today. Call out to key press saying same thing about Scooter as Karl. Not going to protect one staffer and sacrifice the guy"—then "the pres" is crossed out—"that we asked to stick his neck in the meat grinder because of the incompetence of others."

And in the Grand Jury they explained the meat grinder is because Libby had to go out and address others. And the incompetence of others is the incompetence of the CIA for letting the sixteen words get into the State of Union address.

It is a critical, important piece of evidence in this case because it shows his state of mind . . . And he is fighting to get cleared . . . And you know what? If you thought you had done something, the last thing in the world you are going to do is go to Andy Card: "Clear me." You're rejected. Go to Scott McClellan: "Clear me." You're rejected. And then go to the Vice President and say, "Doggone it; it's unfair." Only an innocent person would do that. Only an innocent person.

I will break for lunch, Your Honor.

THE COURT: Very well. We will recess and we will come back at 20 minutes to 2:00 and we will proceed at that time. I would ask everybody to be back in the courtroom, however, at 25 to 2:00 so that we can get started on time.

WALTON AGAIN ADVISES THE JURY about contact with others, and court recesses for lunch.

JEFFRESS TAKES UP THE DEFENSE'S closing argument after lunch, although Wells takes the very conclusion:

MR. JEFFRESS: May it please the Court, Government counsel, Mr. Libby, members of the jury, I'm going to talk for about an hour or so, and I know the devil is in the "or so." But I'm sure Mr. Wells is going [to] keep me to it.

But, ladies and gentlemen, the most important thing I have to say to you this afternoon is going to take me about two minutes. The Government asked you to find that Scooter Libby deliberately made up a false story that could, if he went and told the FBI in the Grand Jury, could mean the loss of his freedom. It could mean the loss of his career.

The Government asked you to find that he made up that story, that he then went and told it to the FBI, risking prosecution for obstruction of justice, perjury and loss of his freedom. They want you to find that, in making up this story, Mr. Libby chose as his source for this information the world's most famous television newsman when he had to know that the FBI could go right out and ask Mr. Russert about that and find out whether it was true or not. This is what they asked you to find.

They asked you to find that, in making up this story, Mr. Libby decided he would say, I forgot the conversation with the Vice President, and I didn't have any other conversations with anybody else about Wilson's wife . . . When he knew that the FBI would go out and talk to all of the people, all of the government officials that he had discussions with about Wilson's wife.

And, ladies and gentlemen, they asked you to find that Mr. Libby did all this . . . to protect himself from prosecution for a crime he did not commit, to protect himself from losing his job or his security clearance, which were . . . never truly in jeopardy for anything that he actually did . . . [T]hese are the things the Government asked you to find in this case. And your standard in finding whether Mr. Libby is guilty or not is beyond a reasonable doubt.

Ladies and gentlemen, . . . common sense alone tells you that they did not carry that burden. As a matter of fact, the witnesses that were called in this case taught you a lot more about the fallibility of human memory than they did about the truth of anything that the Government contends is true in this case.

And a remarkable thing that you heard . . . from Government counsel this morning was a statement that, in our everyday lives, we have no difficulty remembering conversations. That was said with respect to Mr. Fleischer as I recall.

Well, let's talk about our everyday lives. I mean . . . this is the middle of February. Somebody brings you in and says, you know, back before Thanksgiving, do you remember having a meeting with X, Y, or Z? What did you say? What did he say? Did this come up or did this not come up? We don't have any problem remembering that when we have no notes to refresh our recollection. It's simply not so, ladies and gentlemen, it's not so.

The Government tells you this is not a case about memory, but, of course, it's a case about memory. It's not just a case about Mr. Libby's memory. It's a case about the memory of all the other witnesses that came in.

And that's the two-minute summary. I've got other subjects and other witnesses to cover this morning. And I'd like to start, if I may, with reporters who testified in this case. I'm going to start with a number of conversations you learned about, primarily in the defense case, but some in the prosecution case, that Mr. Libby had during June and July of 2003.

The Government, remember in opening statement, told you that Mr. Libby was a leaker. That he set out to leak information about Mr. Wilson's wife, apparently to combat the story that Mr. Wilson was telling. I'm going to go into that story in a little while.

And you were told in opening statement . . . that this investigation by the FBI and the Grand Jury was about who may have broken the law by leaking classified information.

Remember, Ms. Bond testified to that. Now, this case of course isn't about those things. Mr. Libby isn't charged with breaking any laws by leaking to any reporters, by leaking any classified information. But the answer as to what the FBI and the Grand Jury were supposedly investigating [is] relevant here. So, let's look at who did and who didn't talk to reporters.

Now, you remember that we, I think we're in agreement on something with Government counsel this morning, that Mr. Libby first learned about the fact that the former Ambassador's wife worked for the CIA. First learned that on June 11th.

And do you have Government Exhibit 104? You've seen this already this morning. Now, if you look under the first line over to the right you'll see "took place at our behest." That's the CIA talking to the Vice President and the Vice President relaying it to Scooter Libby. The CIA is saying, "took place at our behest, functional office, CP," meaning Counterproliferation, "his wife works in that division." Now, that's Mr. Libby's note of when he learned about this information from the Vice President.

Now, sit back and ask yourself something about this note. Mr. Libby has absolutely no notes of any of these conversations that he's charged with misremembering or forgetting or lying about. And this is the one note that he has that shows that, look, I was told back in June that Mr. Wilson's wife actually works at the CIA in the Counterproliferation Division.

Now, I guess if he was the dishonest person that the Government thinks he is, if he set out to obstruct justice and to hide his conduct, he would have ditched that note, if he were that kind of a person, but he didn't. As a matter of fact, he came into the FBI and told them about it the very first time that he was interviewed.

So he learns about it on June 11 . . . We now know . . . Mr. Grossman, Ms. Martin, Mr. Grenier, . . . all . . . say that they told Mr. Libby the same information at or about that same time that he learned it from the Vice President. In any event he learns about it on June 11.

He talks to a reporter that day. Remember this note that I just showed you was a note that he prepared in talking to the Vice President about what he should say to Walter Pincus about a story that . . . Pincus was writing . . . Let me talk about Walter Pincus for a moment. [He] wrote a story based, in part, on . . . all the sources he had, including Mr. Libby. He wrote a story and it was published on June 12. You have it, and it's about the former ambassador without naming him . . .

Later, after this investigation begins, Mr. Pincus, along with a co-author, wrote an article. It's in evidence. It's in October of 2003. What Mr. Pincus says is that a *Washington Post* reporter was . . . told by a government official on July the 12th of 2003, about the wife.

Now, . . . Scooter Libby is asked in the Grand Jury these kinds of questions about that conversation. "Do you know whether, on the 11th of June, you talked to Mr. Pincus about Mr. Wilson's wife?" "No, I believe I did not, sir." "Can you rule out the possibility that you told Mr. Pincus about Wilson's wife during that conversation?" Mr. Libby says, "I have no recollection of having discussed it with Mr. Pincus and I don't think I did."

Come back[:] "Can you rule out the possibility that you did in your mind?" "I don't think I did." "And I understand that it's very clear that you don't think you did. I'm just saying, can you rule out that you didn't do that when you spoke to Mr. Pincus?" Answer: "I don't know quite what to say, sir. I don't think I did. I have no recollection of doing it. It's just not what I set out to do. I don't believe I did. Just rule out the possibility of an odd phrasing to me. I'm reasonably certain I did not."

It doesn't end there . . . "So I'm simply asking that, even though you think you didn't talk to Pincus about it, is it possible that you did? Is it possible you did?"

Ladies and gentlemen, I put this up there to show you that spending eight hours in a Grand Jury room is not easy. It's not like spending 22 minutes in your lawyer's office with your lawyers there to object and protect you. You remember listening to the tape. I think it took us three days . . . or portions of three days to get through the entire tape of Mr. Libby's appearance. Over eight hours, over eight hours on two occasions.

You know, at the end there, you can barely hear Mr. Libby. Whether he's not speaking into the microphone or whether he's just worn down after all of this questioning, it's understandable that that happens to people if you spend eight hours in a Grand Jury under questioning like this, under questioning like that. I'll come to the October 12 article later because that involves Mr. Kessler.

Okay . . . Now, I'm going to show you a timeline of the reporters between the time that Mr. Libby learns about this information and the time that Mr. Novak's article comes out in July. And the first is Walter Pincus, and that's on June 11.

Now, the next person that you've heard that Mr. Libby talked to in part about the sixteen words controversy is Bob Woodward of *The Washington Post,* June 27th. Mr. Woodward came in and told you, he may have asked because he knew. He knew from Rich Armitage. He may have asked Mr. Libby about that, but he's quite certain Mr. Libby didn't say anything about Wilson's wife.

All right. Next, David Sanger on July 2nd. Again, we brought him in here to tell you, yes, he was writing an article in part about the sixteen words controversy. He interviewed Mr. Libby. Mr. Libby did not say a thing about Mr. Wilson's wife.

Robert Novak, we called in Mr. Novak to say he talked to Scooter Libby during that week. You know, Mr. Libby doesn't recall it being that week. Mr. Libby said to the Grand Jury, . . . [he] recalls that as being later. But in any event, Mr. Novak recalls that it was that week and he is certain. He may have asked because he knew it from Richard

Armitage. He may have asked Mr. Libby about it, but he is certain Mr. Libby said nothing about Wilson's wife.

If you go back, there were two other reporters we didn't call. One of them was Andrea Mitchell of NBC. One of them was David Martin of CBS. You know about the conversation on July the 8th, because you remember Cathie Martin . . . She testified that Mr. Libby had talked to Andrea Mitchell and talked to David Martin the night before. She was upset because Steve Hadley was accusing her of having . . . said some uncomplimentary things about the CIA. So you know about those conversations. Ladies and gentlemen, we haven't heard any evidence that Mr. Libby said anything to either one of these reporters.

And there are two more. Glen Kessler of *The Washington Post.* Again, we brought him in. Mr. Kessler recalls the conversation and recalls clearly Mr. Libby said nothing about Mr. Wilson's wife.

Evan Thomas, . . . of *Newsweek*, he doesn't remember the conversation[,] frankly. But he came in and he looked at the phone record and he saw that, yes, obviously from Andrews Air Force Base a call was placed to my number. I work on Saturdays. I would have returned that call. He's not going to make something up. But the one thing he is sure, . . . whatever we talked about, Mr. Libby did not mention Wilson's wife.

So during this time that the Government says that Mr. Libby remembered . . . that Wilson's wife worked at the CIA and may have been involved in sending him on the trip, he says nothing to any of these reporters that he's dealing with in trying to defend his boss the Vice President in connection with the sixteen words controversy.

Now, there were a lot of reporters who were hearing from government officials about Wilson's wife. Richard Armitage talked to Bob Woodward. You heard a tape recording of that conversation. Richard Armitage talked to Bob Novak—[y]ou heard him testify about it—on July the 8th approximately.

Mr. Rove, the high-ranking White House official, talked to Mr. Novak. Ari Fleischer has told you . . . he spoke to David Gregory of NBC News. John Dickerson of *TIME* magazine, and Mr. Cooper told you that Karl Rove told him. All of this is on or about July the 11th. And finally, in a conversation I'm going to deal with a little more fully later, Ari Fleischer called Walter Pincus on July 12.

Mr. Cooper, after talking to Mr. Rove, reports to his editors on the conversation. Tells a double, super-secret background or something like that. And there are three of them, Jay Carney, Michael Duffy, Adi Ignatius, all reporters for *TIME* magazine, all of them know it by now.

Mr. Novak tells you his story is on the wires July 11th by 1:00 o'clock to a hundred newsrooms. So, maybe we haven't proven that all of the reporters knew it, but we've come mighty close. There were an awful lot of reporters who knew this information by July 11, 2003.

Now, the Government called three reporters. The Government called three reporters, Miller, Tim Russert, and Matt Cooper to tell you about conversations they had with Mr. Libby . . . Mr. Wells has already started talking about Tim Russert, and I'm going to cover . . . the conversations with Matt Cooper and with Judith Miller.

We'll get to those in a moment. But first I want to deal with another subject because the Government says well, you know, Mr. Libby is not just putting this story out through reporters . . . Eleven different reporters that he talked to about this sixteen words controversy, there is one, one, and that's Judy Miller, who claims that Mr. Libby volunteered anything about Mr. Wilson's wife. Cooper says he asked Mr. Libby. So there is one.

Ladies and gentlemen, the Government then wants you to believe that Mr. Libby took another route in getting out this information for reporters. He told it to the White House Press Secretary, supposedly hoping, I guess, that the White House Press Secretary would tell it to the reporters.

. . . That's Ari Fleischer. He's the man, of course, who told two reporters, David Gregory, John Dickerson, about where Mr. Wilson's wife worked. He's the person who told Walter Pincus about where Wilson's wife worked and that she was involved in sending him on the trip.

He was the White House Press Secretary. He told three different reporters . . . the information about Wilson's wife. This was an investigation, remember, that, as Agent Bond told you, was supposed to be who . . . may have committed a crime by disclosing possibly classified information to reporters.

So what happened to Ari Fleischer? Well, he was given . . . immunity from prosecution in exchange for his testimony. The date of that order is interesting. The date of that order is February 16th, [then] he testified before the Grand Jury, February 24, 2004, . . . one week before Mr. Libby was scheduled to . . . testify.

So Ari Fleischer goes in under an order of immunity and testifies to the Grand Jury that he had this conversation with Scooter Libby, and Scooter Libby told him that Wilson's wife works in the Counterproliferation Division.

And Mr. Libby then goes in a week later, he's already told the FBI that that didn't happen. By the way, it was an interesting part of Ms. Bond's testimony. What Mr. Libby . . . actually said, according to the notes of the FBI interview when he was first asked about Mr. Fleischer, . . . "I don't remember such a conversation." And then they type up a memo and it comes . . . adamantly denied that it happened.

So Fleischer gets immunity, . . . and says, "Oh, yeah, it happened." Mr. Libby goes in and gets asked about it under oath now in front of the Grand Jury, says the same thing he said to the FBI. They have another building block for a perjury case against Mr. Libby. That's the way it happened. That's the way it happened. Just put together the dates and the testimony and you'll find that out.

[T]he judge will give you an instruction. It has to do with the testimony of immunized witnesses, and Mr. Fleischer is the only immunized witness in this case.

The judge, as I understand, is going to give you all these instructions in writing, so you don't need to write them down here.

But part of that instruction is going to be that "the testimony of a witness, as to whom immunity has been granted, should be received with caution and scrutinized with care."

Now, let's go on about Mr. Fleischer. You know Mr. Fleischer had two and half years as the Press Secretary for the President. You know he had a lot of experience with a lot of hostile questions and selling the President's program. He's smooth. I will admit that . . .

[I]n [his] opening statement, Mr. Fitzgerald told you that, when Scooter Libby told Ari Fleischer on July 7th about Wilson's wife, the seed that was planted worked. The seed that was planted worked, as if what he told Ari Fleischer is what Ari Fleischer went and told reporters. Let's go with that. Mr. Libby has lunch with him on July 7 and, according to Ari Fleischer, says something about Wilson's wife.

Well, Ari Fleischer left that afternoon on a plane with a whole bunch of reporters and a second plane with tons of reporters, and they left on a presidential trip to Africa.

Does Mr. Fleischer tell any of those reporters on July 7 anything about the wife? Does he tell the reporters at any time on July 8th, when the whole party is traveling to Africa, . . . about Wilson's wife? Remember, this was a big controversy this week. Mr. Wilson had published his article in *The New York Times* and . . . gone on TV on *Meet the Press* on July the 6th. And so does Mr. Fleischer say anything to these reporters?

He's the White House Press Secretary. He's spending his time with reporters. Does he say anything to any of those reporters on July 8th? No. Does he say anything on July 9th? They're in South Africa. July 10th they're in Botswana. They're going back and forth. There are reporters all over the place. This is a big issue. He's the Press Secretary. Does he say anything? No, no.

And then what happens on July 11? Well, Mr. Fleischer said that he's sitting on the plane, on Air Force One, and he's reading a document. That document happens to be the cable. When Wilson came back from his trip, the CIA interviewed him. They prepared a cable that contains the only report on what he found on his trip to Niger back in 2002.

Mr. Fleischer says that he's sitting there reading it, and in walks his boss, White House Communications Director Dan Bartlett. He is on the trip . . . And he announces, I can't believe they're saying the Vice President sent Wilson on the trip. His wife sent him. She works there.

You talk about a seed sprouting. Within an hour, within two hours anyway, Mr. Fleischer sees two reporters on the side of the road, David Gregory and John Dickerson, and tells them exactly what Mr. Bartlett just told him. Is he telling them something he learned from Scooter Libby? Or is he telling him something he learned from his boss, Dan Bartlett?

Now, one of the oddest parts about Mr. Fleischer's testimony was this. He says, when Mr. Bartlett came to his cabin and made this announcement, he was venting. Can't believe it. They're saying the Vice President sent Wilson on the trip. His wife sent him. She works there.

Well, I asked Mr. Fleischer on cross-examination, . . . "So did you tell Mr. Bartlett, ['H]ey, I know that; Scooter Libby told me?'" He said, "No, no, [I] didn't say that . . . I didn't say anything. I was too busy reading my document." . . . His boss walks in venting, telling him this information and he [says]: "Leave me alone, I'm reading my document." Does that sound credible to you? Does that sound like something that actually would have happened? Picture that.

And then Mr. Fleischer, . . . remembers talking to Walter Pincus. There is a phone record to prove . . . that he called from the plane on July 12 . . . and talked to Mr.

Pincus. And I asked him, . . . "So did you tell Walter Pincus about Wilson's wife?" He says "no."

Can you put up that testimony?

Q: "Mr. Fleischer, did you tell Walter Pincus during that conversation, July 12, that Wilson's wife worked at the CIA?"

A: "No, sir, I have no recollection of telling that to [him]."

Q: "No recollection of telling him that at all? You would remember if it happened?"

A: "Sure I would. I did not."

Now, the Government has got three possibilities about this I suppose. One is that Walter Pincus is lying. You don't believe that. You saw Mr. Pincus. The other is that Mr. Fleischer is lying. The Government doesn't want you to believe that.

So, what's their third alternative? Their third alternative is to say . . . Mr. Fleischer forgot. Yet, they want to tell you that, you know, they make the argument I've mentioned earlier about Mr. Zeidenberg [that] we all remember conversations. And yet they want to tell you that he forgot Pincus, but he sure does remember Mr. Libby.

Now, ladies and gentlemen, in a case where the standard is reasonable doubt that doesn't cut it. That just doesn't cut it. When you've heard witnesses like you've . . . heard in the last four weeks, and heard about the fallibility of those witnesses' memories, that just doesn't cut it beyond a reasonable doubt.

And there's one more thing I want to say about Mr. Fleischer before I turn to something else. And that's remember what he actually told Walter Pincus. ...

What Mr. Fleischer told you that Mr. Libby told him about Wilson's wife was she works at the CIA and works in the Counterproliferation Division. But then what did Mr. Pincus tell you? He had notes, remember? He told you that what he learned on July 12 from Mr. Fleischer was that she was a WMD analyst . . . Mr. Pincus was quite certain that what Mr. Fleischer told him was an analyst on WMD, not what he claims Mr. Libby told him, somebody who works in the Counterproliferation Division.

So, is Fleischer telling Pincus something he learned—as well as Gregory and Dickerson—from Scooter Libby? Or something he learned from Dan Bartlett?

NOW, LET ME GO TO THE ARTICLE that I mentioned before that Walter Pincus and Mike Allen wrote on October 12th . . . Walter Pincus and Mike Allen said that a *Washington Post* reporter had learned from an Administration official on July 12, had called and said that Wilson's wife was involved in sending him on the trip.

So, when Mr. Libby came to the Grand Jury, he was asked about this . . . Apparently there was a theory that Glenn Kessler was *The Washington Post* reporter.

This is the questioning in the Grand Jury of Mr. Libby[:] . . . "When you read this October 12th [article], did you think that was describing your conversation with Glenn Kessler on the 12th?" "No, sir." "No, sir? Did it even dawn, dawn on you that reading this on October 12th, that the conversation being described in that article is occurring between a *Washington Post* reporter and an Administration official on July 12 was your conversation meaning with Kessler?"

Answer: "I had a conversation on July 12 with a *Washington Post* reporter and that dawned on me, as you say[.] But what this described was not my conversation."

Question: "Let's go through it then... And it says here, on July 12, a *Post* reporter was told by an Administration official that the White House had not paid attention to the former ambassador's CIA-sponsored trip to Niger because it was set up as a boondoggle by his wife, an analyst for the Agency working on mass destruction. [sic] Did you indicate at any time to Mr. Kessler that people weren't paying attention to the report, to the report by Wilson[,] because it was a boondoggle set up by his wife?" . . .

And you'll have all this back in the jury room. But the reason I put it there is, again, to say it's not easy in the Grand Jury room . . . . And Mr. Libby was there for eight hours undergoing this kind of questioning. And, you know, he didn't get the basic facts wrong . . . . He had a clear memory of the Russert conversation. He's got a clear memory of it. He didn't get the basic facts wrong.

But if he got something wrong at some time in eight hours of testimony, that's understandable. Which witness came in here and didn't get something wrong? What witness?

Now, one other thing I want to say before I leave that reporters' timeline, you remember I put up those public officials in red who talked to reporters about Mr. Wilson's wife? The defense does not contend that those people did anything wrong. They didn't know she was covert any more than Mr. Libby did.

You heard the tape of Mr. Armitage. [He] was the number-two person in the State Department. He was a very responsible guy. Did he sound like somebody who was leaking a covert . . . agent's identity to a reporter? We do not contend that those people did anything wrong.

You know, on that subject, let me deal with what Mr. Zeidenberg described as the government's motive argument. What the Government says is that, Mr. Libby thought he could be prosecuted for a crime in exposing the identity of a covert CIA agent.

But you know he didn't do that. We put in this morning a copy of the statute, the law that punishes people who go out and deliberately disclose the names of . . . covert agents at the CIA. That only punishes you if you know that the person is covert and if the CIA is taking active measures to protect the identity of that agent . . .

Ladies and gentlemen, what do you know about whether the CIA was taking active measures? And what do you know about whether Mr. Libby had any reason to believe that Ms. Plame was covert? The fact of the matter is . . . all of these witnesses who have come in and testified about conversations, whether with Mr. Libby or with somebody else, about lying, any facts concerning Mr. Wilson's wife, not a one of them has come in here and said to you I think she was covert, or I told somebody she was covert.

Certainly all of those people who said anything to Mr. Libby about Mr. Wilson's wife, not a single one of them claimed to have said that this was any kind of classified or covert information . . . [Y]ou heard Mr. Libby explain to you what he thought about whether Ms. Wilson had any kind of covert capacity . . . .

He was asked, "Did you have any sense that if you revealed the person's identity out at the CIA you may be compromising the identity of a covert person?" He says, "Any person? No, sir. I mean, my understanding is that most of the people at the CIA are not covert and their employment there is open and above board."

At another point he says this. "In general, there are a lot of people I know who work at the CIA who, you know, I play softball with or football with and they tell everybody in the game they work at the CIA. I mean, a lot of people work at the CIA and it's not a secret that they work at the CIA. If it is a secret, they don't go tell everybody at the softball game that they work at the CIA."

Now, this is what Mr. Libby understood about the CIA. Where is the evidence to contradict that? . . .

[Let's take a look at] Mr. Novak's article on July 14th.

. . . Mr. Novak reports in his article, and Scooter Libby read this, Mr. Novak reports that the CIA says, presumably tells him that its Counterproliferation officials selected Wilson and asked his wife to contact him.

Now, I'm sorry, but does this sound like a CIA that is trying to protect a covert agent? Look, it's a very important thing, and I don't mean to demean it at all. When we have a true covert agent who risks their life, risks their life by doing clandestine operations overseas on behalf of the United States, those people need to be protected.

But that's not what Ms. Wilson was as far as Mr. Libby knew or as far as what anybody else knew in this case. And as Judge Walton has told you many times, it's irrelevant whether she was or wasn't. We're not trying that issue. All that matters is what Mr. Libby believed.

Okay. So, let's put aside the question about Mr. Libby fearing prosecution. What other theories does the Government give you? They say that, well, Mr. Libby might have gone and risked years in prison for obstruction of justice by making up this elaborate story and telling it to the FBI because he feared losing his job if he didn't.

Well, what evidence is there that Mr. Libby would actually lose his job for anything that he actually did, anything you've heard in the evidence in this case? Have you heard in the evidence that anybody lost their job? Cathie Martin tells [us] Karl Rove still works in the White House. Have you heard any evidence that Mr. Armitage lost his job?

Ladies and gentlemen, that's a theory searching for evidence. The same is true of the non disclosure agreement. Mr. Zeidenberg talks about, well maybe he was afraid he would lose his security clearance because there is some provision in there about negligently disclosing classified information.

You didn't hear one word, not from David Addington, not from anybody in the case, that Mr. Libby had any concern about a security clearance. Mr. Libby testified for eight hours in the Grand Jury. He wasn't asked one question about the security clearance form. This is a newly thought of theory by the Government that's searching for evidence . . .

So, let me turn to the reporters. I'm going to talk about Ms. Miller and Mr. Cooper and I'm going to start with Judith Miller. Mr. Libby testified to the Grand Jury, you heard it, that he did…say something to Ms. Miller. But he remembers that was on July 12th. On July 12th, he recalls it came up in the conversation[:] "I told her we were hearing from reporters that Wilson's wife worked at the CIA."

He did not recall saying anything to her on July 8th . . . Mr. Libby was asked, when he went into the Grand Jury, whether he recalled anything about the meeting, about meeting with Judith Miller before the St. Regis meeting on July 8th. Mr. Libby said, yes, he does recall a meeting some weeks before. My recollection is we had a meeting in my office some weeks before July 8th, but he's never asked any other questions about it. So he's simply never asked about what occurred on the June 23rd meeting.

But Ms. Miller, after spending 85 days in jail and having plenty of time to think about it, having fought a subpoena that's for her testimony about all of this and having plenty of time to think about who did she talk to and when did she talk to them and what did they say, she comes to the Grand Jury, the first time she appeared and says, she has absolutely no memory of any meeting with Mr. Libby concerning the sixteen words, Joe Wilson, et cetera, prior to July 8th of 2003. No memory. She says that under oath. This is a case about memory, ladies and gentlemen.

Judy Miller then comes in to testify to you . . . that she came in and took the stand and testified to you and she had an amazing recovery of memory . . . She told you, she not only remembers the meeting, she remembers it in great detail.

Line one. "Can you describe Mr. Libby's demeanor during that meeting?" Answer: "Yes, Mr. Libby appeared to be agitated, frustrated and angry."

Next. "Did he indicate to you what he was annoyed at?" "Yes. He was concerned that the CIA was beginning to back-pedal to try and distance itself from the unequivocal intelligence estimates it had provided before the war through what he called a perverted war of leaks."

SO HERE'S MS. MILLER, who has a total lack of memory of any meeting on June the 23rd. She accidentally finds some notes, and all of a sudden she can tell you that Mr. Libby was agitated and about his demeanor and exactly what he said, and a perverted war of leaks and so forth and so on. It's pretty amazing, pretty amazing for somebody testifying about a conversation of which they had absolutely no memory for two years.

Now Mr. Libby has . . . no notes of any of these conversations. He's got exactly one note. Of all of the documents that he was able to look at before he went to see the FBI, before he testified in the Grand Jury, he's got exactly one note of any conversation about Mr. Wilson's wife, and that's the one he takes to the FBI the first time that he sees them. It's a conversation with the Vice President. But he's got no notes to go back and look at, whether it's about the July 8th conversation with Judy Miller or any other subject.

But looking at her notes, Ms. Miller says, well, Mr. Libby did mention the wife on June the 23rd because she's got some entry and pages of notes about this meeting that says, in parentheses, wife works in Bureau, question mark, wife works in Bureau, question mark. And I asked her, "Does the CIA have any bureaus?" She couldn't think of any. She said she took that to mean the non proliferation bureau at the CIA. But I showed her the Web site. The non-proliferation bureau is actually the Bureau of Non-Proliferation at the State Department, not the CIA.

Now, where did this come from? Ms. Miller told you on cross-examination, she says that she uses parentheses to mean either something the source said or something that she knows and wants to ask the source about. And she admitted she talked to . . . lots of people about Joe Wilson before she ever met with Scooter Libby.

She didn't just have Joe Wilson's name in her notebook. She had his telephone number and his extension. She said, I never really talked to Joe Wilson. But where did she get this extension? Who is she talking to about Joe Wilson before she ever goes to see Scooter Libby? What does she learn? Well, she's got a bit of a memory problem . . .

She admitted that, when she testified at the Grand Jury, after she found notes of this June 23rd meeting, . . . "I might have been confused because there's a question mark there". Remember, "wife works in bureau," question mark. But, once again, it's in a parentheses that he seemed to have said. "So I think, this is very hard but I, because my memory is so bad on this, but I think he was suggesting that he thought she may work in the bureau question mark. He wasn't sure . . . "

Now this was me questioning, and I said, "Right. That was your testimony. And that's still true, correct, as far as you're concerned?" "Yes, because I had forgotten this meeting entirely," she says.

So, ladies and gentlemen, she doesn't know. She's reconstructing by coming in here and testifying to you as if she has a clear memory of this meeting that occurred three and half years ago. It's just not so.

Let's go to the meeting on July 8th. Mr. Zeidenberg points out correctly that this was a two-hour meeting. That Mr. Libby, as busy as he is and [with] things of enormous importance to the country, things of an enormous importance to him, of all of the things on his plate he has time to go to see Judy Miller for two hours, and this was an important meeting. Yes, he does because his boss told him to do it. Yeah, we make time. I think we all do, when your boss tells you to do it.

So, he made time, despite everything else that he had to do, to go and . . . defend the sixteen words, defend the credibility of the President and the Vice President concerning the reasons we went to war in Iraq.

And ladies and gentlemen, I'm sure I don't need to point this out again, but it doesn't matter how you feel about that issue. In this case, Mr. Libby had a job to do, and he did it. And it was his responsibility. And he's an honest man, not a dishonest man.

Well, I told you that Judy Miller is somebody with a bit of a memory problem . . . This was just her speaking naturally about her memory . . .

I asked [her in cross-examination], "I want you to tell the jury, it's not what I want you to say. I want you to tell the jury, whether it is true, as you told Mr. Goodale, that you talked to senior government officials, other than Mr. Libby, about Mr. Wilson and Valerie Plame?" Answer. "I don't remember whether the people I talked to about Mr. Wilson and Ms. Plame were senior or not so senior. I know I had several conversations. But unfortunately, there is no reference to them in my notebooks and there is no independent memory of them."

She told you she had a memory of talking to a lot of different officials, and I just asked her to name one . . .

I asked, "Is it fair to say that you might have talked to other officials about Wilson's wife during that time-frame, that is after July 6?" The witness, "After July 6, after the article, I certainly would have asked people about that article and about Mrs., no, no, wait a minute. I'm not sure I knew—I can't remember exactly when I began discussing it with people."

So, you know, that's her testimony on that subject, and her notebook has references. She told you her notebook has references to Valerie Flame, Valerie Plame, V.F. She says, she is pretty certain Mr. Libby was not the source of any of those things. And I asked her about, well, who was?

She either can't or won't tell you the name of a single other source, not a single other person she talked to, even though she said she talked to many people, talked to as many people as she could think of, how Mr. Wilson could come [to] write an article, even though she's got entries in her notes referring obviously to Mr. Wilson's wife. She won't tell you the names of any of those people.

That's mighty interesting. Because in the summer of 2004, when the Court overruled her objections and enforced the subpoena, you heard Ms. Miller tell you that she and her lawyer made an offer to Mr. Fitzgerald. She would come in and . . . testify about Scooter Libby . . . . He had waived any confidentiality, affirmatively requested reporters to come forward and tell the investigators about any conversations that he had had with them about this subject.

But Ms. Miller says... to Mr. Fitzgerald, "I'll talk about Scooter Libby, but I want an agreement that you won't ask me about my other sources. And you won't call me back to the Grand Jury the second time." Mr. Fitzgerald refused that offer. We don't criticize Mr. Fitzgerald for that, but he refused that offer.

Finally, she takes it to the Court of Appeals, and the Supreme Court, and she spends 85 days in jail, and she finally comes out, . . . testifies, and, you know, there was an agreement. She said I got out of jail because Mr. Fitzgerald did agree that he wasn't going to ask me about my other sources. But the defense didn't agree to that, and so we did ask her who else did you talk to. And she says, I don't remember. Wow. She spent 85 days in jail to avoid saying she doesn't remember? That's amazing.

Now remember, ladies and gentlemen, Judith Miller [is not the subject] of the counts that remain, because this allegation that was once in the indictment about the July 12 conversation is gone, as [has been] explained to you. The allegations in the case concern . . . conversations with Mr. Cooper and Mr. Russert.

But Judith Miller is somebody, according to Mr. Zeidenberg's argument, that they still rely on to try to prove that this story that Mr. Libby told to the Grand Jury was concocted, was false. And ladies and gentlemen, in a case that requires proof beyond a reasonable doubt, Judith Miller is not a reliable witness for that fact.

Now, let me turn to Matthew Cooper. Let me digress just before I talk about Mr. Cooper and discuss one thing that he raised when he claimed that Mr. Libby and others were engaged in disparagement of Joseph Wilson. Remember that? Disparagement, and he wrote an article called "War on Wilson." And he says, well, there was a question mark. "War on Wilson," question mark.

He claimed that what Mr. Libby was doing was disparagement of Joseph Wilson. Where have we heard, anywhere, even in the Grand Jury testimony, in eight hours of Grand Jury testimony by Mr. Libby, where have we heard that Mr. Libby disparaged Joe Wilson?

You remember that Mr. Wilson was the anonymous source for an article by Mr. Kristof in *The New York Times* on May 6, a second article, June 13, Mr. Kristof again, both of them are in evidence . . .

[A]lthough they didn't name Mr. Wilson, they talked about an unnamed former ambassador who was Mr. Wilson. Here's what Mr. Wilson was saying. First, he was saying, "I was sent to Niger at the behest of Vice President Cheney." Well, Mr. Libby was charged by the Vice President in June of 2003 to say, what is this story all about? Did I know? What are the facts?

Mr. Libby starts investigating, and he finds the truth about that. The Vice President had no knowledge of the trip. Mr. Wilson was sent to Niger by the CIA, after the Vice President, State Department and Defense Department ask questions. The second thing that Mr. Wilson . . . says he reported, after he went to Niger, that the documents on which this intelligence was based were forgeries. When you know from the Tenet statement, George Tenet, head of the CIA, his statement which is in evidence, that the truth is Wilson never saw any documents. The report of his trip says nothing about documents, forged or otherwise.

The next thing he's saying is that his report, when he came back from Niger and reported to the CIA, he debunked the intelligence that Iraq had sought significant quantities of uranium from Africa. That's the sixteen words. The truth? The CIA's own report, based on the debriefing of Wilson, said that in 1999, an Iraqi delegation had met with the then prime minister of Niger who interpreted, the Prime Minister interpreted the approach as an effort to acquire uranium.

Now, they didn't sell any, but the sixteen words was they were trying to get it. Why were they trying to get it? Because it was the belief of the intelligence community that Iraq was trying to reconstitute its nuclear program. That was being said prewar.

Wilson was also saying that his report…would have been seen by the Vice President. But the truth is, the Vice President never saw it, nor was he told about Wilson's report.

Now, ladies and gentlemen, you've seen talking points in this case, where Mr. Libby is trying to get the truth out. He's trying to get the facts out in response to what Mr. Wilson is saying. There [are] at least five different sets of talking points prepared at different times. Not a one, not a one mentions anything about Wilson's wife.

What it mentions is the facts, and it's not just, you know, some arguments that Mr. Libby is making. These are facts that are established by the documents that are in evidence in this case. That's disparagement of Mr. Wilson? When Mr. Libby is out defending his boss and trying to get out the true facts about what Mr. Wilson is saying, that's disparagement? But that's what Mr. Cooper says.

Now, let's turn to this conversation with Mr. Libby on July 12th. Mr. Cooper has been calling in to Cathie Martin, . . . trying to get his questions answered. Mr. Libby has got all these things to do. And he goes down to Norfolk on the plane. This is the first chance he has to call him back. And Mr. Cooper is working on a deadline. And he's been swimming. He comes in. He's falling on the bed. He's got his laptop. He's talking on the telephone. He's taking notes on his laptop at the time he does it.

Now, when Mr. Libby is asked about this conversation, three months after it occurred, for the first time by the FBI, he . . . recalls that he did say something. As a matter of fact, he recalls that he volunteered something about Mr. Wilson's wife. He doesn't recall Matt Cooper actually asked him the question.

You know, it's funny, . . . the way [Mr. Cooper] describes this conversation. "I asked him, . . . 'Have you heard that Wilson's wife was involved in sending him on the trip?'" Sounds very much like what Mr. Libby recalls Mr. Russert saying. Could he have been recollecting Russert when he should have been recollecting Cooper? That's not the way he recalls it. He has a distinct recollection that it was Mr. Russert. But could he be wrong? Of course he could. We all could on something like that.

LADIES AND GENTLEMEN, . . . here's why the Government asks you, as far as Mr. Cooper, to convict Mr. Libby of three different crimes, perjury, false statements, and part of an obstruction of justice charge about Matt Cooper.

Here's what Mr. Libby said to the Grand Jury . . . about his conversation[:]… "In that context, I said, you know, off the record, reporters are telling us that Ambassador Wilson's wife works at the CIA and I don't know if it's true."

Mr. Cooper, on the other hand, and this is his testimony in this Court[:] "Mr. Libby said words to the effect of, 'Yes, I have heard that too.' Or 'Yes, I have heard something like that, too'". . . [O]n [this] the Government asks you to find Mr. Libby guilty of two counts and a portion of a third.

Now, these are based, of course, on two recollections, three months later for Mr. Libby, some over a year later for Mr. Cooper. And one thing you know. You know from the evidence that is whatever Mr. Libby said to Mr. Cooper, it wasn't considered important by Mr. Cooper at the time. And the reason you know that is a document that's in evidence . . .

I'm not going to read this. But this is Mr. Cooper's, after he finishes talking to Mr. Libby, remember they're working on a story. They're working on a story about this whole matter, and he writes to his editors and co-authors, "I spoke this afternoon with I. Lewis Scooter Libby, the Vice President's Chief of Staff."

And he goes on and he gives the on-the-record statement that Mr. Libby gave. He talks about everything that Mr. Libby said. It was a long report. This is information to go into the article. And there's not one single word about Mr. Wilson's wife. This is something he wrote within minutes, as he told you, of the conversation he had with Scooter Libby on July 12th.

Compare this with what he wrote, and this is an e-mail version of what he wrote. After he talked to Karl Rove, the day before, July 11, [on] "double, super-secret background." It was Karl Rove [who] said Wilson's wife apparently works at the Agency on WMD issues who authorized the trip. This was a big deal.

They were discussing how to source this information, how to put it into the article. This was something that they thought that they had something really newsworthy that they were going to report. So he puts it in this report on his conversation with Karl Rove, and doesn't put it in a report of his conversation with Scooter Libby.

The reason he didn't report it is Mr. Libby didn't tell him anything . . . that would be confirmation of the story that he was writing. When . . . somebody asks you a question . . . —"Have you heard that Wilson's wife was involved in sending him on the trip[?]", and you say "I've heard that from other reporters, but I don't even know if it's true," that's not confirmation and you don't put that in your memo to your editor. And you don't put that in your story. And you don't source that person, and you don't put it in your notes . . .

Well, you know, apparently, nobody ever really seriously looked at those notes, nobody ever seriously tried to figure it out before they testified in this courtroom. There is a reason for that. You know, if anybody wanted to give Scooter Libby the benefit of the doubt, anybody ever wanted to start, you know, from a presumption of innocence, they might take a close look at the notes and see if those notes might just support what Mr. Libby is saying. But nobody ever did that . . . They didn't do it, you know, in his lawyer's office where he's testifying about his conversation with Mr. Libby with prosecutors. Apparently, he didn't do it in preparation for his direct examination at trial, but, you know, he was asked about it on cross.

And Mr. Wells says something about a Perry Mason moment. Look, it doesn't take Perry Mason to figure out that, you know, he says something happened. Mr. Libby agrees something happened . . . These are his notes of that conversation.

So, you know, I asked him about [it] . . . We looked at all kinds of notes, and we found that he types R's when he means N's, and he leaves things out and leaves sentences uncompleted. I guess it's particularly hard when you're sprawled on the bed with a phone in one hand and a laptop, you know, in front of you.

I SUBMIT TO YOU, ladies and gentlemen, the conversation is in his notes. And it's not accurately recorded in his notes but, as between what Mr. Libby's recollection of the conversation is and what you can infer and what you can deduct from Mr. Cooper's own notes, tells you that this charge, which the Government has to prove beyond a reasonable doubt that Mr. Libby lied about his conversation with Cooper, is simply not true. Now, the Government tells you, you don't have to rely entirely on Mr. Cooper. You can rely on Cathie Martin because you remember Cathie Martin was there at Andrews Air Force Base. She was in the room where Mr. Libby was making phone calls. And she testified, she testified that she doesn't remember Mr. Libby saying anything about reporters.

Now, you know, there are three possibilities concerning Ms. Martin's testimony. She could have actually been there during the whole conversation and heard the whole conversation. She could be right. That's always a possibility. Possibilities don't cut it in a criminal case but that's a possibility.

But there are two other possibilities. One possibility, you remember, she said she went to take a phone call . . . and she came back and Mr. Libby was still reading from his card. We showed you that card, the card with talking points for this conversation, including an on-the-record statement.

So she came back and she heard him reading from his card, and then the conversation wound up. That was her recollection about it. But, you know, if you look at . . . an exhibit in evidence, which is the telephone record from Andrews Air Force Base . . . I showed it to Mr. Cooper, and he did recall.

There wasn't just one conversation with Mr. Cooper that day. There were two. Cathie Martin didn't remember that. She apparently only heard the first conversation . . . There's one about 14-minute call, and there's a two-and-a-half-minute break, and then there's another four-and-a-half, five minute call. And you'll find that on the phone record.

And I suggest to you, ladies and gentlemen, one of the explanations for Cathie Martin's testimony is that she simply didn't hear the second part of the call. Remember, Matt Cooper said this came up toward the end of the call. But the other thing is Cathie Martin was listening only to Scooter Libby's end of the conversation.

She wasn't on the phone. She wasn't listening to what Mr. Cooper said. She was only listening or in the room at least where she was hearing Mr. Libby's end of the call. But when she is asked months later to recall that, you know, she could have simply forgotten. And I submit to you, ladies and gentlemen, that based on the evidence, with respect to what you heard from Mr. Libby, he's not trying to protect himself here. I mean he says, look, I did talk to these reporters. I did say something. It turns out to be wrong as far as Matt Cooper is concerned. Cooper asked him, he didn't volunteer to Cooper. But, ladies and gentlemen, Mr. Libby got it right as he remembered it.

And the testimony of Matt Cooper, the testimony of Cathie Martin, such as it is with respect to this matter, does not lift that mantle of presumption of innocence, that mantle of reasonable doubt for Scooter Libby on the charges in this case . . .

[Y]ou know, it's not fair to flashback Mr. Libby's Grand Jury testimony. I mean I know he said, ["L]ook, I think I told Matt Cooper that I didn't even know Wilson had a wife." Well, you know, number one, it's obviously not so. Mr. Libby couldn't have been trying to hide anything. He already admitted that he heard from Karl Rove the day before about Mr. Wilson's wife. He admitted that he heard from Mr. Russert two days before or one day before about Mr. Wilson's wife. He's not trying to hide anything.

Look, the charge in this case, fundamentally,... is that Mr. Libby set out to concoct, deliberately concoct a false story to protect himself from prosecution or losing his job or whatever else. Either he did or he didn't . . .

And it wouldn't be fair to go down and pick some little statement that he made in the Grand Jury and say, well, that's not true. You know he must have meant to lie.

. . . The charge is that Mr. Libby is a dishonest man, let's face it. It's a charge that he would commit serious crimes.

Ladies and gentlemen, you're the first people that have ever looked at this case through the lens of presumption of innocence. You're not journalists, not prosecutors.

You're not grand jurors. You're an American jury sworn to give Mr. Libby a presumption of innocence and to enter on that verdict form, that you're going to receive at the end of this case, five times not guilty unless you conclude that the Government has proven guilt of any one of those charges beyond a reasonable doubt.

They haven't, and it's not even close. I'll turn this argument back to Mr. Wells and I'll thank you very much.…

(A brief recess was taken.)

MR. WELLS: Good afternoon.

I have 50 minutes left to speak to you. That's not enough time for everything I have to cover. So I'm going to have to be quick and cut some things out.

When I finished before the break, I had talked about the relevancy of the meatgrinder note in terms of showing Scooter Libby's state of mind because, if you look at the top part of that note, you will see Scooter Libby is saying in his own handwriting, he did not leak classified information. He did not leak to Novak.

That's a note he's given to the Vice President of the United States. Those are notes nobody—you know, that really shows how he feels. I think that's consistent with everything you've heard in this case, in this courtroom. Scooter Libby did not leak any classified information. He did not. And that note is consistent with his state of mind back then.

Also, the prosecution, during their summation, played a clip of Mr. McClellan when he finally comes out and talks about, well, I'm going to clear Scooter Libby and we're all on the same team. My response to that is give me a break. For Scooter Libby to get on the team, he had to go to McClellan, get rejected. He had to go to Andy Card and get rejected.

Finally, he had to go to the Vice President of the United States, "Can you get me on the team?" That's not a team I think he should want to be on. And they sure didn't treat him like he was part of the team.

Now, in terms of Mr. Russert, I didn't have time to cover all of my Russert materials. But, in terms of the telephone calls, to the extent you decide it's important in terms of what time was Mr. Libby's call with Mr. Russert on the 11th, the record is very confusing. That's what you're going to find. Mr. Russert says that he thinks there was one call. That's what he said in the courtroom. Under my questioning he said, well, the call could have been any time on the 10th, the 11th or the 12th.

When he was interviewed in the Grand Jury—and you will see it in the Eckenrode stipulation that I put in—he says, it's possible that there were two calls. Mr. Libby has been consistent that he always thought it was probably two calls, one on the 10th, one on the 11th . . . [T]hey don't have phone records to nail it down.

I'm going to give you a homework assignment. I'm going to… show Mr. Libby is questioned about his call with Mr. Russert repeatedly in the Grand Jury, and I'm going to ask you did you look at Mr. Libby's Grand Jury on March 5. If you read Pages 143 through 162, you will see Mr. Libby is all over the place, whether it's the 11th and what time on the 11th.

Mr. Fitzgerald [asks] well, is it possible that . . . you talked to Russert before you talked to Rove? Mr. Libby says, yes. Well, could it have been earlier in the day, because I'm telling you what if I told you Mr. Rove left early that day. Mr. Libby said, well, if that's what you're saying maybe it would have been in the morning. But remember number one of the rules Judge Walton gave you, the questions by the lawyers are not evidence. There's no evidence to say what time Mr. Rove left. That's just in Mr. Fitzgerald's question.

Also, it may turn out that Mr. Libby is totally confused. Maybe he talked with Mr. Rove first and Mr. Russert second. Nobody really knows. But what you will see is mass confusion because there are no phone records.

But in a case where what is at stake is a man's reputation and a man's freedom, when you have this type of imprecision, this type of confusion, the benefit of the doubt must be given to Mr. Libby. That's part of the problem with this case.

I mean it is built at the end of the day on all sorts of theory that does not have, as a foundation, hard evidence. There's a lot of speculation going on. They're asking you, I submit, to speculate, to make a whole lot of jumps without any proof. Because, as I told you when I opened, there's no witness who has come and given you any direct evidence that Mr. Libby lied.

A lot of cases you'll have . . . somebody who is a co-conspirator. A co-conspirator gets on the stand and says, well, Mr. Libby said he was going to lie or Mr. Libby told me he lied. Well, there is no such witness in this case. You might have a smoking-gun document, some kind of document that makes it clear: Ah-hah! This is it. He lied. There is nothing like that in this case.

There is nothing wrong with circumstantial evidence. Circumstantial evidence, you'll be told by Judge Walton, is as good as direct evidence. But whether it's direct or circumstantial, it's got to be powerful evidence. It's got to be built on a strong foundation if you're going to change a person's life, if you're going to brand somebody a criminal. And they don't have it in this case.

Now, one point, one more point before I go to my next area. I want you to look at GX-65, and that's the letter from the Department of Justice that says what the investigation is about. That's GX-65.

What it says is that, the investigation—and it's dated I think September 30, 2003—that the government's investigation involved an investigation into the possible unauthorized disclosure of classified information in a July 14, 2003, syndicated article published by Novak in the *Chicago Sun-Times* and also something in *Newsday*.

Agent Bond said Mr. Libby had nothing to do with the *Newsday* article. But the investigation was about, when it first started, it was about Novak. That was Mr. Libby's state of mind because you saw that letter was part of the packet that Mr. Addington gave to Mr. Libby . . .

They said that's what the investigation was about. Now, they don't like it. So they say, well, maybe Mr. Libby should have read a newspaper article and thought it was about something else. Mr. Libby had every right, as everybody does, if given a letter by the Department of Justice saying this is what the investigation is about, to rely on the doggone letter.

Now, I want to go to another area. I want to talk very quickly about how the fact that Mr. Libby was greatly involved in responding to the Wilson charges doesn't mean, in any way, that he viewed the wife, Mrs. Wilson, as anything of any great importance. That there is a total disconnect between responding to the allegations by Ambassador

Wilson, responding on the merits and saying, well that means, you had to remember what you knew about the wife or that means you would have done something about the wife. There is a disconnect.

Everybody has had problems in this case remembering things about Mrs. Wilson because, the truth of the matter is, Mrs. Wilson did not become important until there was a criminal investigation many months later. That's when she became important . . .

We do not dispute that people like Ms. Martin told Mr. Libby on or about June 11th that the wife worked at the CIA. We don't dispute that. Ms. Martin doesn't have any reason to lie.

Mr. Libby told the FBI from day one, he learned it from the Vice President on or about June 11th. So he doesn't recollect it. But all of those dates, except if you put Mr. Fleischer to the side, and Mr. Addington, all the other witnesses really cluster around about three days, around June 10, June 11, or June 12. They're all clustered around the same date.

We don't dispute that he told the FBI. He learned it from the Vice President. We don't dispute that he would have heard it at least from Ms. Martin because we don't think she would have any reason to lie. So he heard it. But then, by time he's in the Grand Jury, he has forgotten that Ms. Martin told him. There is nothing wrong with that.

He saw a note that the Vice President told him. Okay? So nobody is disputing that there is a period in June when Scooter Libby learns that Mrs. Wilson works for the CIA. He didn't dispute that from day one with the FBI. He went in the first day. He brought the note . . . that showed that the Vice President had told him.

Mr. Jeffress said, if he's such a bad guy, he should have put the note in the trash can. But he's not a bad guy. He's a honest man, a good person, and brought the note. He said, I looked at the note to refresh my recollection.

Now, I think the government, through its questions, really tried to put a cloud over Vice President Cheney. During their questioning of Ms. Martin, the prosecutors questioned [her]: Well, you weren't with Mr. Libby and the Vice President all the time. Some things could have happened when you weren't there.

And the clear suggestion by the questions were, well, maybe there was some kind of skullduggery, some kind of scheme between Libby and the Vice President going on in private, but that's unfair. It's unfair on the facts of this case because, one thing we know, Scooter Libby wasn't out pushing any stories on the wife. It didn't happen . . .

[W]e brought in all these reporters. And they said to a person Mr. Libby didn't say anything about the wife. The only person who says anything about Mr. Libby and Mrs. Wilson, in terms of Mr. Libby volunteering information, is Judith Miller. And I don't think it happened. I don't think it happened on July 8th. She's got a note that says WINPAC. [Mrs. Wilson] didn't work at WINPAC . . .

The prosecution has focused on [the] July 8th meeting with Judith Miller at the St. Regis Hotel. They said, [how] could Mr. Libby, . . . if he was so busy, . . . have two hours to go out and have lunch with Ms. Miller on July 8th.

The reason he took two hours to have lunch with Ms. Miller is that Mr. Libby understood that the Vice President of the United States had directed him to go meet with Ms. Miller and that . . . President Bush was behind it too. Not to say anything about Valerie Wilson, but to discuss with Judith Miller of *The New York Times* information that President Bush had privately, lawfully declassified concerning the National Intelligence Estimate.

This is what Mr. Libby said in the Grand Jury on that issue. "He,"—mean[ing] the Vice President— ". . . told me . . . that we should go ahead and talk to the press about the NIE. I don't remember whether he said Judith Miller at that point or, or we should go ahead and talk about it. And, you know, I said, the President clear it? And he said yes or something. I didn't use those words necessarily, but that was—I made sure that he had talked to the President. The President said that we should talk about it." . . .

The testimony by government witnesses about conversations Libby may have had in June and July does not answer the question whether he lied or made an innocent mistake in October 2003. Let me explain what I'm saying. They put seven, eight witnesses on the stand that say, well, we had conversations with Scooter Libby in June or July. That's in real time.

But not one of those witnesses said anything about whether Libby had a misrecollection in good faith in October or was Mr. Libby lying in October. Those witnesses can't help you, in any material way, I submit, try to figure out what Libby's state of mind was in October . . .

There is no evidence that Libby was engaged in intentional lying as opposed to he just forgot like all of us forget things. All of us forget things. We misconstrue things. We misrecollect things. It happens to everyone . . . You can be as confident as all get-out that something happened a particular way and you can find out later you just had it wrong. It happens to everybody, everybody . . .

Those witnesses, . . . they don't help you in answering the question [of] what . . . Mr. Libby remember[ed] in October. Did he have a good-faith misrecollection? Or did he lie? . . . No witnesses come into the courtroom and say that in October he lied. Again, there is no smoking gun document. There is no expert testimony that he could not have forgotten . . .

Mr. Fitzgerald conceded appropriately during the trial that there is no allegation that any documents were withheld or any documents were missing. It's not a situation where somebody ditched some documents. You've got all the documents and, of all the documents you have, Mr. Libby only had one note… dealing with the wife; one note. It shows both that she was not important to him and therefore, . . . it's easy for him to have forgotten exactly what he knew when or about her. Also he had hundreds of other notes. We didn't put the notes in because the notes are all sorts of classified information that can't be put in the record.

But Mr. Addington told you, Mr. Libby had hundreds and hundreds and hundreds of pages of notes. That was his life-line. He didn't have a great memory but he was smart and he knew how to have mnemonic devices to support him. The way he supported himself was with notes and with his staff . . .

They said, "No, the criminal system works a different way." He says "Okay. But I'm telling you, for me to handle all this national security stuff, all the domestic policy stuff,

I had to develop a different system and it worked. And I'll walk you through it."

. . . You are going to get a memory instruction from Judge Walton. It is an important instruction. It tries to give you some guidance from the court as to certain things that you might want to consider in trying to figure out did Mr. Libby make a good faith misrecollection or did the Government prove that he was lying beyond a reasonable doubt . . .

And some of the things Judge Walton points to is your assessment based on your life experiences. Ask yourself, if you've been in situations where you had a full plate or you've had a high stress job, is it more likely that you might get confused or you might forget things? Okay? And Mr. Libby, we learned, he had one of the highest stress jobs in the country . . .

[Consider] the amount of time between when a person said or heard something and the impact the passage of time had on the person's memory to accurately recall those events. So, we're talking about, in terms of the FBI interview, a three-month period, in terms of the Grand Jury, we're talking about nine months.

[Think] about the circumstances that existed when the person was exposed to the events he or she is asked to recall, the circumstances that existed.

Mr. Hannah told you, when all of this was going on in June and July, there was some of the most high-stress moments in the history of the United States of America. This country, not only were we at war, not only did we have 100,000 kids on the ground in harm's way, but they hadn't found any weapons of mass destruction.

The country was starting to turn against the Bush administration. The country was saying, hey, you lied to the American public. You lied in the State of the Union. The CIA and the White House are shooting at each other . . .

You listen to those security briefings he got, they make your toes curl. I mean it's frightening. That's how he started his day every day. So use your life experiences. Nothing wrong with using your common sense and your life experiences to put things in context, give him the benefit of the doubt and be fair.

And be fair and ask what did the Government give me that gives me the certainty that he was lying, that I can pronounce him guilty beyond a reasonable doubt? They haven't given you anything . . .

Four. The nature of the information or the event the person is called upon to remember. The wife was not important to Scooter Libby . . .

If you go to the State Department and talk to Mr. Armitage, that might be a different thing. If you talk to Mr. Fleischer who, after he talks to Mr. Bartlett, that might be a different thing. You talk to Mr. Rove, that might be a different thing. But in terms of the Office of the Vice President, in terms of Scooter Libby, the evidence is to the contrary. The wife was never part of the message . . .

Mr. Hannah said Mr. Libby had two jobs. He was a Chief of Staff of the Vice President of the United States. That's the job Mr. Addington [has now]. And he was the National Security Advisor to the Vice President of the United States. That's the job Mr. Hannah [has now] . . .

Mr. Fitzgerald, on his opening statement, said, well[,] how could you be talking to Mr. Fleischer on Monday or Tuesday and be startled when you talked to Mr. Russert on

Thursday? In all due respect, that is not a fair characterization of the model, the issue, that you have to confront.

Nobody is saying that Mr. Libby forgot something in two days. Mr. Libby, that's his testimony in the Grand Jury, he said himself. I don't mean to say that if she told me that I forgot it in those two days. The question is—what did he remember three months later . . .

Next slide.

I DON'T HAVE TIME TO go through all of the witnesses in detail. But in terms of what we saw in this courtroom, there were memory problems with every witness. I mean, Mr. Grenier, he said, "My recollection of a lot of conversations from that time is pretty vague. I will say that, in fact, my recollection of my conversations with Mr. Libby has a fair amount of vagueness attached to it as well."

He goes on to say, "I was saying what I believed to be true at the time and subsequently had a different recollection." Though he said one thing, had a different recollection later: "As I went back over the conversation that I had with Mr. Libby, I really didn't remember anything new from that conversation. But what I did remember that was new over time was the way that I felt immediately after the conversation."

Then we have Ms. Miller. She said, "I have searched my memory and I just can't remember specific discussions with people about Valerie Wilson." She described her memory as note-driven . . . She tries to use her notes, [which] did not prove that trustworthy in this case, but at least she tries to rely on her notes . . .

Each of these witnesses may have a different initial recollection in this trial and then they had a later recollection. And they changed. Either they found the note or something to jog a memory. But initially what they thought was something else.

I mean, Ms. Martin, she thought she learned about Mrs. Wilson, initially in her first FBI interview, she thought she learned about it in July. Turned out, when I cross-examined her and we put all the evidence in front, she learned it in June. She forgot a whole month during which she had known it—an entire month. She wasn't lying. She had a misrecollection in good faith. When enough evidence was presented, she realized what she had said to the FBI was off by an entire month.

. . . Mr. Hannah told you that Mr. Libby had an awful memory for some things, like sources of information, where he got certain information from. One of you jurors, you asked a great question: How did Libby do his job if he had such a poor memory? Did it affect his job? And the answer to the question is that Mr. Libby had a system for remembering information because Mr. Hannah made clear that he thought Mr. Libby did a good job.

What Mr. Libby told the Grand Jury was that, to cope with the numerous amount of information he received every day, was that he pooled the collective recollections of his people together. He would bring people together. They had a concept called back benchers. Where they go to all these meetings, but they always take one person whose job was to be the repository of the information. Okay . . .

What you also saw from Addington, that Mr. Libby took pages and pages of notes. Again, the notes were not entered, but he took pages, hundreds and hundreds and hundreds of pages of notes, that they had these back benchers. He kept files. They had drawers and drawers full of material, and at the end of the day, they would review the concepts and ideas with the staff.

And again, there's this inherent conflict between his mnemonic devices and the criminal justice system. They said, in the Grand Jury investigation, you are to talk to no one. That's okay. There is nothing wrong with that concept as to how criminal justice investigations should be done. But, in this case, there was a collision with a guy who had a different system. And it was a different system. It was a good system. It was an important system because it was about doing his job, which was to be the National Security Advisor to the Vice President of this country . . .

So what Mr. Hannah told you was that Mr. Libby had two full-time jobs. He worked 13 to 14 hours a day. He left home before 6:30 in the morning. He would be in the office until 8:00 or 9:00. He had as many as four meetings by mid-morning. Mr. Grossman said that preparing for those meetings was like cramming for five or six exams in a row. And Mr. Libby had a much bigger job.

...DX 1031, that's the schedule for Mr. Libby on June 11. Look at it. It's in evidence. Just show you that's the day he's supposedly getting all this information about Mrs. Wilson.

The June 14th morning intelligence briefing, that stipulation is in evidence. It will be in the jury room. I urge you to look at it. And that briefing, that's just an example, he got one six days a week. Just read it, discuss it. Try to put yourself in his shoes and figure out how that might impact on your memory. Just be fair . . .

I mean all of these things were going on in real time. In addition to being sent to the St. Regis by the President of the United States on this NIE secret mission, to deal with the Tenet statement where George Tenet was saying the CIA was responsible for the sixteen words . . . It is a crazy period. Now, they're talking about, what did he remember about Valerie Wilson? That was his world, all those people, not just the witnesses in this case. Everybody from Bin Laden on toward North Korea, I mean, it's all in the record.

MR. LIBBY made a lot of mistakes in that Grand Jury. For example, he said that he told Cooper about Wilson's wife. Cooper told Libby. Mr. Libby, if he was trying to help himself, has the conversation going the wrong way, but he's just confused. He's confused about a lot of things. He said he told Kessler about Wilson's wife. Kessler came in here and said, . . . "Libby didn't tell me anything. He's just confused." Again, that wouldn't help him.

Libby said he didn't know Wilson's name until [the] Wilson July 6th op-ed. I don't think that's right. I think Libby did know the name going as far back as some time in June. He didn't know, but he got it wrong. Mr. Libby said he had no recollection of talking to Novak during the week of July 6th. Novak said, no, I talked to Libby. If he had remembered, that would have helped him.

He was trying to give his best recollection. Remember, a lot of this stuff is taking place [over] eight hours, intense questioning. How do you evaluate his Grand Jury testimony? Remember, he had no notes. He had no tape recordings.

It's unfair to expect him to remember the exact words. He remembers concepts. The concept of not confirming information is consistent with Libby's recollection, that he may have said to reporters, ["R]eporters are telling us about Wilson's wife. I don't know if it's true. I don't even know if he has a wife." . . .

All I ask is [that you] use your common sense [and] life experiences. [D]on't base your verdict on speculation. Common sense will tell you that the Government has not established guilt beyond a reasonable doubt.

He gave his best good-faith recollection. Any mistakes were innocent mistakes. He had no knowledge that Wilson's job status was classified. He did not push reporters to write about Valerie Wilson. He did not leak to Robert Novak. Richard Armitage did. He is an innocent person. He had no motive to lie . . .

All I can do is trust in you. I told you that when we chose you, we had already accomplished the most important part of the case. We made a decision that you and you alone would be the judges.

For some of you, this is probably one of the most important jobs you'll ever have in terms of sitting in judgment of another human being. It's an enormous task. It's an enormous responsibility. All I will say to you is follow Judge Walton's instructions . . . Trust in the evidence and trust in each other.

Be the protector of the integrity of your deliberation process. If somebody begins to go off track and starts to have a situation where Mr. Libby has to prove his innocence as opposed to the Government has to prove his guilt, help that person. Somebody starts to speculate, help that person. If somebody starts to say, oh, you know, he's a Republican. He worked for Cheney. You know, let's . . . help that person.

We started off talking about protecting Karl Rove [and] sacrificing Scooter Libby. That's written in the Vice President's own handwriting. I say to you, don't . . . sacrifice Scooter Libby for how you may feel about the war in Iraq or how may feel about the Bush administration. Don't sacrifice Scooter Libby.

Treat him the way he deserves to be treated. He got up every morning and worked 12 hours a day to be the National Security Advisor to this country. You look at what he did. You give him a fair shake. You analyze it. You analyze it fairly. And fight any temptation of filtering how you analyze the evidence through your views, be you Democrat or whatever party.

This is a man with a wife, with two children, and nobody has come in here and said, he's been a bad person, done anything wrong. He is a good person. He has been under my protection for the last month. I give him to you. I ask you at the end of the case, vote not guilty on each and every count and give him back to me. Just give him back.

(End of Wells closing statement.)

WELLS SOBS AUDIBLY as he concludes his closing statement. The court takes a brief recess and then Fitzgerald proceeds with the prosecution's rebuttal, which opens as dramatically as the defense's concluded. One of the notable features of his rebuttal, which also seeks to bolster some of the prosecution's key witnesses and which makes the case that the heart of Libby's obstruction was lying about how he effectively learned that Wilson's wife worked at the CIA, is it's focus on the role of the Vice President, both during July 2003 and during the opening of the investigation in fall 2003. Rebutting the defense's contention that he had put a cloud over the Vice President, Fitzgerald argues that it was Libby's own conduct that had put the cloud over the Vice President as well as over the White House.

News reports at the time noted that Fitzgerald moved very quickly through his rebuttal. He spoke with great haste, and those listening in the courtroom later reported that, at times, he was almost incoherent.

THE COURT: Mr. Fitzgerald.

MR. FITZGERALD: Good afternoon.

THE JURORS: Good afternoon.

MR. FITZGERALD: Madness, outrageous, the Government brought a case about two phone calls with no corroboration, two witnesses, nothing to back it up and they just want us to speculate. The defense wishes that were so.

Saying it, saying it loudly, saying it pounding the table doesn't change the facts, doesn't change the law, and doesn't change the evidence. Let's talk about the facts. Let's get busy.

. . . Is this case about two reporters and two phone calls[?] That's it[?] . . . They wish it were so. This case is not a one-on-one he said/she said. It's a he said, he said, she said, he said, he said, she said, he said, he said, she said, he said and the defendant made it up.

Each of these people talked about conversations. You've heard about conversations where they discussed Wilson's wife. Is this the world's greatest coincidence that nine conversations with eight people, all misremembering the same way, that the defendant is talking about Joseph Wilson's wife?

Is it the greatest coincidence that the one person he said he actually talked to Wilson's wife about [was] the reporter, Tim Russert, [who] forgot it? You know the greatest conspiracy, the scapegoat get replaced by NBC, Tim Russert? No. It's not one on one. It's not he said/she said. It's all the evidence taken together. Maybe the best example is to focus on what Mr. Wells said about Tim Russert.

When he focuses on the Tim Russert count, he wants you to believe that it all depends on Tim Russert. That Tim Russert has to be proved beyond a reasonable doubt himself. First of all, I'll tell you he is. You have every right as a jury to decide the facts as you saw them. You saw the witnesses up on the stand. You saw them look you in the eye. You saw them answer questions on direct and answer on cross.

I'll tell you that Tim Russert alone could be proved beyond a reasonable doubt. But let me make a different point. You don't need Tim Russert's evidence to find the defendant guilty, even on the Tim Russert count.

Now, you're thinking, "He's gone too far. He has lost it. It's a long day." But I haven't gone too far. Think about this. One part of the Tim Russert count says that

Defendant Libby said he was surprised on July 10th or July 11th when he heard this information about Wilson's wife. Struck, as if he were learning anew. Remember? . . .

No one wishes this, but if Tim [Russert] were run over by a bus a month ago and went to that great news desk in the sky instead of coming in here to testify, you would have had no evidence from Tim Russert. You could still find plenty of evidence that the defendant was not surprised on July 10th or 11th.

Because he learned it from the Vice President. He learned it from Bob Grenier of the CIA. He learned it from Cathie Martin. He learned it from Marc Grossman. He shared it with Craig Schmall. The first day he got briefed by Craig Schmall after learning from all those people is a Saturday. [Schmall] told him about it. He told Judith Miller on June 23rd. He told Ari Fleischer on July 7th. He told Judith Miller on July 8th. [He] discussed the spouse with David Addington July 8th.

You know you're not surprised about something on Thursday when you give it out Monday and Tuesday and repeated times. Without Tim Russert ever coming here, you could convict on that count about surprise. If Tim Russert, standing alone, could be proved beyond a reasonable doubt, without Tim Russert at all, you have proved beyond a reasonable doubt. That's the powerful evidence that's talked about in the charges. Something that gives you a firm conviction of what's been proven.

Now, let's talk about importance. Because one of the myths in this case is that Wilson's wife was unimportant. That's why he forgot. Let me make one thing clear. As a person, to the defendant and others who talked about her, she wasn't important. Her name is Valerie Wilson. She was a person. She had a life before she met Joe Wilson, much less before she met this case.

But to them, she wasn't Valerie Wilson. She wasn't a person. She wasn't the CIA employee that she was. She was an argument, a fact to use against Joe Wilson. [when] Joe Wilson dared to criticize.

The two things that Mr. Jeffress keeps pointing out with Mr. Wilson, Mr. Wilson says about himself. Read his op-ed. He said he wasn't sent by the Vice President. He was sent as a result of the question. But in any event, he raised the question and they thought the fact that his wife worked at the CIA was important for a couple of reasons. One, it casts suspicion of who Joe Wilson was. How he got the job. He got sent because of the wife. That's the way of looking at undercutting it. That's one way to look at it, and that was a fact they looked at. The second thing was, what was all the hullabaloo about? What were they really angry about? People kept saying or people kept thinking or people kept interpreting [that] the Vice President sent him. What was important? Who sent him. The question [of] who sent him was hugely important [to them] because they wanted everyone to know it wasn't the Vice President.

What was the answer to the important question who sent him? The wife. That's what they understood. That's what he had been told. That's what he understood. So Wilson's wife was an answer, a fact, an argument—the type of thing that the defendant remembers.

So, was she important as a person? No. But don't buy into this false spread. Oh, Wilson was . . . important, a devastating attack [on] the Administration, a direct attack on the credibility for the White House, the Vice President and the defendant . . . Wilson was important. Wilson's credibility was important. Karl Rove talking about it at White House meetings, attacking his credibility is important. But the wife argument—somehow that's separate.

Let's talk about that. Let's look first at Government Exhibit 702-A. There is an argument made in [the defense's] opening, repeat[ed] again, there is no scientific proof like no fingerprints . . . Government's Exhibit 702-A . . . does two things.

First, it corroborates witnesses I'll just talk about briefly . . . Grossman says that he knew the name Joe Wilson. He gave it to the defendant. Then he told him that his wife works there. Grenier said he was asked by name about Joe Wilson. And he told the defendant his wife works there. Cathie Martin says [she] knew the name before the op-ed, and she told the defendant the wife works there.

The defendant said, "I don't remember these conversations." He testifies in the Grand Jury that he learned the name Joe Wilson at the time of the op-ed, July 6th. He says, "I talked about the wife later with the Vice President, maybe late July even August". . .

[W]ith all the terror threats you've heard about from June 14th, all the things going on in the world from Al-Qaeda, Iraq, Iran, A.Q. Khan, nuclear proliferation, the war in Afghanistan, all that stuff going on, yet they're talking about Tom Cruise, Penelope Cruz, what does the defendant want to talk about?

That's a fingerprint. That's a fingerprint of the defendant's brain. It says "defendant Libby has been here." He's wrapped himself around this issue. He's wrapped himself around the issue of Joe Wilson. He's wrapped himself around the issue of who told him there was a question. He wrapped himself around the issue of Valerie Wilson . . . Now, let's jump ahead. That's because I want to go back to see how important this is. It's important on June 14th. That's what [Libby's] telling the briefer. [The brief is] trying to tell about all the terrorism stuff; [Libby's] bringing up Joe Wilson, Valerie Wilson.

What's July 14th? We all know that's the day that Wilson's wife is written about in the paper by Novak, the Novak column, July 14th. What do we know about that?

Government Exhibit 414. [You] may have seen it during the trial. This comes from the Vice President's file. Remember he sometimes rips out articles of interest. Whatever else was going on in the world, the war with everything else on July 14th, the Vice President rips out the Novak column that talks about Wilson's wife.

Here's a paper copy that he kept in his files. It was found later in the fall. The Vice President kept it for some reason . . .

[Exhibit] 412 is a Maureen Dowd column from July 13th, the day before the Novak column. If you look at it in the jury room, you'll see down at the bottom, he's spending his time on July 14th, you'll know it's after July 13th, writing little points to respond to Maureen Dowd. She is very critical of the administration. She talks about the Office of the Vice President, Dick Cheney, and Joe Wilson. So he's scribbling notes.

One of the things that refutes what she says, the defendant Libby cites, "Novak, 7-14." In fact, I won't pull it up now. But Government Exhibit 413 is a sheathe of articles that goes with this that he kept and he hand wrote Novak at the bottom. So July 14th, he's writing down on a column from the day before, a response. He's focused on the Novak column . . . sitting there ripping out the Novak column. What else do we have? 703-A, Government Exhibit 703-A, which is Schmall. He's the eyewitness, who wasn't into this issue, doesn't read about the Novak column . . . [T]he Vice President and the defendant are both together at a briefing on Monday, July 14th. What do [they ask] Schmall? "Did you read the Novak article?" That's what comes to mind. The Novak article is about Wilson's wife. I'm sorry to call her that. But that's what she's unfortunately been reduced to. "Did you read about the Novak column?" . . .

Let's assume the best-case scenario, the Vice President asked the question, not Mr. Libby, since he did most of the talking. This is a fingerprint that says on July 14th, the Vice President has read the Novak column. The other exhibit shows you, around July 14th, the defendant read the Novak column. And this is a fingerprint that says the brains of the Vice President and defendant Libby are wrapped around the Novak column on July 14th.

Now, was it important before? Well, we've heard about talking points. We've heard how there weren't talking points that talked about Mr. Wilson's wife. So, therefore, it couldn't have been important. After all, they're just running around trying to tell people that the Vice President didn't send him. They wouldn't want to share or focus anyone on who did send him . . .

Let's pull up Government Exhibit 540 . . . [R]emember these talking points Mr. Wells said were very, very important evidence in this case? We agree. [Exhibit] 540 [is] the talking points from July 7th. This is what Cathie Martin said to Ari Fleischer. You can see what they are, four simple talking points.

"The Vice President's office did not request the mission to Niger." "The Vice President's office was not informed of the mission." "The Vice President's office did not receive a briefing about the mission after he returned." "The Vice President's office was not aware of the mission until recent press reports accounted for it." Four points you've seen before. You also heard that the talking points changed.

They changed the following day, July 8th.

They changed when the Vice President is in his office on Capitol Hill. They both talk to Cathie Martin. She wants to talk to him. And he dictates, doesn't discuss. He dictates talking points. The handwritten talking points are in evidence. I think they're 522. She has a yellow sheet or whatever it was, when eight talking points, one is a question mark. She retyped it, screwed up the exhibit numbers. The retyped version is 524. The final version is 523. Light editing by Cathie Martin to defendant Libby.

Now we're good at talking points. There are eight of them. If you look at the second one, the second talking point, it looks like the talking points from the day before. Yesterday's talking points become number two. It said "the Vice President did not request the mission to Niger. The Vice President's office was not informed of Joe Wilson's mission. The Vice President's office did not receive a briefing about Mr. Wilson's mission after he returned."

Now, let's go back and focus on what is the first point that the Vice President dictates to Cathie Martin that he wants her to make to the press on July 8th, two days after the Wilson op-ed. "It is not clear who authorized Joe Wilson's trip to Niger." Any discussion on the annotated 402 of who might have been responsible for sending him on this trip?

Let's go back. "Or did his wife send him on a junket?" A day or two after he writes this, after the Vice President is thinking, did his wife send him on a junket, he makes the number one talking point that Cathie Martin should put out there. It's not clear who authorized the travel. The question of who sent Wilson is important. It is a number one question on the Vice President's mind when he tells Cathie Martin to get it out.

But there is something funny about how they want to talk about who sent him because they don't want to talk about the wife. There is something about it that's strange because what's going on the same two days? Look at Fleischer, look at Addington, and look at Miller together. Fleischer at lunch. He says it's a weird lunch. He only had lunch with the defendant once before. But the defendant gave him no information. He always said go see Dr. Rice.

But on this day he tells him, hush hush, QT, the wife works at the CIA, Counterproliferation Division. Isn't that interesting? The day after the Wilson op-ed, around the time the Vice President [speculated that] Wilson's wife sent him on a junket . . .

What happens the next morning? Addington . . . he had to talk about declassification, so maybe it's July 7th or maybe it's July 8 . . . In a room with a door closed, he tells Addington to lower his voice, won't mention the name Wilson. He said, ["W]hat paperwork is there if a spouse works at the CIA, or a person at the CIA sends his spouse on a trip?"

The defense said, "Well maybe he didn't say 'spouse' when he was first interviewed." What reason would he have to tell David Addington, perhaps the most soft spoken witness we've seen, to lower his voice in a room with the door closed if he is just talking about Wilson and not the spouse? Wilson has been on *Meet the Press*, NBC, *The Washington Post*, *The New York Times*. He is out . . . "Lower your voice" for Addington. "Hush hush QT" for Ari Fleischer.

That's the morning that the defendant is off with Judith Miller, two hours, St. Regis Hotel. That's one of the times that the defendant shared the employment of Wilson's wife with the CIA with Judith Miller. There was a focus of who sent Wilson on this trip. There was an obsession with Wilson. So the focus was on who sent him. They felt the wife was responsible. Any effort to tell you the wife is just [a] separate, unrelated issue, [and] didn't matter [is] try[ing] to take your attention away from what the facts are.

I submit to you, on June 14th, the defendant thought Wilson's wife was important. Couldn't wait to ask the questions of the CIA briefer. July 14th, Vice President ripping the column out of the paper. The defendant is marking it up. They're asking the CIA briefer. And the week before it was important. It was important enough that the Vice President he wanted to question up number one, unclear... who authorize[d] it.

. . . The question of who authorized becomes number one. That's a question that would lead to the answer: Valerie Wilson.

Now, let's talk about the witnesses. Let's talk about Judith Miller. You know what? Let's figure it out. Did what Judith Miller say happened on July 8th happen? Why is she talking about the wife? Why does WINPAC come up? Is this amazing recovery? You have a lab experiment that might tell you what she says is true? Well, we can.

Let's put up on the screen what Judith Miller testified about for July 8th. Remember one thing, her initial Grand Jury testimony was, look, I know I talked about the wife working at WINPAC with the defendant on July 8th. I do have some memory that I talked about it with someone before I can't place. Then she goes back and she finds the notebooks.

She did talk about it before. It [was] June 23rd with the defendant. The only entries in her notebook, she told you, that tied to a discussion of Valerie Wilson by whatever name or description, specifically to an interview, there were only two, the defendant, June 23rd and July 8th.

Let's pull up, and I'll warn you in advance, this will prove I'm a geek. I'll get a lot of grief for it. When you go through this, I want to tell you why I'm going through it because I'll show you three things. I'm going to show you Judith Miller's memory. I'm going to show you the defendant's memory.

I'm going to show you the defendant's focus, because you're going to find out where the information came from. The defendant shared with Judith Miller on July 8th. I'll give you the punch line. It was some of those CIA faxes sent a month before on June 9th. You'll see how much of an amazing recall the defendant had on July 8th [of] what was faxed to him on June 9th.

. . .When you see this, you will see her memory is accurate, and Mr. Libby's memory was accurate and boy was he focused on Wilson.

All right. Here we are. Here's the testimony. She says he told her about two reports. There were two reports about getting uranium from Niger for Iraq. Then there's a third report that talked about the arrival in Niger of delegations of Iraqi officials in 1999. This all had to do with Iraq's interest in acquiring uranium.

So then she mentioned that this report had been up to the Hill, and then it says credit due by the CIA. She indicated that the author of the report was Joe Wilson. Whether she was inaccurate or the defendant was inaccurate because Wilson didn't say until July 6th, she had a written report. This was a report about Wilson.

All right. Now let's look at the exhibit. The exhibit is Defendant Exhibit 64 [which] they've placed in evidence. You'll see it's a fax sent on June 9th to back Iraq-Nigerian uranium, Congressional notification. Remember she said it went up to the Hill. Down below it says please pass to Hannah and Libby. Remember Hannah said he was focused on Wilson. Libby was focused on Wilson at this time. The defense put this exhibit in through Craig Schmall. The briefer sent these materials over to the defendant Libby on June 9th.

Let's go to the next page. This page, it focuses on paragraphs 2 and 3 of a long document. You actually have the exhibit. It's pretty long. Paragraph 2 talks about a report. The CIA's directorate of operations issued a report. Niger planned to send several tons of uranium to Iraq. Then it talks about a second report, paragraph 3. Directorate of operations issued a second report. Niger and Iraq had signed an agreement. Okay. Let's go to the next page.

Now, we see the third report. You remember, she said, he associated the third report with Joseph Wilson. Here we are in Paragraph 6. There's a different copy we'll show you where the 6 is clearer. 8 March 2002, the directorate of operations disseminated information obtained independently for a sensitive source. Goes on to discuss that the sub-source, someone he spoke to, believed Iraq was interested in discussing yellowcake purchases when it sent a delegation to Niamey in mid-1999.

There it is. The Iraq trade delegation 1999. This is a Joe Wilson trip. How do you know that? You know it in two ways. First, it says 8 March 2002. He went—in the Wilson op-ed, he said he went over to Niger in late February, came back in early March. You also know that he reported what he had found out about this 1999 trip . . .

How do you know that the defendant knew that? How do you know that he had focused so much in the weeds in Paragraph 6 that he would know the sensitive source was Wilson. Well, you do know it because of a different exhibit in evidence . . . Grand Jury Exhibit 2-A . . .

The page is Bates Stamped 1784. Low and behold next to the sensitive source there's an arrow that says Joe Wilson in print, Wilson in script . . . [I]f you look at

1784 in the Grand Jury testimony, the defendant says that's his handwriting. He's figured out that . . . the sensitive source is Wilson.

Now, this is where it gets interesting. Go back to Judith Miller's testimony once again. She says, in terms of how Mr. Wilson's wife came up, she said, well Mr. Libby was discussing what he called two streams of reporting on uranium and efforts by Iraq to acquire sensitive materials and components.

He said the first stream was a report like that of Joe Wilson. Then he said the second stream. At that point he said, once again, as an aside, that Mr. Wilson's wife worked at WINPAC. By the way, you see down below, WINPAC stands for Weapons Intelligence of Non-Proliferation and Arms Control. There's a non proliferation in there. And I think when the defense argued this morning that they were saying there is a Non-Proliferation Bureau of State, it's actually Bureau of International Assistance in Non-Proliferation . . .

Let's go with that one. See where this might come from. Here we are in Paragraph 25, when you look at page 7, deep in this document that was sent by Mr. Schmall on June 9th. What does it say? Two streams of reporting, the exact phrase.

Remember on June 23rd, he had the clandestine guy? Now it's two streams of reporting. Two streams of reporting suggest that Iraq has attempted to acquire uranium from Niger. That says that two streams of reporting he referred to in this briefing came from the sensitive source described in paragraph 6 of this notification.

[Also] remember the issue is what is the wife's role? You were told that the wife worked in the unit that sent him on the trip, counterproliferation, non-proliferation, bureau, whatever it is. Remember that one of the things tied up, whether or not there were forged documents involved.

What do you see in the same document? CIA WINPAC received some translated documents in the State Department. CIA WINPAC is dealing with the forged documents. Now, did Ms. Miller get it wrong when [she] came up with WINPAC [for the wife]? Or did Mr. Libby assume that non-proliferation and everything [she] was dealing with. Right after the two streams of reporting, that's when WINPAC comes up.

They want to tell you he got it all wrong. I suggest to you the documents show he was focused. He had a memory. He had a memory for documents, and he knew that they referred back and forth. Remember two streams of reporting. Judith Miller told you what happened. The defendant told her what he knew happened in the CIA documents he received the month before.

Remember he talked to you about a full recollection? Remember how he has the full recollections. He was alone with Ms. Miller at the St. Regis Hotel. What are the streams of reporting? Where do they come from? How do they focus? This is him, by himself, with amazing focus on Wilson at that time.

LET'S MOVE FORWARD to talk about another witness. By the way, if you think there's any doubt in your mind that this whole non-proliferation, counter-proliferation stuff is nonsense in terms of which agency, the best intelligence reporter you can think of testified for the defense, [is] Walter Pincus, 1,000 intelligence articles, Pulitzer Prize, Stewart Alsop Prize.

If you go to his October 12th article, if you go to page 2, first full paragraph, first sentence, he talks about the CIA's non-proliferation section. There is none. Small case. Non-proliferation, counter-proliferation, even this thing about WMD analyst, who works in a counter-proliferation division? Wouldn't you have Weapons of Mass Destruction analysts there? Let's not focus on word splitting. If non-proliferation section is good enough for Walter Pincus, it could work for others.

Let's talk about Matt Cooper. We've heard about this Perry Mason [moment].. We've heard about how it was blown away by this document. If anyone had just been fair minded, just at the time anyone in the government who really cared, would just look at the document, they know it happened the way they said it happened. Really? Let's pull . . . up . . . that document up . . .

"Mr. Libby seemed to want to get off the phone. I was just throwing it out. I should have followed up." It happened at the end of the conversation. What we all know, the defendant was trying [to] get off the phone. He was trying to leave the airport. Trying to go with his kids to the party. That's exactly right . . .

They talked about the Tenet statement. After they talked about the Tenet statement, Wilson says or Cooper says, but why does he say he was sent on the trip. Remember he was saying I can't believe it. The Vice President says he was not sent on the trip. The director said he was not sent on the trip. He says, the defendant said this conversation about Wilson's wife came up after discussion of the Tenet statement.

If you put back up 816, Defense Exhibit. What was so important for the defendant to get in the Tenet statement? They kept wanting to get in this 1999 trip. Again, it's their argument on the merits, but think about it.

His 1999 trip [was] when Wilson said, . . . "Look, there's no way you could have gotten uranium from Niger. You just can't. Well one person told me in 1999 someone asked [about yellowcake, but] it went nowhere." That's supposed to be the thing that [kept] the sixteen words in the State of the Union. That's not what you put in the State of the Union . . .

Well, one thing you know, if you listen carefully to his Grand Jury testimony, the defendant remembers that the first time that the 1999 trip and the Wilson report was declassified was the Tenet statement. It had never been put out there publicly before. The defendant remembered that in March 2004.

He said in the Grand Jury, there was a Wilson cable. I'm not sure if I can talk about it. It's classified. Oh, it was declassified in the Tenet statement. That was the first time. Not true it was ever said before. The 1999 trip was something new. . . .

The third witness, think about the discrepancy between what Cooper is saying and what the defendant is saying. The defendant is saying, I never thought Wilson's wife sent him on the trip until after I read it in the Novak column. That's when the thought first occurred to me. That's in his Grand Jury testimony.

What does Cooper say? He said, I asked, have you heard his wife sent him on the trip. What do we know? Fleischer testified, on the Monday lunch, he's being told by Libby about the wife sending him on the trip. Did Cooper just get lucky, remember wrong, and say something consistent with Fleischer's testimony?

Addington testified being asked some time that week what paperwork would there be if a CIA employee sent a spouse on the trip. Cooper got lucky again. He's got to see ahead that Libby's Grand Jury testimony is going to put it at the end of the conversation. Fleischer will corroborate him. Addington will corroborate him. And who else?

Cathie Martin. Cathie Martin, one call or two calls [with Cooper], she knows when she came back, the defendant was still reading that long prepared statement. She remembered the end of the call, not what was said but she remembered she was there.

Do you think for a moment that the conversation that the defendant described where he's saying reporters are telling us that Wilson's wife worked at the CIA, I don't know if it's true. But this long explanation of why [Wilson] got bad skinny could happen in front of Cathie Martin and she not remember it? She is very careful.

What did she tell you? Whenever someone, the defendant discussed the NIE on July 8th with Andrea Mitchell and again didn't bother to tell her it was declassified, she got nervous. So she left the room in part for that reason. When the Vice President added the NIE stuff to the talking points, she put a question mark because she got nervous.

When Mr. Wells asked her on the witness stand, hey, Novak column, that was no big deal. You knew it already. What did she say? It wasn't a huge revelation to me because I knew. But I knew it was a huge revelation that he was putting it out there. So I mean, I knew it was a big deal [that] he disclosed it. She saw that Novak column, the one the Vice President ripped out of the paper. When she saw it, she said that's a big deal.

When she hears about the NIE, she thinks that's a big deal. Do you think she's going to sit there and listen to Mr. Libby talk on the phone about Wilson's wife working at the CIA and she's not going to have a reaction? Cathie Martin corroborates. Fleischer corroborates. Addington corroborates. Libby's Grand Jury testimony corroborates it happened at the end of the call.

If you think that the Vice President and the defendant Scooter Libby weren't talking about the wife during the week where the Vice President writes that his wife sent him on a junket [on a clipping of] the July 6th column, the Vice President moves the number-one talking point, not clear who authorized the travel. Defendant Libby is telling Fleischer on Monday, Addington on Monday or Tuesday, and Miller on Tuesday about the wife. If you just think that's a coincidence, well, that makes no sense . . .

And you know what? They said something here that we're trying to put a cloud on the Vice President. We'll talk straight. There is a cloud over what the Vice President did that week. He wrote those columns. He had those meetings. He sent Libby off to Judith Miller at the St. Regis Hotel. At that meeting, . . . the defendant talked about the wife. We didn't put that cloud there. That cloud remains because the defendant has obstructed justice and lied about what happened.

Did he come in straight and say here's what really happened? He came in and . . . told the Grand Jury, "I don't remember anything. I remember learning about the wife. I learned it from Russert as if it were new. I was sitting around thinking I don't even know if Wilson's married. How do we know he has a wife?"

He's put the doubt into whatever happened that week, whatever is going on between the Vice President and the defendant, that cloud was there. That's not something that we put there. That cloud is something that we just can't pretend isn't there.

By the way, there is some suggestion that maybe Russert and Cooper got confused and [it's] pretty ridiculous . . . I suggest to you, how would the conversation have happened on July 11 with Karl Rove?

Would Karl Rove have said, hey, I just found out from Novak that he knows that Wilson's wife works at the CIA. And Libby says, yeah, Tim Russert just told me. What would he have said? Oh, Matt Cooper told me tomorrow because he spoke on Saturday because Cooper and the Rove conversation was on Friday.

Let's talk about Tim Russert. Tim Russert is a devastating witness. He puts the lie to the lie. He comes in and says, wait a minute, what are you talking about? I didn't tell him. Not only do I not remember telling him, but just like Glenn Kessler, I couldn't have told him because I remember when I learned.

He remembers being struck by reading the Novak column about this information. And he testified that he remembers asking people, did you know that. And everyone said, quite to the contrary. He remembers the following week trying to think about whether or not NBC should publish about the wife even though Novak has. That's critical testimony.

What we have has thrown anything up against the wall to make it stick. Saying, well, we're not calling Mr. Russert a liar. We're just saying he's saying things different than the way they happened because of all sorts of reasons. Okay, you forgot about the *Buffalo News* article. The *Buffalo News* article, I'm sure Mr. Russert has been criticized before. It was four years old.

By the time this thing happened in 2004, he remembered writing the guy a letter.

Doesn't remember giving a phone call. Let's get over it. This issue in the deposition, he went in. He took a deposition that allows lawyers, okay, so do a lot of other people.

One thing we should point out, Mr. Wells's argument in his opening and his closing, if this was not a First Amendment-protected conversation, he had to assume this was out, no problem, we're going to learn about it real easy. Everyone agrees. Not a protected conversation. What's the issue?

Well, that's a good argument. You assume that the defendant is lying. The defendant testified in the Grand Jury quite differently. Mr. Wells told you this morning, he told you the defendant testified it wasn't a protected conversation. So I had to pull out the indictment and see if I had a memory lapse.

Count V, Count IV perjury. In the charged language it says, "Now, I had said earlier in the conversation, which I omitted to tell you, that this, you know as always, Tim, our discussion is off the record if that's okay with you. He said that's fine." So the defendant's testimony under oath was this was an off-the-record conversation. That off-the-record conversation triggered all the things that an off-the-record conversation does. We'll come back to that a little later.

So we have Russert. Now, we heard about a report, . . . when he was first interviewed where he was called by the FBI . . . Talks about a prior visit . . . He basically is put on the spot because the FBI tells [him], "Hey, I talked to Mr. Libby. He knew the source, this information about the wife." His reaction was, "That's a false statement." . . . He says, "Wait a minute, someone says I gave out information about the wife, and he didn't."

It's a very different story when NBC gets subpoenaed. You've heard about that. We'll come back to that in a moment. To get subpoenaed, that's a very different thing to compel someone who is a journalist. The first time in his career, Mr. Russert's. But you saw from the witness stand, don't let arguments, don't let distractions take away from your judgment of the witness you saw.

He doesn't remember being on the *Today* show. He goes on the *Today* show a lot. If we were all on the *Today* show with Katie Couric, we'd remember it. He's on there all the time. He used the word huge. I'm sure lots of people use the word huge. You can't remember the last time you used the word huge. He didn't remember what happened. The indictment happened. He heard his name coming out of someone's mouth talking about the indictment. That made an impact. So let's not play memory games on this. What he said to you, you can judge for yourself.

There also was that day that, in essence, an allegation that he misled the court because of an affidavit. What he told you a certain fact wasn't in his affidavit. He told you he didn't know what was in the other affidavits. So I want to throw out that the court was misled. You have no knowledge of what the court was told by other people in the litigation . . . That's speculation.

Now, we're asked, why Russert? Why make up this story? One version is why not rely upon Novak. Really? In a case he wants you to believe he thought was only about Novak . . .

He thinks, oh, maybe it was an innocent switch, Russert, Novak, switched. Really?

He told you he doesn't remember the conversation. Novak doesn't remember telling him about the wife. But suddenly we should leap to a conclusion. It's an immaculate reception. Somehow this happened like the pass in the Super Bowl. How does it happen? Suddenly he learns from Novak. Tim Russert and Novak get switched.

And also, two other problems, besides the fact that they're not quite in the same business, print versus media, don't quite look the same. Two other problems with that, how would that explain his story about having this dilemma he talked to Andrea Mitchell? He didn't know whether he could tell Andrea Mitchell that Wilson's wife worked at the CIA. Because if he did, even though he thinks everyone knows it, [s]he might ask him how he knew. He might say I learned it from Tim Russert, get Tim Russert in trouble. If Novak told him, we wouldn't have that dilemma . . .

Why Russert? The sad truth is sometimes when people lie, it looks dumb when they get caught. So you look back and say why did you tell that lie. I'm sure if people knew they were going to get caught in a lie they would have told it differently. What do you know about a couple of things?

First of all, the one thing he had to do, knowing that there was an investigation focused on him talking to reporters, and there was things out there by *TIME* magazine that were underlined. *TIME* magazine heard about the wife and knew it was out there. He's got to worry that Cooper wrote this thing, so Cooper doesn't seem friendly. So he doesn't want to say I've never had a conversation with him before. But he's got to make the conversation clean. He needs a blocker. He needs a story to cut off all those conversations with people, including the Vice President.

He better make it a reporter because if it's a reporter, he can say it's a rumor. He can say I didn't know it was true. I completely forgot. Also, if it's a reporter, there's a much better chance the protections that will kick in for talking to a reporter might affect things.

So he's got to pick a reporter. It's got to be a reporter late in the day because he wants the reporter to be as far out as possible so the likelihood that a reporter might know it was better. If he had picked Bob Woodward and got lucky, it might have been different because Woodward would say, I don't remember telling him, but I knew so maybe I did.

He picks somebody high up in NBC News. That makes sense. Maybe the higher up you go, the more likely you heard. And he picks someone and he talks to him. He talked to him late in the day. I submit to you that, what you have to think about, is that when he gave the interview on October 14, 2003, his mind would be focused on making her, Agent Debbie Bond, go away.

Remember the situation in which he was. There was an interview. What has happened? There is an interview. FBI Agent Bond and her colleagues are there. The White House said Libby was not involved. Rove was not involved. Others were not involved. Let's pull up Government Exhibit 20.

Government Exhibit 20, the Attorney General guidelines in dealing with the media, you look at Government Exhibit 20, I'll go through it quickly because I don't have much time. It says, "No subpoena may be issued to any member of the news media without the express authorization of the Attorney General. In criminal cases, there should be reasonable grounds to believe, based on information obtained from non leaking sources, that a crime has occurred, that the information sought is essential to a successful investigation."

If he can convince Agent Bond and the others there, there is nothing here, move along, no crime, I just gave out a rumor late in the day when everyone else knew it[,] [i]t goes away.

It could have worked, but he told enough of a story to tell the FBI agents that there's nothing here. He's just passing out rumors. It have been enough . . . to get the Attorney General to issue a subpoena, which was the only subpoena in his career. It could have worked if people didn't enforce the subpoenas and go through all that litigation. It could have worked if Russert never talked.

But the thing about it is, when you look back at something that happened, history always looks inevitable. At the time he was sitting there with a motive to lie. He had a problem. There was an investigation; [he's] got security clearances, going to lose his job, they're talking about firing people, and he planted his feet and told the Vice President, I did not leak to Novak. I did not leak classified information.

We've got to come up with somebody to put it behind. Remember when he told the story, he made sure to say, under oath, Tim Russert, this is off the record. That gets the protections. Then just ignore that in the opening and make it up in their closing. Let me testify it wasn't protected. Really? Under oath he said it was off the record.

… Let's talk about memory. When you look at the evidence, you have all the evidence taken together and you realize that nine witnesses can't all misremember wrong the same way, the same thing—that Mr. Libby was focused on something, asking questions about a topic, focused on the issue—and still have a document like Schmall's notes from June 14th saying, hey, he's wrapped around this issue.

Still have documents on July 14th that people are focused on. Still have those talking points that show people want to focus on who sent him on the trip. You can't explain how nine people misremember the same way. And you remember a conversation that didn't happen with Mr. Russert. Now, we're into the memory defense.

Let's talk about it. When they want to compare the defendant to the other witnesses, remember, none of the other witnesses you saw testify have the intent and focus Mr. Libby had on Wilson's wife. Grossman, he gets a request from the Vice President's Chief of Staff. He follows up. Grenier, he thinks the defendant really wants to know. He follows up. Schmall is sitting there at a briefing. He follows up. Many people follow up on what he was interested in.

Judith Miller didn't want to talk about it. She wanted to find out what went wrong with the hunt for weapons of mass destruction in Iraq. "I'm over there. We find nothing. What's going on?" He's doing the inside basics. Yet all of them can remember but he forgets. None of them invented a conversation that didn't happen.

Now, we also talk about the fact that he couldn't talk to others. Well, it leaves out one small fact. He did talk to one person. I want you to think about this. Why in the fall of 2003, when he wants to get cleared, does he not tell McClellan, by the way, you ought to know I did talk to reporters about the wife. I can't do that. The FBI doesn't want you talking to people.

Doesn't tell McClellan, by the way, when I say it's ridiculous about Karl, it's ridiculous about me, you should know that Rove told me that he and Novak spoke about the wife, although Rove told me that Novak told him. But just so you know, he couldn't tell him that . . .

What's the one thing he told one person in the fall of '03? He went and told the Vice President his recollection was that he learned this from Russert. So, one person, he learned about Wilson's wife from in the first place, at a time when he's not supposed to be talking to other people, he goes and he tells the person who told him, I learned it from Russert.

Why is that one fact so important to him if he's this innocent man trying to get a clearing statement? Why is the one thing, of all the facts in this case, does he want to share with [Cheney], not that I heard about Novak through Rove. Not that I talked to Miller. Not that I talked to Cooper or anything else. Just want to let the Vice President know it was Russert. He wanted to go back and tell him when he saw the note.

Whoever found the note in the Office of the Vice President, he saw it, and he knew that note was there. The fact he told the Vice President—when I told you I learned from Russert, I really learned from you. The Vice President cocked his head.

He can't tell McClellan anything. He can't tell Rove anything. He wanted to tell the Grand Jury he can't talk with anybody. Why is the only fact that he got out to anybody else involved in the case, the Russert conversation, the change in the Russert conversation because of the note. And the only person he told was the Vice President. Think about that.

Well, what about his memory? Hannah was an earnest, hard-working guy. But Hannah does want to help out the defendant. He was looking to say things that would be helpful to him. That's fair. He wanted to say he worked hard. Do you believe that a guy with an awful memory is the National Security Advisor to the Vice President, Chief of Staff during time of war, do you really think he's going around with a string around his finger trying to remember what's going on?

What did tell you? What did Hannah tell you? With all the war, threats, terror, and this other stuff, he doesn't remember those memos, but he knows he focused on Wilson. And he also knows that they focused on arguments. The defendant can remember an argument. That's what Valerie Wilson, as a person, got reduced to. She was an argument.

She was an argument that the wife sent him on a junket, and she was an argument that if she sent him, the Vice President did not. Do you really believe that [in] the weeks of July 6th and July 14th, [the] defendant suddenly forgot that so much that nothing could ring a bell? After talking about it Monday and Tuesday several times, that Thursday he's perplexed. I wonder if Wilson is married. I wonder if he has a wife.

Now, moving forward. How many examples do you have of how good Mr. Libby's memory was in March of 2004? Well, Mr. Zeidenberg went over it this morning. He told you that he has a phenomenal memory for somebody else talking to a reporter about Wilson's wife.

Isn't that precious? You have nine conversations with eight reporters about Wilson's wife and you can't remember any of them. But, he had a conversation about Wilson's wife with a reporter and he can tell you chapter and verse. [He talked about] the green room. Remember how Novak described it? Novak couldn't remember if he told his opinion about Wilson to Rove. The defendant had a better memory of Rove's conversation with Novak than Novak did. And Novak didn't even talk to Wilson. He just had this impression of all the things in the green room. Here is Mr. Libby painting that portrait, the green room. He remembers things. He remembers things quite well in March.

And you were asked a couple of questions about how you would be, if you were back in your 21-year-old days, laying on the beach in the summer remembering things. If I told you now, you know what, why don't you tell me what conversation you had on the day of the week about anything on the second week of June 2006. You'd look at me like I was nuts. If I asked you what day of the week a series of articles you read the last week of April last year, you'd look at me like I was nuts, and I would be.

But you know what? In March 2004 in the Grand Jury, Mr. Libby was very precise. When asked about Pincus articles, he said, you know what? There was a Pincus article about the Office of the Vice President in the fourth week of May last year . . . [T]hat's why we showed Mr. Pincus, when he took the stand, some articles. He said, yes, I did write articles about the Office of Vice President at the end of May 2003. Mr. Libby could remember the articles. He could remember the week in May 2003 in March 2004, which also shows you his focus on the press.

REMEMBER THE DISCUSSION about the leak to *The Wall Street Journal*? By the way, some of the things they wanted to show his state of mind, recall his editorial about *The Wall Street Journal*, that he seemed to have a good relationship with *The Wall Street Journal*, because when the Vice President wanted the NIE out, defendant Libby talks about how to get it in *The Wall Street Journal*. They just go to Paul Wolfowitz and lo and behold it's on the editorial page.

What does defendant say in March 2004? Yes, the Vice President and I talked about it on Tuesday, and got it in the editorial page on Thursday. He described it as being the second week of July. He can give the day of the week that he talked to the Vice President about placing information in the newspaper many, many months ahead. Think about that. You heard his testimony.

Now, I will say one thing about the Grand Jury testimony. One [thing] you should be aware about is time frame. During the Grand Jury phase, certain facts were known, certain facts were not. The testimony shows that Kessler had not yet testified. So, was [Libby] questioned closely on whether or not he had leaked to Mr. Kessler about the wife where he was the person in *The Washington Post* that was described on October 12? Sure he was.

What are people supposed to do? When someone is in the Grand Jury, they've already told investigators they learned this stuff from Russert as if it were new . . . The investigators already know that Russert said, hey, that never happened.

Why did they go through reporter by reporter and ask, what about Kessler, what about Pincus, what about Miller, what about Cooper? He wasn't charged for leaking to Kessler. That would be a great defense if someone were stupid enough to charge with leaking to Kessler. But he wasn't.

Of course, he was questioned closely. Was someone making up a story about how they learned the information? Being in the Grand Jury with them is like being in a house of mirrors. You try to figure out where you are, who did you tell, what did you tell.

One side note. We never said he pushed this to every reporter in sight. They'd like you to believe it's devastating that all these people weren't told. What did Cathie Martin tell you? The best way to leak something is an exclusive. Give it to one person. They could have held a press conference. They could have said, "You know, the President just declassified the NIE through the Vice President. Why don't we have all reporters in town come down, go to a press room and we'll hand out Xeroxes?" That's not how it works. They decided Judith Miller was a place to go. They decided she was the one to get this exclusive.

So what did he do, Matt Cooper? There was an opportunity. There was no doubt he had no plan to talk to Matt Cooper about the wife. He was sitting there with two other witnesses. Well, Matt Cooper puts it up in the phone and he said, what have you heard about the wife. He can get away with, "I heard that too." Why not nudge it along? But he wasn't going to tell these other reporters.

In June, the issue wasn't as hot. He was busy telling Pincus a lie because the whole trip came about because of a question by the aide to the Vice President. [Woodward] writes books, not articles. Sanger had Cathie Martin sitting there. He picked a particular reporter, Judith Miller, for a reason. The Vice President picked Judith Miller to get the NIE for a reason.

They went to the St. Regis Hotel for two hours for a reason. The best way to get a story out is to leak an exclusive. Showing that others didn't get it doesn't matter. This case is about perjury, nothing else.

Now, let me focus on two things when it comes to memory. The two things they don't want you to focus on, three things, uniqueness, importance and anger. We remember the unique. We all know we remember the unique. When something is unique, it sticks in your head. That's why a lot of witnesses remembered things they discussed with Libby.

What was unique about July 8th? Think about it. The first time in his government career Mr. Libby ever heard anyone talk about declassifying something privately for the President to the Vice President and then given to Miller. That was unique. He's the only one in the government, other than the President and the Vice President[,] who knew about this. Chief of Staff isn't told. The National Security Advisor isn't told. The head of the CIA isn't told. How unique is that? Never happened to him before. Never happened since. That imprints.

. . . I just want to quickly touch upon some of the issues of importance. We went through the talking points and showed you why it was that they are talking points [and] show importance. But remember the other things that were going on. He had ten conversations with nine people about the wife. Two being meetings with Miller at the St. Regis Hotel, one with Fleischer . . . When you focus that much time and attention that shows importance. 702-A shows importance. He's asking Schmall about it despite all the seriousness of briefing. 703-A, a July 14th note, shows importance, the Vice President is asking him. He's monitoring *Hardball* to see what's going on, what people are saying about him. He's not watching other things.

Do you remember Rove telling you about Novak? Why is that an imprint? Because it was important. Rove telling him that fact that Novak knows about the wife goes to his brain because it's important.

The Vice President cuts out the article. That's important. The Vice President makes the note about the wife. That's important. Government Exhibit 412, he makes the note, the Maureen Dowd column. That's important.

You know what else? One thing that's really important is what Mr. Schmall told him. Craig Schmall told him after the Novak column, after he read it, this is a big deal. He focuses on Valerie Wilson. Schmall says it's bigger than that. Every intelligence service that thinks she was overseas will figure out who was in contact with her and, whether innocent or not, they will look at them. They could arrest them. They could torture them. They could kill them.

Now, we heard about the 21-year-old on the beach trying to remember in September what happened in the spring. You are sitting on a beach as a 21-year-old, I don't care [about] how good a time you're having. Someone said, by the way, what you did recently, did you talk to somebody about [something] that, that may get people killed. I think every 21-year-old would remember it. Every National Security Advisor would remember it.

When you do something that's brought to your attention later that you're discussing something with people that could lead to people being killed, that better be important. That better imprint on your brain, 21-year-old, 4-year-old, whatever you're doing, college kid, certainly a National Security Advisor to the Vice President during a time of war. That's important.

Now, let's talk about anger. You talked about—

MR. JEFFRESS: Approach the bench, Your Honor?
(Bench conference is sealed and redacted.)

THE SIDEBAR EVIDENTLY has to do with Fitzgerald's references to Plame's status, which Judge Walton has repeatedly ruled is not relevant, and the potential damage that could result from her outing. Fitzgerald resumes:

MR. FITZGERALD: Just so we're perfectly clear, I'm talking about Mr. Libby's state of mind. And Mr. Libby's state of mind wants you to believe that the wife was unimportant. It's like a 21-year-old kid not remembering things after the summer. The evidence is Schmall did not know anything about Valerie Plame in particular. But he told the Vice President and the defendant, he said, this is not good. If someone is outed, people can get in trouble overseas. They can get arrested, tortured, or killed.

One of the articles in the fall, from October 4. [T]hey point you to a September 29th online column by Cliff May. October 4 is an article by Walter Pincus. For a state of mind, not whether it's true or false, but you're the defendant, you're reading Walter Pincus, write an article about a front company being exposed and other people being endangered.

Don't you think that imprints? Isn't that important? And that's something. You have every right to consider when people want to tell you that something about a wife wasn't important till later. She was certainly important enough on June 14th.

Important enough for the Vice President to change his talking points on July 8th in a subtle way. Important enough for the defendant to talk to people on July 7th and 8th. Important enough to read about on July 14th and go to the briefer and say[,] you read the Novak article. Important enough when someone tells you harm can happen. Important enough when an investigation starts, but unimportant when the facts proved the defendant told a lie.

NOW, LET'S TALK ABOUT ANGER. What do we know about anger? We know from different witnesses about Mr. Libby's demeanor. It started in June. Mr. Grenier said a little bit [aggrieved], slightly accusatory tone. Craig Schmall, pretty annoyed, annoyed, upset. Remember he was angry on June 14th?

With all the terror threats going on in the world, he was angry that someone in the intelligence community, was at the briefing, not the Schmall briefing, but he was talking. And he brought up Valerie Wilson and Joe Wilson. He was pretty annoyed, annoyed, upset. Judith Miller, agitated, frustrated, angry, annoyed, perverted war of leaks, really unhappy and irritated. Wilson was ruse and irrelevancy . . .

Tim Russert, agitated, damn it, what the hell, upset. That's what sticks in his mind, because you don't get many calls from the Vice President's Chief of Staff like that. What do we all know? We all know when you're angry at someone, you remember. You remember why. You remember things.

Whether you're a Chief of Staff, whatever you do for a living, people remember what they're angry about. He was angry about Wilson. And he may have reason to be angry about Wilson. Whatever the truth of the matter is about the debate about the war, what Wilson said was that the country got lied into a war or raised that specter. One of the people he blamed was the Vice President. One of the people being blamed on *Hardball* was the defendant.

I don't for a moment think, whatever else happened in this case, the defendant would sit down and deliberately lie someone into a war. So if you think you've been wrongly accused of something like that, it gets you angrier. He was angry about Wilson.

When you think it's important, when you're focused on it, when you're angry about it, those are the things you remember. You all have been through life. You know the things that you forget. You know the things you remember. We all know we forget. We look deeper than ourselves. We know at times we've all told a lie and gotten caught at it. You know how to tell the difference. That's your common sense.

Now, just remember this notion that he assumed that everyone would talk.

Remember, to talk, two things have to happen. First you have to be asked. Second, you have to talk. Pretty elementary. But remember the mindset that was going on in the fall of '03? First of all, you had to be asked.

I went through the A.G. guidelines about how the Attorney General is required to approve a subpoena. I went through the fact that Russert had never been subpoenaed before. Go to the mindset of either the person asked to approve a subpoena to the media, and think about whether it would meet those standards, those rare standards, the criticism, the fight in court, the litigation, the prospect of someone going to jail. And that is not a likely prospect.

Think about that from the perspective of someone doing an investigation, like Agent Bond and her colleagues, sitting in a room with someone who sits behind the Vice President at staff meetings. Whether or not the Bureau Chief or the head of NBC News or the Washington Bureau is going to be subpoenaed by the Attorney General, John Ashcroft, to investigate the Vice President's Chief of Staff when it has already been proclaimed from the White House podium he has nothing to be involved.

The mindset is the hope that people will go away and don't ask the questions. The mindset is to make sure that Agent Bond is satisfied there is nothing here . . . Move along people, nothing to look at. And that's why you tell the story about a rumor. He made his bed. He planted his feet and then he's stuck. From then on, he is going to tell the same story. That's what he did.

You also have to assume that people will talk. I won't go through it all, but you saw all the reporters were reluctant to talk. Some were held in contempt. Judith Miller did 85 days in jail. [If] FBI agent doesn't catch Russert at home with his son going off to school, he doesn't hit a chord with Russert . . .

Russert feels compelled to say I've got to knock down that false allegation. I didn't tell them. Things might be different. Don't be confused by looking at history backwards, to say, well, it had to be obvious it would happen this way.

Similarly, whatever happened to people being fired or not, you saw the McClellan video. Any sane person would think, based upon what McClellan said in October 2003, anybody involved in this is getting fired. That's the time frame. You want to focus on October 2003. If you were sitting in the shoes of someone who discussed with the paper was reporting might be a covert operative. You would be very, very rational to think you would get fired if you had done something like that.

There has been a lot of talk about reference to Mr. Armitage and Mr. Rove. Don't be distracted by persons not on trial. The one thing you do know is you were told that Mr. Armitage told Mr. Grossman pretty quickly that he had told the FBI that he had talked to Novak.

You have no evidence to indicate that either Mr. Armitage or Mr. Rove walked in and told the Grand Jury that they learned something all anew from Tim Russert. They learned it anew. They didn't remember anything else, struck them, they were sitting around wondering whether Wilson was married or had a wife. Don't be distracted by people not on trial.

Now, I'm sure when I sit down my partners will tell me I forgot a lot of things.

I WANT TO END THIS CASE with this one note. What's this case about? This is about a madman picking on two conversations, or something bigger? . . . Is it about someone to whom Wilson's wife was important, not as a person but as an argument? As a defense to someone who made him pretty angry, and who focused on it on June 14th. He focused on it July 14th.

He focused on it on June 23rd when he told Judith Miller. He focused on it on July 8th when he told Judith Miller. He focused on it on July 7th when he told Fleischer. He focused on it when he talked [to] Addington. He focused on it and thought it was important for quite a long time.

His boss thought it was important. You know, when his boss first told Mr. Libby, one of the first things in his notes, his wife works out there, did his boss forget about the wife with all the things the Vice President was doing? Well, the first he writes in the Wilson op-ed, he said his wife sent him. He was busy too.

Did he forget about it when the Novak column came out? They both read it. Libby marked up something else. They both talked to a briefer about it. It was important.

You can't believe, I submit you can't believe that nine witnesses remembered ten conversations exactly the same wrong way to put it in there. That's not a coincidence. The conspiracy is gone. If I opened in any way that led you to believe there is some scapegoating conspiracy, I apologize, because the evidence didn't bear it out. I suggest to you that's not what I said at all.

There is no conspiracy. There is no memory problem. This was something important. Something he was focused on. Something he was angry about. He remembers a conversation that did not happen and he remembers the conversation that somebody else had with a reporter, but forget all of this conveniently in a way that wipes the slate clean and takes him out of the realm of classified information.

He had a motive to lie. And a motive to lie matched up exactly with the lie. That's where your common sense kicks in. You don't get surprised on Thursday by something you're giving out on Monday and Tuesday. You don't forget a fact in your argument that is important. He wasn't sitting around saying this is the week the Vice President and I save ourselves. We save ourselves and discuss the wife later.

Right now I'm confused about Wilson, whether he's ever married or whether he had a wife. He made up a story and he stuck to it. You know, there is talk about a cloud over the Vice President. There is a cloud over the White House as to what happened. Don't you think the FBI, the Grand Jury, the American people are entitled to a straight answer?

The critic of the war comes out, he points fingers at the White House, fairly or unfairly. It's not like that editorial he marked. He is fair game. Anything goes. That result is his wife had a job with the CIA. She worked in the Counterproliferation Division, that was stipulated. She gets dragged into the newspapers. Some may think that's okay. That's not.

If people want to find out was the law broken, were the laws broken about the disclosure of classified information? Did somebody do it intentionally or otherwise? People want to know who did it. What role did they play? What role did the defendant play? What role did others play? What role did the Vice President play because he told you early on, he may have discussed sharing this information with the press, with the Vice President, but of course only after the Novak column.

Don't you think the FBI and the Grand Jury are not mad to want straight answers? They deserved straight answers. This defendant was focused on it. It was unique circumstances. It was important. He was angry at Wilson and knew those answers. I submit to you, when you go in that jury room, your common sense will tell you that he made a gamble. He said I'm going to tell them the story about the rumors. Hope it goes away. He lied.

He threw sand in the eyes of the Grand Jury and the FBI investigators. He obstructed justice. He stole the truth from the judicial system. When you return to that jury room, you deliberate, your verdict can give truth back. Please do.

THE COURT: Approach for a minute.
(Bench conference is sealed and redacted.)

WALTON CAUTIONS THE JURY against a couple of possible misunderstandings from Fitzgerald's rebuttal closing:

THE COURT: Ladies and gentlemen, sometimes during the course of argument, lawyers say things that they don't mean to say. And I just want to say a couple of things to you to make sure that you don't inappropriately use information that was presented to you.

In reference to the Attorney General guidelines, those guidelines were admitted for a limited purpose. And that was to put before you those guidelines so you could assess whether the special prosecutor's interaction with the media and with reporters was consistent with those guidelines. That was the sole purpose for which they were admitted.

So, the argument that was being made, if it was made, or a suggestion that was made that Mr. Libby would have been aware of those guidelines and that would have had some impact on his willingness to talk to the press, you have to disregard that argument. There is no evidence to that effect before you that you could consider in that regard.

Also, I am going to give you another cautionary instruction I ask that you comply with. The truth of whether someone could be harmed, based upon a disclosure of information about people working in a covert capacity, is not what is at issue in this case. And you must therefore not let that matter impact your deliberations.

Remember what I have told you several times. Mr. Libby is not charged with leaking classified information or information about anyone's covert status. What is relevant here is what, if any, impact things Mr. Libby read or was told had on his state of mind. In other words, whether it provided a motive for Mr. Libby not to tell the truth when he spoke to the FBI agents and when he testified before the Grand Jury.

Please keep that instruction in mind when you deliberate in this case.

Considering the hour, we'll recess at this time.

WALTON EXPLAINS TO THE JURY that he will give them instructions for their deliberations the next day, and excuses them for the day. The defense requests, and is granted, a written repetition for the jury of the cautionary instruction Walton has just given them. Court is recessed for the day.

*

FEBRUARY 21, 2007

INSTRUCTIONS TO THE JURY

THE NEXT DAY, FEBRUARY 21, Judge Walton reads the instructions for the jurors to follow during their deliberations. Included are the descriptions of the charges and what the Government needs to have proven for Libby to be convicted on each count, starting with Walton's brief explanation that the Judith Miller part of the obstruction charge had been removed:

THE COURT: Now, when this trial started, I described to you the charges against Mr. Libby. I told you that count 1, which charges obstruction of justice, alleged that Mr. Libby falsely testified to the Grand Jury concerning conversations with three reporters: Mr. Russert, Mr. Cooper, and Ms. Miller.

As I told you earlier, one of these allegations—that Mr. Libby lied about his conversation with Judith Miller on July 12, 2003—has been dismissed. The fact that Mr. Libby was charged with obstructing justice by allegedly providing false testimony about his July 12th, 2003, conversation with Ms. Miller, and the fact that this part of the obstruction of justice charge has now been dismissed must be of no further concern to you and cannot in any way influence your verdict regarding the guilt or innocence of Mr. Libby on the remaining allegations of all five counts of the indictment.

Count 1, the obstruction of justice count, is now based solely on the allegations that Mr. Libby falsely testified to the Grand Jury concerning his conversations with two reporters: Mr. Russert and Mr. Cooper. You may, however, consider evidence presented at trial related to all of Mr. Libby's conversations with Ms. Miller in evaluating whether the Government has proven the remaining allegations against Mr. Libby in the indictment beyond a reasonable doubt, including the allegations that now comprise count 1 of the indictment . . .

The defendant is charged in count 1 of the indictment with obstruction of justice. Section 1503 of Title 18 of the United States Code states, "Whomever corruptly endeavors to influence, obstruct or impede, the due administration of justice" is guilty of an offense against the United States.

Count 1 of the indictment charges that on or about March 5 and March 24, 2004, in the District of Columbia, the defendant corruptly endeavored to influence, obstruct or impede the due administration of justice in a federal judicial proceeding, specifically proceedings before a federal Grand Jury, by knowingly and deliberately misleading and deceiving the Grand Jury as to when or how he acquired or thereafter disclosed to the media information concerning the employment of Valerie Wilson by the Central Intelligence Agency, which is also known as the CIA.

In order to prove the offense charged in count 1 of the indictment, the Government must prove the following four elements beyond a reasonable doubt:

One, that there was a proceeding pending before a federal Grand Jury in the District of Columbia concerning the possible unauthorized disclosure of Valerie Wilson's affiliation with the CIA;

Two, that the defendant knew the judicial proceeding just described was pending;

Three, that the defendant specifically intended to mislead or deceive the Grand Jury as to when or how he acquired or thereafter disclosed to the media information concerning the employment of Valerie Wilson by the CIA; and

Four, that in doing what was just described as element three, the defendant corruptly endeavored to influence, obstruct or impede the due administration of justice.

According to count 1 of the indictment, Mr. Libby carried out this corrupt endeavor by making the following three allegedly false statements to the Grand Jury:

One, that when Mr. Libby spoke with Tim Russert of NBC News on or about July 10, 2003, Mr. Russert asked Mr. Libby if Mr. Libby knew that Joseph Wilson's wife worked for the CIA, and that Mr. Russert told Mr. Libby that "all the reporters knew" it;

Two, that when Mr. Libby spoke with Tim Russert of NBC News, on or about July 10, 2003, Mr. Libby was surprised to hear that Mr. Wilson's wife worked for the CIA; and

Three, that Mr. Libby advised Matthew Cooper of *TIME* magazine on or about July 12, 2003, that he had heard that other reporters were saying that Mr. Wilson's wife worked for the CIA, and further advised him that Mr. Libby did not know whether this assertion was true.

TO ACT "CORRUPTLY," as this word is used in these instructions, means to act voluntarily and deliberately and with an evil motive or improper purpose or intent to influence, or obstruct, or interfere with the administration of justice.

The term "endeavors" as used in these instructions means to knowingly and deliberately act or to knowingly and deliberately make any effort which has a reasonable tendency to bring about the desired result. It is not necessary for the Government to prove that the endeavor was successful or, in fact, achieved the desired result.

To prove that the defendant's conduct corruptly endeavored to influence, obstruct, or impede the due administration of justice, the Government must show beyond a reasonable doubt that the defendant's corrupt acts related to a pending federal judicial proceeding. You are instructed that a federal Grand Jury investigation is a federal judicial proceeding.

As to count 1 of the indictment, three allegedly false statements or representations, as set forth earlier in this instruction, are alleged to have been made by the defendant. The Government is not required to prove that all of the statements or representations alleged in count 1 are, in fact, false. To find the defendant guilty of count 1 of the indictment, the Government must prove beyond a reasonable doubt that at least one of the alleged statements or representations contained in count 1 was false.

And, as to count 1, all of you must agree on which statement or representation was false. If you are unable to reach unanimous agreement that at least one and the same statement or representation alleged in count 1 was falsely made by Mr. Libby with specific intent to mislead or deceive the Grand Jury, then you must find him not guilty of count 1.

THE DEFENDANT IS CHARGED in counts 2 and 3 of the indictment with knowingly and willfully making false, fictitious, or fraudulent statements or representations concerning a material fact within the jurisdiction of the executive branch of the United States government, specifically, the Federal Bureau of Investigation, which is commonly referred as the FBI.

Section 1001(a)(2) of Title 18 of the United States Code states, "Whoever, in any matter within the jurisdiction of the Executive Branch of the Government of the United States knowingly and willfully makes any materially false, fictitious, or fraudulent statements or representations" is guilty of an offense against the United States.

In order to prove this offense, the Government must prove the following four elements beyond a reasonable doubt:

One, that the defendant knowingly made a false, fictitious, or fraudulent statement or representation to the Government of the United States, namely, the FBI;

Two, that the statement or representation was made in a matter within the jurisdiction of the Executive Branch of the United States government;

Three, that in making the false, fictitious, or fraudulent statement or representation, the defendant acted willfully, knowing that the statement or representation was false;

And four, that the statement or representation made by the defendant was material to the investigation being conducted by the FBI.

According to count 2 of the indictment, the alleged false statements made by Mr. Libby are the following:

One, Mr. Libby falsely told the FBI on October 14 or November 26, 2003, that during a conversation with Tim Russert of NBC News on or about July 10 or 11, 2003, Mr. Russert asked Mr. Libby if Mr. Libby was aware that Joseph Wilson's wife worked for the CIA; that Mr. Libby responded to Mr. Russert by saying that he did not know that information about Mr. Wilson's wife, and that Mr. Russert replied that "all the reporters knew it"; and

Two, Mr. Libby falsely told the FBI on October 14 or November 26, 2003, that during a conversation with Tim Russert of NBC News on or about July 10 or 11, 2003, that Mr. Libby was surprised by Mr. Russert's statement because, while speaking with Mr. Russert, Mr. Libby did not recall that he previously had heard about Mr. Wilson's wife's employment from Vice President Cheney.

Count 3 of the indictment alleges that Mr. Libby falsely told the FBI on October 14 or November 16, 2003, that during a conversation with Matthew Cooper of *TIME* magazine on July 12, 2003, Mr. Libby told Mr. Cooper that reporters were telling the administration that Mr. Wilson's wife worked for the CIA, but that Mr. Libby did not know if this was true.

A false or fictitious statement or representation is an assertion which is untrue when made or when used and which is known by the person making it or using it to be untrue.

A fraudulent statement or representation is an assertion which is known to be untrue and which is made or used with the intent to deceive.

A statement or representation is material if it had the natural tendency to influence or be capable of affecting or influencing a governmental function.

As related to this case, the question for you to answer in determining whether the statement or representation is false is whether it had the capacity to affect or influence the actions of the FBI. The test is whether the false, fictitious, or fraudulent statement or representation had the capacity to impair or pervert the investigation that was being conducted by the FBI.

In other words, a false, fictitious, or fraudulent statement or representation is material if it relates to an important fact that had the capacity to affect or influence the investigation being conducted by the FBI as distinguished from some unimportant or trivial fact that did not have the capacity to affect or influence the investigation being conducted by the FBI.

You may consider the nature of the FBI's investigation, including the possible crimes that were being investigated, in determining whether the alleged false statements and declarations were material to the investigation.

HOWEVER, YOU SHOULD UNDERSTAND that the alleged false statement or representation need not actually have influenced the actions of the FBI, and the FBI agents need not actually have been deceived.

A person acts knowingly, as this term is used in the indictment, if the person acts consciously and with awareness and comprehension, and not because of ignorance, mistake, misunderstanding or other similar reasons.

A person acts willfully, as the term is used in these instructions, when the person acts deliberately, voluntarily, and intentionally.

As to count 2 of the indictment, two false, fictitious or fraudulent statements or representations, as set forth above in this instruction, are alleged to have been made by the defendant. The Government is not required to prove that each of the statements or representations alleged in count 2 are, in fact, false, fictitious, or fraudulent.

To find the defendant guilty of count 2 of the indictment, the Government must prove beyond a reasonable doubt that at least one of the alleged statements or representations contained in count 2 was false, fictitious, or fraudulent. And, as to count 2, all of you must agree on which statement or representation was false, fictitious, or fraudulent.

If you are unable to reach unanimous agreement that the defendant knew that at least one and the same statement or representation alleged in count 2 was false, fictitious, or fraudulent when the statement was made by Mr. Libby, then you must find him not guilty of count 2.

Finally, the defendant is charged in counts 4 and 5 of the indictment with the offense of perjury. Perjury is made a federal crime by section 1623(a) of Title 18 of the United States Code. This statute states, "Whoever, under oath, in any judicial proceeding, before any Grand Jury of the United States, knowingly makes any false material declaration" is guilty of an offense against the United States.

In order to prove the defendant guilty of perjury, the Government must prove the following four elements beyond a reasonable doubt:

One, that the defendant made a statement to the Grand Jury while he was under oath;

Two, that the statement was false in one or more respects;

Three, that the defendant knew when he made the statement that it was false; and

Four, that the false statement was material to the matter that was being investigated by the Grand Jury.

Count 4 of the indictment alleges that a portion of Mr. Libby's Grand Jury testimony was false. This Grand Jury testimony was played to you, along with the showing of the transcript of this testimony during the trial.

That portion of the Grand Jury transcript, which the indictment alleges in count 4 was false, is being provided to you as part of this perjury instruction, with those portions of the testimony that are allegedly false underlined. You must review this testimony when evaluating this count of the indictment.

Count 5 of the indictment also alleges that a portion of Mr. Libby's Grand Jury testimony was false. This Grand Jury testimony was played to you, along with the showing of the transcript of the testimony, during the trial. That portion of the Grand Jury testimony which the indictment alleges in count 5 was false, is also being provided to you as part of this perjury instruction, with those portions of the testimony that are allegedly false underlined. Again, you must review this testimony when evaluating this count of the indictment.

A STATEMENT UNDER OATH is a false statement if it was untrue when made and the person making it knew it was untrue at that time. The making of a false statement under oath is not an offense unless the falsity relates to a material fact.

A false statement is material if it has a natural tendency to affect or influence, or is capable of affecting or influencing, the exercise of the Grand Jury's decision-making process. The test is whether the false statement had the capacity to impair or pervert the functioning of the Grand Jury.

In other words, a false statement is material if it relates to an important fact that had the capacity to affect or influence the decision of the Grand Jury as distinguished from some unimportant or trivial detail that did not have the capacity to affect or influence the decision of the Grand Jury.

You may consider the nature of the Grand Jury's investigation, including the possible crimes that were being investigated, in determining whether the alleged false statements were material to the Grand Jury investigation. However, you should understand that it is not necessary for the Government to prove that the Grand Jury was, in fact, misled or influenced in any way by the false statement.

In reviewing the testimony that is alleged to have been false, you should consider that testimony in the context of the series of questions asked and the answers given, and the words used should be given their common and ordinary meaning unless the context clearly shows that the questioner and the witness mutually understood the words to have different meaning.

If you should find that a particular question was ambiguous or capable of being understood in two different ways and that the defendant truthfully answered one reasonable interpretation of the question under the circumstances, then such answer would not be false.

Similarly, if you should find that the question was clear, but the answer was ambiguous, and that one reasonable interpretation of the answer would be truthful, then the answer would not be false.

As to count 5 of the indictment, four false statements are alleged to have been made by the defendant. The Government is not required to prove that all of the statements alleged in count 5 are, in fact, false.

To find the defendant guilty of count 5 of the indictment, the Government must prove beyond a reasonable doubt that at least one of the alleged false statements contained in count 5 was false. And, as to count 5, all of you must agree on which statement was false.

If you are unable to reach unanimous agreement that the defendant knew he was giving false testimony to the Grand Jury as to at least one and the same statement as alleged in count 5, then you must find the defendant not guilty of count 5.

WALTON ALSO INSTRUCTS THE JURY on the theory of the defense:

Now, Mr. Libby contends that the Government has not proven beyond a reasonable doubt that he intended to or did obstruct justice, make intentionally false statements to the FBI, or make intentionally false statements to the Grand Jury. Mr. Libby contends that he told the FBI and the Grand Jury his honest recollection at the time, and to the extent any of those recollections were incorrect, his mistakes were innocent.

He contends that he lacked any notes of the conversations about which he was questioned and that he was unable to refresh his recollection by reviewing the notes of other people and discussing with them their recollection of the events.

He further contends that the amount and scope of vital national security issues and information confronting him on a daily basis during June and July 2003 affected his memory of any brief conversations about the employment of Ambassador Wilson's wife when he talked to the FBI agents in October and November 2003, three or four months after the conversations are alleged to have occurred, and when he testified to the Grand Jury in March 2004.

Mr. Libby further contends that when the investigation began, he knew that he had not provided any information about Ms. Wilson to Mr. Novak. He also contends that he did not know that Ms. Wilson's employment status was covert or classified and that he did not knowingly disclose classified information about Ms. Wilson to any reporters.

Further, Mr. Libby contends that he was well aware, when he was first interviewed by the FBI and when he testified before the Grand Jury, that the investigators could likely and would attempt to talk to government officials and the journalists he spoke with concerning Ambassador Wilson. Mr. Libby submits that he had no reason to lie to the FBI or the Grand Jury and did not do so.

AFTER WALTON FINISHES WITH THE INSTRUCTIONS and dismisses (conditionally) the alternate jurors, the jury is led away to begin deliberations and court is recessed for lunch and the day.

Deliberations continue over the next several days. The following Monday a juror is dismissed for having been exposed to media coverage; deliberations continue with 11 jurors.

On February 28, the jury poses what would be the first of several questions to the judge, and each one heightens the media speculation—much of it driven by impatience, and much of it wrong, as it turned out—about what the jury is up to. In this case, the jury communicates to the judge that it has clarified the question for itself without the input of the parties and the judge. Deliberations continue through the end of that week and into the next.

*

MARCH 6, 2007

THE VERDICT

JUDGE WALTON CALLS THE LAWYERS into the courtroom at 9:15 a.m. briefly to discuss a question from the jury regarding count three—that of making false statements to the FBI. Walton asks whether all parties agree that "Mr. Libby would have made the same statement to the FBI agents on the two dates," and Wells confirms there has been no request for a unanimity instruction, as the defense is not challenging that fact. They are then dismissed, as the jurors continue to deliberate.

Then. at 11:45, word goes out that court will reconvene at noon, and the lawyers rush back to the courthouse for Walton to announce that the jurors have finally come to a verdict.

THE COURT: The jury at 11:15 sent a note saying that they had reached a verdict on all five counts . . . As the jury renders its verdict, there should be no response from anyone in the courtroom.

(Jury in.)

THE COURT: You may be seated . . . Has the jury reached a unanimous verdict in the case of the United States of America versus I. Lewis Libby?

THE FOREPERSON: We have.

THE COURT: As to count one of the indictment, charging obstruction of justice, is your verdict guilty or not guilty?

THE FOREPERSON: Guilty.

THE COURT: As to count two of the indictment, charging making a false statement to the Federal Bureau of Investigation, is your verdict guilty or not guilty?

THE FOREPERSON: Guilty.

THE COURT: As to count three of the indictment, charging making a false statement to the federal bureau of investigation, is your verdict guilty or not guilty?

THE FOREPERSON: Not guilty.

THE COURT: As to count four of the indictment, charging perjury, is your verdict guilty or not guilty?

THE FOREPERSON: Guilty.

THE COURT: As to count five of the indictment, charging perjury, is your verdict guilty or not guilty?

THE FOREPERSON: Guilty.

THE COURT: Do all of you agree with the verdict?

THE JURORS: Yes, Your Honor . . .

THE DEFENSE REQUESTS that the jury be polled, and so each juror is asked for his or her individual vote. They verify their unanimity, and Walton takes a moment to thank them for their service:

THE COURT: Ladies and gentlemen, I would like to thank you. I will personally thank you back in my chambers after, but, publicly, I would like to thank all of you for the time that you have given to this case. We know it's a significant inconvenience to have citizens like yourself come and serve as jurors, but it is the way our system works. And I have had the opportunity in the long time I have been a judge to watch a number of jurors. And I can't say I have seen a better group of jurors who, obviously, conscientiously listened to the evidence and went about the business of deciding this case as instructed.

So I commend you for your service, and I think it epitomizes what our judicial system is supposed to be about as it relates to the obligation of jurors who serve as jurors throughout this country.

(Jury leaving courtroom at 12:10 p.m.)

FOLLOWING A SHORT DISCUSSION setting the conditions of bail (Libby was released on his "personal promise" to appear back in court) and the date of his sentencing (for June 5th), the trial was adjourned.

(Whereupon, at 12:15 P.M., the above-entitled matter was adjourned.)

* * *

APPENDIX

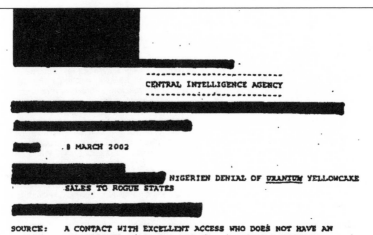

CENTRAL INTELLIGENCE AGENCY

8 MARCH 2002

NIGERIEN DENIAL OF URANIUM YELLOWCAKE
SALES TO ROGUE STATES

SOURCE: A CONTACT WITH EXCELLENT ACCESS WHO DOES NOT HAVE AN
ESTABLISHED REPORTING RECORD. (SENSITIVE CONTACT)

TEXT: 1. (HEADQUARTERS COMMENT: THE SUBSOURCES OF THE FOLLOWING
INFORMATION KNEW THEIR REMARKS COULD REACH THE U.S. GOVERNMENT AND
MAY HAVE INTENDED TO INFLUENCE AS WELL AS INFORM.) FORMER NIGERIEN
GOVERNMENT OFFICIALS CLAIMED THAT SINCE 1997 THERE HAD BEEN NO
CONTRACTS SIGNED BETWEEN NIGER AND ANY ROGUE STATES FOR THE SALE OF
URANIUM IN THE FORM OF YELLOWCAKE. THE FORMER OFFICIALS ALSO
ASSERTED THERE HAD BEEN NO TRANSFERS OF YELLOWCAKE TO ROGUE STATES.

2. FORMER NIGERIEN PRIME MINISTER IBRAHIM ((MAYAKI)), WHO WAS
NIGER'S FOREIGN MINISTER FROM 1996-1997 AND NIGER'S PRIME MINISTER
FROM 1997-1999 AND WHO MAINTAINED CLOSE TIES TO THE CURRENT NIGERIEN
GOVERNMENT, STATED HE WAS UNAWARE OF ANY CONTRACTS BEING SIGNED
BETWEEN NIGER AND ROGUE STATES FOR THE SALE OF YELLOWCAKE DURING HIS
TENURE AS BOTH FOREIGN MINISTER AND PRIME MINISTER. MAYAKI, HOWEVER,
DID RELATE THAT IN JUNE 1999 BARKA ((TEFRIDJ)), A NIGERIEN/ALGERIAN
BUSINESSMAN, APPROACHED HIM AND INSISTED THAT MAYAKI MEET WITH AN
IRAQI DELEGATION TO DISCUSS "EXPANDING COMMERCIAL RELATIONS" BETWEEN
NIGER AND IRAQ. ALTHOUGH THE MEETING TOOK PLACE, MAYAKI LET THE
MATTER DROP DUE TO THE UNITED NATIONS (UN) SANCTIONS AGAINST IRAQ AND
THE FACT THAT HE OPPOSED DOING BUSINESS WITH IRAQ. MAYAKI SAID THAT
HE INTERPRETED THE PHRASE "EXPANDING COMMERCIAL RELATIONS" TO MEAN
THAT IRAQ WANTED TO DISCUSS URANIUM YELLOWCAKE SALES. MAYAKI SAID HE
UNDERSTOOD ROGUE STATES WOULD LIKE TO EXPLOIT NIGER'S RESOURCES,
SPECIFICALLY URANIUM, BUT HE BELIEVED THE NIGERIEN GOVERNMENT'S
REGARD FOR THE UNITED STATES (U.S.) AS A CLOSE ALLY WOULD PREVENT

SECRET

A COPY of Ambassador Joseph Wilson's trip report which the OVP claimed they never saw.

SALES TO THESE STATES FROM TAKING PLACE DESPITE *NIGER'S* ECONOMIC
WOES. MAYAXI CLAIMED THAT IF THERE HAD BEEN ANY CONTRACTS FOR
YELLOWCAKE BETWEEN *NIGER* AND ANY ROGUE STATE DURING HIS TENURE, HE
WOULD HAVE SEEN THE CONTRACT.

3. BOUCAR ((MAI MANGA)), *NIGER'S* FORMER MINISTER OF ENERGY AND
MINES UNTIL 9 APRIL 1999, A FORMER DIRECTOR OF THE NIGERIEN COMENAC
MINE AND CURRENTLY HONORARY PRESIDENT OF COMENAC, STATED THAT THERE
WERE NO SALES OUTSIDE OF INTERNATIONAL ATOMIC ENERGY AGENCY (IAEA)
CHANNELS SINCE THE MID-1980S. MAI MANGA SAID THAT HE KNEW OF NO
CONTRACTS SIGNED BETWEEN *NIGER* AND ANY ROGUE STATE FOR THE SALE OF
URANIUM. HE ADMITTED THAT YEARS AGO A PAKISTANI DELEGATION VISITED
NIGER AND OFFERED TO PURCHASE *URANIUM* BUT THAT NO SALES RESULTED FROM
THESE TALKS. MAI MANGA ALSO SAID THAT (FNU) ((BLASCHER)), THE FORMER
DIRECTOR GENERAL OF SOMAIR AND CURRENTLY A DIRECTOR AT COGEMA, CAME
TO HIM IN 1998 WITH AN IRANIAN DELEGATION TO DISCUSS BUYING 400 TONS
OF YELLOWCAKE FROM *NIGER*; HOWEVER, THE ONLY RESULT WAS A MEMORANDUM
OF CONVERSATION, WITH NO CONTRACT BEING SIGNED AND NO YELLOWCAKE
TRANSFERRED TO IRAN. MAI MANGA THEORIZED THAT *NIGER'S* MINES COULD
HAVE INCREASED PRODUCTION TO SUPPLY IRAN WITH THIS AMOUNT OF
YELLOWCAKE BUT THIS WOULD HAVE REQUIRED OPENING ADDITIONAL MINING
FACILITIES THAT HAVE BEEN MOTHBALLED FOR SEVERAL YEARS. MAI MANGA
THEREFORE CONCLUDED THAT A SALE TO A ROGUE STATE SUCH AS IRAN WOULD
HAVE BEEN DIFFICULT GIVEN THE NEED OPEN MORE FACILITIES. (SOURCE
COMMENT: MAI MANGA APPEARED TO REGRET THAT *NIGER* EVEN DISCUSSED
URANIUM SALES WITH IRAN IN LIGHT OF THE INTERNATIONAL PRESSURE THAT
RESULTED.)

4. MAI MANGA STATED THAT *URANIUM* FROM *NIGER'S* MINES IS VERY
TIGHTLY CONTROLLED AND ACCOUNTED FOR FROM THE TIME IT IS MINED UNTIL
THE TIME IS LOADED ONTO SHIPS AT THE PORT OF COTONOU, BENIN.
ACCORDING TO MAI MANGA, EVEN A KILOGRAM OF *URANIUM* WOULD BE NOTICED
MISSING AT THE MINES. ON-SITE STORAGE IS LIMITED AND HE SAID THAT
EACH SHIPMENT OF *URANIUM* IS UNDER NIGERIEN ARMED MILITARY ESCORT FROM
THE TIME IT LEAVES ONE OF THE TWO NIGERIEN MINES UNTIL IT IS LOADED
ON TO A SHIP IN COTONOU. AIR TRANSPORT IS TOO EXPENSIVE TO SHIP
YELLOWCAKE AND TRUCKING BARRELS OF YELLOWCAKE NORTHWARD WOULD REQUIRE
AN EXPERIENCED GUIDE AND MANY ARMED GUARDS, DUE TO THE SHIFTING DUNES
AND BANDITS IN THAT REGION. MAI MANGA THEREFORE BELIEVED THAT IT
WOULD BE DIFFICULT, IF NOT IMPOSSIBLE, TO ARRANGE A SPECIAL SHIPMENT
OF *URANIUM* TO A PARIAH STATE GIVEN THESE STRICT CONTROLS AND THE
CLOSE MONITORING BY THE NIGERIEN GOVERNMENT AND THE TWO MINING
COMPANIES. MAI MANGA ALSO SAID THAT THE MINE AND YELLOWCAKE WORKERS
ARE TOLD THAT *URANIUM* IS DANGEROUS SO THEY DON'T KNOW HOW TO HANDLE
THE MATERIAL OUTSIDE OF THE STANDARD PROCEDURES.

5. MAI MANGA PROVIDED AN OVERVIEW OF THE TWO *URANIUM* MINES IN
NIGER, SOMAIR AND COMENAC. SOMAIR IS AN OPEN PIT MINE THAT PRODUCES
ROUGHLY 1000 TONS OF YELLOWCAKE PER YEAR. THIS HAS BEEN THE AMOUNT
PRODUCED FOR YEARS AT THIS MINE WHICH IS JOINTLY OWNED BY FRANCE AND
NIGER. COMENAC IS AN UNDERGROUND MINE THAT PRODUCES ROUGHLY 2000
TONS OF YELLOWCAKE PER YEAR. THIS MINE IS JOINTLY OWNED BY FRANCE,
JAPAN, SPAIN AND *NIGER*. IN THE EARLY 1980S THE COMBINED OUTPUT WAS
INCREASED FROM 3000 TONS TO NEARLY 4000 TONS OF YELLOWCAKE PER YEAR,
BUT PRODUCTION WAS CUT IN THE 1980S WHEN THE *URANIUM* PRICE FELL AND
SEVERAL YELLOWCAKE PRODUCTION LINES WERE MOTHBALLED AND HAVE YET TO
RESTART. *NIGER* DOES NOT TAKE ITS OWN PERCENTAGE OF THE PRODUCT; ALL
THE YELLOWCAKE IS SHIPPED TO FRANCE, JAPAN OR SPAIN. FRANCE'S COGEMA
OVERSEES THE PRODUCTION FROM BOTH MINES AND SETS THE PRODUCTION

CO 293 (Rev. 8/91) Subpoena to Testify Before Grand Jury

United States District Court

FOR THE _____ DISTRICT OF _____ COLUMBIA

TO: Office of the Vice President
The White House
1600 Pennsylvania Avenue, NW
Washington, DC 20502
ATTN: Mr. David Addington
Counsel to the Vice President

SUBPOENA TO TESTIFY BEFORE GRAND JURY

SUBPOENA FOR:
☐ PERSON   ☒ DOCUMENT(S) OR OBJECT(S)

YOU ARE HEREBY COMMANDED to appear and testify before the Grand Jury of the United States District Court at the place, date, and time specified below.

PLACE	COURTROOM
United States District Courthouse 3rd and Constitution Avenue, NW Washington, DC 20001	Grand Jury 03-3
	DATE AND TIME
	February 6, 2004

YOU ARE ALSO COMMANDED to bring with you the following document(s) or object(s):*

SEE ATTACHMENT A.

☐ Please see additional information on reverse.

This subpoena shall remain in effect until you are granted leave to depart by the court or by an officer acting on behalf of the court.

U.S. MAGISTRATE JUDGE OR CLERK OF COURT	DATE
Nancy M. Mayer-Whittington, Clerk	January 22, 2004
(BY) DEPUTY CLERK	

This subpoena is issued upon application of the United States of America

NAME, ADDRESS AND PHONE NUMBER OF ASSISTANT U.S. ATTORNEY
Ronald Roos
Deputy Special Counsel
U.S. Department of Justice
Washington, D.C. 20005

FITZGERALD SUBPOENAS the OVP. One of a number of subpoenas to the Office of the Vice President early in the investigation.

DECLASSIFIED

SECRET

5. ▮ In early March 2002, the Directorate of Intelligence prepared an analytic update (an e-mail to intelligence briefer) that reported on a meeting between the U.S. Ambassador to Niger, the Deputy Commander-in-Chief of the US European Command, and President Tandja of Niger. The update noted that in this late February 2002 meeting, President Tandja indicated that Niger was making all efforts to ensure that its uranium would be used only for peaceful purposes. We also reported that President Tandja had asked the US for unspecified assistance to ensure Niger's uranium did not fall into the wrong hands. Our analytic update also stated that we had requested additional information from the ▮▮▮ service that provided the original reporting on this topic and that the service currently was unable to provide new information.

6. ▮ On 8 March 2002, the Directorate of Operations disseminated information—obtained independently from a sensitive source—that indicated a former Nigerien government official claimed that since 1997, there had been no contracts signed between Niger and any rogue states for the sale of uranium in the form of yellowcake. While also asserting there had been no transfers of yellowcake to rogue states, one subsource—a former senior Nigerien official we are confident would have known of uranium sales—also said that he believed Iraq was interested in discussing yellowcake purchases when it sent a delegation to Niamey in mid-1999. The Directorate of Operations collected this information in an attempt to verify or refute, ▮▮ reporting on an alleged Iraq-Niger uranium deal. The Directorate of Operations assesses their sensitive source to be highly reliable▮▮ The subsources, however, were described in the disseminated report as knowing their remarks could reach the US Government and noted these individuals may have intended their comments to influence as well as inform.

7. ▮ On 25 March 2002, the Directorate of Operations released the third and final report on the Iraq-Niger uranium issue▮▮

8. ▮ On 24 September 2002, the British Government published a dossier titled "Iraq's Weapons of Mass Destruction," which stated that "...there is intelligence that Iraq has sought the supply of significant quantities of uranium from Africa." CIA avoided making a similar reference in providing text for the U.S. White Paper entitled "Iraq's Weapons of Mass Destruction Programs" and expressed concerns about the credibility of the reporting to the British▮▮ prior to publication of their assessment. ▮▮ prior to publication of the dossier, the British countered CIA concerns regarding credibility of the reporting by claiming they had corroborating evidence that Iraq sought uranium from Africa. This alleged corroborating information, however, was not shared with us.▮▮

dates noted by Iraq in one section of its 1998 "Full Final and Complete Declaration" on its nuclear program. These discrepancies in dates have been flagged to the Department of State.

001538

SECRET
DECLASSIFIED

LL01(

A CIA REPORT only referring to its source as "a sensitive source." Cheney tentatively identified Wilson as the unnamed official on the trip.

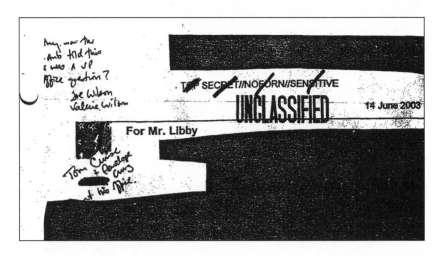

A NOTE MADE BY LIBBY'S CIA briefer Craig Schmall during his June 14, 2003 briefing. "Why was the Amb. told this was a VP office issue? Joe Wilson. Valerie Wilson." During the trial, Schmall testified that he recorded questions posed by the official he was briefing, indicating that, by June 14, Libby knew about the Wilsons and was asking about them by name.

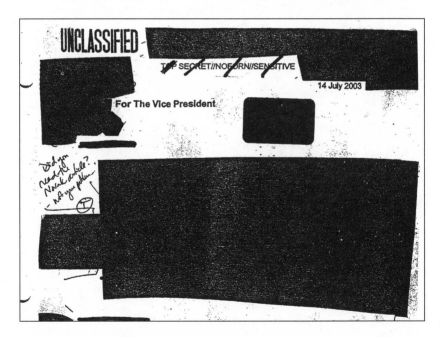

ANOTHER NOTE OF SCHMALL'S, from his July 14, 2003 briefing of Libby and Cheney. "Did you read the Novak article?—Not your problem." When asked during the trial, Schmall was unsure whether Cheney or Libby had posed the question.

Office of Deputy Director for Intelligence
President's Analytic Support Staff

Briefer's Tasking for Richard Cheney on 02/13/2002

Briefer:
David D. Terry
Principal:
Richard Cheney
Attendees:

Briefing Date:
02/13/2002

Tasking:
The VP was shown an assessment (he thought from DIA) that Iraq is purchasing uranium from Africa. He would like our assessment of that transaction and its implications for Iraq's nuclear program. A memo for tomorrow's book would be great.

Tasking met: No

A FEBRUARY 13, 2002 tasking reported by Vice President Cheney's CIA briefer. Cheney's questions about a report of an agreement for Iraq to purchase uranium from Niger played a key role in prompting the CIA to get Joe Wilson to travel to Niger to look into the report. The report subsequently turned out to be based on forged documents.

CATHIE MARTIN'S JULY 7, 2003 talking points regarding Wilson. On July 7, Cathie Martin sent an email to Ari Fleischer with talking points instructing Fleischer how to respond to questions about the role of the Office of the Vice President in Wilson's Niger mission. Following Fleischer's use of them in a gaggle (deemed disastrous for other resaons by many) that morning, he lunched with Libby. It was at that lunch that Libby told Fleischer about Plame.

CIA's ~~prestu~~ NIE stated that all agreed Iraq trying
to reconstitute Nuclear weapons

- unequivocally stated Iraq was vigorously
  trying to acquire uranium.
- wire we sd we didn't know
- ~~doubts of a~~

CIAs
CIA's NIE did not express doubt re Niger intel
~~MOBS~~ VP, CONDI, ~~PLLAY~~, ~~SLTTER~~

OPTIONS
- **MTP** — VP
- **LEAK** to Sanger Pincus/Newsmag.— sit down + give to him
- **PRESS** conference — CONDI/RUMSFELD
- **Op-ed**

MTP	
pro	con
- BEST	- too weeds
- control message.	- too defensive
	- raises bar

BOB WOODWARD. all intell
sit in a room + debate
NIE — We do there when not sure —
what is threat?
- It is an estimate — make judgments —
- both press + fragments.
Sorry serious mistake
Bush needs to explain

002878

LL005-09441

NOTES CATHIE MARTIN made on the back of a draft of Tenet's July 11 statement, which Libby and Cheney were working on late on July 10. Part of Martin's possible plan of attack is a list of "to-do" items including having the VP appearing on *Meet the Press* (where she felt they could "control message," as she writes in the 'pro' column), leaking to Sanger or other reporters, and having someone write a friendly op-ed. She also wrote that the NIE "stated that all agreed Iraq trying to reconstitute nuclear weapons," which was actually not the case.

Addington, David S.

From: Mayfield, Jennifer H.
Sent: Wednesday, October 01, 2003 1:57 PM
To: Martin, Catherine J.
Subject: RE: Today's gaggle w/ highlights

thanks

-----Original Message-----
From: Martin, Catherine J.
Sent: Wednesday, October 01, 2003 1:55 PM
To: Mayfield, Jennifer H.
Subject: Today's gaggle w/ highlights

EXCERPT RE SCOOTER:

Q -- one more question. You said the other day,
emphatically, that you had received assurances from Karl Rove
that he had nothing to do with this. Have you since then
received similar assurances from the Vice President's Chief of
Staff?

MR. McCLELLAN: John, I'm not going to go down -- I made
this clear the other day -- I'm not going to go down a list of
every single member of the staff in the White House --

Q That's just one name. (Laughter.)

MR. McCLELLAN: I'm not going to go -- and there was a
specific accusation made, and I responded to that. But I'm not
going to go down the list from this podium.

Thanks.

Q It's a short list, though.
-----Original Message-----
From: Suntum, Margaret M.
Sent: Wednesday, October 01, 2003 11:29 AM
Subject: resend: gaggle 10/1

THE WHITE HOUSE

Office of the Press Secretary

Internal Transcript   October 1,
2003

009801

2/2/2006

AN EXCERPT of the October 1, 2003 White House gaggle during which Press
Secretary McClellan refused to publicly exonerate Scooter Libby (as he had done for
Karl Rove), instead saying, "I'm not going to go down a list of every single member of
the staff in the White House." The excerpt was e-mailed by Cathie Martin to Libby's
assistant, Jennifer Mayfield.

7/12/03

f- Uranium

On the Record

- The Vice President heard in his regular intelligence briefing that Iraq was trying to acquire Uranium from Niger. As part of the regular briefing process, the Vice President asked a question about the implication of Iraq trying to acquire Uranium from Niger. (Note: During the course of the year, the Vice President asks the Agency many questions.) The Agency responded within a day or two. The Agency said that they had reporting suggesting the possibility of such a transaction but the reporting lacked detail. The Agency pointed out that Iraq already had 500 tons of yellowcake, portions of which came from Niger according to the IAEA.

- The Vice President was unaware of the Joe Wilson trip and did not know about it until June of this year, when it was first discussed in the press.

- The Vice President did not see Wilson's trip report until recently.

- The Vice President saw the NIE last fall, which he took to be authoritative.

Deep Background (as Administration Official)

- The only written record of Joe Wilson trip included that "the former Prime Minister of Niger said he had been approached by and met with a delegation of Iraqi officials in what he believed to be an effort to acquire more Uranium in 1999."

Notes

- Give straight report on NIE.

- Mention "vigorously pursue."

DECLASSIFIED

Treated as
~~SECRET/SCI~~

002891
LL005-09454

TALKING POINTS that Cheney dictated to Libby on Air Force One on July 12, 2003 (and that were later typed by Cathie Martin). Libby read verbatim from them during his phone conversation later that day with Matthew Cooper of *TIME* magazine.

Talking Points re Joe Wilson

1. It is not clear who authorized Joe Wilson's trip to Niger.

2. He did <u>not</u> travel to Niger at the request of the Vice President.

    - The Vice President's office did <u>not</u> request the mission to Niger.

    - The Vice President's office was <u>not</u> informed of Joe Wilson's mission.

    - The Vice President's office did not receive a briefing about Mr. Wilson's mission after he returned.

3. According to Mr. Wilson's own account, he was unpaid for his services.

4. Mr. Wilson never saw the documents he was allegedly trying to verify on his trip to Niger.

5. Mr. Wilson provided no written report of his trip to Niger when he returned.

6. Mr. Wilson has said he was convinced that Niger could not have provided uranium to Iraq but, in fact, Niger did provide uranium to Iraq in the 1980's – which is currently under IAEA seal.

7. The Vice President was unaware of Joe Wilson, his trip or any conclusions he may have reached until this spring when it was reported in the press – over a year after Mr. Wilson's trip.

8. Six months after the Joe Wilson trip, the considered judgment of the intelligence community was that Saddam Hussein had indeed undertaken a vigorous effort to acquire uranium from Africa according to the National Intelligence Estimate.

A REVISED VERSION of "Talking Points re Joe Wilson" indicated that the uncertainty about the origin of authorization for Wilson's trip had gained in importance within the OVP. Fitzgerald argues in his rebuttal closing that the emphasis on this point stems from the fact that Libby and Cheney believed they held the answer, and that the answer was "Wilson's wife."

LIBBY TOOK NOTES of his conversation with Cheney in June 2003 when Cheney originally told him that Wilson's wife worked at the CIA (transcribed opposite).

CONSOLIDATED CIPA § 5 NOTICE

Exhibit 84
LL005-09429
≈

6/12/03   Telephone -- VP re "Uranium in Iraq" – Kristof NYT article
     ·) Took place at our behest – functional office
               CP/ – his wife works in that division
         Debriefing took place here
         & was meeting in region
VP: hold →   4) OVP and Defense and State – expressed strong interest in issue
get agency   1) didn't know about mission
to answer   2) didn't get report back
that   3) didn't have any indication of forgery was from IAEA

              Treated as
              ~~**SECRET/SCI**~~

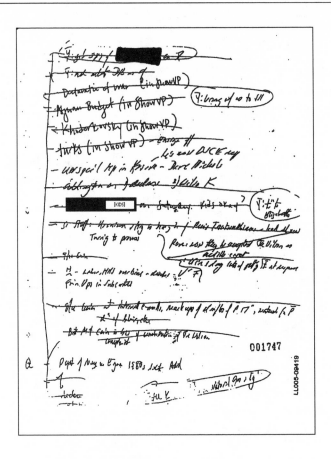

SOME OF LIBBY'S NOTES from around July 7 or 8, 2003. A note reading, "Addington on 1) declas 2) Wilson K," bears on a key conversation in which Libby asked the OVP's counsel, David Addington, about the president's declassification power and about documentation at the CIA regarding Wilson's trip (Addington testifies that "K" stands for "contract"). Libby's notes farther down (from a senior staff meeting probably on July 8) record the gist of Karl Rove's complaints about Wilson and the inadequacy of the White House's response to that point. (Transcription opposite.)

--VP: Get copy of ████████ on Iran
--VP: need meet DR on Iraq
--Declaration of War (in Show VP)   VP: bring with us to SH
--Afghan Budget (in Show VP)
--Khodorkovsky (in Show VP)
--Turks (in Show VP)
--UN Special Representative in Kosovo (he's now OSCE rep) Dave
Nichols
--Addington on 1) declass 2) Wilson Contract
-- [Kids] on Saturday. Kids okay?   VP: talk to Elizabeth
-- Senior Staff: Uranium story is becoming question of President's
trustworthiness & leads all news. Turning to process: Rove: now they
have accepted Joe Wilson as credible expert. We're 1 day late with
getting CIA right response
-- 9/11 Commission
-- House -- Labor, HHS overtime & disclos -- Veto threat
. Foreign Ops in Subcommittee
-- 9/11 Commission wants internal e-mails, mark-up of drafts of
   President's speech, materials for President's discussions with Blair, etc.
-- British Mil Commission is because of combination of Joe Wilson
   complaint
--Dept. of Navy v. Egan 1980s Supreme Court Addington
-- A Q Khan
-- Declassify
-- Khodorkovsky's deep interest in exporting gas from Murmansk
   VP: See k in office on Natural Gas & Energy

Scooter Libby's Schedule
Office of the Vice President
Tuesday, July 8, 2003
3 Draft

6:15am	Depart Private Residence en route Naval Observatory
6:50am	Arrive Naval Observatory
7:00am	**Intelligence Briefing with Vice President Cheney** Location: Naval Observatory
7:35am	**Meeting with Vice President Cheney** (10 minutes) Location: Naval Observatory
8:00am	Depart Naval Observatory en route White House
8:15am	Arrive White House
8:30am	Office Time (3 hours) *Private Meeting @ St. Regis*
11:45am	NSC DC Meeting (45 minutes) Location: Situation Room
12:40pm	Depart White House en route Capitol Building
12:55pm	Arrive Capitol Building
1:00pm	Senate Policy Lunch (1 hour) Location: Room S-207, Capitol Building
2:05pm	Depart Capitol Building en route White House
2:15pm	Arrive White House
3:30pm	Meeting with Vice President Cheney and Cathie Martin (30 minutes) Location: VP's Office, West Wing
4:00pm	VP's Phone Call with Turkish Prime Minister

009117

11:52 AM 07/09/03

	(20 minutes) Location: VP's Office, West Wing
4:30pm	CIA Briefing on Kashmir (1 hour) Location: Your Office, EEOB
6:00pm	Interview with Billy O'Brien (20 minutes) Location: Your Office, EEOB
6:30pm	Office Time (TBD)
TBDpm	Depart White House en route Private Residence
TBDpm	Arrive Private Residence
POTUS:	Tuesday: Dakar, Senegal and Pretoria, South Africa Wednesday: Pretoria, South Africa Thursday: Pretoria, South Africa and Gaborone, Botswana Friday: Pretoria, South Africa and Entebba, Uganda

LIBBY'S SCHEDULE for Tuesday, July 8, 2003. Though the period from 8:30 to 11:30 was officially listed as "office time," a handwritten note on Libby's schedule for that day adds that the time was specifically alloted for a "private meeting" at the St. Regis Hotel. This was Libby's breakfast meeting with then *New York Times* reporter Judith Miller.

7/10/03 T·MM

001739

LL005-09411

A NOTE LIBBY WROTE to himself on July 8, 2003. Libby testified to the Grand Jury on March 24, 2004 that this was "the Vice President telling me to go ahead and talk to Judith Miller."

From: Cooper, Matthew - Time U.S. <matt_cooper@timemagazine.com>
Sent: Friday, July 11, 2003 11:07 AM
To: Duffy, Michael - Time U.S. <michael_duffy@timemagazine.com>
Cc: Carney, James - Time U.S. <jay_carney@timemagazine.com>
Subject: Rove/P&C

Spoke to Rove on double super secret background for about two mins before he went on vacation....his big warning....don't get too far out on wilson....says that the DCIA didn't authorize the trip and that Cheney didn't authorize the trip. it was, KR said, wilson's wife, who apparently works at the agency on wmd issues, who authorized the trip. not only the genesis of the trip is flawed ans suspect but so is the report. he implied strongly there's still plenty to implicate iraqi interest in acquiring uranium fron Niger.....some of this is going to be dclassified in the coming days, KR said. don't get too far out in front, he warned. then he bolted....will include in next file.....

please don't source to rove or even WH but have TB check out with Harlow

---

Matthew Cooper
TIME magazine
555 12th Street N.W., Suite 600
Washington, D.C. 20004-1200
Phone:
Mobile:
Pager:

MATTHEW COOPER'S e-mail to his *TIME* magazine colleagues, Michael Duffy and James Carney, on July 11, following his conversation with Karl Rove during which Rove, on "double super secret background," alleged Wilson's wife was responsible for the mission to Niger. Cooper was careful to note that Rove had asked that neither he nor the White House be listed as a source.

press and din't notice wherther nao had been asked and it's hard to believe that the secretary to nato and doesn't know and after coming back and check it out....and came it and we did ask nato back in october and what about after the war and have to check and I find that difficult to accept...

No....

Tenrs to accept aintelligence.....my initial reaction to this is and maybe I'm being too forgiving and this is a major embarassmanet and including in his speech a flat out falsehood that's anbad thing and we ought to get and and I don't know why there's not more outrage from the administration and the president himself and the chances that they intentionally including a knowing and that would be so stupid and I can't imagine that it happened and the broader case of weapons of mass destruction and criticize them for presenting intel information as gospel and the big vulnerability on emphasizing the wmd too much is that tomorrow we could discover something and so that's the vulnerability and the real vulnerability and the planning for the aftermath and which I fine to be rather breathtaking and we all knew we'd win the war and the hardest part was going to be the aftermath and stabilize the country and build a democracy and I think a major blunder and weakness for the administration....and the next few weeks in any event...

There's a recognition that it's a state of embarrassment but probably doesn't have much legs to it and a greater concern about the inadequacy...of postwar iraq and building crescendo.....

Don' t get too war on Wilson and not sent by the director of the cia and when it comes out whoand it was the agency and somebody at the agency atinvolved in wmd and like his wife.....notable...and this guy was not an emissary and did not and his report is nowhehre near and there's nowhere andiragis have not and it's the

MATTHEW COOPER'S NOTES from his interview wth Karl Rove. Entered as an exhibit by the defense to show that Rove was the one who had disclosed to Cooper that Wilson was "not sent by the Director of the CIA" but instead "someone at the agency…like his wife."

The vice president heard about the possibility of iraq
trying to acuqire iran from niger in feb 2002 as part
of his regulkar intel the vioce president aske an
question about the implication of the report...during
the course of a year the vice president asked many
such questions and the agency responded within a day
or two the agency said they had reporting suggesdting
the possibility of such a traqnsaction. but rhe
agencye noted that the reporting lacked detail. the
agency pointed out that iraq already had 500 tons of
uranium, portions of which came from niger according
to the IAEA. The vice president was unaware of the
trip by AMbassador Wilson. And didn't know about it
until this year when it became public in the last
month or so.

on the record...

off the record and i did not state of the union......and did
he from his langley...i don';t recall it coming up on our
trips and in some of them we taliked about iraq and in some
we etalked about weapons of mass destruction and don't want
to deal with it definitively....and i don';t recall and any
of our trips out there and i don't recall him asking or me
asking...

we were not involve in part of that speech process drafting
and we maha d and more focus on project bioshield and
different spee

we would try and get thed bioshield language and not
engagaed...in a particular subject...of

had somethine and about the wilson thing and not sure if
it's ever

there's only one written record of the wilson trip and it
included a statement of the former prime minister and
wilson asked a former prime minister of niger and the guy
said no we haven't and he also said that he had been
approached by the iraqis and they sent a delegation to
niger and met with him.....for expanded drelations which he
understood to be and to acuqire...the net import of wilson
niger-eans denied it and but they also but he;d also
reporteds swomething fairly consisten with thwat the

```
..president..said..in..the..speech..and..the..iraqis..were............ ...........
  trying..saying the iraqis had approached him and the
  uranium and credible on that....


  some piece he saw that was circulated...

3019817358
```

MATTHEW COOPER'S NOTES of his interview with Libby. Nowhere in his notes was there a mention of Wilson's wife.

[People have made too much of the difference in how I described Karl and Libby] .

I've talked to Libby.

I said it was rediculous about Karl and it is rediculous about Libby Libby was not the source of the Novak story.

And he did not leak classified information.

Tenet Wilson memo

Has to happen today
Call out to key press saying same thing about Scooter as Karl

Not going to protect one staffer + sacrifice the guy ~~that~~ that was asked to stick his neck in the meat grinder because of the incompetence of others .

009502

LT 001-00099

NOTES FROM BOTH LIBBY AND CHENEY after White House spokesman McClellan publicly cleared Karl Rove of any wrong-doing and refused to do the same for Libby. Libby's notes detail what he wanted Cheney to order McClellan to say, namely, "I said it was ridiculous about Karl and it is ridiculous about Libby. Libby was not the souce of the Novak story. And he did not leak classified information." Below the line are Cheney's notes, including the enigmatic line the defense used to suggest that Libby was being scapegoated to save Rove.

GOVERNMENT
EXHIBIT
11
05 Cr. 394 (ID)

FEDERAL BUREAU OF INVESTIGATION

STATEMENT AND WAIVER

I, _Lewis "Scooter" Libby_ have been advised by Special Agents

Jack Eckenrode and _Deborah Bond_

of the Federal Bureau of Investigation that they are conducting an investigation into

the possible disclosure to unauthorized persons of classified information in connection with

Ambassador Joseph Wilson, his trip to Niger in February 2002, and matters relating thereto

("the subject matters under investigation").

I have informed the Federal Bureau of Investigation of my recollection of any communications I have had with members of the media regarding the subject matters under investigation. I hereby waive any promise of confidentiality, express or implied, made to me by any member of the media in connection with any communications that I may have had with that member of the media regarding the subject matters under investigation, including any communications made "on background," "off the record," "not for attribution," or in any other form. I request any member of the media with whom I may have communicated regarding the subject matters under investigation to fully disclose all such communications to federal law enforcement authorities. In particular, I request that no member of the media assert any privilege or refuse to answer any questions from federal law enforcement authorities on my behalf or for my benefit in connection with the subject matters under investigation.

Signed: _____

Witness: _____

Witness: _____

Date: _1/5/04._

ON JANUARY 5, 2004, Libby signed a waiver surrendering "any promise of confidentiality, express or implied, made to me by any member of the media in connection with any communications that I may have had with that member of the media." Many members of the media—most notably, Judith Miller—believed this waiver was coerced. Later, in a personal note, Libby wrote to the jailed Miller, "You went into jail in the summer. It is fall now. You will have stories to cover—Iraqi elections and suicide bombers, biological threats and the Iranian nuclear program. Out West, where you vacation, the aspens will already be turning. They turn in clusters, because their roots connect them. Come back to work—and life. Until then, you will remain in my thoughts and prayers. With admiration, Scooter Libby." Miller then relented, agreed to testify, and was released from prison.

[Handwritten annotations across top of page:] Have they done this sort of thing before? Send an Amb. to answer a question? Do we ordinarily send people out pro bono to work for us? Or did his wife send him on a junket?

What I Didn't Find in Africa

By Joseph C. Wilson 4th

WASHINGTON

Did the Bush administration manipulate intelligence about Saddam Hussein's weapons programs to justify an invasion of Iraq?

Based on my experience with the administration in the months leading up to the war, I have little choice but to conclude that some of the intelligence related to Iraq's nuclear weapons program was twisted to exaggerate the Iraqi threat.

For 23 years, from 1976 to 1998, I was a career foreign service officer and ambassador. In 1990, as chargé d'affaires in Baghdad, I was the last American diplomat to meet with Saddam Hussein. (I was also a forceful advocate for his removal from Kuwait.) After Iraq, I was President George H. W. Bush's ambassador to Gabon and São Tomé and Príncipe; under President Bill Clinton, I helped direct Africa policy for the National Security Council.

It was my experience in Africa that led me to play a small role in the effort to verify information about Africa's suspected link to Iraq's nonconventional weapons programs. Those news stories about that unnamed former envoy who went to Niger? That's me.

In February 2002, I was informed by officials at the Central Intelligence Agency that Vice President Dick Cheney's office had questions about a particular intelligence report. While I never saw the report, I was told that it referred to a memorandum of agreement that documented the sale of uranium yellowcake — a form of lightly processed ore — by Niger to Iraq in the late 1990's. The agency officials asked if I would travel to Niger to check out the story so they could provide a response to the vice president's office.

Joseph C. Wilson 4th, United States ambassador to Gabon from 1992 to 1995, is an international business consultant.

After consulting with the State Department's African Affairs Bureau (and through it with Barbro Owens-Kirkpatrick, the United States ambassador to Niger), I agreed to make the trip. The mission I undertook was discreet but by no means secret. While the C.I.A. paid my expenses (my time was

There was no Iraq-Niger uranium deal.

offered pro bono), I made it abundantly clear to everyone I met that I was acting on behalf of the United States government.

In late February 2002, I arrived in Niger's capital, Niamey, where I had been a diplomat in the mid-70's and visited as a National Security Council official in the late 90's. The city was much as I remembered it. Seasonal winds had clogged the air with dust and sand. Through the haze, I could see camel caravans crossing the Niger River (over the John F. Kennedy bridge), the setting sun behind them. Most people had wrapped scarves around their faces to protect against the grit, leaving only their eyes visible.

The next morning, I met with Ambassador Owens-Kirkpatrick at the embassy. For reasons that are understandable, the embassy staff has always kept a close eye on Niger's uranium business. I was not surprised, then, when the ambassador told me that she knew about the allegations of uranium sales to Iraq — and that she felt she had already debunked them in her reports to Washington. Nevertheless, she and I agreed that my time would be best spent interviewing people who had been in government when

the deal supposedly took place, which was before her arrival.

I spent the next eight days drinking sweet mint tea and meeting with dozens of people: current government officials, former government officials, people associated with the country's uranium business. It did not take long to conclude that it was highly doubtful that any such transaction had ever taken place.

Given the structure of the consortiums that operated the mines, it would be exceedingly difficult for Niger to transfer uranium to Iraq. Niger's uranium business consists of two mines, Somair and Cominak, which are run by French, Spanish, Japanese, German and Nigerian interests. If the government wanted to remove uranium from a mine, it would have to notify the consortium, which in turn is strictly monitored by the International Atomic Energy Agency. Moreover, because the two mines are closely regulated, quasi-governmental entities, selling uranium would require the approval of the minister of mines, the prime minister and probably the president. In short, there's simply too much oversight over too small an industry for a sale to have transpired.

(As for the actual memorandum, I never saw it. But news accounts have pointed out that the documents had glaring errors — they were signed, for example, by officials who were no longer in government — and then there's the fact that Niger formally denied the charges.)

Before I left Niger, I briefed the ambassador on my findings, which were consistent with her own. I also shared my conclusions with members of her staff. In early March, I arrived in Washington and promptly provided a detailed briefing to the C.I.A. I later shared my conclusions with the State Department African Affairs Bureau. There was nothing secret or earth-shattering in my report, just as there was nothing secret about my trip.

Though I did not file a written report,

there should be at least four documents in United States government archives confirming my mission. The documents should include the ambassador's report of my debriefing in Niamey, a separate report written by the embassy staff, a C.I.A. report summing up my trip, and a specific answer from the agency to the office of the vice president (this may have been delivered orally). While I have not seen any of these reports, I have spent enough time in government to know that this is standard operating procedure.

I thought the Niger matter was settled and went back to my life. (I did take part in the Iraq debate, arguing that a strict containment regime backed by the threat of force was preferable to an invasion.) In September 2002, however, Niger re-emerged. The British government published a "white paper" asserting that Saddam Hussein and his unconventional arms posed an immediate danger. As evidence, the report cited Iraq's attempts to purchase uranium from an African country.

Then, in January, President Bush, citing the British dossier, repeated the charges about Iraq efforts to buy uranium from Africa.

The next day, I reminded a friend at the State Department of my trip and suggested that if the president had been referring to Niger, then his conclusion was not borne out by the facts as I understood them. He replied that perhaps the president was speaking about one of the other three African countries that produce uranium: Gabon, South Africa or Namibia. At the time, I accepted the explanation. I didn't know that in December, a month before the president's address, the State Department had published a fact sheet that mentioned the Niger case.

Those are the facts surrounding my efforts. The vice president's office asked a serious question. I was asked to help formulate the answer. I did so, and

I have every confidence that the answer I provided was circulated to the appropriate officials within our government.

The question now is how that answer was or was not used by our leadership. If my information was deemed inaccurate, I understand (though I would be very interested to know why). If, however, the information was ignored because it did not fit certain preconceptions about Iraq, then a legitimate argument can be made that we went to war under false pretenses. (It's worth remembering that in his March "Meet the Press" appearance, Mr. Cheney said that Saddam Hussein was "trying once again to produce nuclear weapons." At a minimum, Congress, which authorized the use of military force at the president's behest, should want to know the assertions about Iraq were warranted.

I was convinced before the war that the threat of weapons of mass destruction in the hands of Saddam Hussein required a vigorous and sustained international response to disarm. Iraq possessed and had used chemical weapons; it had an active biological weapons program and quite possibly a nuclear research program — all of which were in violation of United Nations resolutions. Having encountered Mr. Hussein and his thugs in the run-up to the Persian Gulf war of 1991, I was only too aware of the dangers he posed.

But were these dangers the ones the administration told us about? We have to find out. America's foreign policy depends on the sanctity of its information. For this reason, cherry-picking the selective use of intelligence to justify the war in Iraq is nothing short of sniping no "revisionist history" as Mr. Bush has suggested. The act of war is the last option of a democracy, taken when there is a grave threat to our national security. More than 200 American soldiers have lost their lives in Iraq already. We have a duty to ensure that their sacrifice came for the right reasons.

CHENEY'S COPY of Wilson's op-ed. Cheney made his annotations on a physical copy of *The New York Times.* He wrote, "Have they done this before? Send an Amb. to answer a question? Do we ordinarily send people out pro bono to work for us? Or did his wife send him on a junket?"

DECLASSIFIED

Treated as

~~TOP SECRET/SCI~~

003079

LL013-11563

"PRESIDENT: STATE OF THE UNION – KRISTOF REPORT." Libby's note from June 9, 2003, he later testified to the Grand Jury, indicated that President Bush expressed interest in Nicholas Kristof's month-old column. The day before, the ABC program *This Week* had confronted Condoleezza Rice with the apparent contradiction between the sixteen words from Bush's State of the Union and Kristof's report on the mission to Niger. Rice was not well prepared with a response.

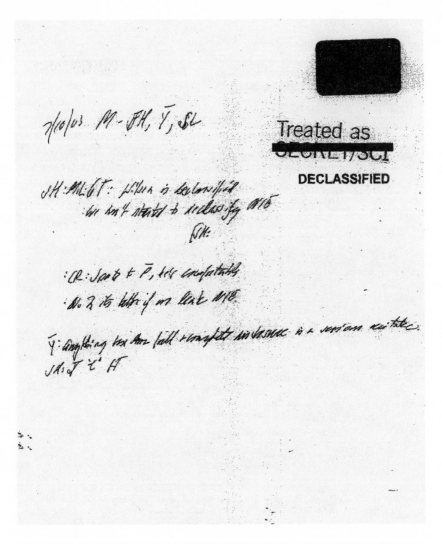

LIBBY'S NOTES FROM A JULY 10, 2003 MEETING with then-Deputy National Security Adviser Stephen Hadley and Vice President Dick Cheney in the context of pressing George Tenet to come out with a statement about the sixteen words controversy. Stephen Hadley reports that while CIA Director George Tenet had apparently declassified the trip report from Wilson's mission, he hadn't yet declassified the October 2002 NIE; and Hadley says it's better to leak the NIE in an exclusive to a reporter. Neither Cheney nor Libby told Hadley that in fact President Bush had already authorized Libby to leak the NIE, which they understood constituted a presidential declassification, and that Libby had leaked it to Judith Miller. Cheney tells Hadley that "anything less than full and complete disclosure is a serious mistake," and Hadley responds, "I will—I told that to George Tenet." (Hadley also reports that Condoleezza Rice told him the President was "comfortable"—it is not clear with what.)

.Analyzing the Iraq-Niger controversy
involving the State of the Union

THE VICE PRESIDENT
HAS SEEN.

SUMMARY

Key documents written by the Intelligence Community in late
2002 and early 2003 show that the White House would have been
reasonable in believing prior to the State of the Union Address
that Iraq had sought uranium from Africa. In fact, these
documents show that, only days before the speech, the
Intelligence Community stood behind its judgment that, "Iraq
began to vigorously attempt to procure uranium" from Africa..

These documents include relevant sections of the
Intelligence Community's October 2002 NIE and a CIA submission
to the White House on January 24, 2003. Both contain the flat
assertion that Iraq was vigorously attempting to procure
uranium, and cite examples from Africa. In addition, the report
of Amb. Joe Wilson has been distorted by the press and Mr.
Wilson.

None of these documents have been declassified and
presented fairly to the public. But less probative oral
discussions and inferences have been readily thrown about. This
should be corrected

The Problem. Recent leaks, Director Tenet's July 11 public
statement, Amb. Joe Wilson's claims and the media have left the
public with the misimpression that the Intelligence Community
was expressing widespread doubts about the Iraq-African uranium
connection before the State of the Union. From this, some
assert that the President or Vice President knew or should have
known about these doubts before the President delivered the
speech.

The Truth. The complete record -- including especially the
written record -- shows that the CIA was communicating directly
to the President, Vice President, and other Senior White House
officials that the Intelligence Community *credited* the reports
of the Iraq-African connection.

 1.   THE OCTOBER 2002 NIE FLATLY ASSERTS THAT IRAQ WAS
VIGOROUSLY TRYING TO OBTAIN URANIUM. The 1 October 2002 NIE

OVP Staff Secretary Received
7/8/03

001528

LL010-10487

A DOCUMENT PRODUCED in the Vice President's office sometime shortly before July 18, 2003. This document, seen and perhaps used by the Vice President, shows the focus Cheney maintained on pushing back against both Wilson and the CIA even after Novak's column. Of particular note is the emphasis on a CIA fax sent to the National Security Council shortly before Bush's 2003 State of the Union which simply reprinted the October 2002 NIE's claim about Iraqi pursuit of uranium in Africa.

FBI Agents Tracing Linkage Of Envoy To CIA Operative

The Washington Post
By Walter Pincus and Mike Allen
October 12, 2003

WASHINGTON, DC -- **FBI** agents investigating the disclosure of a CIA officer's identity have begun by examining events in the month before the leak, when the CIA, the White House and Vice President Cheney's office first were asked about former ambassador Joseph C. Wilson IV's CIA-sponsored trip to Niger, according to sources familiar with the probe.

The name of Wilson's wife, Valerie Plame, a clandestine case officer, was revealed in a July 14 column by Robert D. Novak that quoted two unidentified senior administration officials. In their interviews, **FBI** agents are asking questions about events going back to at least early June, the sources said. That indicates investigators are examining not just who passed the information to Novak and other reporters but also how Plame's name may have first become linked with Wilson and his mission, who did it and how the information made its way around the government. Administration sources said they believe the officials who discussed Plame were not trying to expose her, but were using the information as a tool to try to persuade reporters to ignore Wilson. The officials wanted to convince the reporters that he had benefited from nepotism in being chosen for the mission.

What started as political gossip and damage control has become a major criminal investigation that has already harmed the administration and could be a problem for President Bush for months to come. One reason investigators are looking back is that even before Novak's column appeared, government officials had been trying for more than a month to convince journalists that Wilson's mission was not as important as it was being portrayed. Wilson concluded during the 2002 mission that there was no solid evidence for the administration's assertion that Iraq was trying to acquire uranium in Niger to develop nuclear weapons, and he angered the White House when he became an outspoken critic of the war. The **FBI** is trying to determine when White House officials and members of the vice president's staff first focused on Wilson and learned about his wife's employment at the agency.

One group that may have known of the connection before that time is the handful of CIA officers detailed to the White House, where they work primarily on the National Security Council staff. A former NSC staff member said one or more of those officers may have been aware of the Plame-Wilson relationship. White House press secretary Scott McClellan said in response to a query for this article: "I think it would be counterproductive during an ongoing investigation for me to chase rumors and speculation. The president has directed the White House to cooperate fully, and that is exactly what we are doing." Investigators are trying to establish the chain of events leading to the leak because, for a successful prosecution under the law prohibiting unauthorized disclosure of a covert U.S. officer's name, the disclosure must have been intentional, the accused must have known the person was a covert officer and the identity must not have been disclosed earlier.

The first public mention of Wilson's mission to Niger, albeit without identifying him by name, was in the New York Times on May 6, in a column by Nicholas D. Kristof. Kristof had been on a panel with Wilson four days earlier, when the former ambassador said State Department officials should know better than to say the United States had been duped by forged documents that allegedly had proved a deal for the uranium had been in the works between Iraq and Niger. Wilson said he told Kristof about his trip to Niger on the condition that Kristof must keep his name out of the column. When the column appeared, it created little public stir, though it set a number of reporters on the trail of the anonymous former ambassador. Kristof confirmed that account. The column mentioned the alleged role of the vice president's office for the first time.

That was when Cheney aides became aware of Wilson's mission and they began asking questions about

A COPY of an October 12, 2003 *Washington Post* article by Walter Pincus and Mike Allen that Libby had underlined. The article discussed the outing of Valerie Plame.

The New York Times
nytimes.com

July 6, 2003

What I Didn't Find in Africa

By JOSEPH C. WILSON 4th

WASHINGTON

Did the Bush administration manipulate intelligence about Saddam Hussein's weapons programs to justify an invasion of Iraq?

Based on my experience with the administration in the months leading up to the war, I have little choice but to conclude that some of the intelligence related to Iraq's nuclear weapons program was twisted to exaggerate the Iraqi threat.

For 23 years, from 1976 to 1998, I was a career foreign service officer and ambassador. In 1990, as chargé d'affaires in Baghdad, I was the last American diplomat to meet with Saddam Hussein. (I was also a forceful advocate for his removal from Kuwait.) After Iraq, I was President George H. W. Bush's ambassador to Gabon and São Tomé and Príncipe; under President Bill Clinton, I helped direct Africa policy for the National Security Council.

It was my experience in Africa that led me to play a small role in the effort to verify information about Africa's suspected link to Iraq's nonconventional weapons programs. Those news stories about that unnamed former envoy who went to Niger? That's me.

Those are the facts surrounding my efforts. The vice president's office asked a serious question. I was asked to help formulate the answer. I did so, and I have every confidence that the answer I provided was circulated to the appropriate officials within our government.

The question now is how that answer was or was not used by our political leadership. If my information was deemed inaccurate, I understand (though I would be very interested to know why). If, however, the information was ignored because it did not fit certain preconceptions about Iraq, then a legitimate argument can be made that we went to war under false pretenses. (It's worth remembering that in his March "Meet the Press" appearance, Mr. Cheney said that Saddam Hussein was "trying once again to produce nuclear weapons.") At a minimum, Congress, which authorized the use of military force at the president's behest, should want to know if the assertions about Iraq were warranted.

I was convinced before the war that the threat of weapons of mass destruction in the hands of Saddam Hussein required a vigorous and sustained international response ~~to~~ possessed and had

and I agreed that my time would be best spent interviewing people who had been in government when the deal supposedly took place, which was before her arrival.

I spent the next eight days drinking sweet mint tea and meeting with dozens of people: current government officials, former government officials, people associated with the country's uranium business. It did not take long to conclude that it was highly doubtful that any such transaction had ever taken place.

Given the structure of the consortiums that operated the mines, it would be exceedingly difficult for Niger to transfer uranium to Iraq. Niger's uranium business consists of two mines, Somair and Cominak, which are run by French, Spanish, Japanese, German and Nigerian interests. If the government wanted to remove uranium from a mine, it would have to notify the consortium, which in turn is strictly monitored by the International Atomic Energy Agency. Moreover, because the two mines are closely regulated, quasi-governmental entities, selling uranium would require the approval of the minister of mines, the prime minister and probably the president. In short, there's simply too much oversight over too small an industry for a sale to have transpired.

LIBBY PRINTED OUT a copy of Joseph Wilson's op-ed in *The New York Times* and made notes in the margins.

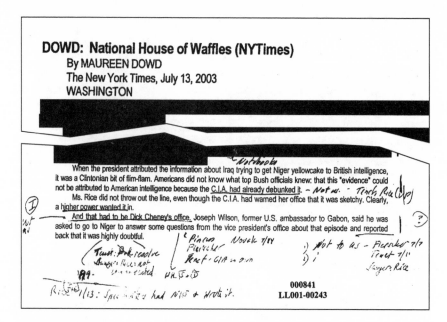

DOWD: National House of Waffles (NYTimes)
By MAUREEN DOWD
The New York Times, July 13, 2003
WASHINGTON

When the president attributed the information about Iraq trying to get Niger yellowcake to British intelligence, it was a Clintonian bit of flim-flam. Americans did not know what top Bush officials knew: that this "evidence" could not be attributed to American intelligence because the C.I.A. had already debunked it.

Ms. Rice did not throw out the line, even though the C.I.A. had warned her office that it was sketchy. Clearly, a higher power wanted it in.

And that had to be Dick Cheney's office. Joseph Wilson, former U.S. ambassador to Gabon, said he was asked to go to Niger to answer some questions from the vice president's office about that episode and reported back that it was highly doubtful.

LIBBY'S NOTES on a July 13, 2003 *New York Times* column by Maureen Dowd. Though Libby's handwriting is somewhat difficult to decipher, his notes show just how detailed Libby was in tracking media commentary about the story and preparing to respond to critics.

A)   A Question Of Trust (Time)

B)   After the War Intelligence (NYT) *Single*

C)   WMDs Inquiry Urged (AP)

D)   White House mea culpa prompts new calls for probe of
     prewar intelligence (AP) ....

E)   Ari Fleischer Gaggle

F)   Retired Envoy: Nuclear Report Ignored (WPost) *Pincus 7/6*

G)   Report Cast Doubt on Iraq-Al Qaeda Connection (WPost) *Pincus. 6/22*

H)   Rice on Fox News Sunday

   I   *Novak*

THE TABLE OF CONTENTS from an OVP collection of articles on the sixteen words controversy. The Office of the Vice President was tracking the developing story of Valerie Plame and Joseph Wilson closely. They collected and circulated a group of articles on the prewar intelligence controversy, thereby illustrating how engaged on the issue the OVP was.

2. I hereby acknowledge that I have received a security indoctrination concerning the nature and protection of classified information, including the procedures to be followed in ascertaining whether other persons to whom I contemplate disclosing this information have been approved for access to it, and that I understand these procedures.

3. I have been advised that the unauthorized disclosure, unauthorized retention, or negligent handling of classified information by me could cause damage or irreparable injury to the United States or could be used to advantage by a foreign nation. I hereby agree that I will never divulge classified information to anyone unless: (a) I have officially verified that the recipient has been properly authorized by the United States Government to receive it; or (b) I have been given prior written notice of authorization from the United States Government Department or Agency (hereinafter Department or Agency) responsible for the classification of the information or last granting me a security clearance that such disclosure is permitted. I understand that if I am uncertain about the classification status of information, I am required to confirm from an authorized official that the information is unclassified before I may disclose it, except to a person as provided in (a) or (b), above. I further understand that I am obligated to comply with laws and regulations that prohibit the unauthorized disclosure of classified information.

4. I have been advised that any breach of this Agreement may result in the termination of any security clearances I hold; removal from any position of special confidence and trust requiring such clearances; or the termination of my employment or other relationships with the Departments or Agencies that granted my security clearance or clearances. In addition, I have been advised that any unauthorized disclosure of classified information by me may constitute a violation, or violations, of United States criminal laws, including the provisions of Sections 641, 793, 794, 798, and *952, Title 18, United States Code, *the provisions of Section 783(b), Title 50, United States Code, and the provisions of the Intelligence Identities Protection Act of 1982. I recognize that nothing in this Agreement constitutes a waiver by the United States of the right to prosecute me for any statutory violation.

5. I hereby assign to the United States Government all royalties, remunerations, and emoluments that have resulted, will result or may result from any disclosure, publication, or revelation of classified information not consistent with the terms of this Agreement.

6. I understand that the United States Government may seek any remedy available to it to enforce this Agreement including, but not limited to, application for a court order prohibiting disclosure of information in breach of this Agreement.

7. I understand that all classified information to which I have access or may obtain access by signing this Agreement is now and will remain the property of, or under the control of the United States Government unless and until otherwise determined by an authorized official or final ruling of a court of law. I agree that I shall return all classified materials which have, or may come into my possession or for which I am responsible because of such access: (a) upon demand by an authorized representative of the United States Government; (b) upon the conclusion of my employment or other relationship with the Department or Agency that last granted me a security clearance or that provided me access to classified information; or (c) upon the conclusion of my employment or other relationship that requires access to classified information. If I do not return such materials upon request, I understand that this may be a violation of Section 793, Title 18, United States Code, a United States criminal law.

8. Unless and until I am released in writing by an authorized representative of the United States Government, I understand that all conditions and obligations imposed upon me by this Agreement apply during the time I am granted access to classified information, and at all times thereafter.

9. Each provision of this Agreement is severable. If a court should find any provision of this Agreement to be unenforceable, all other provisions of this Agreement shall remain in full force and effect.

10. These restrictions are consistent with and do not supersede, conflict with or otherwise alter the employee obligations, rights or liabilities created by Executive Order 12356; Section 7211 of Title 5, United States Code (governing disclosures to Congress); Section 1034 of Title 10, United States Code, as amended by the Military Whistleblower Protection Act (governing disclosure to Congress by members of the military); Section 2302(b)(8) of Title 5, United States Code, as amended by the Whistleblower Protection Act (governing disclosures of illegality, waste, fraud, abuse or public health or safety threats); the Intelligence Identities Protection Act of 1982 (50 U.S.C. 421 et seq.) (governing disclosures that could expose confidential Government agents), and the statutes which protect against disclosure that may compromise the national security, including Sections 641, 793, 794, 798, and 952 of Title 18, United States Code, and Section 4(b) of the Subversive Activities Act of 1950 (50 U.S.C. Section 783(b)). The definitions, requirements, obligations, rights, sanctions and liabilities created by said Executive Order and listed statutes are incorporated into this Agreement and are controlling.

(Continue on reverse.)

009726

NSN 7540-01-280-5499
Previous edition not usable.

312-102

STANDARD FORM 312 (REV. 1-91)
Prescribed by GSA/ISOO

OCT-20-2005 09:05

98%

P.02

11. I have read this Agreement carefully and my questions, if any, have been answered. I acknowledge that the briefing officer has made available to me the Executive Order and statutes referenced in this Agreement and its implementing regulation (32 CFR Section 2003.20) so that I may read them at this time, if I so choose.

SIGNATURE	DATE 1/23/01	SOCIAL SECURITY NUMBER (See Notice below)

ORGANIZATION (IF CONTRACTOR, LICENSEE, GRANTEE OR AGENT, PROVIDE: NAME, ADDRESS, AND, IF APPLICABLE, FEDERAL SUPPLY CODE NUMBER) (Type or print)

OFFICE OF THE PRESIDENT

WITNESS	ACCEPTANCE
THE EXECUTION OF THIS AGREEMENT WAS WITNESSED BY THE UNDERSIGNED.	THE UNDERSIGNED ACCEPTED THIS AGREEMENT ON BEHALF OF THE UNITED STATES GOVERNMENT.
SIGNATURE / DATE 1/23/01	SIGNATURE / DATE 1/23/01
NAME AND ADDRESS (Type or print)	NAME AND ADDRESS (Type or print)
DOJ/SSC	DOJ/SSC

LIBBY'S NDA. (here and opposite) In January of 2001, Libby had signed a nondisclosure agreement certifying he understood that, as part of his job, he would be granted access to classified information which he would be obligated to protect. Libby had an affirmative obligation not to be negligent and confirm the status of information with classification status of which he was uncertain.

1:14	WOODWARD: ...What's Scowcroft up to?
1:15	ARMITAGE: [ ] Scowcroft is looking into
1:16	the yellowcake thing.
1:17	WOODWARD: Oh yeah?
1:18	ARMITAGE: As the PFIAB
1:19	WOODWARD: Yeah. What happened there?
1:20	ARMITAGE: They're back together. [coughs] They
1:21	knew with yellowcake, the CIA is not going to be hurt by this
1:22	one---
1:23	WOODWARD: I know, that's---
1:24	ARMITAGE: -- Hadley and Bob Joseph know. It's
1:25	documented. We've got our documents on it. We're clean as a
2:1	[ ] whistle. And George personally got it out of the
2:2	Cincinatti speech of the president.
2:3	WOODWARD: Oh he did?
2:4	ARMITAGE: Oh yeah.
2:5	WOODWARD: Oh really?
2:6	ARMITAGE: Yeah.
2:7	WOODWARD: It was taken out?
2:8	ARMITAGE: Taken out. George said you can't
2:9	do this.
2:10	WOODWARD: How come it wasn't taken out of the State
2:11	of the Union then?
2:12	ARMITAGE: Because I think it was overruled by
2:13	the types down at the White House. Condi doesn't like being
2:14	in the hot spot. But she ---
2:15	WOODWARD: But it was Joe Wilson who was sent by
2:16	the agency. I mean that's just ---
2:17	ARMITAGE: His wife works in the agency.
2:18	WOODWARD: --- Why doesn't that come out? Why does ---
2:19	ARMITAGE: Everyone knows it.
2:20	WOODWARD: ---that have to be a big secret?
2:21	Everyone knows.
2:22	ARMITAGE: Yeah. And I know [ ] Joe Wilson's
2:23	been calling everybody. He's pissed off because he was
2:24	designated as a low-level guy, went out to look at it. So,
2:25	he's all pissed off.
3:1	WOODWARD: But why would they send him?
3:2	ARMITAGE: Because his wife's a [ ] analyst at

3:3	the agency.
3:4	WOODWARD: It's still weird.
3:5	ARMITAGE: It---It's perfect. This is what she
3:6	does she is a WMD analyst out there.
3:7	WOODWARD: Oh she is.
3:8	ARMITAGE: Yeah.
3:9	WOODWARD: Oh, I see.
3:10	ARMITAGE: [ ] look at it.
3:11	WOODWARD: Oh I see. I didn't [ ].
3:12	ARMITAGE: Yeah. See?
3:13	WOODWARD: Oh, she's the chief WMD?
3:14	ARMITAGE: No she isn't the chief, no.
3:15	WOODWARD: But high enough up that she can say, "Oh
3:16	yeah, hubby will go."
3:17	ARMITAGE: Yeah, he knows Africa.
3:18	WOODWARD: Was she out there with him?
3:19	ARMITAGE: No.
3:20	WOODWARD: When he was ambassador?
3:21	ARMITAGE: Not to my knowledge. I don't know.
3:22	I don't know if she was out there or not. But his wife is in
3:23	the agency and is a WMD analyst. How about that [ ]?

THE TRANSCRIPT OF AN EXCERPT from the recording that Bob Woodward made of his conversation with Richard Armitage on July 13, 2003, during which Armitage blows Plame's cover. This is significant because it is the first known occasion where an admininstration official leaked Plame's identity to a reporter. What's also interesting is that it shows Armitage knew all about the White House's pointed decision to ignore warnings not to use the uraninum claim in the 2003 State of the Union address.

MONDAY, JULY 14, 2003 **A21**

Robert D. Novak

Mission To Niger

The CIA's decision to send retired diplomat Joseph C. Wilson to Africa in February 2002 to investigate possible Iraqi purchases of uranium was made routinely at a low level without Director George Tenet's knowledge. Remarkably, this produced a political firestorm that has not yet subsided.

Wilson's report that an Iraqi purchase of uranium yellowcake from Niger was highly unlikely was regarded by the CIA as less than definitive, and it is doubtful Tenet ever saw it. Certainly President Bush did not, before his 2003 State of the Union address, when he attributed reports of attempted Iraqi uranium purchases to the British government. That the British relied on forged documents made Wilson's mission, nearly a year earlier, the basis of furious Democratic accusations of burying intelligence, though the report was forgotten by the time the president spoke.

Reluctance at the White House to admit a mistake has led Democrats ever closer to saying the president lied the country into war. Even after a belated admission of error last Monday, finger-pointing between Bush administration agencies continued. Messages between Washington and the presidential entourage traveling in Africa hashed over the mission to Niger.

Wilson's mission was created after an early 2002 report by the Italian intelligence service about attempted uranium purchases from Niger, derived from forged documents prepared by what the CIA calls a "con man." This misinformation, peddled by Italian journalists, spread through the U.S. government. The White House, the State Department and the Pentagon, and not just Vice President Cheney, asked the CIA to look into it.

That's where Joe Wilson came in. His first public notice had come in 1991 after 15 years as a Foreign Service officer when, as U.S. chargé in Baghdad, he risked his life to shelter in the embassy some 800 Americans from Saddam Hussein's wrath. My partner Rowland Evans reported from

BY MARGARET SCOTT

...ade the strategic
...th of negotiation.
...e of peace will take
...ng the systematic
...ed struggle, the el-
...the notion that kill-
...e accomplished al-
...mined government
...tement in govern-
...tional curriculums.
...are taught about Is-
...i maps of Israel ap-
...s as the place next
...onquered, when co-
...e jihad kindergarten
...oorstep. For as John
...Peace does not lie in
...t. It lies in the hearts

_____

...ster of Israel._

...th

...ion about the study been
...etter signed by 138 mem-
...the NAS president, warn-
...000 appropriation was not
...olicy changes that would
...hol industry.
...and Human Services ad-
...e study's program officer
...l industry be allowed to
...before it was released.

CHENEY'S COPY of Bob Novak's July 14, 2003 syndicated column publicly blowing Plame's cover. Fitzgerald argued the fact that Cheney ripped it out and kept it indicated the attention the Vice President was paying to the matter.

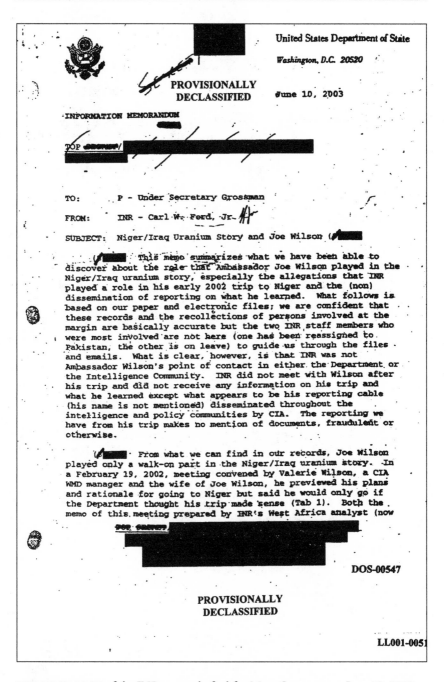

United States Department of State

Washington, D.C. 20520

PROVISIONALLY DECLASSIFIED

June 10, 2003

INFORMATION MEMORANDUM

TOP ~~SECRET~~/

TO: P - Under Secretary Grossman

FROM: INR - Carl W. Ford, Jr.

SUBJECT: Niger/Iraq Uranium Story and Joe Wilson (

This memo summarizes what we have been able to discover about the role that Ambassador Joe Wilson played in the Niger/Iraq uranium story, especially the allegations that INR played a role in his early 2002 trip to Niger and the (non) dissemination of reporting on what he learned. What follows is based on our paper and electronic files; we are confident that these records and the recollections of persons involved at the margin are basically accurate but the two INR staff members who were most involved are not here (one has been reassigned to Pakistan, the other is on leave) to guide us through the files and emails. What is clear, however, is that INR was not Ambassador Wilson's point of contact in either the Department or the Intelligence Community. INR did not meet with Wilson after his trip and did not receive any information on his trip and what he learned except what appears to be his reporting cable (his name is not mentioned) disseminated throughout the intelligence and policy communities by CIA. The reporting we have from his trip makes no mention of documents, fraudulent or otherwise.

From what we can find in our records, Joe Wilson played only a walk-on part in the Niger/Iraq uranium story. In a February 19, 2002, meeting convened by Valerie Wilson, a CIA WMD manager and the wife of Joe Wilson, he previewed his plans and rationale for going to Niger but said he would only go if the Department thought his trip made sense (Tab 1). Both the memo of this meeting prepared by INR's West Africa analyst (now

~~TOP SECRET~~

DOS-00547

PROVISIONALLY DECLASSIFIED

LL001-0051

THE FIRST PAGE of the INR report drafted for Marc Grossman on June 10, 2003 to inform his response to Libby's questions about the mission to Niger. The report on "the role that Ambassador Joe Wilson played in the Niger/Iraq uranium story" identified Valerie Wilson as Joe's wife and a CIA employee.

ACKNOWLEDGMENTS

MURRAY WAAS would like to thank his co-equal partner in this endeavor, Jeff Lomonaco. Jeff's knowledge of this case is unparalleled perhaps by anyone except the lawyers who tried it in court.

This book was originally conceived by the editorial director of Union Square Press, Philip Turner. It was his original conception of the idea for this book and his drive and determination that made this book possible. I am also grateful for good humor and hard work while trying to meet an impossible deadline.

This book would have also been impossible without the enthusiasm and hard work of Iris Blasi, who made sure the trains ran on time as we attempted to meet the deadline. Because of that deadline, both Philip Turner and Iris Blasi did both editing of the transcript and original writing for the book, for which Jeff and I are eternally grateful.

I would like to thank the many journalists and bloggers whose own reporting enlightened our writing and editing of this book. I would like to thank many as well for their personal insights and reflections, some for their camaraderie during their trial, and several for friendships that go back as long as twenty years and others that are more recent—the result of covering this enormously difficult and complex story. They include Tom Hamburger and Peter Wallensten of the *Los Angeles Times*; Knut Royce and Tom Brune of *Newsday*; James Gordon Meek of the *New York Daily News*; Neil Lewis, Scott Shane, Frank Rich, and Paul Krugman of *The New York Times*; Rich Leiby and Peter Eisner of *The Washington Post*; Laura Rozen, whose work on this subject appeared in the *American Prospect* and *Mother Jones*; Emma Schwartz of *Legal Times*; David Shuster of MSNBC; Joshua Micah Marshall and Justin Rood of Talking Points Memo Media; Graham Messick of *60 Minutes*; Michael Wolff of *Vanity Fair*; Amy Goodman of *Democracy Now*; and Dan Froomkin, whose columns on the Bush White House for Washingtonpost.com's "White House Watch" were fearless and without peer.

Among bloggers my reporting and knowledge of the case was regularly enlightened by John Amato of Crooksandliars.com; Jeralyn Merritt of Talkleft.com; Jane Hamsher, Parachutec, TRex, Phoenix Woman, and Christy Hardin Smith at firedoglake.com; Swopa; Joe Gandleman at themoderatevoice.com; Tom McGuire at JustOneMinute.com; Marcy Wheeler, aka Emptywheel at TheNexthurrah.com; Greg Sargent at several blogs, his most recent home being with TPM media; Jay Rosen at Press Think; everyone at Dailykos.com; and eriposte and Steve Soto at theleftcoaster.com.

I would like to thank the many exceptional editors who have edited my original stories on both the prewar intelligence issue and the Fitzgerald investigation: Charlie Green, Robert Gettlin, and Pat Pexton of the *National Journal*; Michael Tomasky, Tara McKelvey, and Jeff Dubner of the *American Prospect*; Laura Conaway of the *Village*

Voice; and Ariana Huffington, Colin Sterling, Elinor Shields, Michael Owen, and both Katharines at the *HuffingtonPost*.

Brian Beutler was an indefatigable research assistant and colleague during my reporting on the Plame affair. Brian will undoubtedly, someday, as have all of most assistants, be a great journalist in his own right and more successful than his former boss.

Thanks most of all to my family who have endured my long working hours and have been my most avid readers.

And thanks always to Peggy Daley.

FROM JEFF LOMONACO: It's a pleasure to recognize the people who have helped me understand the Libby case and the CIA leak investigation. Bloggers Tom Maguire, Jane Hamsher, Christy Hardin Smith, Swopa, Jeralyn Merrit and Polly have done remarkable research and analysis on a case that often turned on fine points. No one knows the case better than Marcy Wheeler, and I've benefited not only from her blogging but also from endless email correspondence with her. Many of the journalists who have provided excellent coverage have generously responded when I emailed them out of the blue over the last two years. Laura Rozen's reporting on the larger context of the debate over prewar intelligence has been consistently outstanding. Murray Waas has not only produced extraordinary reporting on the case, he's been great to work with on the book. My friend Colin Kahl has listened to me talk on this subject more than he might have liked, but always offered an intelligent response. My lawyer friends Adam Grumbach, Hank Lanman and Paul Winke have helped me understand the specifically legal dimensions of the case, as well as how they interacted with the political. And I'd like to give a special thanks to Juliet, August and Gabe for everything.

THIS BOOK would not have been possible without the efforts of Tilman Reitzle of Oxygen Design, Sterling staff Edwin Kuo, Rachel Maloney, Elizabeth Mihaltse, Chuck Bloodgood, Sara Cheney, Mary Hern, Amy Lapides, Becky Maines, Andrea Santoro, and Pip Tannenbaum, and freelancers Josh Karpf, Nancy Delia, Sherman Johnson, Jay Kreider, Patricia Nicolescu, Marina Padakis, Crystal Velasquez, and Paul Witcover.

INDEX

ABOUT THE EDITORS

MURRAY WAAS is an investigative journalist based in Washington, D.C. His ground-breaking reporting on the CIA leak case has been published in the *National Journal.* His reporting was cited by Special Counsel Patrick Fitzgerald in a letter to Scooter Libby's lawyers, leading to the end of Judith Miller's eighty-five day jail term. He blogs regularly for the *Huffington Post* and at www.whateveralready.blogspot.com. His investigative reporting has appeared in the *Los Angeles Times*, the *Boston Globe*, the *New Yorker*, *Salon*, the *Nation* and the *American Prospect*. His reporting on the Arkansas Project and the roots of the Whitewater scandal first brought him to the notice of many readers in the 1990s. In his late teens, he worked for the legendary Jack Anderson, and he was a Pulitzer Prize finalist in 1993. He has also been a winner of Harvard University's John F. Kennedy School's Goldsmith Prize for Investigative Reporting. Douglas Frantz of the *Los Angeles Times*, who shared reporting credit with Waas on the Pulitzer-nominated stories, says, "He's a dogged reporter with an amazing capacity to get sensitive documents."

JEFF LOMONACO is an assistant professor political science at the University of Minnesota. He received his Ph.D. from Johns Hopkins University in 1999 and his B.A. from Amherst College in 1991. His writing has appeared in *American Prospect*, the journal "Ethics and International Affairs," and the *Journal of the History of Ideas.*